About the ...

Ron Person

Ron Person is the owner of Ron Person & Co., Software Training Consultants, operating out of San Francisco and Santa Rosa, California. Ron Person & Co. supports clients with standardized and tailored personal computer training that improves the efficiency, production, and quality of their work.

The author teaches courses in both the business use of personal computers and in training techniques for data trainers for the Business and Management Department of the University of California, Berkeley Extension and for Sonoma State University, Extension. He has an MS in physics from The Ohio State University and has an MBA from Hardin-Simmons University.

Ron's 10 computer books include *1-2-3 Business Formula Handbook* and *Using Microsoft Windows*. He was contributing author for *1-2-3 QueCards* and revision author for the best-selling *Using WordPerfect*, 3rd Edition.

Mary Campbell

Mary Campbell is president of Campbell & Associates, a consulting firm in Gates Mills, Ohio. A frequent speaker at seminars and conferences, Ms. Campbell has more than 20 years of experience in the computer field and was author of Que's *Using Excel* and *Excel Macro Library*.

Content Overview_____

Using Excel:
IBM® Version

Ron Person
and Mary Campbell

Que™ Corporation
Carmel, Indiana

Library of Congress Catalog Number: 86-63979
ISBN 0-88022-284-0

91 90   8 7

Interpretation of the printing code: the rightmost double-digit number is the year of the book's printing; the rightmost single-digit number, the number of the book's printing. For example, a printing code of 88-4 shows that the fourth printing of the book occurred in 1988.

Using Excel: IBM Version is based on Version 2.0 of Microsoft® Excel.

Screen reproductions in *Using Excel: IBM Version* were created with HotShot® Graphics by SymSoft Corp.

Table of Contents

I Installing Excel and Operating Windows

II Excel Worksheets

10 Using Multiple Windows and Linking Worksheets

III Excel Charts

15 Creating and Enhancing Charts 383

V Excel Macros

27   Troubleshooting Macros 625

VI Advanced Techniques

Trademark Acknowledgments

Que Corporation has made every effort to supply trademark information about company names, products, and services mentioned in this book. Trademarks indicated below were derived from various sources. Que Corporation cannot attest to the accuracy of this information.

1-2-3, Lotus, and VisiCalc are registered trademarks of Lotus Development Corporation.

3Com is a registered trademark, and EtherSeries is a trademark of 3Com Corporation.

Apple II and LaserWriter are registered trademarks of Apple Computer, Inc.

AST Premium and AST Rampage are registered trademarks of AST Research, Inc.

AT&T is a registered trademark of American Telephone & Telegraph Company.

dBASE II, dBASE III, and MultiMate are registered trademarks of Ashton-Tate Corporation.

COMPAQ and Deskpro are registered trademarks of COMPAQ Corporation.

DynaComm is a trademark of Future Soft Engineering

Epson is a registered trademark of Epson Corporation.

Hercules Graphics Card is a trademark of Hercules Computer Technology.

Hewlett-Packard is a registered trademark, and LaserJet is a trademark of the Hewlett-Packard Co.

IBM and Personal System/2 are registered trademarks, and OS/2 and PS/2 are trademarks of International Business Machines Corporation.

Intel is a registered trademark and Above Board is a trademark of Intel Corporation.

Microsoft, Microsoft Excel, Microsoft Windows, Microsoft Windows Write, Microsoft Word, Microsoft Works, MS-DOS, and Multiplan are registered trademarks, and Mach 20 is a trademark of Microsoft Corporation.

Netware and Novell are registered trademarks of Novell, Inc.

Omnis Quartz is a trademark of Blythe Software.

PageMaker is a registered trademark of Aldus Corporation.

Paradox is a trademark of Ansa Corporation.

PostScript is a registered trademark from Adobe Systems, Incorporated.

Quattro is a registered trademark and Reflex: The Analyst is a trademark of Borland International, Inc.

Star is a registered trademark of Star Micronics America, Inc.

Ungermann-Bass is a registered trademark of Ungermann-Bass, Inc.

Windows GRAPH is a trademark of Micrografx, Inc.

WordPerfect is a registered trademark of WordPerfect Corporation.

Development Director
David Paul Ewing

Product Director
David Maguiness

Editorial Director
David F. Noble, Ph.D.

Acquisitions Editor
Terrie Lynn Solomon

Editors
Gregory Croy
Kathie-Jo Arnoff
Rebecca Kenyon

Technical Editor
Pat Leary

Book Design and Production
Dan Armstrong
Sharon Hilgenberg
Jennifer Matthews
Cindy Phipps
Joe Ramon
Dennis Sheehan
Mae Louise Shinault
Peter Tocco
Carrie L. Torres

Introduction

I feel as though I've just put another well-worn tool in the back of the tool shed.

The old tool served its purpose, as did the tool before it, and I'm indebted. But the new tool I'm using now is better than anything that's come before. It's easier to use, yet it has significantly greater flexibility and performance. With the new tool, I can get more done in less time, with less effort, and make it look better.

The tool of course, is the next generation of electronic worksheet, Microsoft® Excel.

I'm left with mixed feelings, a little sorrow for leaving the old, but elation as I look forward to what's possible with the new. It has happened before. Let me explain.

Back in 1978, I would covertly sneak home during work at a large minicomputer manufacturer. The clandestine trips were worth it. A few minutes with VisiCalc® on an Apple® II at home equaled a day's worth of recalculating and repricing computer components by hand. The trips were semisecret because official company policy forbade such "toys" as an Apple II in the plant—even to increase productivity. VisiCalc and the Apple II worked great on small, simple problems but quickly reached their limit on larger business problems.

When the computer manufacturer introduced its own personal computer, a PC and Lotus® 1-2-3® quickly took over a corner of my desk. After I thoroughly devoured a copy of *Using 1-2-3* by Que Corporation, the world of 1-2-3 opened to me, and the shortcomings of VisiCalc and the Apple II were alleviated.

Now, after four successful years of consulting, training, and writing about 1-2-3, I've watched many people come up against 1-2-3's inherent barriers to business solutions. 1-2-3 is difficult for many people to learn. It's unforgiving of mistakes. And some real business problems that should be easy to solve aren't; they require arcane worksheet trickery. Worst of all, the majority of people never get to use what power there is in a 1-2-3 database or macro. People don't have the time to learn all the rules and nuances.

In April of 1987, I saw the bridge that passed over the barriers in 1-2-3 and the original MS-DOS® computers. That's when I joined the prerelease testing of Excel on the new generation of personal computers.

What Is Excel?

Excel is part of the new generation of software that takes advantage of the power and capabilities of personal computers using 80286 and 80386 processors. As part of this new generation, Excel is both easier to use and more powerful than older electronic worksheets.

Excel gives you the ability to enter text, numbers, and formulas into cells within a grid that is 256 columns wide and 16,384 rows deep. These entries show Excel how you want mathematical problems solved.

In addition to solving mathematical problems, Excel automatically creates charts in any of 44 predefined formats. With Excel, you can customize charts and produce presentation quality graphics.

You do not need to learn a lot of hocus-pocus to use the Excel database. Excel automatically generates a database form that you use to enter, edit, delete, and retrieve information.

Along with its greater functionality, Excel gives you the power to communicate with authority. From a laser printer, your charts, worksheets, and database reports look like they just came from the art department's typesetting equipment.

Excel includes a macro recorder that makes repetitive tasks easier. Turn on the recorder, and it records the keys you press and the commands you choose. Later, you can repeat the recorded actions at the press of a key. (After you have gained some experience, you can use the macro language to build completely automated business systems. You can even use macros, for example, to link Excel worksheets to other applications.)

As part of the new generation of software, Excel operates in MS-DOS under the Microsoft Windows environment and in OS/2™ under the Presentation Manager environment. This gives you a common menu structure and operating style with other programs operating in Windows or the Presentation Manager. That's important. It means that 60 percent of your learning on one Windows or Presentation Manager application carries over to the next application.

Another advantage stemming from Windows and the Presentation Manager is that applications can easily exchange data. You can have many applications available in memory at one time, and you can cut and paste data between the applications. Some Windows applications, such as Microsoft Excel, Blyth Software's Omnis® Quartz relational database, Micrografx Windows GRAPH, and Future Soft Engineering's DynaComm communications, can even link "live" data using Dynamic Data Exchange. As linked data in one application changes, it automatically updates the data in the other applications.

Using this new generation of software requires a new generation of hardware, machines built around 80286 and 80386 processor chips. If your current personal computers prevent you from taking advantage of the new generation of software, you have two options. You can add an accelerator board to your computer, such as Microsoft's Mach 20 board, or you can stay within the limits of older generation worksheets such as Microsoft Works, Borland's Quattro®, or 1-2-3.

Accelerating up the Productivity Curve

Many companies are concerned about the training time necessary to learn the new generation of software like Excel. In the case of Excel, those companies should consider three factors beyond the short term.

1. For beginners, Excel is easier to learn than 1-2-3.

2. For users of 1-2-3 or Multiplan®, Excel is extremely easy to learn.

3. Given the same experience level, Excel users work at a higher level on the productivity curve than do 1-2-3 users.

After teaching both Macintosh Excel and 1-2-3 in courses for the California State University system, it is obvious to me that new users learn Excel nearly twice as fast as they learn 1-2-3.

If you already know 1-2-3, you will learn Excel quickly. Nearly all concepts are the same. In addition, Excel reads and writes 1-2-3 Release 1A and Release 2 worksheets. Excel translates 1-2-3 macros and has help screens that show you the Excel commands that are equivalent to 1-2-3 commands. Depending upon your experience level and learning method, Excel operators can select commands with the mouse, arrow keys, touch typing, or Ctrl and Alt key combinations. If you already know 1-2-3, you will find yourself more productive in Excel within a week. In this book, Chapter 30, "Making the Switch from 1-2-3 to Excel," is especially designed to raise your Excel learning curve by taking advantage of your 1-2-3 knowledge. If you have 1-2-3 experience, read Chapter 30 first.

The real bottom-line question is this: how much can you learn about Excel that you can use to improve your job performance? The additional productivity and quality available from Excel over a year exceeds the time necessary to learn it.

Look at one example for a moment. Novice users do not have to have extensive training to learn how to use Excel databases or charts. When the database range is set, Excel automatically creates a form for data entry, editing, deleting, and searching. Also, Excel automatically creates charts with labels and titles using the numbers and text in the selected range. The user can then select from one of the 44 predefined formats, without ever having to use the many custom features available. Both of these capabilities put beginning Excel operators at the same level as intermediate 1-2-3 operators.

As another example, users of 1-2-3 Release 2 must know arcane printer control codes to change character fonts for a printed line. These printer codes vary with each printer, and when put in a worksheet, render the worksheet confusing for normal work. In addition, the results cannot be seen until printed.

By comparison, even brand new Excel operators can select character fonts, sizes, and styles from options in a dialog box. Operators need not remember or understand mysterious printer codes. And because the enhancements are displayed on-screen, the page can be previewed exactly the way it will print.

Intermediate-level 1-2-3 users can begin doing the equivalent of advanced work when they move to Excel. One reason for this is the macro recorder. Everyone can create command macros using the macro recorder. Users with a little experience can also easily link worksheets together and create complex charts.

Where does this leave the advanced 1-2-3 users who switch to Excel? With even more power. They can link Excel worksheets to other Windows applications, control other Windows applications from within Excel, write macros with the extensive macro language, and create complete application packages with custom menus, dialog boxes, and help files.

Installing Excel and Operating Windows

Windows applications, like Excel, all operate with the same concepts and procedures; and often, Windows applications have quite similar commands. When you learn one Windows application, you are well on your way to learning another. Procedures like making selections from a menu or choosing options from a dialog box work the same in different Windows applications.

This similarity between Windows applications means that you can often learn one Windows application, then immediately begin productive work with a different application that you have never used before. The common procedures among Windows applications provides an immense savings in time and frustration.

Part I contains three chapters that help you install Excel and learn some of the fundamental commands necessary to use Windows applications effectively. The commands and concepts you will learn can be transferred to most Windows applications.

The installation process for Excel is extremely easy, but there are a few tricks you should know. Chapter 1 explains these tricks, which make Excel run at peak performance.

Chapter 2 is the first of five Quick Starts. Quick Starts are mini-tutorials that guide you through a short, hands-on session. They teach the fundamental concepts found in their respective Parts. The Quick Start in Chapter 2 teaches you how to start Excel, move and size windows, choose commands, and select options. More detail about operating Windows applications is provided in Chapter 3.

If you are a Lotus 1-2-3 user, you will find it helpful at this point to skip forward to Chapter 30, "Making the Switch from 1-2-3 to Excel." Chapter 30 is designed to help people familiar with Lotus 1-2-3 understand Excel's compatibility, differences, and enhancements.

Chapter 1
Installing and Running Excel

Chapter 2
Windows Quick Start

Chapter 3
Operating Windows

1

Installing and Running Excel

Excel is one of the new generation of software that runs under Windows 2.0, Windows/386 or higher, or the OS/2 Presentation Manager environments. In this chapter, you learn how easy it is to install and run Excel. In addition, you find tips that make Excel's performance even more impressive.

Finally, the last part of this chapter helps you decide how to use the rest of the book most effectively to learn about Excel's features.

Before You Install Excel

Before you install Excel, you must have the appropriate hardware and the right software. Because Excel asks you for the names of your equipment during installation, making a list before you start makes the task go faster.

To provide optimum performance in either the OS/2 Presentation Manager or the Windows environments, these environments must have the following minimum hardware requirements:

- IBM Personal System/2®, AT, COMPAQ® 386 Deskpro®, or compatible. Computers with 8088 or 8086 processors do not normally have sufficient computing power for Excel to operate efficiently.

- 640K of memory

- IBM VGA, Extended Graphics Adapter, CGA graphics cards, Hercules Graphics Card™, or other graphics cards and monitors compatible with Windows 2.0 or greater. The quality of display and performance of Excel may vary significantly with the graphics card.

- hard disk with at least five megabytes of free storage

9

- at least one 360K, 1.2M, or 1.44M floppy disk drive

- DOS 3.0 or higher (as required by your system and network) or OS/2

In addition, Excel supports the following:

- a wide range of printers and plotters, including the Hewlett-Packard® LaserJet™ and PostScript®-compatible laser printers

- a mouse

- expanded memory (EMS or EEMS). Excel automatically takes advantage of expanded memory to store large worksheets. The SMARTdrive software may also be installed to use part of expanded memory as disk cache; this significantly increases performance. (Appendix C describes the SMARTdrive software and how to install it.)

- extended memory, when used with the SMARTdrive disk cache to increase Excel operating speed if expanded memory is either unavailable or needed for program space

- math coprocessors (Intel 80287 and 80387) to decrease math recalculation time

- major personal computer networks such as IBM PC Network, IBM Token Ring Network, AT&T® STARLAN, Novell® Netware®, 3Com® 3+, 3Com EtherSeries™, Ungermann-Bass®/One, and networks supporting Windows version 2.0 or higher

Excel can run by itself (under the Windows Single Application Environment), with Windows 2.0 and higher, or with Windows/386. Windows 2.0 and Windows/386 give Excel the capability to operate with other applications and exchange data.

Before you install Excel, you should make a list of the following:

- manufacturer and type of computer (If your computer is a clone, choose the closest compatible from a major vendor.)

- display card type and monitor type

- printer manufacturer and model

- laser printer cartridge being used

- printer port (connection) to which the printer is connected

- printer communication information for serial printers (connected to COM1 or COM2), such as baud rate, number of data bits, stop bits, and parity. Find this information in your printer manual, from the dealer, or the manufacturer.

- mouse manufacturer and type
- port connection of the mouse
- name of directory in which you want to install Excel

If you are unfamiliar with any of these items, check your equipment manuals, sales receipt, the dealer (with the date of purchase), or your corporate MIS hot-line.

If you are running both Excel and Windows 2.0 or higher, Excel should be under the Windows directory. Install Windows 2.0 (or Windows/386) before you install Excel. (You can install Windows after installing Excel.) You do not have to create the directories before installing Excel or Windows, because the setup program prompts you for the directory name and creates the directory for you if necessary.

If you will be running Excel by itself (you're missing out), you can install Excel under any directory name but preferably off the root directory.

Installing Excel

After you have created a list of your system configuration and checked it twice, it is time to install Excel.

1. Protect your original disks from accidental change. On 5 1/4-inch disks put a sticky write-protect tab over the square cut notch on the edge. On 3 1/2-inch disks slide the write-protect notch so that it is open.

2. Put the Setup Disk (disk 1) into drive A, and type:

    a:setup

3. Press Enter.

4. Read and follow the directions that appear on the screen. As you go through the installation process, you will be given the opportunity to make corrections or to quit and start over.

> **NOTE**
>
> ### Installing Excel with "Early" Versions of Windows
>
> Excel does not run with Windows versions previous to Windows 2.0. You will get the best performance in Windows/386 with version 2.03 or higher. (Contact Microsoft for an upgrade if your versions are older than these.) If you have these environments on your hard disk, install Excel in a different directory. The Excel setup program asks you for the name of the directory in which you want to install Excel.
>
> Make sure you contact Microsoft for an upgrade to your older Windows software. Being able to share information between Excel and other Windows or standard DOS applications is a major benefit.

Improving Excel Performance

You can make some manual changes that will greatly improve Windows and Excel performance. These changes require that you use a text editor or word processor (with a Text save command) to edit lines in the AUTOEXEC.BAT and CONFIG.SYS files.

Before you make any changes to these files, use the DOS COPY command to create a backup copy of the original file. If something doesn't work as planned, you can always recopy the backup to the correct file name. For example, to create a backup of the CONFIG.SYS file, type the following at the DOS prompt:

    copy config.sys config.old

Then press Enter.

Begin by creating a directory for Windows temporary files with the following command:

    MD C:\TEMP

Then use your text editor or word-processing program to modify your AUTOEXEC.BAT file so that it includes the following lines:

    PATH C:\WINDOWS;C:\EXCEL;C:\PM;C:\DOS;C:\UTIL
    SET TEMP=C:\TEMP

or to modify similar lines that already exist.

By dictating which directories to look in and in what order to look, the PATH command helps DOS find files. If you installed Excel within the Windows directory, you will not have to list the Excel directory separately in the PATH command.

Save the AUTOEXEC.BAT file as a text file. It will take effect the next time you restart the computer.

The CONFIG.SYS file, which is located in your hard disk's root directory, also needs to be changed. Check your CONFIG.SYS file to make sure that it contains the lines:

```
BUFFERS =20
FILES =10
```

If your CONFIG.SYS file does not have these lines, add them. Note that these are minimum numbers for BUFFERS and FILES. Adding the BUFFERS line can make a significant improvement in performance. Some applications (such as databases, accounting packages, and PageMaker®) require a higher number of buffers. Setting buffers higher (unnecessarily) may not improve performance, but will use up memory.

Windows comes with SMARTdrive caching software that improves the performance of many applications. But you must install SMARTdrive. You will find installment instructions in Appendix C of this book and in the README files on the original Windows and Windows/386 installation disks. Because 80386 computers do not use expanded memory, you will need to install SMARTdrive so that it uses extended memory. (You will *not* use the /A option when you enter the SMARTdrive device line in the CONFIG.SYS file.)

TIP

Accidentally Erasing Excel Application Files

If you accidentally erase Excel files that contain parts of the application or contain temporary information, the program may freeze or may not restart. If this occurs, don't panic. (You have backup copies of your data, right?) Use your duplicate copies of the originals to reinstall Excel in the same directory, and press on.

Starting Excel

You can start Excel from DOS if you do not have Windows. To start Excel from DOS, do the following:

1. Change to the directory containing Excel. If Excel is in the Windows directory, you would use the command:

   cd \windows

2. Type **excel**, then press Enter.

If you have Windows or Windows/386 installed, you can start Excel from Windows. To start Excel from Windows, do the following:

1. Start Windows or Windows/386 by typing **win** or **win386**, and pressing Enter.

2. Change to the directory containing the file EXCEL.EXE, if necessary, and choose the file name EXCEL.EXE.

   Mouse: Rapidly click the pointer twice (double-click) on the name EXCEL.EXE.

   Keyboard: Type the letter **e**, or press the arrow keys to select the file name EXCEL.EXE, then press Enter.

When Excel runs under Windows, you can start Excel and a selected worksheet together. All you need to do is choose the worksheet file name from the MS-DOS Executive instead of the EXCEL.EXE file name. (An Excel worksheet file name ends with .XLS.)

You can also start Excel from Windows so that it appears with exactly the worksheets, charts, and macros that you want on the screen. To do this, you must arrange the Excel screen the way you want it to be when you restart, then save your work with the **File Save Workspace** command. You will be asked to name this workspace.

When you want to restart, choose that workspace name from the MS-DOS Executive. (Workspace files end with .XLW.) Excel starts, loads, and positions all the documents. The workspace file expects to find the original documents in the same directories and with the same file names they had when you saved the workspace.

Performance Enhancements

Excel is one of the new generation of software that requires an 80286 or 80386 processor. But even with one of these fast processors, there are ways to increase Excel's speed.

Accelerator Cards

If you have an 8088, 8086, or 80286-based computer, you can add an 80286 or 80386 accelerator board so that it will run Windows, Excel, and OS/2 applications faster. Check with the manufacturer to ensure that the accelerator board you buy is compatible with OS/2 so that you can upgrade from DOS to OS/2 should you need to in the future.

Disk Organizers

Over time, hard disks store data in a less and less organized fashion. Eventually, data is so scattered over the hard disk that retrieving information is like retrieving a report that has each page stored in a different folder. Software utilities known as disk optimizers can reorganize and restructure your hard disk so that data is read much faster. Make sure you thoroughly review the different commercially available disk optimizer packages before reorganizing your disk. As an added precaution, you should back up your hard disk before reorganizing it.

Expanded Memory

Excel and Windows take advantage of EMS and EEMS memory and compatible memory systems that support Lotus/Intel/Microsoft specification version 4.0. The file named READMEEM.TXT contains information on how to add the Windows expanded memory manager.

If you have only 640K of memory, Excel stores part of itself on disk and retrieves that part when needed. However, with the addition of expanded memory, Excel can store formulas and cell tables in expanded memory, leaving more room in main memory (the first 640K) for the application. Because this reduces the amount of reads from the disk, the program speeds up. Of course, it also lets you run much larger worksheets.

Disk Caching

Excel and other Windows applications are not compatible with other RAM disk or disk-caching utilities. If you are running Windows or Windows/386 however, you can install SMARTdrive. SMARTdrive is disk cache software that comes with Windows 2.0 or higher, and Windows/386. SMARTdrive enables extended or expanded memory to improve the effective performance of the hard disk. Because part of the Excel application is read from disk during certain operations, this speeds up Excel performance. Refer to Appendix C for information on installing SMARTdrive.

Using Excel Help Files

Excel has a good system for giving you help when you need it. But you can also use the Help feature as a way of exploring new territory in Excel.

To get general help in Excel:

1. Choose the **Help Index** command, or press F1.

   Mouse: Click the pointer on **Help,** then click on **Index** when the menu appears.

   Keyboard: Press Alt, then H, then I.

2. Choose the subject area, then the specific item from the Help index shown in figure 1.1.

   Mouse: Click on the subject area of interest. When items underneath that subject appear, click on the specific item.

   Keyboard: Press Tab or Shift+Tab, or type the first letter of the subject or item name until the subject or item you want is selected, then press Enter. Use this method to select the specific item.

Fig. 1.1. Help index window.

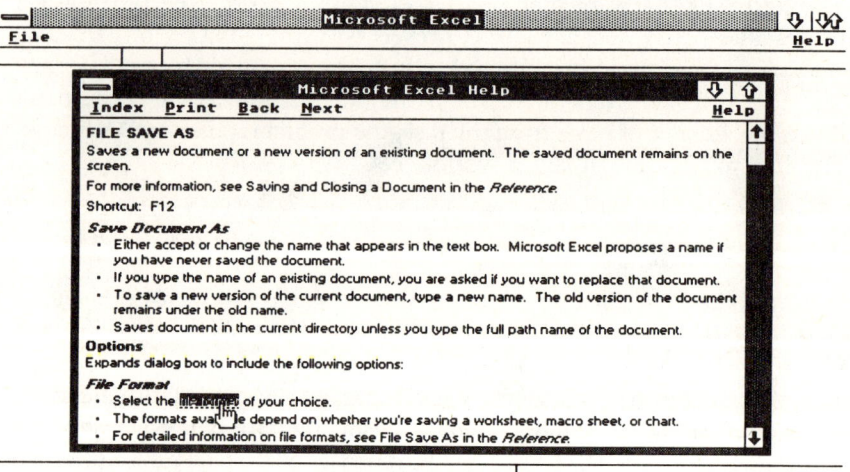

3. Scroll through a page of help information with PgDn or PgUp. Press F1 or Esc to return to your document.

To get specific help within the context of your work, press F1 when a command is selected or a dialog box displayed.

TIP

Exploring Your Way through Excel

When you press Shift+F1, the mouse pointer changes to a question mark. If you have no mouse, a large question mark appears. The next command or area of the screen you select will display a Help window describing that command or screen area. Press F1 or Esc to put away the Help window.

Shift+F1 is important. Whenever you come across a menu command or feature with which you are not familiar, use Shift+F1 to do a little exploring. Those occasional 30-second explorations can reveal features about Excel that could help you in the future.

1-2-3
TIP

Do You Speak Lotus 1-2-3?

If you are familiar with Lotus 1-2-3, you may want to begin learning about Excel by turning to Chapter 30, "Making the Switch from 1-2-3 to Excel." That chapter contains a number of topics relating Excel to Lotus 1-2-3. Make sure you become familiar with Excel's help command for Lotus 1-2-3 users. This command asks you for a Lotus 1-2-3 command, such as /File Save, and it shows you the equivalent Excel commands and explanation. Figure 1.2 shows the Lotus 1-2-3 help box with a request entered for the Excel equivalent to the Lotus 1-2-3 /fs commands.

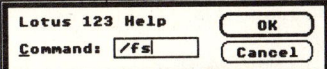

Fig. 1.2. Lotus 1-2-3 help window.

From Here . . .

After you install Excel, complete the Windows Quick Start and the Worksheet Quick Start. From there, you can skip to any of the other Quick Starts.

When you have completed a Quick Start for a section, you will be able to knowledgeably skim through the chapters in that section.

You may find Excel commands easiest to learn if you follow this procedure. When looking for a command, do the following:

1. Learn the menu commands by first selecting the menu that you think contains the command, then pressing the right- or left-arrow

key to open adjacent menus if the one you have chosen does not actually contain the command.

2. When you become familiar with frequently used commands, you can save time in selecting commands by pressing first Alt, then the underlined menu letter, and then the underlined command letter. You need not wait for the menu to appear before choosing the command letter. (Note that in this book, the underlined letter is indicated with boldface type.)

3. When you are confident of what you want to do, you can take real shortcuts with Shortcut Keys, keys that provide immediate shortcuts through commands. Some Shortcut Keys appear next to each command on the pull-down menus. An extensive list of Shortcut Keys can be found on the Quick Reference Card.

TIP

Stay out of Ruts

Do not be satisfied with constantly keying the same commands month after month, year after year. Complacency can prevent you from learning other functions in Excel that can save you time and work. Occasionally, flip through this book, scan the index, peruse the Table of Contents, scour the Tips and Notes, and explore the Excel Help files. See if there is an idea that can reduce your work load or improve the quality of your end results. Try an interesting idea on a simple and small scale before using it in your work.

Probably the fastest method of learning Excel is to follow these steps:

1. Work through the Quick Starts that precede each section. Keep the completed Quick Start on the screen.

2. Skim through the chapters following the Quick Start so that you know the available features. As you skim through a section, experiment in your completed Quick Start worksheet, chart, or macro sheet with features that look valuable.

3. Every few weeks, skim through the Table of Contents, the Table of Tips (Appendix A), and the Index. When you skim through sections this time, imagine how you can apply tips and techniques to make work easier. As you become more familiar with Excel, your mind will be able to synthesize new uses for Excel in your work.

2

Windows Quick Start

Microsoft Excel operates within an application known as Microsoft Windows. In the next 15 minutes, you can learn the important features of operating Excel in the Windows environment. If you are familiar with Windows, this chapter will be easy for you. You should, however, work through the exercises anyway to learn keystroke shortcuts and other information that may improve your efficiency when operating Excel.

Under Windows, you have the ability in Excel to see and work simultaneously with multiple worksheets, charts, and macros. There are many important reasons for using Windows as the "environment" for Excel. Two of the most important reasons are that all Windows applications operate similarly, and much of what you learn from one application transfers to another. Also the appearance and control techniques you use in Windows under MS-DOS are the same as that used by the Presentation Manager under the new operating system OS/2. That means that applications running Windows on an MS-DOS computer will look the same as the next generation of applications running under Presentation Manager on OS/2 computers.

Microsoft Excel runs two ways under Windows. You can install and run Excel by itself, and it will operate in a version of Windows that only allows you to operate Excel and no other application. This is the Single Application Environment version (SAE). However, if you also have a full version of Windows installed along with Excel, then you can run Excel with other applications, switch rapidly between applications, and transfer data between applications. There are many advantages to running Excel under the full version of Microsoft Windows.

If you haven't yet installed Excel, go back to Chapter 1 and follow the installation instructions before you continue. If you already have installed Excel, now is the time to get started by working through this "Quick Start." Before you begin, you should take time to understand the terms used throughout this book to describe important actions (see table 2.1).

Table 2.1
Excel Actions

Action	Description
Select	Highlight or mark a menu selection, option, or cell location with either keyboard or mouse actions.
Choose	Make a final selection that executes or cancels a command.

Mouse procedures

Click	Select a single item by moving the mouse pointer (the on-screen arrow, cross, or I-beam indicating the current mouse location) so that the tip of the pointer is on the item; then quickly press the left mouse button one time.
Double click	Choose or execute an item by quickly clicking the left mouse button twice.
Drag	Move the tip of the mouse pointer onto the first item; then hold down the left mouse button as you move the mouse pointer.

Keyboard procedures

Type	Type, but do not press the Enter key.
Enter	Type, and then press the Enter key.
Alt	Press the Alt key.
Alt, *letter**	Press the Alt key, release it, and then press the underlined letter or number shown in the menu or command.
letter	Press only the underlined letter shown in the menu or command.
Alt+*letter*	Hold down the Alt key as you press the underlined letter.
Alt, hyphen	Press the Alt key, release it, and then press the hyphen key.
Alt, space bar	Press the Alt key, release it, and then press the space bar.

Action	Description
Tab	Press the Tab key.
Esc	Press the Esc key.

*Note that in this text, the letters that appear underlined on the Excel screen are printed in boldface type.

If you have a mouse, try using both mouse actions and keystrokes to perform commands and tasks. The exercises in this Quick Start provide instructions for using both options. You soon will find that the keyboard works well for some commands and features, and the mouse works well for others. Which method you use depends on your preference and the task at hand.

Starting Excel without Windows

If you do not have Windows, you can start Excel from DOS by following these steps:

1. Type **cd \excel** and press Enter to change to the Excel directory. (If you installed Excel into a different directory, use the name of the directory containing the file EXCEL.EXE.)

2. Type **excel** and press Enter.

The Excel application will run in the Single Application Environment (SAE) version of Windows. You can run Excel, but you won't have all the capabilities of Windows.

Starting Excel with Windows

If you are operating Excel with Windows, start Excel from the MS-DOS Executive just as you would start any Windows application. Follow these steps:

1. Change to the directory containing the file EXCEL.EXE.

   Mouse: First click on the backslash (\) following C: at the top of the MS-DOS Executive screen. In the dialog box that appears, type the path (directory) where the EXCEL.EXE is located, and click OK.

   Keyboard: Press Alt-S to select the **S**pecial menu. Press C to select the **C**hange Directory command. Enter the name of the path (directory) where the Excel program is located, and then press Enter.

2. Select the EXCEL.EXE file.

   Mouse: Rapidly click twice on the EXCEL.EXE file name.

   Keyboard: Press E (the first letter of the file name) until EXCEL.EXE is selected (highlighted), and then press Enter.

The Windows MS-DOS Executive provides two alternative ways to select a file. With the mouse, you can immediately execute the EXCEL.EXE file by double clicking on the name. From the keyboard, you can use the up-, down-, left-, or right-arrow keys to move the selection through the list of names to the file name EXCEL.EXE, and then press Enter.

Learning the Parts of the Excel Screen

When Excel appears, you will see a screen like the one shown in figure 2.1. The Excel *application window* fills the entire screen, and a smaller *document window* displays a blank worksheet. (If you started Excel from Windows, the application window may not fill the screen.)

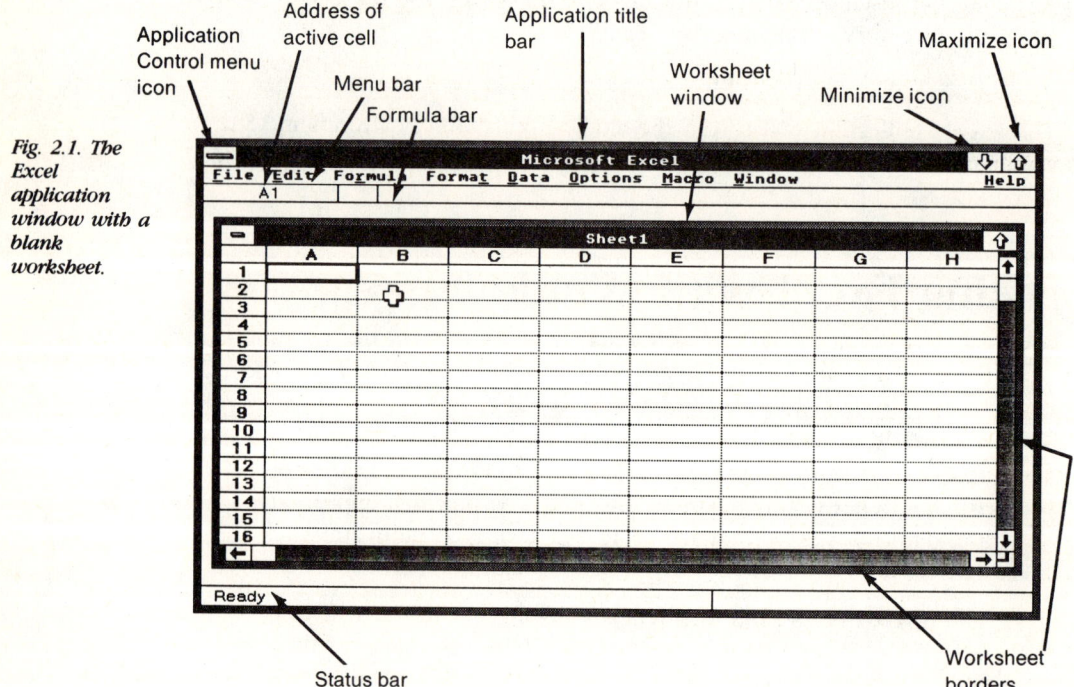

Fig. 2.1. The Excel application window with a blank worksheet.

The document window, Sheet1, has a solid *title bar*, indicating that it is the active document window (see fig. 2.2). You can have multiple worksheets, charts, or macros open at the same time, but you can enter data and commands only into the active document window. Title bars of nonactive windows normally appear a lighter shade unless they have been customized.

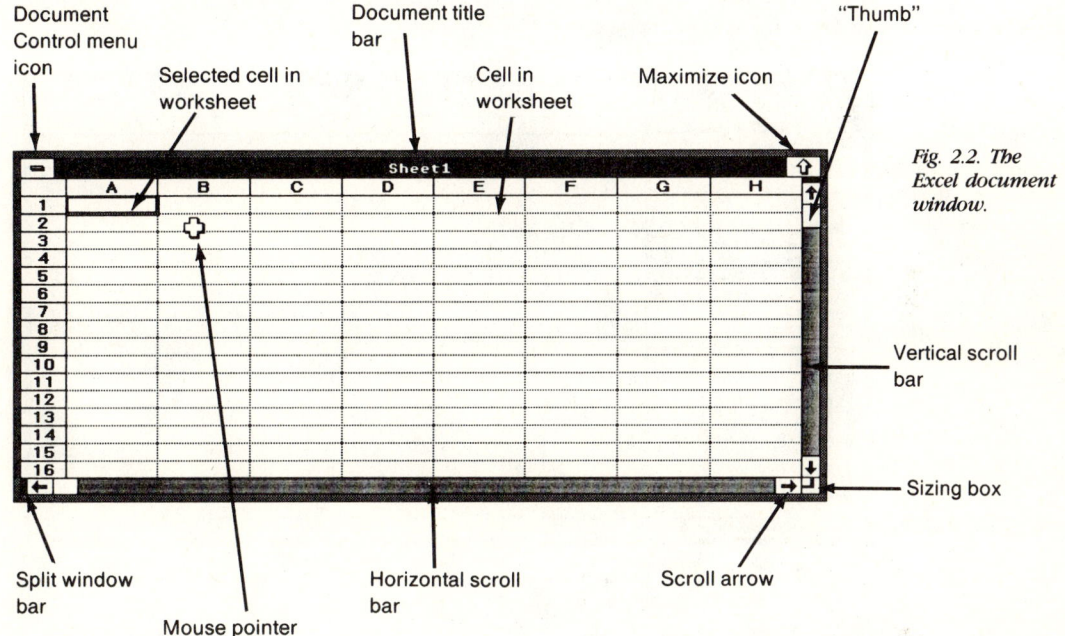

Fig. 2.2. The Excel document window.

Look over the names of the different parts of the Excel application and document windows shown in figures 2.1 and 2.2. These names are used throughout the rest of the book.

Exploring the Menus

Excel provides different ways to execute a command or accomplish a task. The method you use depends on the task and your personal preference. In most cases, the Quick Start chapters of this book use the most basic, but not necessarily the shortest method. However, by reading the tables of shortcut keystrokes, the chapters following each Quick Start, and the Tip boxes within each chapter, you will learn many shortcuts.

Windows and Excel commands are displayed in pull-down menus that appear below menu headings, such as File and Edit. Figure 2.3 shows the File menu pulled down. The application window and the document window each have a Control menu that controls the window's location, size, and status. The application Control menu appears at the top left of the Excel application window; the document Control menu appears at the top left of each document window. Each Control menu is shown in figures 2.1 and 2.2.

Fig. 2.3. The File menu displayed on a full screen.

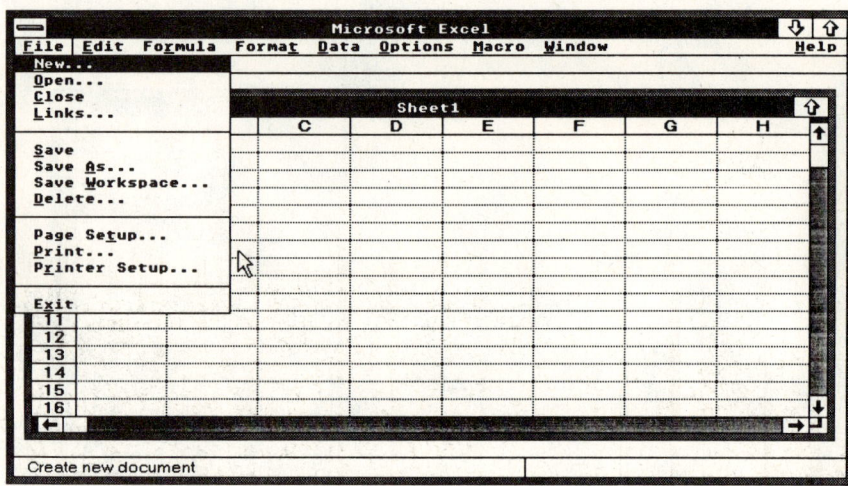

Changing the Active Mouse Button

Throughout *Using Excel: IBM Version*, the left mouse button is referred to for clicking on commands or making selections. Chapter 28, "Using Excel with Windows Applications," describes how to use the Control Panel application to activate the right mouse button.

Scanning Excel Menus

Windows applications are easier to learn than other applications because what you learn from one Windows application will help you learn the next one. In Windows applications, you can see what commands are available by scanning through the menus. When you forget where an Excel command is located, you can easily scan through the menus to see the commands they contain. Follow these steps to scan through the Excel menus:

1. Select the File menu, and then scan the menus to its right.

   Mouse: First click once on the word File in the Excel menu bar. Then drag slowly from File to Window by putting the mouse pointer on File, holding down the left mouse button, and moving the tip of the mouse pointer over the menu names.

   Keyboard: Press Alt and then F to open the File menu. Then press the right-arrow key to open each menu in turn.

2. Remove the menus without choosing a command.

   Mouse: Click the mouse pointer on the worksheet or background, but outside the pull-down menu.

   Keyboard: Press the Esc key.

Notice that each name in the menu bar and each item in a menu have an underlined letter. These underlines clue you to which letter to press from the keyboard in order to select a menu or command. (In this text, these underlined letters are printed in boldface type.)

Choosing from a Menu

Usually, you execute commands by opening a menu and then choosing an item from that menu. For example, you might choose the Save As command from the File menu.

First you select the File menu, and then you select the Save As command. With the mouse, click on File, and then click on Save As. From the keyboard, press Alt then F to open the File menu, and then press A to select Save As.

The File menu shown in figure 2.4 is displayed. Observe that the command Save As is followed by an ellipsis (. . .). When you choose commands followed by an ellipsis, a dialog box appears asking you for additional information.

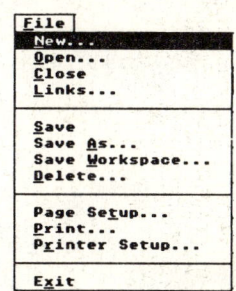

Fig. 2.4. The File menu.

Notice that you did not have to press Alt from the keyboard before typing the A in Save **As**. After you have opened a menu, you need only press the letter of the command to make a selection from the menu. The sequence you use to select any menu command is Alt, the underlined menu letter, then the underlined command letter.

TIP

Displaying Shortened or Full Menus

Excel gives you the option of seeing all the commands available through the menus or a shortened version of the menus that is more appropriate for learning or casual Excel users. If you want to see a shortened version of the menus so that only fundamental commands show, then choose **Options Short Menus**. When you want to see all the commands that are available through the menu, choose **Options Full Menus**.

Entering Information in a Dialog Box

Excel asks for additional information by displaying a dialog box, such as the one shown in figure 2.5. Dialog boxes contain areas where you can type text or numbers, turn options on or off, and select from lists of options or names. The currently active button or box is enclosed in a dashed line. When a text box used for typed entries is active, the text appears selected (highlighted) or contains a flashing vertical cursor.

Fig. 2.5. The Save Worksheet dialog box.

Save Worksheet as:	Ok
SHEET1.XLS	Cancel
C:\EXCEL	Options >>

When the **S**ave Worksheet dialog box appears, the file name SHEET1.XLS appears selected within a text box. If you enter a new name for the worksheet, your entry will replace SHEET1.XLS because the new entry will be selected.

Follow these steps to change parts of the **S**ave Worksheet dialog box:

1. Type the word **TEST** as the name for this blank worksheet. TEST will replace the selected SHEET1.XLS worksheet.

2. Select **Options**.

   Mouse: Click inside the **O**ptions command button.

> **Keyboard:** Press Alt+O by holding down the Alt key as you press
> O, and then release both keys.

Selecting the **Options** button extends the dialog box to display additional
alternatives (see fig. 2.6). Notice that the **Options** button appears gray on the
screen because it is no longer available for selection.

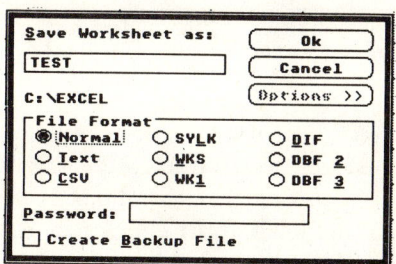

*Fig. 2.6. The
extended Save
Worksheet
dialog box.*

NOTE

Gray Commands on Menus

Commands, buttons, and options that are not available for selection appear
in gray.

The option buttons in the File Format area of the **Save Worksheet** dialog box
turn on or off the format used to save the Excel worksheet. You can turn on,
or darken, only one option button at a time. By choosing one of these option
buttons, you can save your Excel worksheet so that it can be read by 1-2-3
Releases 1A or 2, dBASE II® or dBASE III®, two different forms of text formats,
and in other formats. The **Normal** option saves the worksheet in Excel format.

Using the mouse, click on the **WK1** option button so that the worksheet will
be saved in Lotus 1-2-3 Release 2 format. From the keyboard, press Alt+1, or
press the arrow keys until that button darkens.

Each time you press the Tab key in a dialog box, the surrounding dashed line
moves to another part of the box. The part of the box containing the dashed
line is where you can make changes. Notice that the .WK1 file name extension
automatically has been added to the TEST file name you entered (see
fig. 2.7).

The small square box labeled Create Backup File is a *check box*. Any number
of check boxes can be selected at the same time. An X in the box indicates
that the box is selected.

Fig. 2.7. The
Save Worksheet
dialog box with
.WK1 added to
the file name.

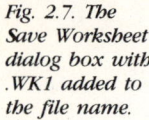

```
┌─────────────────────────────────────────────────┐
│ ‾Save Worksheet as:      (    Ok    )             │
│ ┌─────────────┐                                   │
│ │TEST.WK1     │          (  Cancel  )             │
│ └─────────────┘                                   │
│ C:\EXCEL                 ( Options >> )            │
│ ┌File Format────────────────────────┐             │
│ │ ○ Normal    ○ SYLK     ○ DIF       │             │
│ │ ○ Text      ○ WKS      ○ DBF 2     │             │
│ │ ○ CSV       ◉ WK1      ○ DBF 3     │             │
│ └────────────────────────────────────┘            │
│ Password:    ┌─────────────────────┐              │
│              └─────────────────────┘              │
│ □ Create Backup File                              │
└─────────────────────────────────────────────────┘
```

For example, you can select the Create **B**ackup File check box so that a backup file is automatically created during the save operation. With the mouse, click inside the small square check box. To select the check box from the keyboard, press Alt+B or press Tab until the dashed line surrounds Create **B**ackup File. Then press the space bar to select the check box.

Executing or Canceling a Command

After you have set the dialog box with the names and options you need for the File Save **A**s command, you can execute the command in a number of ways. With the mouse, you can click inside the OK button. From the keyboard, you either can press Enter, or you can press the Tab key until OK is enclosed in a dashed line and then press the space bar.

Notice that after the worksheet is saved, the title in the title bar changes to agree with the file name. The title bar now says TEST.WK1 instead of Sheet1.

Instead of executing the command, suppose that you decide to cancel the command and put away the dialog box. To do so, you select the Cancel button or press Esc.

Moving a Document Window

The application and document control menus allow you to move, resize, and control the status of Excel windows. You probably will prefer to use a mouse, if you have one, for these actions. In the following steps, notice that window size, location, and status can be changed with mouse shortcuts. From the keyboard, the Control menu must be used. Complete the following steps to drag the TEST document window up and left:

1. Display the document control menu.

   Mouse: Move the tip of the mouse pointer into the title bar.

Keyboard: Press Alt, release it, and then press the hyphen key (-). The hyphen is to the right of the zero key at the top of the keyboard. (Notice the small hyphen icon at the top of the document window.)

2. Highlight the edge of the window and reposition it.

Mouse: Hold down the mouse button, and you will see that the edge of the window darkens as a shadow border overlaps the edge of the window. Continue holding down the button and drag the shadow up and left to the new location. Release the button after the shadowed border is relocated.

Keyboard: Press M to select Move from the document Control menu. A four-headed arrow will appear in the title bar, as shown in figure 2.8, and the edge of the window will become a shadow. Use the arrow keys to reposition the shadow border. Press Enter to "fix" the shadow and to redraw the window at its new location.

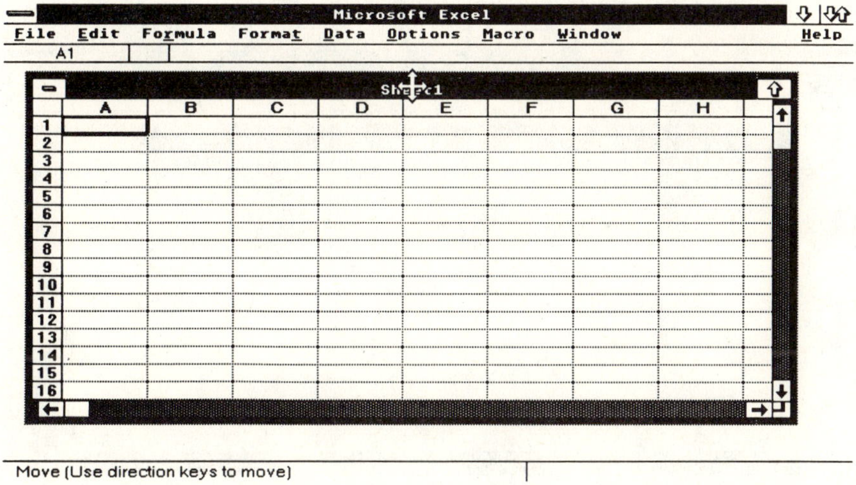

Fig. 2.8. A four-headed arrow, indicating that the window may be moved with the arrow keys.

Changing the location of the Excel application window is just as easy as moving the document window. With the mouse, drag the title bar that displays Microsoft Excel. From the keyboard, press Alt and then the space bar to display the application control menu. From that menu, type M to choose Move, and then use the arrow keys to move the application window. You cannot move the Excel application window if it fills the full screen.

Resizing Windows

In the preceding section, you saw how easily you can move a window. Changing its size is just as easy. Here again the mouse may be more convenient to use than the keyboard. Follow these steps to make the TEST document window smaller by moving its right side to the left:

1. Open the document Control menu, and then select the right edge of the window to be resized.

   Mouse: Move the mouse pointer onto the right edge of the window until the mouse pointer changes to a two-headed arrow as shown in figure 2.9.

   Keyboard: Press Alt and then hyphen. Choose the Size command. The window edges darken with a shadow, and a four-headed arrow appears in the middle of the screen. The arrow key you press next determines which edge will be resized. Press the right-arrow key to select the right edge. A small two-headed arrow like the one shown in figure 2.9 appears at the right edge of the window.

Fig. 2.9. A two-headed arrow at the right edge of the window.

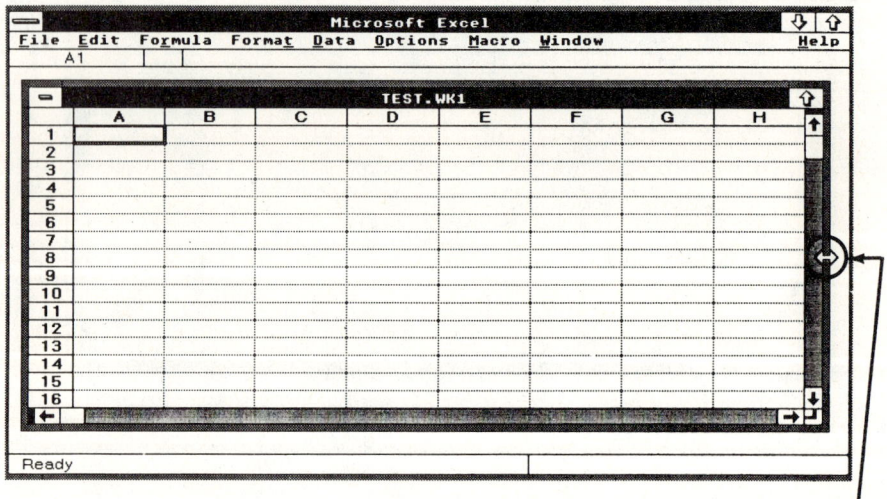

Two-headed arrow for resizing

2. Move the right edge of the window to the left.

   Mouse: Drag the right edge to the left, releasing the mouse button when the shadow is where you want it.

Keyboard: Press the left-arrow key to move the edge to the left. After the edge is positioned, press the Enter key.

You can move any edge or corner with either the mouse or keyboard commands. To move a corner (two sides at once), drag the corner to its new location with the mouse. Or from the keyboard, press Alt, hyphen, S, and then the two arrow keys that point to the corner you want to move. For example, to move the upper right corner, you would press Alt, hyphen, S, the right arrow, and then the up arrow. The two-headed arrow appears at the upper right corner; the two-headed arrow appears diagonally to show that the corner is being moved.

Exiting Excel and Closing Windows

After you finish experimenting with Excel, you will need to exit the program. To do this, click on **File** and then on **Exit**. From the keyboard, press Alt, F, and X.

If you made changes to the worksheet since the last save operation, a dialog box will appear asking whether you want to save again. Choose the **No** button to exit without saving.

If you started Excel from Windows, you can leave Windows and return to the DOS prompt or continue operating DOS and Windows applications from within Windows. To leave Windows, you need to choose **Close** from the MS-DOS Executive control menu. With the mouse, click on the MS-DOS Executive's control menu at the upper left corner of the MS-DOS Executive window, and then click on **Close**. From the keyboard, press Alt and then the space bar to select the MS-DOS Executive's Control menu. Then press C to choose **Close**.

This Quick Start shows you some of the steps used to control Windows applications such as Excel. But there are many shortcuts when using the mouse and the keyboard. To learn more about controlling Excel, its menus, dialog boxes, and windows, read Chapter 3, "Operating Windows." Make sure you look through the tables that list different methods of control.

If you feel comfortable controlling windows and menus, then you should begin Chapter 4, "Worksheet Quick Start." It shows you how to apply the general concepts covered in Chapters 2 and 3 toward building a worksheet that forecasts sales and profits.

3

Operating Windows

This chapter is the place to start if you are not familiar with Microsoft Windows. You will use the ideas and concepts you learn here in all your Excel operations. In fact, what you learn in your first Windows application will carry over to other Windows applications.

You will learn how to control not only Excel's menus and dialog boxes but also the windows that contain Excel and its worksheets, charts, and macro documents. By the end of this chapter, you should be able to choose commands from menus, select options from dialog boxes, and manipulate windows on the screen. Of course, you need to know how to choose from menus and select options in dialog boxes in order to run the application. In addition, you also should be able to organize windows so that you can access and use multiple worksheets at the same time or "clear away your desktop" to concentrate on just one job.

Understanding the Excel Screen

One advantage of Windows applications is the capability to run several applications and display them on the screen simultaneously. Chapters 28 and 29 describe how you can run Excel and other Windows or DOS applications together and transfer on-screen information between them. This can save you time when you transfer numbers into or out of Excel, transfer charts to graphics applications for further enhancements, or create automatically updated links between Excel worksheets and certain Windows applications.

Each Windows application, such as Excel, runs in its own application window. Some application windows can contain multiple document windows, each of which contains a different type of result. For example, Excel displays document windows that contain worksheets, charts, or macro sheets. Figure 3.1 shows the Excel application window along with a worksheet and a chart document window.

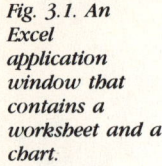

Fig. 3.1. An Excel application window that contains a worksheet and a chart.

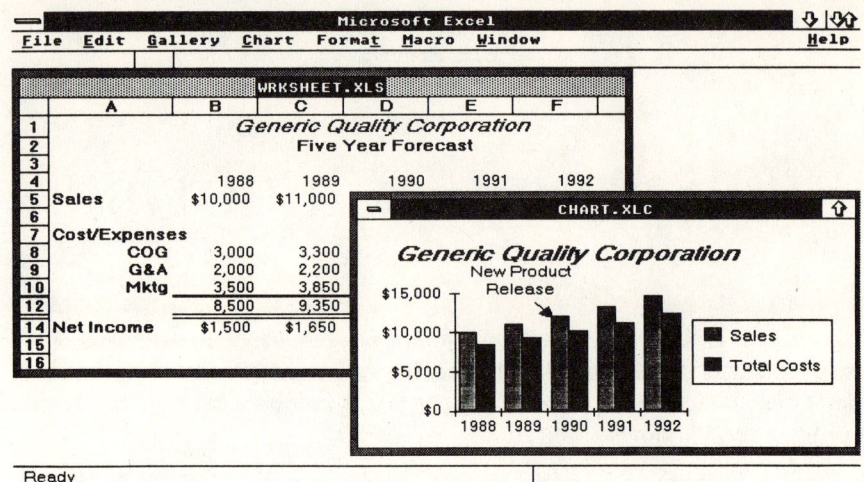

Take some time to go back to the "Windows Quick Start" (Chapter 2) and look over figures 2.1 and 2.2 so that you become familiar with the different parts of the Excel screen. Then study the components of the Excel screen described in table 3.1.

Table 3.1
Parts of the Excel Screen

Part	Description
Application window	The window within which Excel runs
Document window	The window within which worksheets, macro sheets, and charts are displayed
Application Control menu	The menu that lets you manipulate the application window; access the menu by pressing Alt and then the space bar.
Document Control menu	The menu that lets you manipulate the active (top) document window; access the menu by pressing Alt and then the hyphen key.
Active window	The window that accepts entries and commands; has a solid title bar and is normally the top window
Mouse pointer	The on-screen arrow, cross, or I-beam indicating the current mouse location.

Part	Description
Title bar	The bar at the top of the window.
Menu bar	A list of menu names displayed beneath the title bar of a window; to display a pull-down menu, click on the name or press the Alt key followed by the underlined letter.
Command	A function or procedure you perform by choosing from a pull-down menu; either click the mouse on the command's name or press the underlined letter in the command's name.
Formula bar	The area of the screen where you enter text, numbers, or formulas. The formula bar is below the menu bar.
Minimize icon	A symbol that you can click on to store an application as a small symbol at the bottom of the screen; it's the same as the application Control Minimize command.
Maximize icon	A symbol that you can click on to fill the screen with the active window; it's the same as the application Control Maximize command.
Scroll bar	The area of the screen that contains arrowheads you can click on to scroll the window in the direction of the arrowhead and a square (sometimes called an "elevator") you can drag to change the window's relative location to the sheet it contains. Horizontal and vertical bars at the right and bottom of each document window.
Status Line	A bar at the bottom of the screen that shows what Excel is prepared to do next; watch it for prompts and guidance.

Using the Mouse

The *mouse* is an optional piece of hardware that attaches to your PC and enables you to move the on-screen pointer by moving the mouse with your hand. In Excel, you can control the application with either mouse movements or keystrokes. Each approach works well depending on the task at hand (for example, windows are easier to size and move with the mouse) and your personal preference. You will find that using a combination of mouse, touch typing, and shortcut keys is the most productive way to work.

Moving the Mouse

The mouse, shown in figure 3.2, is a small hand-held device that lies on your desktop and fits comfortably under your palm. As you move the mouse across your desk, the *mouse pointer*—a shape on the screen—moves in the same relative direction across the screen. You will find that using the mouse to "point" at an item on the screen with the mouse pointer becomes a very natural process. The mouse is especially useful for selecting large cell areas, copying and pasting cells, exploring menus, changing the sizes and locations of windows, and moving objects on charts.

Fig. 3.2. The mouse.

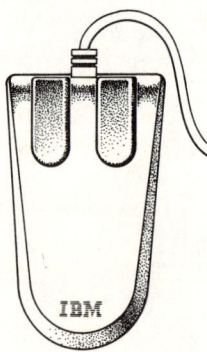

When you hold the mouse, the wire should project forward, away from your arm, so that the buttons are under your fingers. A mouse may have two or three buttons; however, Excel uses only the left button.

TIP

For Left-Handed Operators Controlling Right-Handed Mice . . .

If you are left-handed, you should check out the Control Panel application described in Chapter 28, "Using Excel with Windows Applications." The Control Panel application lets you switch the mouse button control from the left button to the right. (Among the many other Excel features you can customize with the Control Panel are screen colors, border width, cursor flash rate, mouse reactions, and international character sets.)

As you move the mouse pointer on the screen, the mouse may run out of clear space on your desktop. This does not mean that you need a larger desk or that you need to find a shovel to clear away the work that has stacked up. Instead, when the mouse collides with something, just pick up the mouse, move it to a clear area, put it down, and continue the motion. Usually, about one square foot of clear desk space gives you enough room to control the mouse.

The best practice is not to operate the mouse on a dusty or dirty surface or over paper. The mouse senses its movement with a ball on its underside. Rolling over a dirty surface or paper gets dirt and paper lint on the ball, causing the mouse pointer to skip or hesitate when moving. If this happens, refer to the mouse manual for cleaning instructions.

Understanding the Changing Mouse Pointer

The mouse pointer shows the relative position of the mouse on the screen. The pointer changes appearance depending on its location. You usually will see the mouse pointer as an arrow when it is in the menus or as a cross when it is in the worksheet. Each different appearance is a signal to you of the type of power you have at that location. The different shapes of the pointer are shown and explained in table 3.2.

Table 3.2
Mouse Pointer Shapes

Mouse Pointer	Location	Function
⌀	Menu, scroll bar, chart	Select by moving the tip of the arrow onto an item, then clicking the mouse button.
I	Text boxes, formula bar	A vertical flashing line (the cursor) inside text or formulas indicates where typed characters will appear. To move the cursor's location, move the I-beam to the location, and then click.
⬌	Between column headings, edge of window	Drag to change column width or window edge.

Table 3.2
Mouse Pointer Shapes

Mouse Pointer	Location	Function
✛	Between row headings, edge of window	Drag to change row height or window edge.
▨	Window corners	Drag to size two window edges at one time.
✛	Inside worksheet	Select cells in worksheet when mouse button is clicked.
⇨	Split bar in scroll bar	Drag to split window.
⌕	Print preview	Select document area for closer review.
☝	Help window	Select items for more information.
⌛	Any screen location	Please wait.

Selecting with the Mouse

Windows and Excel are designed so that you can take many command short-cuts with the mouse. You will use three basic selection techniques with the mouse:

Click   Click to select an item such as a menu, command, cell, or chart object.

To click, move the tip of the mouse pointer inside a name or item and quickly press and release the mouse button once.

Double click   Double click to execute selected commands from within a dialog box without having to choose the OK button.

To double click, click twice in rapid succession on a name or item.

Drag   Drag to select multiple text characters, to select a range of cells, to move the scroll bar, or to move an item.

To drag, put the tip of the mouse pointer on the item, hold down the mouse button, and move the mouse pointer to the new location. In some cases, the item will move with the mouse pointer; in others, you will see the area covered by the mouse pointer become highlighted or selected. Release the mouse button to complete the drag operation.

You can change the active button on the mouse, the double click rate, and screen movement rate with the Control Panel application. This application is described in Chapter 28, "Using Excel with Windows Applications."

Using the Keyboard

You have full control over Windows and Excel from the keyboard as long as you understand the sequence in which keys are pressed. This section tells you how *Using Excel: IBM Version* describes the order in which keys are pressed. You will learn the alternative ways you can use the keyboard to choose commands from a menu. You also will learn how to accelerate the selection process with shortcut keys.

As a Windows application, Excel follows the conventions set down for all Windows applications. When you learn how to select menus and choose items in Excel, you will know how to control other Windows applications that follow the recommended conventions.

Choosing Commands from a Menu

Usually, at least two ways exist for accomplishing any task in Excel. If you are not familiar with the Excel menu structure, you will want to use the following steps to choose commands by looking for them and reading an explanation about them:

1. Press Alt to select the menu bar.

2. Press the right or left arrow to highlight the menu name. Notice that the status line at the bottom of the screen explains the menu's function.

3. Press the Enter key to display the selected menu.

4. Press the up or down arrow to select (highlight) a command. Read the status line for an explanation of each command.

5. Press the right or left arrow to move from one menu to another.

6. Select the command you want, and then press Enter; or press Esc to back out without selecting.

When you become more familiar with the Excel menus, you can rapidly choose commands with only three keystrokes:

1. Press Alt to select the menu bar. (If you are used to Lotus 1-2-3, you can press / instead).

2. Press the underlined letter in the menu name you want—for example, **File**.

3. Press the underlined letter in the command name you want—for example, **Open**, if you want to open an existing worksheet, chart, or macro.

You do not need to wait for the menu to appear when using this second method for choosing commands from the keyboard.

1-2-3 TIP

You Already Know the Three Most Important Keys

If you are familiar with the three most important keys in Lotus 1-2-3, then you already are familiar with the three most important keys in Excel:

/	Activate the menu
Esc	Back out of the menu or dialog box
F1	Help

Throughout this book, you will see combinations of keys indicated with a plus sign (+), such as Alt+F. This means that you must hold down the Alt key while you next press F. After pressing F, you can release both keys. (Just press the F key; do not hold down the Shift key for the capital F unless the directions indicate otherwise.) Keystrokes that appear separated by commas can be pressed in sequence. For example, Alt, space bar, is accomplished by pressing and releasing Alt, then pressing the space bar. Table 3.3 describes the keystrokes, combinations, and sequences of keystrokes you will use for making selections from Windows and Excel menus.

Table 3.3
Keystrokes for Selecting from Windows and Excel Menus

Keystroke	Action
Alt	Activate the menu.
letter	Choose the command from the pull-down menu.
Alt+*letter*	Choose a pull-down menu or select the option or button with the underlined letter in a dialog box.
Alt, space bar	Display the application Control menu to manipulate the Excel window.
Alt, hyphen	Display the document Control menu to manipulate the active worksheet, chart, or macro.
up and down arrows	Move the selection up or down arrows in the menu; move between option buttons in a dialog box.
left and right arrows	Select the menu adjacent to the current menu; move between option buttons in a dialog box.
Enter	Choose the selected (highlighted) name or command. In a dialog box, choose the button with bold edges.
Esc	Back out of a command or dialog box without choosing.
Tab	Activate the next group of options in a dialog box.
Space bar	Choose the button or check box in a dialog box that is surrounded by a dashed line.

Using Shortcut Keys for Accelerated Selections

You can greatly speed your Excel operation by using shortcut keys. Shortcut keys produce results without going through the menus. Many involve key combinations, such as Alt+F6 or Shift+Alt+F6. The keys that control Excel application and document windows are described in table 3.4. There are many other shortcut keys for commands and functions. A complete list of shortcut keys is provided on the Command Reference Card.

> **TIP**
>
> ### Speeding Up with Touch Typing Selections
>
> If you know which commands and options you want, press the keys—you don't have to wait for menus and dialog boxes to appear.

Table 3.4
Shortcut Keys for Excel Control

Function	Document window command	Excel window command
Close	Ctrl+F4	Alt+F4
Restore	Ctrl+F5	Alt+F5
Activate next	Ctrl+F6	Alt+Tab
Activate prior	Ctrl+Shift+F6	Alt+Shift+Tab
Move	Ctrl+F7	Alt+F7
Size	Ctrl+F8	Alt+F8
Minimize	N/A	Alt+F9
Maximize	Ctrl+F10	Alt+F10

Example: Ctrl+F6 activates the next document window. Hold down Ctrl while you next press F6. Where indicated, hold down both Shift and Ctrl or Alt before pressing a function key.

Save Time with Keyboard Shortcuts

Excel has many keyboard shortcuts that are built-in and others that you can design yourself. In each chapter, you will find the built-in shortcut keys that pertain to the subjects being discussed. An entire list of quick keys for Excel appears in the Command Reference Card.

You can create your own shortcut keys with command macros. After you work through the "Worksheet Quick Start" (Chapter 4), you will be able to run the "Macro Quick Start" (Chapter 25). You will be pleased at how easy macros are to create, and elated about how much time they can save you.

Manipulating Windows

When you use Excel with Windows, you can display and run more than one application or multiple sets of data within one application. Seeing that much information on your screen can be confusing unless you keep your windows organized. Just as you organize folders and papers on your desk, you can organize your Windows applications and Excel documents.

You will see two types of windows on the screen. An *application* window contains an application such as the MS-DOS Executive, Excel, or Microsoft Windows Write. Some applications display their data in separate windows referred to as *document* windows. For example, Excel can have multiple document windows, each window containing a worksheet, chart, macro sheet, or other information. With Excel, you can link information between the different documents or between Excel and certain other applications.

Selecting the Active Window

You can work in an application or document only when its window is active. You can tell that a window is active by the solid title bar that appears. If windows are overlapping, the active window is usually the one on the top. Notice in figure 3.3 the difference between the title bars.

If you started Excel from Windows, you can use other applications without exiting Excel. Activate the application you want to use, and Windows will keep Excel ready for you to return to. For example, you can activate Microsoft Windows Write to write a memo and then return to Excel, keeping both applications loaded and running.

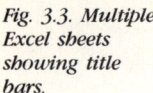

Fig. 3.3. Multiple Excel sheets showing title bars.

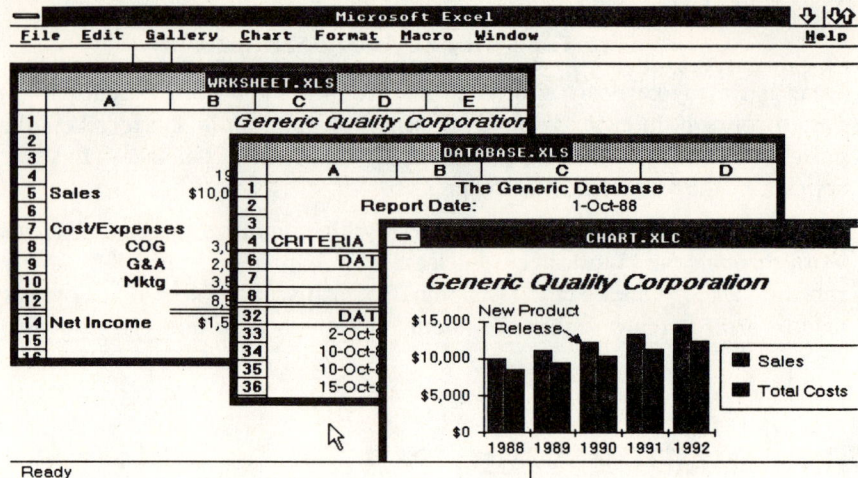

To select between different application windows on the screen, click on the window you want to use. From the keyboard, press Alt+Esc or Alt+Tab to cycle through application windows.

Because Excel makes working with several worksheets and charts easy, you frequently will have more than one document window on the screen. However, you can affect only the active document. From within the Excel window, if you can see the document, you can make it active by clicking on the document with the mouse pointer. If you cannot see the document, move other windows so that you can, or use the mouse to select the same commands as you would with the keyboard method.

To change active windows from the keyboard, you choose the window number from the Window menu. Press Alt, and then press W to open the Window menu. Read the names of the document windows currently available. Press the underlined number in the name of the window you want activated.

The Window menu changes depending on the titles of the sheets that are on the screen. Figure 3.4 shows just one example of how these worksheet titles appear. The title with the check mark is currently the active document.

Moving a Window

With multiple applications or multiple Excel documents on the screen, you will want to move windows for the same reason you reorganize work on your desk. You can move a window with either the mouse or the keyboard.

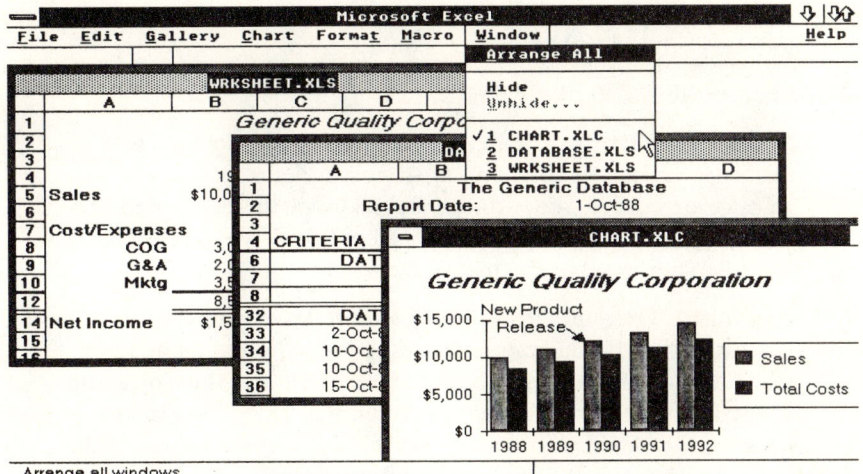

*Fig. 3.4. The
Window menu
with multiple
documents.*

To move a window with the mouse, you first must select the window you will move. Drag the title bar until the shadow border is where you want the window. Then release the mouse button to fix the window in its new location.

From the keyboard, select the application or document Control menu by pressing Alt and then the space bar for the application Control menu, or Alt and then hyphen for the document Control menu. Press M to select Move. A four-headed arrow will appear in the title bar. Press an arrow key to move the shadowed outline of the window. Press Enter to relocate the window, or press Esc to retain the original location.

Sizing a Window

You frequently will want to see only part of an application or document window. You can do this by changing the size of the window. Follow these steps to change the size of a window:

1. Activate the window.

   Mouse: Move the entire window so that the side you want to change is visible. Move the mouse pointer to the edge of the window or corner so that the mouse pointer changes to a two-headed arrow.

   Keyboard: Press Alt and then the hyphen key to select the document Control menu, or press Alt and then the space bar to select the application Control menu. Press S to choose **Size**, and a four-headed arrow will appear at mid-screen.

2. Change the size of the window.

   Mouse: Drag the two-headed arrow in the direction you want that edge or corner to move, as shown in figure 3.5. As you drag an edge or corner, you will see a shadow of the edges that are changing. Continue dragging until the shadow is the size you want it. Then release the mouse button.

   Keyboard: Press the arrow key that corresponds to the edge you want to move. If you want to move a corner, press an arrow key that points to one of the sides of the corner, and then press the arrow key that points to the corner on that side. For example, pressing the down arrow and then the right arrow indicates the bottom right corner. When the double-headed arrow appears, press an arrow key to move the edge or corner. Continue to move the shadow of the window outline until the shadow is the size you want it. Figure 3.5 shows how the shadowed edge indicates the new window size. Press Enter to fix the new window size.

Fig. 3.5. An Excel window being resized.

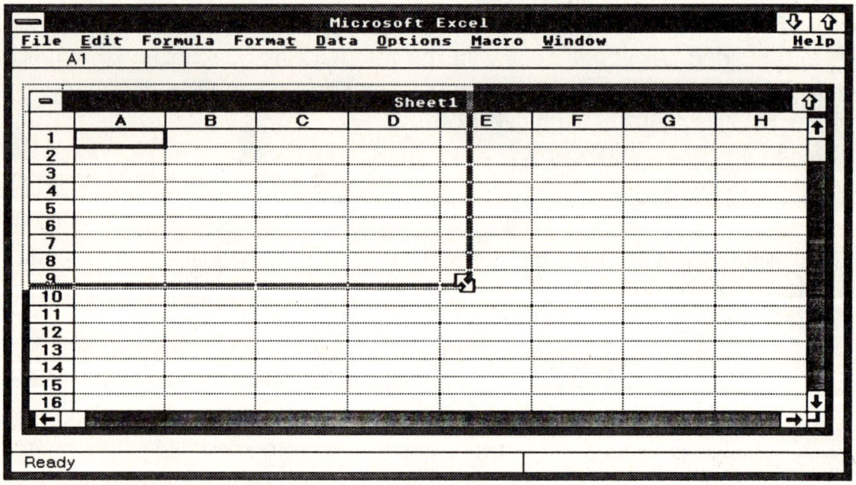

By scrolling in the smaller window, you can look at all the information it contains. Scrolling is described in Chapter 6, "Operating Worksheets."

Shrinking, Expanding, and Restoring Windows

You soon will find that your computer desktop can become as cluttered as your real desktop. To gain more space, you can temporarily put unused applications on hold by *minimizing* them so that they become small symbols (icons) at the bottom of the screen. (Document windows containing worksheets, macros, or charts cannot be minimized to icons. You can, however, hide them using the **Window Hide** command.) When you need one of the applications that has been minimized, you can *restore* its icon in its former application window at the original location and size. When you want a window to fill the entire available screen area, then you will *maximize* it. The icons for minimizing and maximizing space are shown in figure 3.6.

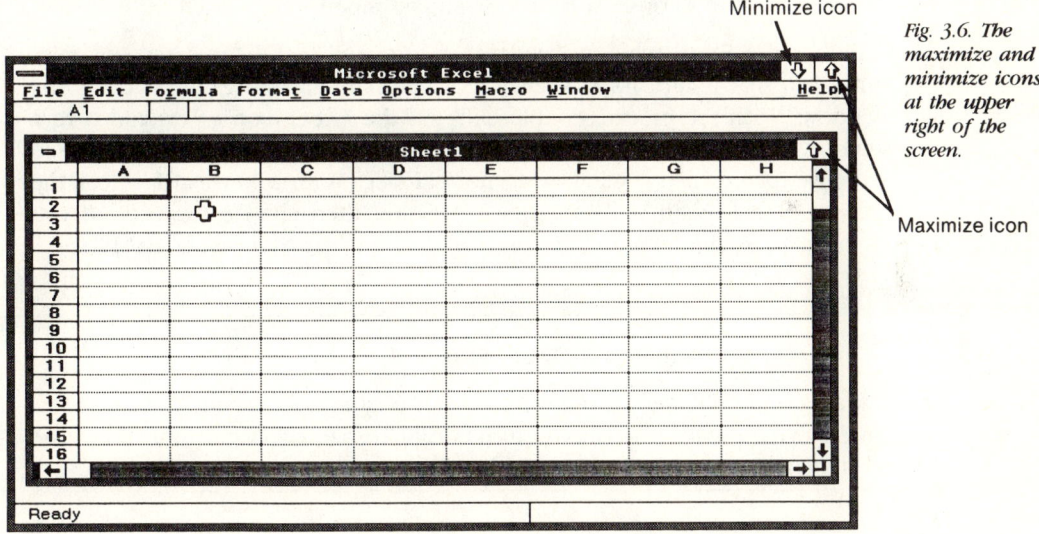

Minimize icon

Fig. 3.6. The maximize and minimize icons at the upper right of the screen.

Maximize icon

To maximize a window with the mouse, click on the maximize icon for the active window or double click in the title bar of the window. To maximize a window from the keyboard, press Alt and then the hyphen key to display the document Control menu, or press Alt and then the space bar to display the application Control menu. Press X to choose Maximize from the menu.

NOTE

Maximizing a Document Window

When you maximize a document window, it fills all the space below the Excel menu and formula bar. As a consequence, the document Control menu (the small dash in the box at the upper left of the worksheet) changes position slightly. It no longer appears at the top left corner of the document. Look for a small dash to the left of the menu.

You can shrink application windows so that they are temporarily stored at the bottom of the screen. Some applications "freeze" when minimized to icons. Other applications, such as DynaComm, a communication application from Future Soft Engineering, continue to work as you work in Excel.

To shrink an application window so that it is stored at the bottom of the screen as an application icon, click on the minimize icon. From the keyboard, press Alt and then the space bar to display the application Control menu. Then press N to choose Minimize from the menu.

Whether the Excel window has been maximized to fill the screen or minimized so that it appears as a small icon, you can always restore it to its last window. With the mouse, double click on the Excel icon to expand it to a window. Click on the double-headed icon at the top right of the maximized window to return the window to normal size. With a keyboard, select the Excel Control menu with Alt, space bar, and then choose **Restore**. (If you have multiple applications running, switch between them with Alt+Tab.)

TIP

Restoring a Document to Its Original Size

A maximized document window will not display a double-headed restore icon. To restore a document window to its original size, choose **Restore** from the document Control menu (Alt and hyphen).

Closing a Document Window

When you finish with the application, worksheet, or chart, you should close the window to remove it from the screen and to free memory. When you close the application, you will not lose your data as you would with Lotus 1-2-3. If you have made a change since the last time you saved the document, Excel displays an alert dialog box, like the one shown in figure 3.7, asking whether you want to save your work before closing.

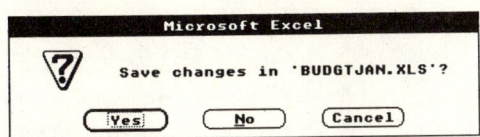

Fig. 3.7. An alert dialog box asking whether you want to save changes.

To close a document window, follow these steps:

1. Close the window.

   Mouse: Double click on the document Control menu icon at the upper left corner of the document window. This icon looks like a hyphen in a square. The document will close if you have made no changes since the last save, or the alert box will appear asking whether you want to save your changes.

   Keyboard: Press Alt and then hyphen to display the document Control menu. Press C to choose **Close** from the menu. The document will close if you have made no changes since the last save, or the alert box will appear asking whether you want to save your changes.

2. Confirm whether or not you want to save your changes.

   Mouse: In the dialog box, click on the **No** command button to abandon the changed version of the file, or click on the **Yes** command button to save your changes.

   Keyboard: In the dialog box, press Alt+N to choose the **No** command button, or press Enter to choose the **Yes** command button to save your changes.

3. If you chose Yes, enter a new file name.

   Mouse: Enter the new name in the **S**ave Worksheet dialog box that appears, and click on the OK command button.

   Keyboard: Enter the new name in the **S**ave Worksheet dialog box that appears and press Enter.

TIP

Saving Your Work

You can avoid frustration and lost work if you save different versions of your work. When you save your document using the same file name, your previous work is replaced by the current work, and you cannot go back to old files.

Instead of using the same file name over and over, reserve two characters at the end of each file name for a version number—for example, BUDGET07, BUDGET08, and so on. If you do this, you can go back to previous work. (Don't retype the entire name; just press the left arrow or backspace to edit the old name.) When you get too many files of the same type, just erase the old ones with the **File Delete** command.

Quitting Excel

When you are finished working for the day or when you need to free memory for other applications, you will want to close or quit Excel. To quit Excel, follow these steps:

1. Quit Excel.

   Mouse: Double click on the application Control menu icon. It appears as a space bar symbol in a box at the left of the Microsoft Excel title bar. Excel quits immediately if you haven't made any changes since the last time you saved your documents.

   Keyboard: Press Alt and then the space bar to display the application Control menu. Press C to choose the **Close** command.

2. Confirm whether or not you want to save your changes.

   Mouse: If you have made changes to any document, Excel displays an alert box asking whether you want to save your current work. Click on the **Yes** command button to save your work, or click on the **No** command button to quit without saving.

   Keyboard: If you have made changes to any document, Excel will display an alert box asking whether you want to save your work since the last file save. Press Enter to choose **Yes** and save your work, or type N to choose **No** and abandon your changes.

3. Repeat steps 1–2 for each document name displayed in an alert box. The alert box will appear for each document you have on the screen that has been changed.

Saving All Your Work Just as It Is

To save all the documents and their window arrangements that you are currently working with, choose the File Save Workspace command before closing Excel. When you want to resume work from the exact point you left off, choose the File Open command and select the file name you assigned the "workspace." The workspace name will be followed by an .XLW extension.

Using Dialog Boxes

When Excel needs more information to complete a command, the application displays a dialog box. In the pull-down menus, commands that require additional information are followed by an ellipsis (. . .). Choosing one of these commands displays a dialog box in which you enter needed information. For example, the Format Number . . . command results in the dialog box shown in figure 3.8.

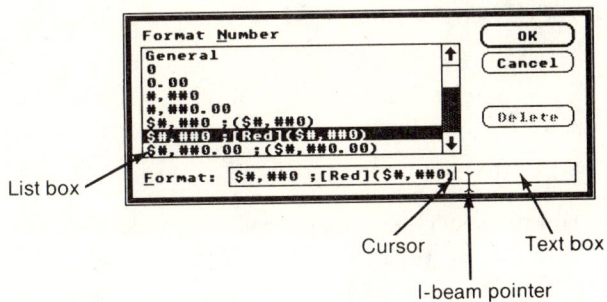

List box

Cursor   Text box

I-beam pointer

Fig. 3.8. The Format Number dialog box.

Dialog boxes can contain a text box for typing text or numbers, option buttons for selecting one of many options, check boxes for checking multiple options, list boxes for displaying a list of alternative names or functions, or command buttons for executing or canceling a command.

The Format Number dialog box shown in figure 3.8 contains both a list box and a text box. You can type a custom numeric or date format into the text box, or you can select an existing format from the list box.

Figure 3.9 demonstrates the types of entries you can make in a dialog box. The Format Font dialog box is used to change the size, style, and appearance of text. In that box, you also can specify which of four fonts are to be available for use in a worksheet or chart.

*Fig. 3.9. The
expanded
Format Font
dialog box.*

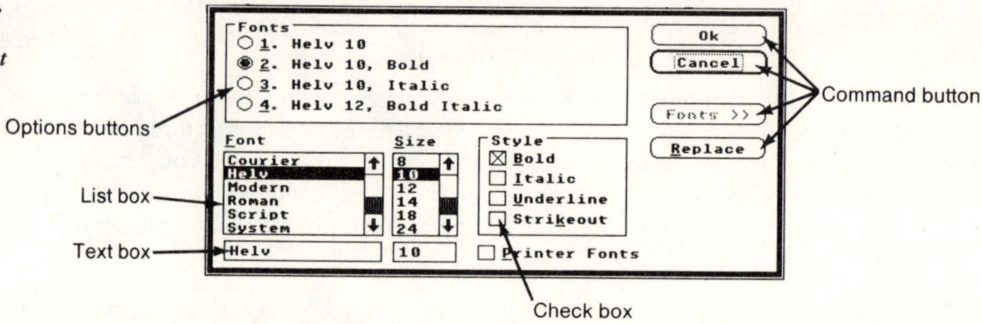

Options buttons

List box

Text box

Command button

Check box

A dashed line surrounds the active item or group of options in a dialog box. For example, in figure 3.9, the Cancel button is active.

You can cycle through different parts of the dialog box by pressing Tab. Each time you press Tab, the dashed line moves in a clockwise direction to the next part. Pressing Shift+Tab moves the dashed line in a counter-clockwise direction.

The dashed line indicates which part of a dialog box can be changed by using the space bar or arrow keys.

Turn an active check box on or off by pressing the space bar. Move between active options buttons with the arrow keys.

Select the active or bold command button by pressing Enter.

You can cancel a dialog box without making a choice by selecting the Cancel button or by pressing Esc.

Text Boxes

Text boxes enable you to type information, such as file names and numbers, into a dialog box. You can edit the text within a text box the same way you edit text elsewhere in Excel.

TIP

Do Not Retype an Entire Section of Text

Typing replaces any text that is selected (highlighted) within a text box. Use one of the techniques described here to edit only the portion of a name or text you want to change.

The mouse pointer will appear as an I-beam, as shown in figure 3.10, when it is in a text box. The actual cursor location is indicated by a flashing vertical bar. (You can use the Replace dialog box shown here to search for and replace text or parts of formulas throughout the worksheet.)

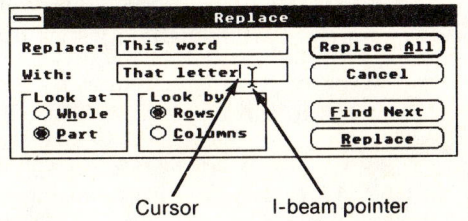

Fig. 3.10. A dialog box with an I-beam pointer indicating that the box is a text box.

Cursor   I-beam pointer

To insert text within a text box, first select the text box by clicking on it. Then position the I-beam by moving the mouse to where you want to insert text, click at the new cursor location and, finally, type the text to be inserted.

To insert text from the keyboard, press Tab until the text box is selected. Then press the left- or right-arrow keys to move the flashing vertical cursor. Type the text to be inserted. You can also select a text box by pressing Alt+*letter* where *letter* is the underlined letter in the name of the text box.

To delete text within a text box, follow these steps:

1. Select the text box.

    Mouse: Click on the text box.

    Keyboard: Press Tab until the text box is selected.

2. Move the cursor next to the text you want deleted.

    Mouse: Reposition the I-beam, and then click at the new cursor location.

    Keyboard: Press the left- or right-arrow keys.

3. Press Del to delete the character on the right of the cursor or press Backspace to delete the character on the left of the cursor.

To replace text or delete multiple characters, follow these steps:

1. Select the text box.

    Mouse: Click on the text box.

    Keyboard: Press Tab until the text box is selected.

2. Select the text you want to replace.

   Mouse: Drag the I-Beam over the text you want to replace. The text will become highlighted just as *mmm* is highlighted in the date format shown in figure 3.11.

   Keyboard: Move the pointer before the first character you want to replace. Then press Shift+right arrow until the text you want replaced is highlighted just as *mmm* is highlighted in figure 3.11.

3. Type the text you want as a replacement, or press Del to delete the selected text.

When the text box is selected, you can use the mouse actions and keys shown in table 3.5 to edit text in the dialog box.

Fig. 3.11. The Format Number box with mmm *selected.*

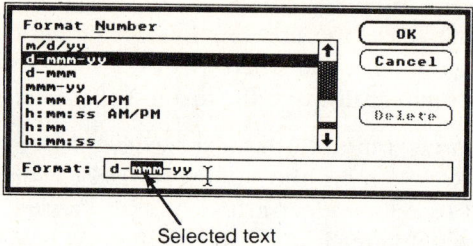

Selected text

Table 3.5
Text Editing Commands

Mouse action	*Result*
Click	Move the flashing cursor to the I-beam (mouse pointer) location
Shift-click	Select text between the flashing cursor's location and the I-beam (mouse pointer) location
Drag	Select all text that the I-beam moves over as you hold down the mouse button
Keyboard action	*Result*
Left arrow	Move the flashing cursor left
Right arrow	Move the flashing cursor right

Keyboard action	Result
Shift+left arrow	Select text as the cursor moves left arrow
Shift+right arrow	Select text as the cursor moves right arrow
Home	Move the cursor before the first character
Shift+Home	Select from the current cursor location to the beginning of the text in the text box
End	Move the cursor after the last character
Shift+End	Select from the current cursor location to the end of the text in the text box

List Boxes

From Excel's list boxes, you can choose file names, functions, formulas, named ranges, and macros. List boxes can save you time and prevent typing errors. Figure 3.12 shows you the **File Open** list box used to select the file to be retrieved.

Text box to select file name or file pattern

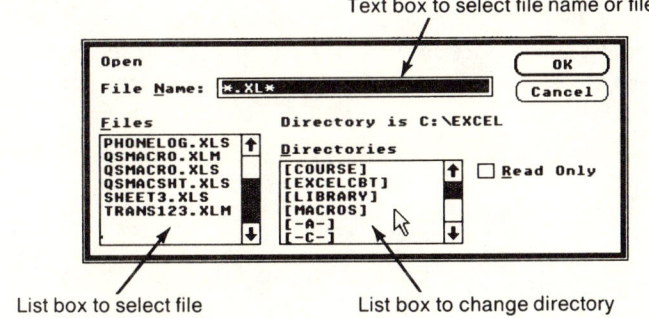

Fig. 3.12. The File Open list box.

List box to select file   List box to change directory

To select a name from a list box, follow these steps:

1. Activate the list box.

   Mouse: Click on the list box.

   Keyboard: Press the Tab key until the list box is activated or press Alt+F.

2. Scroll to the name you want.

   Mouse: Click on the down scroll arrow at the side of the list box and hold down the mouse button.

Keyboard: Press the up arrow, down arrow, Home key, End key, or first letter of the name.

3. Select the name.

   Mouse: Click on the name so that it is highlighted.

   Keyboard: Continue scrolling until the name is highlighted.

4. Select more options in the dialog box if necessary.

5. Choose Cancel to cancel, or choose OK to execute the command.

   Mouse: Click in the OK button to execute the command or click in the Cancel button to cancel.

   Keyboard: Press Enter to choose the OK button when it is bold. Press Esc to choose the Cancel button. Press Alt+*letter* to select any other button.

In most dialog boxes, you can double click on a name in a list box to simultaneously select the name and choose the OK button.

NOTE

Be Sure To Select the Name You Want

Make sure that the name you want to select from the list box is highlighted and not just surrounded by a dashed line before you select a command button such as OK. When you press the Tab key, dashes may surround a name, but the name may not be highlighted.

TIP

Saving Time in List Boxes

When you use the keyboard, you can find names quickly in a list box because they appear in alphabetical order. Press the first letter of the name you are searching for, and the list will scroll to the first name beginning with that letter. You also can scroll with the up- and down-arrow keys or the PgUp and PgDn keys.

Option Buttons and Check Boxes

Excel commands often have a large number of associated options that appear in dialog boxes. The round option buttons allow you to make only one choice from a number of alternatives. The square check boxes let you check off as many features as you need; your result will be a combination of the features you checked. Refer back to figure 3.9, the Format Font dialog box. It contains a number of option buttons and check boxes.

To change an option button with the mouse, click on the button you want. Remember, only one button in a group can be selected.

To change an option button from the keyboard, press and hold the Alt key and then press the underlined letter or number of the option you want, or press Tab until an option in the group is enclosed by dashed lines. Then press the arrow keys to select the option you want to change within that group.

Check boxes are square boxes assigned to a feature such as bold or underline. Unlike option buttons, you can have more than one check box in a group turned on. A check box is on when an X appears in the box.

To select or unselect a check box, click on the check box you want changed. From the keyboard, press Alt+*letter* where *letter* is the underlined letter in the name of the check box.

If you are making a succession of changes in a dialog box, you may find that pressing the Tab key is the easiest way to move between parts of the dialog box. Each press of the Tab key moves to a different part of the dialog box. You can tell which part of the dialog box is active because of the enclosing dashed line. When you have activated a group of option buttons, move the selection between them by pressing the arrow keys. When a check box is enclosed by the dashed line, you can turn the box on or off by pressing the space bar.

Command Buttons

Command buttons usually appear at the upper right corner of dialog boxes and enable you either to execute or cancel the command. Occasionally, as you can see in figure 3.9, command buttons let you expand a dialog box or display an additional box. For example, choosing the Format Font command displays only the upper portion of the dialog box in figure 3.9. Choosing the Fonts>> command button expands the box to appear as shown.

The upper right corner of the dialog box in figure 3.9 contains the command buttons OK, Cancel, Fonts, and **R**eplace. OK will always execute the command and put away the dialog box. Cancel removes the dialog box without executing the command.

Notice that the **F**onts button appears gray to show that it is not currently available for selection. A command that appears gray is not available.

With the mouse, you can choose a command button by clicking on it. From the keyboard, you can choose a command button using a couple of methods. If the command button contains an underlined letter, for example, **R**eplace, then choose the button by pressing Alt+R (holding down the Alt key as you press R). Choose OK when it is bold by pressing Enter. Choose Cancel by pressing Esc. You can select any command button by pressing Tab until the button name is enclosed in dashed lines and then pressing Enter.

From Here . . .

You should work through the "Windows Quick Start" (Chapter 2) if you have not already done so, even if you are familiar with Windows. In addition, review the shortcut keys that are listed in tables throughout this Chapter.

After this Chapter, you should go through the "Worksheet Quick Start" (Chapter 4). It will take you step-by-step through a small practice worksheet. If you are already familiar with Lotus 1-2-3, you should first read about Excel's improvements and differences from Lotus 1-2-3 in Chapter 30, "Making the Switch from 1-2-3 to Excel."

Skim through the worksheet chapters and look for examples of work you might want to do in Excel. Experiment with a few small test worksheets and basic features such as formatting and editing before you attempt to build a large worksheet. Follow the worksheet design steps in Chapter 5, "Designing Worksheets," as you build your first worksheets.

Part II

Excel Worksheets

The worksheet is the heart of Excel. It is like a giant sheet of columnar paper almost 11 feet wide and 340 feet tall on which you can place text, numbers, and formulas. What makes the worksheet indispensable to business is that when you change a number, all formulas that depend on that number automatically recalculate their results. In your work this automatic recalculation means that budgets, forecasts, cost estimates, and other number-intensive jobs suddenly become easier and more accurate. Jobs that you used to have to calculate each time from scratch now only need to be calculated once. Changes to a job can be recalculated by just entering the changed number. Excel does all the recalculation.

What you learn in the first five chapters of Part II is a foundation for your later work with Excel. For example, entering and editing data is the same for a worksheet as for a database or macro. And editing a formula in the worksheet is the same as editing a series formula in a chart.

The 10 chapters in this Part comprise the foundation of the worksheet. Chapters are segmented as functional topics except for the Quick Start and the last chapter, which discusses troubleshooting.

The Worksheet Quick Start in Chapter 4 is a good place to start this section because it gives you a quick hands-on overview of the features and commands discussed in detail in the rest of the chapters. The Quick Start guides you through exercises that build a forecasting worksheet. You get a quick look and feel at how Excel operates. When you finish the Quick Start, you can read sections of the following chapters to learn specific features or commands in detail.

Other chapters in Part II provide in-depth discussions about designing and operating worksheets, entering and editing worksheet data, formatting worksheets, using functions in worksheets, and printing worksheets. There are chapters on using multiple windows and linking worksheets and building advanced worksheets. Finally, a chapter on troubleshooting worksheets provides help when you run into problems.

Chapter 4
Worksheet Quick Start

Chapter 5
Designing Worksheets

Chapter 6
Operating Worksheets

Chapter 7
Entering and Editing Worksheet Data

Chapter 8
Formatting Worksheets

Chapter 9
Using Functions in Worksheets

Chapter 10
Using Multiple Windows
and Linking Worksheets

Chapter 11
Building Advanced Worksheets

Chapter 12
Printing Worksheets

Chapter 13
Troubleshooting Worksheets

4

Worksheet Quick Start

Whether you are new to electronic worksheets or you want to learn some of Excel's advantages over the worksheet you currently use, you will find the Quick Start for worksheets a good introduction to Excel. Even if you are experienced with other worksheets, you should work through this Quick Start. You may discover some new features and shortcuts available in Excel.

This Quick Start should take about 45 minutes to complete and will give you enough information to begin building simple worksheets on your own. Because you may not have enough time to work through the entire Quick Start at one sitting, a midway break is included. Before the break, the text tells you how to save your work so that at a later time you can start from where you left off.

As you complete this Quick Start, write down the questions you have. The Quick Start teaches only the fundamentals. Your questions about Excel's many features, functions, and shortcuts will be answered in other chapters in this section of the book.

After you have completed the Quick Start, take a few minutes to skim through the other worksheet chapters. The Notes, Tips, and 1-2-3 Tips will show you where to find the answers to many of your questions. Later, when you begin to build your own worksheets, you will be able to find the information you need in the worksheet chapters. To find the exact information you need, look for the subject listing in the index.

Creating a Forecasting Worksheet

All companies need some type of forecast no matter how small they are. Suppose that you are the president of a company called the Generic Quality Corporation. GenQ is a small company with accounts that have only three expense items and a single source of revenue. You have determined that you need a forecast worksheet for entering this year's sales and calculating the estimated sales for the next four years. The three cost and expense items will be entered as a percentage of each year's sales.

After a few experiments and some pencil sketches, you realize that you need to create a worksheet that looks like the one shown in figures 4.1 and 4.2. The upper rows of the worksheet, in figure 4.1, show the calculated results of the forecast while the lower rows, in figure 4.2, contain an area to enter assumptions and data. When you change the assumption numbers and data in figure 4.2, you immediately will see the recalculated results in figure 4.1.

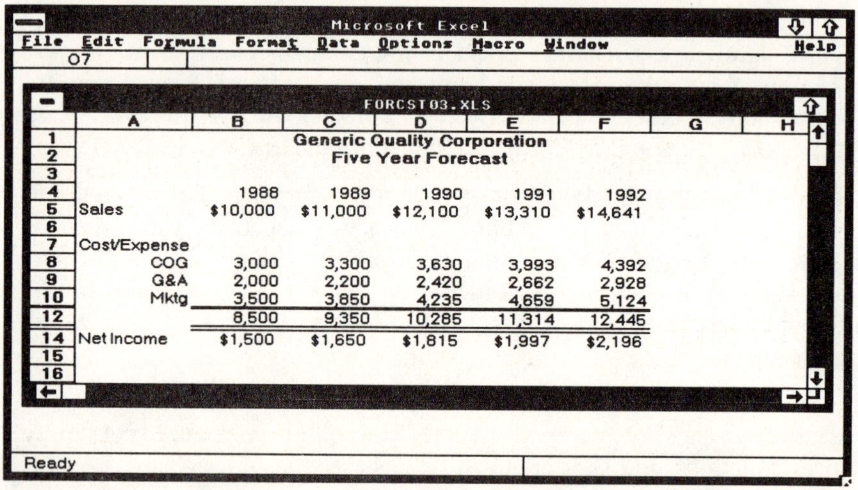

Fig. 4.1. The forecast portion of the worksheet.

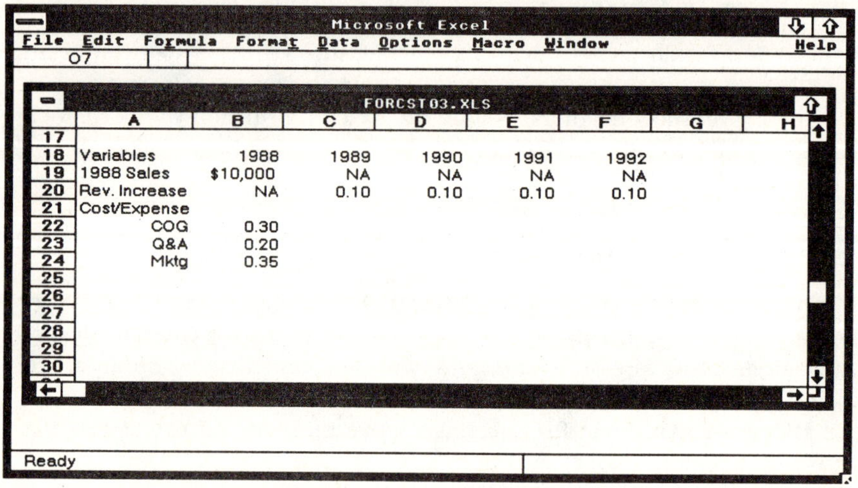

Fig. 4.2. The assumptions and data entry portion of the worksheet.

Note: If you haven't yet started Excel, do so before you continue. For instructions on starting the program, see Chapter 2, "Windows Quick Start."

The Blank Worksheet

Excel opens with a blank worksheet titled Sheet1. Sheet1 appears in its own document window. Figure 4.3 points out important parts of the Excel and document window.

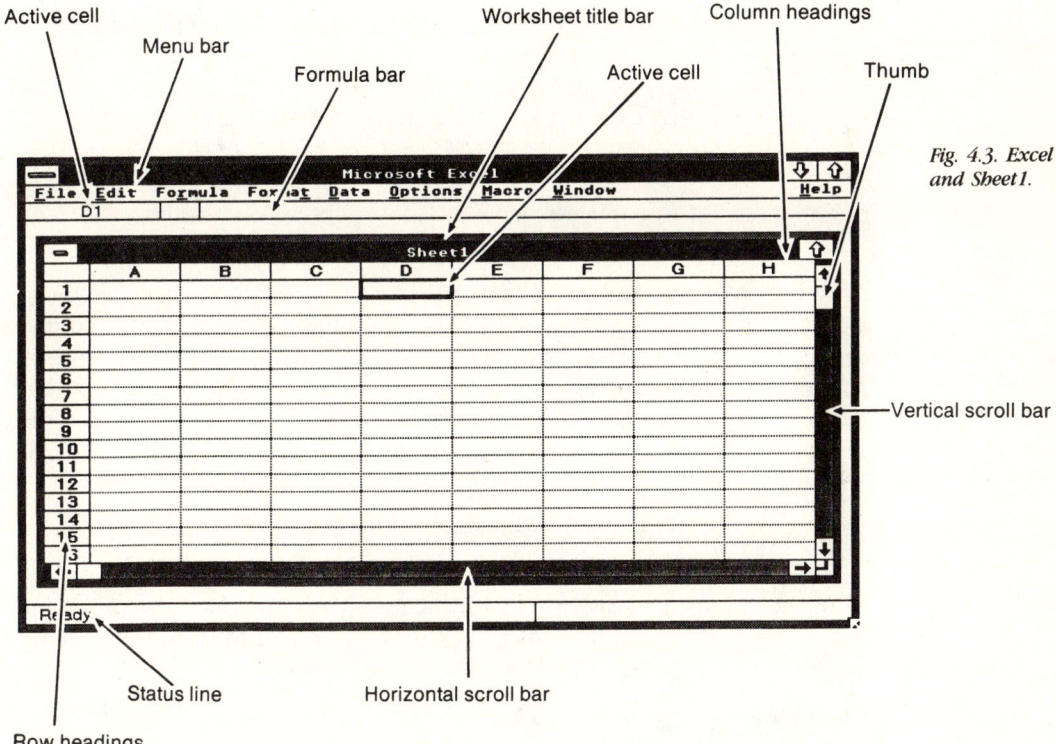

Fig. 4.3. Excel and Sheet1.

The worksheet contains 256 columns with alphabetic headings and 16,384 numbered rows. Each intersection of row and column is a unique *cell* that can be referenced by its row and column, for example, cell D1. (Excel also can display worksheets in the R1C1 style cell reference, if you prefer; that style is explained in Chapter 6, "Operating Worksheets.") In each cell, you can type a number, text, or a formula.

Moving Around in the Worksheet

In figure 4.3, cell D1 is the *active cell*. The active cell has a border around it. You can change this cell with a menu command, or you can enter data into it.

From the keyboard, you can activate a different cell by pressing the arrow keys or by pressing the PgUp or PgDn key. To activate cells that are an entire screen to the left or right, press Ctrl+PgDn or Ctrl+PgUp.

To move your view without moving the active cell, press the Scroll Lock key, and then press an arrow key. Press Scroll Lock again when you want to move the active cell.

> **TIP**
>
> ### Activating Cell A1
>
> When you want to move the active cell to A1, press Ctrl+Home.

With a mouse, you activate a different cell by clicking once on it. If the cell is not visible, move the window by clicking on the scroll bar arrowhead that points in the direction you want to move. You can click in the scroll bar itself to move a page at a time, or drag the white box (thumb) in the scroll bar for large moves. After you have moved the window so that you can see the cell you want, click once on the cell to activate it.

Building a Text Skeleton

Worksheets are much easier to build when you have a text skeleton or outline as a guide. This part of the Quick Start shows you how to build the skeleton for the Generic Quality Corporation's forecast worksheet.

The following steps show you how to build a text skeleton that serves as a map for entering data and formulas. Building a text skeleton helps organize your work. You build a text skeleton by moving the active cell to the cell you want to enter text in. After typing and entering text, you can widen columns as necessary to display text. Text and numbers can then be aligned to the left, right, or center so that the text skeleton is easier to read. Because the text skeleton is just used as a guide during building, you can wait until later to enhance the worksheet by changing character fonts, using characters in color, changing row height, and so on.

TIP

Learning To Use Any Windows Application

All Windows applications use the same convention for making changes. The steps in any Windows application are

1. Select the text, cell, or graphic item to be changed.

2. Choose the command or press the shortcut key to make the change.

Text and cells display in reverse when selected. Graphic items show small rectangular "handles" at the edges when selected.

Commands that need additional information display a dialog box, in which you can choose options or enter more information.

In most cases the selected text, cells, or graphic item remains selected after step 2. This makes it easy to immediately execute another command to affect the same selected items.

Selecting Cells and Entering Text

Before you can enter data into a cell or change a cell with a command, you must select the cell or cells. Follow these steps to select cells for the text entries in your sample worksheet:

1. Select cell A1.

   Mouse: Click on the scroll bar arrowheads until you have moved the window so that cell A1 is visible. Then click on cell A1 to make it active.

   Keyboard: Press Ctrl+Home to make A1 active. (Be sure to hold down the Ctrl key as you press Home, and then release both keys.)

2. Select cell D1.

   Mouse: Click on cell D1.

   Keyboard: Press the right-arrow key to move the active cell to D1.

   Notice in figure 4.3 that the active cell D1 appears to the left of the formula bar.

3. Type the title: **Generic Quality Corporation**. Your typing should appear in the formula bar, as shown in figure 4.4.

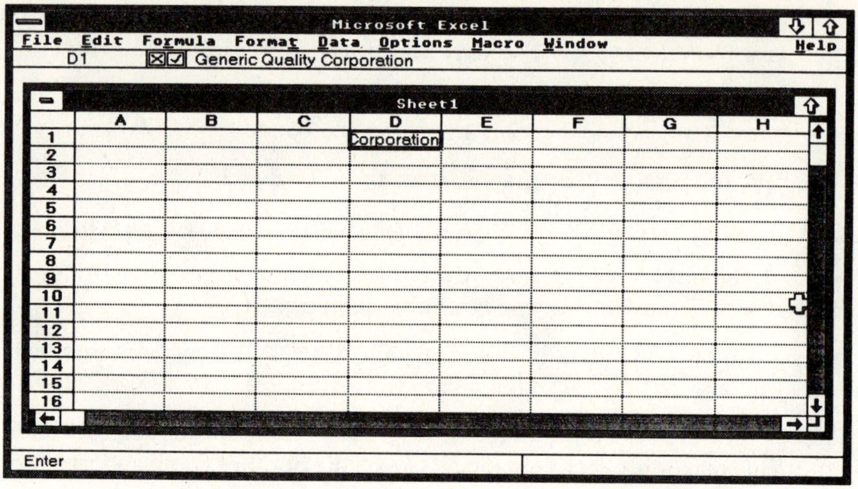

Fig. 4.4. The worksheet title displayed in the formula bar.

4. Enter the title in cell D1.

   Mouse: Click on the check mark at the left of the formula bar. (Note: Clicking on the X cancels your typing.)

   Keyboard: Press Enter. (Note: Pressing Esc cancels your typing.)

5. Select D2 and enter the title **Five Year Forecast**. Then select D1 again.

6. Select both cells D1 and D2 so that the worksheet looks like figure 4.5.

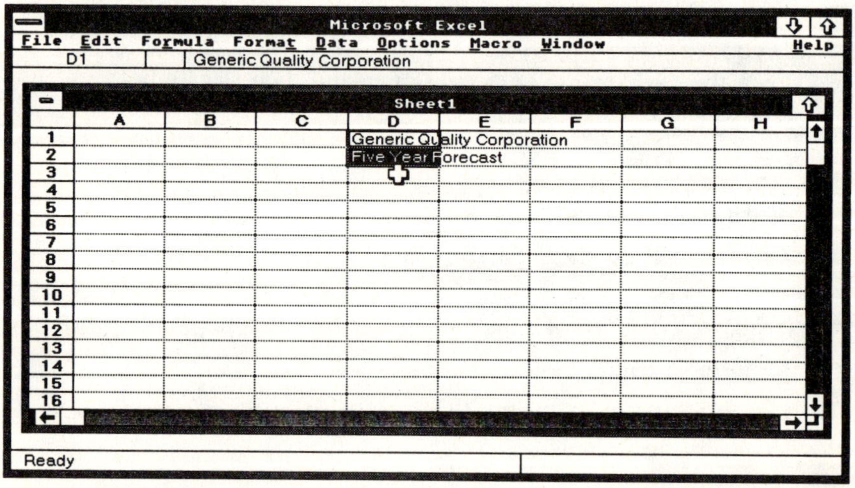

Fig. 4.5. Cells D1 and D2 selected.

Mouse: First click on cell D1. Then hold down the left mouse button and drag the mouse pointer from D1 to D2 so that both cells are highlighted. Release the mouse button.

Keyboard: Press Shift+down arrow to highlight both cells. Note: Holding down the Shift key as you move the active cell selects multiple cells.

Notice that cell D1 is still active, but cell D2 is also selected. To unselect multiple cells, select a single cell outside the highlighted area by clicking or pressing an arrow key by itself.

NOTE

Selecting Multiple Cells

If you hold down the mouse button as you move the pointer, you will select multiple cells. To return to a single active cell, click once on a single cell.

Although multiple cells may be selected, only the active cell (the cell with the heavy border) receives entered data. However, all selected cells are affected by a command such as **Edit Copy** or **Format Number**.

TIP

Erasing Cell Contents

If you make a mistake or enter something incorrectly during the Quick Start, do not worry. You can erase a cell's format or contents easily. Select the cell(s) you want to erase, and then press Del. A dialog box appears with option buttons from which you can select the type of items you want erased. Press the arrow keys to select among option buttons, and then press Enter.

Changing Text Style and Alignment

You now can use the following steps to change the text alignments and style of the selected cells D1 and D2 at the same time:

1. Select the Format menu.

   Mouse: Click on Format in the menu bar.

   Keyboard: Press Alt, release it, and then press T (the underlined letter in the Format option).

The Format menu shown in figure 4.6 appears underneath Format. Notice that an ellipsis (. . .) follows the Font command on the menu. This indicates that the command produces a dialog box requesting more information.

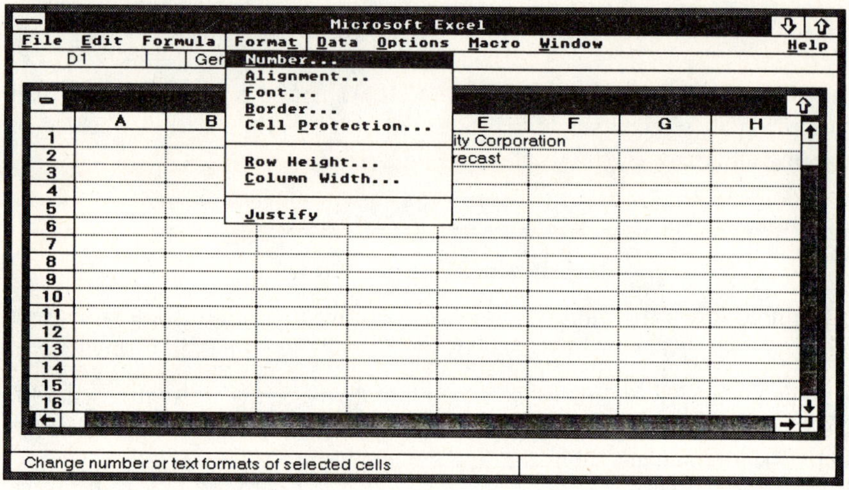

Fig. 4.6. The Format menu.

2. Select **Alignment**.

   Mouse: Click on the Alignment command.

   Keyboard: Press A for the Alignment option.

   The Alignment dialog box appears, displaying an option button for each type of text alignment in a cell (see fig. 4.7).

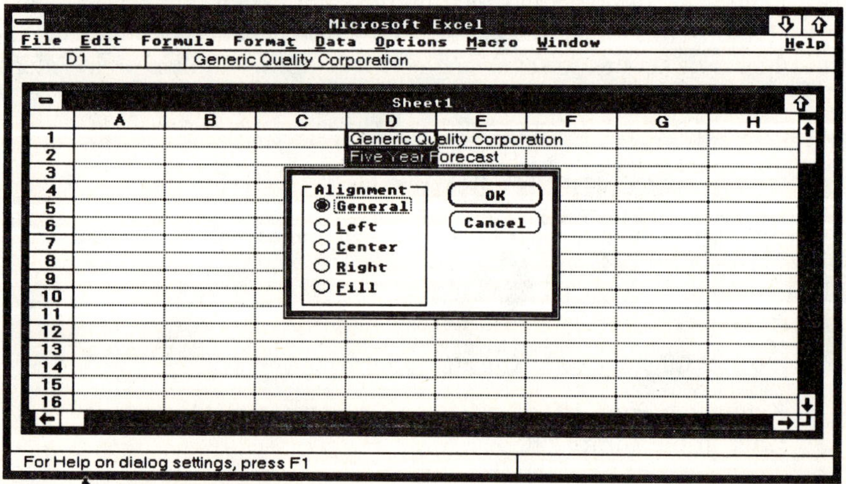

Fig. 4.7. The Alignment dialog box.

3. Select **Center.**

   Mouse: Click on the Center button, and then click on the OK button.

   Keyboard: Press Alt+C to select **Center,** the button with a title containing an underlined C. Press Enter to choose OK, the command button encircled in bold. (Note: OK is not always the bold button.) As an alternative, press Tab until OK is enclosed in dashes, and then press the space bar.

Both titles center on column D the cells containing the text. This type of centering is different than in Lotus 1-2-3, which does not allow centering of text wider than a column's width.

To Choose and To Select

The word *select* means to display a menu or highlight a cell or group of cells. The word *choose* means to specify the appropriate menu and then issue the command from the menu.

Because both cells remain selected, you can continue to choose commands to change the appearance of the text. Follow these steps to change the two headings you have entered to boldface type:

1. Choose the Format Font command.

   Mouse: Click on Format, and then click on Font.

   Keyboard: Press Alt and then T to open the Format menu, and then press F to choose the Font command.

   Figure 4.8 shows the Fonts dialog box.

2. Select option 2 (Helv 10, Bold) to display the text in cells D1 and D2 in the 10-point Helvetica bold font.

   Mouse: Click on option button **2.**

   Keyboard: Press Alt+2.

3. Choose OK or press Enter.

   Complete the text skeleton as shown in figures 4.9 and 4.10. To enter the text, move the active cell in turn to each cell location that has an entry in the figures, type the entry, and then press Enter.

Fig. 4.8. The Fonts dialog box with the first option button selected.

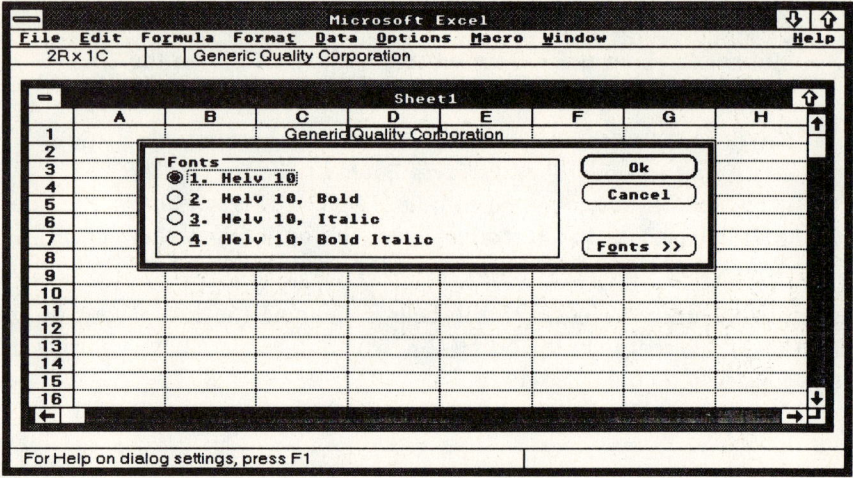

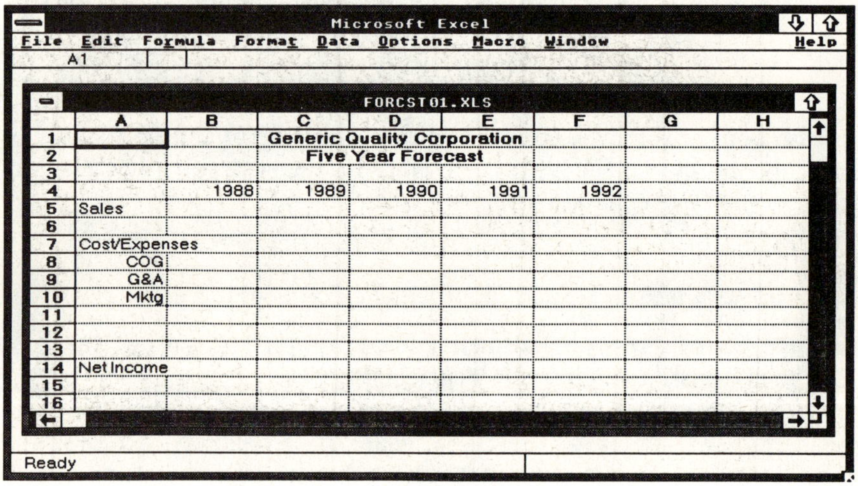

Fig. 4.9. The top half of the text skeleton before formatting column A.

Type the complete entry cell A20 as **Rev. Increase**, although you can't see the full text in figure 4.10. Then type **NA** in cell B20. Notice how the contents of cell B20 overlap the contents of cell A20. (Column A will be widened later to display the full text in cell A20.)

Note that NAs (Not Applicable) must be typed into the cells. Also, *do not* put spaces in front of the entries COG, G&A, or Mktg. Type the years as numbers. They do not have to be preceded by an apostrophe as in Lotus 1-2-3.

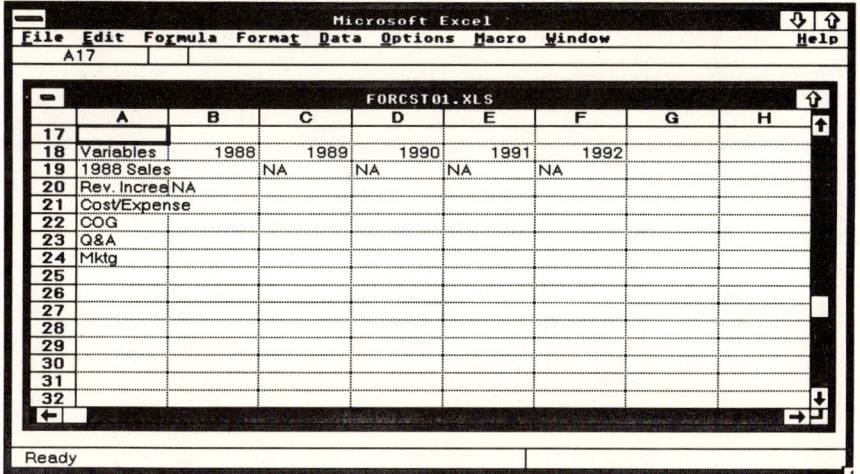

Fig. 4.10. The bottom half of the text skeleton before formatting column A.

If you make a mistake while typing you can press the Backspace key to remove characters if you have not yet entered the mistake in the cell. If you have entered a mistake in a cell, select the cell and enter the correction over the top. (Editing is covered in Chapter 7, "Entering and Editing Worksheet Data.")

Widening a Column

After entering the text, you probably noticed that some of the text is wider than the default column width. To widen column A, follow these steps:

1. Select any cell in column A, and then choose the Format Column Width command.

   In the dialog box that appears, notice that the text box is completely selected (highlighted). This means a number you type will replace the selected number.

2. Type **13** into the column width text box, and then choose the OK button or press Enter.

After column A is widened, you can see that Excel normally aligns text against the left edge of the column. (Numbers and dates align against the right edge.) In Chapter 8, "Formatting Worksheets," you will learn a much faster method of widening columns with the mouse.

Aligning Items in a Column

To make the worksheet more clear, you can align the three expense items—COG, G&A, and Mktg—against the right column edge. To do so, follow these steps:

1. Select the range A8:A10.

   Mouse: Drag the mouse pointer from A8 to A10, and then release the mouse button.

   Keyboard: Select A8 by pressing arrows keys until it is active. Then press Shift+down arrow twice to select A9 and A10 while A8 remains active.

2. Choose the Format **Alignment** command.

   Mouse: Click on Format and then click on **Alignment**.

   Keyboard: Press Alt and then T to open the Format menu, and then press A to choose the **Alignment** command.

3. Select the **Right** option.

   Mouse: Click on the **Right** option button.

   Keyboard: Press Alt+R.

4. Choose the OK button or press Enter.

   Figure 4.11 shows the three selected cells after being right aligned.

Fig. 4.11.
Selected cells
A8:A10 after
aligning text to
the right.

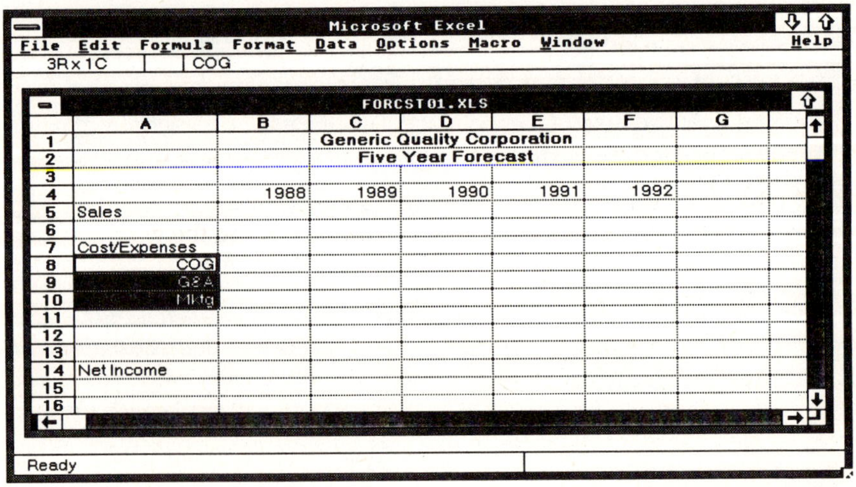

5. Use the procedure given in Steps 1–4 to align the cells in A22:A24 and all of the NAs at the right edge.

NOTE

Excel Colons

Notice that the colon (:) is used throughout Excel and this book to indicate a rectangle of selected cells. The cell address preceding the colon marks the first corner of the rectangle; the cell address after the colon marks the opposite corner.

Saving Your Worksheet

After you have completed this amount of work, you might begin to worry about possible power failures, or maybe you just want to take a break. Before you continue working or get up from the computer, you should take a moment to save your worksheet. Saving temporary versions of your worksheets as you build them is always a good practice. Give each version a unique name so that you can return to it at a later date. To save your partially completed worksheet, follow these steps:

1. Choose the **File** **Save As** command.

   Mouse: Click on **File**, then click on Save **As**.

   Keyboard: Press Alt and then **F** to open the **File** menu; and then press A to choose the Save **As** command.

2. Type the name **FORCST01** (it will replace the name Sheet1 in the text box).

3. Choose the OK button or press Enter.

Notice that the worksheet name in the title bar has changed from Sheet1 to FORCST01.XLS, the name you specified.

Now you can take a break and know that you will not lose the work you have completed. When you return, you can continue the Quick Start at the "Entering Simple Data" section.

If you decide to exit Excel at this point, you can follow the instructions for exiting provided at the end of this Quick Start. In that case, when you return to the Quick Start, you will need to start Excel again and begin with the next topic on opening saved worksheets.

Opening Your Saved Worksheet

After starting Excel, you can reopen worksheets that you previously saved. If you saved the FORCST01 worksheet and exited Excel, you can reopen the worksheet with the following steps:

1. Choose the **File Open** command to display the **Open** dialog box (see fig. 4.12).

```
 Open
 File Name:  [*.XL*                      ]          (  OK  )
                                                    ( Cancel )
 Files              Directory is C:\EXCEL
 FORCST01.XLS  ↑    Directories
 PHONELOG.XLS
 QSMACRO.XLM        [..]          ↑    ☐ Read Only
 QSMACRO.XLS        [BUSINESS]
 QSMACSHT.XLS       [COURSE]
 SHEET3.XLS         [EXCELCBT]
 TEST.XLS           [LIBRARY]
 TRANS123.XLM  ↓    [MACROS]     ↓
```

2. Select the list files box.

   Mouse: Click inside the box at the lower left containing file names.

   Keyboard: Press Tab until a name in the box is enclosed with dashes.

3. Select the file name FORCST01.XLS.

   Mouse: Click on the file name FORCST01.XLS. If you need to scroll through the files, click on the arrows at the side of the box.

   Keyboard: Press the down arrow until FORCST01.XLS is highlighted.

4. Choose the OK button or press Enter.

Entering Simple Data

You now have a text skeleton that makes seeing where to enter data and formulas easier. Entering simple data before entering formulas helps you see which cell contains the value needed in a formula and produces an immediate result when you enter a new formula. This approach can help pinpoint errors when a formula you have just entered results in an obviously wrong answer. If you had not entered simple, sample data, you would not have recognized the unreasonable result.

Excel automatically formats cells for dates, currency, and percentages if the first number entered in the cell contains an acceptable Excel format. Follow these steps to begin entering data:

1. Select B19.

2. Type **$10,000** and press Enter.

Notice that Excel accepts the number and retains the currency format with no decimal places. Only the number without formatting appears in the formula bar.

Enter the rest of the numeric data shown in figure 4.13 with the two sets of steps that follow. To make entering large areas of data easier, Excel has a number of data entry shortcuts. For example, use this shortcut to enter a row of data:

1. Select C20:F20.

   Mouse: Drag from C20 to F20, and then release the mouse button.

   Keyboard: Move the active cell to C20, then press Shift + right arrow to select from C20 to F20.

2. Type **.1** in C20 and press Tab.

3. Type **.1** in each of the following cells, pressing Tab after each entry: D20, E20, and F20.

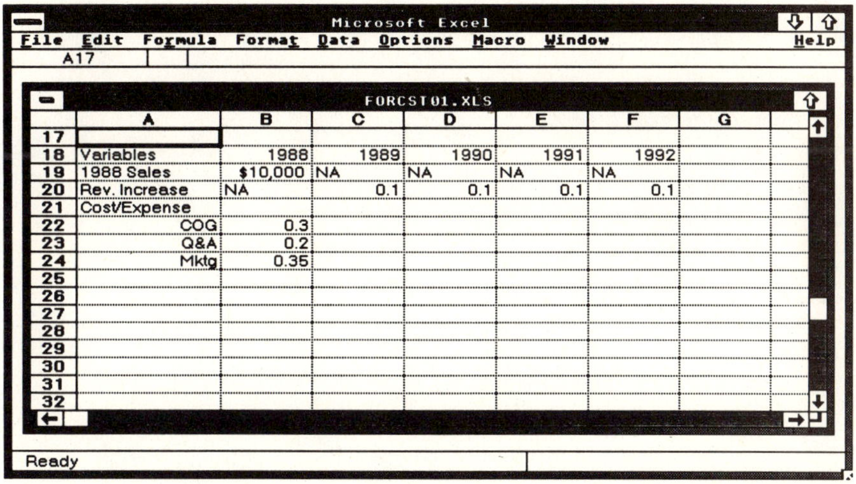

Fig. 4.13. The bottom half of the worksheet with simple sample data entered in rows 19 and 20, and column B.

When you have rows of data to enter, pressing Tab enters what you type in the active cell and moves the active cell one to the right. When the active cell is at the right edge, pressing Tab wraps the active cell back to the beginning of the next line or to the first cell in a range of cells.

When you select a range of cells, pressing Tab enters the data and moves the active cell one column to the right. Pressing Enter enters the data and moves the active cell one row down. When it reaches an edge, the active cell wraps around the selected range of cells.

Use the following steps to enter a column of simple data:

1. Select B22:B24.

2. Type **.3** in B22 and press Enter.

3. Type **.2** in B23 and press Enter.

4. Type **.35** in B24 and press Enter.

The Excel worksheet would look better if the Rev.Increase rate and Cost/Expense percentages appeared with two decimal places. To alter the format in this way, follow these steps:

1. To format the Rev.Increase percentages, select C20:F20.

2. Choose the Format Number command.

   The Format Number dialog box appears showing a text box at the bottom and a list box of prebuilt formats on the left side (see fig. 4.14). In Chapter 8, "Formatting Worksheets," you learn how to create custom number and date formats in the text box.

Fig. 4.14. The Format Number dialog box.

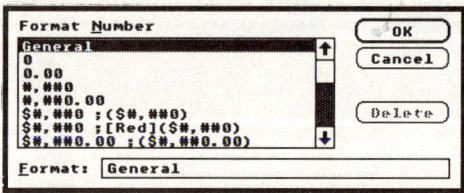

3. Select the 0.00 format.

   Mouse: Click on the 0.00 format in the list.

   Keyboard: Press the down-arrow key until 0.00 is highlighted. (Press the Tab key if the list box is not active with a selected format.)

4. Choose the OK button or press Enter.

The Rev.Increase numbers are reformatted to display two decimals, and the range C20:F20 remains selected.

5. To format the expense percentages, move to B22, select B22:B24, and repeat Steps 2–4.

The simple data portion of your worksheet now should look like figure 4.15.

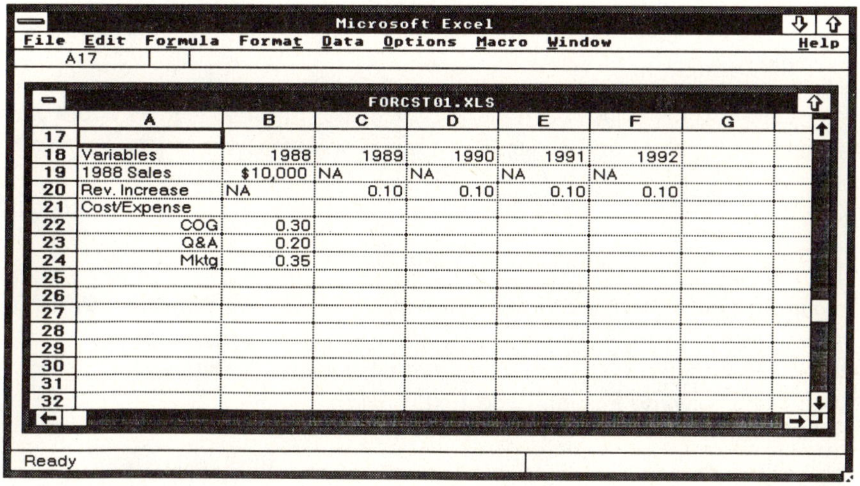

Fig. 4.15. The completed bottom half of the worksheet with text and simple data entered and formatted.

Entering Formulas

The usefulness of electronic worksheets comes from the formulas entered in cells. These formulas produce new answers whenever the data the formula depends upon changes.

Cells may contain simple formulas that refer only to the value stored in another cell, or they may contain complex formulas that include built-in functions, custom functions, and numerous references to data in cells. Formulas begin with an equal sign (=). If you are more familiar with Lotus 1-2-3, you can begin formulas with a plus sign (+).

Entering Formulas by Typing

Because you have built a text skeleton and entered simple sample data it is easy to see which cells need formulas. You will be moving the active cell to the cell where you want to enter a formula; then you will type the formula, and press Enter. As the following steps show, you don't have to type every formula in the worksheet. Excel has a number of methods for copying a formula into other cells.

One way to enter a formula is to type it. Use the following steps to enter a simple formula that copies the value $10,000 from cell B19 to cell B5:

1. Select B5.

2. Type the formula =**B19**

3. Press Enter or click on the check mark immediately to the left of the formula bar.

The number 10000 from B19 will appear in B5. Because cell B5 is not formatted, however, no dollar signs or commas will appear.

NOTE

Errors in Your Formulas

During the Quick Start, if you make mistakes when typing a formula, go ahead and enter the formula. Then reenter the corrected formula on top of the mistake. In Chapter 7, "Entering and Editing Worksheet Data," you will learn how to edit existing formulas and text.

Entering Formulas by Pointing

An alternative to typing a formula is to enter it by "pointing" to the cells you want to reference in the formula. The pointing method reduces typographical errors. The next steps show you how to build a formula by pointing to the cell references involved in the formula.

The formula you will enter in cell C5 takes the value in B5 and adds to it the amount of sales increase according to the percentage in cell C20. The formula you will be entering is =B5+B5*C20.

TIP

Building Formulas the Easier Way

After you have a text skeleton and simple, sample data, formulas built by "pointing" are much less prone to typographical errors. The general rules for building formulas by pointing are,

1. Select the cell or cells to contain the formula.

2. Type an equal sign (=).

3. Point to the first cell address in the formula by pressing arrow keys or clicking.

4. Press the F4 key to change the absolute reference of this address if necessary.

5. If the formula is complete, press Enter.

If the formula continues, type a math operator such as +, -, *, /, (, or). Return to step 3.

Remember, you can't point to the next cell address until you type a math operator.

Follow these steps to enter the formula using the pointing method:

1. Select C5.

2. Type an equal sign (=) to let Excel know that a formula is being entered.

3. Select B5.

   Mouse: Click on cell B5.

   Keyboard: Press the left-arrow key.

   Notice that B5 is now enclosed in a "marquee" of moving dashes, and cell C5 is still the active cell. The B5 cell reference appears in the formula just as though you had typed it (see fig. 4.16).

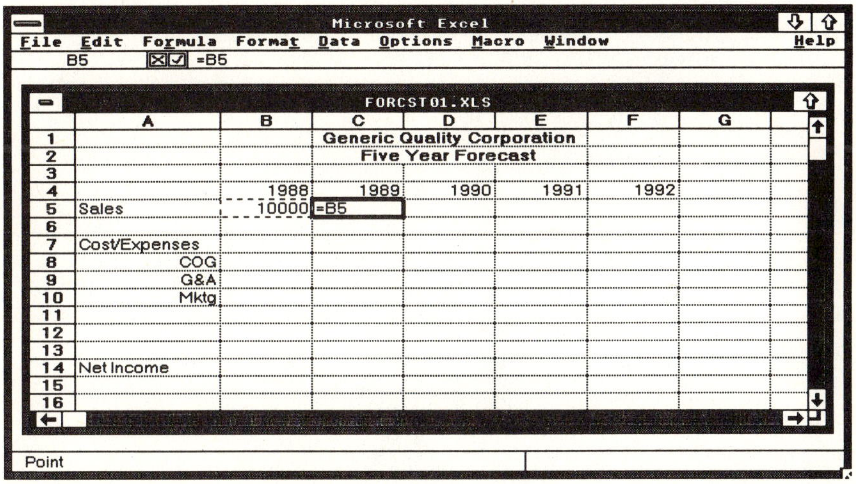

Fig. 4.16. The beginning of a formula entered in cell C5 by pointing.

4. Type the next operator—the plus sign (+).

   The formula now should look like =B5+. Entering a math operator tells Excel to freeze the cell you pointed at (B5) so that you can point to the next cell reference to be included in the formula.

5. Select B5 again by clicking on it or pressing the left arrow, and the formula should look like =B5+B5.

6. Type the multiplication operator (*).

7. Select cell C20 (the last cell reference in the formula).

   Mouse: Click on the down scroll arrow so that you can see cell C20, and then click on C20.

   Keyboard: Press the down-arrow key until you see cell C20, and then select it.

8. If the formula bar displays =B5+B5*C20, enter the formula by pressing Enter or clicking on the check mark immediately to the left of the formula bar. If the formula is not displayed correctly, press Esc or click on the X box, and then rebuild the formula.

You can see that the result of the formula in cell C5 is 11000. That result appears to be correct, because you expected a 10 percent increase over 1988's value of 10000.

Copying and Pasting Formulas

If you had to go through the process of typing or pointing for every formula, building a worksheet would take a long time. Instead, you can use the Copy and Paste functions to duplicate the formula you entered in cell C5 in cells D5, E5, and F5. Follow these steps:

1. Select C5, the cell containing the formula you want to copy.

2. Choose the **Edit** Copy command.

   Notice that the Status line at the bottom of the screen prompts you for the next step. This step stores a copy of the cell's contents in the *clipboard*. The clipboard acts as a temporary storage area for information being moved or copied.

3. Select cells D5:F5, as shown in figure 4.17.

   Mouse: Drag from D5 to F5.

Keyboard: Press the right-arrow key to activate D5. Then hold down the Shift key and press the right-arrow key until cells D5 to F5 are selected.

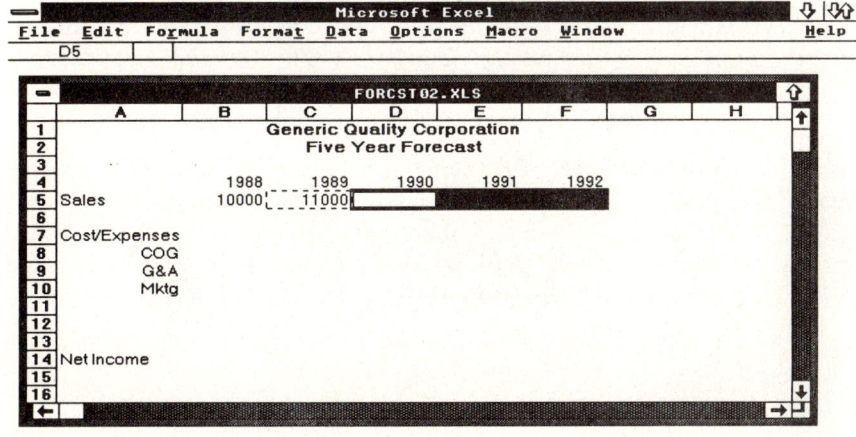

4. Choose the **Edit Paste** command.

The **Edit Paste** command transfers the contents of the clipboard into cells D5 through F5. The marquee around C5 will remain until the next command, next entry, or until you press Esc.

Using Absolute and Relative Cell References

When Excel pastes an existing formula from one cell into a new location, the program also adjusts the cell references in the formula to reflect the formula's new location. Move to each of the formulas in cells C5 through F5 and notice the difference between the original formula and the copies.

Original formula

C5   =B5+B5*C20

Copies

D5   =C5+C5*D20

E5   =D5+D5*E20

F5   =E5+E5*F20

Cell references that adjust to their new location are known as *relative references*. Excel normally enters cells using their relative reference. The formula actually *references* a cell by its *relative* position to the formula.

In some formulas, you will *not* want Excel to change a cell reference when the formula is copied and pasted into a new location. This is the case for the formula in cell B8 for the Cost of Goods (COG): =B5*B22. Copying this formula from B8 and pasting it into C8 results in the adjusted formula =C5*C22; this formula is incorrect because no number exists in cell C22.

Instead, you want the B22 address to stay the same no matter where the formula is copied to. References that stay the same are known as *absolute references*. (The reference stays "absolutely" the same wherever it is copied.) To copy the contents of B22 as an absolute reference, you put a dollar sign in front of the row and column address: $B$22. Use the following Excel shortcut to make an address absolute:

1. Select B8.

2. Use the typing or pointing method to enter the formula =B5*B22. *Do not press Enter.*

3. Press F4 (Absolute Reference) so that B22 appears as $B$22.

    Notice that the flashing cursor in the formula bar is next to B22.

4. Press Enter or click the check mark to enter the formula =B5*$B$22.

The result, 3000, in cell B8 appears reasonable because COG was 30% of the 10000 in first year sales.

Use the previous four steps to enter the formulas in cells B9 and B10:

Cell	Formula	Result
B9	=B5*$B$23	2000
B10	=B5*$B$24	3500

TIP

When To Use Absolute Reference

If you copy a formula, and the copied formulas produce wrong results, then one or more of the addresses in the original need to use an absolute reference.

If the formula you are about to copy contains a reference to an isolated, single cell, then that cell address should probably be an absolute reference.

Summing a Column of Numbers

The sample worksheet needs to display in cell B12 a total of the expenses in cells B8:B10. You could enter a formula in B12, such as =B8+B9+B10, but then additional expense items later inserted into the column would not be included in the total. A much better method for writing this formula uses Excel's SUM function. SUM totals all the values that are within the range of cells you specify. To enter the formula for the total in cell B12, follow these steps:

1. Select B12.

2. Type the formula **=SUM(B8:B11)** and press Enter.

The result, 8500, appears to be the correct total. You also can enter the SUM formula with the pointing method by typing **=SUM(** and then selecting the cells from B8 to B11. When pointing, you still must close the SUM function by typing **)** and pressing Enter.

By including B11 as the bottom of the range of numbers to be summed, it ensures that if a number is inserted below the 3500 in B10, the new number will still be included in the total.

Finish the calculations for column B by inserting in cell B14 a formula that calculates the Net Income. The Net Income is the Sales minus the total Cost/Expenses. Follow these steps to enter the formula:

1. Select B14 by moving the active cell to it or by clicking on it.

2. Type the formula **=B5-B12**.

3. Press Enter or click on the check mark.

Entering Single and Double Underlines

Make your worksheets look more professional by using underlines to set off columns of numbers from their subtotals or totals. Use a solid single line for subtotals and a double line for final totals. Excel creates solid lines for these underlines. If you want to use dashes or equal signs instead, select the Format Alignment Fill option to fill cells with single or double dashes.

The following steps draw borders around a row of cells. When the height of the row is collapsed, the borders become solid lines.

1. Select cell B11.

2. Choose the Format **B**order command to display the Border dialog box (see fig. 4.18).

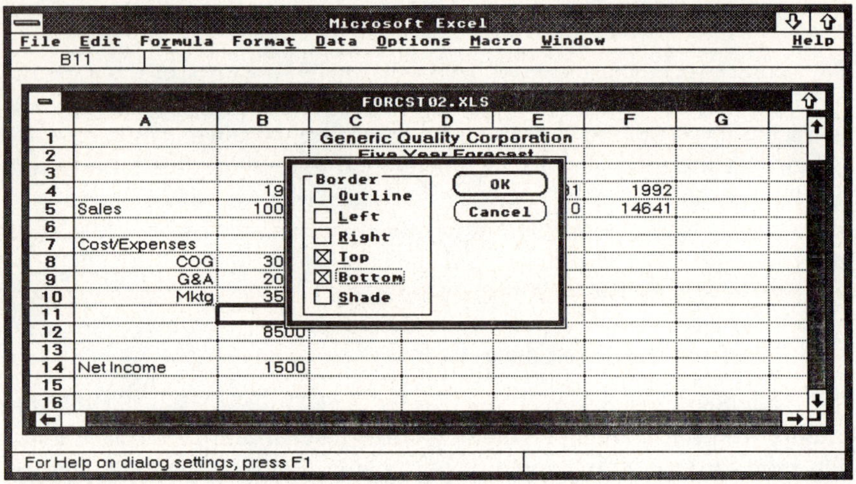

Fig. 4.18. The Border dialog box.

3. Select the **Top** and **Bottom** check boxes.

   Mouse: Click on both check boxes.

   Keyboard: Press Alt+T and then Alt+B.

4. Choose the OK button or press Enter.

5. Choose the Forma**t** **R**ow Height command to change the height of the active cell's row. Cell B11 should still be selected.

6. Type **1** to make the row height 1 point high.

7. Choose OK or press Enter.

8. Move to B13 so that you can see the solid single underline in B11 and prepare for the next underline.

Make cell B13 into a double underline by selecting B13 and repeating the procedure used in the preceding steps. Use a row height of 3 to create a double underline. The result of your nearly completed worksheet appears in figure 4.19.

TIP

Unselecting Check Boxes

You can unselect a check box in a dialog box like the Border dialog box by selecting the check box again. For example, if the **T**op box has an X, then pressing Alt+T or clicking on it will unselect the box.

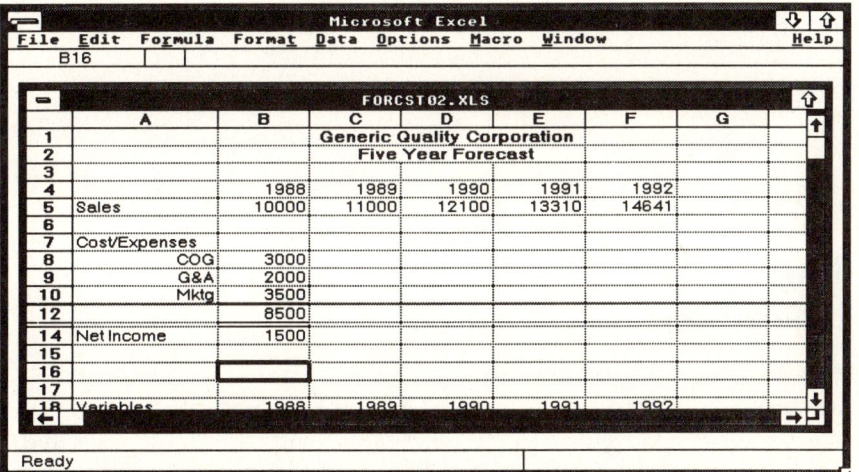

Fig. 4.19. The top half of the worksheet with underlines for totals added.

Formatting Formula Results

You will want to format some of the results of the formulas in your sample worksheet as currency with dollar signs and commas. Other numeric data should be formatted with commas only.

To format cells B5:F5 and cell B14 as currency, follow these steps:

1. Select B5:F5.

2. Choose the Format Number command.

3. Select the $#,##0 ;($#,##0) format from the list box.

   Mouse: Click on the $#,##0 ;($#,##0) format.

   Keyboard: Press the down arrow until you highlight the $#,##0 ;($#,##0) format.

4. Choose OK or press Enter.

5. Repeat the procedure in Steps 1–4 to format cell B14 with a currency format.

Format with commas other cells in the sample worksheet by following these steps:

1. Select B8:B12.

   Mouse: Drag from B8 through B12.

Keyboard: Select B8. Press Shift+down arrow to highlight from B8 through B12.

2. Choose the Format Number command.

3. Select the #,##0 format.

4. Choose the OK button or press Enter.

Filling Adjacent Cells with Formulas and Formats

Besides cutting, copying, and pasting formulas from one cell to another, you also can fill entire areas with formulas and formats from adjacent cells. For example, the cell range B8:B14 has the formulas and formats you want in the range C8:F14. Instead of repeating all the formula entry and formatting steps for each cell, use the following steps to fill the C8:F14 range with the formulas and formats in B8:B14:

1. Select B8:F14 so that the formulas and formats to be copied are on the left edge of the selection as shown in figure 4.20.

   Mouse: Drag from B8 to F14.

   Keyboard: Select B8, and then hold down Shift as you use the arrow keys to move to F14.

Fig. 4.20.
Selected cells
B8:F14 about to
be filled.

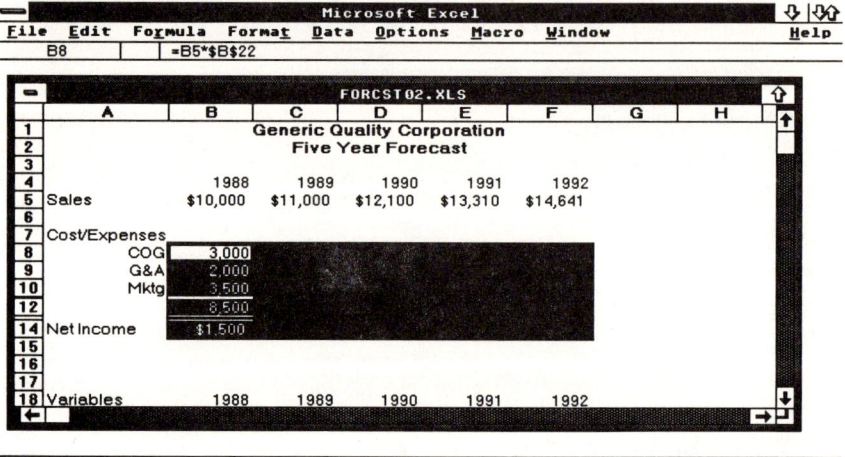

2. Choose the **Edit** **Fill** **Right** command.

3. Press Ctrl+Home to move the active cell to A1 so you can more easily read the formulas.

The formulas and formats from the left column fill the cells in the columns to its right. Later chapters describe how you also can fill columns up, down, and left. You even can use a quick key to fill a selected area as soon as you press Enter.

The upper portion of your worksheet now should look like figure 4.21. All that is left to do is to save the worksheet and cross-check it for errors.

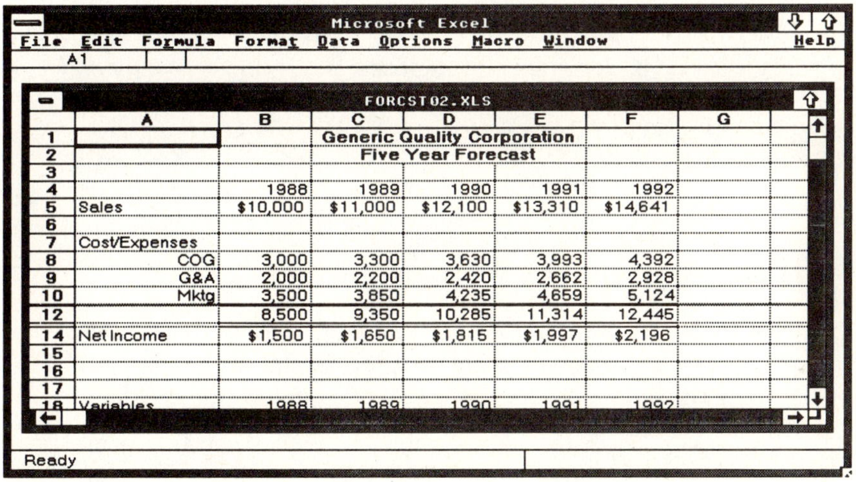

Fig. 4.21. The completed top half of the worksheet.

If you wish to remove the gridlines from the worksheet so that it appears like figure 4.1, then choose the **Options** **Display** command, select the Gridlines check box with Alt+G, then press OK.

Saving and Backing Up Your Worksheet

You must save your work in a magnetic recording on a hard disk or diskette if you want to reuse it later. For important work, you will want to have a working copy on your hard disk and a backup copy on diskette for safety.

Before testing your worksheet, save it. This worksheet is used as a basis for the quick start on charting in Chapter 14. Follow these steps to save the worksheet:

1. Choose the **F**ile Save **A**s command.

2. Type the file name FORCST03.

3. Choose OK or press Enter.

These steps save your worksheet to the hard disk directory shown in the lower left corner of the dialog box. For valuable worksheets, you also will want to complete the following steps to save a copy to diskette:

1. Make sure a formatted diskette is in drive A or B.

2. Choose the **F**ile Save **A**s command.

3. Press Home to use the same file name used during the save to hard disk. The cursor moves to the front of the file name.

4. Type **A:** or **B:** depending on the drive you want to save the file to. The file name now will be displayed as A:FORCST03.XLS or B:FORCST03.XLS.

5. Choose OK or press Enter.

Testing Your Worksheet

Test your worksheet by entering new numbers into the data entry and assumptions area in the lower portion of the worksheet. Notice how Excel immediately recalculates formula results as you enter new data.

Although Excel recalculates fast, extremely large worksheets may take some time. With Excel you can continue doing data entry and making changes as the recalculation continues.

NOTE

Manually Cross-Check Your Worksheets

Never use a worksheet until you have manually cross-checked its results.

Exiting Excel

To exit Excel, follow these steps:

1. Choose the **F**ile E**x**it command.

   If you have made changes to the worksheet since the last time you saved it, an alert box will ask whether you want to save the worksheet (see fig. 4.22).

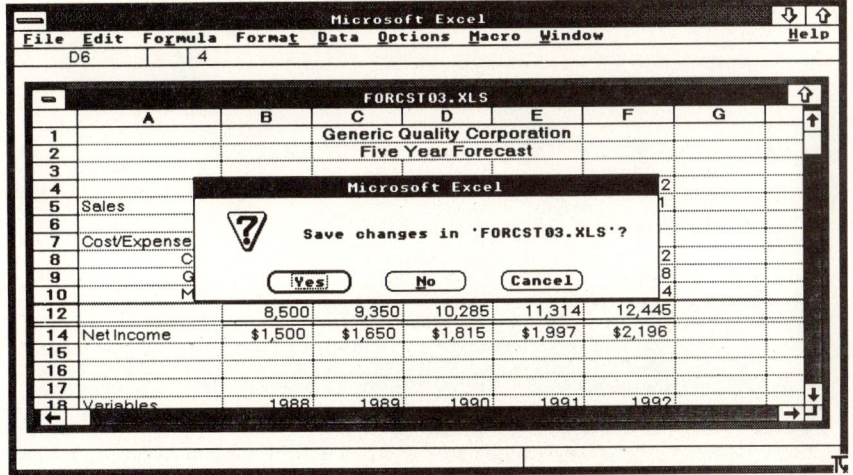

Fig. 4.22. An alert box asking whether you want to save the worksheet before exiting.

2. Choose **Yes** if you want to save the worksheet or **No** if you do not.

3. If you chose **Yes** in Step 2, you will be asked to supply a file name.

If you started Excel with Windows, you will return to the MS-DOS Executive. If you do not have a full Windows application, you will return to the DOS prompt.

From Here . . .

This Quick Start covered only a few of Excel's basic techniques. Excel has many more features and functions, and you can use many more techniques than those demonstrated. You may want to use the worksheet you have built as an experimental tool when reading through other worksheet chapters. When you find an interesting technique or feature, test it on the Generic Quality Corporation forecast worksheet.

5

Designing Worksheets

You have two choices when you start a new worksheet. You can spend a little time planning ahead in the beginning, or you can spend a lot of time repairing and restructuring the worksheet later on. For small, one- or two-screen worksheets, planning and design methods are helpful. For anything larger, planning and building the worksheet in the correct order is essential to save you time and effort. Moreover, planning will increase the flexibility of the system if you need to change it.

The correct worksheet design and construction steps can save you time, increase your alternatives when changing completed worksheets, and reduce the likelihood of errors. Designing a good worksheet involves at least 14 steps:

1. Understand the problem and the desired solution.

2. Make thumbnail sketches.

3. Enter global formats.

4. Build a text skeleton.

5. Adjust and enhance text.

6. Enter simple, sample data.

7. Enter formulas.

8. Check for reasonable results.

9. Format numeric data and results.

10. Cross-check your worksheet.

11. Document the worksheet.

12. Save different versions of the worksheet.

13. Store a backup copy off-site.

14. Run and compare both old and new systems.

1. Understand the problem and the desired solution.

You must understand the problem and the desired solution before starting to create a worksheet. Regardless of whether you are creating a worksheet for yourself or for someone else, you must know precisely what the finished sheet will do and how it will be used.

One way to prevent miscommunication is to create prototype data-entry screens and reports. Use a word processor to create sample data-entry screens and examples of report formats. From these examples, the real users can tell you what changes are needed.

Many questions need to be answered before you design a worksheet. What solution are you seeking? What input do you need in order to find that solution? What is the best design for entering data? How do you want the output to look? Will you or management actually use the output or will it just provide more paper for the office files?

2. Make thumbnail sketches.

Every great artist from Michelangelo and Leonardo da Vinci to Picasso has made thumbnail sketches (small practice exercises) and sample drawings before starting a major work. You will find that thumbnails are helpful when designing worksheets too.

You may want to test smaller versions of your worksheet before attempting to establish a final version. Drawing charts of the work flow and maps of the worksheet layout such as shown in figure 5.1 is also helpful. These flowcharts and maps can pinpoint problems before you have committed yourself to a specific design.

Before laying out a worksheet map, read through the discussions in this book on conserving memory, linking multiple worksheets, and improving performance. Your worksheet map should show blocks that indicate the data entry areas, calculation areas, the database, database extract areas for printed reports, and other major parts of the worksheet.

Keep data entry cells separate from calculation areas. This practice reduces the chance of errors and allows room for instructions and entry-checking formulas. You should try to make the data entry screen appear like a paper form. You will want to keep assumptions, such as growth rates, outside of formulas. To make them easy to change, put assumptions together in one area of the worksheet.

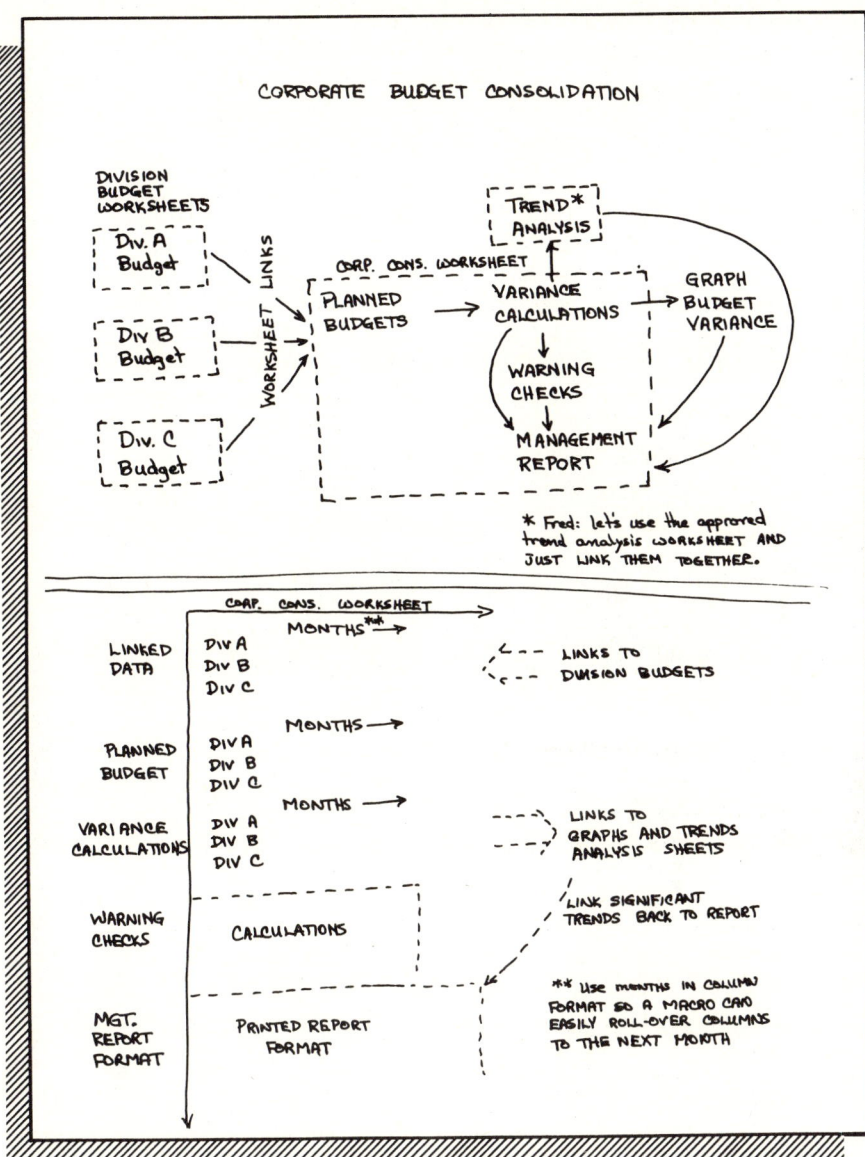

Fig. 5.1. A "thumbnail" sketch for a worksheet map.

3. Enter global formats.

You can save yourself work during worksheet construction if you first format the entire worksheet with the most frequently used numeric format, text alignment, row height, and column width. Select the entire worksheet either by pressing Ctrl+Shift+space bar or by clicking the mouse pointer in the blank heading cell at the upper left corner of the row and column headings. Then use the Format Number, Format Align, and Format Row Height, and Format Column Width commands to change all these settings for the entire worksheet.

4. Build a text skeleton.

One of the easiest ways to design a worksheet is to create a framework on which you can build (see fig. 5.2). Your framework will be the text and labels that show where data will be entered, where formula results will appear, and so on. After you have created the text skeleton, entering data and formulas in the correct locations is easier. Having a text skeleton to show screen locations significantly reduces your chance of entering an incorrect cell address in a formula. If you later decide that you don't like your original layout, Excel's editing commands make moving and copying cell contents easy.

Fig. 5.2. A text skeleton.

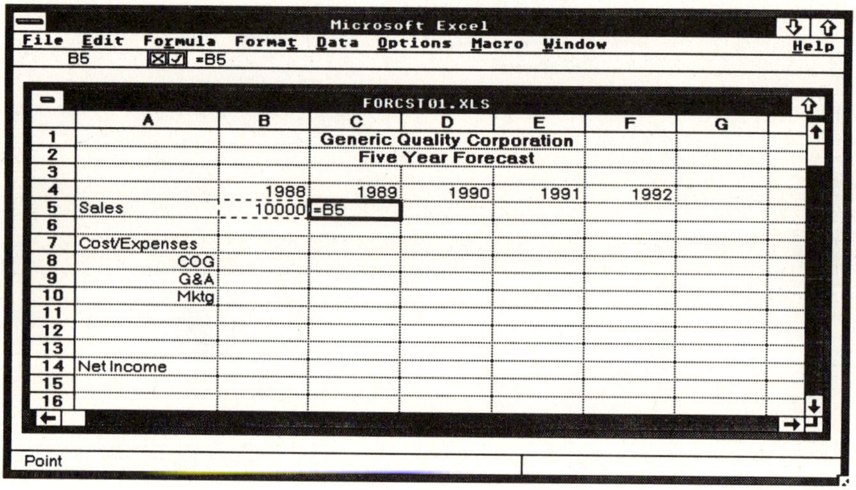

5. Adjust and enhance text.

Use the Format Column Width command to set the width of each column for the text and data in it. Then use the Format Alignment command to align text within the columns or to fill areas. To add emphasis to headings or output, use the other Format menu commands to change borders, text size, and text style.

6. Enter simple, sample data.

After you have a text skeleton, you can see where to enter simple, sample data. Use simple data such as .1 and 200 so that you can immediately recognize whether the results of formulas are correct. Figure 5.3 shows the simple data used to build the worksheet FORCST01. If you enter simple data before entering formulas, you can tell as soon as you enter the formula whether the result is correct. Using simple, sample data increases the odds that you will detect an error. Formulas are also easier to enter after data is entered in cells. The data makes picking the correct cell address much easier. (During step 10, you will replace the simple, sample data with real data.)

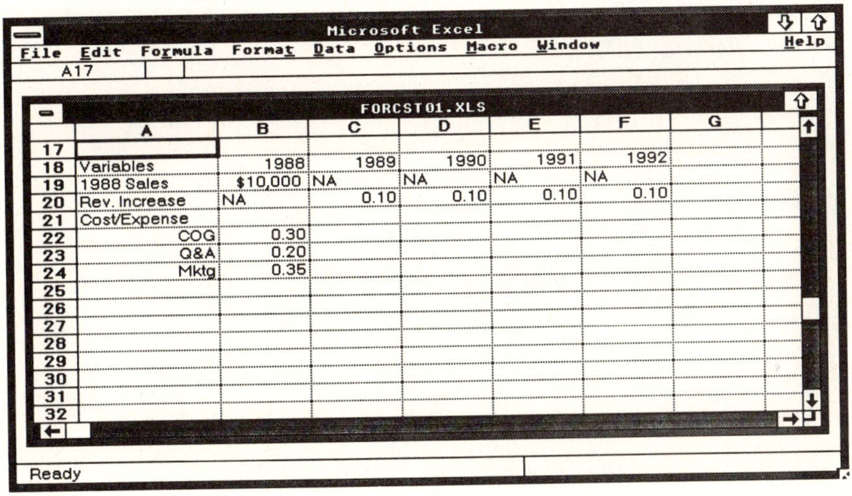

Fig. 5.3. Simple, sample data entered in a worksheet.

7. Enter formulas.

When you enter formulas, start with the simple ones and work toward the more complex formulas that depend on the results of other formulas. Never enter numbers that could change, such as an interest rate, directly in a formula. Enter the number in a cell, then use the cell address in the formula. By keeping variables out of the formulas, you increase the reliability of your worksheet and reduce your work. In this way, you can make changes by typing a new number in one cell rather than editing formulas throughout the worksheet.

8. Check for reasonable results.

Because you enter simple, sample data first, most of your formulas produce a result as soon as you enter them. And because the data is simple, you should be able to judge whether the formula is correct. Ask yourself if the answer seems reasonable.

9. Format numeric data and results.

Use the Format Number command to select the way you want to display numbers in your worksheet. In Excel, you can create custom numeric and date formats. You can save time by selecting all the cells and ranges with the same format and formatting them at once. The selected cells do not need to be adjacent.

Keep in mind that formatting rounds the displayed number but not the number used in Excel's internal calculations. To round a formula result to a specific number of decimal places, use the ROUND function or the Options Calculations command followed by the Precision as Displayed option.

10. Cross-check your worksheet.

Compare the worksheet results against more than one hand-calculated answer from previously solved problems. *Never* trust a new worksheet.

11. Document the worksheet.

Enter a date and version number in the top left corner of a completed worksheet along with the creator's initials and the initials of the audit team. You also may want to write a macro that automatically enters the version number into the page footer when the worksheet is printed.

Use the Formula Note command to attach to cells notes like the one shown in figure 5.4. In these notes, you can explain formulas and assumptions as well as add instructions. Notes can help you and others remember how your worksheet works, why you used certain numbers, or how a formula was derived. Without notes, even you might forget how your own worksheets work. You can print your notes as an aid to further documentation.

12. Save different versions of the worksheet.

To coin a new computer phrase, "There are those who back up their work and those who wished they had backed up their work."

Save copies of your worksheets about every 15 minutes as you build them. Use different version numbers for each one so that you can refer back to previous versions—for example, FORCST12, FORCST13, FORCST14, and so on. You later can erase outdated versions with the File Delete command.

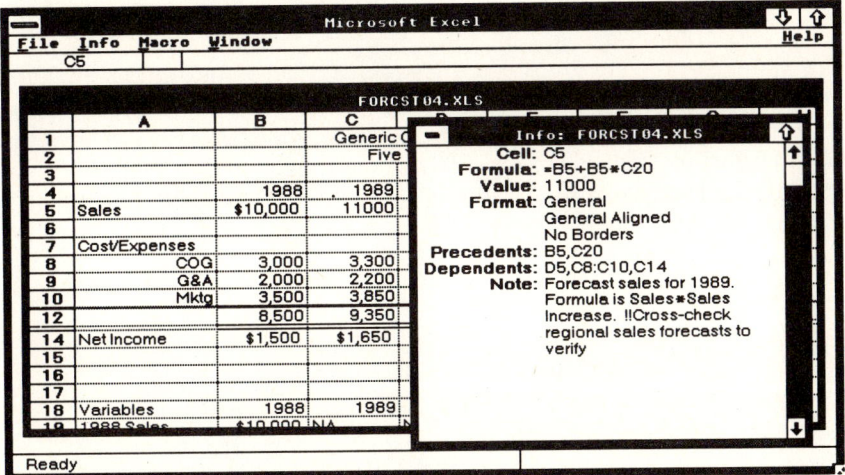

Fig. 5.4. A cell note with documentation.

13. Store a backup copy off-site.

If your worksheets and data are important, store copies of them in physically separate locations. If the building burns or a thief steals the computer and disks, you do not want to lose both your original and backup disks.

14. Run and compare both old and new systems.

Just as editing your own writing is difficult, so is verifying your own worksheets. If the worksheets are critical to your business, operate "parallel" business functions running both worksheet and manual calculations until you are sure that the worksheets work correctly. Some worksheets and their databases are so complex that you won't be able to verify their correctness during the cross-check in step 10. Although doing work twice, once the old way and again with the new Excel system, seems like extra work, it can prevent disaster. In a few rare cases companies have gone bankrupt because they didn't continue manual accounting during the first few months a computerized accounting system was installed.

From Here . . .

This short chapter has given you a few general guidelines toward building worksheets and databases. If you haven't gone through the worksheet tutorial in Chapter 4, please do so. Chapters 6 through 12 describe the details of the many alternatives available in Excel. When you come across a snag, check the tips and notes in the appropriate chapter and check Chapter 13, "Troubleshooting Worksheets."

6

Operating Worksheets

This chapter teaches the basics of using Excel. If you had to read one chapter about Excel and had to discover the rest on your own, this is the chapter you should read.

In this chapter, you learn how to choose Excel commands and operate dialog boxes. When you learn how to choose commands, you can use Excel's Help command to learn more about Excel on your own. When you begin moving around in the Excel worksheet, you can enter text, numbers, dates, and formulas.

An important section on cell references (cell addresses) explains how to prevent formulas from changing when they are copied. The closing portion of the chapter describes how to change hard disk directories, as well as save, open, and close files.

Before you continue with this chapter, take a moment to review the following basic procedures.

To affect any portion of a worksheet:

1. Select the cells you want to change.

2. Choose the command or press the shortcut key.

3. Select options from the dialog box if one appears, then choose OK or press Enter.

4. Choose another command if necessary to affect the area still selected in step 1.

To choose a command from a menu:

Mouse: Move the pointer onto the menu heading and click. Then point to the command you want in the pull-down menu and click.

Keyboard: Press the Alt key to activate the menu. Press the underlined letter in the menu heading you want. Then press the underlined letter of the command you want in the pull-down menu.

To select options in a dialog box:

Mouse: Move the pointer onto the option button, check box, or text box you want and click.

Keyboard: Press Alt+letter where letter is the underlined letter in the name of the option or group of options you want. Move between items in a list box by pressing the up- or down-arrow key.

To complete a command from a dialog box:

Mouse: Click on the OK command button or double click on the item you want in a list box.

Keyboard: Press Enter or press Tab until a dashed lines appears around OK, then press the space bar.

To back out of a menu or dialog box:

Mouse: Click on the Cancel command button.

Keyboard: Press the Esc key to escape or press Tab until the dashed line surrounds Cancel, then press the space bar.

Choosing Excel Commands

Excel uses the same menu selection methods used by Windows and other Windows applications. Frequently, a task can be accomplished with more than one Excel or Windows method. With Excel, you can learn easier methods first and graduate to methods that best fit your work style and the function you want to perform. The various methods you can use to choose commands from Excel menus illustrate the program's versatility. You can control the menus with the mouse, keystrokes, cursor keys, or shortcut keys. In many cases, you can mix your methods of menu selection, starting with one method and finishing with another.

To choose a command from a menu with a mouse, click first on the menu heading, then on the command that appears in the pull-down menu. When you click on the menu heading, the menu will pull down and stay as shown in figure 6.1.

To choose a command using the keyboard, press the Alt key to activate the menu bar, then press the underlined letter in the menu heading you want. When the pull-down menu appears, as shown in figure 6.1, press the underlined letter in the command you want.

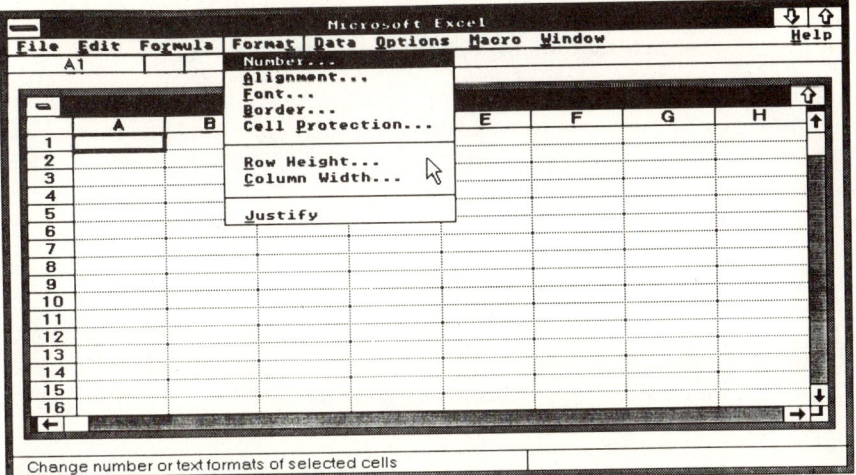

Fig. 6.1. An Excel window with a pull-down menu.

Use the Slash Key To Access Excel's Menus

You can activate Excel's menu bar by pressing the slash key (/) instead of the Alt key. This method may be more convenient if you are accustomed to using Lotus 1-2-3 or Reflex: The Analyst™.

If you are unsure of which menu or command to use, then explore the menus and commands with this procedure. Press Alt to activate the menu, then press Enter. This pulls down the File menu. If you do not see the command you are interested in, press the right- or left-arrow key to see an adjacent menu. Move sideways through the different menus by pressing the right- or left-arrow key until you see a command that looks correct. Press the up- or down-arrow key to select that command. Check the Status line at the bottom of the screen to see what that command does. If it appears to do what you want, complete the selected command by pressing Enter.

Faster Command Selections

You do not have to wait for the menu to appear before pressing the next key. You can rapidly choose the Format Alignment command, for example, by touch typing Alt, T, A. (Do not press Shift when typing the menu or command letters.)

NOTE

Backing Out of Menu Selections with Esc

Not often can you explore new territory and then escape when you need to. But in Excel, you can. You can back out of any menu or dialog box by pressing Esc (Escape). Remember: When you are in trouble, Escape from it.

Showing All or Partial Menus

Excel uses either full or partial menus. For infrequent or beginning operators, a short menu that only shows the most important commands may be easier to use and learn. More experienced and knowledgeable operators will want to use the full menus that show all the commands available.

To show full menus, choose the Options Full Menus command. If you are already in full menus and want to return to partial menus, then choose the Options Short Menus command. The Options menu displays either the Full Menus command or the Short Menus command so that you can switch to a menu length that is opposite the length in use.

Getting Help While You Work

Excel contains an extensive system to help you learn more by yourself. A context-sensitive help system even lets you learn about a command or dialog box that you are about to use. In addition, Excel contains a tutorial that guides you through some of the basic features. (Help facilities for Lotus 1-2-3 users are described in Chapter 30, "Making the Switch from 1-2-3 to Excel.")

TIP

Getting Help on Help

To get help on using Help, press F1, then press Alt, H or click on Help.

To use the Help menu, select the Help menu. You will see a number of different Help alternatives. Your choices are

Index	A list of subjects and words that have help files available
Keyboard	Helpful and shortcut keystrokes
Lotus 1-2-3	Help for Lotus 1-2-3 users
Multiplan	Help for Multiplan users

Tutorial	A guided tour of Excel capabilities
Feature Guide	Demonstrations of different Excel capabilities
About	Shows Excel version, available conventional and expanded memory, and whether a math coprocessor is installed

If you choose **Index**, a help window will appear showing an index of general topics. Click on the topic you want or type the first letter of the topic until it is selected, then press Enter. A list of subtopics appears. When you reach the information level for the topic you're interested in, the window fills with help information as shown in figure 6.2.

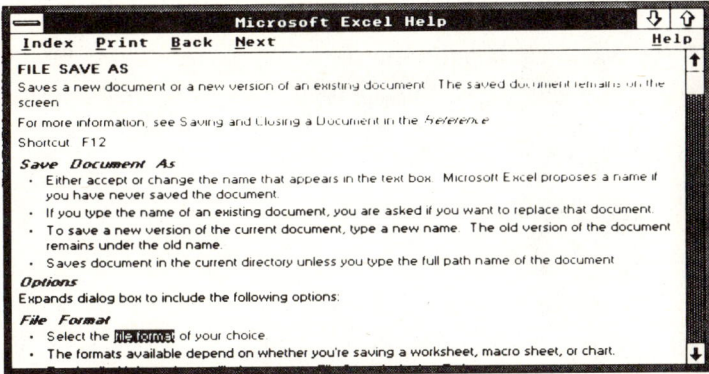

Fig. 6.2. An Excel Help window.

Scroll through the help window using normal scroll bar procedures for the mouse, or with up or down arrows or PgUp or PgDn keys. Go to the beginning of a topic with Ctrl+Home or the end with Ctrl+End.

From the Help windows menu, you can choose **Print** to print a topic on the current printer, **Back** to return to the previous topic, or **Next** to go to the next topic.

Within a Help window, you may see terms underlined with a solid or dashed line. Terms underlined with a dashed line contain a *hidden* definition behind them. Terms with a solid underline are *jumps* to another help window with additional help about that related topic. In figure 6.2, the selected *file format* near the bottom of the window is a glossary term that contains a definition.

To see a glossary term or jump to a related topic with the mouse, just click on jump words (underlined), or click and hold on glossary terms (dashed underlined). Choose the **Back** menu heading to return from your jump to a related topic.

To see a glossary term or jump to a related topic with the keyboard, press the Tab key until the topic is selected, then press Enter. (Hold the Enter key down to see a glossary item.) To return from a jump to a related topic, press Alt+B to select Back from the menu.

TIP

Getting Help in the Middle of Your Work

When you are about to choose a command or when you are in the middle of a dialog box, you may want help specific to what you're doing. Press Shift+F1 to get context-sensitive help.

If you are in a dialog box and press Shift+F1, a Help window appears describing the dialog box and its options.

If you want help about a specific command, press Alt, press the right or left arrow to the menu heading, then press Enter. Press the down arrow to select the command in question, and then press Shift+F1. A Help window appears describing the command you selected.

To close a Help window, press the Esc key or double click on the Help window's document Control icon. (The document Control icon appears as a hyphen symbol at the upper left corner of the Help window.)

Choosing Commands with Shortcut Keys

A good practice is to learn Excel by using the menus. While you are learning, you can open the menus and search for the command you need. This practice reinforces command locations in your mind and lets you discover commands that you did not know were available. After you are comfortable and confident with Excel, you will want to work even more quickly. At that point, you may want to use shortcut keys that accomplish a command with a Ctrl or Alt key combination.

You will notice key combinations listed on the right side of some pull-down menus. These key combinations execute the command immediately without going through the menu and menu item. For example, instead of choosing the Edit Clear command, you can press Del to clear a cell or group of cells.

TIP

Creating Custom Shortcut Keys

If you use the same commands frequently and a shortcut key is not available, you can create your own shortcut key with a command macro. After you are familiar with Excel menus, work through the Macro Quick Start (Chapter 25) to learn how to create simple macros easily.

Each function key, when pressed alone, has an assigned action. Some of the shortcut keys use combinations of function keys with the Alt, Shift, or Ctrl keys to duplicate menu commands. When you are supposed to press a combinations of keys, this book shows the keys joined by a plus sign (+). The hyphen means "hold down the first key(s) as you press the last key." For example, Ctrl+F6 means that you hold down the Ctrl key as you press F6. Ctrl+Shift+right arrow means you hold down Ctrl and Shift as you quickly press the right-arrow key.

The function keys and their Alt, Shift, and Ctrl key combinations follow this general pattern:

Function key	Duplicates a menu command (most are similar to Lotus 1-2-3 function keys)
Shift	A slight variation or reverse action from the function key
Ctrl	Controls the document (worksheet, chart, macro) window
Alt	Controls the Excel application window

Many shortcut key combinations use keys other than the function keys. These are discussed in later sections of this chapter. The Command Reference Card contains a complete listing of shortcut keys.

Addressing Cells

In Excel, you can refer to cells in the worksheet in one of two styles: A1 or R1C1. If you are used to Lotus 1-2-3, use the A1 style; if you are familiar with Multiplan, use the R1C1 style. Throughout this book, the A1 style is used.

The A1 Reference Style

In the A1 style, columns are labeled with letters, and rows are numbered. The first cell in the upper left corner (known as *Home*) is A1. A worksheet has 256 columns, designated A through IV, and 16,384 rows. You can locate or refer to any cell's contents by the address of the cell's column and row. Figure 6.3 shows a single cell, selected at B4 (column B, row 4).

Fig. 6.3. A worksheet with cells selected in A1 style.

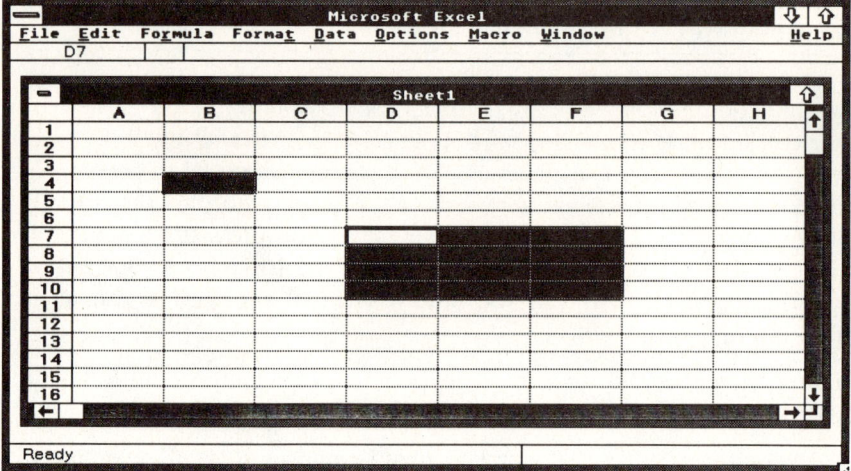

You can refer to ranges or rectangular groups of adjacent cells, such as the one shown in figure 6.3, with the notation D7:F10. The opposite corners of the range (D7 and F10) are separated by a colon (:). A range of cells must be contiguous; it cannot have holes in it. However, in Excel, you can select multiple ranges at one time. You will use ranges when you want a command to affect multiple cells or when you want to apply a function to several values.

The R1C1 Reference Style

The R1C1 style of cell addressing takes a slightly different approach. The worksheet still contains 256 columns by 16,384 rows, but columns as well as rows are numbered. You will need to be familiar with the R1C1 style if you plan to manually create macros.

In R1C1 style, you refer to a cell by its row and column number. For example, the single upper left selected cell in figure 6.4 is R4C2 (row 4, column 2). You also can designate a range in R1C1 style. For example, in figure 6.4, the first corner of the range is R6C4, and the opposite corner is R9C6. Using a colon to separate the corners, the complete range is designated as R6C4:R9C6. In R1C1 style, as in A1 style, all cells in a range are selected.

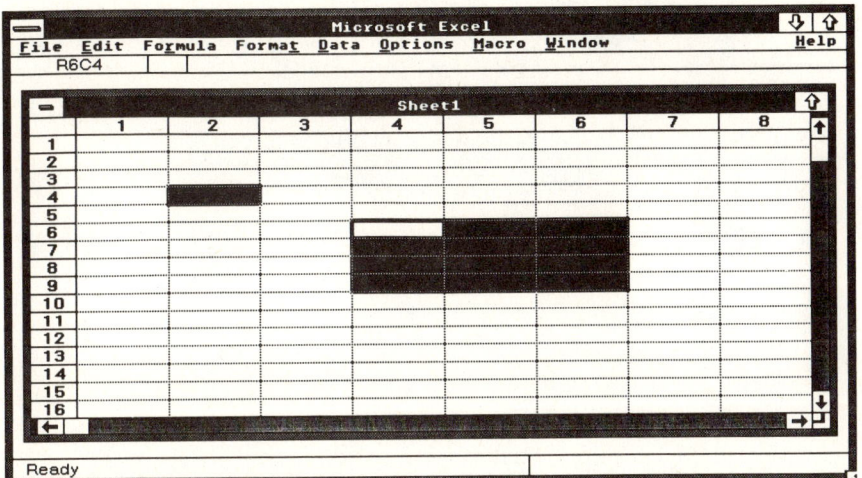

Fig. 6.4. A worksheet with cells selected in R1C1 style.

Selecting Cells

Selected cells are highlighted or reversed from the rest of the worksheet. If you select a range of cells, such as those shown in figures 6.3 and 6.4, all the cells will be highlighted, but one cell will have a bold border and white background.

The cell with the bold border and white background is the *active cell*. Commands affect all selected cells; data and formulas are entered in the active cell.

Selecting a Single Cell

Use either the mouse or the arrow keys to select cells. Selecting a cell with the mouse is easy; just move the mouse pointer to the cell and click the mouse button.

To select a single cell from the keyboard, press the appropriate arrow key to move the active cell. For example, to move the active cell to the next cell right, press the right-arrow key. To move the active cell one screen down, press PgDn.

Table 6.1 shows the keys that move the active cell. To issue key combinations, such as Ctrl+PgUp, hold down the first key (Ctrl) as you press the second key (PgUp).

Table 6.1
Keys That Move the Active Cell

Key	Movement
Up arrow	Move the active cell up one cell
Down arrow	Move the active cell down one cell
Right arrow	Move the active cell right one cell
Left arrow	Move the active cell left one cell
Tab	Enter data and move the active cell right
Shift+Tab	Enter data and move the active cell left
Enter	Enter data and move the active cell down in the selected range
Shift+Enter	Enter data and move the active cell up in the selected range
Ctrl+arrow	Move the active cell in the direction indicated until the cell content changes from empty to filled or from filled to empty
Home	Move the active cell to column A of the same row
Ctrl+Home	Move the active cell to the first cell in the worksheet (A1)
End	Move the active cell to the end of the row as far as the rightmost column
Ctrl+End	Move the active cell to the last cell in the used portion of the worksheet
PgUp	Move the active cell up one full window
PgDn	Move the active cell down one full window
Ctrl+PgUp	Move the active cell one screen width left
Ctrl+PgDn	Move the active cell one screen width right

Ctrl keys can be real time-savers when you need to move across a worksheet or when you need to move up or down a column. The Ctrl+ arrow key combinations act as express keys that move the active cell as if the cell were on an expressway or an elevator. The Ctrl+arrow combinations move the selected cell in the direction of the arrow until the cell contents changes in one of the following ways:

- If the active cell is blank, it will move in the direction of the arrow until it reaches a filled cell.

- If the active cell is filled, it will move in the direction of the arrow until it reaches a blank cell.

You can make your worksheet more efficient by building expressways and elevators. Fill rows with dashes to make horizontal expressways. Use columns of data as vertical elevators.

TIP

Don't Stop Short

When you use Ctrl+up arrow or Ctrl+down arrow to move through columns, make sure that the active cell has not accidentally stopped before reaching the top or bottom of a column like this. An accidental blank cell may stop the active cell before reaching the true end of the columns.

Selecting a Range of Cells

Select a range of cells when you want to change an area of cells with a single command or when you want to define a space in which to enter data. You also use ranges to describe to Excel such things as which cells are to be printed.

To select a range of cells with the mouse, follow these steps:

1. Click on the cell at the top left corner of the range, as shown in figure 6.5, and drag to the bottom right cell in the range.

   As you drag, the selected cells will be highlighted. The first cell selected will be the active cell.

2. When you reach the lower right corner of the range, as shown in figure 6.6, release the mouse button.

To select a range of cells with the keyboard, follow these steps:

1. Move the active cell to the cell at the upper left of the rectangular area of cells you want to select, as shown in figure 6.5.

2. Hold down the Shift key and press the arrow or movement keys to move the selection area down to the lower right corner of the area you want selected. The active cell stays at the top left corner as shown in figure 6.6.

Fig. 6.5. The top left corner of a range—the active cell.

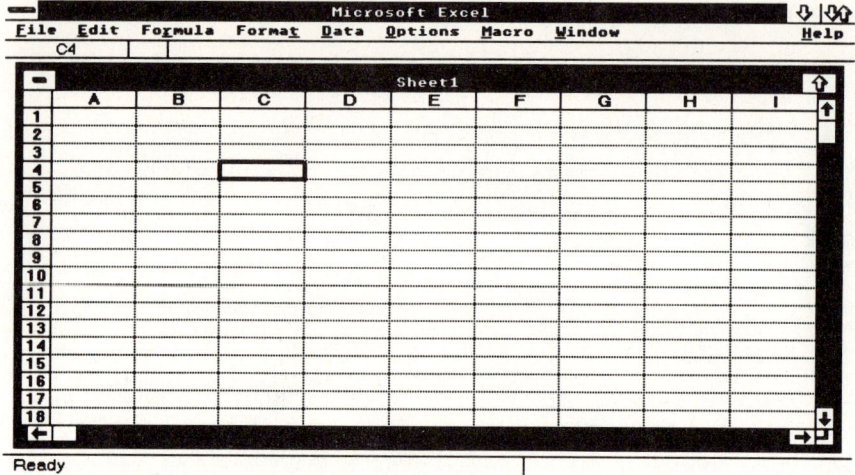

Fig. 6.6. The lower right corner of a range; selection completed.

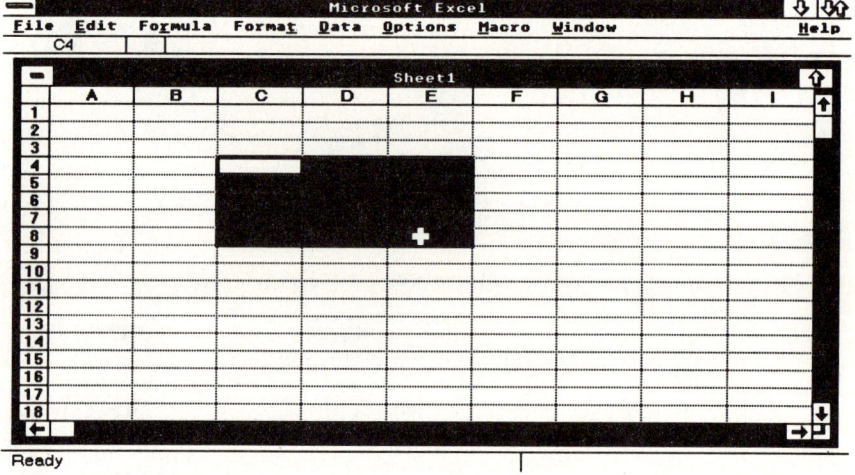

If the lower right corner of the range is off the screen, move the mouse pointer against the document window's edge in the direction you want to move. The window will scroll over the worksheet. (See the "Scrolling the Window over the Worksheet" section later in this chapter.)

In some cases, a range is so large that scrolling from one corner to another takes a long time. A quick method for selecting a large range is to use the following steps:

1. Select the upper left corner of the range.

   Mouse: Click on the cell at the upper left corner of the range.

Keyboard: Press the arrow keys to position the active cell at the upper left corner of the range.

2. Select the lower right corner of the range.

   Mouse: Click in the scroll bars to move the window to the opposite corner of the range (do not click inside the worksheet). Then hold down Shift while you click on the cell at the opposite corner of the range. All cells in between the first click and the Shift-click are selected.

   Keyboard: Hold down the Shift key while you press the keys listed in table 6.1 to move to the lower right corner of the range. All cells in between the first position and the current position are selected as you move the arrow keys with the Shift key held down.

TIP

Selecting Large Ranges from the Keyboard

If you have a large range to select, using the keyboard follow these steps:

1. Select the upper left corner of the range.

2. Choose the Formula Goto command.

3. Type the cell address of the lower right corner for the range.

4. Hold down the Shift key, and press Enter.

By convention, *Using Excel: IBM Version* always instructs you to select ranges from upper left to lower right. However, you can click on any corner and drag to its opposite corner. Notice that the cell you start on becomes the active cell.

You also can select ranges using the F8 function key to turn on Extend mode. Extend mode produces the same result as continuously holding the Shift key down. In figure 6.7, you can see the EXT (Extend) indicator in the status line at the bottom of the screen.

To select a range such as the one shown in figure 6.7, follow these steps:

1. Select a corner of the range then press F8.

   Mouse: Click at one corner of the range you want, and then press F8.

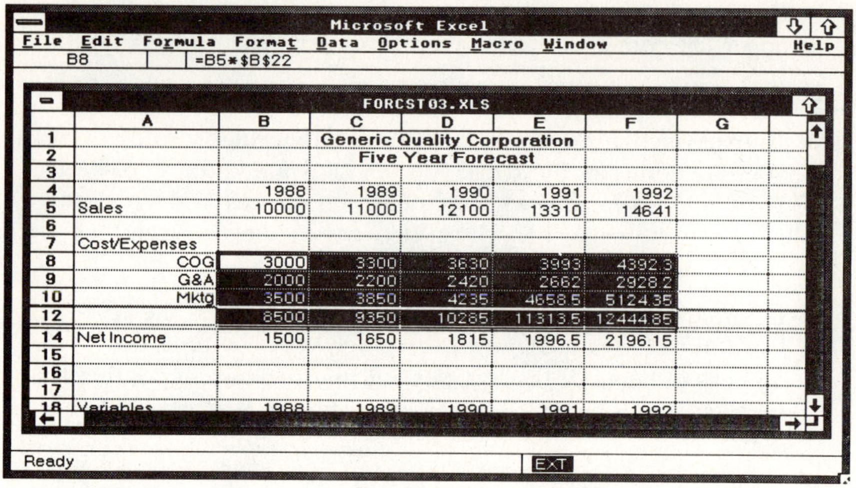

Fig. 6.7. A range selected with the worksheet set in Extend mode.

Keyboard: Move to one corner of the range you want, and then press F8.

2. Select the opposite corner of the range.

   Mouse: Click in the cell at the opposite corner of the range, and then press F8 a second time to turn off Extend mode.

   Keyboard: Move to the opposite corner of the range, and then press F8 a second time to turn off Extend mode.

As long as EXT is displayed in the status line, the first corner selected remains anchored. The opposite corner of the selected range moves under mouse or key control (see table 6.1).

Keep in mind that you can use all the movement keys shown in table 6.1 to select a range with the keyboard. To speed your range selections, use the shortcut keys listed in table 6.2.

Table 6.2
Shortcut Keys for Selecting Ranges

Key	Extend selection from active cell to
F8	Last cell selected
Shift+arrow	Last cell selected
Shift+Home	Beginning of row
Shift+Ctrl+Home	Beginning of worksheet (A1)

Key	Extend selection from active cell to
Ctrl+End	Las cell used in worksheet
Shift+space bar	Entire row of active cell
Ctrl+space bar	Entire column of active cell
Shift+Ctrl+space bar	Entire worksheet
Shift+PgUp	Cell in same column one window up
Shift+PgDn	Cell in same column one window down
Shift+Ctrl+arrow	Next change from filled cell to unfilled or unfilled to filled

To keep a range selected and reposition the corner that the active cell is on, press Ctrl+period (.). Each press of Ctrl+. moves the active cell to another corner.

TIP

Adjusting a Range that Is Already Selected

If you've selected a range, but then decide you want to move a corner or side, you can do so with these steps:

To change a corner, and keep the selection:

1. Press Ctrl+. until the active cell is in the corner opposite the one being moved.

2. Hold down the Shift key and use the keys in table 6.1 to move the corner opposite the active cell.

Selecting Multiple Ranges of Cells

Excel has the capability to select multiple ranges simultaneously. With this feature, you can do such things as format multiple cell ranges with a single command, print different parts of the worksheet as though they were one continuous document, or erase different areas of the worksheet.

To select multiple ranges with the mouse, follow these steps:

1. Select the first range.

2. Hold down the Ctrl key as you select each additional range.

3. Release the Ctrl key and choose a command from the menu or enter data in the selected range.

From the keyboard, you can select multiple ranges by entering Add mode with Shift+F8. To select multiple ranges from the keyboard, follow these steps:

1. Select the first cell.

2. Press Shift+arrow and select the first range.

3. Press Shift+F8. Notice that the status line indicates Add mode.

4. Move to the first corner of the next range.

5. Press Shift+arrow and select the second range. Notice that Add disappears from the Status line.

6. Repeat steps 3, 4, and 5 until you have selected all the ranges you need.

As long as the ADD indicator appears at the bottom of the screen, you can move to and make new selections.

TIP

Selecting the Whole Worksheet

If you want to select the entire worksheet in order to format all cells at one time, first press Ctrl+Shift+space bar. Then select the Format command you want.

When you need to format or print more than one range with the same command, select all the ranges at once, and then give the command. For example, in the Worksheet Quick Start (Chapter 4), you selected one range at a time and had to issue the same formatting commands more than once.

Figure 6.8 shows how two rows of currency formatting could have been performed at once by selecting multiple ranges. In this example, the range B5:F5 was selected first, using the normal procedure. With the mouse the lower row was selected by holding down the Ctrl key and dragging from B14 to F14. The lower row could have been selected with the keyboard by pressing Shift+F8 and pressing arrow keys to move the active cell to B14. Then Shift+right arrow was pressed to select B14:F14.

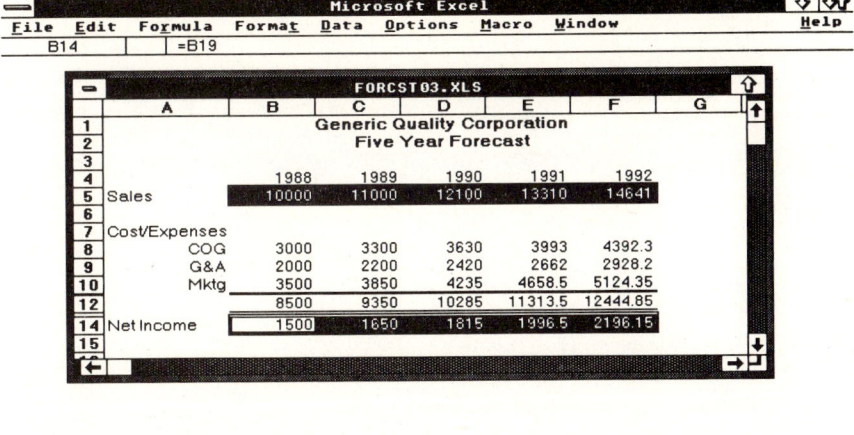

Fig. 6.8. Multiple ranges selected for formatting.

Scrolling the Window over the Worksheet

In the preceding sections, you learned how to move the active cell. At times, you will want to keep the active cell at the same location and *scroll* the window over the worksheet. Scrolling is a handy way of keeping a cell or range selected while looking at a different part of the worksheet.

Scrolling with the Mouse

To scroll the window with the mouse, use the scroll bars located at the right side and bottom of each worksheet (see fig. 6.9). The arrows in the scroll bars show the direction the window moves over the worksheet. (Remember: imagine the window moving over a stationary worksheet.)

To scroll the worksheet in single row or column increments, click on the arrowhead in a scroll bar. The arrowheads point in the direction the window moves over the worksheet. To scroll continuously, point at a scroll arrow and hold down the mouse button.

To move through the worksheet in larger increments, drag the "thumb" through the scroll bar. Release the thumb to display the worksheet at that relative location. As you can see in figure 6.9, the position of the thumb in a scroll bar shows the relative position of the window on the worksheet.

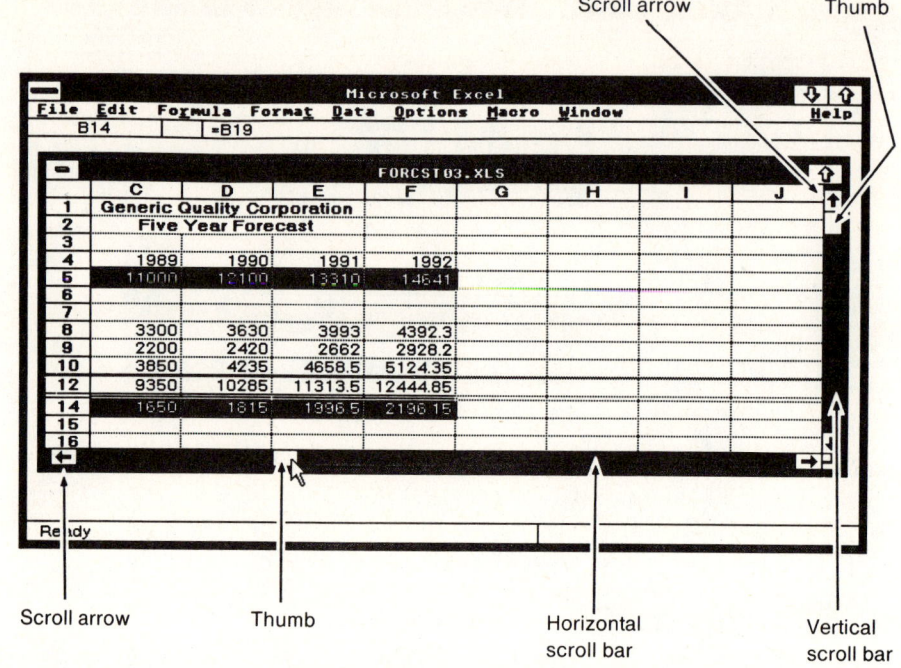

Fig. 6.9. A
worksheet with
scroll bars and
thumb labeled.

Scrolling from the Keyboard

From the keyboard, you scroll the window over the worksheet with the same keys you used to move the active cell. You can use all the movement keys listed in table 6.1, but you must press the Scroll Lock key before you press the movement keys. Keep in mind that the rectangular thumb in the horizontal and vertical scroll bars on the edge of the window will show you the position of the window with respect to the entire worksheet. On some keyboards, the Scroll Lock key lights up when scrolling is enabled. Do not forget to press the Scroll Lock key a second time after you are finished scrolling.

TIP

When Work Disappears from the Screen . . .

If your work suddenly disappears from the screen, do not panic too quickly. You may have accidentally scrolled to a new location. Check the row and column headings, and move back to your original work area.

Moving Quickly with Formula Goto

The Formula **G**oto command moves the active cell to any address you request. To use the Goto command, follow these steps:

1. Choose the Formula **G**oto command to display the Goto dialog box (see fig. 6.10).

2. Type the cell address you want to go to, or select from the list box the named location you want to go to.

3. Choose the OK button or press Enter.

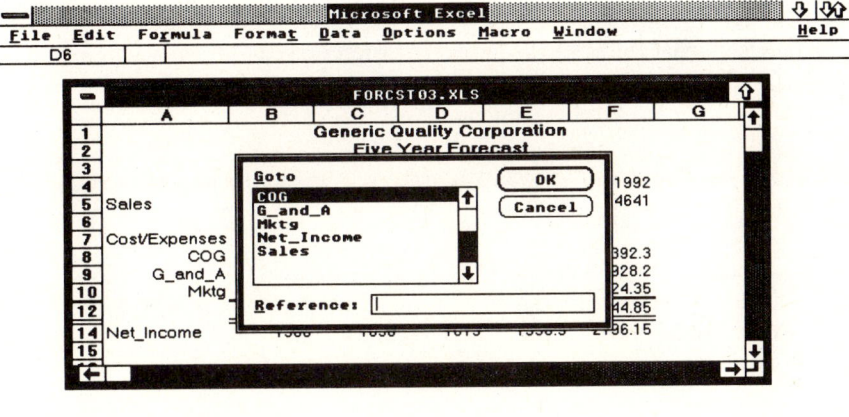

Fig. 6.10. The Goto dialog box.

For Help on dialog settings, press F1

If you choose a named cell or range with the Goto command, the entire range is selected. (Named ranges are cells or ranges that have been given a text name such as REVENUE; ranges are discussed in detail in Chapter 7, "Entering and Editing Worksheet Data.")

TIP

Selecting Frequently Used Ranges

Use the **G**oto command to select frequently used ranges quickly. For example, if you print different areas of the worksheet in sequence, these steps will reduce the time required for the task.

Prepare the worksheet by using the Formula **D**efine Name or Formula **C**reate Names commands to name your frequently used ranges. You can use names such as QTR1REPORT and QTR1_FORCST, for example.

When it comes time to print the frequently printed areas, follow these steps:

1. Choose the **Formula Goto** command, select the named range you want to print, and press Enter.

2. Choose the **Options Set Print Area** command.

3. Choose the **File Print** command to print the named range.

4. Repeat steps 2 and 3 for each range you need to print.

For more information on printing, refer to Chapter 12, "Printing Worksheets."

When you know what you are seeking, but not where it is located, use the **Formula Find** command to search for it. Formula Find locates numeric or text values, partial or whole formulas, or the contents of a note attached to a cell. Chapter 7, "Entering and Editing Worksheet Data," contains more information about the **Find** command.

Managing Files and Worksheets

Excel saves each document (worksheet, chart, or macro sheet) in a separate file. This arrangement allows you, for example, to create a single chart and link it to multiple worksheets, or to create a macro sheet and use it with different worksheets.

In the text that follows, you learn how to save, open, clear, and delete individual Excel documents. You find out how to save your work in progress so that you can restore it exactly as you last left it—with all windows and documents in the same locations and sizes.

Chapter 10, "Using Multiple Worksheets," describes how to open linked worksheets. Saving or retrieving non-Excel program files is covered in Chapter 29, "Using Excel with Standard DOS Applications."

Opening a New Document

When you start Excel with the EXCEL.EXE file, the program opens with a blank worksheet titled Sheet1. You can open additional new worksheets, charts, or macro sheets at any time by following these steps:

1. Choose the **File New** command.

2. Select the **Worksheet**, **Chart**, or **Macro Sheet** option button (see fig. 6.11).

3. Choose OK or press Enter.

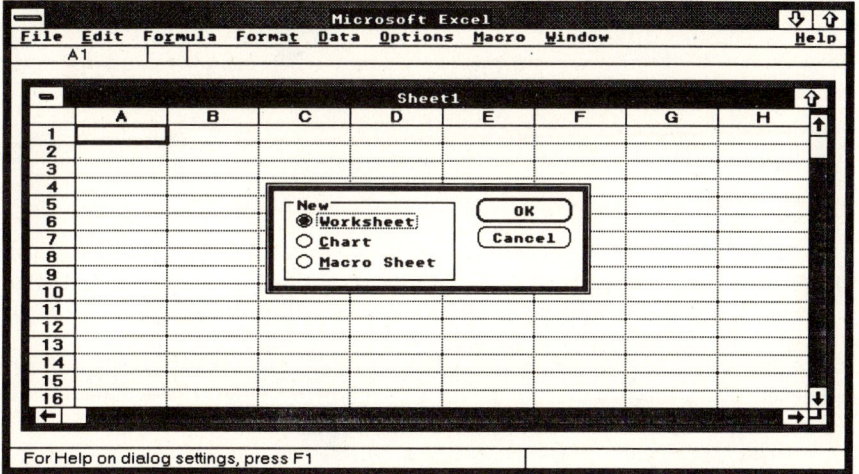

Fig. 6.11. The new file dialog box.

Each additional window reduces the available memory. This memory reduction limits the file size you can later retrieve and lowers performance. Closing nonessential windows frees memory.

Opening an Existing Document

To open an existing document while Excel is running, follow these steps:

1. Choose the **File Open** command (see fig. 6.12).

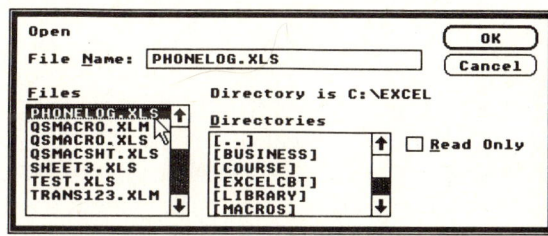

Fig. 6.12. The Open dialog box.

2. Select the file name.

   Mouse: Type the file name and extension in the text box, or select the file name from the list box by scrolling the list box and clicking on the name.

   Keyboard: Type the file name and extension in the text box, or press the Tab key until the file name list box is selected. Then press the up- or down-arrow key or type the first letter of the file name until the name is highlighted.

3. Choose OK or press Enter.

NOTE

Finding Files That Are Not Listed

If you don't see the file you want after scrolling through the list box, change the file name search pattern in the text box from *.XL* to a pattern that matches your files. The pattern *.* allows you to find all files.

If you still don't see the file name you are looking for, it may be located in a different directory. Changing directories from the **Open** dialog box is covered in this chapter's "Changing Disk Directories" section.

The file extension can be a clue to finding the file you want. Excel files use different file extensions for each type of file. These extensions are described in table 6.3.

Table 6.3
Excel File Extensions

Extension	File type
.XLS	Worksheet
.XLC	Chart
.XLM	Macro sheet
.XLW	Workspace (a list of documents all in use at one time)

A quick method of opening files from the dialog box is to double click on the file name in the list box. Double clicking simultaneously selects the name and chooses OK. If you are in the Windows MS-DOS Executive application and Excel is not running, you can simultaneously start Excel and a worksheet by double clicking on the worksheet's file name or by selecting the file name and pressing Enter.

Changing Disk Directories

Excel displays files in the current directory in the **File Open** and **File Save** dialog boxes. You can change the directory and disk that Excel uses for saving and retrieving.

To change the current disk or directory, either use the mouse pointer to traverse the directory tree or type the disk and directory directly. To change the current directory using the directory list box, choose the **File Open** command, select the new disk or directory name from the **Directory** list box, and then choose OK or press Enter. You do not have to open a file after changing directories. When the files in the new directory display in the box, choose Cancel or press the Esc key. Future files you save or open will be in the last directory you saw.

For example, in the **O**pen dialog box shown in figure 6.13, the current directory is C:\EXCEL. Examples of listings in the **D**irectory box are described in table 6.4.

Fig. 6.13. The Open dialog box.

Table 6.4
Directory List Box Options

Directory box	Path name
[-A-]	A:, the diskette drive
[-C-]	C:, the current directory
[..]	The parent directory of the current directory; in this case, C:\ ([..] is out of view in figure 6.13)
[COURSE]	C:\EXCEL\COURSE
[MACROS]	C:\EXCEL\MACROS

To change the current directory from the keyboard, press Alt+D to select the **D**irectory list box. Press the up or down arrow to select the desired directory, then press Enter.

To save a file to a different directory or drive but remain in the current directory, type the drive and directory (path name) in front of the file name you enter in the dialog box. Figure 6.14 shows a Save **A**s dialog box with the current directory listed as C:\EXCEL. The file, however, will be saved in the C:\CLIENT directory.

Fig. 6.14. The Save As dialog box.

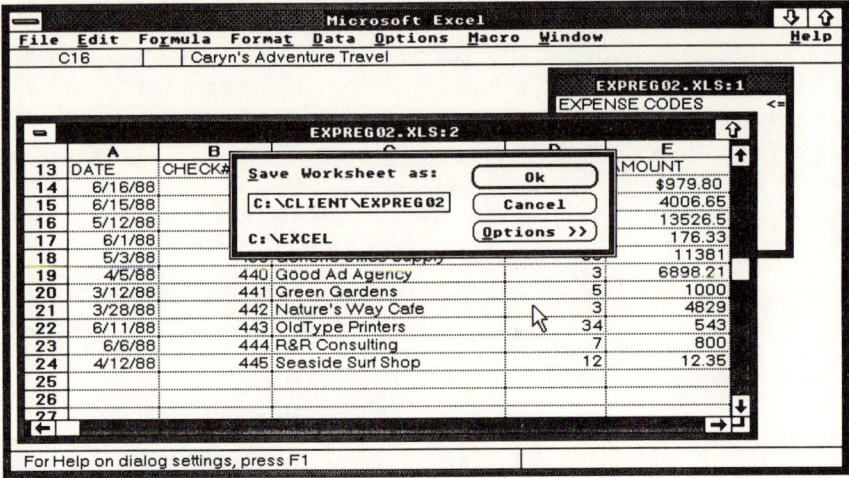

Using a similar procedure, you can retrieve a file from another directory while staying in the current directory. In the **O**pen dialog box, type the temporary path name in front of the file name being retrieved.

Saving Documents

You should save your documents regularly to a file name that includes a version number. For example, save your work to FORCST03.XLS; then in 15 or 20 minutes or after a major change, save it to FORCST04.XLS. In this way, you always can return to previous versions of your work. If you save to the same file name each time, the previous work is replaced. (Delete old versions of work with the **File Delete** command.)

To save the active worksheet to the current directory, follow these steps:

1. Activate the document you want to save. (Any of a document's multiple windows can be activated.)

2. Choose the **File Save As** command.

3. Enter a new name or edit the existing name in the name box. Do not type a file extension.

4. Choose OK or press Enter.

Use file names with one to eight characters. File names can include letters, numbers, and some symbols. Because only some symbols can be used, the best practice is to use only the underline (_) and the hyphen (-). Use these symbols in place of spaces.

Never Use Spaces in File Names!

File names never can include spaces. Spaces confuse DOS's capability to store the file with the name you want. Also, don't use periods, other than the one before the extension, in file names.

Use the Save **As** command instead of the **S**ave command, because the Save **A**s command gives you a chance to change the file name for each save. The **F**ile **S**ave command saves the document under the last name used.

Chapter 29 explains how to save files in formats that you can use with other programs, such as Lotus 1-2-3 and dBASE II or dBASE III.

Protecting Your Work

If your work is important, keep the original and backup copies in two different physical locations. In that way, a fire or vandal won't destroy both your original and your backup.

Saving All Your Work at Once

Excel can save all your windows exactly as they appear on the screen so that you can begin the next session exactly where you left off. This capability also gives you a method of "packaging" Excel worksheets, charts, and macros so that others can start all the documents at once with windows in the layout you have arranged.

When you need to save all the work in progress exactly as it appears on the screen, choose the **F**ile **S**ave **W**orkspace command. Type the name you want the work saved under, and choose OK or press Enter. When you are ready to resume work, choose the **F**ile **O**pen command and choose the file name you specified.

Keeping Your Workspace Files Together

The **F**ile **S**ave **W**orkspace command saves a list of file names rather than the documents themselves in the .XLW file that the command creates. Nonetheless, all the document files to be saved at one time with this command must be available with the same names and in the same disk or directory.

Deleting Files

You can delete individual files from within Excel with the **File Delete** command. Choose the **File Delete** command, select the file you want to delete from the list box and choose OK or press Enter. An alert box appears asking you to confirm the deletion; choose **Yes** to delete.

To delete multiple files at one time, switch to the Windows MS-DOS Executive application, and use it as a file manager. On the screen shown in figure 6.15, multiple file names were selected by holding down the Shift key as selections were made. After files are selected, you can choose MS-DOS Executive's **File Delete** command to delete all the selected files at one time. The MS-DOS Executive is only available when you run Excel with a full copy of Windows. (*Using Microsoft Windows*, published by Que Corporation, explains how to use MS-DOS Executive as a file manager.)

Fig. 6.15. The Windows MS-DOS Executive application with multiple files selected.

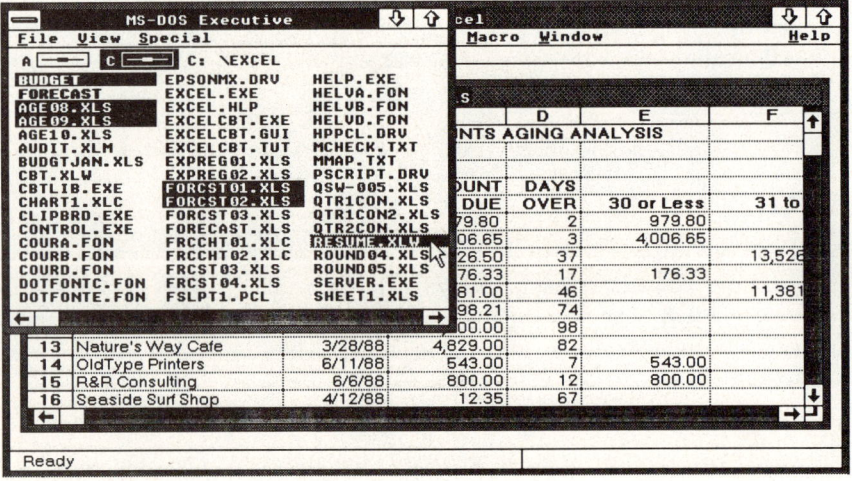

After you have deleted files, you cannot use the **Edit Undo** or **Esc** commands to restore them. Choosing the Cancel button does not undo a file you have deleted; Cancel only removes the dialog box. Files can be retrieved if you stop work immediately and use a commercially available file recovery program. Saving any work to disk after you have accidentally deleted a file may destroy your chance of recovering the file.

Closing Document Windows and Exiting Excel

You can close a window that contains the active worksheet by doing the following:

1. Activate the window to be closed.

   Mouse: Click on the window you want to close so that it appears on top.

   Keyboard: Select the **W**indow menu, and type the number of the window you want to be active.

2. Close the window.

   Mouse: Double click on the document Control menu (the dash located at the upper left corner of each worksheet's window).

   Keyboard: Press the shortcut key, Ctrl+F4; or press Alt, hyphen to open the document Control menu, and type C for **C**lose.

3. An alert box appears if you have made changes since the last time you saved the file (see fig. 6.16). If you want to save the document before closing, choose **Yes**.

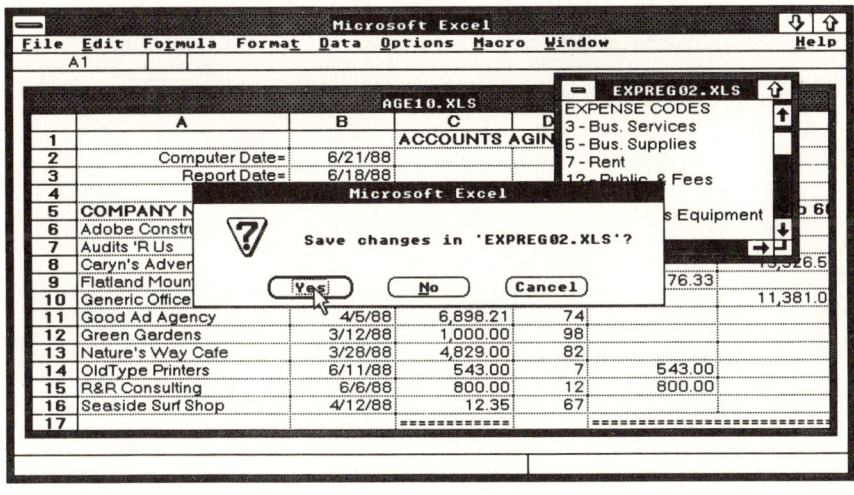

Fig. 6.16. An Excel alert box asks if you want to save changes.

> **TIP**
>
> ### Closing All Document Windows, but Keeping Excel Running
>
> To close all the document windows with a single command, hold down the Shift key as you select the **File** menu. A new command, **Close All**, appears. Choosing **Close All** closes all worksheets and asks you to confirm whether you want changed worksheets saved.

To exit Excel, choose the **File Exit** command. If you have made changes to documents since they were last saved, you will be asked whether you want to save the changes.

From Here . . .

You can operate Excel in any way that fits your style and the task at hand. You can use the mouse, Alt+letter menu selections, Alt+arrow key menu selections, or the ever popular shortcut keys. You should, however, avoid using the same commands over and over, year after year, without considering Excel's additional capabilities. Occasionally, you should take the time to scroll through the commands in menus, highlighting commands with the arrow key, looking at the descriptions in the status line, and pressing the Help key (F1). You can flip through *Using Excel: IBM Version* for new ideas.

The next chapter deals with data entry and editing. If you are familiar with Lotus 1-2-3, you are familiar with Excel's basic data entry and editing concepts. You should skim these chapters anyway, because Excel has many timesaving techniques and special features.

7

Entering and Editing Worksheet Data

Excel's value lies in storing, manipulating, and displaying information. You must enter that information into the cells of the worksheet. This chapter discusses the types of information a cell can contain and explains how to enter numbers, dates, formulas, and text. You also learn how to name cells and how to create formulas that manipulate information, and you discover some tips on speeding up data entry.

In addition to telling you how to enter information, this chapter covers two types of editing: editing the contents of a cell in the formula bar and editing the architecture and arrangement of the worksheet. You learn how to correct formulas and text that need editing as well as how to insert and delete cells, rows, and columns. You can save considerable time in building worksheets after you learn how to move or copy text or formulas.

The techniques you learn in this chapter are fundamental to building even simple worksheets.

Entering Information in Cells

Excel worksheet cells can contain values or formulas. The four types of constant values they can contain are numbers, text, dates, and times. In addition to constant values, cells can contain two other types of values: logical values and error values. A logical value, such as TRUE or FALSE, is the result displayed after a formula is tested for correctness. Error values, such as #NUM!, occur when Excel cannot properly handle the contents of a cell.

When you type a value or formula in an Excel worksheet, the entry appears in the formula bar near the top of the screen (see fig. 7.1). As you type, two boxes appear to the left of the formula bar. If you are using a mouse, clicking on the X box cancels an entry while clicking on the check box enters an entry. Your typing appears in the long text box on the right side of the formula bar.

*Fig. 7.1. A text
entry displayed
in the formula
bar.*

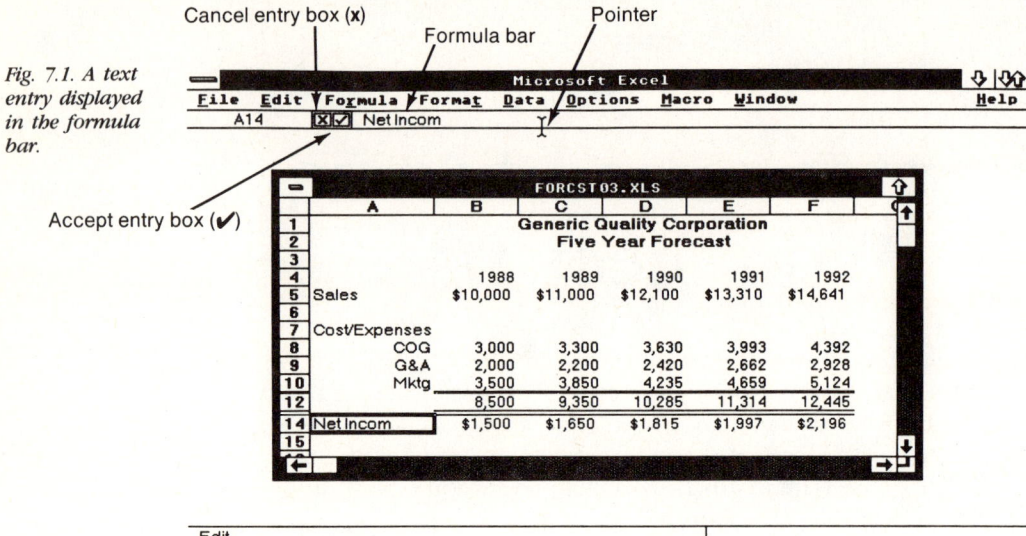

Cancel entry box (**x**)

Formula bar

Pointer

Accept entry box (✔)

Edit

To make any type of entry in a worksheet, follow these steps:

1. Select the cell in which you want to enter data.

2. Type the entry.

   The entry appears in the formula bar as you type. If you decide
   that you want to cancel the entry in the formula bar, click on the
   X box in the formula bar or press Esc.

3. Enter your typing.

   Mouse: Click on the check box in the formula bar.

   Keyboard: Press Enter.

Entering Text

Text can be alphabetical characters, numbers, and symbols. To enter text in
a cell, select the cell, type the text entry, and then enter the text by clicking
on the check box or pressing Enter.

You can type as many as 255 characters in a cell. (Note that all the characters
may not show in a cell if an adjacent cell contains data and the column isn't
wide enough.) When you enter text in a cell that still has the original General
format, the text automatically aligns on the left side of the cell.

You can make Excel accept numbers as text by beginning the numbers with an equal sign and enclosing them in quotation marks. For example, suppose that you enter what Excel would normally consider as a number, as follows:

="$45,000"

Excel treats the entry as text. The entry has no value in a formula and is displayed according to the text format for that cell. (If you need to display quotation marks on-screen, then you must use three quotation marks on either side of the text—for example,

="""The Absolute Best""")

TIP

Mixing Text and Numbers in an Entry

Unlike Lotus 1-2-3, Excel allows you to type phrases beginning with a number directly into the worksheet. For example, the following address is accepted by Excel as text because it contains letters:

45 Oak Ridge Trail

Entering Numbers

Numbers are constant values containing only the following characters:

1 2 3 4 5 6 7 8 9 0 - + . E e

To enter a number, you select the cell, type the number, and then press Enter or click on the check box. You can enter integers, such as 135 or 327; decimal fractions, such as 135.437 or 327.65; or scientific notation, such as 1.35437E2.

As you create worksheets, Excel may display newly entered numbers or formulas as ######### (see fig. 7.2). A cell filled with # signs indicates that the column is not wide enough to display the number in its current format. In this case, you need to change the numeric format or widen the column with the Format Column Width command.

When you enter a number in a cell with General format (a cell's original format), Excel tries to establish from your entry how the number should be formatted. For example, Excel accepts and displays the entries listed in table 7.1 with the formats indicated.

The second example—7999 Knue Rd.—illustrates that if an entry is not a number or date, then Excel stores it as text. This feature is convenient when you are entering database information such as inventory codes or street addresses.

Fig. 7.2. A cell filled with # signs, indicating that the column is too narrow to display the numeric entry.

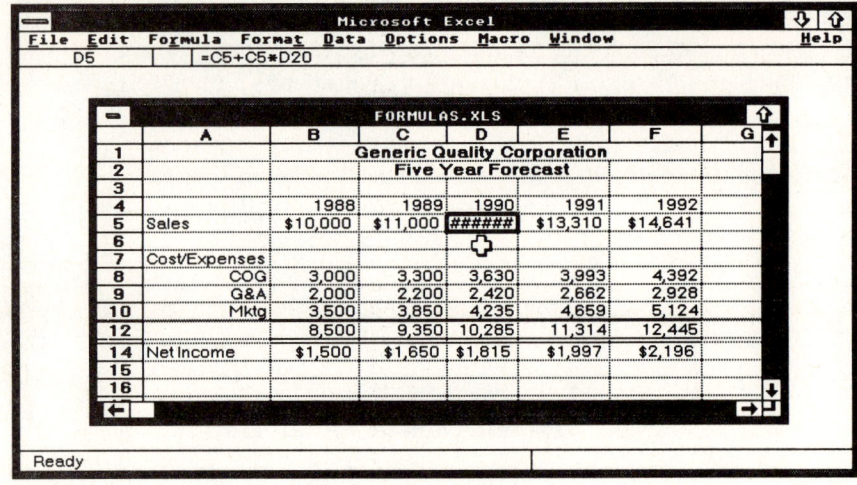

Table 7.1
Excel Formats

Typed entry	Excel's automatically chosen format	Displayed result
897	Number, General	897
7999 Knue Rd.	Text, left aligned	7999 Knue Rd.
$450.09	Number, dollar format	$450.09
54.6%	Number, percent format	54.6%
45,600	Number, comma format	45,600
-678	Number, negative	-678
(678)	Number, negative	(678)
4/5/87	Date, m/d/yy	4/5/87

TIP

How Many Digits Does Excel Store?

Excel stores numbers with as many as 14 digits. You can change the format to display fewer digits, but the full number is still used in calculations. This can cause problems. It means that the number used in calculations may be slightly different from the number displayed. To solve this problem, review the **Options Calculation Precision as Displayed** command and the ROUND function, both discussed in Chapter 8, "Formatting Worksheets."

Excel sets a limit on the size of numbers it can store. Numbers in decimal and scientific notation format can be from 1.789E308 down to and including 2.225E-308.

Entering Dates and Times

Excel recognizes dates and times typed the way you are used to writing them. However, Excel takes each date or time you enter and converts it to a *serial* number. The serial number represents the number of days from the beginning of the century until the date you type. Excel records each time with a serial number that represents the decimal fraction part of a day. Excel does not display this serial number unless you change a cell's format from a date format to General format.

When you enter a date into a cell Excel automatically changes the cell's format from General to the date format that matches your entry.

To enter a date, type the date into the cell with any of these formats:

7/8/87

8-Jul-87

8-Jul   (The year from the system date is used.)

Jul-87   (Only the month and year show.)

In any of these date formats, you can use either a / or - to separate elements.

Enter times in any of these formats:

13:32

13:32:05

1:32:05 PM

1:32 pm

1:32 p

The first two examples are from a 24-hour clock. If you use a 12-hour clock, follow the time with a space and A, AM, P, or PM (in either upper- or lowercase). Be sure that you leave a space before the AM or PM. Do not mix a 24-hour clock time with an AM or PM.

For information about formatting or changing the formats of dates and times, refer to Chapter 8, "Formatting Worksheets."

> **TIP**
>
> ### When the Date or Time Does Not Automatically Format
>
> In some cases when you enter a correctly formatted date or time, the displayed result is not in a date or time format. This occurs when the cell has been previously formatted to others than the default, General. To reformat for the correct display, select the cell, choose Format Number, select the date or time format from the list box, and choose OK or press Enter.

Entering Formulas

Formulas perform the calculations that are the heart of Excel. These formulas automatically recalculate new results when you update data the formulas depend on. Formulas refer to the contents of a cell by its address, such as B12. Math operators such as + or -, as well as prebuilt functions like SUM or PMT (payment), can be used in formulas.

In this section, you learn how to build formulas, how to use different types of cell references so that formulas can be copied, and other concepts important to more complex formulas.

Normally, a cell displays the results of a formula rather than the formula itself; the formula itself is displayed in the formula bar. Figure 7.3 shows the active cell as C5 and its formula displayed in the formula bar.

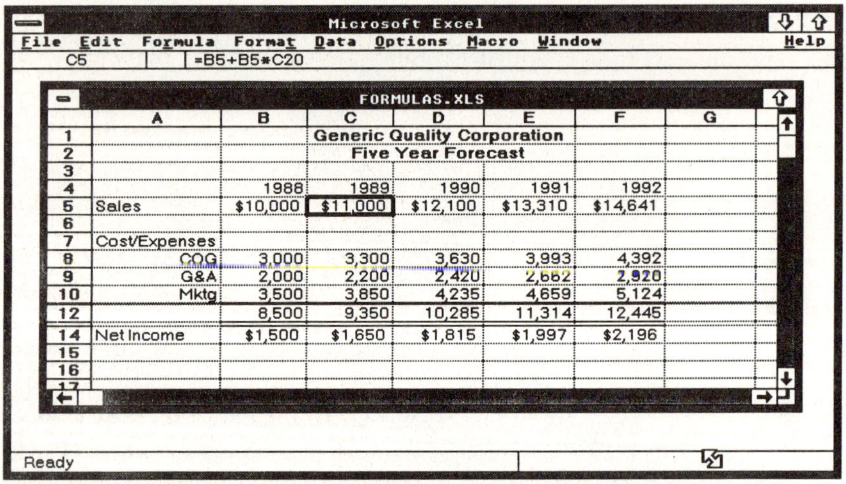

Fig. 7.3. The formula for active cell C5 displayed in the formula bar.

	A	B	C	D	E	F	G
1			Generic Quality Corporation				
2			Five Year Forecast				
3							
4		1988	1989	1990	1991	1992	
5	Sales	$10,000	$11,000	$12,100	$13,310	$14,641	
6							
7	Cost/Expenses						
8	COG	3,000	3,300	3,630	3,993	4,392	
9	G&A	2,000	2,200	2,420	2,662	2,920	
10	Mktg	3,500	3,850	4,235	4,659	5,124	
12		8,500	9,350	10,285	11,314	12,445	
14	Net Income	$1,500	$1,650	$1,815	$1,997	$2,196	
15							
16							
17							

Cell C5: `=B5+B5*C20`

FORMULAS.XLS

Figure 7.4 shows another way to view formulas: displaying two windows on the same worksheet. One window displays the results while the other displays the formulas. The formulas are displayed in the lower window with the **Options Display Formulas** command. The method of displaying and controlling multiple windows onto the same worksheet is described in Chapter 10, "Using Multiple Windows and Linking Worksheets."

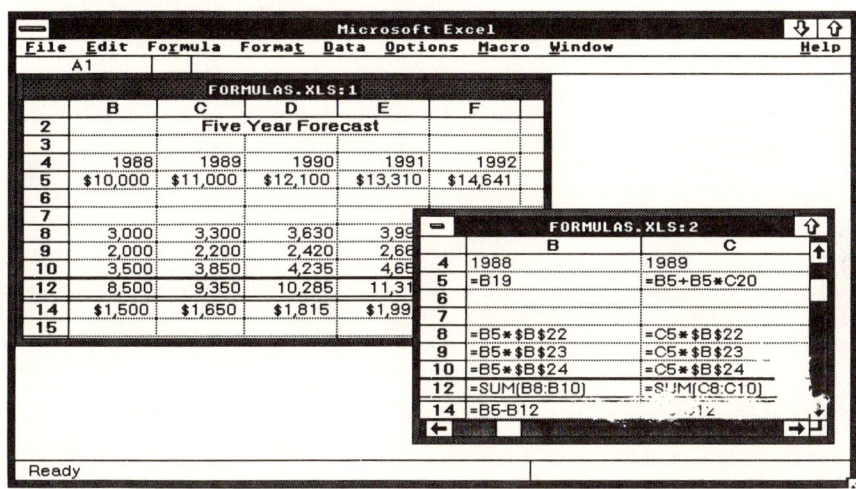

Fig. 7.4. Two windows on the same worksheet: one with formulas, the other with results.

To prepare to enter a formula in an Excel cell, you first select the cell and then type an equal sign (=). You can follow the equal sign with a formula that contains values (numbers, text, logical values, and so on), cell addresses, and operators. Formulas also can include prebuilt formulas (called functions) and names that specify cell ranges. Do not type spaces in formulas.

To enter a formula, follow these steps:

1. Select the cell.

2. Type an equal sign (=).

3. Type a value, address, function, or name.

4. Type an operator.

5. Return to step 3 unless the formula is complete.

   Always separate terms in a formula with operators. Do not leave any spaces in the formula.

6. To enter the formula, click on the check box or press Enter.

Before a formula has been entered, you can clear it from the formula bar by clicking on the X box. From the keyboard, press Esc.

TIP

Filling a Range with a Value or Formula on Entry

If you need to fill a range of cells with the same value or formula, follow these steps:

1. Select the cells to contain the entries.

2. Type the value or formula that is appropriate for the active cell.

3. Press Ctrl+Enter.

The Ctrl+Enter key combination both enters your typing in the active cell and copies it into other cells in the selection. By holding down the Ctrl key as Enter is pressed, the formula enters into the active cell and copies to the selected cells.

Any formulas you enter with Ctrl+Enter adjust their relative cell references to their new locations just as though you had copied them or filled them into the selected cells.

Entering Addresses by Pointing

The most accurate method of entering addresses in a formula is by pointing. Although you can type an entire formula, using the active cell to point to the cell or range you want to include in a formula is often more convenient and always more accurate.

To enter an address into a formula by pointing, follow these steps:

1. Select the cell for the formula.

2. Type an equal sign (=).

3. Point to the cell you want in the formula.

    Mouse: Click on the cell you want included in the formula.

    Keyboard: Press the movement keys to move the dashed "marquee" around the cell you want included in the formula.

    The address of the cell you point to appears at the cursor location in the formula bar. The cell pointed to is enclosed in a dashed line.

4. Enter an operator.

5. Point to the next cell.

6. Repeat step 4 to continue the formula, or enter the formula by clicking on the check box or pressing Enter.

Using Cell References in Formulas

You can refer to a cell's location in Excel with either a *relative reference* or an *absolute reference*. You should be careful that you use the correct type of cell reference in each formula you create. If you understand the difference between the two types of cell references (or two ways you can refer to a cell address) used in Excel, you can avoid one of the most common mistakes made in worksheets.

Everyone uses both relative references and absolute references every day. Suppose, for example, that you are in your office and you want someone to take a letter to the mailbox. Using a relative reference, you would tell the person: "Go out the front door, turn left and go two blocks, turn right and go one block." These directions are *relative to* or determined by your office location. When you move to a different location, these directions do not work anymore. Your letter could end up in an ice-cream parlor.

To make sure that your letter gets to the mailbox no matter from where you give the directions, you must say something like this: "Take this letter to the mailbox at 2700 Mendocino." No matter where you are speaking from, the mailbox will be at one *absolute* location: 2700 Mendocino. The address *absolutely* will not change. And you absolutely will not end up with an unexpected ice-cream cone.

Relative References: Copying or Filling Formulas

Excel assigns a relative reference, such as B12, to a cell address when you enter addresses in a formula, unless an absolute address is explicitly indicated. This means that cell references in a formula change when you copy the formula to a new location or when you fill a range with a formula.

In figure 7.5, the formula in cell C5 is =B5+B5*C20. Only relative references are used in this formula. The formula, translated into English, would read as follows:

Take the contents of the cell 1 column left of C5 and add it to the contents of the cell 1 column left of C5 multiplied by the contents of the 15th cell below C5.

Fig. 7.5. Relative references used in a formula in cell C5.

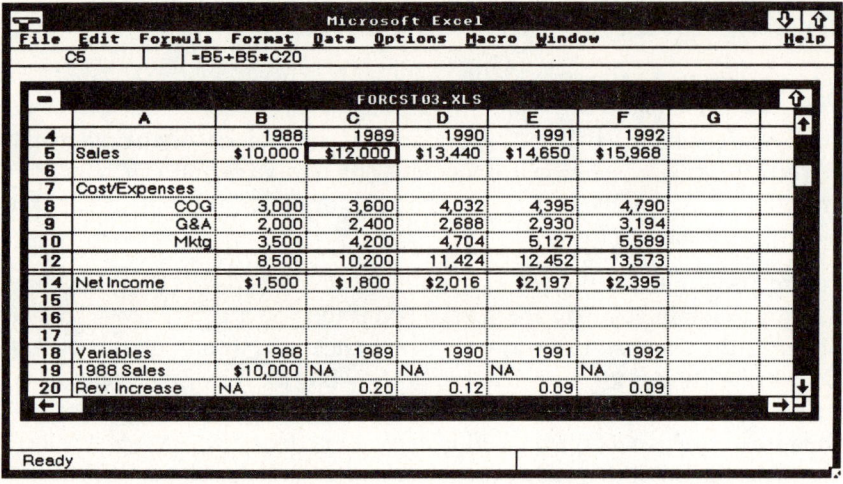

When you copy this formula across row 5, the formula automatically adjusts the B5 and B20 terms to their new positions. The copied formulas therefore look like this:

Cell	Formula
D5	=C5+C5*D20
E5	=D5+D5*E20
F5	=E5+E5*F20

Most of the time, this is the kind of result you intend to achieve. But what would happen if the worksheet didn't have a row of values all the way across row 20? What if row 20 had a single value that each copied formula had to use? What if your worksheet had only a single Rev. Increase number in C20 to be used for each year's revenue increase? Each of the copied formulas in these cases would have been wrong. When you must copy a formula and you must make sure that some terms in the formula do not adjust to their new locations, you must designate those terms as absolute references.

Absolute References: Freezing Cell Addresses during a Copy or Fill

To keep cell references from changing when you copy or fill a formula to new locations, use absolute references. Indicate absolute references by putting a dollar sign ($) in front of the column letter and row number that you want to freeze. (This is the same principle as using the 2700 Mendocino address to locate the absolute address of the mailbox.)

In figure 7.6, the worksheet from Chapter 4, "Worksheet Quick Start," an absolute reference address for $B$22 must be used in the formula in cell B8. The dollar sign in front of each part of the address, B and 22, prevents that part from changing during a copy or fill operation.

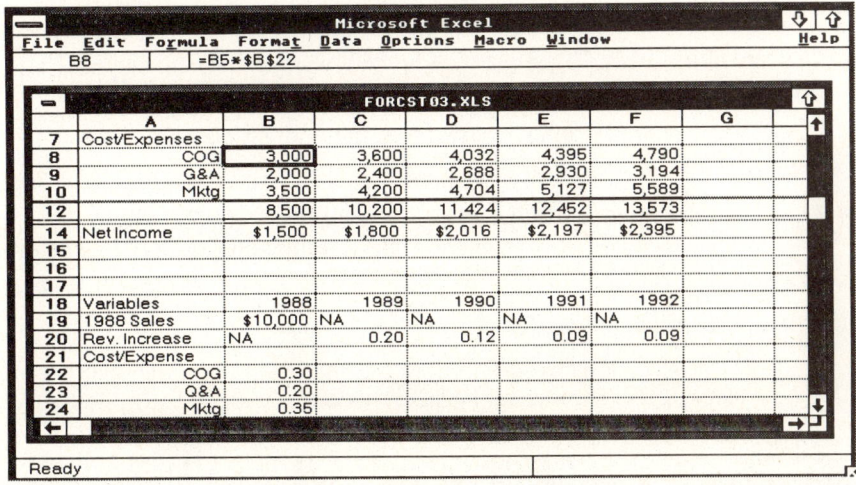

Fig. 7.6. The absolute reference, $B$22, won't change when copied.

The formula in B8, for example, was copied into cells C8, D8, E8, and F8. Cell B8's formula is =B5*$B$22. When copied, only the B5 term was adjusted; the $B$22 term stayed the same because it used an absolute address. The copied formulas still referred to the single unique number: .30 in cell B22. (If B22 was used instead of $B$22, then the copied formulas would contain C22, D22, E22, and F33 respectively.)

TIP

When To Use Absolute References in Formulas

Any formula that contains a reference to a unique single cell should refer to that cell by absolute reference. The fastest way to insert the dollar signs for an absolute reference is to press F4 when the cursor is on the cell reference in the formula bar. You can change the reference of an address in a formula when you are entering the formula or when you edit it.

Press F4 until a dollar sign appears in front of the row or column portion of the cell address you want fixed.

You can enter the dollar signs for an absolute reference in any of three ways:

• Type the dollar sign as you enter the formula in front of the row or column that you want to remain the same.

- Choose the Formula **Reference** command after typing a cell address.

- Move the cursor in the formula bar to the cell address and press F4, the absolute reference key. (If the formula already has been entered, select its cell and press F2 to edit it.)

To enter an absolute reference using the Formula **Reference** command or F4 key, follow these steps:

1. Enter the formula as far as including the address you want to be absolute.

2. Choose the Formula **Reference** command or press F4, the absolute reference key, until the right combination of dollar signs appears.

3. Type the next operator and continue to enter the formula.

You can use the Formula **Reference** command or F4 key when editing an existing formula.

Mixing Absolute and Relative References in Formulas

On some occasions, you will want only the row to stay fixed when copied or only the column to stay fixed. In these cases, you need to use a *mixed reference*, one that contains both absolute and relative references. For example, $B5 prevents the column from changing but the row changes relative to a new copied location. In B$5 just the opposite occurs. The column adjusts to a new location but the row always stays fixed at 5.

You can create mixed references in the same ways you can create absolute references. Type the dollar signs, choose the Formula **Reference** command, or press F4. Each choice of Formula **Reference** or each press of F4 cycles the cell reference to a new combination.

Each time you select the Formula **Reference** command or F4, Excel changes the reference to the next combination in its cycle of combinations of $ signs in the cell address. Press F4 four times, for example, and you cycle through B22, $B$22, B$22, $B22, and B22.

Using R1C1 Style in Absolute and Relative References

In earlier electronic spreadsheets, two types of cell addressing were used: the A1 style familiar to Lotus 1-2-3 users and the R1C1 style familiar to Multiplan users. In Excel, you can use either. When you write custom macros, some macro functions require R1C1 style.

You can switch between the A1 and R1C1 styles of displaying cell references by choosing the **Options Workspace** command, selecting the R1C1 button, and then choosing OK (see fig. 7.7). To switch from R1C1 style back to A1 style, select the R1C1 button again and choose OK.

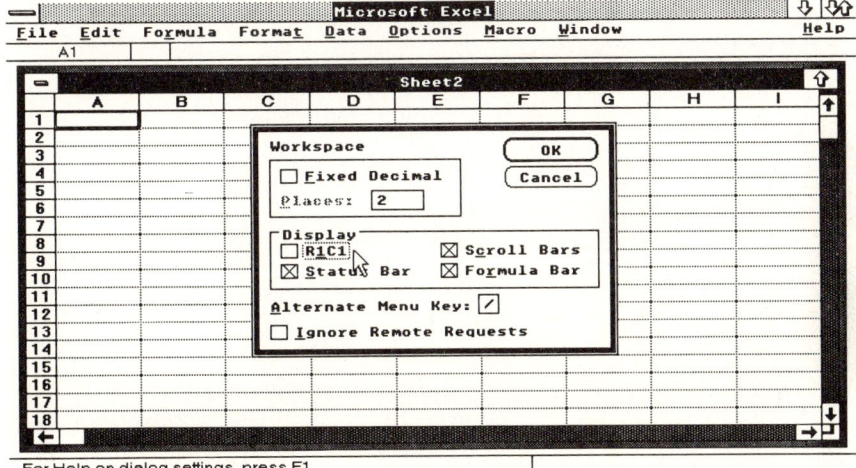

Fig. 7.7. The Workspace dialog box.

In R1C1 style, Excel automatically uses relative references, but displays the relative location by enclosing the number of the row or column in square brackets. For example, R[-3]C[2] defines a cell that is three rows up and two columns to the right of the cell that contains the formula. If no row or column number is specified, then the same row or column as the formula cell is assumed.

In R1C1 style, absolute references appear without the square brackets. For example, R3C2 is the cell at row 3, column 2. This reference does not adjust when copied to a new location. Just as in A1 style, you can mix absolute and relative references, such as R[5]C, R3C[-20] or R[-1]C3.

Using Operators in Formulas

Operators tell formulas what operations to perform. Excel uses four types of operators:

Arithmetic	+, -, *, /, %, ^
Text	&
Comparative	=, <, <=, >, >=, <>
Reference	colon (:), comma (,), space ( )

Table 7.2 illustrates with examples how each of the arithmetic operators can be used in formulas.

Table 7.2
Arithmetic Operators

Operator	Formula	Result	Type of operation
+	=5+2	7	Addition
-	=5-2	3	Subtraction
-	-5	-5	Negation (takes the negative of the number)
*	=5*2	10	Multiplication
/	=5/2	2.5	Division
%	5%	.05	Percentage
^	=5^2	25	Exponentiation (raised to the power of)

Excel can work with more than just arithmetic formulas. The program also can manipulate text, do comparisons, and relate different ranges and cells on the worksheet. For example, the ampersand (&) operator joins text within quotation marks or text contained in referenced cells. Table 7.3 illustrates how text operators can be used.

Table 7.3
Text Operators

Operator	Formula	Result	Type of operation
&	="Ms. "&"Gibbs"	Ms. Gibbs	Text is joined
&	=A12&" "&B36	Ms. Gibbs	Text is joined when A12 contains *Ms.* and B36 contains *Gibbs*

When you need to compare results, you can create formulas using comparative operators. These operators return a TRUE or FALSE result depending on how the formula evaluates the condition. Table 7.4 lists the comparative operators.

Here are some examples of comparative operators in formulas:

=A12<15	TRUE if the content of A12 is less than 15; FALSE if the content of A12 is 15 or more
=B36>=15	TRUE if the content of B36 is 15 or more; FALSE if the content of B36 is less than 15

Table 7.4
Comparative Operators

Operator	Type
=	Equal to
<	Less than
<=	Less than or equal to
>	Greater than
>=	Greater than or equal to
<>	Not equal to

If a cell contains the text TRUE or true, Excel evaluates the cell as TRUE; if a cell contains the text FALSE or false, the cell is evaluated as FALSE. The number 0 is always evaluated as FALSE while any nonzero number is TRUE.

Another type of operator is the reference operator (see table 7.5). Reference operators do not make changes to constants or cell contents. Instead, they control how a formula groups together cells and ranges of cells when the formula calculates. Reference operators let you combine absolute and relative references, and named ranges.

Table 7.5
Reference Operators

Operator	Example	Type	Result
:	SUM(A12:A24)	Range	Evaluates as a single reference the cells in the rectangular area between the two "corners"
,	SUM(A12:A24,B36)	Union	Evaluates two references as a single reference
space	SUM(A12:A24 A16:B20)	Intersect	Evaluates the cells common to both references (if no cells are common to both, then #NULL results)

TIP

Save Work with the Range Operator (:)

Use the range operator (:) to reduce your work in formulas. For example, if you want a formula to refer to all cells in column B, type **B:B**. Similarly, the range that includes all cells in rows 5 through 12 is entered as **5:12**.

1-2-3 TIP

Multiple Ranges

Excel uses a colon (B12:C36) to designate a range in the same way that 1-2-3 uses two periods (B12..C36). Excel has one added benefit: you can use a comma to select multiple ranges (B12:C36,F14:H26) for many functions.

Excel follows a consistent set of rules when applying operators in a formula. Working from the first calculation to the last, Excel evaluates operators in the order shown in table 7.6.

Table 7.6
The Order in Which Excel Evaluates Operators

Operator	Definition
:	Range
space	Intersect
,	Union
-	Negation
%	Percentage
^	Exponentiation
* and /	Multiplication and division
+ and -	Addition and subtraction
&	Text joining
=, <, <= >, >=, <>	Comparisons

You can change the order in which calculations are performed by enclosing in parentheses the terms you want Excel to calculate first. Notice, for instance, the difference between these results:

Formula	Result
=6+21/3	13
=(6+21)/3	9

Changing Formulas to Values

In some situations, such as calculating a number as you enter it in a worksheet, you may want to type a formula, but change it to a value upon entry. To "freeze" a formula into its resulting value, follow these steps:

1. Type the formula in the formula bar, or select the cell of an existing formula and press F2 (the Edit key).

2. Choose the Options Calculate Now command.

   The formula in the formula bar is replaced by its calculated value.

3. Choose OK or press Enter.

You can change part of a formula into a value by selecting from the formula bar the part of the formula you want changed, then choosing the Options Calculate Now command. For example, typing the formula =8*2.5 and then choosing the Options Calculate Now command changes the formula in the formula bar to 20.

Naming Cells for Easier Use

If you get tired of trying to decipher the meaning of B36 or F13:W54 in a formula, you can use names to refer to cells, ranges, and multiple ranges. For example, you can give the range F19:L65 an easily recognizable name such as SALES_REPORT. Named cells and ranges in Excel are similar to range names in Lotus 1-2-3, but in Excel you can paste names into formulas, create compound names, and even assign names to formulas and constants that you use frequently.

Advantages of Naming Names

Using names in worksheets has many advantages in Excel:

- Names reduce the chance for errors in formulas and commands. You and Excel both can recognize that you mistyped SAELS_REPORT when you meant to type SALES_REPORT, but you might not recognize an error in typing F19:L65.

- You can name any frequently used constant or formula and use the name in formulas. (The named constant or formula does not have to reside in a cell as it does in 1-2-3.) For example, you can enter a name such as RATE in a formula and then at any later time use the Formula Define Name command to assign a new value to the word RATE. The new assignment changes the value of RATE throughout the worksheet.

- Named ranges expand and contract automatically to adjust to inserted or deleted rows and columns. This feature lets you conveniently name print or database ranges that expand or contract as you work.

- Names make finding your way around the worksheet easy. You can choose the Formula Goto command and enter the name of the location you want to go to. Choosing the Formula Goto command and then selecting DATA or REPORT is a convenient technique.

- Using names in macros when referring to specific locations on worksheets helps make your macros more versatile. If you rearrange a worksheet, a cell address referenced within a macro does not change automatically. However, if you use a named cell reference in the macro, the name remains correct and the macro works. If you use the same name on different worksheets, you also can use the macro on more than one worksheet.

- Names make formulas easy to recognize and maintain. For example, the formula

    =REVENUE-COST

is much easier to understand than the formula

    =A12-C13

- Names make typing references to other worksheets easy. You do not need to know the cell reference in the other worksheet. If the other worksheet has a named cell reference, then you can type a formula such as

    =YTDCONS.XLS!SALES

This formula brings the information from the SALES cell in the worksheet with the file name YTDCONS.XLS into the cell in your active worksheet.

- Names are easier to remember than cell references. After you name cells or ranges, you can look at a list of names and paste the names you want into formulas with the Formula Paste Name command (see this chapter's "Pasting Names and Functions" section).

Rules for Naming Names

When the time comes to name names, you must remember a few rules:

- Names must start with a letter, but you can use any character after that *except a space*. Do not use a space in a name; instead use an underline (_), hyphen (-), or period (.). Be careful when using a hyphen; it may be mistaken as a minus sign, as in SALES-EXPENSES.

Correct names	*Incorrect names*
SALES_EXPENSES	SALES EXPENSES
YR1989	1989
RATE	%

- Although names can be as long as 255 characters, you will want to make them shorter. Because formulas also are limited to 255 characters, using long names in a formula leaves you less room for the rest of the formula. Also, the longer the name, the harder you may find remembering it. Conversely, do not make names so abbreviated that you feel like you are playing a word game trying to figure them out.

- Names can be typed in either upper- or lowercase letters. Excel changes them to uppercase.

- Do not use names that look like cell references, such as B13 or R13C2.

Naming a Cell, Range, or Multiple Ranges

To name a cell, range of cells, or multiple range, follow these steps:

1. Select the area you want to name.

2. Choose the Formula Define Name command.

3. Leave the name Excel proposes, if it is acceptable, or type the name you want in the Name box.

4. Leave the cell reference in the **Refers To** box, if it is acceptable, or type an equal sign (=) followed by the correct reference.

5. Choose OK or press Enter.

You can see in figure 7.8 that Excel proposes a name to use when the cells you select contain text. Excel looks at the left edge for a text name in a row or looks above for a text name in a column. If you select a range, Excel checks for a name in the upper left cell of the range. Notice that Excel automatically replaced the blank between Mo and Increase with an underscore to make the name legal. (In figure 7.8, cell B4 could have been selected by itself and the name typed in.)

Fig. 7.8. A range name and cell reference proposed by Excel for the selected cells on the worksheet.

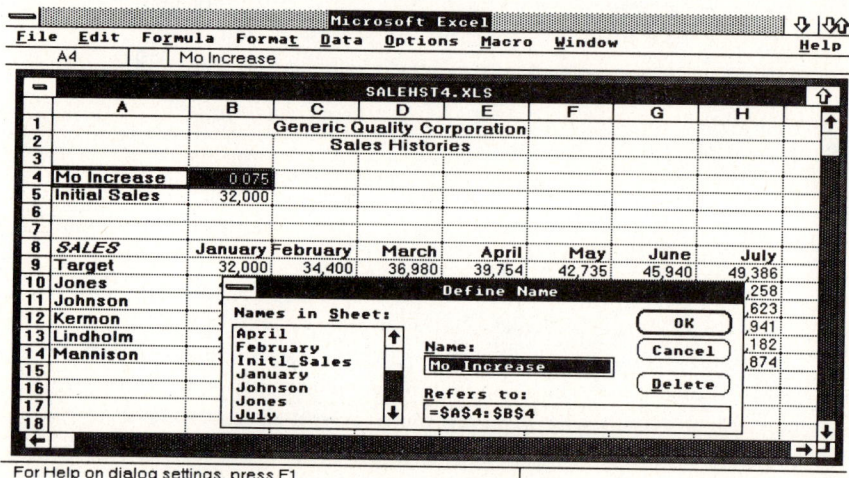

For Help on dialog settings, press F1

TIP

Printing Multiple Ranges Quickly and Easily

If you frequently must print the same areas of the worksheet, select those areas as a multiple range and give them a name. When you print, use this name to indicate that you want to print all those ranges at the same time.

1-2-3 TIP

Why Range Names Don't Show in Formulas

Excel does not immediately replace existing cell addresses in formulas with range names. You have the advantage of specifying the areas of the worksheet where formulas show the range names. This procedure is described in the "Applying Names" section later in this chapter.

Creating Names from Existing Text

If you have built a text skeleton for your worksheet (as described in Chapter 5, "Designing Worksheets"), you can use the text on the worksheet to assign names automatically to adjacent cells. Moreover, by selecting a range of cells, you can assign a number of names at the same time.

To assign a number of names at the same time, you use the Formula Create Names command. This Excel command works like the /Range Name Labels command in Lotus 1-2-3, but you can do more with Formula Create Names. You specify the range to which you want names applied, and Excel uses the text along the top or bottom rows or in the left or right columns to name adjacent cells or ranges.

To create names from existing text, follow these steps:

1. Select the range of cells you want to name. Be sure to include the row or column of text cells that compose the names.

2. Choose the Formula Create Names command.

    The dialog box shown in figure 7.9 appears.

Fig. 7.9. The Create Names dialog box.

3. Select the Top Row option to use text in the top row as names for the columns. Similarly, the Bottom Row option uses the bottom row of text as names for the columns. The Left Column option uses text in the left column to name the rows to the right of the text; and the Right Column option uses the text in the right column to name the rows to the left of the text.

4. Choose OK or press Enter.

In figure 7.10, the cells in the columns are named with the names at the top of each column. In figure 7.11, each of the selected rows is named with the names down the left column of the selected area.

If you attempt to assign a duplicate name, a dialog box appears, warning you that the name is already in use. Choose the Yes button to update the name to the new references; choose the No button to retain the old name and references; or choose the Cancel button to retain the old name and back out of creating new names.

Fig. 7.10. Names created from the top row of text.

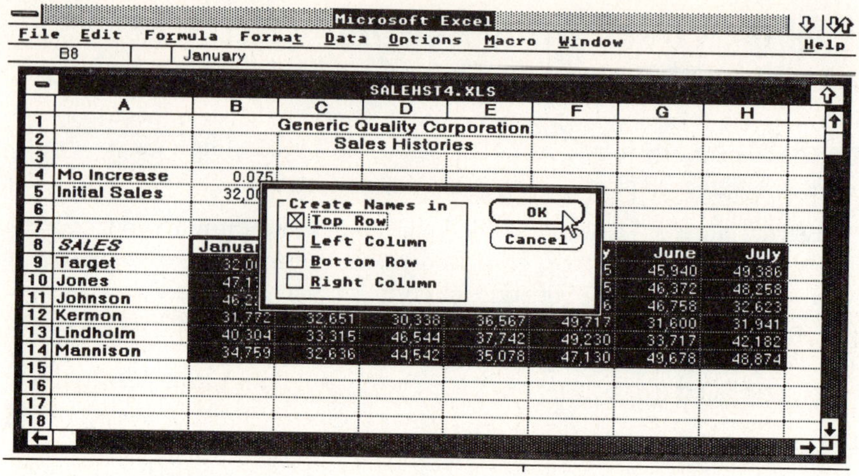

Fig. 7.11. Names created from the left column of text.

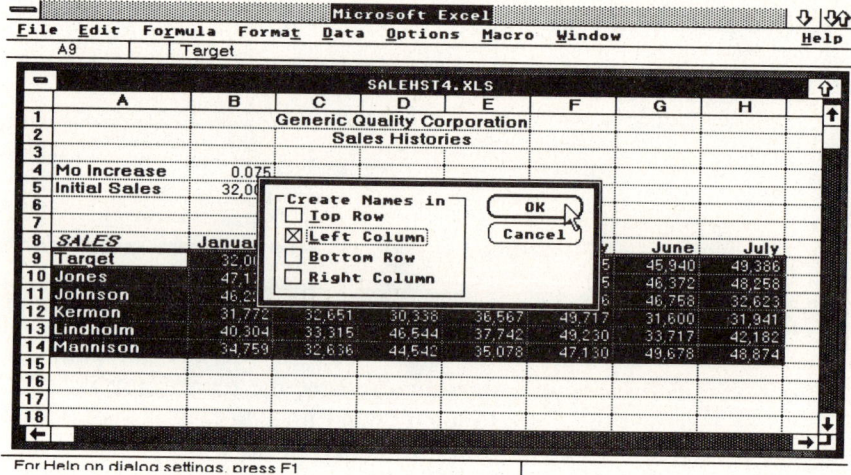

Automatic Naming

If you use Formula Create Names to name cells, make sure that the text in the cells does not violate the rules for names. An alert box appears to tell you when text cannot be accepted as a name.

Text in cells used as names can have spaces. Excel automatically replaces the space with an underscore mark in the created name. For example, Sales Rate in a cell becomes the name Sales_Rate.

You can select more than one box from the Create Names dialog box. As a result, you can name cells in different orientations with different names. If you select two options that overlap, then any text in the cell at the overlap is used as the name for the entire range. For example, if you select both the Top Row and Left Column options, then the text in the cell at the top left of the selected range is the name for the entire range. In figure 7.12, the name SALES applies to the entire range while the names apply to the rows and the months apply to the columns.

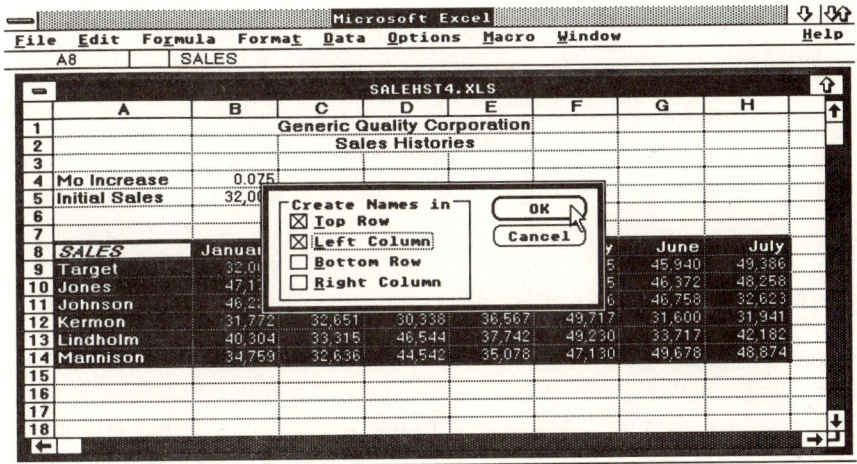

Fig. 7.12. In Excel you can create column and row names simultaneously.

TIP

Pasting a List of Names

As part of your worksheet documentation, you should include a list of the names used. Excel can paste into your worksheet a complete list of names and the cells they name. Move the cursor to a clear area and choose the Formula **Paste** Name command followed by the Paste **List** button. A list of all the names and corresponding cell addresses appears in your worksheet.

Changing or Deleting Names

Sometimes you will want to change a name or the cells that the name refers to. Also, from time to time, you may want to delete names that are no longer needed. Deleting unneeded names keeps your list of names free of clutter.

To change a name or the cells that the name references, follow these steps:

1. Choose the Formula **D**efine Name command. (This is the same command you use to name a cell or range of cells manually.)

2. Select from the list box the name you want to change.

3. Select the **N**ame box or the **R**efers To box.

    Mouse: Click on the box you want to change.

    Keyboard: Press Tab until the answer appears in the box you want to change.

4. Edit the name or cell reference in the appropriate text box. Use the arrow keys, backspace, and Del keys to edit in the text box.

5. Choose OK or press Enter.

To delete a name, select the name you want to delete. Then choose the Delete button. Caution: After you have deleted a name, selecting Cancel does not undelete it.

Applying Names

When you create or define names, they are not automatically distributed to formulas throughout the worksheet. Excel gives you the ability to select where you want names applied with the Formula Apply Names command (see fig. 7.13).

Fig. 7.13. The Apply Names dialog box.

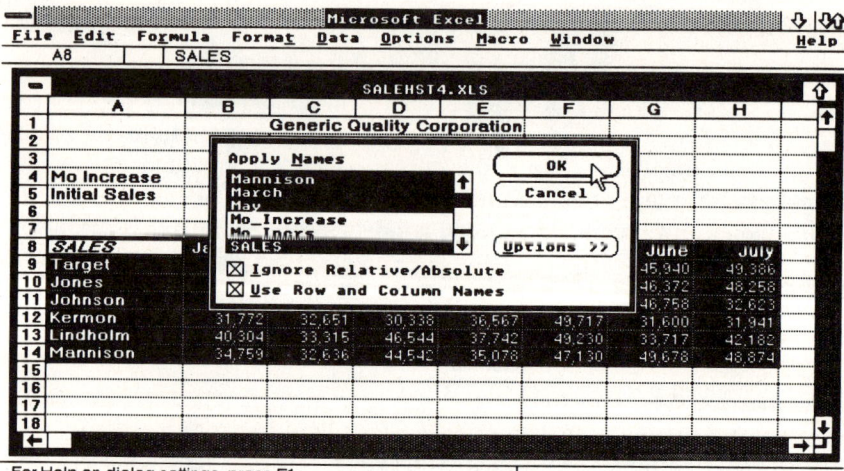

To apply existing names to formulas containing named cell references, follow these steps:

1. Select a single cell if you want to apply names to the entire worksheet, or select a range to apply names to formulas within the range.

2. Choose the Formula Apply Names command.

3. Select names to apply from the Apply Names dialog box.

    Mouse: Hold down Ctrl as you click on each name you want to apply. Ctrl enables you to select multiple names.

    Keyboard: Press the up- or down-arrow key to move through the list. Hold down Ctrl to keep previous selections as you move. Press Shift+arrow to select multiple contiguous names.

4. Select the **Ignore** Relative/Absolute check box if you want names to replace absolute and relative references. Unselecting this box matches absolute names to relative references.

5. Select the **Use Row and Column Names** check box if you want Excel to rename cell references with range names that are appropriate for the cell's location. Unselect this box if you want only individual cell names to apply to cell references.

6. Select the **Options** button to omit names in the same row or column.

7. Choose OK or press Enter.

TIP

The Conservative Approach to Applying Names

If you want to be conservative when you apply names to cell references, then unselect both the **Ignore** Relative/Absolute and the **Use Row and Column Names** check boxes. With these two boxes unselected, names replace only exact matches with absolute or relative references.

NOTE

When To Use Ignore Relative/Absolute

If you do not plan to copy any formulas, leave the **Ignore** Relative/Absolute check box selected. If you still have a lot of formula copying to do, unselect the **Ignore** Relative/Absolute check box.

Creating Your Own Named Formulas and Values

Your worksheets are much more readable and understandable if you use names for commonly used constants or frequently used formulas. You can name any number or formula and then use that name in a cell or formula. The number or formula does not have to be in a cell.

Use these steps to name a value or formula you enter:

1. Choose the Formula Define Name command.

2. Select the Name text box and enter the name.

3. Select the **Refers to** box.

   Mouse: Click on the **Refers to** box.

   Keyboard: Press Tab until the **Refers to** box is selected.

4. Delete unwanted characters with the backspace or Del key.

5. Type the constant number or the formula. Begin by typing an equal sign (=) and enter the formula as you would in the formula bar. You can edit in the **Refers to** box as you edit in the formula bar. (Use the backspace or Del keys to erase. Press F2 and then the arrow keys to move in the text.)

6. Choose OK or press Enter.

Figure 7.14 illustrates how a formula is assigned a name. Type the formula or constant value into the **Refers to** box, just as you would have typed a new cell reference. Because this name is not tied to a cell reference, you can use the name anywhere in the worksheet. Because the formula or constant stored in the name does not have to be stored in a cell, your worksheets stay neater and are easier for inexperienced people to use. (The names in the list box show names that already have been created.)

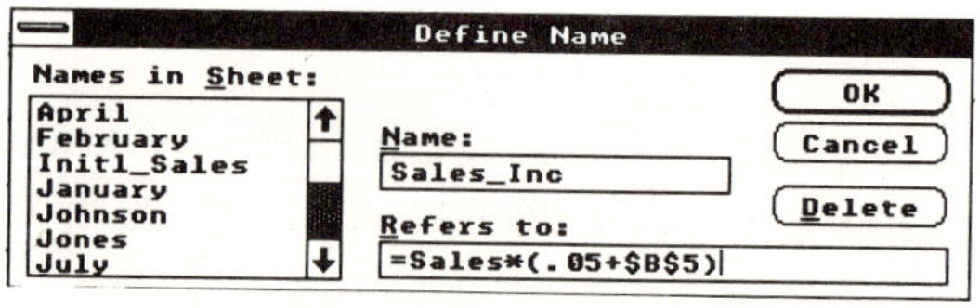

Fig. 7.14. The Define Name dialog box.

If you build formulas in the **R**efers to box by pointing to cell references, Excel supplies only absolute references (such as $D$15). These references are absolute because a name usually applies to one specific location on a worksheet. You can type relative references or edit out the dollar signs to make names that act like relative references. For example, if the active cell is C6, you might type the formula =C12 in the **R**efers to box. You could give the formula the name RIGHT6. You then can use the name RIGHT6 in a formula or cell in order to pick up the contents of the cell six cells to the right of the cell containing the name RIGHT6. If the Define Name dialog box is in the way of a cell you want to select, then move the dialog box. Use the mouse to drag the box to a new location; or from the keyboard, press Alt and then the space bar. Then choose the **M**ove command.

1-2-3 TIP

Be Careful with Relative References in Named Formulas

Beware when using names that contain formulas with relative references. The relative references change if the name is copied to a new location.

TIP

Formula Macros Save Even More Time

If you have formulas that you want to use in multiple worksheets, you should create formula macros. Try the Macro Quick Start in Chapter 25, "Macro Quick Start," and then learn how easily you can create function macros in Chapter 26, "Building Command and Function Macros."

Increasing Data-Entry Efficiency

Data entry is usually tedious, but it must be done correctly. The following sections show you how to speed up the data-entry process.

Entering Data for Accounting

If you are accustomed to using a 10-key pad where the decimal point is entered automatically, you will appreciate the fixed decimal feature of Excel. If you choose the **O**ptions **W**orkspace command, Excel enters the decimal point automatically for you. When the Workspace dialog box appears, select the **F**ixed Decimal box. In the **P**laces text box, enter the number of decimal places you want (2 is normal). Choose OK or press Enter.

Now, for example, to enter the number 345.67, you can type **34567**. When you press Enter, Excel enters the number and inserts the decimal point. If you want a particular entry to have a decimal place different than 2 digit, you can type the decimal manually. For example, you can type **34.567** to enter the number 34.567.

Excel continues to operate with the fixed decimals even when you quit and restart Excel. To turn off the feature, you must unselect the **Options** Workspace **Fixed Decimal** box.

NOTE

Choose the Correct Decimal Place Command

When you want the decimal place entered automatically, make sure that you choose the **Options Workspace** command and select **Fixed Decimal**. A command that appears similar, but that alters the numbers stored in memory, is the **Options Calculation Precision as Displayed** command, discussed in Chapter 8, "Formatting Worksheets."

Entering Data in a Range

Selecting the range in which you want to enter data speeds your data-entry process. After you insert additional cells in the middle of a database, as shown in figure 7.15, the data-entry range is automatically selected. In Excel, the inserted cells remain selected and retain a format appropriate to their column.

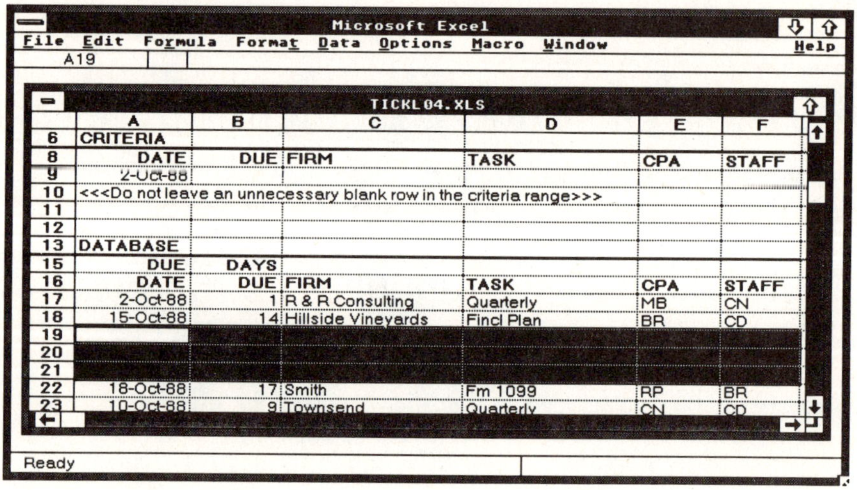

Fig. 7.15. Cells inserted in the middle of a database.

	A	B	C	D	E	F
6	CRITERIA					
8	DATE	DUE	FIRM	TASK	CPA	STAFF
9	2-Oct-88					
10	<<<Do not leave an unnecessary blank row in the criteria range>>>					
11						
12						
13	DATABASE					
15	DUE	DAYS				
16	DATE	DUE	FIRM	TASK	CPA	STAFF
17	2-Oct-88	1	R & R Consulting	Quarterly	MB	CN
18	15-Oct-88	14	Hillside Vineyards	Fincl Plan	BR	CD
19						
20						
21						
22	18-Oct-88	17	Smith	Fm 1099	RP	BR
23	10-Oct-88	9	Townsend	Quarterly	CN	CD

With the active cell in the selected area, you can type an entry, and then press one of these keys:

Key	Action
Tab	Enters data and moves right in the selected area; at the right edge of the selected area, wraps to the left
Shift+Tab	Enters data and moves left in the selected area; at the left edge of the selected area, wraps to the right
Enter	Enters data and moves down in the selected area; at the bottom of the selected area, wraps to the top
Shift+Enter	Enters data and moves up in the selected area; at the top of the selected area, wraps to the bottom

When the active cell reaches the edge of the selected area, it automatically wraps around to the next appropriate cell. For example, if you are pressing Tab repeatedly, the active cell reaches the right edge and then jumps to the first cell in the next row of the left edge.

Using Data-Entry Shortcuts

As you enter data in a database, you may want to copy down information from the cell above the active cell or insert the current date and time. Excel has shortcut keys that make this easy and convenient to do. You also can use these shortcut keys when you are working in selected ranges like the ones shown in figure 7.15:

Key	Action
Ctrl+' (apostrophe)	Copies the formula and value from the cell above (cell references are not adjusted to the new location)
Ctrl+" (quotation mark)	Copies the format from the cell above
Ctrl+; (semicolon)	Inserts the time
Ctrl+: (colon)	Inserts the date

Ctrl+1	Format Font 1
Ctrl+2	Format Font 2
Ctrl+3	Format Font 3
Ctrl+4	Format Font 4

Working While Excel Recalculates

Most worksheet applications calculate the entire worksheet during any re-calculation. Excel knows which cells depend on each other and only recal-culates those cells that are affected by a change. The benefit of this Excel function for you is less time spent waiting for the worksheet to recalculate.

When it recalculates, Excel incorporates two additional features that can in-crease your productivity. First, you can continue entering data, changing for-mulas, or giving commands as the worksheet recalculates. Excel incorporates the changes you make as it recalculates. No more do you have to stare at a WAIT signal wondering how long the recalculation will take before you can make a change.

Secondly, you can start a recalculation on a worksheet, and then activate other Windows applications and work in those as Excel continues recalculating the worksheet in the "background." This capability allows you to continue work-ing on other projects while the worksheet is recalculating. This feature is almost like having two personal computers.

Choosing When To Recalculate

Excel normally recalculates applicable portions of the worksheet as soon as you make a change. If you are entering data into a database or if your worksheet has large tables, data entry may slow down. In these cases, you may want to disable automatic recalculation.

To disable automatic recalculation, follow these steps:

1. Choose the **Options Calculation** command to display the dialog box shown in figure 7.16.

2. Select the **Manual** button for manual recalculation, or select **Automatic except Tables** to recalculate the worksheet, but not tables.

3. Choose OK or press Enter.

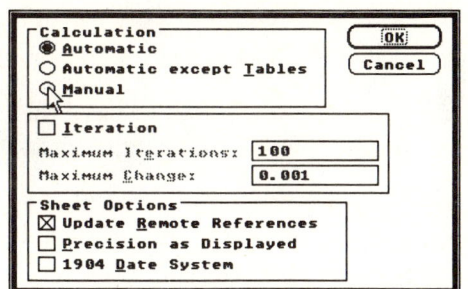

Fig. 7.16. The Calculation dialog box.

After manual calculation is selected, a Calculate message appears at the bottom of the screen whenever you make an entry to indicate that a manual recalculation must be performed before the results are accurate.

NOTE

Watch for the Calculate Message

When manual recalculation is turned on, the worksheet does not automatically recalculate. What you see on the screen or print to paper could be wrong. If the Calculate message appears at the bottom of the screen, make sure that you choose the **Options Calculate Now** command (F9) or the **Options Calculate Document** command (Shift+F9) before you use the worksheet results.

To recalculate all your open worksheets manually, choose the **Options Calculate Now** command or press F9. To recalculate only the active document, choose the **Options Calculate Document** command or press Shift+F9.

Editing in the Worksheet

You can edit a worksheet in two ways: by editing the contents of a cell in the formula bar and by editing the architecture and arrangement of the worksheet. Here are the basic procedures:

- Edit the contents of a cell by selecting it, then clicking in the formula bar (or pressing F2). Use the edit keys to make changes, and then press Enter or click the check to enter the changes in the cell. Press Esc or click the X box to back out of a formula edit.

- Edit the arrangement of cells in the worksheet by selecting areas of cells, and then cutting or copying them. Select a cell at the upper left corner where you want the copy to appear. Use the **Edit Paste** command to paste the cells into the new location (or press Shift+Ins). Be sure to check the formulas for correctness.

- You can undo your last worksheet edits with **Edit Undo**.

If you have edited text in other Windows applications, then you already know how to change text in Excel. However, you should read this chapter's material on editing formulas to learn the commands and shortcuts available in Excel. The shortcut keys for editing in the worksheet are summarized in table 7.7.

Table 7.7
Shortcut Keys for Editing in the Worksheet

Key	Action
Formula bar editing	
F2 (or click in bar)	Moves the cursor into the formula bar for editing
F4	Cycles the address next to the cursor in the formula bar between absolute and relative references
Ins	Toggles between Insert and Typeover modes
Del	Clears the character or selection to the right of the cursor
Backspace	Clears the character or selection to the left of the cursor
Ctrl+Del	Clears all characters to the end of the line
Shift+Del	Cuts the character or selection to the right of the cursor
Shift+Ins	Pastes the text at the cursor or into the selected area
Home	Moves the cursor to the front of the formula bar
End	Moves the cursor to the end of the formula bar's contents
Shift+Home	Selects all characters from the cursor to the front of the formula bar
Shift+End	Selects all characters from the cursor to the end of the formula bar

Key	*Action*
Shift+arrow	Selects characters during a move
Worksheet editing	
Del	Clears selected cells; same as **Edit Clear**
Ctrl+Del	Clears selected formulas; same as **Edit Clear Formulas**
Backspace	Clears the formula bar; activates and clears formula bar
Ctrl+Ins	Copies the selection; same as **Edit Copy**
Shift+Del	Cuts selected cells; same as **Edit Cut**
Shift+Ins	Pastes at the selected cell; same as **Edit Paste**
Alt+backspace	Undoes last command from **Edit** menu
Ctrl+backspace	Repositions the worksheet so that the active cell is in view

Editing the Contents of a Cell

Whether you are editing a text box in a dialog box or a formula, you use the same basic principles. Before you can edit text, use the following steps to select the cell, display its contents in the formula bar, and open the text box for editing:

1. Select the cell.

    Mouse: Click on the cell.

    Keyboard: Move to the cell.

2. Move the cursor into the formula bar.

    Mouse: Position the I-beam pointer where you want the cursor to appear, and then click the mouse button to create an insertion point (cursor).

    Keyboard: Press F2 (Edit).

    or

1. Select a text box within a dialog box.

    Mouse: Click on the text box you want to make active.

Keyboard: Press Tab until the text box you want is active, or press Alt and the underlined letter within the name of the text box.

Editing the Formula Bar Before You Enter

You are not limited to editing text or formulas after they are entered. You can edit the work you are currently typing in the formula bar by pressing F2. After you press F2, you can use the arrow, Home, and End keys to move through text. You can insert or delete characters as you would in any Windows application.

Inserting Text

To insert information in a text box or formula bar, follow these steps:

1. Select the text box or display the cell contents in the formula bar by pressing F2.

2. Position the cursor within the text at the point where you want to make the insertion.

   Mouse: Position the I-beam pointer at the appropriate point, and then click the mouse button.

   Keyboard: Press the arrow, Home, or End keys to position the cursor.

3. Type your text. Any existing text or formula moves to make room.

When you need to insert the same text in several places, select the text and copy it to the clipboard (temporary memory) with the Edit Copy command. Then move the flashing cursor where you want the copy placed and choose Edit Paste. The Formula Replace command, described in this chapter's "Making Multiple Changes" section, is designed to replace multiple occurrences throughout the worksheet.

Excel normally is in Insert mode. If you want to type over existing text, position the I-beam, press Ins (Insert), and then type. You are in Typeover mode. Pressing Ins a second time toggles you back to Insert mode.

You can delete single characters to the left of the cursor by pressing backspace. Delete single characters to the right of the cursor by pressing Del.

When Excel beeps and does not let you edit, the problem may be that the cell is protected against changes. Protection is described in Chapter 8, "Formatting Worksheets."

Deleting or Replacing Text

You do not need to make corrections one character at a time. You can use the following steps to select blocks of text and delete or replace them in text boxes and formula bars:

1. Select the text box or display the cell contents in the formula bar by pressing F2.

2. Position the cursor to the left of where you want to make the deletion.

    Mouse: Position the I-beam pointer to the left of the first character of the text block and click the mouse to position the insertion point (cursor).

    Keyboard: Press the arrow, Home, or End keys to position the cursor to the left of where you want text replaced.

3. Select the characters you want to delete.

    Mouse: Drag over the appropriate characters.

    Keyboard: Press Shift+right arrow to select text to the right of the cursor.

4. Press Del to delete the selected text or type new text (selected text is automatically replaced).

TIP

Delete to End of Line

Delete from the cursor's current location to the end of the line with Ctrl+Del.

Editing Formulas

You can edit Excel formulas with the same techniques you used to build them. For example, you can paste named ranges and functions into formulas or refer to cells and ranges by pointing to them. Excel even has a find-and-replace function to help you repeat changes throughout the worksheet. You may not need all the formula editing techniques described in this chapter at one time, but knowing what is available saves you time and effort later.

TIP

Putting Problem Formulas "on Hold"

The time may come when you know that a formula contains an error, but you cannot seem to find it. Although Excel does not let you enter the formula, you hate to press Esc and lose it. Instead, put the incorrect formula "on hold" until a later time.

With the formula still in the formula bar, press F2 to make sure that you are in Edit mode. Then press Home and the space bar to insert a single space before the equal sign (=) at the front of the formula. Press Enter. Because the formula now starts with a space instead of an equal sign, Excel accepts it as text. You can come back later to fix your errant formula. (When you correct the formula, remember to delete the space at the beginning of the line.)

TIP

Seeing Double with Formulas

Editing a formula is sometimes easier when you can see both the formula and its result. You can do this by opening a new window onto the same worksheet. Format one window with Options Display Formulas to show formulas, and the other can be left to show results. Changes in one window automatically appear in the other.

Finding Formulas That Need To Be Changed

The Formula Find command finds whatever you want in the worksheet (or database), including text or formulas. You can use the Formula Find command to find formulas that contain a unique term, a specific text label, a cell note containing a specific word, or error values. The Formula Find command is especially helpful when you are correcting a worksheet with which you may not be familiar.

To find text or a value with Formula Find, follow these steps:

1. Select the cells you want to search. If you do not select a range of cells, then the entire worksheet is searched from the active cell's location.

2. Choose the Formula Find command to display the Find dialog box (see fig. 7.17). In the Find What box, type the text for which you are searching.

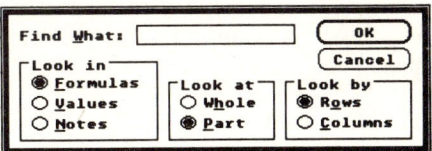

Fig. 7.17. The
Find What
dialog box.

3. From among the Look In options, select one button that describes the items you want to search through:

   Formulas   Search through formulas in the cells indicated.

   Values   Search through values in the cells indicated.

   Notes   Search through notes attached to the cells indicated. (Notes are hidden descriptive text that can be attached to cells.)

4. Select one Look At option that describes how much of the cell contents must match:

   Whole   The text in the Find What box must match the entire formula or value in the cell.

   Part   The text in the Find What box can match any part of the formula or value in the cell.

5. Select the Look By option that describes the direction in which you want the search to proceed:

   Rows   Search through each row, and then proceed to the next row.

   Columns   Search through each column, and then proceed to the next column.

6. Choose OK to find the next match, or press Shift and choose OK to find the previous match. Choose Cancel to stop finding items.

After you have completed step 6 and found the item, edit the formula with normal editing procedures.

To find the next cell that satisfies the same conditions, choose Formula Find and then OK to search for the next occurrence of the item. For even quicker results, press F7 (Formula Find) to search for the next occurrence, or press Shift+F7 to search for the previous occurrence.

Formula Find cannot be used with comparative operators such as =, <, and >=. For example, entering <12 in Cell Find creates a search for the text *<12* rather than for numbers less than 12.

A similar command, Formula Select Special, is a valuable tool for finding worksheet errors. Chapter 13, "Troubleshooting Worksheets," contains a description of the Select Special command.

Making Multiple Changes

The Formula Replace command is a big help when you have to do a major overhaul on a worksheet. The command works the same as a search-and-replace command does in a word-processing program. You tell Excel what text to replace and what text replaces it. Excel finds the text you are looking for and asks whether you want it replaced. If you want, you can go immediately to the next occurrence of the same text and replace it also.

Formula Replace can save you from dreadful financial problems. If you must make major changes to a term or formula used throughout a worksheet, missing a single formula can have dire consequences. With Formula Replace, you can be sure that you have found and replaced all the incorrect formulas or terms.

TIP

Be Safe Before You Replace

In Excel, you can "undo" some mistakes, but you can't undo an incorrect search-and-replace. Before you replace, you may want to make a backup copy of your work using the File Save As command.

To search and replace, follow these steps:

1. Select the cells you want to search.

   If you do not select a range of cells, then the entire worksheet is searched from the active cell forward.

2. Choose the Formula Replace command to display the Replace dialog box (see fig. 7.18).

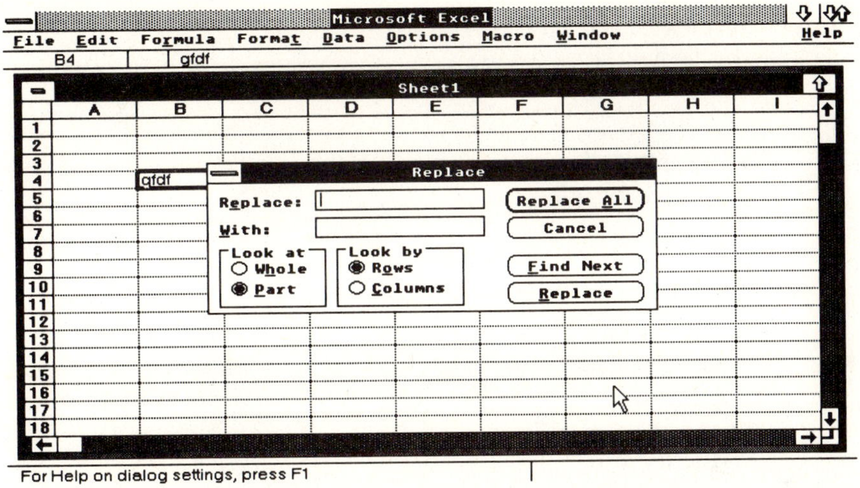

Fig. 7.18. The Replace dialog box.

For Help on dialog settings, press F1

3. Select the **R**eplace box and type the text to be replaced.

4. Select the **W**ith box and type the replacement text.

5. Select the Look At option that describes how much of the cell contents must match:

Whole   The text in the Find What box must match the entire formula or value in the cell.

Part   The text in the Find What box can match any part of the formula or value in the cell.

6. Select the Look By option that describes the direction in which you want the search to proceed:

Rows   Search through each row, and then proceed to the next row.

Columns   Search through each column, and then proceed to the next column.

7. Choose the Replace **A**ll button to find and replace all matches, **F**ind Next to find the next match, or **R**eplace to replace the current found item. Choose Cancel to stop the Replace command and put away the dialog box. Choosing Cancel does not undo replacements that already have occurred.

Editing Absolute and Relative References

To change an absolute or relative cell reference that is already entered into a formula, follow these steps:

1. Select the formula.

   Mouse: Click on the cell containing the formula. Then click in the formula bar.

   Keyboard: Move to the cell, and then press F2 (Edit).

2. Move the cursor to the cell reference in the formula that you want changed. The cursor can be alongside or within the cell reference.

3. Press F4 to cycle through combinations of absolute and relative cell references. Or choose the Formula Reference command to accomplish the same thing as pressing F4.

4. When the formula is displayed correctly, press Enter.

Figure 7.19 shows a formula bar with the cursor in a cell reference before F4 was pressed. Figure 7.20 shows the effect of pressing F4 one time.

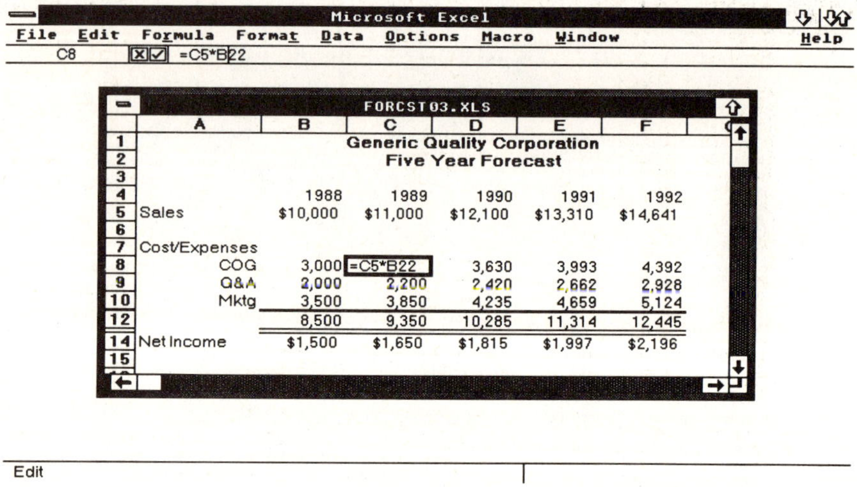

Fig. 7.19. A formula with relative references and the cursor within B22 in the formula bar.

	A	B	C	D	E	F
1			Generic Quality Corporation			
2			Five Year Forecast			
3						
4		1988	1989	1990	1991	1992
5	Sales	$10,000	$11,000	$12,100	$13,310	$14,641
6						
7	Cost/Expenses					
8	COG	3,000	=C5*B22	3,630	3,993	4,392
9	G&A	2,000	2,200	2,420	2,662	2,928
10	Mktg	3,500	3,850	4,235	4,659	5,124
12		8,500	9,350	10,285	11,314	12,445
14	Net Income	$1,500	$1,650	$1,815	$1,997	$2,196
15						

C8 =C5*B22

Edit

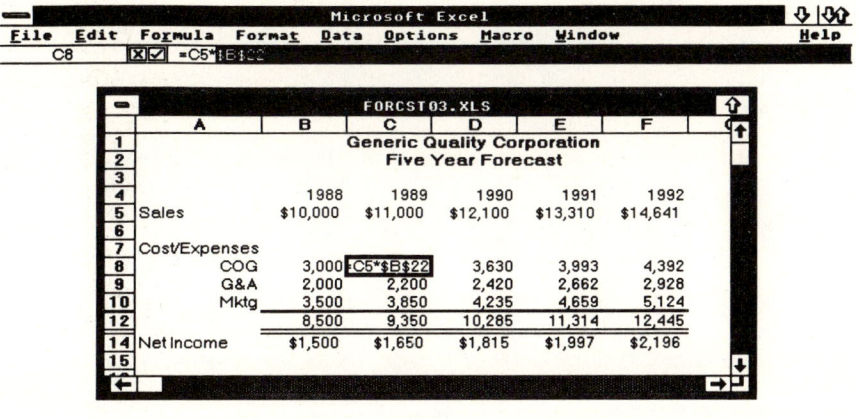

Fig. 7.20. The same formula after pressing F4.

Entering New Cell References

Using the same techniques you used to create formulas, you can edit them to create new cell references. You are not limited to typing cell references in existing formulas. For example, to insert new cell references, you can use the cell pointer to point to cells and ranges on the worksheet just as you did when you first created the formula.

To insert a new cell reference or range into an existing formula, follow these steps:

1. Position the cursor in the formula bar where you want the new cell reference or range. If you are replacing one reference with another, select the portion of the formula you want to replace.

2. Type or point to the new cell reference.

   Mouse: Type or click on the new cell reference. If your new reference is a range, click on the top left corner and drag to the lower right corner.

   Keyboard: Press the arrow keys to move the cell enclosed by dashes to the cell you want included in the formula. To include a range in the formula, press the arrow keys to move the cell enclosed by dashes to the upper left corner of the range. Then press Shift+arrow to select the range.

   Watch the formula bar as you perform step 2. You see the new cell references appear in the formula.

3. If you want to add another cell reference, first type an operator (such as + or *) and then repeat step 2. When the formula is complete, choose OK or press Enter. (If you decide to back out of the formula bar without making a change, press Esc.)

All the worksheet movement keys are available for pointing when you edit. If the worksheet does not display the cells you need to point to, scroll the worksheet so that you can see the cells.

Pasting Names and Functions

If you have named cell ranges or are using Excel's ready-made functions, you doe not have to do much work to edit those names or functions in formulas. Excel lets you choose the name or function you want from a list and then paste it into a formula. Pasting a name or function is an easier and more accurate method than typing one.

To paste a name or function into an existing formula, follow these steps:

1. In the formula bar, move the cursor to the point in the formula where you want the name or function inserted or select the part of the formula you want replaced.

2. Choose either Formula **P**aste Name to display the dialog box shown in figure 7.21 or Formula Paste Function to display the dialog box shown in figure 7.22.

3. From the list box, select the name or function you want to paste.

   Mouse: Scroll the list box until the name or function you want is displayed, and then click to select it.

   Keyboard: Press Tab to move the dashed line to the list box, and then press the first letter of the name or function or use the up- or down-arrow keys to highlight the name or function you want.

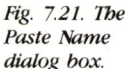

Fig. 7.21. The Paste Name dialog box.

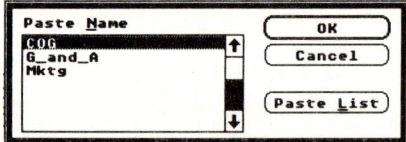

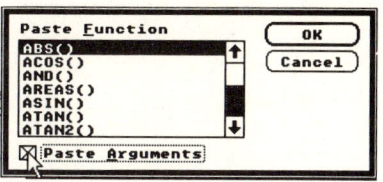

Fig. 7.22. The Paste Function dialog box.

4. Choose OK or press Enter.

5. Type an operator before inserting the next entry. When the formula is completed, click on the check box or press Enter. (If you decide to cancel all edit changes, click on the X box or press Esc.)

TIP

Choosing Quickly with the Mouse

If you are using the mouse, you can select from a list box and choose the OK button simultaneously by double clicking on your selection in the list. Try double clicking on different dialog boxes that require a list selection or text entry.

Editing the Arrangement of Cells in the Worksheet

After you have drafted and tested your worksheet, you may find that you need to do some reorganizing or restructuring. When you restructure, you may need to delete or insert cells, rows, and columns. In the following sections, you also learn how to selectively clear cells, move or copy cell contents or formats, and undo incorrect changes.

Clearing Cell Contents

Excel gives you alternatives when clearing or erasing cells. You can erase everything in a worksheet macro sheet cell or range, erase the current format, erase just the formulas, or erase notes.

When many people first use Excel, they make the mistake of using the wrong technique for erasing or clearing cells. To clear a cell's contents, use the **Edit Clear** command rather than the **Edit Delete** command. The **Edit Delete** command is described later in this chapter.

> **NOTE**
>
> ### Beware of the Space Bar When Erasing
>
> Novice worksheet users commonly erase a cell's contents by typing a blank space and then pressing Enter. Beware! Sometimes you can do this without harm; but in some situations, this procedure creates problems. For example, in some worksheet functions and database commands, Excel sees that cell not as blank, but as a cell containing a blank character. Finding those blanks can be a real headache.

When you want to clear a formula, value, or format from a cell or range of cells, follow these steps:

1. Select the cell or range of cells you want to clear.

2. Choose Edit Clear to display the Clear dialog box (see fig. 7.23).

Fig. 7.23. The Clear dialog box.

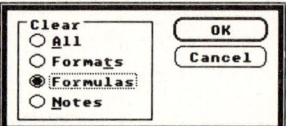

3. Select the button that describes what you want cleared:

All	Clears any cell contents and notes; returns the format to General format
Formats	Returns the format to General format
Formulas	Clears formulas but does not change formats or notes
Notes	Clears notes but does not change formulas or formats

4. Choose OK or press Enter. (If you decide not to clear the cell or range, choose Cancel or press Esc to ignore the Clear command.)

If you accidentally clear a cell's contents, *immediately* choose the Edit Undo command. This command undoes your most recent edit.

> **TIP**
>
> ### Clearing Cells Quickly
>
> The quickest way to clear cells is to select the cells to be cleared, press Del to activate the Edit Clear command, and then choose from the Clear dialog box. If you know that you want to clear the formula but retain the format, then press Del followed by Enter.

This procedure is the same as selecting **Edit Clear** from the menu. You do not have to wait for the Clear dialog box to appear before pressing the keys.

Cells that have been cleared appear as zeros to formulas. Clearing cells may cause formulas that depend on those cells to produce errors. To find formulas with errors, choose the Formula Select Special command, and select the Formula option. Turn off all the check boxes, but leave the **Errors** check box selected; then choose OK or press Enter. All cells containing error values (such as #NAME?) are selected. Press Tab to move between the selected cells. Watch the formulas the cells contain in the formula bar.

Deleting and Inserting Cells, Rows, and Columns

In Lotus 1-2-3, you can insert or delete rows or columns that pass through the entire worksheet. One problem inherent with that technique is that deleting a row or column affects other areas of the worksheet through which the row or column passes. You may accidentally delete a formula that is not immediately visible to you.

With Excel, you can delete or insert entire rows or columns, or you can just as easily delete or insert cells leaving the rest of the same row or column unaffected. The **Edit Delete** command completely removes the selected cells and "slides" in adjacent cells to fill the gap. You choose the direction from which cells slide in to fill the vacancy.

Deleting Cells, Rows, and Columns

The **Edit Delete** command removes cells, rows, or columns from the worksheet. This command is useful when rearranging your worksheet to give it a more suitable layout.

Edit Delete is different than the **Edit Clear** command. The **Edit Clear** command clears a cell's contents or format, but leaves the cell intact. **Edit Delete** completely removes the selected cells and "slides in" other cells to fill the gap. You can choose the direction that cells will slide. Figures 7.24 and 7.25 show a worksheet before and after cells were deleted and the lower cells moved up to fill the gap. Notice that the worksheet area to the right of the deleted cells was not affected. **Edit Delete** is an excellent command for sliding rows or columns into a new location without affecting adjacent cells.

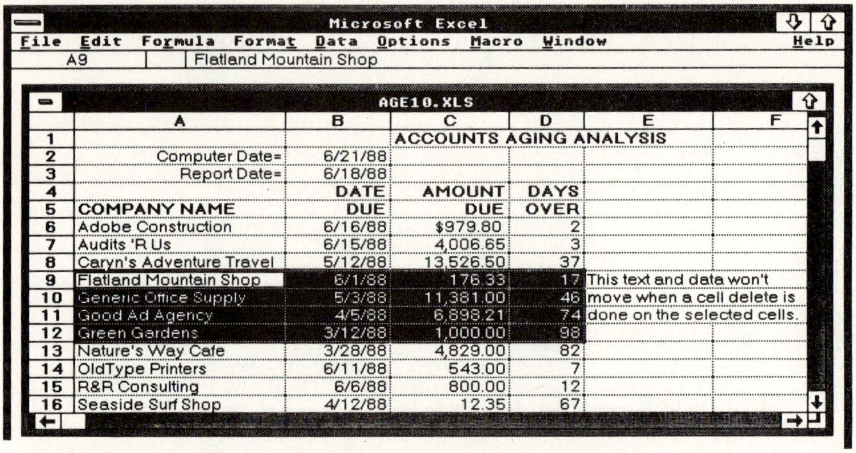

Fig. 7.24. A worksheet with cells selected for deletion.

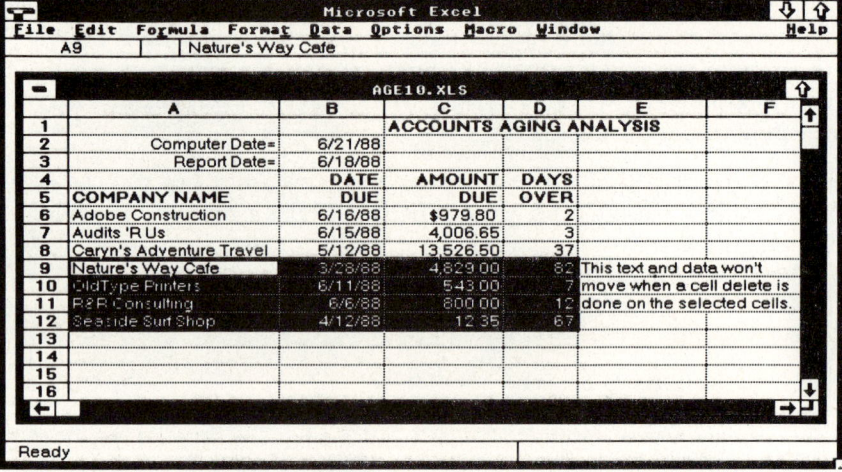

Fig. 7.25. A worksheet with selected cells deleted.

When you need to *remove cells* from the worksheet, follow these steps:

1. Select the cells or range of cells you want to delete.

2. Choose the **Edit D**elete command.

3. Select the button for the direction you want cells to move into the gap left by the deleted cells:

   Shift Cells **L**eft   Cells to the right of the deleted cells move left.

   Shift Cells **U**p   Cells below the deleted cells move up.

4. Choose OK or press Enter.

To undo an incorrect deletion immediately after making it, choose **Edit Undo Delete.**

When you need to *remove an entire row or column*, follow these steps:

1. Select the row number or column heading you want to delete.

   Mouse: Click on the row number or column heading you want to delete. Drag down the row numbers or across the column headings if you want to delete multiple rows or columns.

   Keyboard: Move to the top row or leftmost column you want to delete. Press Ctrl+space bar to select the current column or press Shift+space bar to select the current row. To select multiple rows, press Shift+down arrow; to select multiple columns, press Shift+right arrow.

2. Choose the **Edit Delete** command.

3. Choose OK or press Enter.

Figure 7.31 shows a worksheet with a row selected before deletion. Notice that the row heading 21 is selected. This is the row that is deleted across the entire worksheet.

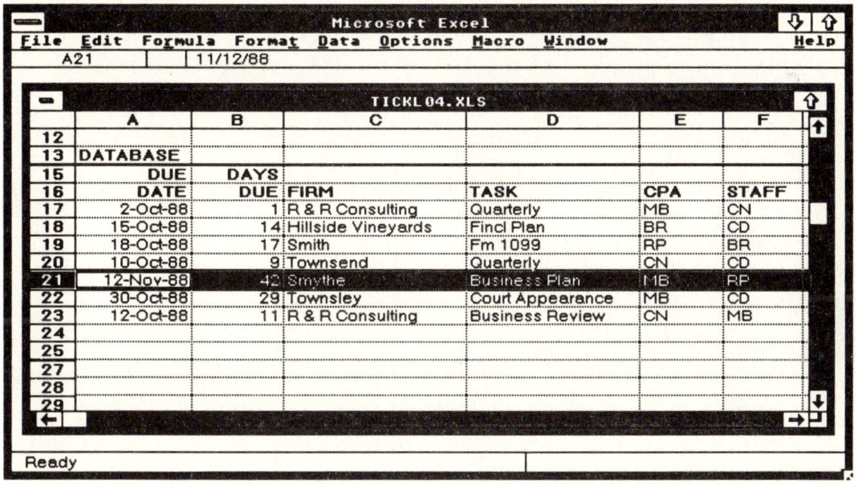

Fig. 7.26. A database with row 21 selected for deletion.

Depending on the design and layout of the worksheet, deleting cells, rows, or columns that contain information used by formulas can cause errors. Because the cell and its contents no longer exist (the deleted cell is not just blank; it's gone), the formula cannot find anything at that reference. Formulas that try to use the nonexistent cells display the #REF! error value. Use the Formula Select Special command to search for #REF! errors.

Excel Preserves Ranges If You Delete a Range Boundary

In Lotus 1-2-3, deleting a row or column that acts as the edge of a range "blows up" functions that depend on that range and loses ranges stored in menus. In Excel, if you delete a row or column on the edge of a range, Excel adjusts that range to compensate. In other words, in Excel, you can delete the last row of a database or SUM column without producing errors and destroying your worksheet.

Inserting Cells, Rows, and Columns

Sometimes you must insert cells to make room for new formulas or information. You can insert cells, rows, or columns as easily as you can delete them. Inserting rows and columns helps you reorganize your worksheet.

To insert cells, rows, or columns, follow these steps:

1. Select a cell or range of cells of the size and shape that you need to insert. Select as many rows or columns as you need to insert.

   Mouse: Select cells where you want cells inserted. If you want to insert entire rows or columns, then click on the row number or column heading where you want the insertion. Drag down the row numbers or across the column headings if you want to insert multiple rows or columns.

   Keyboard: Select cells where you want cells inserted. If you want to insert entire rows or columns, then move to the top row or leftmost column where you want to insert. Press Ctrl+space bar to select the current column, or press Shift+space bar to select the current row. To select multiple rows, press Shift+down arrow; to select multiple columns, press Shift+right arrow.

2. Choose the **Edit Insert** command.

   If you selected a cell or range of cells, a dialog box appears (see fig. 7.27).

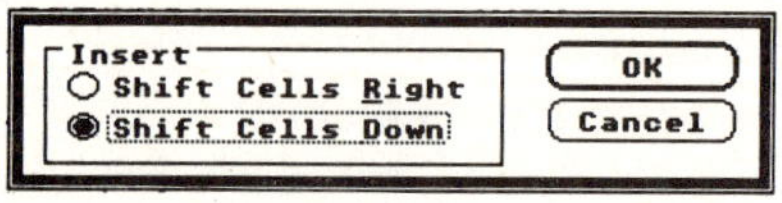

Fig. 7.27. The Insert cells dialog box.

```
┌─Insert────────────────┐   ┌──────────┐
│ ○ Shift Cells Right    │   │    OK    │
│ ◉ Shift Cells Down     │   │  Cancel  │
└───────────────────────┘   └──────────┘
```

3. Select the button that describes the direction existing cells should slide:

Shift Cells **Right**   Move the existing cells to the right to make room for the new cells.

Shift Cells **Down**   Move the cells down to make room for the new cells.

4. Choose OK or press Enter.

In figure 7.28, a range of cells has been selected where blank cells will be inserted. Figure 7.29 shows the results after insertion. Notice that the data in the cells to the right of the inserted area have not moved. Only the cells below the insertion move down to make room for the inserted cells.

	A	B	C	D	E	F	
12							
13	DATABASE						
15	DUE	DAYS					
16	DATE	DUE	FIRM	TASK			
17	2-Oct-88	1	R & R Consulting	Quarterly			
18	15-Oct-88	14	Hillside Vineyards	Fincl Plan			
19	18-Oct-88	17	Smith	Fm 1099	This won't move		
20	10-Oct-88	9	Townsend	Quarterly	even when cells are		
21	12-Nov-88	42	Smythe	Business Plan	inserted into the		
22	30-Oct-88	29	Townsley	Court Appearance	database on the		
23	12-Oct-88	11	R & R Consulting	Business Review	left.		
24							
25							
26							
27							
28							

Fig. 7.28. A worksheet with a range of cells selected for an insertion.

Excel takes some of the work out of inserting. In most cases, when you insert a row or group of cells, you want that group to have the same format in each column as the row above. Excel automatically formats the inserted row or cells for you.

TIP

Quickly Removing the Format After Inserting

If you want to remove the format that Excel automatically copied into the inserted area, insert the row or cells and immediately press Del to activate the Edit Clear command. Press T to select Formats, and then press Enter. You don't have to wait for the dialog box to complete the typing.

Fig. 7.29. The worksheet after the insertion.

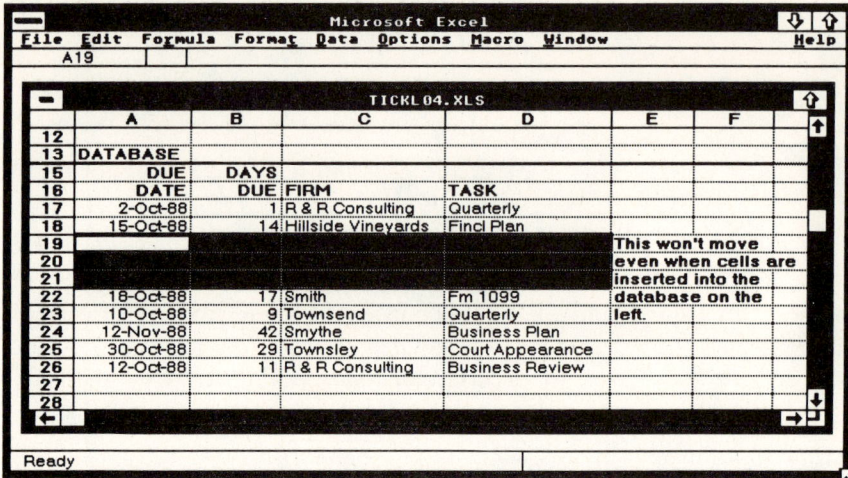

Be sure that you examine your worksheet to see the effect of inserting cells, rows, and columns. Formulas in the worksheet automatically adjust their references for the changes made by inserting. However, the insertions may have rearranged data-entry forms, database rows, or printed areas. To repair the worksheet, use the **Edit Cut** and **Edit Paste** commands to move areas back to their correct locations.

Moving Cell Contents

Cutting and pasting is a valuable function for reorganizing your worksheet. You "cut out" a range of cells and "paste" them elsewhere. This operation moves cell contents from one location to another.

Formulas remain the same after they are moved. You do not need to worry about relative and absolute cell references. (You do need to be concerned about cell references when "copying" formulas.)

To move a cell or a range of cells to a new location, follow these steps:

1. Select the cell or range of cells you want to move.

2. Choose **Edit Cut** or press Shift+Del. The cells you have selected appear surrounded by a *marquee*—a moving dashed line like the one shown in figure 7.30.

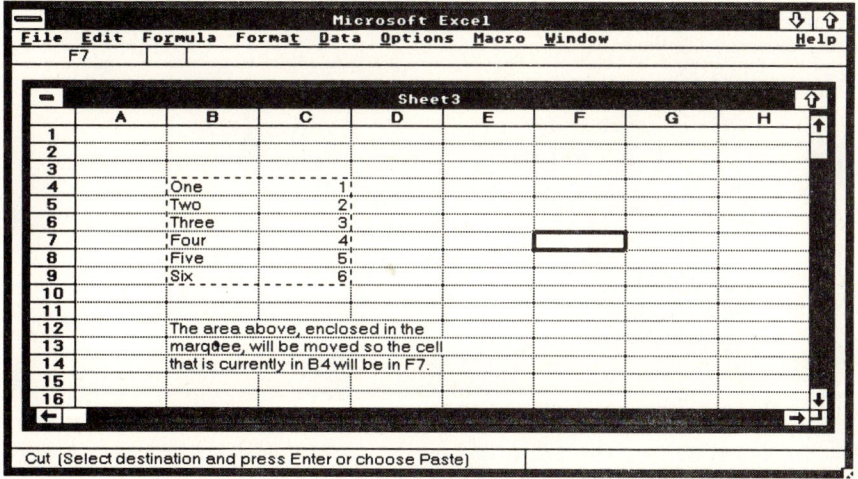

Fig. 7.30. The area to be cut enclosed in a marquee and the upper left corner of the paste area specified.

3. Move the active cell to the upper left corner of the new location.

4. Choose **Edit Paste** or press Enter.

   The cells you selected in step 1 are cut out and moved to the location you indicated. The area from which they were cut is blank and has a General format.

You need to show Excel only the upper left corner of the new location. The move procedure is similar to moving a picture from one place on a wall to another. You do not need to describe where all four corners of the picture go; you need to specify only one corner of the new location.

TIP

Moving Entire Rows or Columns

You can move entire rows or columns by selecting the row or column headings you want moved. (Click on the heading or press Ctrl+space bar or Shift+space bar. Choose the Edit Cut command. Move the active cell to the row or column where you want to insert them, and choose Edit Paste.

NOTE

Getting Out of a Wrong Move

Moved cells replace the cell contents of any cells they cover. If you do not want to complete the move because you discover that you will cover existing cells, press Esc until the marquee around the cut cells disappears. If you already have made the move and accidentally have covered existing cells, select **Edit Undo Paste**.

Copying Cell Contents

You can save yourself a lot of data-entry and creation time with Excel's copy commands. Instead of typing each formula in a worksheet, you can type a few formulas and copy them into other cells. You even can copy the formula and format at the same time.

If you need to change formulas into their resulting values, transpose rows and columns, or paste a format, be sure to read this chapter's "Power Pasting with Special Effects" section. This chapter also covers methods for moving cells, copying by "filling" in adjacent cells, and how to check whether a copy seems to give the correct results.

Filling Any Direction

Worksheets would take a long time to build if you had to type every formula. In most cases, the same or similar formula can be used across a row or down a column. The Edit Fill command lets you copy formulas to where they are needed. These commands fill a row or column with the formula on the edge of the row or the top of the column. In many cases, **Edit Fill** commands are quicker and easier to use than copy commands.

Figure 7.31 shows a worksheet that was used as an example in Chapter 4, "Worksheet Quick Start." In the Quick Start, cell C5 was copied and then pasted into the rest of the row. Figure 7.32 shows the result of using the single command **Edit Fill Right** to fill the cells to the right with the formula in cell C5.

You can fill cells left or right across a row and up or down a column. The cell that contains the formula or value you are filling with must be on the outside edge of the selected area, as shown in figure 7.31. To fill cells to the right or down, follow these steps:

1. Select the row or column you want to fill.

   The cell containing the formula being used to fill the other cells must be on the left edge of the row or at the top of the column.

2. Choose **Edit Fill Right** to fill right, or choose **Edit Fill Down** to fill down from the dialog box.

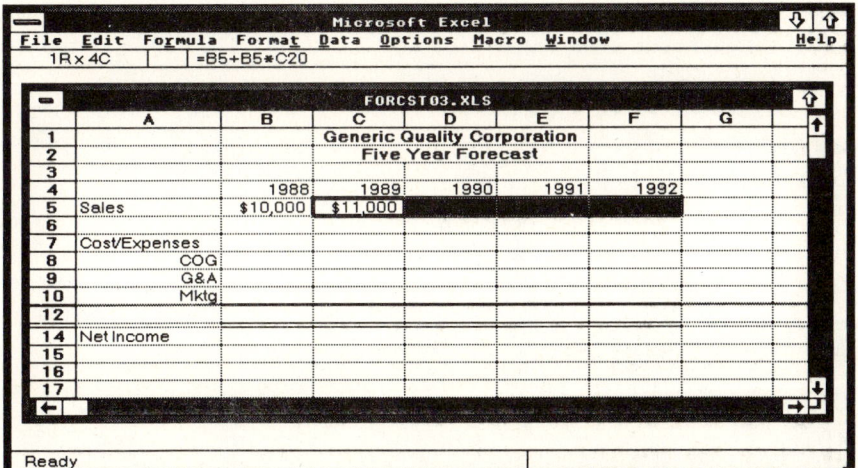

Fig. 7.31.
Selected cells
before filling
cells to the right
with the
formula in
cell C5.

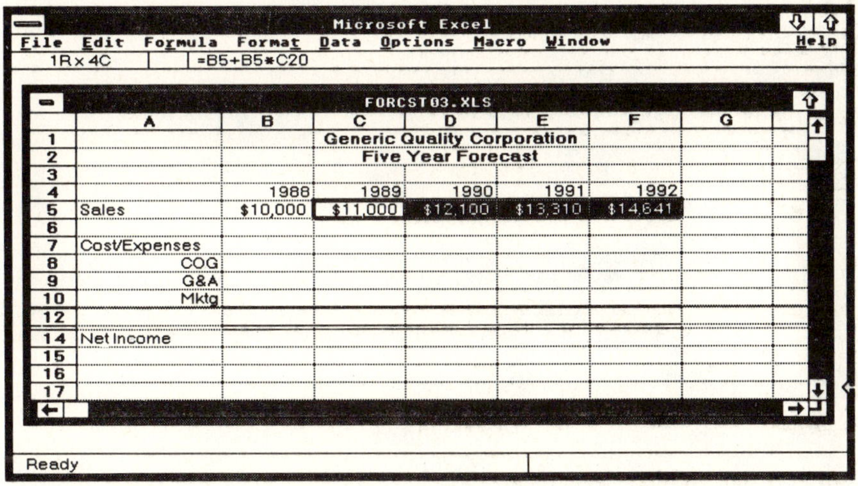

Fig. 7.32.
Selected cells
after filling cells
to the right with
the formula in
cell C5.

3. Check to see that the filled formulas have produced reasonable answers. If the answers are not reasonable, check to see that the formulas for those cells have cell references that refer to the correct cells. Cell references in the formulas may have adjusted incorrectly to their new locations. Review the subjects of relative and absolute cell references, discussed earlier in this chapter, to correct this problem.

The result of an Edit Fill command is the same as copying. Duplicated formulas or values replace any cell contents they cover.

To see the Fill Left (**h**) and Fill Up (**w**) commands on the Edit menu, hold down the Shift key when you select the Edit menu. These two commands only appear on the **Edit** menu when the Shift key is held as **Edit** is selected. Press **h** or **w** to choose the command. If you are filling left, then the original must be on the rightmost cell in the selected row. If you are filling up, then the original must be at the bottom of the selected column.

After you are familiar with the Edit Fill commands, you can fill multiple columns or multiple rows with a single command. For example, in figure 7.33, the column of formulas on the left side of the selected area fill across the rest of the selected area. (Select the cells as shown in figure 7.33, then choose **Edit Fill Right**.)

Fig. 7.33.
Multiple
formulas to fill
the cells to the
right.

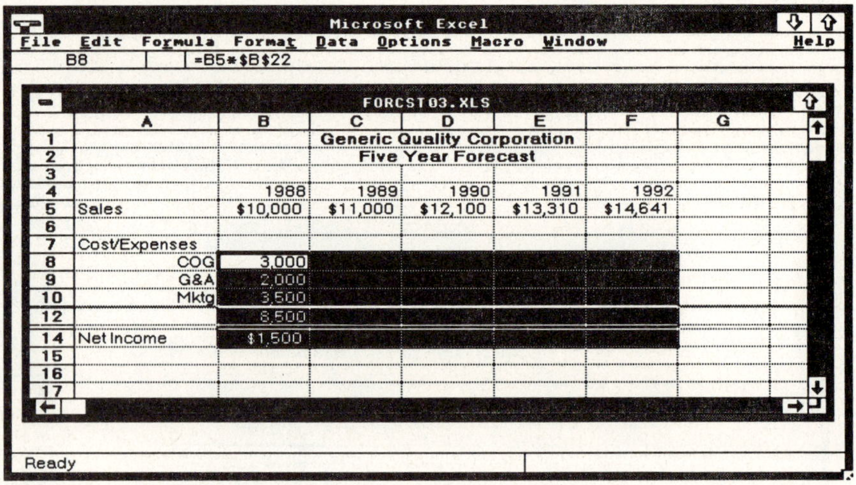

Copying and Pasting

Copying is similar to moving. The primary difference between copying and moving is that when you copy, a duplicate is created in the new location and the original remains; copying also lets you create more than one duplicate.

Copying adjusts formulas to their new locations. Therefore, if you are unsure how the formulas will adjust, you should save a copy of your work before copying formulas. If the copied formulas give you reasonable answers, you can continue. If the copied formulas produce wrong answers, you can correct them or return to your original.

To copy a cell or range of cells and paste the copy into a new location, follow these steps:

1. Select the cell or range of cells you want to copy. Check the size of the range you are copying.

2. Choose the **Edit Copy** command or press Ctrl+Ins. The cells to be copied appear surrounded by a marquee (a moving dashed line).

3. Move to the area of the worksheet where you want your copy to appear and see whether enough room is available to receive the duplicate.

   Copied cells replace the cell contents of the cells they cover. If you need to stop the copy command at this point, press Esc, and the moving dashed line surrounding the copied area disappears.

4. Select a cell that marks the position of the upper left corner for the duplicate. You do not need to select the entire area.

5. Choose **Edit Paste** or press Shift+Ins. A copy appears with its upper left corner in the cell you selected in step 4.

6. Repeat steps 4 and 5 to continue pasting copies into other locations.

The range of cells you copy remains in memory, so you can continue to paste it until the next time you cut or copy.

Because Excel knows the size and shape of the area you are copying, the program needs to know only the upper left corner of the location for the duplicate. Figure 7.34 shows the cells to be copied and the upper left corner of the area selected to receive the duplicate. Figure 7.35 shows the result of the single copy operation.

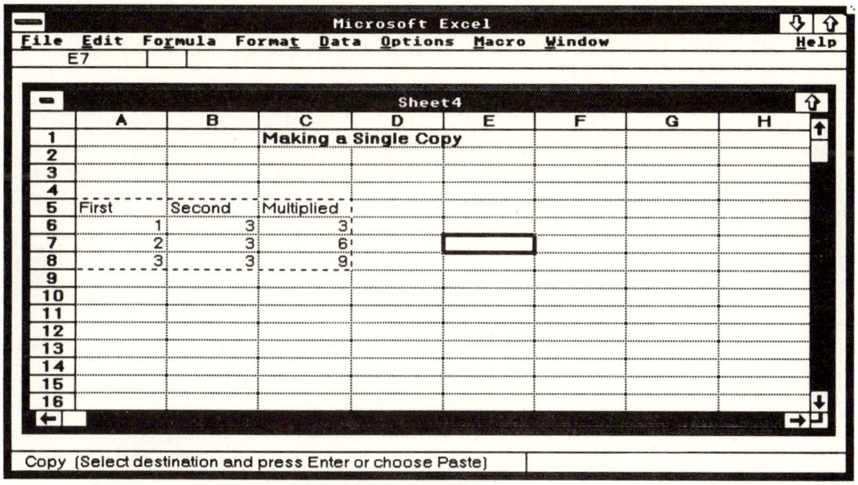

Fig. 7.34. A selected range of cells to be copied and the upper left corner of the duplicate.

Fig. 7.35. The
result of the
single copy
operation.

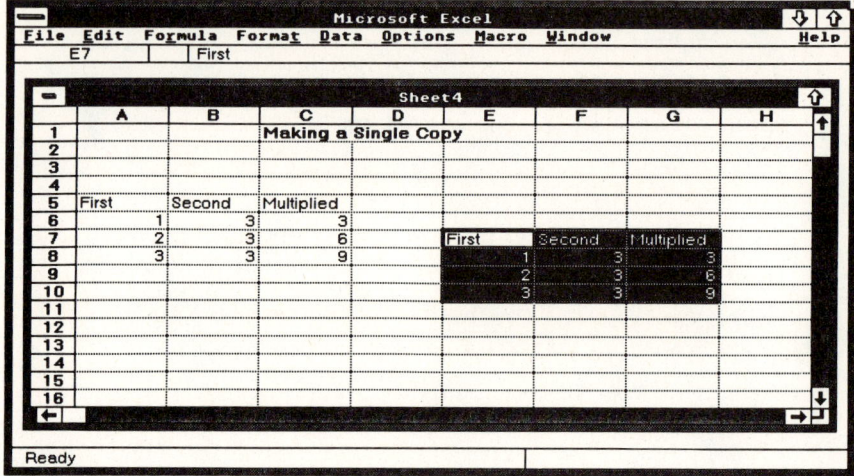

Frequently, you will want to make multiple copies of selected cells. For example, you may want to duplicate an entire column of formulas in multiple locations. In that case, you need to select only the upper left corner of where each copy will be duplicated. Figures 7.36 and 7.37 show how a column of formulas is copied to multiple columns. In figure 7.36, the column has been cut and is surrounded by a marquee. The top left corner where each duplicate will be pasted is selected. Figure 7.37 shows the result after pasting. In the example, the top left corner of each duplicate is simply the top of the duplicate's column. (Note that because the formulas use a relative reference, the values in the duplicate cells are different from the values in the original cells. To keep the same values, it would be necessary to convert the relative reference to an absolute reference.)

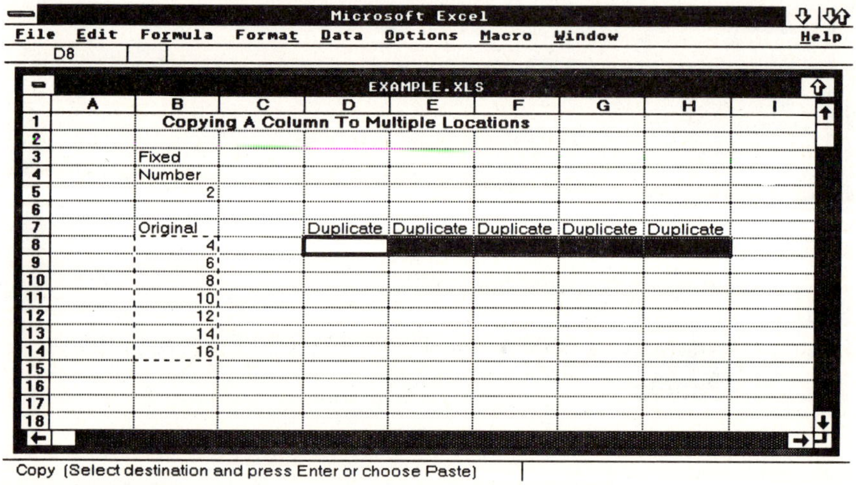

Fig. 7.36. A
column of cells
after Edit Copy
and locations
selected for
multiple copies.

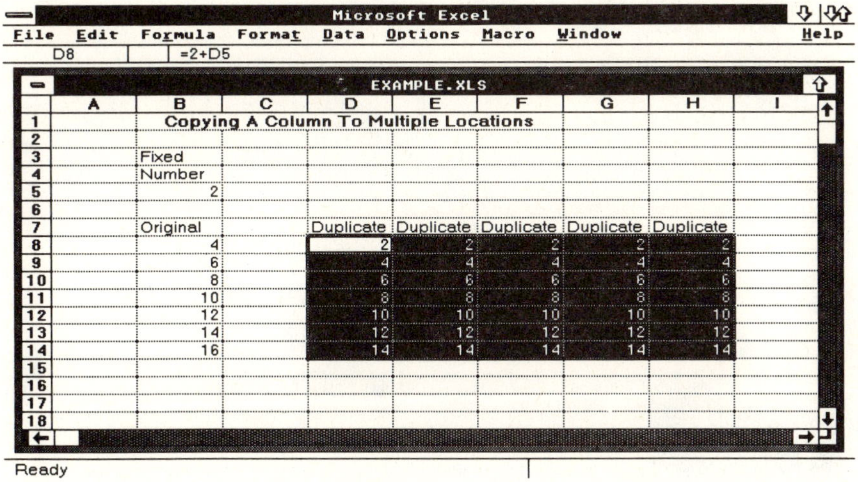

Fig. 7.37. The result of copying a column to multiple locations.

Figures 7.38 and 7.39 show how a row of formulas can be copied into a number of other rows at the same time. Notice that you can skip rows or columns by selecting cells wherever you want a duplicate. You still select the upper left cell where you want a duplicate row to be pasted. In this case, the upper left corner of the duplicate is the far left cell of the duplicate row. (Note that because the formulas use an absolute reference, the values in the duplicate cells are the same as the values in the original cells.)

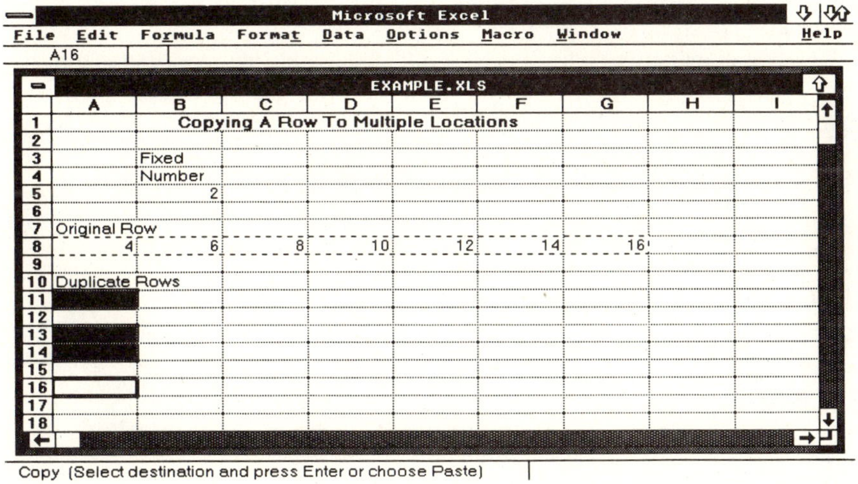

Fig. 7.38. A row of cells after Edit Copy and locations selected for multiple copies.

Fig. 7.39. The result of copying a row to multiple locations.

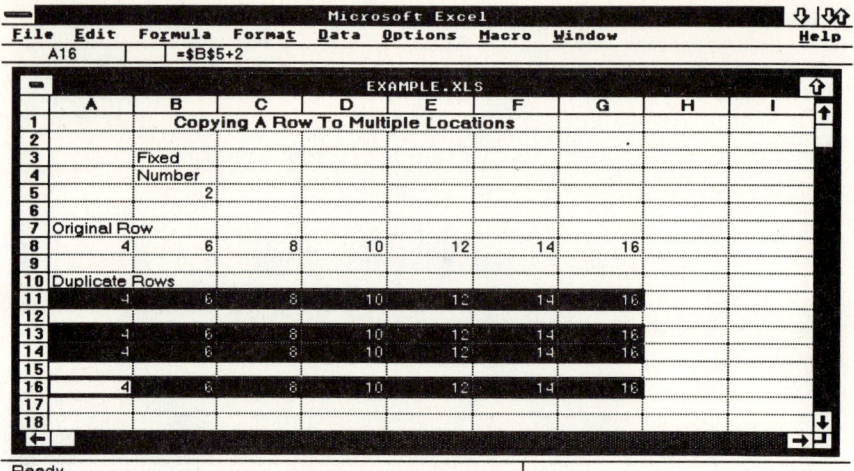

Power Pasting with Special Effects

At first, the **Edit Paste Special** command appears to be just a handy helpmate for pasting the characteristics of a cell onto other cells. For example, you can paste the format from one cell onto others or change a formula into a fixed value.

But Paste Special hides a couple of powerful functions. You can use this command to combine sections of a worksheet. All you need in order to add, subtract, multiply, or divide one area of a worksheet by another area is to paste copied areas on top of each other using the Paste Special command. It's an excellent way to consolidate results from multiple worksheets into one worksheet. With Paste Special, you even have the power to transpose rows of data into columns or vice versa. For information on how to use Paste Special across multiple worksheets, refer to Chapter 10, "Using Multiple Windows and Linking Worksheets." (Paste Special does not link worksheets. For information on linking worksheets so that they automatically update each other, refer also to Chapter 10.)

To use the **Edit Paste Special** command for any of the operations just described, follow these steps:

1. Select the cell or range of cells that contain the characteristics or information you want to transfer or transpose.

2. Choose the **Edit Copy** command.

   Edit Paste Special works only with the **Copy** command, and not with **Cut**.

3. Select the upper left corner of each area that will receive information.

   Make sure that you are not pasting over cells you want to leave untouched. (If you are transposing rows and columns, be sure to consider which cells will be covered when the copied area is rotated 90 degrees.)

4. Choose **Edit** Paste **S**pecial to display the dialog box shown in figure 7.40.

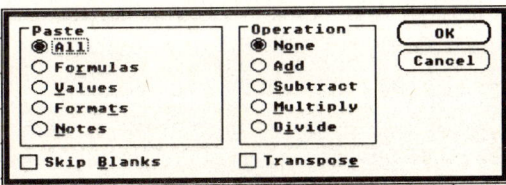

Fig. 7.40. The Paste dialog box.

5. Select from the dialog box the characteristics you want transferred:

All	Transfer all of the original's contents and characteristics.
Formulas	Transfer only the formulas.
Values	Transfer only the values and formula results. (This option converts formulas to values.)
Formats	Transfer only the cell format.
Notes	Transfer only note contents.

6. Select from the dialog box how you want the transferred characteristics or information combined with the receiving cells:

None	Replace the receiving cell.
Add	Add to the receiving cell.
Subtract	Subtract from the receiving cell.
Multiply	Multiply by the receiving cell.
Divide	Divide into the receiving cell.

7. Select the Skip **B**lank check box if you do not want to paste blank cells on top of existing cell contents.

8. Select the Transpose check box if you want rows changed to columns or columns changed to rows.

9. Choose OK or press Enter.

TIP

Freeze Formulas into Values

You can freeze formulas into values so that they do not change by copying the range of formulas you want to freeze. Then without moving the active cell, use Paste Special with the Values and None check boxes checked to paste the values over the original formulas.

The Transpose option in the Paste Special dialog box may save you time and work if you use database information in your worksheets or worksheet data in your database. The Transpose option rotates a row of database values into a column for use in a worksheet. Conversely, the option can rotate a column of worksheet values into a row for insertion into a database.

Checking Results for "Reasonableness"

After you copy a formula, make sure that you always do a check for "reasonableness." Copying a formula adjusts the formula's cell references to the formula's new location. The cell references of the duplicate formula may adjust incorrectly when copied. The result may be incorrect answers that are not immediately obvious. For more information on building worksheets that help you find errors, read Chapter 5, "Designing Worksheets." For information on how cell references adjust when copied, refer to this chapter's "Using Cell References in Formulas" section.

If the copied formulas produce incorrect answers, check the cell references of the duplicate formulas to make sure that they refer to the correct cells. If a cell reference has changed incorrectly, go back to the original formula and change that cell reference to an absolute cell reference. Then repeat your copy procedure.

Undoing Worksheet Edits

The wrong move, copy, insert, or delete in your worksheet could be disastrous. Although Excel cannot correct every wrong move automatically, the Undo command can help in most cases. When you want to "undo" your last worksheet edit, choose Edit Undo. If the last change you made was a deletion, then the menu item reads Undo Delete; if the last change you made was a paste, then the menu item reads Undo Paste. Undo does not work with all types of edits.

Tagging Notes onto Cells

You attach notes to cells for two reasons: to preserve your sanity and to preserve your business. Notes are messages attached to worksheet or database cells (see fig. 7.41). They appear in special Info windows or are printed at your request. You can display notes with the **Window Show Info** command.

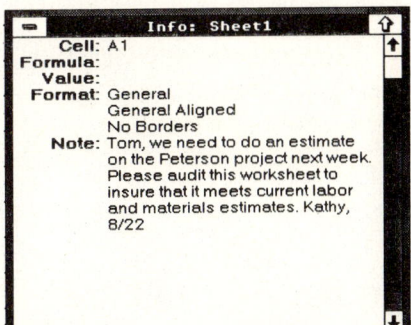

Fig. 7.41. A note attached to cell A1.

What Should You Note?

Include in notes any information that is helpful to the next person using the worksheet. That next person might even be you in two months, after you have forgotten how and why the worksheet operates.

You can put many things in a note. Some suggestions follow.

In cell A1, put the following:

- the author's name
- the auditor's names
- the date of the last review for accuracy

In data input cells, put the following:

- the origins of the worksheet's assumptions (history, guess, management's mandate, and so forth)
- limits to the data-entry values

- the historical significance of a value (such as the high sale of the year)

In formula cells, put the following:

- the origin and rationale behind a formula

- how the formula relates to other formulas

- an analytical comment about a result ("Pete, this profit margin is too low!")

In a cell in which you type the word Help, put the following:

- the names of helpful macro sheets

- a discussion of the macro keys used in the worksheet

- important keystrokes for that section of the worksheet

Take time to put notes on a worksheet as you build it. These notes prevent you from having to spend time in the future to figure out how the worksheet was built.

Adding, Editing, and Deleting Notes

To add a note to a selected cell, follow these steps:

1. Choose the cell you want the note attached to.

2. Choose Formula Note or press Shift+F2 to display the Cell Note window (see fig. 7.42).

Fig. 7.42. The Cell Note dialog box.

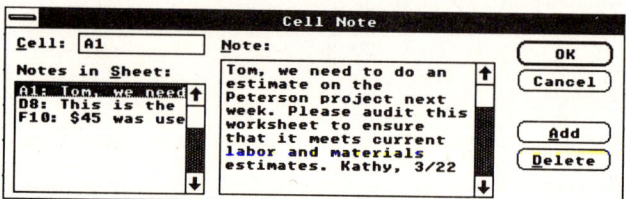

3. Enter text in the notepad in the center of the dialog box.

4. Press Enter or choose OK when the note is completed.

The Notes in Sheet list box lists all the notes in the worksheet preceded by their cell references. The cell reference for a note also shows in the Cell box. You can select another note by selecting from this box.

The **Add** button adds information from the **Note** box to the cell shown in the **Cell** box. This lets you add notes to cells whose address you enter in the **Cell** box without having to return to the worksheet.

To edit a note, select the cell and choose the Formula **Note** command. Then edit the note as you normally edit text in Excel. To delete a note, select it from the Notes in **Sheet** box, and choose the **Delete** button.

Displaying and Finding Notes

You can display notes and other important cell information by choosing **Window Show Info**. Chapter 13, "Troubleshooting Worksheets," describes this command in greater detail.

Find which cells contain notes by choosing the Formula **Select Special** command and selecting the **Notes** option. Move between the cells containing notes with Tab or Shift+Tab.

Use the Formula **Find** command to search quickly through cells and find a note that contains a pertinent word. Select the Note button in the Find dialog box, and choose the Part option to find any occurrence of the word in context.

TIP

Reading Notes Quickly and Easily

If you know that a cell contains a note, double click on the cell, or press Shift+F2 to see the Cell Note window as shown in figure 7.42.

If you want to read through notes but aren't sure where they are located, choose Formula **Select Special** with the **Notes** option. All the cells with notes are selected. Traverse through them with Tab or Shift+Tab. To read the one that is active, press Shift+F2, or press Shift and click on it.

From Here . . .

You can use the worksheet you created in Chapter 4, "Worksheet Quick Start" to experiment further with different methods of entering formulas and data. If you already have worked through the Quick Start, reopen the worksheet (FORCST03.XLS) and try some of the data-entry and editing techniques described in this chapter. For example, use Shift+arrow or drag to select a data-entry area, or use the Add key (Shift+F8) to select multiple cells for data entry. After you have selected cells, use Tab and Enter to enter data and move within the selected cells. Also, experiment with the shortcut keys that copy information down from the cell above or that automatically enter the date and time.

Chapter 18, "Database Quick Start," uses a number of the data-entry tips described in this chapter. For more practice on entering data in rows or columns, you may want to try that Quick Start.

As you have learned, Excel has extensive editing capabilities for both cell contents and worksheet architecture. The Formula Find and Replace command features are especially handy for making multiple changes more convenient.

When you begin editing, you probably will use the Edit menu primarily, but do not stop with the menus. As you gain confidence, try the shortcut keys listed in table 7.7. You will find that you quickly can cut, copy, or paste with just a few keystrokes.

At this point, you will want to work through the next chapter, Chapter 8, "Formatting Worksheets." That chapter shows you how to "dress up" your worksheets. After you have experimented with some of the ideas that chapter contains, you should be ready to build and format your own worksheets.

When you are ready to print your worksheets, you should review Chapter 12, "Printing Worksheets." If you are concerned with building complex formulas, check through the prebuilt functions available in Excel (see Chapter 9, "Using Functions in Worksheets"). You may find that a lot of your work already has been done by a prebuilt function. When you need to edit or build formulas that link worksheets, read Chapter 10, "Using Multiple Windows and Linking Worksheets." And when you're faced with problems using Excel, don't forget Chapter 13, "Troubleshooting Worksheets," or the Help key, F1.

8

Formatting Worksheets

Appearance isn't everything, but it counts for a lot when you need to communicate with confidence. Your worksheet has no merit if important information is obscured. The value of information is evident when it is communicated and used effectively.

Excel has format and style features that will make your worksheets easier to read, understand, and believe. In addition to standard formatting commands for changing column widths or selecting a numeric format, you can create your own formats, change the height of rows, change the font and style of characters in a cell, hide the grid, and shade areas for emphasis. With Excel, your printed worksheet or database can look as though it just came from the typesetter. You can get your point across with emphasis.

In this chapter, you learn how to control the displayed and printed appearance of individual cell contents as well as the overall worksheet.

1-2-3 TIP

Use Excel To Print Lotus 1-2-3 Worksheets

Excel's formatting and printing abilities are so easy to use yet produce such excellent output that Excel can be put to good use polishing up worksheets from Lotus 1-2-3 so that they can be printed with an "annual report quality" look. To open 1-2-3 worksheets, use the **File Open** command as described in Chapter 30, "Making the Switch from 1-2-3 to Excel."

Changing Character Fonts, Sizes, and Styles

You see different character fonts and styles every day. *Fonts* are the various typefaces used in printed materials. For example, Times Roman appears frequently in newspapers and magazines, while Helvetica, the straight upright typeface, commonly appears in signs and headings. Font heights are measured in *points*; there are 72 points per inch.

You can change the emphasis given a font by changing its *style*. Styles used in Excel are plain, bold, italic, underline, and strikeout. Figure 8.1 shows examples of many different fonts with various point sizes and styles.

Fig. 8.1. Examples of Excel fonts, point sizes, and styles.

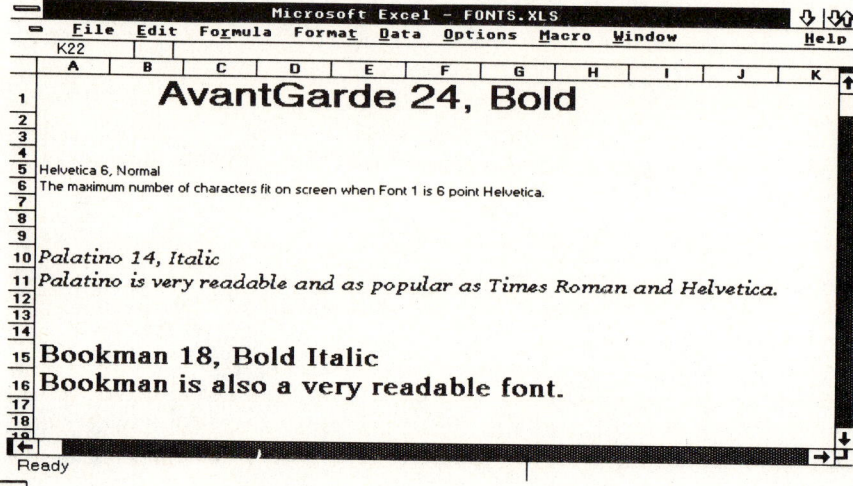

TIP

Reduce Your Work When Formatting

When you need to copy an entry or formula, format its cell first. That way the duplicates will also be formatted. If you want to copy and paste only the format or only the contents without the format, then copy using the **Edit Copy** command and paste with the **Edit Paste Special** command.

Excel worksheets can hold four different combinations of fonts, point sizes, and styles at one time. Using the **Format Font** command, you can redefine the four available fonts.

TIP

Get More on the Screen

If you need to see a lot of data at one time, you can visually compress large worksheets before you work in them. Choose the **Format Font** command, select Fonts>> and change Font 1 to Helvetica 6 point. Font 1 is the default font and determines most row heights and column widths. If you want the entire worksheet to change to Font 1, select the worksheet with Ctrl+Shift+space bar; then choose the **Format Font** command and select Font 1.

Changing a Font, Size, or Style

To change the font, size, or style of the contents of a cell or range of cells, first select a cell or range of cells. Next, choose Format Font. The Fonts dialog box (see fig. 8.2) shows four combinations of font, size, and style. Only four combinations are available at a time. Select the button for the combination you want, and choose OK or press Enter.

Fig. 8.2. The Fonts dialog box showing four font combinations.

> **NOTE**
>
> ### Changing Fonts Changes Your Previous Formatting
>
> Other combinations can replace one of the four shown in figure 8.2, but no more than four combinations can be used at a time. If you replace a combination, characters assigned to the old combination take on the font, pitch, and style of the new combination. For example, if Font 1 is Helvetica 10 and you change choice 1 to be Courier 10 Bold, then all cells previously formatted with Helvetica 10 will become Courier 10 Bold.

To quickly format selected cells with the current font choices 1 through 4, press these shortcut keys

Shortcut key	*Font choice from font dialog box*
Ctrl+1	1
Ctrl+2	2
Ctrl+3	3
Ctrl+4	4

Changing the Available Fonts

To replace one of the four font combinations, follow these steps:

1. Choose Format Font and select the Fonts>> button on the lower right side of the dialog box.

   The dialog box expands to appear as shown in figure 8.3 and includes a list of fonts, point sizes, and styles that can replace one of the four Excel fonts.

Fig. 8.3. The
expanded Fonts
dialog box.

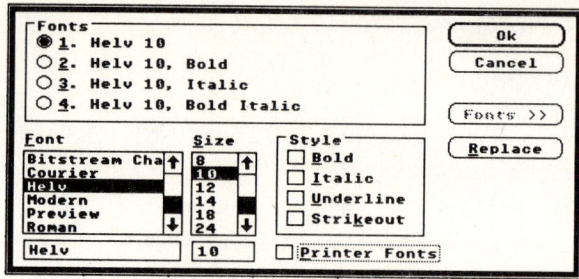

2. Select the **Printer Fonts** box if you want to use only the screen fonts that match those available with your current printer. With **Printer Fonts** selected, the list box only shows fonts that your current printer will print with. If you are formatting the worksheet to be printed elsewhere, then leave this box unselected.

3. From the Fonts box, type the number of the font you want to replace.

4. From the **Font** list box, select the font you want as a replacement for the font chosen in step 3.

5. Select the replacement point size.

   Mouse: Click on the list box of point sizes, and then click on the replacement point size. (You may have to scroll the list to find it.)

   Keyboard: Press Tab until the Size list box is selected. Type or select the new point size.

6. Select the check boxes for the style or combination of styles you want.

7. Choose the **Replace** button to replace the original font with the new font.

8. If you want to make more replacements, repeat steps 3-6.

9. Choose OK or press Enter to complete the process.

Mixing and Matching Fonts

Mixing too many fonts can be aesthetically offensive. A single font such as Helvetica used throughout a worksheet gives it a consistent appearance. Use the different styles (bold, italic, underline) and sizes to emphasize or define particular information. A large Helvetica font works well as the main title for a worksheet.

If you do not see the font you want, it may not be available for the current printer selection or it may not be installed in Windows. Unselect **Printer** Fonts to see fonts that are available on the screen but do not match your printer fonts. Use the Control Panel program, CONTROL.EXE, (available under **Run** in the application system menu when you press Alt+space bar) to load additional fonts. The Control Panel is described in Chapter 28, "Using Excel with Windows Applications."

Font 1 is the default font for all cells in which another font has not been specified. Replacing font 1 may change the majority of your worksheet. Font 1 is used as the standard for measuring column widths. If you replace Font 1 with a new font, column widths may change. Check your worksheet after substituting a new font. You may find headings and text that do not look good in the replacement font.

Aligning Numbers and Text within the Cell

To dress up the appearance of your worksheet, you can display numbers, formula results, or text against the left or right edge of a cell or around the cell. You also can easily fill cells with a character you specify (such as a dash or equal sign) in order to create lines across your worksheet.

You use the Format Alignment command to align numbers, formula results, and text. The alignment options align text with the column, whether or not the text fits within the column. For example, centering text centers text in the column, even if the ends of a text line squeeze out the sides of the column. This means that you don't have to change column widths to get text aligned the way you want.

When you first type text in a cell, it aligns against the left edge of the column. Numbers align on the right. To change the alignment of cell contents, follow these steps:

1. Select the cell or range of cells you want to format. If you want to fill a row of cells with a character(s), enter a character(s) at the left cell of each row to be filled.

2. Choose Format Alignment to display the Alignment dialog box (see fig. 8.4).

Fig. 8.4. The Alignment dialog box.

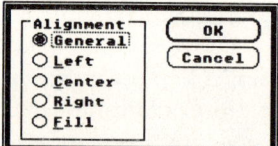

3. Select one of the alignment buttons:

General   Aligns text to the left and numbers to the right (the default)

Left   Aligns entries so that the first character is against the left edge (the text default)

Center   Centers characters around the cell. The characters may extend past either side of the cell.

Right   Aligns entries so that the last character is against the right edge (the numeric default)

Fill   Fills the indicated cell or range of cells with the character in the leftmost cell

4. Choose OK or press Enter.

You can save time when formatting by selecting multiple cells and ranges. Then choose the format you want to apply to all the cells you selected.

Fill alignment creates underlines for headers, section dividers, and double bottom lines. The Fill command fills a cell or horizontal range of cells with the characters you specify, regardless of the column widths. When you change the column width, the characters automatically compensate to fill the column. Other methods for filling cells, rows, and columns are discussed throughout this chapter and in the Worksheet Quick Start (Chapter 4).

Figure 8.5 shows a double bottom line being added to the FORCST03.XLS worksheet (from the Worksheet Quick Start). A single equal sign (=) has been entered in B13. Next, cells from B13 to F13 were selected, and the

Format **Alignment** command was chosen. After the Fill option is selected and Enter is pressed, Excel uses the equal sign in B13 to display equal signs across all the selected cells. Note, however, that the only cell that actually contains anything is B13.

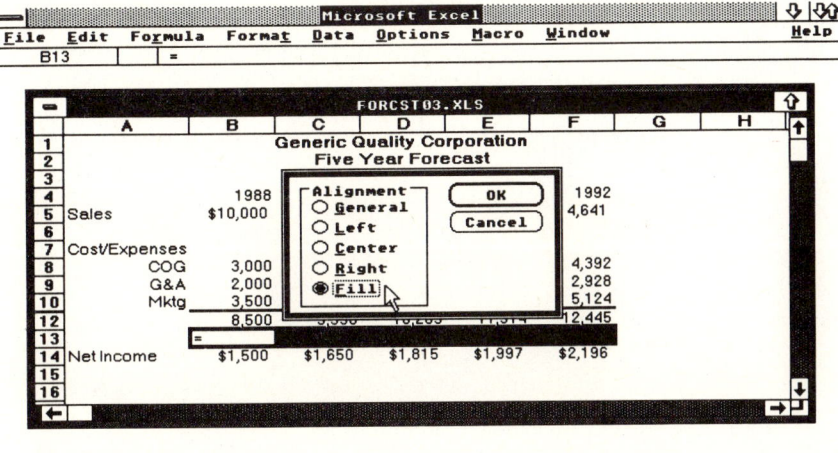

Fig. 8.5. The FORCST03.XLS worksheet with Fill alignment selected.

NOTE

Formatting Blank Cells

Be careful that you do not format blank cells with the Fill option. If you enter a character in the blank "fill" cell, that character will fill all the cells. This result can be confusing if you are not expecting it. If you see this happen, select the leftmost filled cell, and choose the Format **Alignment** command to see whether the **Fill** option is selected.

One disadvantage to using the Fill format emerges when you use the express keys (Ctrl+arrow) to move the active cell around the worksheet. The express keys normally move the active cell until it "bumps" into something. Filled cells do not stop the active cell because a filled cell may not actually contain anything.

TIP

Create a Filled Line

If you want to include a filled line in your worksheet, but you still want to have a character in every cell so that you can use express moves (Ctrl+arrow), create lines with **Edit Fill**. Follow these steps to produce a filled line that contains a character in every cell:

1. Enter the fill character, such as a hyphen (-) or an equal sign (=) in the first cell of the row.

2. Select only the single cell containing the character.

3. Choose the Format **A**lignment command.

4. Choose the **F**ill button.

5. Choose OK to fill the single cell.

6. Select the filled cell and the cells to its right that make up the row.

7. Choose **E**dit **F**ill **R**ight.

You can create better solid single and double lines with the Format **B**order command. The Worksheet Quick Start (Chapter 4) demonstrates how to use Format **B**order and Format **R**ow Height to create solid single and double lines.

Justifying Paragraphs

Excel has a primitive word-processing function in its Format **J**ustify command. This command takes long text entries and wraps them to the next line so that they fit neatly into the area you specify. Use the Justify command if you want to make instructions fit neatly on a worksheet to rearrange text that is cut off because not enough room is available, or to justify short memos. (If you want to position text or numbers within a cell, use the Format **A**lignment command described earlier in this chapter.)

To justify text, you select the area where you want the text to fit. Then you choose the Format **J**ustify command. All the text you want justified must be included in your initial selection.

The worksheet shown in figure 8.6 has some long rows of text that are about to be justified. Cells A2, A3, A4, A6, and A7 contain the text. The selected range, A2 through D12, defines how much space the justified text can occupy. After applying Format **J**ustify, the text appears as shown in figure 8.7. If you don't select an area large enough to hold the justified text, a dialog box with a message appears.

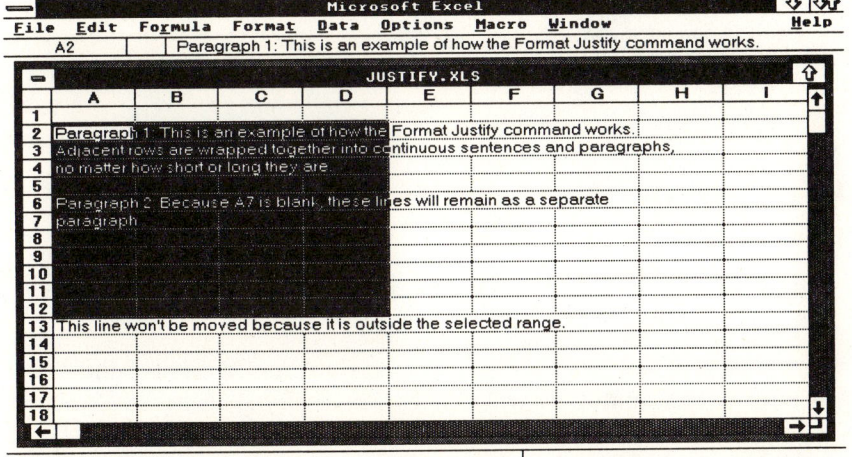

Fig. 8.6. Text selected before justifying.

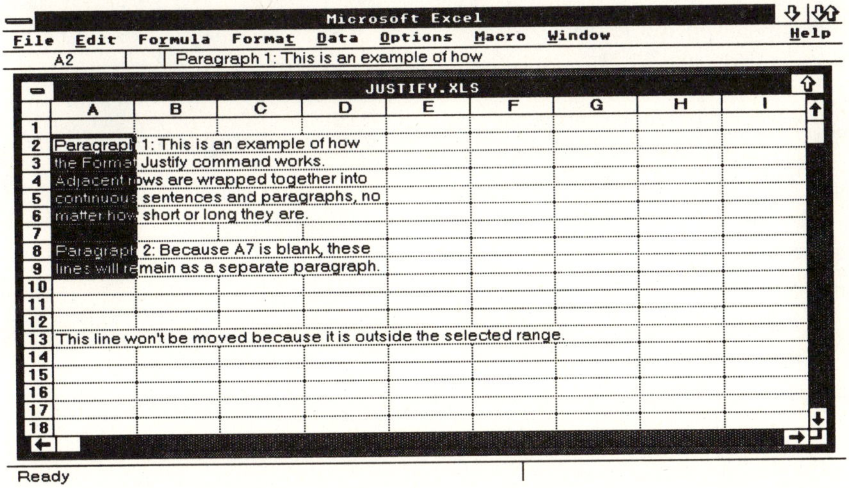

Fig. 8.7. Text after justifying.

Blank lines between text remain blank after justifying. This feature keeps paragraphs separated before and after justifying. Text in adjacent rows, no matter how short a line, merge together to form continuous sentences and paragraphs. Data outside the range you specify does not move when you issue the Justify command. (Notice that the text in A13 did not move between figs. 8.6 and 8.7.)

Excel prevents justified text from overwriting nontext cells that are in the area you select. You can, however, overwrite existing data in one special case. If the text will not justify within the range you specify, Excel displays an alert box. If you choose OK rather than Cancel, the text justifies even though it won't fit in the area you specified. Information may be covered by the resulting spillover.

Formatting Numbers

Excel has 12 numeric and predesigned formats. In addition, you can design your own custom formats. If you have a color monitor, you even can format cells to display their contents in color.

Cells that have not been used or that have been cleared have the General numeric format. In this format, numbers are displayed unaltered. If you enter a number with its own format, such as $12.95, into a General format cell, Excel automatically formats the cell for currency ($x,xx0.00). Enter a percentage as 15%, and you will see it in the worksheet as 15% (even though it appears in the formula bar as .15).

TIP

Numeric Formats For Financial Reports

In most financial reports, you will want to use one of the $#,##0 formats for the top and bottom dollar amounts. Use a format like #,##0 for the body of the numeric column.

To format numeric displays using the predefined formats or existing custom formats, follow these steps:

1. Select the cells you want to format. Keep in mind that you can select multiple cells and ranges and format many cells with a single command.

2. Choose Format Number to display the Format Number dialog box (see fig. 8.8).

3. From the Format Number list box, select the format you want.

4. Choose OK or press Enter.

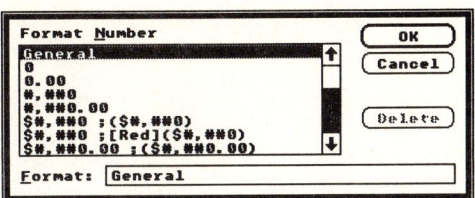

```
Format Number                    (    OK    )
General                      ↑
0                                (  Cancel  )
0.00
#,##0
#,##0.00                          ( Delete  )
$#,##0 ;($#,##0)
$#,##0 ;[Red]($#,##0)
$#,##0.00 ;($#,##0.00)        ↓

Format:  General
```

Fig. 8.8. The Format Number dialog box.

Predesigned numeric fonts and their results are

Format from list	*Number entered and used in calculation*		
	2500	*-2500*	*.5*
General	2500	-2500	.5
0	2500	-2500	1
0.00	2500.00	-2500.00	.50
#,##0	2,500	-2500	1
#,##0.00	2,500.00	-2500.00	.50
$#,##0 ;($#,##0)	$2,500	($2,500)	$1
$#,##0;[RED]($#,##0)	$2,500	($2,500)*	$1
$#,##0.00 ;($#,##0.00)	$2,500.00	($2,500.00)	$1
$#,##0.00 ;[RED]($#,##0.00)	$2,500.00	($2,500.00)*	$1
0%	250000%	-250000%	50%
0.00%	250000.00%	-250000.00%	50.00%
0.00E+00	2.50E+03	-2.50E+03	5.00E-1

Shortcut keys that bypass the Format Number command and immediately format the selected cell include:

Shortcut key	*Format result*
Ctrl+~	General
Ctrl+!	0.00
Ctrl+$	S#,##0.00 ;($#,##0.00)
Ctrl+%	0%
Ctrl+^	0.00E+00

A number or date that is too wide for the column appears as #####. Don't reach for the Format Number command to correct this display; widen the column with the Format Column Width command.

> **NOTE**
>
> ### Changing the Display Format
>
> Changing the display format does not change the number used in calculations. If rounding values makes a difference in calculations, or if numbers on your worksheet do not match your hand calculations, be sure to read about the danger in formatting numbers, described later in this chapter. Remember, what you see may not be what you get!

Designing Custom Numeric Formats

You can design your own numeric formats to use for catalog part numbers, telephone numbers, international currency, and so forth. Anytime you need to display a number in a special way, consider using a custom numeric format.

Type custom numeric formats into the Format text box at the bottom of the dialog box. Use special formatting symbols as well as free-form text to compose the custom formats. When you choose OK or press Enter, the currently active cell is formatted with the custom format you have created, and the custom format is added to the list of available formats. Table 8.1 describes the formatting symbols you can use in designing custom formats. Figure 8.9 shows a custom format being typed into the text box.

Fig. 8.9. A custom numeric format being entered in the text box.

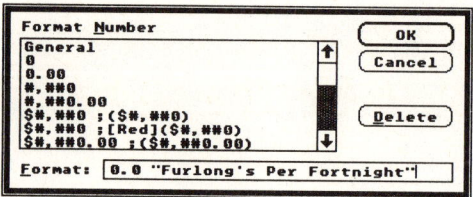

Table 8.1
Formatting Symbols for Custom Formats

Formatting Symbol	Result
0	Marks the location of any numbers and zeros used as place markers. Use a 0 to the left of the decimal point to force decimal fractions to display with a leading zero. Zeros to the right of the decimal point mark where zeros will appear in the display if not enough places are available in the decimal value. For example, the value 3.5 with a format $#,##0.00 is displayed as $3.50, and the number .245 appears as $0.25.

Formatting Symbol	Result
#	Marks the location of a number. Zero is not displayed if a number is absent. Values that have a larger decimal fraction than # signs round up to the number of # signs. For example, the value 3.5 with format $#,###.## is displayed as $3.5, and the number .245 as $.25.
. (decimal)	Marks the location of the decimal point. To ensure that decimal fractions display a leading zero, enter the format with a zero preceding the decimal.
,	Marks the position of thousands when surrounded by 0 or #. You need to mark only the location of the first thousand.
%	Multiplies the entry by 100 and displays the number in percentage format. The number is displayed as a decimal in the formula bar.
E- E+ e- e+	Displays the number in scientific notation. One or more 0's or #'s to the right of the E or e indicate the size of the exponent.
: $ - + () space	Displays the specified character in the position indicated. (Quotation marks are not needed.)
\	Displays the character following the backslash. The backslash is not displayed.
"text"	Displays the text within quotation marks.
*	Fills the remaining column width with the next character (one asterisk per format).
@	If text is typed in a cell using this format code, then the text will appear at the location of @ in the format.

Figure 8.10 shows examples of custom formats and how they can be used. The custom format shown in column B was entered in the Format Number dialog box as a custom format. This format then was used to format the number in column C so that the number displays like the number in column D.

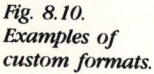

Fig. 8.10.
Examples of
custom formats.

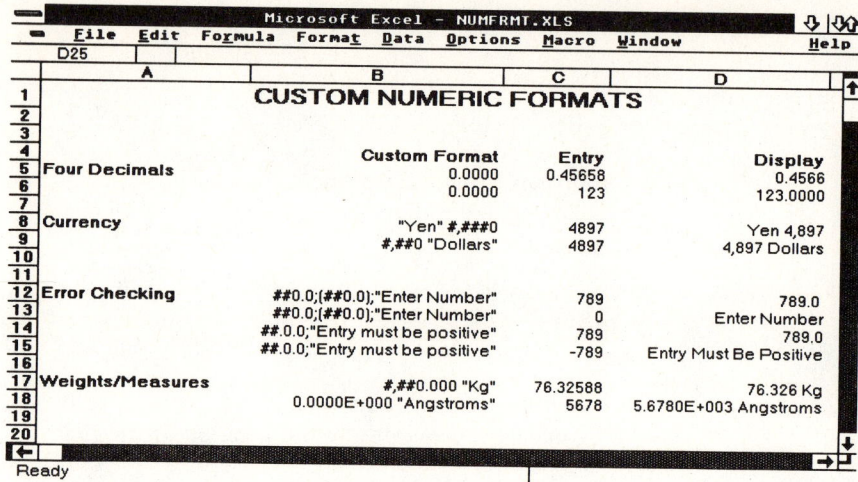

Fig. 8.11 shows uses for custom numeric formats outside of formatting numbers.

Fig. 8.11.
Examples of
non-math
custom formats.

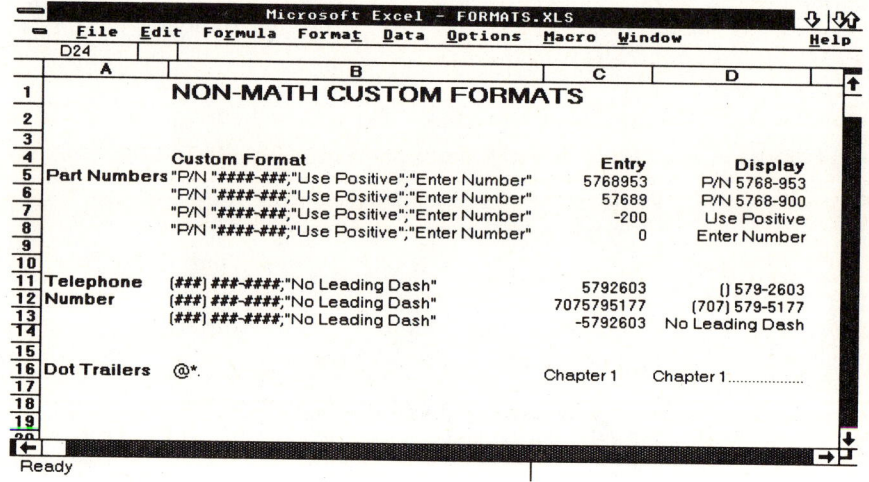

TIP

Save Time by Editing Predefined Formats

If the custom format you want is similar to an existing format, select the existing format from the Format **N**umber list box. It appears in the **F**ormat text box at the bottom of the dialog box. Use normal Window editing procedures to edit it. The custom format you create does not replace the predefined format. The custom format displays as one of the last selections in the list box.

Excel uses a semicolon (;) to separate the formats for positive, negative, and zero formats:

positive format;negative format;zero format

For example, the custom format $#,##0 ;($#,##0);"Zero" displays a positive number in the $#,##0 format, a negative number in the ($#,##0) format, and the text *Zero* for a zero.

Display text by inserting the text enclosed in quotation marks at the appropriate locations between colons. If you want a part number always to appear preceded by P/N and to have a hyphen before the last three numbers, you would create a custom format like the following:

"P/N "####-###; "Use Positive"; "Enter Number"

With this format the number 5768953 displays as P/N 5768-953. Entering a negative number displays the text *Use Positive*, and entering a zero produces the text *Enter Number*.

To hide numbers, don't put a format between colons where Excel expects one. For example in table 8.2 the third example hides negative numbers and zeros.

A single semicolon hides all values. Hidden numbers are still in the worksheet and can be used by other formulas. You will see them in the formula bar if you select a cell containing one of them. Select and reformat cells to redisplay hidden numbers.

Negative numbers enclosed in parentheses will be out of alignment with positive numbers in the same column because of the parentheses around the negative number. You can compensate for this by leaving a blank space after the positive number and before the first semicolon. Leave as many blanks as necessary to align numbers that use different formats.

Table 8.2 gives some examples of ways you can use text and the semicolon to your advantage.

Table 8.2
Custom Numeric Formats

Custom Format	Positive	Negative	Zero
$#,### ;($#,###)	$2,500	($2,500)	$0
$#,### ;($#,###);	$2,500	($2,500)	
$#,### ;;	$2,500		
$#,### ;($#,###);"Zero"	$2,500	($2,500)	Zero
$#,### ;"Negative "$#,### ;	$2,500	Negative $2,500	
;	All values hidden		

TIP

Setting Formats For Your Country

If your entire worksheet uses non-U.S. currency formats, currency symbols, and date/time formats, then use the Control Panel application described in Chapter 28, "Using Excel with Windows Applications," to display your country's formats in the Format **Number** list box.

NOTE

Watch for the ####

A formatted number may require more spaces than are available in the column. When this happens, Excel fills the cell with ####. Use the Format Column Width command to widen the column.

Formatting Cells with Color

If you use a color monitor and have installed Excel or Windows for color, you can format cells to display in color. The color format works on a cell along with the numeric or date formats. You can format text in color by combining the General format and a color.

You must type the color formats as custom formats. Do this just as you would custom number formats. First choose the Format Number command. In the Format text box, specify the color of the cell contents by entering one of the following color formats along with the numeric or General format:

[BLACK]
[WHITE]
[RED]
[GREEN]
[BLUE]
[YELLOW]
[MAGENTA]
[CYAN]

Then choose OK or press Enter. The active cell will be formatted with that color. You then can choose the color from the list box. Some examples of color formats are:

$#,##0 ;[RED] ($#,##0)
[BLUE] General

Color formats also change the color of text in the cell.

Deleting Custom Formats

Remove custom formats by choosing the Format Number command and selecting the custom format from the Format Number list in the dialog box and choosing the Delete button.

You cannot delete predefined formats.

Hiding Zeros

Hiding zeros often makes worksheets easier to read. In Excel, you have three options for hiding zeros: hiding them throughout the worksheet, creating a custom format, or using an IF function.

To hide zeros throughout the entire worksheet, choose the Options Display command, and unselect the Zero Values box. Reselect the Zero Values box when you want to see the zeros.

Use a custom format to hide zeros if you want to selectively format number cells so that positive and negative numbers show, but zeros do not. One such format is

$#,### ;($#,###);

This format defines the positive format as $#,###, the negative format as ($#,###), and the zero format as nonexistent. Zeros are not displayed in cells with this format.

In formulas, use an IF function to hide a zero with a formula such as the following:

=IF(A12+B12=0,"",A12+B12)

This formula says that if A12+B12 equals zero, Excel displays what is between the quotation marks, which is nothing. If A12+B12 does not equal zero, Excel displays the result of the formula.

Understanding the Danger in Formatted Numbers

The formatted values that display on the screen may not be the same values used in calculations. This discrepancy can cause the displayed or printed result to be different from manually calculated answers.

Figure 8.12 illustrates this problem. Column B contains the actual numbers entered. Cell B14 contains the formula =SUM(B11:B13). Column D contains references to the first column; for example, cell D11 contains the formula =B11, and column D has been formatted for two decimal places. Notice that the total for column D does not agree with the total of the displayed numbers because the full three decimal places are used for calculations, while the display shows the rounded numbers. What you see on the screen is not necessarily what is used for calculations.

Fig. 8.12.
Displayed values
that differ from
values used in
calculations.

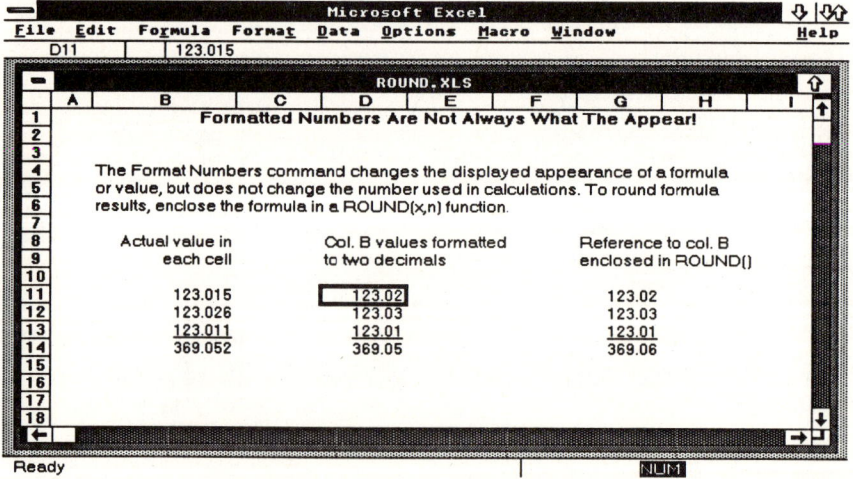

You can use two techniques in Excel to handle this problem. The ROUND function solves the problem by rounding formula results in a specific cell, while the **P**recision as Displayed option solves the problem by rounding worksheet values. Each of these solutions is discussed in the text that follows.

Rounding Formula Results To Match the Display Format

You can round a formula result so that it matches the displayed precision by using the ROUND function. In figure 8.12, column G contains a ROUND function that rounds the simple reference to column B. The effect of the rounding is that the result of the calculations matches the display format. The ROUND function rounds formula results or values—for example:

   =ROUND(B11,2)

This function rounds the number stored in B11 to two decimal places and displays the result in cell G11. If you want to round the result of a more complex formula, put the formula inside the ROUND function—for example:

   =ROUND(B12*5,2)

If you want to round the precision of *all* the values and formulas on the worksheet, then choose the **O**ptions Calculation command, and select the **P**recision as Displayed option. With this option selected, the calculations use the number that's displayed for calculations.

Rounding Worksheet Values To Match the Display Format

Precision as Displayed *permanently* rounds the constant value stored in worksheet cells so that the number used in calculations matches the displayed format. For example, in a normal worksheet, **P**recision as Displayed is off. When you enter the number .3456 into a cell formatted for two decimal places, your entry is displayed as .35, but the number used for calculations is still .3456.

When you enter a number such as .3456 while **P**recision as Displayed is selected, the number will be displayed as .35. The number used for calculations, however, is actually .35. This is also the number stored in Excel's memory.

To select **P**recision as Displayed, choose **O**ptions Calculation. Reselect the **P**recision as Displayed box to turn off the feature. Note that when you have selected **P**recision as Displayed, you cannot return constant values to their original precision without reentering them.

In addition to making the numbers used in calculations match the display, **Precision as Displayed** reduces the amount of memory needed to store the numbers. However, selecting this option may make formulas take slightly longer to recalculate.

Formatting Date and Time

When you enter dates and times, you do not use any special functions or format cells. You type the date or time in the way you are used to reading or writing it. Excel recognizes dates and times entered in any of the formats shown in table 8.3. For example, if you type the date 1/12/89 into a cell with the General (default) format and press Enter, the cell will automatically be formatted as m/d/yy format.

Table 8.3
Predefined Excel Date and Time Formats

Format	Example
m/d/yy	12/24/88
d-mmm-yy	24-Dec-88
d-mmm	24-Dec
mmm-yy	Dec-88
h:mm AM/PM	9:45 PM (12-hour clock)
h:mm:ss AM/PM	9:45:15 PM (12-hour clock)
h:mm	21:45 (24-hour clock)
h:mm:ss	21:45:15 (24-hour clock)
m/d/yy h:mm	12/24/88 21:45 (24-hour clock)

You don't need to use a special DATE or DATEVALUE function when you enter the date. If the cell is in General format (the default), you do not even need to format the cell. Excel changes the General format automatically to agree with the date and time format you first enter. Later, you can change the cell's format to display the time and date as you want. When you reformat, you can use one of the nine predesigned date/time formats or design your own.

When Excel accepts a date or time, the program automatically calculates the serial number—the number of days from the beginning of this century to the date you enter. (This serial number can be used to perform date arithmetic; see Chapter 9, "Using Functions in Worksheets.") Time is calculated as the decimal portion of 24 hours. To see the serial number in a date/time cell, reformat the cell to General format.

The following shortcut keys can save you time when entering and formatting dates and times:

Shortcut Key	*Format Result*
Ctrl+;	Insert current time
Ctrl+: (Shift+;)	Insert current date
Ctrl+@	Format h:mm AM/PM
Ctrl+#	Format d-mmm-yy

Predefined Date and Time Formats

Regardless of how you entered or calculated the date and time, you can display the date and time in any predefined format. You also can select a different color for the cell's contents as described earlier.

To change the date and time format of a cell, select the cells or range of cells you want to format. Then choose Format Number. From the list box, select the date and time format. Choose OK or press Enter.

Custom Date and Time Formats

If you can't find the date or time format you want, you may be able to create it. Use the following steps and the examples throughout this section as guides for creating your own custom date and time formats:

1. Choose the Format Number command.

2. Select the Format text box at the bottom of the dialog box.

3. Type the date and time symbols to create the format.

    An alternative procedure here is to select an existing format from the list box and then edit it in the text box. You will not lose an existing format that you use as a base for editing.

4. Choose OK or press Enter.

The custom formatting characters you can use for date and time are shown in table 8.4.

Table 8.4
Date and Time Characters for Custom Formats

Type	Display result
General format	Serial date/time number
	Days
d	1 to 31. Day number. No leading zero.
dd	01 to 31. Day number. Leading zero.
ddd	Mon to Sun. Three-letter abbreviation.
dddd	Monday to Sunday. Full name of the day.
	Months*
m	1 to 12. Month number. No leading zero.
mm	01 to 12. Month number. Leading zero.
mmm	Jan to Dec Three-letter abbreviation.
mmmm	January to December. Full name of month.
	Year
yy	00 to 99. Two-digit year number.
yyyy	1900 to 2078. Full year number.
	Hours
h	0 to 24. Hour number. No leading zeros.
hh	00 to 24. Hour number. Leading zeros.
	Minutes*
m	0 to 59. Minutes. No leading zeros.
mm	00 to 59. Minutes. Leading zeros.
	Seconds
s	0 to 59. Seconds. No leading zeros.
ss	00 to 59. Seconds. Leading zeros.
AM/PM am/pm A/P a/m	Display the hour using the 12-hour clock
	Dividers
–	Dash divider between parts
/	Slash divider between parts
:	Colon divider between parts

*Excel interprets *m* characters that follow an *h* as minutes.

Some examples of custom date formats are shown in table 8.5.

Table 8.5
Custom Date and Time Formats

Format	Display
mmmm d, yyyy	April 1, 1988
d mmm, yy	1 Apr, 88
yy/mm/dd	88/04/01
[blue] d mmm, yy	1 Apr, 88 (in blue)

TIP

International Date And Time

If you want the entire worksheet to reflect a country's date, time, and currency formats, you can set them all at once using the Control Panel. Chapter 28, "Using Excel with Windows Applications," describes Control Panel operation.

Controlling the Worksheet Display

You can change many characteristics of Excel's worksheet display. In addition to changing common elements such as column width and row height, you can customize your worksheet and emphasize certain features by removing grids and worksheet headings and by drawing borders.

TIP

Give Yourself a Break

If you find yourself using certain display or format commands frequently, take a side trip to Chapter 25, "Macro Quick Start." Macros reduce your frequently used commands to a single keystroke.

Excel worksheets come preset for the most commonly used settings for characteristics such as column width, text alignment, and numeric format. If the majority of cells in your worksheet use a different setting, you will want to establish new worksheet settings before you begin.

Changing Formats in the Entire Worksheet

One of the first steps you want to take after planning your worksheet and drawing thumbnail sketches is to set the entire worksheet to the most common formats you plan to use. To set formats for the entire worksheet *before* you make any other entries, follow these steps:

1. Select the entire worksheet.

   Mouse: Click on the blank square at the intersection of the row and column headings as shown by the pointer location in figure 8.13.

   Keyboard: Press Ctrl+Shift+space bar.

2. Choose the format commands you want to apply to the entire worksheet.

3. Move the active cell to unselect the worksheet.

Fig. 8.13. A blank worksheet with all cells selected.

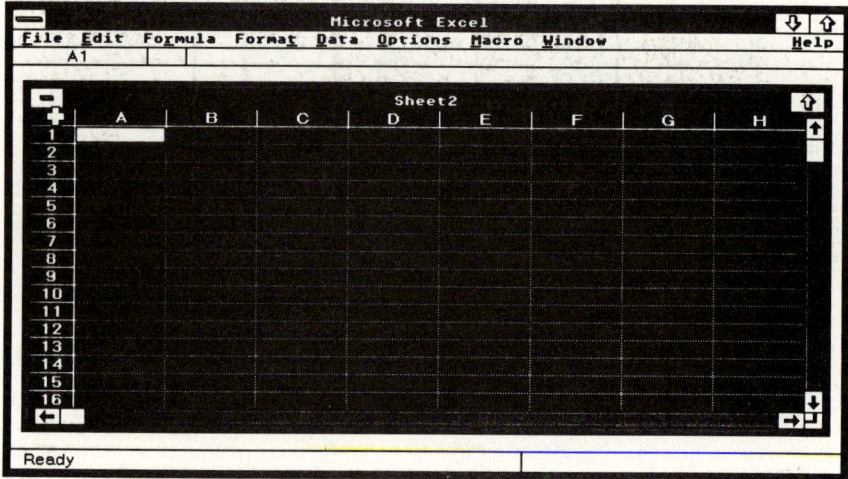

How To Lose All Your Original Formats

The previous three steps replace any formats or settings that existed in the worksheet. You could lose spacing, widths, and formats you labored over. That's why it's best to use these three steps before making any formats or settings.

Change the worksheet's appearance, gridlines, headings, and so on, with **Op**tions **D**isplay or **O**ptions **W**orksheet. These can be chosen at any time during worksheet construction.

Adjusting Column Width

You should adjust the worksheet column widths so that you fit the most information on the screen while maintaining an organized appearance. If sufficient room isn't available in a column to display a number or date, Excel lets you know by displaying ###### in the cell.

You easily can change one or more column widths with the mouse by using these steps:

1. Select the column(s) you want to change by dragging the pointer across the column headers. If you are changing a single column, as in figure 8.14, you do not have to select it.

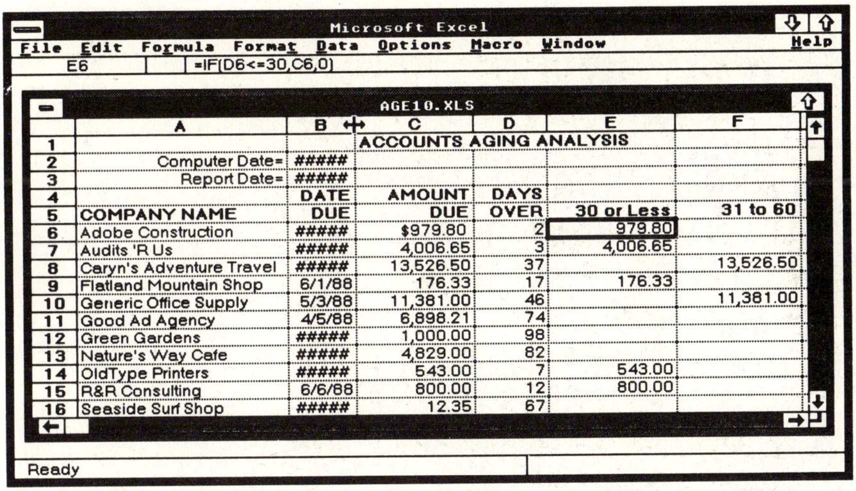

Fig. 8.14. The width of column B ready to be changed with the mouse pointer.

2. Move the pointer onto the vertical line separating two columns. When correctly positioned, the mouse pointer changes to a two-headed horizontal arrow. Figure 8.13 shows the mouse pointer positioned to change the width of column B.

3. Drag the two-headed arrow left or right to change the column width. Release the mouse button when the shadow of the right column wall is correctly positioned.

Changing multiple column widths can be done faster from the keyboard by using these steps:

1. Select cells in the columns you want to change.

2. Choose Format Column Width.

3. Enter the column width as the number of characters. (The width of a character in Font 1 is used as the standard for a unit width of 1.)

4. Choose OK or press Enter.

Hiding Columns

When you generate a database or worksheet for multiple users, you may not want to print all the information. You can selectively display and print columns by temporarily hiding unwanted columns.

Hide selected columns with the keyboard by choosing Format Column Width and entering zero as the desired column width.

Hide columns with the mouse by dragging the shadow of the right column edge past the left column edge. Then release the mouse button. This procedure reduces the column width to zero. (Refer to this chapter's "Adjusting Column Width" section for greater detail.)

To return hidden columns to view, follow these steps:

1. Select a range of cells that cross the hidden column(s).

   Figure 8.15 shows cells in columns D and G selected. Notice that these two cells span the hidden E and F columns.

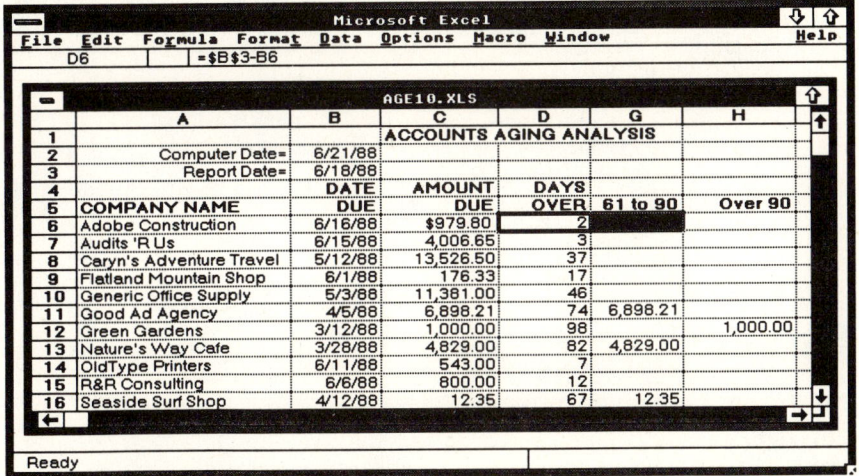

Fig. 8.15.
Hidden columns
about to be
revealed.

2. Choose Format Column Width.

3. Enter the column width number used by the columns adjacent to the hidden columns, or select the Standard Width box if you aren't sure.

4. Choose OK or press Enter.

5. Adjust the width of each newly revealed column individually.

Adjusting Row Height

The procedure for changing the height of rows is similar to that for changing column widths. Row heights change automatically to accommodate the tallest font in the row. You can shrink row heights to less than the height of one character.

To change the height of a single row with the mouse, follow these steps:

1. Select each row you want changed by Ctrl+clicking on the row number. If you want to change a single row height, as in figure 8.16, you do not need to select the row.

Fig. 8.16. The height of row 2 ready to be changed with the mouse pointer.

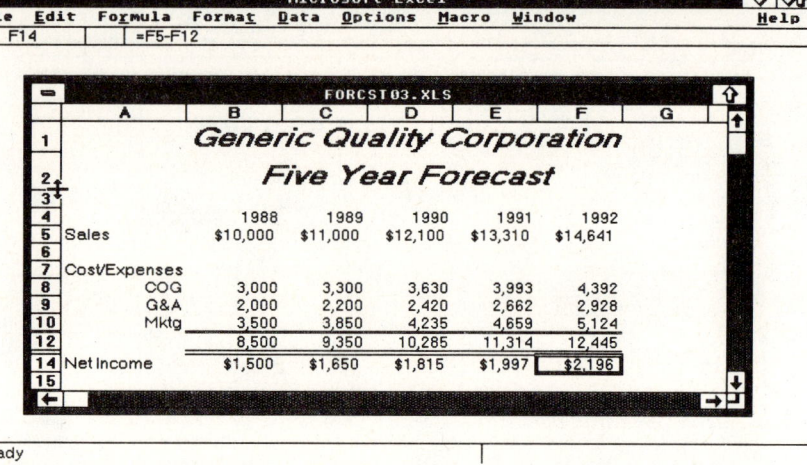

2. Move the mouse pointer onto the line below the row heading of the row you want to change, as shown in row 2 of figure 8.16. When correctly positioned, the mouse pointer changes to a two-headed vertical arrow.

3. Drag the two-headed arrow up or down to change the row height, and then release the mouse button.

Before changing one or more rows using the keyboard, you may want to check the font size with the Format Font command. Row heights are measured in the same units, picas, as font heights.

You can change the height of multiple rows by completing these steps from the keyboard:

1. Select a cell in the row(s) you want to change.

2. Choose Format Row Height.

3. Enter the height that you want the rows to be.

   If you want to return the rows to normal height, select the Standard Height box.

4. Choose OK or press Enter.

Hiding Rows

You can hide rows of information using the same steps that you use to change the row height. Change the row height to zero, and the rows will be invisible on the screen and in print.

To display a hidden row, follow these steps:

1. Select the rows on either side of the hidden row.

2. Choose Format Row Height.

3. Enter a row height greater than zero.

4. Choose OK or press Enter.

   When the hidden rows reappear, the hidden rows and the rows immediately above and below them will all be the same height. Therefore, you will have to adjust the individual heights of these rows.

5. Adjust the height of each revealed row individually.

Hiding Row and Column Headings

Some Excel displays, such as data-entry forms, information, and help screens, do not need row and column headings. Choose Options Display, and unselect the Row & Column Headings check box to turn off headings.

You also have the option of keeping the headings on the screen, but not printing them. Turn off row and column headings in your printed copies by choosing File Page Setup and making sure that the Row & Column Headings check box is not selected.

Turning Off Gridlines and Changing Grid Color

Turning off the gridlines displayed on the screen is convenient when you are typing memos, using data-entry forms, and displaying information and help windows.

To turn the screen gridlines on or off, follow these steps:

1. Choose Options Display.

2. Select the Gridlines check box.

3. Make additional display selections if needed.

4. Choose the OK button or press Enter.

Figure 8.17 illustrates how a data-entry form without headings or gridlines appears more like a paper form. This kind of display can make data entry easier and reduce mistakes. (The entry areas shown in the figure were outlined with the Format Borders command.)

Fig. 8.17. A text data-entry form without gridlines.

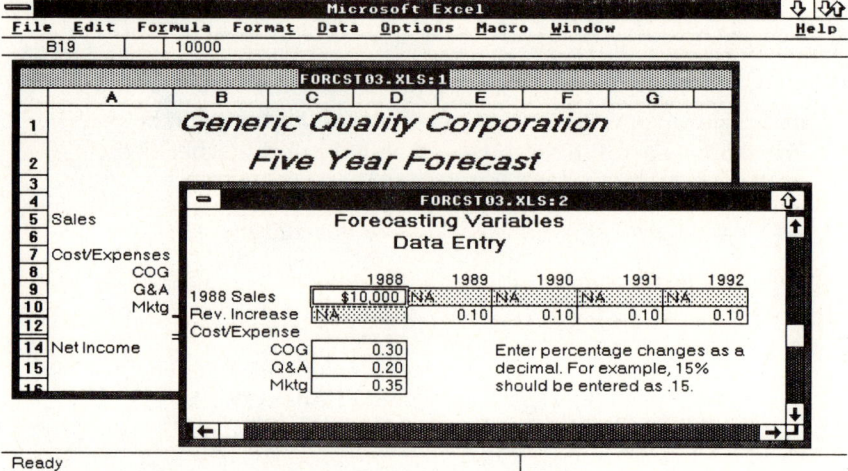

To change the color of the grid display, follow these steps:

1. Choose **Options Display.**

2. Select Gridline & Heading Color.

   Mouse: Click on the color button you want.

   Keyboard: Press Alt-C, and then press the left- or right-arrow key until the rectangle surrounds the color you want.

3. Make additional display selections if needed.

4. Choose the OK button or press Enter.

If you want to color individual cell or range contents, use the Format **Number** command described in this chapter's "Formatting Cells with Color" section.

Shading and Bordering Cells

You can shade cells or put borders around them to add emphasis or to define data-entry areas. Final results in printouts are easier to find when enclosed in borders.

Data-entry cells stand out on the screen if you turn the gridlines off and put borders around the entry area. If you put the data-entry part of the worksheet in a separate window, you can format the entry form differently from the rest of the worksheet. Figure 8.17 shows a screen form that uses borders to mark where data is to be entered.

To border or shade selected cells, follow these steps:

1. Select the cells you want bordered or shaded.

2. Choose Format **B**order to display the dialog box shown in figure 8.18.

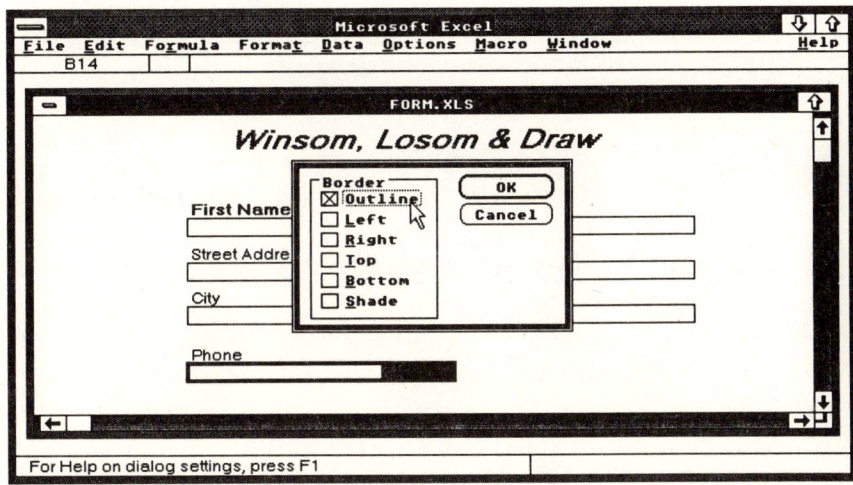

Fig. 8.18. The Border dialog box on a data-entry form.

3. Select the check boxes for the type of border and shading you want.

   You can outline a box by selecting the **Outline** box. You don't have to build a frame by constructing the sides, top, and bottom separately.

4. Choose OK or press Enter.

Figure 8.19 shows examples of single and double vertical and horizontal lines created with the Border command. To create a double vertical line, you select a column of cells and then use the Border command to create the left and right borders. To move the lines closer, you shrink the column width. Notice the width of column C.

Use the same process to create a double underline. Select the row of cells for the double underline and then create the line by choosing **T**op and **B**ottom from the Border dialog box. To bring the top and bottom lines closer together, reduce the row height with the Format **R**ow Height command. Notice the height of row 7. The Worksheet Quick Start (Chapter 4) demonstrates how to create bottom lines with this technique.

Fig. 8.19. Lines and shading on a worksheet.

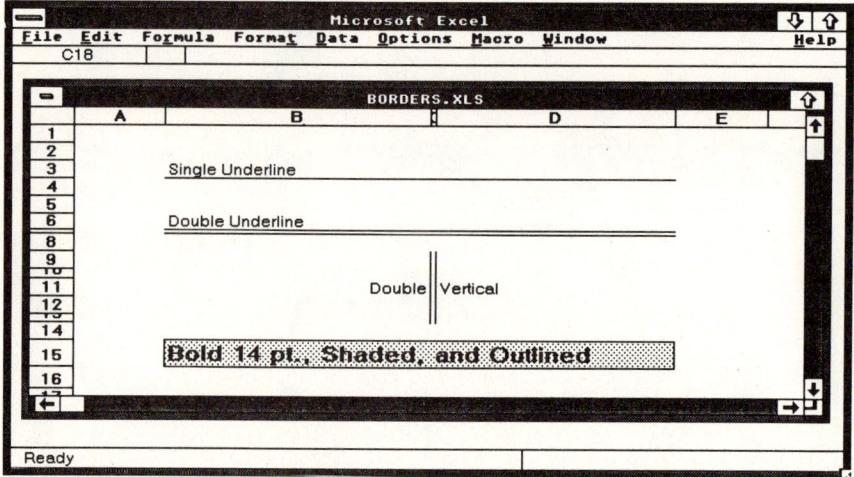

Displaying Formulas

You will want to display formulas on the screen or in your printout at particular times: when debugging your worksheet (finding and correcting problems), when reviewing an unfamiliar worksheet, or when printing a documentation copy of the worksheet for future reference.

Excel displays all formulas in the worksheet and increases the column width when you follow these steps:

1. Choose **O**ptions **D**isplay to display the dialog box shown in figure 8.20.

Fig. 8.20. The Display dialog box.

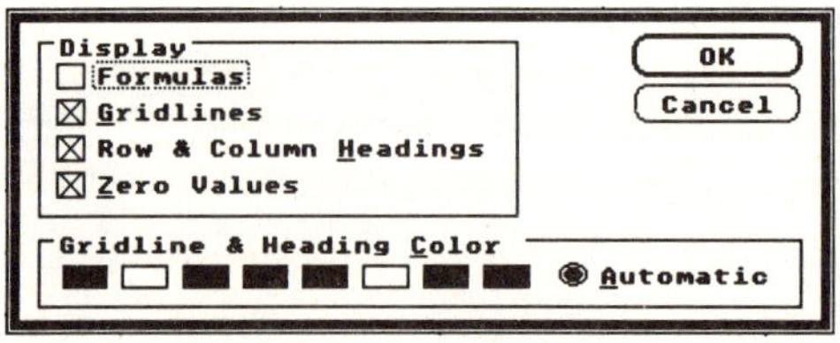

2. Select the **Formulas** check box.

3. Make additional display selections if needed.

4. Choose OK or press Enter.

Column widths double and each formula appears in its cell. You can use Format **Column** Width to widen columns further if necessary to show a complete formula. You will not be able to align formulas within their cells.

When printing a spreadsheet to show the formulas for documentation, check the Formulas, Gridlines, and Row & Column Headings boxes in the Display dialog box. Make sure that columns are wide enough to display each formula completely.

Protecting Worksheets from Change

If you develop Excel worksheets for use by inexperienced operators, create worksheets for sale, or work in the mistake-filled hours after midnight, then you will find this section interesting. The procedure described here protects the worksheet from accidental entry errors.

Excel lets you protect cells, documents, and windows. If you need to protect confidential or proprietary information, you can also hide formulas so that they do not appear in the formula bar. You can use a password to prevent unauthorized people from changing the protection status or the display of hidden information.

Protecting Cell Contents

Cell protection is a valuable feature for preventing someone from accidentally entering data over the top of a formula, and for preventing unauthorized users from changing your formulas. When your worksheet finally has completed the 57 levels of audit and review required by your company, you want to make absolutely, positively sure that careless or unauthorized users don't change the formulas.

An invisible cell format specifies how a cell reacts when the worksheet as a whole is protected. By changing this invisible format from locked (its normal setting) to unlocked, you allow the cell contents to be changed even though the rest of the worksheet is protected from change.

Two different commands are used to specify the cell format and the worksheets protection status. Before you protect a worksheet, you must use the Format **Cell** **P**rotection command to format cells that you want to be changeable. These changeable cells must be formatted as unlocked. After you indicate which cells will remain changeable, you use the **Options Protect Document** command to turn on the worksheet protection.

The steps to follow are:

1. Select all cells that you want to remain changeable.

    Use multiple cell selection techniques to select all the cells at once so that they all can be formatted with a single command.

2. Choose Format Cell **P**rotection to display the dialog box shown in figure 8.21.

Fig. 8.21. The Cell Protection dialog box.

3. Unselect the Locked check box so that selected cells will remain changeable.

4. Choose OK or press Enter.

5. Choose **O**ptions **P**rotect Document and enter a password if desired in the **P**assword text box. Select the **C**ontents check box.

    Step 5 turns on worksheet protection. Only cells formatted as "unlocked" can be changed when worksheet protection is on. If you don't enter a password, anyone can unprotect the worksheet with the proper commands.

6. Choose OK or press Enter.

Take a look through some of the menus after locking the cells. Because the cells cannot be changed, most of the commands are grayed and unusable.

Don't forget your password! If you do, you won't be able to get back in and change the worksheet.

To unprotect the worksheet, follow these steps:

1. Choose **O**ptions **U**nprotect Document.

2. Enter the password if you used one to protect the worksheet.

3. Choose OK or press Enter.

Using Functions in Worksheets

Excel uses prebuilt worksheet functions to perform complex operations on data. You should use functions rather than writing your own equations. Functions are fast, take up less space in the formula bar, and reduce the chance for typographical errors.

Functions act on data in much the same way equations act on numbers. Functions accept numeric or text input, referred to as *arguments*, and return a *result*.

Two of the most widely used functions, which were described previously in the worksheet section, are SUM and ROUND. The SUM function adds a column or row of numbers, and the ROUND function rounds values to a specified number of decimal places. Other functions manipulate text, logical values, financial equations, arrays, and databases.

In this chapter, you will learn what functions are and the two methods of entering a function: manually typing the function or pasting the function into a cell or formula by selecting the function from a list. You also will learn how to get Excel to prompt you for arguments that functions use.

The latter part of the chapter is a directory of Excel's 131 different functions and descriptions of the arguments that the functions use. The directory is segmented by types of functions and includes examples for many of the functions.

Entering Functions

You pass data to functions through arguments contained within the function's parentheses. Each function takes a specific type of argument, such as numbers, references, text, or logical values.

Enter functions into the formula bar as you would enter a term in an equation. You could look at the function as a shorthand method that replaces part of an equation. For example, instead of entering

=(A12+A13+A14+A15)*2

use the function

=SUM(A12:A15)*2

If you forget which functions are available, use the Formula Paste Function command to enter a function in a formula:

1. Position the cursor within the formula in the formula bar, and choose the Formula Paste Function command to display the dialog box shown in figure 9.1.

2. Select the function from the list box by pressing the up- or down-arrow key or the first letter of the function.

3. Select Paste Arguments from the Paste Function dialog box if you want Excel automatically to insert a reminder for each argument.

4. Choose OK or press Enter.

Fig. 9.1. The Paste Function dialog box.

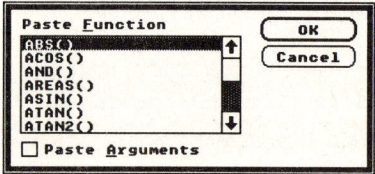

After you select the function you want from the Paste Function list box, it will appear at the cursor location in the formula bar.

TIP

Finding Functions Quickly

You can quickly scroll to a function in the Paste Function list box by pressing its first letter. Excel scrolls the list to the first function beginning with that letter.

As you enter formulas with Formula Paste Function, you can get help from Excel by turning on the Paste Arguments option box. Text arguments shown in the definitions will appear in the appropriate locations between the parentheses. For example, with Paste Arguments off, when you select

PMT( ) from the list box, the function appears as PMT( ) in the formula bar. When Paste Arguments is turned on, the function appears as PMT(rate,nper,pv,fv,type) in the formula bar. The placeholders *rate*, *nper*, *pv*, *fv*, and *type* remind you which arguments are needed and where they must be located. You must replace the placeholders with actual values or references before using your worksheet; otherwise, the function or formula will return the #NAME? error.

TIP

Editing Pasted Arguments

To edit pasted arguments, press F2, the Edit key. Move to the beginning of the argument text, and press Shift+Ctrl+right-arrow key. This selects from the cursor location to the position past the next comma. Type the value to replace the argument text and its trailing comma.

NOTE

Be Careful When Using Paste Arguments

If you have named cells or references that use the same name as the placeholders in a pasted function, Excel will assume that the placeholder refers to the named cell or range. This feature can save you time, but it also can confuse you if you are not careful.

You can use Excel's predefined functions to create function macros. Functions macros act and are used in the same ways as predefined worksheet functions, except that you define them. Function macros are described in Chapter 25, "Macro Quick Start," and in Chapter 26, "Building Command and Function Macros."

Entering Function Arguments

Each Excel function accepts specific types of data, known as arguments. Many argument names refer to the type of data to be entered. The basic types of arguments used by functions are listed in table 9.1.

Table 9.1
Excel Function Argument Types

Argument	Meaning
Value	A number, value, formula, or reference to one of these
Logical	A logical value
Number	A number or numeric formula
Text	A text or text formula
Array	An array of values
Serial number	A date and time number
Reference	A cell or range of cell's address

The Excel function dictionary that follows lists each function name and its arguments. The names of the arguments in the function dictionary are the same as the arguments pasted when you choose Paste Arguments from the Paste Function dialog box. Arguments appear differently depending on how they are to be used:

Argument entry	Interpretation
argument	A mandatory argument
argument	An optional argument
argument . . . (ellipsis)	An argument that can be repeated. Most functions have a limit of 14 arguments.

In this book, arguments within a description appear in italics for easy identification. Within a description, therefore, the italics does not mean that the argument is optional.

Arguments must be separated by commas; otherwise, Excel cannot distinguish between them. If you do not insert an argument between two commas, Excel usually interprets the missing argument as zero or FALSE. Do not put spaces between the parentheses that enclose function arguments or anywhere else in a function.

Make sure that you enclose text within quotation marks. Do not enclose range names in quotation marks. If text contains a quotation within a quotation, use two sets of quotation marks for each internal quotation. Text values, including the quotation marks, can be 0 to 255 characters long.

Displaying Blank Text

To create empty text that produces nothing on the screen, use two double quotation marks with nothing between them—for example:

=IF(A12>15,"","Entry must be greater than 15!")

When A12 is greater than 15, nothing is displayed in the cell because the TRUE portion of the IF function returns " ". When A12 is 15 or less, the message

Entry must be larger than 15!

is displayed.

Excel Function Dictionary

In the function dictionary that follows, each Excel function is displayed with its proper arguments along with explanation, limitations, examples, and tips. Function definitions are grouped by type and are listed in alphabetical order within each group. The functions are grouped as follows:

- Database
- Date
- Financial
- Information
- Logical
- Lookup
- Mathematical
- Matrix
- Statistical
- Text
- Trigonometric

Database Functions

Each of Excel's database functions uses the same arguments: *database*, *field*, and *criteria*. These arguments, as described in the discussion of DAVERAGE, apply to all the database functions. Examples of database functions and tips that help you analyze your database contents are provided in Chapter 23, "Building Advanced Databases."

DAVERAGE(database,field,criteria)

This function averages the numbers in the *field* of the *database* for those records matching the query in *criteria*.

DAVERAGE finds the average in a specific field of those records that meet specifications you set in the criteria range. For the *database* argument, you can specify a range such as B36:D54, a name such as INVENTORY, or the name DATABASE set by the Set Database command.

The *field* argument specifies on which column or row the function acts. You can specify the field by its range name; by its field name; or by number, where 1 is the first field (column or row), 2 the second, and so on. Remember to enclose a field name in quotation marks.

Like *database*, the *criteria* argument can be specified by range, name, or with the name CRITERIA set by the Set Criteria command. You set up criteria as described in the Database section of this book. The *criteria* set for a database function (Dfunction) does not have to be the same criteria range used in Data Set Criteria. If *criteria* is optional and does not contain a search specification, the function will act on all fields. (Chapters 18, 20, and 21 go into greater descriptions of the *criteria*.)

TIP

Dfunctions Can Have Different Databases and Criteria

The *criteria*, *field*, and *database* arguments used in Dfunctions do not have to be the same as those with Data Set Database or Set Criteria. You can have several Dfunctions working at the same time on different databases, and each function can have its own criteria.

You probably will find that DAVERAGE and DSUM are useful database functions for even simple tasks. For example, you can use DAVERAGE to find the average amount owed during the month of April or use DSUM to find the total owed by account ID.

DCOUNT(database,field,criteria)

Counts how many cells contain numbers in the *field* of the *database* for those records matching the specifications you set in the *criteria*.

Limits: If the *field* argument is omitted, DCOUNT counts all records in the database.

DCOUNTA(database,field,criteria)

Counts the number of nonblank cells in the *field* of the *database* for those records matching the query in the *criteria*.

Limits: If the *field* argument is omitted, DCOUNTA counts all nonblank records in the database.

DMAX(database,field,criteria)

Finds the largest number in the *field* of the *database* for those records matching the query in the *criteria*.

DMIN(database,field,criteria)

Finds the smallest number in the *field* of the *database* for those records matching the query in the *criteria*.

DPRODUCT(database,field,criteria)

Multiplies the values in the *field* of the *database* for those records matching the query in the *criteria*. This action is similar to DSUM, but the values are multiplied rather then added.

DSTDEV(database,field,criteria)

Approximates the standard deviation for the numbers in the *field* of the *database* using a sample of the population from those records matching the query in the *criteria*.

DSTDEVP(database,field,criteria)

Calculates the standard deviation for the numbers in the *field* of the *database* from the entire population for those records matching the query in the *criteria*.

DSUM(database,field,criteria)

Totals all numbers in the *field* of the *database* for those records matching the query in the *criteria*.

DVAR(database,field,criteria)

Approximates the variance for the numbers in the *field* of the *database* using a sample of the population from those records matching the query in the *criteria*.

DVARP(database,field,criteria)

Calculates the variance for the numbers in the *field* of the *database* from the entire population for those records matching the query in the *criteria*.

Date Functions

Excel records dates and times as serial numbers. A date is the number of days from January 1, 1900, to the date you specify; and a time is a decimal fraction of 24 hours. Serial numbers provide the math capabilities to calculate elapsed days, future times, and so on.

If the 1904 **Date** System option is on in the **Options Calculation** dialog box, the first day for serial dates is January 1, 1904. You select this when you are reading Excel worksheets created on the Macintosh. The following definitions and examples assume that the 1904 **Date** System option is not selected.

TIP

Typing Date and Time Entries

The same predefined date and time formats you type into a worksheet apply to worksheet functions. When a function's argument is *serial_number*, you can use the serial date number, a reference to a date or time cell, or one of the predefined date or time formats enclosed in quotations marks as text, such as "24-Dec-88".

DATE(year,month,day)

Produces the serial number for a specific date. Use the DATE function to calculate a serial number from formulas that produce a numeric year, month, or day. Enter the *year, month,* and *day* as a number or reference a cell containing a numeric value or formula.

Limits: Serial numbers are returned for dates between January 1, 1900, and December 31, 2078. Enter years between 1900 and 2078 or 00 and 178, months from 1 to 12, and days from 1 to 31.

Example: DATE(1988,7,B11) produces the serial number 32336 if B11 contains the day number 12.

TIP

Find the First Day of Each Quarter

DATE(1987,CHOOSE(QTR,1,4,7,10),1) produces serial numbers for the first day of each quarter when QTR refers to a cell containing the numbers 1 through 4. Use Format **Number** to format the serial number so that it appears as a date.

1-2-3 TIP

Using Excel's @DATE and @DATEVALUE Equivalents

Do not use Excel's DATE and DATEVALUE functions to enter dates as you would with the @DATE and @DATEVALUE functions in 1-2-3. Excel accepts dates as they are normally typed in American and European formats, such as 12/24/88. Use the DATE or DATEVALUE functions inside formulas to calculate serial numbers when performing date math.

DATEVALUE(date_text)

Converts a date written as *date_text* into a serial number. The text can be in any format matching one of Excel's predefined date formats found in the list box of the Format Number command's dialog box. Excel accepts text dates entered either in formulas or directly into cells. The function is most useful with formulas.

Limits: Serial numbers are returned for dates between January 1, 1900, and December 31, 2078. Enter years between 00 and 178, months from 1 to 12, and days from 1 to 31.

Example: DATEVALUE("24-Dec-88") produces 32501.

DAY(serial_number)

Converts a *serial_number* to the number of the day of the month between 1 and 31. Format the cell as a number.

Limits: The serial number must be in the 0 to 65380 range.

Examples: DAY(32501) produces 24.

        DAY("24-Dec-88") produces 24.

        DAY(B11) produces 24 when B11 contains 24-Dec-88.

HOUR(serial_number)

Returns a value for the number of hours in the fractional part of a *serial_number*. This conversion is based on a 24-hour clock. Format the cell as a number.

Examples: HOUR(32501.75) produces 18.

        HOUR("24-Dec-88 18:00") produces 18 hours.

MINUTE(serial_number)

Returns the number of minutes from a *serial_number*. The fractional portion of a day is based on a 24-hour clock. The number of minutes returned is between 0 and 59. Format the cell as a number.

Example: MINUTE(32501.75456) produces 6 minutes.

MONTH(serial_number)

Converts the *serial_number* to the number of the month, 1 to 12. Format the cell as a number.

Examples: MONTH(32501.7546) produces 12.

MONTH(B14) produces 12 if B14 contains "24-Dec-88".

NOW()

Calculates the serial number of the date and time in the computer's clock.

Limits: You must include the empty parentheses when entering this function. NOW() does not use an argument.

TIP

Stamp Your Worksheets with the Date and Time

Use the NOW() function to stamp a worksheet with the date and time it was printed. Enter NOW() in a cell formatted with the Format Number command as a date/time format. Each time you retrieve the worksheet, the cell contents will be updated. Use Edit Paste Special with Values selected to freeze a date or time.

SECOND(serial_number)

Produces the number of seconds from a *serial_number*.

Limits: Seconds are between 0 and 59.

Examples: SECOND(32501.753) produces 19.

SECOND("24-Dec-88 18:04:19") produces 19.

TIME(hour,minute,second)

Calculates the serial number of a specific time as a decimal fraction of a 24-hour clock.

Example: TIME(18,4,19) produces .752998.

TIMEVALUE("time_text")

Converts a time written as *text* into a serial number.

Limits: You must enclose the text in quotation marks and use one of Excel's predefined date or time formats.

Examples: TIMEVALUE("18:04:19") produces .752998.

TIMEVALUE("12:00 PM") produces .5.

WEEKDAY(serial_number)

Converts the *serial_number* to the day of the week. The result is a number from 1 (Sunday) to 7 (Saturday).

Example: WEEKDAY("24-Dec-88") produces 7 (Saturday).

YEAR(serial_number)

Converts the *serial_number* into the year.

Example: YEAR(32501) produces 1988.

Financial Functions

Excel's financial functions can replace financial formulas you would have to enter manually. Excel functions operate faster and with less chance of error than typed formulas.

Excel provides a family of functions that solve annuity problems. Annuities are a series of even cash flows over a period of time. Cash flows may be rent coming in according to a regular time period or payments you make to a retirement fund. The following functions involve annuities:

FV(rate,nper,pmt,pv,type)

NPER(rate,pmt,pv,fv,type)

PMT(rate,nper,pv,fv,type)

RATE(nper,pmt,pv,fv,type,guess)

The periodic interest is the *rate*. Its period must be in the same units as *nper*—the number of periods (such as months) in the life of the cash flow. For example, the annual interest rate should be divided by 12 if payments or receipts are monthly.

The *pmt* (payment) is the constant amount paid or received in each period on an investment or amortized loan such as a mortgage. Normally, *pmt* contains both principal and interest. The worth of something at the end of the last period is called *fv* (future value), and *pv* (present value) is the worth of something at the beginning of the period.

Some functions perform different tasks depending on the number you enter as the *type* argument. When *type* equals zero, cash flow is assumed to be at the end of the period. If *type* equals 1, cash flow is assumed to be at the beginning of the period. If no value is entered for *pv* or *type*, each is assumed to be zero.

Enter a negative *pmt* (payment), cash you pay out, as a negative amount in the function.

Guess is your best estimate at the final rate. Usually, a *guess* between 0 and 1 will produce an answer. If *guess* is not entered, then a *guess* of 10 percent is assumed. If your *guess* is too far off, Excel will not be able to find an answer and #NUM! error will be returned.

NOTE

When #NUM! Appears in Financial Functions

If #NUM! appears after you enter one of the financial functions, you may have incorrectly entered the positive or negative signs on *pmt*, *pv*, or *fv*. Remember, money you are paying out should appear as a negative number.

DDB(cost,salvage,life,period)

Calculates the depreciation for the *period* you indicate using the double-declining balance depreciation method. You must indicate the initial *cost*, the *salvage* value at the end of the economic life, and the *life* of the item.

Limits: The *period* and economic *life* must be in the same terms. Check with your CPA or accountant to determine the appropriate economic life.

The function uses the following equation in its calculations:

DDB=((*cost*-prior total depreciation)*2)/*life*

Example: The lathe in your factory cost $130,000 and will be worth $4,800 at the end of its economic life in 15 years. What is the depreciation amount at different points in the life?

DDB(130000,4800,15,12) results in $3,591.33 for year 12.

DDB(130000,4800,15*12,12) results in $1,277.39 for the 12th month in the first year.

FV(rate,nper,pmt,*pv*,*type*)

Calculates the future value of a series of cash flows of equal *pmt* amounts made at even periods for *nper* (number of periods) at the constant interest *rate*. A lump sum, *pv*, is invested at the beginning of the term.

Limits: If no values are entered for *fv* and *type*, they are considered to be zero.

Example: You invest $2,000 as a lump sum, and you add $100 at the beginning of each month for 5 years (60 months) at an interest rate of 8% compounded monthly. Use the following function to find the worth of the investment at the end of the term:

FV(.08/12,60,-100,-2000,1)

The result is $10,376.36.

Notice that amounts you pay out are negative, and amounts you receive are positive.

IPMT(rate,per,nper,pv,*fv,type*)

Calculates the interest portion of a payment on an annuity (an investment of even periodic cash flows). You can use this function to calculate the interest paid on a mortgage at some period, *per*, within the term of the mortgage, *nper*.

Limits: The value of *per* must be in the range 1 to *nper*. If no values are entered for *fv* and *type*, they are considered to be zero.

Example: A flat-rate mortgage of $150,000 is made at 10% interest for 30 years. How much was paid toward interest in the 14th month? Use this function to calculate the answer:

    IPMT(.10/12,14,360,150000,0,0)

The result is -$1242.44. The interest rate is negative because it is being paid out.

IRR(values,*guess*)

Produces the internal rate of return for a series of periodic cash flows found in *values*. The function uses your *guess* at the rate of return as a starting point for estimation. The result is the rate of return for a single period.

The *values* may be positive and negative cash flows of uneven amounts contained in a range or array of referenced cells. The cash flows must be in the order received.

Guess is your best estimate at the final rate. Usually, a *guess* between 0 and 1 will produce an answer. If *guess* is not entered, then a *guess* of 10 percent is assumed. If your *guess* is too far off, Excel will not be able to find an answer and #NUM! error will be returned.

The IRR function makes continuous estimates of the rate of return until 2 estimates are within .00001%. If this resolution cannot be reached after 20 tries, IRR produces the error value #NUM!.

Limits: The IRR method used by all spreadsheets can produce a different solution for each change of sign in the cash flow. You must try different guesses to find the most accurate solution. The IRR method does not allow you to reinvest positive cash flows or save for negative cash flows at realistic rates. The MIRR function produces more realistic results.

Example: Figure 9.2 shows the forecasted cash flows from an apartment complex. Year 0 is the purchase price plus rehabilitation costs. The internal rate of return function in cell G4 is

IRR(D5:D15,0.1)

The result of the function is 0.1111655 or 11% return.

Fig. 9.2. Forecast cash flows from an apartment complex.

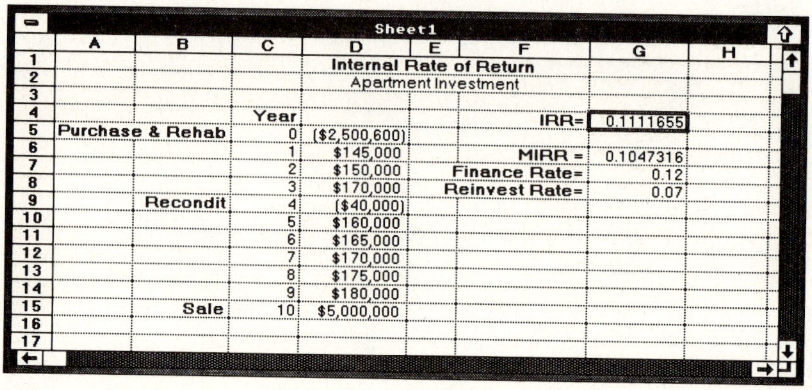

	A	B	C	D	E	F	G	H
				Internal Rate of Return				
				Apartment Investment				
1								
2								
3								
4			Year			IRR=	0.1111655	
5	Purchase & Rehab		0	($2,500,600)				
6			1	$145,000		MIRR =	0.1047316	
7			2	$150,000		Finance Rate=	0.12	
8			3	$170,000		Reinvest Rate=	0.07	
9		Recondit	4	($40,000)				
10			5	$160,000				
11			6	$165,000				
12			7	$170,000				
13			8	$175,000				
14			9	$180,000				
15		Sale	10	$5,000,000				
16								
17								

MIRR(values,finance_rate,reinvest_rate)

Calculates the modified internal rate of return from a series of positive and negative cash flows in the range *values*. The *finance_rate* specifies the rate that investment funding costs. The *reinvest_rate* is the safe rate at which positive cash flows may be invested.

Limits: At least one positive and one negative cash flow must be specified.

Example: Consider the same forecasted cash flows from an apartment complex as used for the IRR function (see fig. 9.2). For this example, a finance rate of 12% and a reinvestment rate of 7% are used to make the calculation more realistic. The function in cell G6 is

MIRR(D5:D15,G7,G8)

The result is .1047316. This result is only a half percent less than it was with the IRR method, but some investments will make a larger difference.

NPER(rate,pmt,pv,*fv,type*)

Calculates the number of periods required to create the annuity determined by the given arguments.

Limits: If no values are entered for *fv* and *type*, they are considered to be zero.

Example: NPER(0.10/12,-500,10000) produces 21.969 or 22 payments.

NPV(rate,value1,*value2*, . . .)

Calculates the net present value of a series of cash flows found in the range or array of *value1*, *value2*, and so on, given a discount rate equal to *rate*. The net present value of a series of cash flows is the value those cash flows represent in a single amount in terms of current money if money currently earns the specified *rate* per period.

Limits: The cash flows are considered to be at the end of each period. Cash flows do not have to be equal amounts. The rate must be the rate per period.

Example: You purchased a piece of equipment for $40,000 cash. You could have invested the cash at 8%. At the end of each of the next 5 years, the equipment will have saved you $9,000, $6,000, $6,000, $5,000, and $5,000, respectively. At the end of the 6th year, the equipment saves you $5,000, and you sell the equipment for $20,000. Is the purchase worth making?

The net present value of the purchase is

    NPV(0.08,9000,6000,6000,5000,5000,25000)

The result is a $41,072.67 savings. The purchase saved you $1,072.67 over what an equivalent amount invested at 8 percent would have earned.

PMT(rate,nper,pv,*fv,type*)

Calculates the periodic payment for different *type*s of investments given the investment's *rate*, term (*nper*), present value (*pv*), or future value (*fv*).

Limits: If no values are entered for *fv* and *type*, they are considered to be zero.

Example: Suppose that you want to purchase a small bungalow in California for $190,000 with a flat-rate mortgage of 30 years at 10%. The monthly payment is

    PMT(0.10/12,360,190000)

The result is -$1667.39. Note: The amount is negative because you will be paying out the mortgage. Make sure the interest rate and term are in the same units as your payment frequency—for example, term in months, interest per months, and one payment per month.

PPMT(rate,per,nper,pv,*fv,type*)

Calculates the principal payment portion of a payment made on an amortized investment. This portion is the part of the PMT function that reduces a loan balance.

Limits: If no values are entered for *fv* and *type*, they are considered to be zero.

Example: Consider the mortgage described in the PMT function example. The payment toward principal in the 12th month will be

PPMT(0.10/12,12,360,190000)

The result is -$92.09, which is negative because you are paying out the money.

PV(rate,nper,pmt,*fv,type*)

Calculates the present value of a series of future cash flows of equal *pmt* amounts made at even periods for *nper* (number of periods) at the constant interest *rate*. PV is the amount in current dollars that an even cash flow in the future will be worth. If the amounts of the cash flow are uneven, use the NPV function.

Limits: If no values are entered for *fv* and *type*, they are considered to be zero.

Example: You know that you can afford a car payment of $220 per month for the next 4 years. Current loans are at 9%. How large a loan can you afford? The function you need for the calculation is

PV(0.09/12,48,-220)

The result is $8,840.65.

RATE(nper,pmt,pv,*fv,type,guess*)

Calculates the interest rate for the annuity determined by the supplied arguments.

Limits: If no values are entered for *fv* and *type*, they are considered to be zero. If you do not enter an estimated interest rate for *guess*, Excel uses 10%. RATE may return more than one solution, depending on the value used for *guess*. If *guess* is too far from the correct value, Excel may not be able to make an estimate and may return #NUM!.

Example: RATE(12,-800,9000) results in an interest rate of 1.007% per month (12.09% per year).

SLN(cost,salvage,life)

Returns the amount used each year for straight-line depreciation when given the initial *cost* of an item, the *salvage* value at the end of the item's economic life, and the economic *life* of the item.

Example: SLN(40000,12000,5) produces $5,600 per year depreciation.

SYD(cost,salvage,life,per)

Calculates the depreciation for the *per* indicated using the sum-of-the-years depreciation method. You must indicate the initial *cost*, the *salvage* value at the end of the economic life, and the *life* of the item.

Examples: SLN(40000,12000,5,1) produces $9,333 depreciation the first year.

SLN(40000,12000,5,2) produces $7,467 depreciation the second year.

Information Functions

Information functions are necessary when cell contents, ranges, or selected areas must be analyzed before performing a function or macro.

AREAS(reference)

Produces the number of areas in *reference*. Use the AREAS function to find how many multiple selections are within an area.

Example: AREAS(PRINTOUT) results in 2 when the range named PRINTOUT contains 2 range selections.

TIP

Use AREAS in Macros

Use AREAS in macros to ensure that the operator has not selected more ranges than allowed for the macro function working on the selected area.

CELL(type_of_info,*reference*)

Returns information about the cell contents of the current or *reference* cell. The *type_of_info* determines what the cell contents are checked for. The possible values of *type_of_info* and result returned by the function are listed in table 9.2.

Table 9.2
Results Returned by the CELL Function

Value of type_of_info	Produces
"width"	The column width in integer numbers, measured in terms of font 1 character widths
"row"	The row number of the *reference*

Value of type_of_info	*Produces*
"col"	The column number of the *reference*
"protect"	Zero if the cell is not locked, otherwise 1
"address"	The reference of the first cell in *reference* in text form; for example, $B$2
"contents"	The value in the *reference*
"format"	The text value showing the cell format. Some examples are

"G"	General
"F2"	0.00 or #,##0.00
"C2"	$#,##0.00;($#,##0.00)
"D4"	m/d/yy

"prefix"	The label prefix for alignments:

'	Left alignment
"	Right alignment
^	Center alignment
\	Fill

"type"	The text value showing the cell format:

"b"	Blank
"l"	Label
"v"	Value

Limits: The CELL function is used primarily with macros translated from Lotus 1-2-3. For greater capabilities with Excel macros, use the GET.CELL macro.

Example: CELL("width",B36) produces 18 if column B is 17.8 characters wide in font 1.

TIP

Use IF with CELL To Display a Message

IF(CELL("type",B12)="b","Enter a name here","") results in the text "Enter a name here" whenever cell B12 is blank. This works well to prompt for data-entry fields.

COLUMN(*reference*)

Produces the column number of the *reference* cell. If *reference* is a range, then the column numbers of each column in the range are produced as a horizontal array. If the *reference* argument is not specified, COLUMN( ) produces the column number of the cell containing the function.

Examples: COLUMN(Print) returns the array {3,4,5} if Print is the range name of the range C5:E20.

   COLUMN(C15) returns 3.

COLUMNS(array)

Produces the number of columns in *array*.

Example: COLUMNS(E4:G6) produces 3.

INDIRECT(ref_text,*type_of_ref*)

Returns the contents of the cell indicated by *ref_text*. The *ref_text* argument must be an A1, R1C1, or cell name. When *type_of_ref* is omitted, TRUE or 1, INDIRECT expects *ref_text* to be R1C1 style. When *type_of_ref* is FALSE or 0, INDIRECT expects A1 style.

Limit: An incorrect *ref_text* produces #REF!.

Example: INDIRECT(A20) produces 5 if A20 contains the text "B35" and cell B35 contains 5.

ISfunction(value)

Excel has nine worksheet functions that examine whether a cell meets certain conditions, such as whether it is blank or contains an error value. Depending on the status of the cell, the IS function produces either a TRUE or FALSE value.

IS functions are most useful when used with IF functions to test whether a cell or range is blank or contains numbers, text, or errors. For example, you might want to prevent the division by zero error, #DIV/0!. Consider the following formula:

   =IF(ISERROR(B12/C13),"C13 must not be zero",B12/C13)

This formula determines whether B12/C13 produces an error. If an error is produced, the formula prints a message. If an error is not produced, the division result appears.

You also can use IS functions to test for the proper type of entry. This example tests to make sure that B36 contains a number:

=IF(ISNUMBER(B36),"Good entry","Entry not a number")

The IS functions and their results are listed in table 9.3.

Table 9.3
Excel IS Functions

Function	Result
ISBLANK(value)	TRUE if value is a blank reference. FALSE if value is nonblank.
ISERR(value)	TRUE if value is any error other than #N/A. FALSE for any other values.
ISERROR(value)	TRUE if value is any error value. FALSE if not an error value.
ISLOGICAL(value)	TRUE if value is a logical value. FALSE if value is not a logical value.
ISNA(value)	TRUE if value is the #N/A error value. FALSE if value is not #N/A.
ISNONTEXT(value)	TRUE if value is not text. FALSE if value is text.
ISNUMBER(value)	TRUE if value is a number. FALSE if value is not a number.
ISREF(value)	TRUE if value is a reference. FALSE if value is not a reference.
ISTEXT(value)	TRUE if value is text. FALSE if value is not text.

N(value)

Translates *value* into a number. N translates numbers into numbers, and logical TRUE into 1. Any other value becomes 0. N is primarily used to provide compatibility with translated worksheets.

Examples: N("9 nine") produces 0.

N(A12) produces 1 if A12 is TRUE.

NA()

Always produces error value #N/A, which means "No value Available." NA() does not take an argument. You can type #N/A directly into a cell for the same result.

Type #N/A Directly into Blank Cells

Enter #N/A into blank data-entry cells. If a data-entry cell has not been filled, the formulas that depend upon this cell result in #N/A.

ROW(*reference*)

Results in the row number of the *reference* cell. If *reference* is a range, ROW produces a vertical array of the row numbers. If you don't specify the *reference* argument, ROW() produces the row number of the cell containing the function.

Examples: ROW(D5) is 5.

ROW(D5:F7) is {5;6;7}

ROWS(array)

Produces the number of rows in *array*.

Example: ROWS(B12:D35) results in 24.

TYPE(value)

Determines the type of a cell's contents and produces a corresponding code (see table 9.4).

Table 9.4
Results of the TYPE Function

Value	Result
Number	1
Text	2
Logical value	4
Error value	16
Array	64

Examples: TYPE(B36) results in 1 if B36 contains a number.

TYPE(B36) results in 16 if B36 contains #N/A.

Logical Functions

The Logical functions may be the most powerful worksheet functions. The IF statement is useful for testing conditions and making decisions. AND and OR functions can test multiple criteria or test conditions for use within IF functions.

AND(logical1,*logical2*, . . .)

Joins test conditions: TRUE if all *logicals* are TRUE; FALSE if any *logical* is FALSE.

Limits: Arguments must be single logical values or arrays containing logical values. AND cannot contain more than 14 *logical* values.

Example: AND(B36,C12>20) is TRUE only when B36 is not zero and C12 is greater than 20.

TIP

Use AND To Test Limits

To test whether an entry value is between an upper and lower limit, use the AND function in a formula such as the following:

=IF(AND(B36>=20,B36<=50),"","Entry out of range")

This formula produces a blank cell if the number in B36 is from 20 to 50. If B36 is less than 20 or greater than 50, the message "Entry out of range" will appear.

1-2-3 TIP

AND Functions in Excel

In 1-2-3, AND functions appear between logical conditions and are separated by # signs, such as in the following formula:

@IF(B36>=20#AND#B36<=50,"","Entry out of range")

The equivalent Excel formula is

=IF(AND(B36>=20,B36<=50),"","Entry out of range")

FALSE( )

Always produces a logical FALSE. You must type the parentheses even though they do not contain an argument.

IF(logical_test,value_if_true,*value_if_false*)

Produces the *value_if_true* when the *logical_test* is TRUE; produces the *value_if_false* when the *logical_test* is FALSE.

One of the most valuable functions in Excel, the IF function can test cells and make decisions based on the cell contents.

TIP

Use IF with Other Logical Functions

Use the AND, OR, and NOT functions with the IF function to make complex decisions. Examples are shown under the definitions of AND and OR functions. Other examples can be found in Chapter 11, "Building Advanced Worksheets."

In macros, *value_if_true* and *value_if_false* can be GOTO functions or action functions—for example:

    IF(counter>10,GOTO(end),GOTO(loop))

Limits: Up to seven IF functions can be nested.

Example: IF(ONHAND<ORDERQNTY,"Reorder","") results in the message "Reorder" whenever the quantity on hand drops below the reorder quantity.

NOT(logical)

Reverses the result of the *logical* from TRUE to FALSE or FALSE to TRUE. Use this function to take the opposite condition of the one stated in an IF statement.

Example: IF(NOT(OR(B36=12,B36=20)),"Not a 12 or 20","Is a 12 or 20"). This statement checks whether B36 does not contain a 12 or 20 and produces the message "Not a 12 or 20" when it does not.

OR(logical1,*logical2*, . . .)

Joins test conditions: TRUE if one or more *logicals* is TRUE; FALSE only when all *logicals* are FALSE.

Limits: OR is limited to 14 or fewer arguments. Arguments cannot be blank cells, error values, or text. Use IS functions within OR functions to test for blank cells, error values, or text.

Example: IF(OR(B36=12,B36=20),"Is a 12 or 20","Not a 12 or 20"). This statement checks whether B36 contains either 12 or 20 and produces the message "Is a 12 or 20" when it does. If B36 contains anything else, the second message appears.

TRUE( )

Always produces TRUE. You must type the parentheses even though they do not contain an argument.

Lookup Functions

The LOOKUP and MATCH functions enable your worksheets to retrieve a value from within a table. Examples of many of these functions are found in Chapter 11, "Building Advanced Worksheets." Index functions enable you to extract specific value from within an array.

CHOOSE(index_number,value1,*value2*, . . .)

Chooses from the list of *values* a value that corresponds to the *index_number*. For example, when the *index_number* is 2, the function chooses *value2*. When used in a macro, the CHOOSE function can have *values* that are GOTO or action functions.

Limits: CHOOSE displays #VALUE when the *index_number* is less than one or greater than the number of items in the list.

Examples: CHOOSE(B12,5,12,32,14) produces 32 when B12 contains 3.

DATE(1987,CHOOSE(QTR,1,4,7,10),1) produces the serial numbers for the first day of each quarter when QTR refers to a cell containing the numbers 1 through 4.

CHOOSE(WEEKDAY(A12),"Sunday","Monday","Tuesday", "Wednesday","Thursday","Friday","Saturday") produces Saturday if A12 contains 12/24/88 because WEEKDAY converts 12/24/88 into the number 7.

HLOOKUP(lookup_value,table_array,row_index_num)

Looks across the top row of the range defined by *table_array* until the *lookup_value* is met, and then looks down that column to the row specified by *row_index_num*.

Limits: Values in the first row of *table_array* must be in ascending order, both alphabetically (A-Z) and numerically (0-9).

If the *lookup_value* is not found, HLOOKUP uses the largest value that is less than or equal to the *lookup_value*.

Row_index_num begins with 1. To return a value from the first row, use 1, from the second row, use 2, and so on. If *row_index_num* is less than 1, HLOOKUP produces the #VALUE! error. If *row_index_num* is greater than the rows in the table, #REF! is displayed.

Examples: Refer to Chapter 11, "Building Advanced Worksheets," for examples using the HLOOKUP function.

INDEX(ref,row_num,column_num,*area_num*)

In the reference form of INDEX, produces a cell reference from within the *ref* specified and at the intersection of the *row_num* and *column_num*. Other functions treat the value returned by INDEX as a cell reference or as the value of the cell contents.

The referenced area is *ref*. If this area contains multiple ranges, enclose the reference in parentheses, as in (B36:D45,G56:H62). If *ref* contains more than one area, *area_num* can choose between areas. In the preceding example, an *area_num* of 2 will choose G56:H62. If you do not include an *area_num*, Excel assumes it is 1.

The arguments *row_num* and *column_num* choose a cell within the area specified. The first row or column is 1. A second form of the INDEX function is used with arrays. The second form follows.

Limits: If either *row_num* or *column_num* is outside the specified area, IN-DEX results in #REF!.

Example: INDEX((B2:C5,E7:G9),1,2,2) produces the reference or value in F7, the second area, first row, second column.

INDEX(array,row_num,column_num)

In the array form of INDEX, *row_num* and *col_num* return the value of a cell within the array. The definitions of *row_num* and *col_num* are the same as described in the reference version of INDEX.

Examples: INDEX({3,4,5;8,9,10},2,3) produces 10.

INDEX({3,4,5;8,9,10},0,3) produces the single column-matrix {5;10} when the INDEX function is entered as an array formula using Shift+Ctrl+Enter.

LOOKUP(lookup_value,lookup_vector,result_vector)

LOOKUP can be either a vector or an array function. This description applies to the vector function. A *lookup_vector* contains a single row or column. This function searches through the *lookup_vector* until *lookup_value* is found. The function then produces the value that is in the same location in the *result_vector*. If the *lookup_value* can't be found, then LOOKUP returns a value corresponding to the largest value less than or equal to *lookup_value*. If *lookup_value* is smaller than any value in *lookup_vector*, then #NA is returned.

Limits: Values in *lookup_vector* can be text, numbers, or logical values. They must be sorted in ascending order to give the correct return.

LOOKUP(lookup_value,array)

The array form of LOOKUP is similar to HLOOKUP and VLOOKUP. HLOOKUP searches for a match to *lookup_value* in the first row; VLOOKUP searches for a match to *lookup_value* in the first column; but LOOKUP searches in the first row or column depending on the shape of the array. If the array is square, or wider than tall, then LOOKUP searches across the first row for the *lookup_value*. If the array is taller than its width, the search proceeds down the first column. LOOKUP always selects the last value in the row or column where the *lookup_value* is found.

Limits: LOOKUP is provided primarily for compatibility with imported spreadsheets. HLOOKUP and VLOOKUP are usually more suitable for use.

MATCH(lookup_value,lookup_array,*type_of_match*)

MATCH returns the position of the match for *lookup_value* in *lookup_array*. The type of match is determined by *type_of_match*. The *look_up* value can be a number, text, logical value, or cell reference. The types of match are

Type_of_match	*Finds*
1, or omitted	Largest value less than or equal to *lookup_value*
0	First value that is an exact match
-1	Smallest value less than or equal to *lookup_value*

Limits: MATCH returns the position of the found item, not its value or cell reference.

Example: Chapter 23, "Building Advanced Databases," contains an example.

VLOOKUP(lookup_value,table_array,col_index)

Looks down the left column of *table_array* until the *lookup_ value* is met, and then looks across that row to the column specified by *col_index*. Values in the first column can be text, numbers, or logical values in ascending order. Upper- and lowercase text are considered the same.

Limits: If VLOOKUP can't find the *lookup_value*, the function searches for the next largest value it can find in the first column. Other limits are the same as specified in the discussion of the HLOOKUP function.

Examples: Refer to Chapter 11, "Building Advanced Worksheets," for examples using the lookup functions.

Mathematical Functions

Mathematical functions provide the foundation for the majority of worksheet calculations. Most scientific and engineering functions are mathematical functions. If you do not find the function you need, you can create your own by referring to Chapter 25, "Macro Quick Start," and Chapter 26, "Building Command and Function Macros."

ABS(number)

Returns the absolute (positive) value of the *number*.

Examples: ABS(-5) produces 5.

ABS(5) produces 5.

EXP(number)

Returns the base of natural logarithms, e, raised to the power of the *number*. EXP is the inverse of the LN function.

Limits: The value of e is 2.71828182845904.

Examples: EXP(0) produces 1.

EXP(10) produces 22026.46579.

FACT(number)

Returns the factorial of the *number*.

Example: FACT(4) produces 24 (or 4 times 3 times 2 times 1).

INT(number)

Rounds a *number* to the nearest integer.

Examples: INT(7.6) produces 7.

INT(-7.6) produces -8.

TIP

Round Numbers in Three Ways

Use INT( ) to round a number to the nearest integer. Use TRUNC( ) to truncate a number to its next lower integer. And use ROUND( ) to round a number up or down.

LN(number)

Returns the natural log of a *number* in base e. LN is the inverse of EXP.

Limits: The value of the *number* must be positive.

Example: LN(3) produces 1.098612289.

LOG(number,*base*)

Returns the logarithm of the *number* in the *base* specified.

Limits: The value of the *number* must be positive. LOG uses base 10 if the *base* argument is omitted.

Examples: LOG(10) produces 1.

LOG(64,2) produces 6.

LOG10(number)

Returns the logarithm of the *number* in base 10.

Examples: LOG10(10) produces 1.

LOG10(100) produces 2.

MOD(number,divisor_number)

Produces the remainder of the *number* divided by the *divisor_number*.

Limits: The #DIV/0! error appears if the *divisor_number* is zero.

Examples: MOD(7,6) produces 1.

MOD(32,15) produces 2.

PI()

Returns the value of π.

Limits: An estimate of π, 3.14159265358979, is used. The parentheses must be included even though the function does not take an argument.

PRODUCT(number1,*number2*, . . .)

Multiplies *number1* by *number2* by the rest of the arguments.

Limits: You can specify up to 14 arguments. Arguments that are blank cells, logical values, error values, or text are ignored. Text that can be converted into a numeric value is converted.

Example: PRODUCT(B12:C14) produces 24 when cells B12 through C14 contains the numbers 1, 2, 3, and 4.

RAND()

Produces a random decimal number from 0 to 1. The function does not take an argument between the parentheses.

Example: RAND( ) produces .8567.

Using Random Numbers

To produce a random number between the starting number, *START*, and the ending number, *END*, use the following formula:

   =START+RAND( )*(END-START)

To choose randomly from a list, use the preceding formula as the index number for a CHOOSE, HLOOKUP, or VLOOKUP function.

To freeze the RAND( ) value, enter RAND( ) in the formula bar, select it, and then choose **Options Calculate Now**.

ROUND(number,number_of_digits)

Rounds the *number* to the *number_of_digits* specified.

Example: ROUND(456.345,2) produces 456.35.

Rounding Up and Down

The ROUND(x,n) function normally rounds the *x* attribute up or down to *n* decimal places, depending on whether the decimal part of the number is equal to or greater than .5. If you want all numbers to be rounded up, add .5 to the numbers you are rounding—for example:

   =ROUND(A12+.5,2)

This statement rounds any value in cell A12 to the next higher number.

SIGN(number)

Produces 1 when the *number* is positive, 0 when it is 0, and -1 when it is negative.

Example: SIGN(B12) produces 1 when B12 contains 5, and -1 when B12 contains -23.

SQRT(number)

Returns the square root of the *number*.

Limits: The value of the *number* must be positive.

Example: SQRT(25) produces 5.

TRUNC(number)

Changes the *number* to an integer by "cutting off" or truncating the decimal fraction portion.

Example: TRUNC(5.6) produces 5.

TIP

Use TRUNC To Truncate or ROUND To Round

If you want to round a number rather than truncate it, use the ROUND function.

Matrix Functions

In all the matrix functions except TRANSPOSE, *array* is a square numeric array stated as a range (such as B36:C37) or as an array constant (such as {3,54;4,65}). The error value #VALUE! is returned if cells contain text or are empty, or if the matrix is not square. Matrix functions are most frequently used for solving problems involving multiple simultaneous equations with multiple unknowns.

Matrix functions are shown with examples in Chapter 11, "Building Advanced Worksheets."

MDETERM(array)

Produces the determinant of *array*. The array can be a reference such as B36:C37 or an array constant such as {1,2,3;5,6,7;8,9,10}. The #VALUE! error is returned if the array contains a zero or is not square.

MINVERSE(array)

Produces the inverse of *array*. Produces the determinant of *array*. The array can be a reference such as B36:C37 or an array constant such as {1,2,3;5,6,7;8,9,10}. The #VALUE! error is returned if the array contains a zero or is not square.

Because the MINVERSE function produces an array as a result, you must enter the MINVERSE function as an array formula by selecting a square range of cells of equivalent size, typing the formula, and then pressing Shift+Ctrl+Enter.

MMULT(array1,array2)

Produces the product of *array1* and *array2*.

Because the MMULT function produces an array as a result, you must enter the MMULT function as an array formula. Entering the MMULT function is described in Chapter 11, "Building Advanced Worksheets."

TRANSPOSE(array)

Transposes the current *array* so that the first row in the current *array* becomes the first column of the new array, the second row of the current *array* becomes the second column of the new array, and so on.

Because the TRANSPOSE function produces an array as a result, you must enter the TRANSPOSE function as an array formula. Entering the TRANSPOSE function is described in Chapter 11, "Building Advanced Worksheets."

Statistical Functions

Statistical functions can help you with simple problems such as finding an average or counting items. Statistical functions can also do simple statistical analysis such as biased or nonbiased standard deviation.

AVERAGE(number1,*number2*, . . .)

Returns the average (mean) of the arguments. The *ranges* can contain numbers, cell references, or arrays that contain numbers. Text, logical values, errors, and blank cells are ignored.

Limits: AVERAGE can take from 1 to 14 arguments.

Examples: AVERAGE(B12:B15) produces 3.5 when B12 to B15 contains the numbers 2, 3, 4, and 5.

AVERAGE(B12:B15,20) produces 6.8 when B12 to B15 contains the numbers 2, 3, 4, and 5.

COUNT(value1,*value2*, . . .)

Produces a count of how many numbers are in the arguments. The *range* arguments can be numbers, cell references, or arrays that contain numbers. Text, logical values, errors, and blank cells are not counted.

Limits: You can include from 1 to 14 arguments in COUNT.

Example: COUNT(B12:B15) produces 4 when B12 to B15 contains the numbers 2, 3, 4, and 5. The statement produces 3 if B12 is blank instead of containing 2.

COUNTA(value1,*value2*, . . .)

Produces a count of how many values are in the arguments. This function counts values of all types, not just numbers. Empty cells within arrays or references are ignored. COUNTA determines the number of nonblank cells.

Limits: You can include from 1 to 14 arguments in COUNTA.

Examples: COUNTA(A12:A20) produces 8 if cell A13 is blank.

> COUNTA(B12:B15) produces 4 when B12 to B15 contain the values 2, "Tree", 4, and "Pine".

GROWTH(known_y's,*known_x's*,*new_x's*)

Calculates the exponential growth curve that best fits the test data contained in the ranges *known_y's* and *known_x's*. GROWTH then uses the *new_x's* values to calculate new y values along the calculated curve.

Because the GROWTH function produces an array, you must enter the GROWTH function as an array formula.

LINEST(known_y's,*known_x's*)

LINEST calculates the straight line equation that best fits the data and produces an array of values that define the equation of that line.

The line has the equation $y=b+m_1*x_1+m_2*x_2+. . . .$ The array returned is of the form $\{m_1,m_2, . . .,b\}$. The constants within that array can be used to calculate y values on the line for any given set of x_1, x_2, and so on.

Examples: Examples of the trend analysis functions are included in Chapter 11, "Building Advanced Worksheets."

LOGEST(known_y's,*known_x's*)

Calculates the growth curve of the form $y=b*(m_1{}^{\wedge}x_1)*(M_2{}^{\wedge}x_2)*. . . .$ When given the text data *known_y's* and *known_x's*, the values for b and m are returned in a horizontal array of the form $\{m_1,m_2, . . .,b\}$.

MAX(number1,*number2*, . . .)

Produces the largest number among the arguments.

Limits: MAX can take up to 14 arguments. Arguments that are error values or text that cannot be interpreted as a number are ignored. Within a referenced array or range, empty cells, logical values, text, or error values are ignored.

Examples: MAX(C2:D4) produces 32 if the numbers in these cells are -2, 4, 32, and 30.

> MAX(C2:D4,50) produces 50 if the numbers in the cells are the same as in the preceding example.

MIN(number1,*number2, . . .*)

Produces the smallest number among the arguments.

Limits: MIN can take up to 14 arguments. Arguments that are error values or text that cannot be interpreted as a number are ignored. Within a referenced array or range, empty cells, logical values, text, or error values are ignored. If the arguments contain no numbers, MIN produces 0.

Examples: MIN(C2:D4) produces -2 if the numbers in these cells are -2, 4, 32, and 30.

MAX(C2:D4,-3) produces -3 if the numbers in the cells are the same as in the preceding example.

STDEV(number1,*number2, . . .*)

Calculates the standard deviation of the numbers in the arguments using the *n-1* or nonbiased method.

Limits: STDEV can take up to 14 arguments. If the arguments include the entire population, then use STDEVP.

Example: STDEV(B2:B12) produces 12.12 when the range from B2 to B12 contains 98, 67, 89, 76, 76, 54, 87, 78, 85, 83, and 90.

STDEVP(number1,*number2, . . .*)

Calculates the standard deviation of the numbers in the arguments using the *n* or biased method.

Limits: STDEV can take up to 14 arguments. If the arguments do not include the entire population, then use STDEV.

Example: STDEVP(B2:B12) produces 11.55 when the range from B2 to B12 contains 98, 67, 89, 76, 76, 54, 87, 78, 85, 83, and 90.

SUM(number1,*number2, . . .*)

Calculates the sum of the numbers in the arguments. Calculated arguments can include numbers, empty cells, logical values, or text numbers. Arguments that cannot be converted from text to numbers or error values are ignored. Only numbers within an argument's referenced cells are totaled.

Example: SUM(B36:B40) produces 25 if the range includes the numbers 3, 4, 5, 6, and 7.

| TIP |

"Fence" a Summed Range

To prevent accidents during data entry or worksheet changes, include a text "fence" on either end of a range that is summed. For example, when totaling a column of numbers from B5 to B15, include a text label at the top of the column and a double-dashed line (=) at the bottom of the column so that the SUM function appears as SUM(B4:B16). The text entries on either end do not affect the total because they have zero numeric value, but they prevent you from accidentally adding numbers that are above or below the summed range.

TREND(known_y's,*known_x's,new_x's*)

Calculates the straight line that best fits the test results in the arrays *known_y's* and *known_x's*. For the *new_x's* array, the TREND function produces an array of corresponding *y* values.

Examples: Examples of the trend analysis functions are included in Chapter 11, "Building Advanced Worksheets."

VAR(number1,*number2,* . . .)

Calculates the variance of the population from a sample of the population given in the *numbers* arguments.

Limits: Use VARP if the arguments contain the entire population.

Example: VAR(B2:B12) produces 146.82 when the range from B2 to B12 contains 98, 67, 89, 76, 76, 54, 87, 78, 85, 83, and 90.

VARP(number1,*number2,* . . .)

Calculates the variance of an entire population from the *numbers* arguments.

Limits: Use VAR if the arguments contain only a sample of the population.

Example: STDEVP(B2:B12) produces 133.47 when the range from B2 to B12 contains 98, 67, 89, 76, 76, 54, 87, 78, 85, 83, and 90.

Text Functions

CHAR(number)

Produces the character corresponding to the ASCII code *number* between 1 and 255.

Example: CHAR(65) is A.

CLEAN(text)

Removes from the specified *text* argument any characters that are lower than ASCII 32 or above ASCII 127. These characters are not printed. Note that upper- and lowercase text have different ASCII code numbers. This function is useful for removing control codes, bells, and non-ASCII characters from imported text.

CODE(text)

Produces the ASCII code of the first letter in the specified *text*.

Example: CODE("Excel") is 69.

DOLLAR(number,*decimals*)

Rounds the *number* to the specified number of *decimals* to the right of the decimal point and converts the number to a textual currency format.

Use the DOLLAR function to incorporate numbers in text. For example, consider the following statement:

="Your reimbursement is "&DOLLAR(A12,2)&"."

When A12 contains the number 2456.78, the result is

Your reimbursement is $2,456.78.

Limits: If you specify a negative number for the *decimal* argument, the function rounds the *number* to the left of the decimal point. If you omit the *decimals* argument, the function assumes two decimal places.

Examples: DOLLAR(32.45,2) results in $32.45.

DOLLAR(5432.45,-3) results in $5,000.

EXACT(text1,text2)

Compares *text1* and *text2*: if they are exactly the same, returns the logical TRUE; if they are not the same, returns FALSE.

Example: EXACT("Glass tumbler",A12) produces TRUE when A12 contains the text "Glass tumbler", but produces FALSE when A12 contains "glass tumbler".

FIND(find_text,within_text,*start_at_num*)

Beginning at *start_at_num*, FIND searches *within_text* to locate *find_text*. If *within_text* is found, the FIND function produces the character location where *find_text* starts. If *start_at_num* is out of limits or a match is not found, the #VALUE! error value is displayed.

Limits: If *start_at_num* is not specified, it is assumed to be 1.

Example: FIND(B12,"ABCDEFGHIJKLMNOPQRSTUVWXYZ") produces 3 if B12 contains "C".

FIXED(number,*decimals*)

Rounds the *number* to the specified *decimals* and displays it as text in fixed decimal format with commas.

Limits: If you do not enter *decimals*, the *number* is rounded to two places. If you specify a negative *decimal*, the function rounds the *number* to the left of the decimal point.

Examples: FIXED(9876.543) produces 9,876.54.

FIXED(9876.543,-3) produces 10,000.

LEFT(text,*number_of_characters*)

Produces the leftmost *number_of_characters* from *text*.

Limits: The value of *number_of_characters* must be positive and greater than zero. If the value is omitted, it is assumed to be one.

Example: LEFT(A17,3) produces "Que" if A17 contains "Que Corporation".

LEN(text)

Produces the number of characters in the *text* string. The LEN function is particularly useful when paired with the LEFT, MID, and RIGHT functions (see the example in the discussion of the MID function).

LOWER(text)

Changes *text* to all lowercase.

Example: LOWER("Look OUT!") produces "look out!".

MID(text,start_number,number_of_characters)

Produces characters from the specified *text*, beginning at the character in the *starting number* position and extending the specified *number_of_characters*.

Example: MID("Excel is the worksheet",10,3) produces "the".

PROPER(text)

Changes *text* to lowercase with initial capitals.

Example: PROPER("excel, the worksheet") produces "Excel, The Worksheet".

REPLACE(old_text,start_number,num_chars,new_text)

Replaces the characters in *old_text*—starting with the character at *start_number* and continuing the specified number of characters (*num_chars*)—with the specified *new_text*.

Limits: The first character in *old_text* is character 1.

Example: REPLACE(A12,8,11,"one") takes the old phrase

"We are many people on an island in space."

in cell A12 and changes it to the better thought

"We are one on an island in space."

REPT(text,number_times)

Repeats the *text* for *number_times*.

Limits: The value of *number_times* must be positive and nonzero.

Example: REPT("__..",3) produces __..__..__..

RIGHT(text,*number_of_chars*)

Produces the *number_of_chars* from the right end of *text*.

Limits: The value of *number_of_chars* defaults to 1 when omitted.

Example: RIGHT("San Francisco, CA",2) produces "CA".

SEARCH(find_text,within_text,*start_at_num*)

Begins at *start_at_num* in the specified *within_text*, searches through it for the *find_text*, and produces the character number where *find_text* begins inside *within_text*.

Limits: The first character position in *within_text* is 1. SEARCH ignores case differences. If *within_text* is not found or if *start_at_num* is out of limits, #VALUE! is returned.

Example: SEARCH("an","Marathoners run long distances",14) produces 26.

TIP

Use Wild Cards in Searches

You can use wild cards within *find_text* to specify any character(s) you aren't sure of. Use a question mark (?) to specify any single character in a specific position. Use an asterisk (*) to specify any group of characters in a specific position.

SUBSTITUTE(text,old_text,new_text,*instance_number*)

Substitutes *new_text* for *old_text* within the specified *text*. If *old_text* occurs more than once, *instance_number* specifies which occurrence to replace.

Limits: If *instance_number* is not specified, every occurrence of *old_text* is replaced.

Example: SUBSTITUTE("The stone age","stone","information") produces "The information age".

T(value)

Returns text when *value* is text; returns blank, " ", when *value* is not text.

Examples: T(B12) produces "Top" if B12 contains "Top".

T(57) produces " " (blank).

TEXT(value,format_text)

Converts the numeric *value* to text and displays it with the specified *format_text*. The result appears to be a formatted number, but actually is text.

Limits: Use one of the numeric or date formats listed in the Format Number list box to specify the format for the *value*. The format cannot contain an asterisk (*) or be General format.

Example: TEXT(4567.89,"$#,##0.00") produces "$4,567.89".

TRIM(text)

Deletes all spaces from *text* so that only one space remains between words.

Example: TRIM("this   is   the   breathy   look") produces "this is the breathy look".

UPPER(text)

Changes *text* to all uppercase.

Example: UPPER(B2) produces "ENOUGH!" when B2 contains "enough!".

VALUE(text)

Converts text numbers or dates in one of Excel's predefined formats into numbers usable in formulas. Because Excel normally converts numeric text into numbers when necessary, this function is primarily used to ensure compatibility with other spreadsheets.

Limits: The text number must be in one of the predefined numeric formats available in Excel.

Example: VALUE(B2) produces 52 when B2 contains the text "$52.00".

Trigonometric Functions

Trigonometric functions use angles measured in radians. Convert between radians and degrees with these equations:

Radians = Degrees*π/180
Degree = Radians*180/π

ACOS(number)

Produces the arccosine of the radian angle *number*. ACOS is the inverse of the COS function. When given a *number*, ACOS produces the original angle measured in radians.

Limits: The *number* must be in the range -1 to 1. The resulting angle will be in the range 0 (0 degrees) to π radians (180 degrees).

Example: ACOS(.2) produces 1.369438406 radians.

ASIN(number)

Produces the arcsine of the radian angle *number*. ASIN is the inverse of the SIN function. When given a *number*, the result of a sine function, ASIN produces the original angle measured in radians.

Limits: The *number* must be in the range -1 to 1. The resulting angle will be in the range -π/2 (-90 degrees) to π/2 (90 degrees).

Example: ASIN(.2) produces .201357921 radians.

ATAN(number)

Produces the arctangent of the radian angle *number*. ATAN is the inverse of the TAN function. When given a *number*, the result of a tangent function, ATAN produces the original angle measured in radians.

Limits: The resulting angle will be in the range -π/2 (-90 degrees) to π/2 (90 degrees).

Example: ATAN(.2) produces .19739556 radians.

ATAN2(x_number,y_number)

Produces the arctangent of the angle from the x-axis to the point with the coordinates *x_number* and *y_number*.

Limits: The resulting angle will be in the range -π (-180 degrees) to π (180 degrees). If *x_number* and *y_number* are both 0, the function displays the divide-by-zero error #DIV/0!.

Example: ATAN2(1,1) produces .785398163 radians.

COS(radians)

Produces the cosine of the radian angle *radians*.

Example: COS(.5) produces .877582562.

SIN(radians)

Produces the sine of the radian angle *radians*.

Example: SIN(.5) produces .479425539.

TAN(radians)

Produces the tangent of the radian angle *radians*.

Example: TAN(.5) produces .54630249.

From Here . . .

Use this chapter as a reference guide. Rather than trying to read through it, look at the headings, such as "Database Functions" and "Text Functions," and return to those sections when you need to manipulate a database or text.

Three functions that you will use often are SUM, DSUM, and ROUND. The use of SUM is demonstrated in Chapter 4, "Worksheet Quick Start." DSUM is demonstrated in Chapter 23, "Building Advanced Databases." And ROUND is described in Chapter 8, "Formatting Worksheets."

10

Using Multiple Windows and Linking Worksheets

Excel has solved a problem everyone has faced at some time: needing to be in more than one place at the same time. Excel does not limit you to one document on the screen. You can have multiple worksheets, charts, and macro sheets open at the same time. You even can see more than one view of the same worksheet or macro sheet. And one worksheet can be recalculating as you work on another.

Excel also solves the problem of linking data and consolidating information between worksheets. With Excel, breaking a large business model into separate worksheets and linking data among them is convenient, easy, and efficient. If you are running Excel under Windows, you even can link Excel to data from other Windows applications. The ability to work with multiple windows and worksheets and to link data between worksheets enables you to see data from many points of view and to work with small, easy-to-understand worksheets that are linked into a more complex system.

After reading and experimenting your way through this chapter, you will see worksheets in a new way. Literally!

You'll be able to look at as many as four different areas of one window by breaking the window into panes. And you can scroll panes independently. It's a handy feature when you need to scroll through a worksheet or database, yet freeze in place rows or columns containing titles.

After breaking windows into panes, you will learn how to open multiple windows onto the same worksheet. Being able to see your worksheet through different windows is helpful in a number ways. For example, you can enter data in one window while watching results in a different window that shows a distant area of the same worksheet, or you can display results in one window and the formulas that produce the results in another window.

The most powerful feature discussed in this chapter is linking and consolidating worksheets. Linked worksheets transfer data changes in one worksheet to another worksheet. When one worksheet changes, the linked cells in the other worksheet change. In many cases, all the linked worksheets don't even need to be open. Some linked worksheets can remain on disk or reside elsewhere in the network. In this chapter, the descriptions on linking use on-screen examples and a step-by-step list so you can follow along and duplicate the keystrokes.

Working with Multiple Documents

When you need to work with multiple worksheets, charts, or macro sheets, use **File Open** just as you open a first document. When you open some documents, such as worksheets with complex links to other worksheets, Excel may request that you also open the documents to which they are linked. If you do not open the linked documents, the worksheet or chart will use its previous values; this is discussed later in this chapter under "Linking and Consolidating Worksheets."

Activating the Window You Want

If you have multiple worksheets or windows on the screen, you can activate the one you want in either of the following ways:

Mouse: Move other windows out of the way by dragging their title bars. Click anywhere on the window you want to activate.

Keyboard: Press Ctrl+F6 until the window you want is active, or choose the window from the **Window** menu.

Organizing and Displaying Multiple Windows

You can manually arrange windows by moving and sizing them as described in Chapter 3, "Operating Windows." If you have many windows to reorganize and you have not resized them, you may want to take advantage of some automated assistance. Choose **Window Arrange All**, and the windows will be resized and rearranged so that you can see them all. Figure 10.1 shows three windows after using **Window Arrange All**. After issuing the command, the active window appears on the left.

Hiding and Unhiding Windows

You do not need to keep all your worksheets, charts, and macro sheets on the screen at one time. You can hide documents from view so that the screen

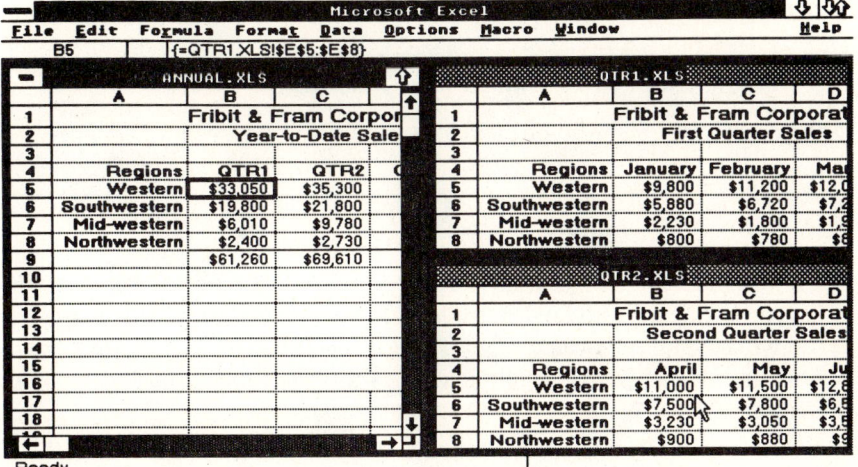

Fig. 10.1.
Arranged
multiple
windows each
with a different
worksheet.

appears more organized and less confusing. A hidden document remains available to other documents with which it is linked.

To hide a window, you activate it and then select **Window Hide** using either of the following methods:

> **Mouse:** Click on the window. Note the title of the window you want to hide, and choose the **Window Hide** command.

> **Keyboard:** Press Ctrl+F6 until the window you want is active, or select the window from the **Window** menu. Note the title of the window you want to hide, and choose the **Window Hide** command.

The window disappears from the screen, and the Unhide command appears as a choice on the **Window** menu.

To reveal hidden windows, follow these steps:

1. Choose **Window Unhide** to display the dialog box shown in figure 10.2.

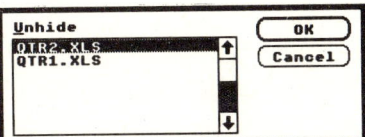

Fig. 10.2. The
Unhide dialog
box.

2. From the list box, select the title of the hidden window you want to reveal.

3. Choose OK or press Enter.

Hidden windows reappear in their former position and size.

TIP

Building Worksheets for Novices

When building a system of multiple linked worksheets to be used by inexperienced Excel users, you may want to hide worksheets that are not necessary to the work being performed. This practice cleans up the display and makes it look less overwhelming, while keeping the linked data available to other worksheets.

If all windows are hidden, the Window menu (along with all other menus aside from the File menu) disappears, and the Unhide command appears under the File menu.

Locking Windows in Position

After windows are sized and in the proper positions, you may want to make sure that they stay there. Locking windows in position is a good idea particularly if the worksheets are used by inexperienced operators or are presented automatically by macros.

To keep all windows that are dependent on the active worksheet from moving or changing size, follow these steps:

1. Position all the windows that belong to the worksheet you want to lock.

2. Activate one window belonging to the worksheet to be locked.

3. Choose Options Protect Document.

4. Select the Windows box.

5. Enter a password if you do not want others to remove protection.

6. Choose OK or press Enter.

You can scroll through windows that are locked, but you will not be able to resize or move them. You still, however, will be able to enter and edit cells unless they are protected with Format Cell Protection and the Contents box has also been selected in step 4.

To unlock a worksheet, activate one of the worksheet windows, and then choose **Options** Unprotect Document. If a password was used to lock the window's position, you will be asked to enter the password.

Viewing a Window through Multiple Panes

Breaking an Excel window into sections enables you to see two or four different views out of the same window. Each section of the window is referred to as a *pane*. The views are synchronized when you scroll. Multiple panes are particularly useful when you work with databases or large worksheets.

You can display both the criteria range and the extract range of a database at the same time. This technique enables you to enter a criteria and see whether the extract matches what you expected. Figure 10.3 shows the criteria and extract ranges of a sample database displayed in two separate panes.

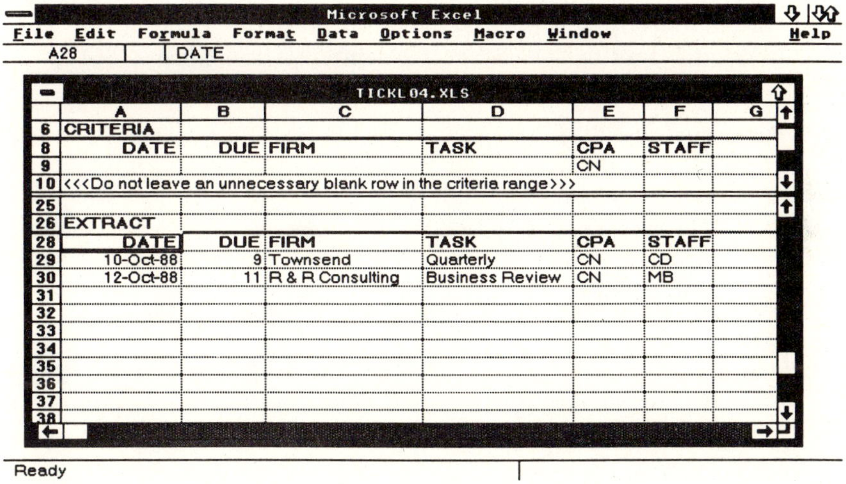

Fig. 10.3. A sample database with the criteria and extract ranges displayed in separate panes.

You can put the data-entry area of a large worksheet in one pane and the results in another. If you divide the worksheet into four panes and use **Options** Freeze Panes to freeze the panes containing the headings, you can scroll through the worksheet but still see the worksheet's row and column headings.

Breaking a Window into Multiple Panes

Figure 10.3 shows a database window divided into two panes. (Notice how the row numbers jump from 10 to 25.) The upper pane shows the criteria range, and the lower shows the extract range.

To break a worksheet window into panes from the keyboard, follow these steps:

1. Activate the window.

2. Press Alt and then the hyphen key to display the document Control menu.

3. Press T to select Split from the menu.

   Two gray bars appear that cross the window at its upper left corner. A four-headed arrow appears where the gray bars cross.

4. Use the left-, right-, up-, and down-arrow keys to move the gray bars so that the window divides as you want it.

   Figure 10.4 shows two gray bars positioned to divide the window into four sections. If the Enter key was pressed in figure 10.4, the window would be split down the right edge of column A and below row 10.

5. Press Enter to divide the windows as shown.

Fig. 10.4. A gray bar in position to divide a window into four panes.

	A	B	C	D	E	F	G
6	CRITERIA						
8	DATE	DUE	FIRM	TASK	CPA	STAFF	
9					CN		
10	<<<Do not leave an unnecessary blank row in the criteria range>>>						
25							
26	EXTRACT						
28	DATE	DUE	FIRM	TASK	CPA	STAFF	
29	10-Oct-88	9	Townsend	Quarterly	CN	CD	
30	12-Oct-88	11	R & R Consulting	Business Review	CN	MB	
31							
32							
33							
34							
35							
36							
37							
38							

Microsoft Excel — File Edit Formula Format Data Options Macro Window — Help

A28 | DATE

TICKL04.XLS

Split (Use direction keys to split)

Moving between Panes

From the keyboard, move the active cell clockwise between panes by pressing F6, or press Shift+F6 to move counter-clockwise between panes. The active cell moves to the same cell it occupied the last time it was in the pane. With the mouse, you can shift between panes by clicking in the pane you want to activate. Note that jumping between panes often causes windows to reposition.

While a window is divided into multiple panes, all the scroll bars and movement keys function normally.

Removing Panes

To remove the panes from windows, simply imagine that you want to shrink the top and left panes as much as possible. Then you will be left with a single window pane that fills the screen.

From the keyboard, you can return to a full window by first pressing Alt and then the hyphen key to display the document Control menu. From the menu, choose Split. When the gray lines and four-headed arrow appear, move the four-headed arrow to the upper left corner as far as it will go. Press Enter to complete the procedure.

If you are using a mouse, drag each split bar (solid black bar in the scroll bar) to its farthest point in the scroll bar.

Viewing One Document through Multiple Windows

If you have worked with a spreadsheet program before, you probably have wanted to see different parts of the current worksheet at the same time. You can do this in Excel by opening new windows onto a single worksheet. These windows can look at the same area or a different area.

Opening Multiple Windows

In figure 10.7, you can see that two windows opened on the same worksheet have the same name in the title bar, but the title of the first window opened ends with :1 and the second with :2. Each window can be located and sized separately.

Choose the **Window New Window** command to create a new window onto the current worksheet. You can move and size the new window in the same

Fig. 10.7.
Multiple
windows on the
same worksheet
have many uses.

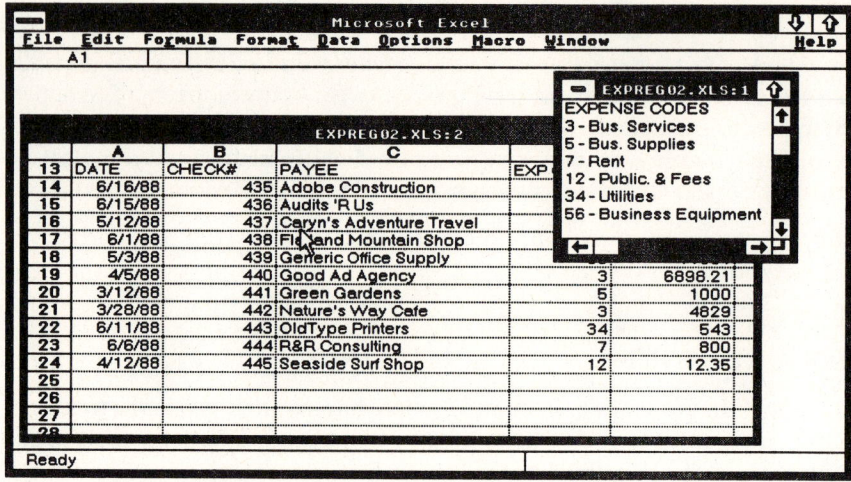

way as the original. Each window can have different formats, column widths, and display arrangements. In fact, each can appear totally different. However, if you change data or formulas in one window, the change affects all the windows belonging to that worksheet. The number of new windows you can open on a single worksheet is limited only by your computer's memory.

Opening additional windows multiplies your power with Excel. The tips that follow show you a few ways you can tap the power of multiple windows.

TIP

Data Entry and Help Windows

Multiple windows make data entry easier, as figure 10.7 illustrates. The left window displays the data-entry area. If you need a reminder about account codes, pressing Ctrl+F6 activates the window that explains those codes. You can scroll through the account code window to find what you need.

You also can use multiple windows to create help screens for your programs. Open a window onto the instruction area, and users can scroll to the instructions they need.

TIP

Debugging and Fixing Problems

Use **Window New Window** to create a second or third window onto the active worksheet when you want to debug it. Use **Options Display Formulas** to format the new window so that it displays formulas. The original window still will display results. This technique lets you see results and formulas at the same time, as shown in figure 10.8. You can see the cell references and the effect of changes more quickly and easily with these two windows.

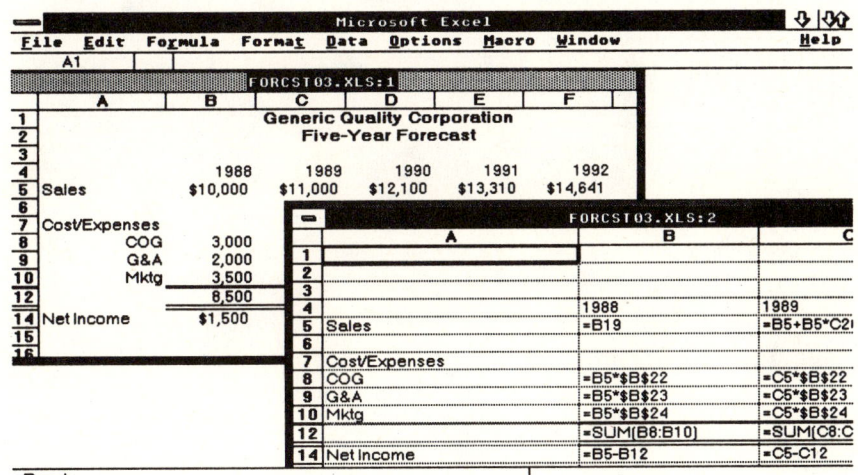

Fig. 10.8. The FORCST03 worksheet with results and formulas displayed in separate windows.

TIP

Database Queries and Reports

You often find yourself jumping between the criteria range, the database range, and the extract range in a database. This movement can slow down your work. Instead, set up a window onto each range. Arrange the windows in some fashion similar to figure 10.9. You can even have the windows maximized to full screen. Whenever you want to use that part of the worksheet shown in another window, press Ctrl+F6 until that window appears on top.

Saving and Closing Multiple Windows

When you save your worksheet to disk, all the windows with their current sizes and shapes are saved. You can set up multiple windows on a worksheet

Fig. 10.9.
Windows open
on the criteria,
database, and
extract ranges
of the same
worksheet.

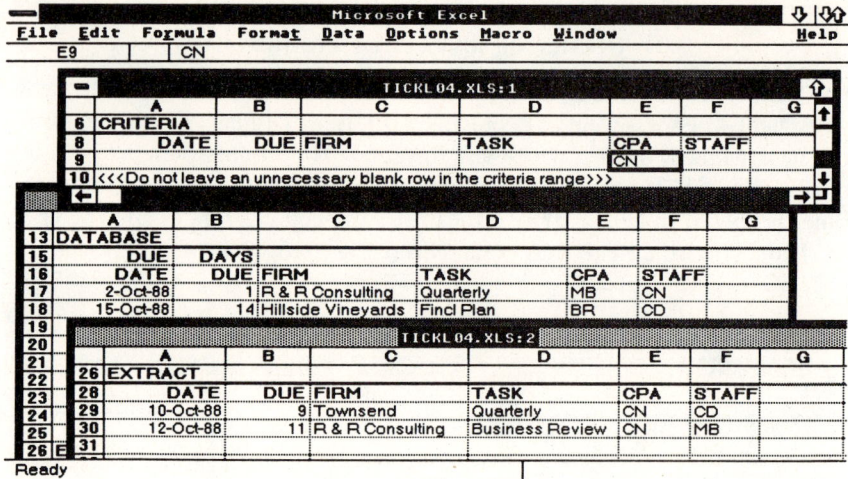

in the arrangement that you use most frequently, and then save the worksheet to disk. When you open the worksheet from disk, all the windows will be arranged and sized as you left them.

If you want to save a worksheet with only one window, make sure that you close the extra windows. To close unwanted windows, activate the window you want to close. Then select the document Control menu and choose Close.

Linking and Consolidating Worksheets

Linked documents share data and the results of formulas. They update automatically when the document they are linked with changes.

Consolidated worksheets accumulate the results of many worksheets into a single worksheet. Consolidations are usually done at a single point in time and won't change when the worksheets they depend upon change. You will find that linking and consolidating can be valuable tools no matter whether you build straightforward monthly budget worksheets or large complex accounting systems.

Small linked worksheets give you the opportunity to get away from some of the problems inherent in large cumbersome worksheets. You can build small worksheets to do specific tasks, and then link all these *modules* together to form a larger *system*.

Here are some of the advantages of building systems composed of smaller worksheet modules:

- Systems require less memory because all worksheets may not have to be open simultaneously. Some worksheets can be linked to other worksheets that remain on disk.

- Modules can be built separately by different people as long as the data transfer between modules is planned and coordinated. This arrangement can mean quicker project completion.

- Systems composed of worksheet modules are flexible and can be updated easily. One module can be redesigned, tested, and implemented without having to rebuild the entire system.

- Worksheet modules run faster than single, large worksheets. You will get your answers more quickly.

- You can create data-entry modules that operate on separate computers. At the end of the day, the completed data-entry modules can be linked or consolidated into the system. This setup has a number of advantages: more people can work on the system at once; people can work in separate locations; the work can be completed faster; and the chance that an inexperienced operator will damage the overall system is reduced.

- Systems are easier to maintain and debug when they are built in modules.

- Worksheet modules can be modified for use in different systems. For example, an expense register module could be linked to separate systems in different divisions.

- The chance of one module's macros "contaminating" or ruining results in another module are greatly reduced.

Consolidation lets you accumulate similar data across separate entities and share data among worksheets. For example, a consolidation of all the division sales forecast worksheets will result in a sales forecast for the entire company. Monthly financial reports can be consolidated into quarterly and annual reports. With Excel, you can add, subtract, multiply, and divide consolidated information between worksheets.

How Linking Works

Linking worksheets enables one worksheet to retrieve the cell or range contents of another. A reference term similar to a normal cell reference or range name links worksheets.

The worksheet that contains the original data is known as the *supporting worksheet*. The worksheet that depends on the linked data is the *dependent worksheet*.

The cell reference that links the supporting worksheet to the dependent worksheet is an *external reference*. When that reference is used in a formula, the formula is known as an *external reference formula*.

Excel uses two types of external reference formulas: simple and complex. A simple external reference formula refers to a cell, range, or name on another worksheet. All this formula does is transfer the information without performing any calculations. Supporting worksheets for simple external references can remain on disk while the dependent worksheet is open on the screen. Simple external references are the preferred method of linking worksheets.

Figure 10.10 shows two worksheets that are linked by a simple external reference formula. The external reference formula appears in the formula bar as =QTR1.XLX!$E$5. Data from E5 on the First Quarter Sales worksheet (QTR1) is linked to B5 on the Year-to-Date worksheet (ANNUAL). Should the contents of E5 in the QTR1 worksheet change, the value of B5 of the ANNUAL worksheet would also change. Here the QTR1 worksheet is supporting the dependent ANNUAL worksheet.

Fig. 10.10. Two worksheets linked by a simple external reference formula.

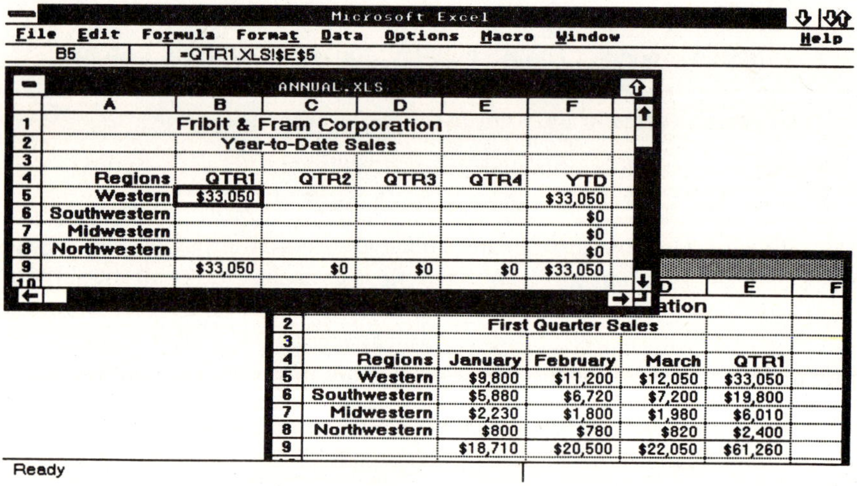

Simple external reference formulas take the following form:

=WorksheetName!CellRef

An exclamation mark (!) separates the supporting worksheet name from the cell reference. External references are initially created as absolute references, using dollar signs ($), but the references can be changed by editing.

Here is an example of a simple external reference formula:

   =QTR1.XLS!$E$5

In this formula, QTR1.XLS is the name of the supporting worksheet containing the data, and $E$5 is the cell being linked.

A complex external reference formula does two things: it links the data and manipulates it in the same formula. The manipulation could be as simple as adding a number to the external reference or as complex as involving multiple external references and complex calculations. Supporting worksheets to complex external reference formulas must be open at the same time as the dependent worksheet.

An example of a complex external reference formula is:

   =QTR1.XLS!$E$5*2

Performing math in the same cell as the link makes it a complex reference. Complex references need the supporting worksheet open.

TIP

Finding External References

To find cells that contain external references, use the Formula Find command and search all formula cells for an exclamation mark (!). This can be helpful when updating your worksheet or when tracing errors.

The appearance of an external reference varies within a cell in the supporting worksheet depending on whether the supporting worksheet is open. Table 10.1 shows some examples of simple external references along with descriptions of their supporting worksheet locations. Notice that references to unopened worksheets have the path and file name enclosed in single quotation marks.

Table 10.2 compares some examples of simple and complex external references.

Notice that a name such as Sales in the last example of table 10.2 can be used in both simple and complex external references. In a simple external reference however, the name can apply only to cells, ranges, or constants. If the name is a formula, then the external reference becomes complex.

Table 10.1
Simple External References
and Their Supporting Worksheet Locations

Simple external reference	Supporting worksheet location
=QTR1.XLS!$E$5	Open
='QTR1.XLS'!$E$5	On disk, same directory as dependent
='C:\BUDGET\QTR1.XLS'!$E$5	On disk, different directory

Table 10.2
Simple and Complex External References

Simple	Complex	Reason formula is complex
=QTR1.XLS!$B$5	=QTR1.XLS!B5	B5 is a relative reference.
=QTR1.XLS!$B$5	=QTR1.XLS!$B$5*2	Formula involves a calculation.
=QTR1.XLS!$B$5:$B$8	=SUM(QTR1.XLS!$B$5:$B$8)	Formula involves a function.
=QTR1.XLS!Sales	=QTR1.XLS!Sales	Sales is a named formula or constant.

In general, you should try to link worksheets using simple external references. With simple external references, a supporting worksheet such as QTR1 does not have to be open. You can leave the supporting worksheet on disk, and the formula in ANNUAL will retrieve the appropriate cell value from the disk file. This technique saves memory, reduces clutter on the screen, and reduces the chance of data-entry errors.

Moreover, a simple external reference lets you see the exact value transferred from the external worksheet. This type of reference gives you a chance to double-check correctness. If you use many simple external references, you may want to place them all in one spot on the dependent worksheet to make them easier to cross-check.

Complex external references let you use values from other worksheets directly in a formula, but they do have drawbacks. Worksheets that support complex external references must be open to be updated. If the supporting worksheets are not open, the external reference formula produces a #REF error.

Having the supporting worksheets open consumes memory. In addition, opening and loading all the supporting worksheets takes time. Moreover, you cannot see the value being transferred from the supporting worksheet because the value is used inside a formula.

TIP

Editing Similar External References

When you create an external reference formula containing many similar names, using **Edit Copy** and **Edit Paste** in the formula bar can be helpful. Copy one of the external references and paste it where it is needed. Then correct the differences in the names between formulas. For example, consider the following formula:

=QTR1.XLS!PROFIT+QTR2.XLS!PROFIT+QTR3.XLS!PROFIT+QTR4.XLS!PROFIT

You can copy QTR1.XLS!PROFIT and paste it in the other three locations. Then correct the numbers.

Linking Worksheets by Pointing

One of the easiest ways to link worksheets is to use the method you use to create formulas: pointing on a single worksheet. When pointing, you build formulas by moving the active cell to the cell you want added to a formula, and then you enter the next math operator. Chapter 4, "Worksheet Quick Start," steps you through this process and Chapter 7, "Entering and Editing Worksheet Data," explains it in more detail.

Follow these steps to create a simple external reference that links a single cell (E5) on a supporting quarterly worksheet (QTR1.XLS) to a single cell (B5) on a dependent annual worksheet (ANNUAL.XLS). This link results in the transfer of the Western region's first quarter total into cell B5 of the ANNUAL worksheet (see fig. 10.11).

1. Open the dependent worksheet, ANNUAL, and the supporting worksheet, QTR1.

2. Activate the dependent worksheet, ANNUAL, so that it is on top by clicking on it or by pressing Ctrl+F6.

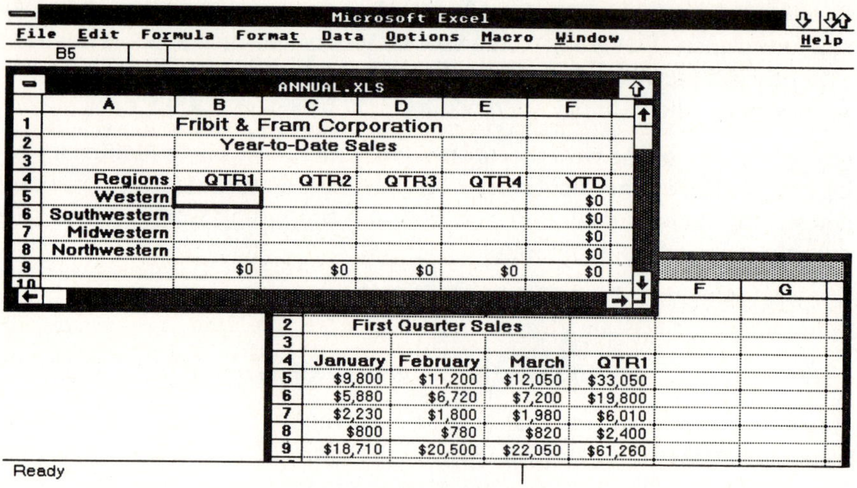

Fig. 10.11. Cell E5 on the supporting worksheet, QTR1, prior to linking with cell B5 the dependent worksheet, ANNUAL.

3. Select cell B5 on the ANNUAL worksheet.

4. Type an equal sign (=) to start a formula in B5.

5. Activate the supporting worksheet, QTR1, by clicking on it or by pressing Ctrl+F6.

6. Select cell E5 on the QTR1 worksheet so that it appears in the formula bar.

   Mouse: Click on cell E5 in QTR1.

   Keyboard: Press the arrow key once to make the dashed marquee appear around a cell. Use the arrow keys to move to cell E5 in QTR1. As you move, the dashed marquee will surround the selected cell on QTR1.

7. Press Enter or click on the check mark to enter the simple external reference formula

   =QTR1.XLS!$E$5

The ANNUAL worksheet will reappear on top with a formula in cell B5 that links the two worksheets. Figure 10.12 shows the resulting worksheets and the simple external reference displayed in the formula bar.

You can use the pointing method to enter complex external references such as the following:

   =QTR1.XLS!$E$5+QTR2.XLS!$E$5+QTR3.XLS!$E$5+QTR4.XLS!$E$5

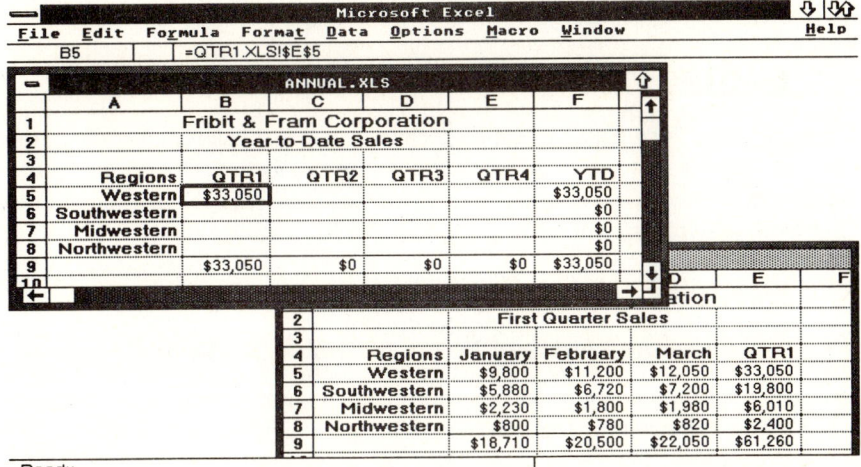

*Fig. 10.12.
Worksheets
linked through
a simple
external
reference.*

Enter the formula as you would enter a single external reference. Then enter an operator, such as the plus sign (+). Activate the next supporting worksheet, and link it to the dependent worksheet.

You can also use pointing to enter ranges in external reference formulas. For example, consider this formula:

=SUM(SUPPORT.XLS!$F$6:$F$8)

After typing =SUM(, you can switch to the supporting worksheet, move to F6, then select the range F6:F8. When you type the closing) and press Enter, you will be returned to the dependent worksheet with the formula.

```
                                                          TIP
```

Linking Databases

Learn how to share information between two or more databases and how to create reports using information gleaned from two or more databases. See Chapter 23, "Building Advanced Databases" for details.

Linking Worksheets by Typing Formulas

Typing external reference formulas is easiest when you already know the exact external references you want. For example, suppose that you have an existing worksheet named QTR1.XLS open on the screen, and that the worksheet has a cell named PROFIT. Then in the ANNUAL.XLS worksheet, you can type this formula:

=QTR1.XLS!PROFIT

When you type formulas containing a simple external reference such as this one, the answer appears as soon as you enter the formula if the supporting worksheet is open. (If you use a range name such as PROFIT, that name must exist on the external worksheet.)

TIP

Reducing Work and Errors in Linked Worksheets

External reference formulas do not automatically adjust when cell contents are moved in the supporting worksheet. In the example used so far, the formula =QTR1.XLS!$E$5 in the ANNUAL worksheet will be incorrect if cell E5 in QTR1 is moved.

To make sure moved cells or inserted or deleted rows and columns do not ruin your links, use named cell or range references. For example, the formula

=QTR1.XLS!PROFIT

in the ANNUAL worksheet will remain correct, no matter where the cell named PROFIT is moved in the QTR1 worksheet.

Suppose that you enter a complex external reference formula such as the following:

=QTR1.XLS!PROFIT+QTR2.XLS!PROFIT

You may be surprised to see a #REF error value appear when you enter the formula. The #REF error appears if a supporting worksheet is not open. Open the worksheet to replace the #REF with the formula's result.

When you type external references, you must tell Excel where the worksheet is located. Type the name of an open supporting worksheet as the name appears in the title bar—for example:

=QTR1.XLS!$E$5

When you type the name of an unopened supporting worksheet that is in the same directory as the dependent worksheet, enclose the unopened worksheet name in single quotation marks, as follows:

='QTR1.XLS'!$E$5

If a supporting worksheet is in a different directory from the dependent worksheet, you must type the path name and worksheet name within single quotation marks, as follows:

='C:\SALES\QTR1.XLS'!$E$5

Path names include the disk, directories, and file name.

Linking Ranges with Paste Link

To link a range of cells in a supporting worksheet to a corresponding range in the dependent worksheet, you use the Edit Paste Link command. First, use the **Edit Copy** command to copy the range from the supporting worksheet. Then use **Edit Paste Link** to paste the copy into the dependent worksheet.

Use the following steps to link the entire range of E5:E8 on the QTR1 worksheet to the QTR1 column on the ANNUAL worksheet:

1. Open the worksheets you want to link: QTR1 and ANNUAL.

2. Activate the supporting worksheet, QTR1.

3. Select the range of cells you want linked, E5:E8, as shown in figure 10.13.

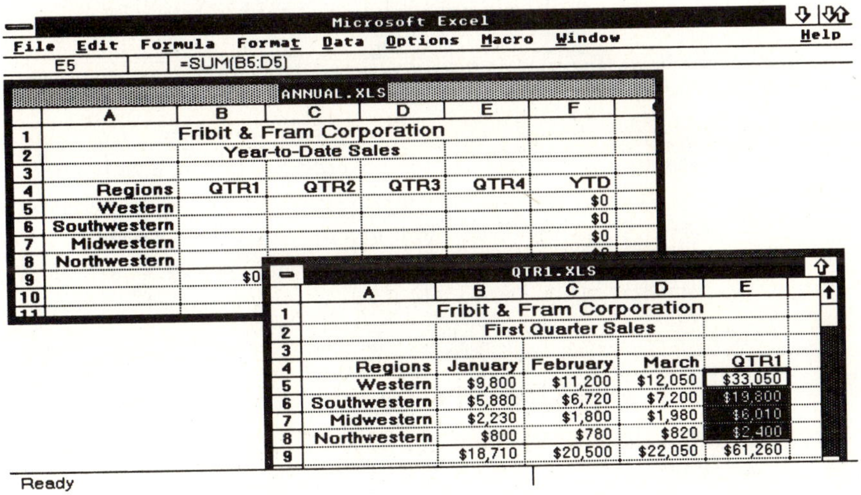

Fig. 10.13. The active supporting worksheet QTR1 with a range of cells selected in preparation of a Paste Link.

4. Choose the **Edit Copy** command.

   This step copies the name of the supporting worksheet and the copied range into the clipboard, a temporary area of memory.

5. Activate the dependent worksheet, ANNUAL.

6. Select cell B5. Do not select an entire range to paste into; doing so is not only unnecessary, but it increases the chance of mistakes. All you need to select is the single cell at the upper left corner of where you want to paste.

7. Choose Edit Paste Link.

The result appears as shown in figure 10.14.

Fig. 10.14. The dependent worksheet ANNUAL with a complex external reference pasted in the formula bar.

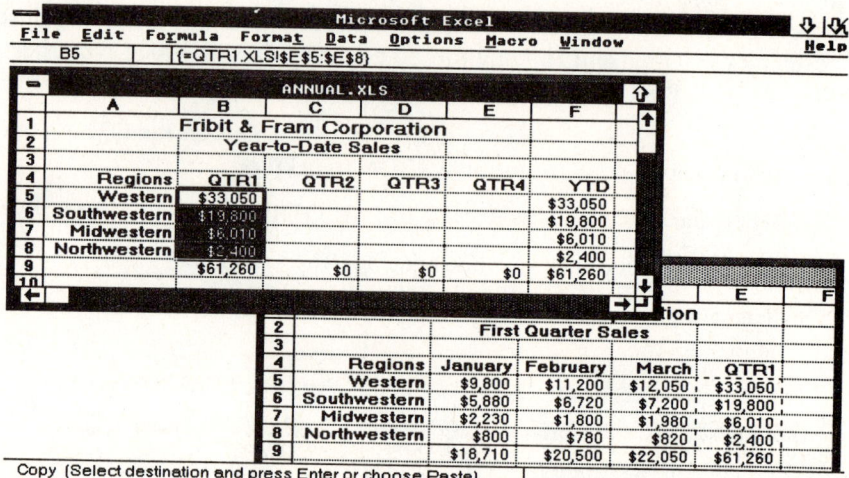

Notice in the formula bar that cells in the linked range are enclosed in braces ({ }). The braces indicate that the linked range is one large array, a complex external reference. Single formulas within the array cannot be changed. (The procedure for creating a range of external formulas that can be treated individually is discussed in the next section.)

NOTE

Treat a Pasted Range as an Array

Formulas pasted with Edit Paste Link are arrays. You cannot change individual formulas in an array.

Linking Many Individual External References

The disadvantage to using **Edit Paste Link** to paste a range of linked cells is that the individual cells cannot be edited. Individual cells cannot be changed because they are all part of an array. Using a trick, however, you can get around this limitation.

In the dependent worksheet, point to or type a single external reference formula. The formula from the ANNUAL worksheet used in the pointing example was

=QTR1!.XLS$B$5

Press the Edit key (F2) and remove the dollar signs so that the external reference changes to a relative external reference. (External references normally are absolute.) The formula now will look like the following:

=QTR1!.XLSB5

Select the cell containing the relative external reference and extend the selection to cover the same number and shape of cells as those being linked from the supporting worksheet. Figure 10.15 shows the formula displayed in the formula bar and the selection highlighted.

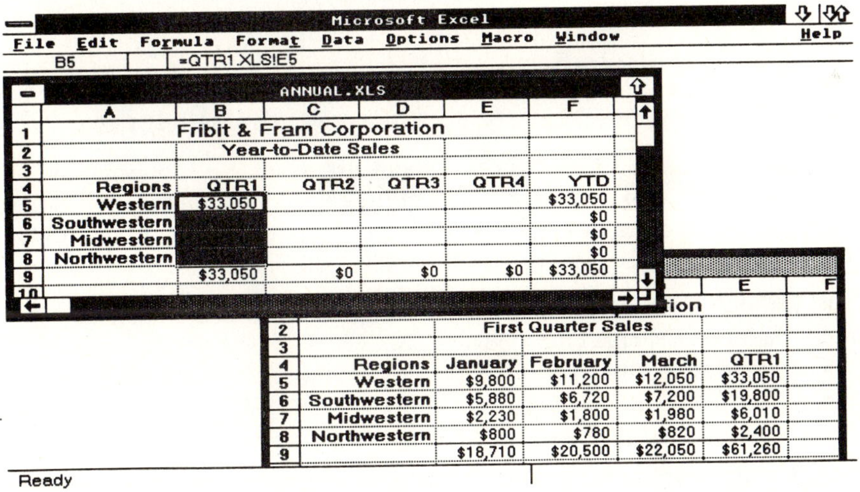

Fig. 10.15. A relative external reference before duplication to other cells.

Choose **Edit Fill Down** to fill the cells down the column. The following formula fills down the range in ANNUAL:

=QTR1!.XLSB5

Each formula adjusts to its new location so that the other formulas become

=QTR1!.XLSB6
=QTR1!.XLSB7
=QTR1!.XLSB8

Each of these external reference formulas is complex because of the relative reference. This means the supporting worksheet, QTR1.XLS, must be open.

NOTE

Be Cautious of Relative External References

Copying a relative external reference to a new location on the same dependent worksheet causes the worksheet to link to different cells. When you copy the relative external reference formula, Excel adjusts cell addresses to their new locations. This adjustment in turn adjusts the link to the supporting worksheet.

Calculating Linked Worksheets

Formulas with simple external reference formulas, such as the following, are updated when you open their worksheet even though the referenced cell is in a worksheet on disk:

=FORECAST.XLS!$R$54

='C:\WINDOWS\EXCEL\BUDGET\FORECAST.XLS'!$B$36:$D$52

If you load a dependent worksheet without first loading a supporting worksheet, an alert box asks whether you want the dependent worksheet updated. Choosing Yes updates the worksheet from the supporting file. Choosing No retains the last values used in the simple external references.

Cells with formulas containing complex external reference formulas (any formulas that aren't simple) are updated only when the supporting worksheet is open. If the supporting worksheet is not open, the complex external formula displays a #REF! error value.

Changing the Layout of Linked Worksheets

Beware! Excel does not automatically adjust external cell and range references when the supporting worksheet changes. If you move areas or insert and delete rows or columns in supporting the worksheet, the referenced cells may be positioned in a different location than the dependent worksheet expects.

You can prevent this problem by using names to reference cells and ranges in external references. Names remain accurate even when the layout of the supporting worksheet changes.

Changing a Link

Renaming a supporting worksheet file or moving it to a different directory leaves the dependent worksheet wondering where the supporting worksheet went. Instead of displaying the value for the line the #REF! error value appears. When you rename or move supporting worksheets, you must update the links with the following procedure:

1. Activate the dependent worksheet.

2. Choose **File Links**.

3. Select from the list box the supporting worksheet whose links you want to update.

4. Choose the **Change** button.

   A new dialog box that looks similar to the File Open dialog box appears. In it, you can see list boxes for file names and paths.

5. Type the path name and file name for the new supporting worksheet in the text box.

6. Choose OK or press Enter.

Saving Linked Worksheets

When you save linked worksheets, use **File Save As** to save the supporting worksheets first. For example, you would save the supporting worksheets QTR1.XLS and QRT2.XLS before you saved the dependent worksheet ANNUAL.XLS. This practice ensures that the dependent worksheet knows the correct names and path names of its supporting worksheets. If you try to save a dependent worksheet that refers to an unsaved supporting worksheet, a dialog box with a warning will appear.

When you choose **File Open** to open a linked worksheet, you may see an alert box with the following message displayed:

    Update references to non-resident sheets?

The formula bar displays the external reference formula that caused the box to appear (see fig. 10.16).

Fig. 10.16. An alert box that displays the Update references message.

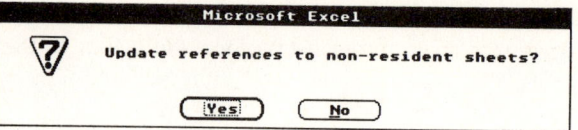

Choosing the **Yes** button reads the data from the supporting worksheet on disk and updates the dependent worksheet. If you choose **No**, the dependent worksheet uses the last value calculated by the formula.

In some cases, you will open a dependent worksheet and leave its supporting worksheets unopened. Later you may want to open the supporting sheets, but you don't know all of their names. You can get around this problem with the **File Links** command. File Links knows which worksheets need to be opened in order to update the active dependent worksheet.

Activate the dependent worksheet, and then select **File Links**. The list box displays all the worksheets that support the active worksheet. Select the worksheet file you want to open, and choose **Open**.

TIP

Selecting All the Linked Worksheets

With the mouse, you can select multiple linked worksheets from the **File Links** list box by holding down Ctrl as you click on each selection. From the keyboard, hold down Ctrl and press the up- or down-arrow key to move through the list box. Press the space bar whenever a name you want to select is enclosed in dashes.

If you are on a network, and you want only to read (not change) information from a supporting worksheet, select the Read Only box from the Links dialog box. This option allows others on the network to read the same worksheet.

Deleting Links

One way of removing a link between worksheets is by using the **Edit Clear** command to eliminate the cells that contain the link. That method, however, is harsh and can create errors in formulas that use the values from the link.

To preserve the values linked by the external formula but remove the external reference, you can freeze the external reference so that it becomes a value. Freeze either the entire formula or just the external cell or name reference.

To freeze an external cell or name reference, select the cell so that the formula appears in the formula bar. Select the external reference within the formula by dragging or using the Shift+arrow key. Choose **Options Calculate Now** to change the selected reference into an unchanging value. Then enter the formula.

You can freeze formulas by selecting the cell or range containing the formulas. Choose **Edit Copy**, and then choose **Edit Paste Special**. Next, select the **Values** box and paste directly on top of the original. This procedure replaces formulas with their values.

Consolidating Worksheet Values with Paste Special

When you need to transfer only values between worksheets and you do not want those values automatically updated, use **Edit Paste Special**. With Paste Special, you combine the values from one worksheet into another. Paste Special enables you to combine data by pasting values, or by adding, subtracting, multiplying, or dividing values with existing cell contents. Because a link is not established, values are not updated when the supporting worksheet changes.

To consolidate data between worksheets, use **Edit Copy** to copy cell contents from one worksheet. Activate the other worksheet, and past with the **Edit Paste Special** command.

> **1-2-3 TIP**
>
> ### How To /File Combine Add and Subtract
>
> Use Excel's **Edit Paste Special** command to perform the same functions as 1-2-3's **/File Combine Add and Subtract**. You can multiply and divide worksheet values when combining data. Use the linking techniques described throughout this Chapter if you want the values updated automatically when the supporting worksheet changes.

From Here . . .

Excel's capability to display multiple views of multiple worksheets and its capability to link data across multiple worksheets gives you a great deal of flexibility in designing your systems. In Excel, you also can link multiple worksheets to a single graph or paste data into a predesigned graphic format.

Linking worksheets to graphs is described in Chapter 16, "Building Advanced Charts."

If you have the added advantage of running Excel under Windows 2.0 or Windows/386, you can dynamically link Excel worksheets and other Windows applications. For example, you can have worksheet data automatically updated by a telecommunications program or have Excel automatically analyze changes to a databases inventory. Linking Excel with other Windows applications is described in Chapter 28, "Using Excel with Windows Applications."

11

Building Advanced Worksheets

Excel contains many commands and features that reduce your workload. This chapter describes a potpourri of commands and techniques that can help you become more accomplished in less time. Once you understand the fundamentals of Excel, the techniques in this chapter will help you reduce your workload and create more advanced forecasting and analysis worksheets.

In this chapter, you will learn how to enter a series of numbers or dates, how to use formulas to manipulate text, and how to write formulas that make decisions based on conditions you specify. You will also learn how to test input values to make sure they are in the correct range, how to use lookup tables to find tax or commission rates, and how to use arrays to enter formulas and save memory. The chapter ends with examples on using forecasting functions such as TREND.

Entering a Series of Numbers or Dates

As you build spreadsheets or databases, you can enter a series of evenly spaced numbers or dates quickly with the **Data Series** command. Rather than typing the name of each of the 12 months into a row of headers, you can instruct Excel to enter a series of dates. If you work with a database, you might want to number records (rows) or automatically enter a series of dates. If you want to test a sequence of different variable values, you can combine the work of the **Data Series** and **Data Table** commands to save you hours.

Figure 11.1 shows examples of numeric and date series entered with the **Data Series** command. (Note that the text entries for the days and months were created with a custom date format described later in this section.)

*Fig. 11.1.
Numeric and
date series
entered with the
Data Series
command.*

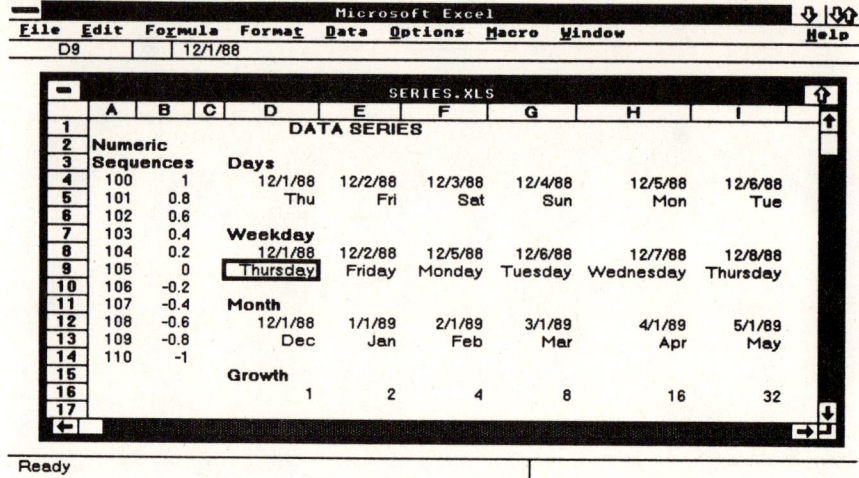

*Fig. 11.1.
Numeric and
date series
entered with the
Data Series
command.*

To create either a series of numbers or dates, begin with the following steps:

1. Enter the first number or date in the first cell of the series.

2. Select the range of cells you want filled with the series. Start with
the leftmost cell of a row or the top cell of a column.

   Figure 11.2 shows a series about to be created in column A. The
   first number in the series will be 100.

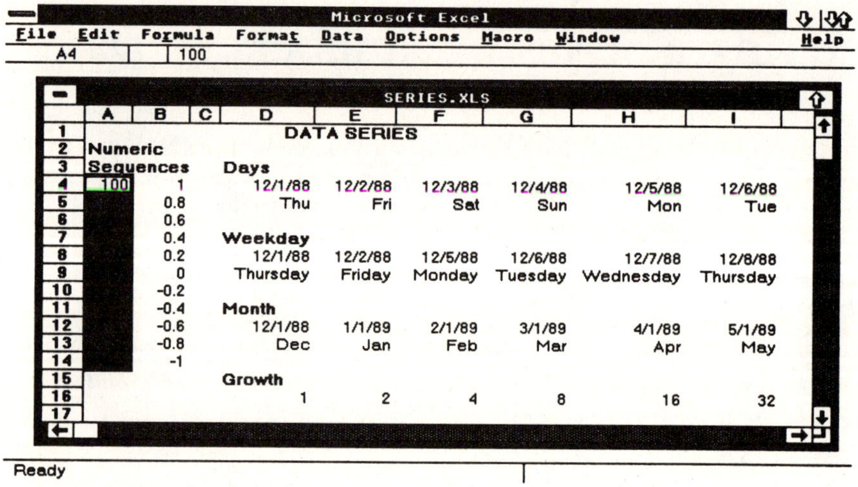

*Fig. 11.2. The
first number in
a series entered
and a selected
range of cells to
be filled.*

3. Choose **Data Series** to display the Series dialog box shown in figure 11.3.

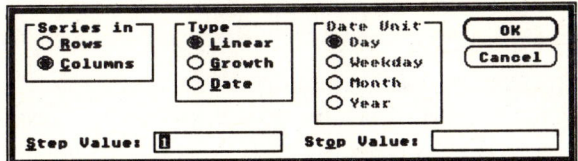

Fig. 11.3. The Data Series dialog box.

4. Verify that the **Columns** or **Rows** option matches the type of range you want filled.

5. Select one of the following Type options:

Linear	Add the **Step Value** to the preceding number in the series.
Growth	Multiply the **Step Value** by the preceding number in the series.
Date	Change to a date sequence.

If you are entering a series of numbers and you chose either Linear or Growth in step 5, continue with the following steps:

1. Enter the **Step Value**. This is the amount by which the series will change from cell to cell. The **Step Value** can be positive or negative.

   Figure 11.1 shows how a -.2 **Step Value** decreases the numbers in column B.

2. Enter the **Stop Value** only if you think you may have highlighted too many cells when you selected the range you want to fill.

   Excel stops the series when it reaches either the end of the selected range or the Stop Value. You cannot use a formatted number or cell reference for the Stop Value. If you use a negative **Step Value**, consider that the Stop Value must be "less" than the starting value.

3. Choose OK or press Enter.

The series fills the selected cells, starting with the value in the first cell of the selection and increasing or decreasing by the Step Value. (If you selected the Growth option, the **Step Value** acts as a multiplier.) The series remains selected after it is generated, letting you change the font, alignment, or numeric format.

If you are entering a series of dates and you chose Date in step 5 of the opening steps for creating a series, continue with the following steps:

1. From the Date Unit area of the Data Series dialog box, select either Day, Weekday, Month, or Year to designate the rate at which you want the starting date to grow.

   (Note that Weekday gives you dates without Saturdays and Sundays.)

2. Enter the Step Value to indicate the amount the starting value grows with each increment.

   For example, if the starting value is 12/1/88 and you choose Month as the Date Unit and 2 as the Step Value, the second date in the series will be 1/1/89, and the next will be 3/1/89.

3. Enter the Stop Value only if you think you may have highlighted too many cells.

   The Stop Value indicates the latest possible date in the series. You can use one of Excel's predesigned date formats, such as the one shown in figure 11.4, as the Stop Value.

4. Choose OK or press Enter.

Fig. 11.4. The Data Series dialog box with a date Stop Value entered.

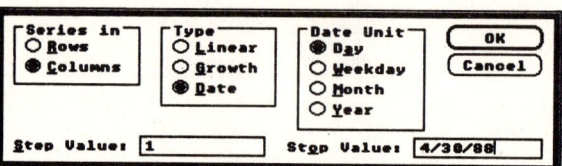

If you want to display only the name of the month or the day of the week as shown in figure 11.1, use custom date formatting to format the date series. Some examples of date sequence formatting appear in table 11.1.

Table 11.1
Date Formats in a Series

Custom date format	Display
mmm	Jan
mmmm	January
ddd	Thu
dddd	Thursday

Use the Format Number command to create custom date and numeric formats as described in Chapter 8, "Formatting Worksheets." The custom date formats shown in table 11.1 should be entered in the Format text box of the Format Number dialog box.

Using Formulas To Manipulate Text

Excel lets you manipulate text as well as numbers and dates. Text manipulation comes in handy for combining text and numbers in printed invoices, or for using data from a database to create a mailing list.

To combine text in order to form a new text string, use the joining operator, & (ampersand), as though you were adding pieces of text together. For example, consider the following formula:

="This "&"and That"

This formula displays the text as follows:

This and That

You also can join text by referring to its cell address. If A12 contains the text "John" and B12 contains the text "McDougall", you can use this formula to combine the first and last names:

=A12&" "&B12

The result of the formula is

John McDougall

Notice that a space between two quotation marks is used to separate the text contained in A12 and B12.

Excel, unlike other spreadsheet packages, also lets you use a number as text. You can refer to a number as you would a cell filled with text. If A12 contains 99 and B12 contains "Stone St.", use this formula to create the full street address:

=A12&" "&B12

The result of the formula is

99 Stone St.

If you want to display a certain text message when specified conditions are present, you can use a formula or function to display the message. This feature enables you to display warnings such as "Quantity Low!" or "Incorrect Entry!". The technique for using text in an IF function is described in the "Using Formulas To Make Decisions" section of this chapter. To learn other ways you can manipulate text with Excel's numerous functions, also see Chapter 9, "Using Functions in Worksheets."

TIP

Using Formatted Numbers and Dates in Text Formulas

When you refer to a number or date in a text formula, the number or date appears in the General format, not as it appears in its formatted display. For example, suppose that cell B23 contains the date 12/24/88 and you enter the following formula:

="Merry Christmas! Today is "&B23

The result of the formula is

Merry Christmas! Today is 32501

You can change the format with the FIXED, DOLLAR, and TEXT functions. These functions change numbers and dates to text in the format you want. For dates, for example, you can use the TEXT function to change the following formula:

="Merry Christmas! Today is "&TEXT(B23,"d-mmm-yy")

Here is the result of the formula with the date formatted as specified by TEXT:

Merry Christmas! Today is 24-Dec-88

You can use any legal predefined or custom numeric or date format between the quotation marks of the TEXT function.

Using Formulas To Make Decisions

Excel's IF function can make decisions based on whether the question you ask is true or false. Use IF to test whether it is time to reorder a part, whether data has been entered correctly, or which of two results or formulas should be used.

The IF function uses the following format:

IF(logical_test,value_if_true,*value_if_false*)

If the *logical_test* (question) is true, then *value_if_true* is calculated; but if the *logical_test* is false, the *value_if_false* is calculated. The true or false results can display text, calculate a formula, or display a cell reference.

Consider the following formula:

=IF(B34>50,B34*2,"Entry too low!")

In this example, the IF function produces the answer 110 if B34 is 55. If B34 is 12, however, the function displays the text

Entry too low!

Making Simple Decisions

IF functions are frequently used to make simple decisions such as comparisons. Figure 11.5 shows an Accounts Aging Analysis worksheet in which Excel checks how long an amount has been owed. Using IF functions and the age of the account, Excel displays the amount in the correct column.

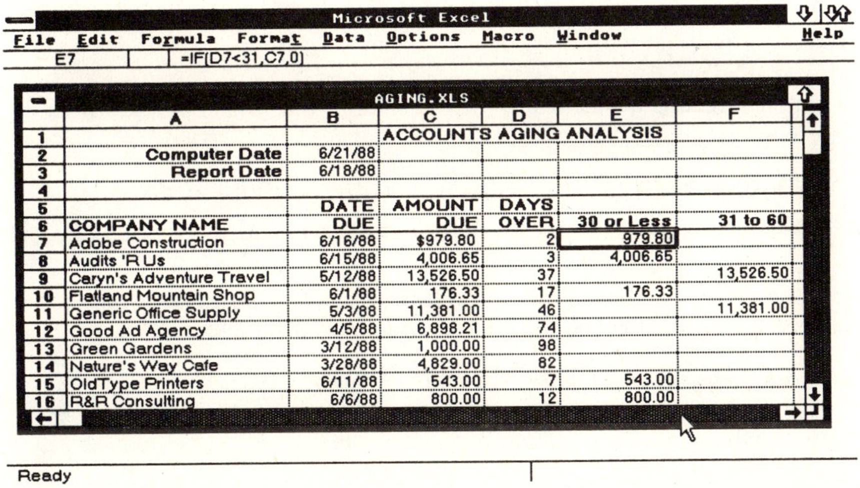

	A	B	C	D	E	F
1			ACCOUNTS AGING ANALYSIS			
2	Computer Date	6/21/88				
3	Report Date	6/18/88				
4						
5		DATE	AMOUNT	DAYS		
6	COMPANY NAME	DUE	DUE	OVER	30 or Less	31 to 60
7	Adobe Construction	6/16/88	$979.80	2	979.80	
8	Audits 'R Us	6/15/88	4,006.65	3	4,006.65	
9	Caryn's Adventure Travel	5/12/88	13,526.50	37		13,526.50
10	Flatland Mountain Shop	6/1/88	176.33	17	176.33	
11	Generic Office Supply	5/3/88	11,381.00	46		11,381.00
12	Good Ad Agency	4/5/88	6,898.21	74		
13	Green Gardens	3/12/88	1,000.00	98		
14	Nature's Way Cafe	3/28/88	4,829.00	82		
15	OldType Printers	6/11/88	543.00	7	543.00	
16	R&R Consulting	6/6/88	800.00	12	800.00	

Fig. 11.5. IF functions used to decide where values should be displayed.

The first few times you use IF statements, you should write an English sentence stating the *logical_test* or question you want to ask. The question also should state the results if true and if false. For each cell from E7 through E16 in the example, the English language equivalent of the needed IF statement for each row is

> IF DAYS OVER is less than 31, show the AMOUNT DUE, but if DAYS OVER is not more than 31, show nothing.

The IF function equivalent of that statement for cell E7 appears in the formula bar as

> =IF(D7<31,C7,0)

In this example, D7 contains the DAYS OVER for row 7, and C7 contains the AMOUNT DUE for the row. Choose Options Display and unselect **Zero** Values to prevent the display of zeros in column E.

TIP

Displaying a Blank Cell

If you want to have zeros in the rest of your worksheet, but not as a result of IF statements, leave Zero Values selected from the Options Display command so that zeros display throughout the worksheet. Modify your IF function so that it looks like this:

> =IF(D7<31,C7,"")

Because nothing is entered between the quotation marks, this function displays a blank cell for the false condition.

Making Complex Decisions

In column F of the worksheet shown in figure 11.5, the IF question needs to be more complex:

> IF DAYS OVER is greater than 30 and DAYS OVER is less than 61, show the AMOUNT DUE; but show nothing if DAYS OVER is outside that range.

The IF functions in F7 through F17 use the following formula to produce a formula that checks for DAYS OVER in the range from 31 to 60:

> =IF(AND(D7>30,D7<61),C7,0)

The AND function produces a TRUE response only when all the elements within the parentheses meet their conditions (D7>30 is true *AND* D7<61 is true). When the AND function produces TRUE the IF formula produces the value found in C7.

Checking Data Entry

IF functions are also useful for verifying that data is within allowable limits. You can put an IF function in a cell adjacent to the entry cell in order to warn the operator when data is out of limits. Consider, for example, the following formula:

=IF(AND(B6>250,B6<500),"","Enter values between 250 and 500")

This formula results in the following warning when the value entered in B6 is not between 250 and 500:

Enter values between 250 and 500

Looking Up Data in Tables

You can build a table in Excel and look up the contents of various cells within the table. Lookup tables provide a handy way of dealing with numbers or text that you cannot produce with a formula. For example, you may not be able to calculate a tax table or commission table. In those cases, looking up values from a table is much easier.

Figure 11.6 shows an example of a VLOOKUP table designed for looking up sales commissions. In this example, the formula that finds the sales commission is in cell D5. The VLOOKUP function, as shown in the formula bar of the example, is the following:

=VLOOKUP(D3,C11:F15,D4+1)

This formula looks down the left column of the table displayed in the range C11:F15 until finding a Sales $ amount larger than D3 ($12,452). VLOOKUP then backs up to the previous row and looks across the table to the column specified by D4+1. The formula D4+1 results in 2, the second column of the table. (Sales $ is column 1. The value 1 is added to D4 so the lookup starts in the Product Class portion of the table.) The VLOOKUP function returns the value .045 from the table. The Commission is calculated by multiplying .045 by the Amount of Sale, $12,452.

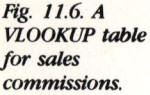

Fig. 11.6. A VLOOKUP table for sales commissions.

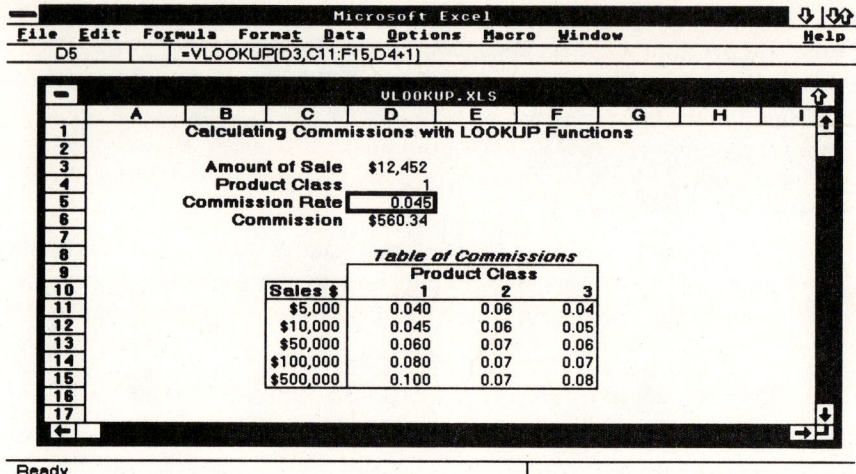

The numeric headings in D10, E10, and F10 are not used by the lookup function but are there for the user.

Columns are numbered from left to right. Sales $ is column 1, the first column of the table. But commissions start in column 2 of the table. So the value 1 is added to D4.

Excel uses three different functions for lookup tables. The one shown in figure 11.6 is a VLOOKUP table because the function looks down the vertical column on the left side of the table. The HLOOKUP function looks across the horizontal row at the top of the table until it finds the appropriate comparison value. The third form, LOOKUP, is described in Chapter 9, "Using Functions in Worksheets."

The VLOOKUP and HLOOKUP functions use the following forms respectively:

VLOOKUP(lookup_value,table_array,col_index)

HLOOKUP(lookup_value,table_array,row_index_num)

The *lookup_value* is the value being matched in the left column of the table for the VLOOKUP function or the top row for the HLOOKUP function. The *table_array* describes the range containing the table and the lookup values. The *col_index* for the VLOOKUP function or the *row_index_num* for HLOOKUP tells the function which column or row, respectively, contains the result. The first column or row in the table is always numbered 1.

The values used for comparison, the cells in C11:C15 in figure 11.6, must be in ascending order for the lookup function to work correctly. The function searches down column one in a VLOOKUP table or across row one in an HLOOKUP table until it meets a value that is larger than the *lookup_value*; therefore, if the *lookup_values* are not in ascending order, the function can be misled. Table 11.2 shows the order in which comparison values must be listed.

Table 11.2
Comparison Value Order in HLOOKUP or VLOOKUP Tables

Type	Ascending order
Numbers	-3, -2, -1, 0, 1, 2, 3
Text	Alphabetical order (upper- and lowercase are considered equal)
Logicals	FALSE, then TRUE (0 represents FALSE; 1 represents TRUE)

Calculating Answers from Multiple Inputs

The "what if" game is one major reason electronic worksheets have become so popular and useful in business. Worksheets provide immediate feedback from questions such as the following:

"What if we reduce costs by .5%?"

"What if we sell 11% more?"

"What if we don't get that loan?"

When you test how small changes affect the result of a worksheet, you are conducting a *sensitivity analysis*. You can use Excel's **Data Table** command to conduct sensitivity analysis across a wide range of inputs.

With **Data Table**, you can automate "what if" analysis to test many different combinations of inputs with a single calculation. Excel will create a table showing the range of conditions you want to test and the results, reducing the need for you to enter all the possibilities manually.

You can use **Data Table** in two ways:

1. Change one variable and see the resultant effect on one or more formulas.

2. Change two variables and see the resultant effect on only one formula.

Testing a Single Input with a Data Table

One of the most frequently used, but still the best introductory example of sensitivity analysis is a data table that calculates the loan payments for different interest rates. The single-input data table described in this section creates a chart of monthly payments for a series of different loan interest rates.

Before creating a data table, you need to build a worksheet that solves the problem you want to test. For example, the FORCST03 worksheet built in Chapter 4, "Worksheet Quick Start," can be used to demonstrate a data table. Any of the inputs in the FORCST03 assumptions area can be used as the input for data table tests.

To create a single-input data table that tests different loan rates, follow these steps:

1. Build a worksheet that solves the problem.

   Figure 11.7 shows a simple worksheet that uses the PMT function in cell D7 to calculate the monthly payment for a car loan of $12,341 at a 9.5% annual interest rate for 4 years. Note that in the formula bar, the annual interest rate is divided by 12, and the 4-year term is multiplied by 12. This puts all the arguments in terms of months.

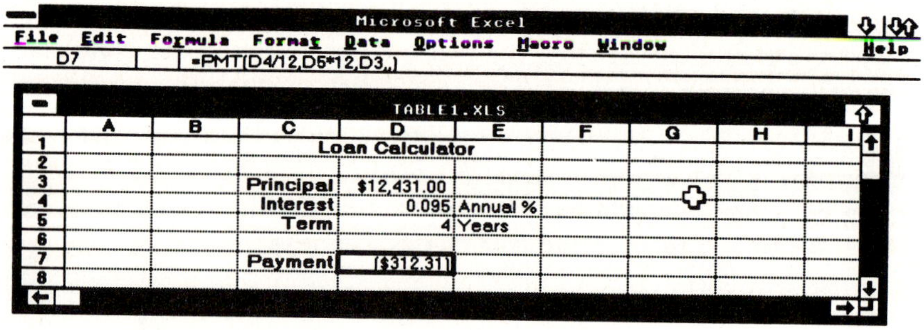

Fig. 11.7. A formula that uses the PMT function to calculate the monthly payment for a car loan.

2. Enter the different values you want tested in the worksheet. (You can enter the values in any sequence.)

   Cells C11:C15 in figure 11.8 show the different interest rates to be tested. Make sure that the upper left corner, cell C10 in the example, of a single input data table with a single input remains clear.

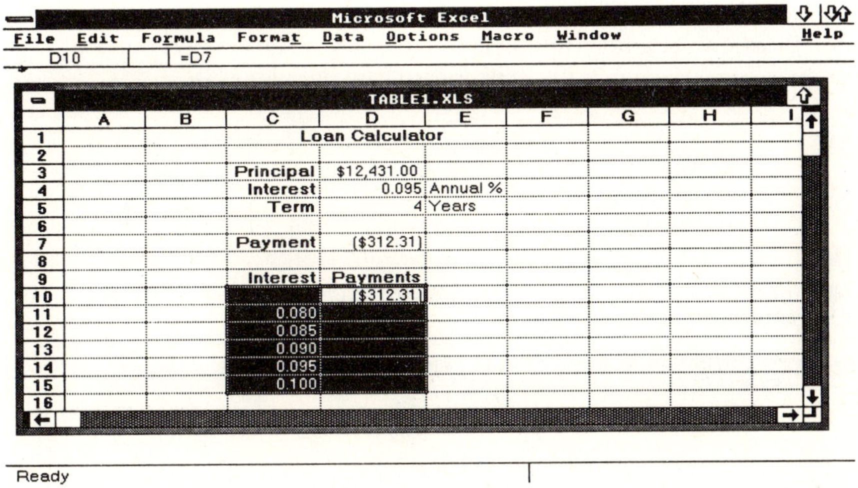

Fig. 11.8.
Interest rates to be tested entered in C11:C15.

3. In the top row of the table, above each blank column enter the address of each formula for which you want answers or enter a complete formula.

   In figure 11.8, cell D10 contains =D7. Therefore, the results for the Payment formula in D7 will be calculated for each interest rate. Enter as many formulas as necessary in the row. For example, additional formulas could be entered in E10, F10, and so on. You can enter a complicated formula or a simple reference to a cell containing a formula.

4. Select the cells enclosing the table. Include the input values in the left column and the row of formulas at the top, as shown in figure 11.8.

5. Choose **Data Table** to display the Table dialog box (see fig. 11.9).

Fig. 11.9. The Table dialog box.

```
┌─────────────────────────────────────────────┐
│ ▬                  Table                      │
│ ┌───────────────────────────────────────────┐│
│ │ Row Input Cell:    [            ]   ┌──OK──┐││
│ │ Column Input Cell: [$D$4        ]   ┌Cancel┐││
│ └───────────────────────────────────────────┘│
└─────────────────────────────────────────────┘
```

6. Enter the **Row** Input Cell or **Column** Input Cell.

   In this example, the **Column** Input Cell is $D$4. This tells Excel to take each value from the column, C11:C15, and substitute them one at a time into cell D4. After each substitution put the resulting answer in the appropriate row of column D.

7. Choose OK or press Enter.

The data table will fill with the payment amounts that correspond to each interest rate (see fig. 11.10).

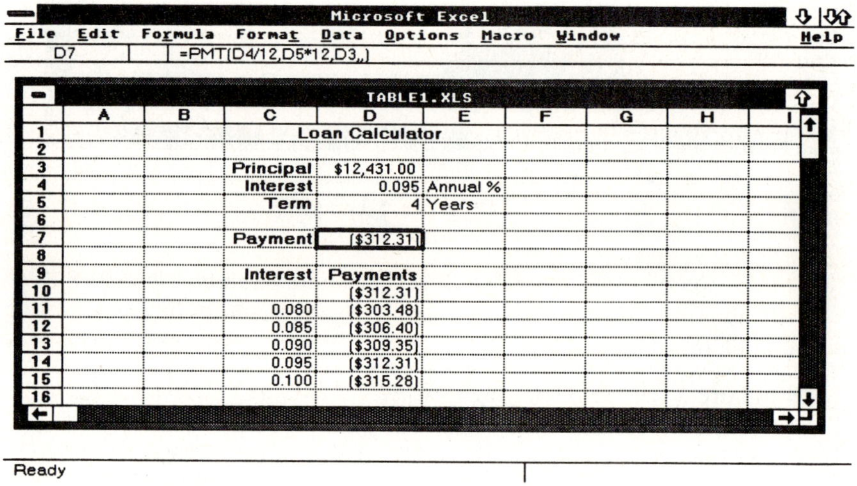

Fig. 11.10. The data table filled with payment amounts that correspond to the interest rates.

```
┌──────────────────────────────────────────────────────────────┐
│ ▬                    Microsoft Excel                    ⇩ ⟨⟩  │
│ File  Edit  Formula  Format  Data  Options  Macro  Window  Help│
│ ┌──D7──┐        =PMT(D4/12,D5*12,D3,,)                         │
│ ┌────────────────────────────────────────────────────────────┐│
│ │ ▬                     TABLE1.XLS                         ⇧  ││
│ │     A     B      C        D        E     F     G     H    I ││
│ │  1              Loan Calculator                             ││
│ │  2                                                          ││
│ │  3          Principal  $12,431.00                           ││
│ │  4          Interest        0.095 Annual %                  ││
│ │  5          Term                4 Years                     ││
│ │  6                                                          ││
│ │  7          Payment    ($312.31)                            ││
│ │  8                                                          ││
│ │  9          Interest  Payments                              ││
│ │ 10                    ($312.31)                             ││
│ │ 11             0.080  ($303.48)                             ││
│ │ 12             0.085  ($306.40)                             ││
│ │ 13             0.090  ($309.35)                             ││
│ │ 14             0.095  ($312.31)                             ││
│ │ 15             0.100  ($315.28)                             ││
│ │ 16                                                       ⇩  ││
│ │ ←                                                        → ││
│ └────────────────────────────────────────────────────────────┘│
│ Ready                                          |               │
└──────────────────────────────────────────────────────────────┘
```

If the Table dialog box covers the cells you want to select as the row or column inputs, move the dialog box by dragging the title bar, or by pressing Alt and then the space bar and selecting Move.

TIP

Entering a Sequence of Input Values

Use **Data Series** to create a sequence of evenly incremented numbers, such as the range C11:C15 of the example shown in figure 11.10.

Testing Two Inputs with a Data Table

Figure 11.11 shows how to create a data table that uses two values as input. The worksheet calculates the result of a formula for all the possible combinations of those values. The top row of the table area contains amounts for cell D3, the Row Input Cell. The left column of the table still contains the sequence of interest rates to be used in cell D4.

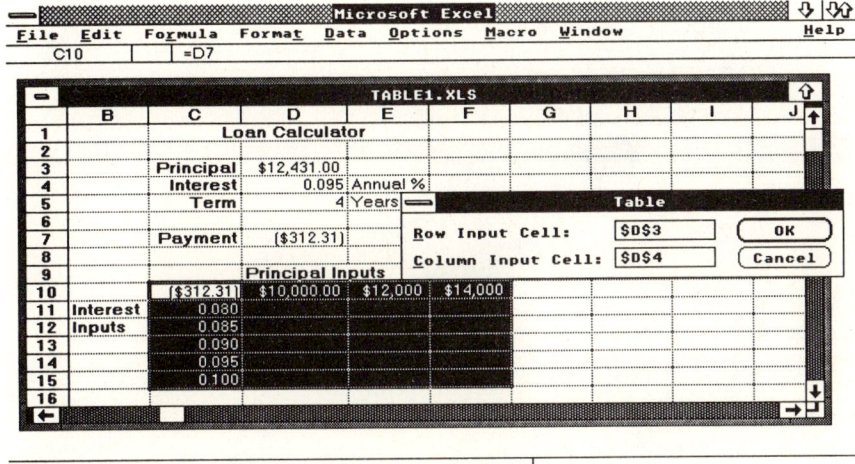

Fig. 11.11. A data table with two input values before calculation.

Notice that when you use two different inputs (one in the left column and the other in the top row), you can test the results from only one formula. That formula or a reference to the formula must be in the top left corner of the table. In figure 11.11, cell C10 contains a reference, =D7, to the payment formula being tested.

Figure 11.12 shows the result of a two-input data table. Each dollar value is the amount you would pay on a loan with that principal amount and annual interest rate. Because each monthly payment represents a cash outflow, the results are displayed in parentheses to show that they are negative amounts.

Editing Data Tables

After your data table is complete, you can change values in the worksheet on which the data table depends. The table will be recalculated automatically using the new values. In the example in figure 11.12, typing a new Term in D5 will cause new Payment amounts to appear.

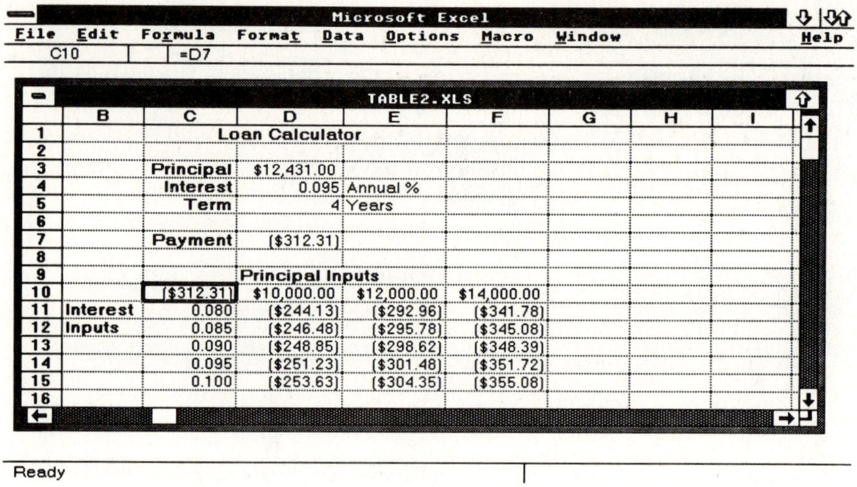

Fig. 11.12. The completed data table with two input values.

The completed data table with two input values.

	B	C	D	E	F	G	H	I
1			Loan Calculator					
2								
3		Principal	$12,431.00					
4		Interest	0.095	Annual %				
5		Term	4	Years				
6								
7		Payment	($312.31)					
8								
9			Principal Inputs					
10		($312.31)	$10,000.00	$12,000.00	$14,000.00			
11	Interest	0.080	($244.13)	($292.96)	($341.78)			
12	Inputs	0.085	($246.48)	($295.78)	($345.08)			
13		0.090	($248.85)	($298.62)	($348.39)			
14		0.095	($251.23)	($301.48)	($351.72)			
15		0.100	($253.63)	($304.35)	($355.08)			
16								

1-2-3 TIP

Data Tables Recalculate Automatically

In 1-2-3, you have to recalculate data tables by pressing Calc (F9). In Excel, data tables recalculate automatically whenever you change a cell that the data table uses in its calculations. If you want, you can turn off Excel's automatic recalculation feature or turn off just table recalculation (see this chapter's "Increasing Data-Entry Speed" section).

After you construct a data table, you also can change the numbers or text in the rows and columns of input values and see the resulting change in the data table output. In the example in figure 11.12, you could type new numbers or use the **Data Series** command to replace the numbers in C11:C15 or in D10:F10. The data table would be updated automatically.

You cannot edit a single formula within the data table result area. All the formulas in that area are array formulas of the following form:

    {=TABLE(D3,D4)}

The array formulas all must be cleared at one time.

Increasing Data-Entry Speed

Data entry will be slowed in some worksheets if the table is recalculated whenever one of its dependent variables changes. To speed data entry, you can temporarily turn off recalculation by choosing the command Options Calculation and selecting the Automatic except Tables option. To recalculate the worksheet, you must return to full automatic recalculation or press F9 to calculate all documents (the shortcut for the Options Calculate Now command). To recalculate only the active worksheet, press Shift+F9.

Calculating with Array Math

Arrays are rectangular ranges of formulas or values that Excel treats as a single group. You will find that arrays are easy to use and can save not only memory, but save time when you enter formulas. Some Excel functions, such as the trend analysis functions discussed in the last section of this chapter, require that you have a slight knowledge of arrays. In some cases, arrays can solve problems, such as multiple linear equations, that would be difficult to solve in any other way.

Excel uses two types of arrays: *array ranges*, a rectangular area sharing a common formula or function; and *array constants*, a rectangular area containing constants for use in array math.

Entering Array Ranges

You can save memory when creating some types of formulas by entering array formulas rather than entering or copying a formula into each cell of a range. (Excel stores array formulas in memory as a single formula even if it is in many cells.) Also, some Excel functions must be entered as arrays because they produce a range of results.

Figure 11.13 shows a worksheet for cost estimating with Price in column D and Quantity in column E. In cell F5, you could enter a formula such as the following:

    =D5*E5

Then you could copy the formula down column F. This process would require memory for each formula in each cell.

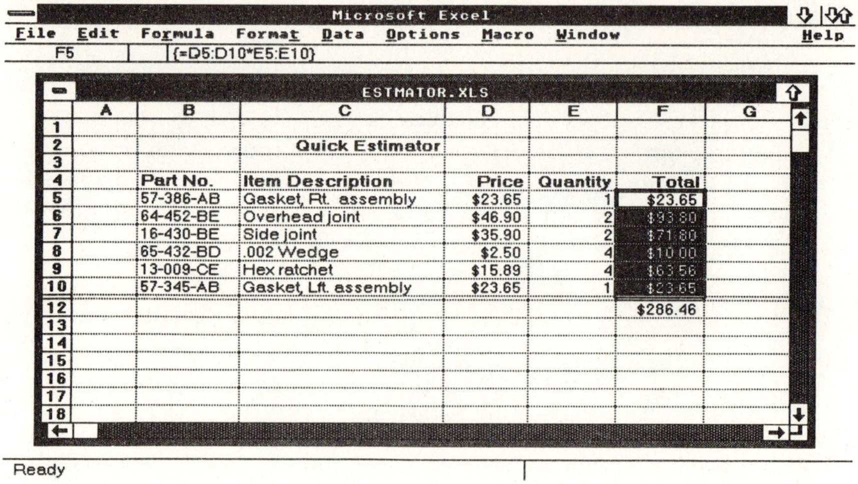

*Fig. 11.13. A
cost estimation
worksheet with
an array
formula in
cell F5.*

	A	B	C	D	E	F	G
1							
2			Quick Estimator				
3							
4		Part No.	Item Description	Price	Quantity	Total	
5		57-386-AB	Gasket, Rt. assembly	$23.65	1	$23.65	
6		64-452-BE	Overhead joint	$46.90	2	$93.80	
7		16-430-BE	Side joint	$35.90	2	$71.80	
8		65-432-BD	.002 Wedge	$2.50	4	$10.00	
9		13-009-CE	Hex ratchet	$15.89	4	$63.56	
10		57-345-AB	Gasket, Lft. assembly	$23.65	1	$23.65	
12						$286.46	
13							
14							
15							
16							
17							
18							

F5 : {=D5:D10*E5:E10}

Ready

Instead, you can use the following steps to enter a single array formula in
cell F5 that will fill the range from F5 through F10:

1. Select the range that will contain the array formula.

   Make sure that the shape of the range is appropriate for the type
   of function or array math being performed (see the section
   "Selecting the Range for an Array" in this chapter). F5:F10 is
   selected in figure 11.14.

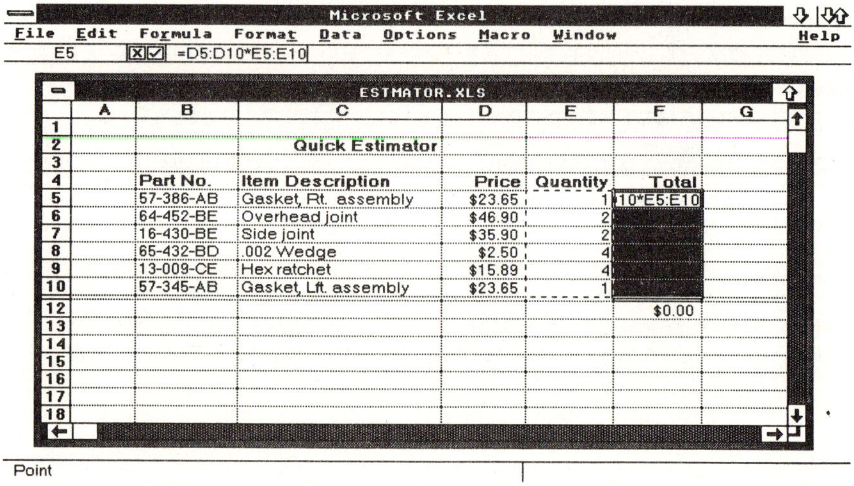

*Fig. 11.14. Array
range selected
and formula
entered.*

E5 : =D5:D10*E5:E10

	A	B	C	D	E	F	G
1							
2			Quick Estimator				
3							
4		Part No.	Item Description	Price	Quantity	Total	
5		57-386-AB	Gasket, Rt. assembly	$23.65	1	10*E5:E10	
6		64-452-BE	Overhead joint	$46.90	2		
7		16-430-BE	Side joint	$35.90	2		
8		65-432-BD	.002 Wedge	$2.50	4		
9		13-009-CE	Hex ratchet	$15.89	4		
10		57-345-AB	Gasket, Lft. assembly	$23.65	1		
12						$0.00	
13							
14							
15							
16							
17							
18							

Point

2. Enter the formula by typing it or pointing with the mouse.

   Instead of multiplying two individual cells at a time, the formula shown in the formula bar of figure 11.14 multiplies the two arrays D5:D10 and E5:E10. (Enter ranges such as D5:D10 by pointing to D5, holding down Shift, and then pressing the down arrow or dragging down to the bottom of the array.)

3. Press Shift+Ctrl+Enter to enter the formula or function as an array.

A single array formula or function will fill the selected array range as shown in figure 11.13.

Notice that the formula in figure 11.13 appears with braces ({ }) around it. Each cell in the array range F5:F10 contains the same formula in braces. The braces signify that the formula is an array formula and that the array range must be treated as a single entity. You cannot insert rows within the array range, delete part of it, or edit a single cell within it.

TIP

Check Each Array Formula after Entry

If you fail to hold down Shift and Ctrl as you press Enter when you issue the Shift+Ctrl+Enter command, Excel still will enter a formula and produce a result. However, the formula won't be an array formula. Check that braces ({ }) enclose the formula to verify that it is an array formula.

You can enter functions with array math that operates on ranges. *Array functions* are functions that use an array of values as an input and produce an array of results as an output. Enter array functions the same way you enter an array formula. Select an array range of the correct size to hold the array result, type the array function, and then press Shift+Ctrl+Enter.

Suppose that you wanted only the total in cell F12 of figure 11.13 and did not need the total price for each part. You could enter this array function in cell F12:

   =SUM(D5:D10*E5:E10)

When you enter this formula with Shift+Ctrl+Enter, Excel calculates the sum of the two multiplied arrays. The SUM formula will be displayed in the formula bar with braces around it.

Selecting the Range for an Array

Generally, the range you select for an array formula or function output should be the same size and shape as the arrays used for input. If the array range you select is too small, you will not see all of the results. If the array range is too large, the unnecessary cells will display #N/A.

In figure 11.14, the array range for each column was 6-by-1 (six rows by one column). The result of multiplying these two arrays is a 6-by-1 array. Therefore, the range from F5 through F10 was selected.

To understand what array shape should be used in function arguments for Excel array math, remember that each input array must have the same number of rows as the largest number of rows in any of the input arrays. Each input array also must have the same number of columns as the largest number of columns in any of the input arrays.

When an array is the wrong size or shape, Excel may expand it during calculation and fill the expanded rows or columns with #N/A. This expansion is what produces #N/A in some of the output array elements. If an array has a single element (cell), a single row, or a single column, then that element, row, or column is repeated to expand the array to the appropriate size.

Editing Array Formulas and Functions

You must treat arrays as a single entity. To edit an array formula or function, follow these steps:

1. Move the pointer within the array range.

2. Press Ctrl+/ (Ctrl+slash) to select the entire array.

3. Press F2 (Edit).

4. Edit the array formula or function so that it still maintains its array qualities.

5. Press Shift+Ctrl+Enter to reenter the array.

You cannot delete or edit part of an array. To clear an array, press Ctrl+/ to select the entire array range, and then press Del or choose **Edit Clear**.

TIP

Selecting the Array Range

You can select the entire array range containing an array formula or function by moving the active cell inside the array and then pressing Ctrl+/ (Ctrl+slash). An alternative method is to move inside the array, choose Formula Select Special, and select the Current Array option.

Entering Array Constants

You can enter constant values in an array in two ways. In the cost estimation worksheet (see fig. 11.13), example constants were entered as *continuous* cell ranges, such as D5:D10.

The other way to enter constants is as constant values within braces ({ }). When you enter constants within braces, separate columns by commas (,) and rows by semicolons (;). For example:

{1,2,3;"Jan","Feb","Mar"}

This constant value is the same as the following array:

1	2	3
Jan	Feb	Mar

Text must be enclosed in quotation marks, and numbers cannot contain dollar signs, parentheses, or percent signs.

Analyzing Trends

Excel has four functions that are designed to calculate a line which passes through a series of data with the least amount of error. You can use these four functions in calculating trends and making near-term forecasts.

These functions work by calculating the equation for either the straight line or exponential growth line that passes through your data. The LINEST and LOGEST functions calculate the parameters for the straight line and exponential growth line equations. The TREND or GROWTH functions calculate (or forecast) the values along the straight line or exponential growth line.

Before you can use the trend analysis functions, you must be familiar with dependent and independent variables. Understanding these variables is quite easy. The value of a *dependent variable* is a function of the value of an *independent variable*. Frequently, the independent variable is time, but it also can be such things as the price of raw materials, growth rates, or the Dow Jones average. In a comparison of time versus population, the time is an independent variable. As time increases, the dependent variable, population, changes. The independent variable's actual data is entered as the *known-x* argument in the function, and the dependent variable's actual data is entered as the function's *known-y* argument.

Calculating a Business Trend

Imagine that you own a concrete business which depends on new residential construction. You want to plan for future growth or decline so that you can best manage your assets and people.

After research (with the help of the local economic advisory boards), you assemble statistics on housing starts in your service area for the last five years. Figure 11.15 shows the housing starts by year in row 4. After discussion with county planners, you are convinced that your area will continue to grow at the same or slightly better rate. But what will the number of starts be in 1988 and 1989?

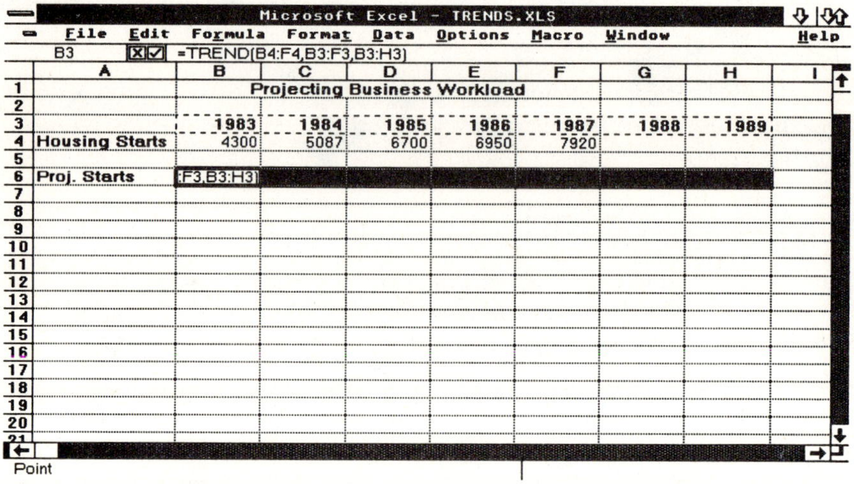

Fig. 11.15. A worksheet that shows housing starts for the last five years.

If the trend from the past five years continues, you can project the estimated housing starts for the next two years with the following steps:

1. Select the number of cells you want your straight-line projection to fill, B6:H6, as shown in figure 11.15.

2. Choose Formula Paste Function.

3. Select TREND from the list box.

4. Select the Paste Arguments option to help you enter the function's arguments.

5. Enter the arguments for the TREND function so that the formula appears the same as in figure 11.15.

   The syntax for the TREND function is

   TREND(*known_y's,known_x's,new-x's*)

   Replace the *known_y's* argument with B4:F4. (Housing Starts are y's because they depend on the Year value.)

   Replace the *known_x's* argument with B3:F3. (Year is the independent variable.)

   Replace *new_x's* with B3:H3 because these are the years for which you want to know the projected Housing Starts.

   Notice that the selected area in figure 11.15 covers the same number of cells as the *new_x's* cells, B3:H3. This area provides enough room for the resulting calculated *y* values.

6. Press Shift+Ctrl+Enter to enter the TREND function as an array function in the selected range.

The result shown in figure 11.16 illustrates that years 1988 and 1989 may have housing starts of about 8922 and 9833 if the trend continues.

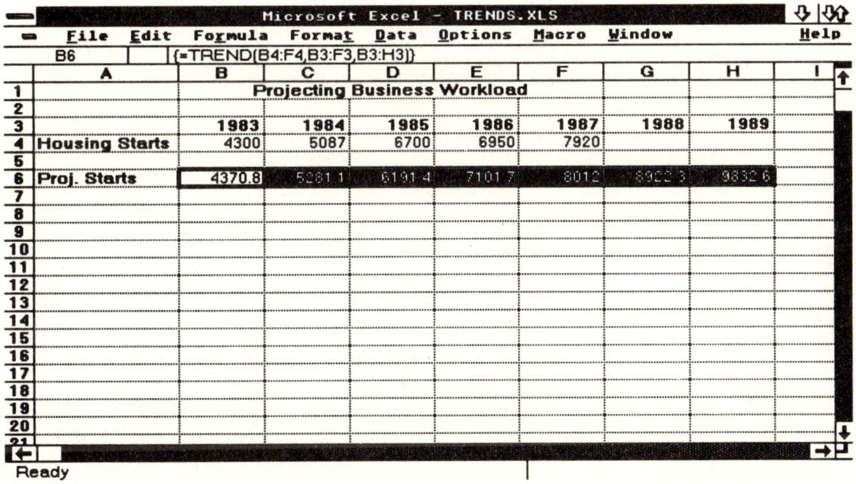

Fig. 11.16.
Projected
housing starts
for 1988 and
1989.

Notice that the new Y values, in cells B6:F6, don't exactly match the known Y values in B3:F3. That is because the TREND function has calculated the housing starts for those years according to its trend equation (a linear regression). The real number of housing starts in each year will undoubtedly be different. The greater the differences between the real housing starts and projected housing starts the less likely that the projection is accurate.

Understanding the Danger of Trend Analysis

Trend analysis is a helpful tool, but it must be used with the awareness that it can be dangerous if misunderstood or misused. Most growth or decline does not occur in a straight line; but a straight line can be used for short-term approximations. In all cases, using trend analysis to understand past trends in light of the historical record is the best practice. If projections are made, they should be kept to short periods of time.

Few problems exist that can be condensed to a few dependent variables. Many problems also have variables that have remained static in the past, but may change in the near future without your knowledge. In the Housing Starts example, a legislated moratorium on building, a major thrust by a competitor, or a layoff by a major employer could affect the forecast. Your judgment and business experience must temper any forecast.

From Here . . .

The techniques described in this chapter work best when synthesized and combined with other commands, functions, and techniques. You can find additional advanced techniques and tips in Chapter 23, "Building Advanced Databases."

12

Printing Worksheets

Excel lets you maximize all the capabilities of your printer. Excel reports from laser printers can come out looking as though they have been sent to the typesetter. Dot-matrix and laser printers alike reflect the font sizes and styles of the worksheet. You will find that you can achieve better quality with your printer than you ever have before.

Figures 12.1-12.4 show samples of what you can produce. Excel can produce the equivalent of preprinted invoices or "annual report quality" financial statements.

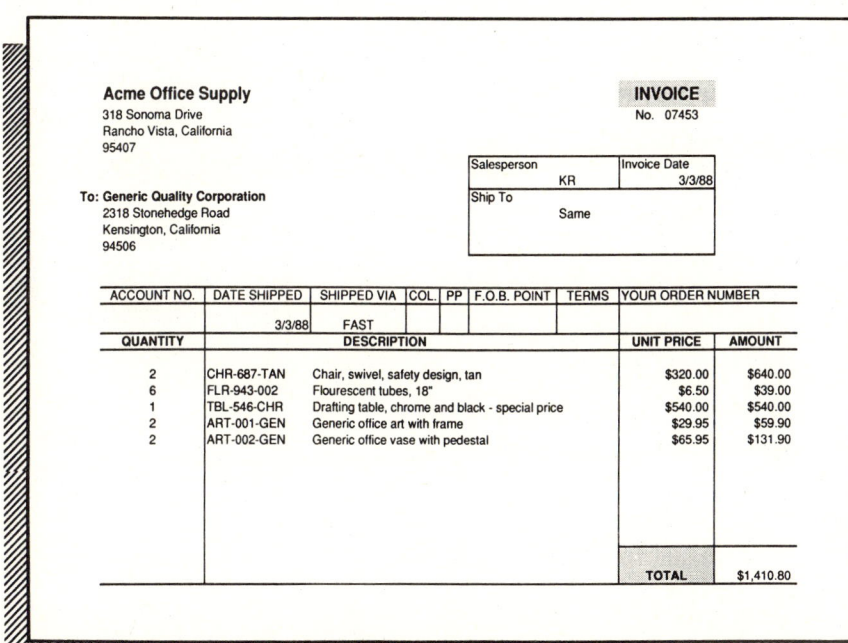

Fig. 12.1. A sample printout of an invoice.

Acme Office Supply
318 Sonoma Drive
Rancho Vista, California
95407

INVOICE
No. 07453

Salesperson		Invoice Date
	KR	3/3/88
Ship To	Same	

To: Generic Quality Corporation
2318 Stonehedge Road
Kensington, California
94506

ACCOUNT NO.	DATE SHIPPED	SHIPPED VIA	COL.	PP	F.O.B. POINT	TERMS	YOUR ORDER NUMBER
	3/3/88	FAST					

QUANTITY		DESCRIPTION	UNIT PRICE	AMOUNT
2	CHR-687-TAN	Chair, swivel, safety design, tan	$320.00	$640.00
6	FLR-943-002	Flourescent tubes, 18"	$6.50	$39.00
1	TBL-546-CHR	Drafting table, chrome and black - special price	$540.00	$540.00
2	ART-001-GEN	Generic office art with frame	$29.95	$59.90
2	ART-002-GEN	Generic office vase with pedestal	$65.95	$131.90
			TOTAL	$1,410.80

Fig. 12.2. A sample printout of a balance sheet.

GENERIC QUALITY CORPORATION
Balance Sheet
March 31 1988

ASSETS

	This Year	Last Year	%
Current Assets			
Cash	14,988	8,253	181.6%
Accounts receivable	504,600	548,478	92.0%
Inventory	245,000	247,475	99.0%
Prepaid expenses	12,300	5,348	230.0%
Investments	97,650	0	0.0%
Total Current Assets	874,538	809,554	108.0%
Fixed Assets (Cost less Depreciation)			
Buildings	420,000	420,000	100.0%
Leasehold improvements	3,800	3,800	100.0%
Furniture & fixtures	25,200	21,356	118.0%
Machinery & Equipment	179,800	168,037	107.0%
	628,800	613,193	102.5%
Less accumulated depreciation	169,800	140,331	121.0%
	459,000	472,863	97.1%
Land	64,000	64,000	100.0%
Total Fixed Assets	395,000	408,863	96.6%
	1,269,538	1,218,417	104.2%

LIABILITIES AND SHAREHOLDERS' EQUITY

	This Year	Last Year	%
Current Liabilities			
Notes payable	354,957	325,649	109.0%
Trade accounts payable	148,900	190,897	78.0%
Accrued liabilities	33,555	35,321	95.0%
Corporate income taxes payable	13,009	5,782	225.0%
Total Current Liabilities	550,421	557,649	98.7%
Long-term debt	180,000	197,802	91.0%
Due to shareholders	5,200	8,525	61.0%
Deferred income taxes	(6,300)	(96,923)	6.5%
Shareholders' equity:			
Capital stock	132,453	131,272	100.9%
Opening retained earnings	567,099	370,653	153.0%
Dividends declared	7,465	2,574	290.0%
Profit or (loss) for the period	12,098	4,514	268.0%
Total Shareholders' Equity	719,115	509,013	141.3%
	$1,269,536	$1,066,662	119.0%

Karen Ross
2314 Warren Road
Sebastapol, CA 95407

Jason Holmes
3033 Cleveland Ave.
Corte Madera, CA 93209

Jean Paul
879 Kurlander Way
Santa Rosa, CA 95403

Anderson & Clark
Accountants
43 Westheimer Dr.
Richardson, TX 57908

Rita Dover
515 Ross Street
Healdsburg, CA 94550

Dennis Smith
105 Settlers Trail
Austin, TX 78769

Ken Darvin
P.O. Box 47
Dallas, TX 57910

Steve Morrison
Service Tech
Fourteen California Street
San Francisco, CA 94111

Nicholas Elga
1820 Gate Road
San Anselmo, CA 94406

Dr. Susan Clarke
4587 Bluesky
Little Rock, AK 98432

Cynthia McDonald
3000 San Jose Ave.
Mill Valley, CA 89000

Lauren Murdock
Foundation Managers
P.O. Box 87
Novato, CA 94607

Steve Enson
659 Sonoma Blvd.
Sonoma, CA 95408

Joyce Dunaway
Business Consultant
1932 Fairview Court
Shasta, CA 97804

Darlene Green
Waxford Communications
617 Waltham Road
Chesterfield, OR 80900

Dr. Larry Hardwhil
University of California
P.O. 156-3
Berkeley, CA 93005

Jonathan McGivers
DataMasters
106 Bennet Valley Rd.
Norton, TX 56832

Kathy Machivey
3304 W. Anderson
Houston, TX 78605

Karen Masterson
498 Tamal Plaza
Vista View, UT 89045

Barbara Malley
227 Parkhurst St.
Oakland, CA 94609

Scott Faren
Trainer
7865 Fairway Dr.
Ashford, OR 89076

Sarah Kirin
55 Cambridge Ave.
Duluth, MN 45300

Janet Tarrant
134 Plum Creek
Cedar Park, TX 78698

Miriam Cassidy
Business Journal
87 Heald Blvd.
Ohi, CA 98970

Fig. 12.3. A sample printout of mailing labels.

Fig. 12.4. A sample printout of an Accounts Aging Report.

Generic Quality Corporation
Accounts Aging Report

Accounts aging report for   18-Jun-87

COMPANY NAME	DUE DATE	CURRENT AMOUNT	DAYS	30 & Under	31 to 60	61 to 90	Over 90
ACCESS COMMUNICATIONS	16-Jun-87	$979.80	2	979.80			
ADOBE CONSTRUCTION	12-Mar-87	$4,006.65	98				4006.65
AMERICAN TYPEWRITER	13-Apr-87	$13,526.50	66			13526.50	
BUENA VISTA METALS	12-Jun-87	$4,649.96	6	4649.96			
COLLINS CARPETERIA	14-May-87	$9,868.16	35		9868.16		
EBER ALUMINUM SIDING	1-Jun-87	$6,958.16	17	6958.16			
GOLDEN GATE SLIDES	3-May-87	$176.33	46		176.33		
J & J PLUMBING	3-Mar-87	$11,381.59	107				11381.59
LA ROCCA POOL & SPA	3-Jun-87	$6,898.21	15	6898.21			
LUCAS FLOORING	24-May-87	$1,000.00	25	1000.00			
LUCAS CLAY TILES	11-Jun-87	$4,829.40	7	4829.40			
MONROE ROOFING CO.	2-Jun-87	$13,464.73	16	13464.73			
SHASTA MECHANICAL	12-Apr-87	$10,701.04	67			10701.04	
T & M TRAVEL TOURS	6-Jun-87	$7,719.64	12	7719.64			
TOTAL		$96,160.17		46499.90	10044.49	24227.54	15388.24
				48.4%	10.4%	25.2%	16.0%
CHECKSUM		$96,160.17					

Excel saves you from the trial-and-error process most applications require in printing because you can preview the printed page on-screen before you send it to the printer. You even can preview added printing features such as headers, footers, and titles.

Another Excel printing feature—the Spooler—also increases your work efficiency. The Spooler queues material to be printed, allowing you to print a job as you continue working on other projects. You also have the option of printing to different printers simultaneously.

An Overview of the Printing Process

Usually, your printing process will consist of the steps that follow. Each of these steps, along with the specific options you can choose along the way, is described in detail later in this chapter.

1. Choose **File Printer** Setup, and select your printer. If you have not printed to this printer before, set the printer setting by choosing the **Setup** button.

2. If you want to change margins, headers, or footers, choose **File Page** Setup, and define the page setup.

3. Select the area to be printed, and then choose **Options Set Print Area**. If you are printing the entire worksheet, use the **Formula Define Name** command to delete the name PRINT_AREA if it exists from a previous print.

4. Set manual page breaks where necessary with **Options Set Page Break**. Remove manual page breaks by moving the active cell below the page break and selecting the **Options Remove Page Break** command.

5. Set row or column titles for each page with **Options Set Print Titles**.

6. Choose **File Print**.

7. Choose the **Preview** option box to preview the appearance of the page on the screen.

8. Choose **File Print**, unselect the **Preview** option, and press Enter to print.

Installing Your Printer

When you installed Excel or Windows, you were asked to define your printers. If you want to add or delete printers, you can do so either by reinstalling Excel or by running the Windows Control Panel. The Windows CONTROL program is available in Excel even if you do not have Windows. See Chapter 28, "Using Excel with Windows Applications," for information about the Control Panel.

Selecting the Printer

You may have installed more than one printer when you installed Excel. To select the printer to be used for the next print job, follow these steps:

1. Choose **File Printer Setup**.

2. Select the printer and printer port you want to use.

3. Select the **Setup** button if you have not used this printer before. A dialog box similar to the one shown in figure 12.5 will appear.

4. Select the appropriate options for the printer you have specified.

5. Choose OK or press Enter.

Excel will continue to print to the printer you selected until another printer is selected.

The Printer Setup dialog box will be different for different printers. Some of the options available are shown in table 12.1.

*Fig. 12.5. The
Printer Setup
dialog box.*

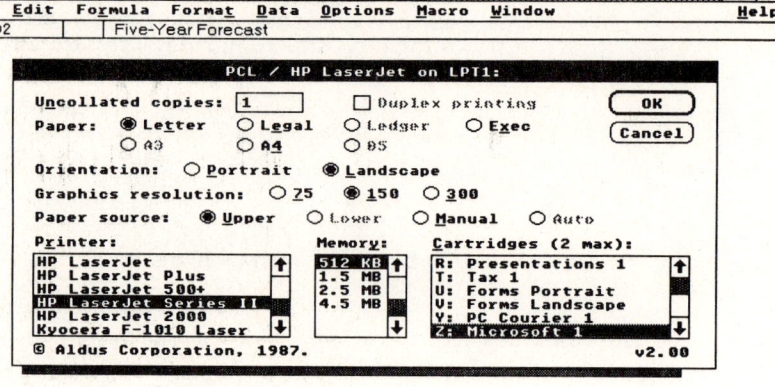

*Fig. 12.5. The
Printer Setup
dialog box.*

Table 12.1
Printer Setup Options

Option	Definition
Copies	The number of copies printed each time you select **File Print**.
Paper	The types of paper sizes. A3, A4, and B5 are European sizes.
Orientation	Portrait prints characters on the page as they appear in a normal letter. Landscape prints sideways on the paper and is useful for making transparencies and charts.
Graphics resolution	Some printers have the option of printing at different degrees of resolution, often defined in dots per inch. Printing at high resolution slows the printer speed, but produces better graphic images.
Paper source	Some printers have automatic paper storage bins or manual feed options.

Defining the Page Setup

The **File Page Setup** command controls the position of print on the page, enables you to print a custom header and footer at the top and bottom of each page, turns on and off the gridlines, and determines whether the row and column headings print.

To use the Page Setup command, follow these steps:

1. Choose File Page Setup.

2. Change the page options as needed in the Page Setup dialog box shown in figure 12.6.

3. Choose the OK button or press Enter.

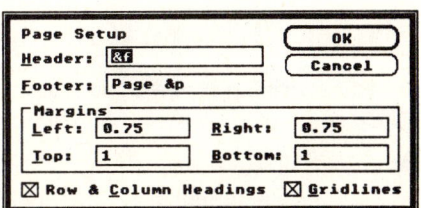

Fig. 12.6. The Page Setup dialog box.

TIP

Printing Sideways

Although you might think that you should be able to select portrait (vertical) or landscape (horizontal) orientation from the Page Setup dialog box, you actually need to choose the File Printer Setup command and select the Setup button (see this chapter's "Selecting the Printer" section).

Setting the Paper Margins

Excel's character width changes with each different font size. Rather than counting characters to set margins, therefore, you need to measure your margins in inches. The default settings for margins are shown in table 12.2.

Table 12.2
Default Margin Settings

Margin	Default in inches
Left	0.75
Right	0.75
Top	1
Bottom	1

Measure the bottom margin from the bottom of the paper up and the right margin from the right edge inward. When you set top and bottom margins, keep in mind that headers and footers automatically print one-half inch from the top or bottom of the paper.

Many laser printers are unable to print to the edge of the paper in at least one direction. Because of this limitation, you may not be able to set margins of less than a quarter inch on some sides of the paper.

Turning Row and Column Headings On or Off

For most printed reports, you will not want to print row and column headings. Turn them off by unselecting the check box for Row & Column Headings.

You will, however, want to print row and column headings when you print worksheet documentation showing the formulas and their cells. In this case, select Row & Column Headings. If you use Options Display, you can display the formulas on-screen so they can be printed (for documentation).

Note that the Row & Column Headings block of the Page Setup dialog box does not affect the screen display while you are working on a worksheet. Turn on or off the row and column headings that appear on-screen with Options Display.

Turning Gridlines On or Off

Remove the gridlines from your printed worksheets by unselecting the Gridlines option in the Page Setup dialog box. Note that this option won't change the screen appearance. You must use Options Display to remove gridlines from the screen display.

Creating Headers and Footers

You can create headers and footers that put a title, date, or page number at the top or bottom of each printed page of your worksheet. For example, managers may require that internal printouts include headers or footers that reveal the author, the date of the printout, and which worksheet was used. This audit trail ensures that old reports aren't misread as new and that old worksheets aren't used instead of newly updated ones. With Excel, you can quickly add headers or footers that automatically enter this data for you.

Excel automatically uses the document name as the header and the word *Page* and the page number as the footer. You can delete these or change them. These elements are centered one-half inch from the top or bottom of the page and three fourths of an inch from the side of the page regardless of margin settings. They print in font 1.

In the **Header** or **Footer** text boxes of the Page Setup dialog box, you can type codes to position the text, change the character style, and automatically insert dates, times, and document names. You enter these codes, shown in table 12.3, before you enter your custom text in the text boxes.

Table 12.3
Header and Footer Codes

Code	Effect
Position Codes	
&L	Aligns text against left margin
&C	Centers text between margins
&R	Aligns text against right margin
Style Codes	
&B	Prints the left, center, or right part of text in bold
&I	Prints the left, center, or right part of text in italic
&&	Prints an ampersand
Automatic Insert Codes	
&D	Inserts the computer's date
&T	Inserts the computer's time
&F	Inserts the name of the worksheet or chart
Page Codes	
&P	Inserts the page number
&P+# or &P-#	Inserts the page number plus or minus an adder (#). Use the page code with the plus sign (+) to start printing at a page number greater than the actual page number. Use the page code with the minus sign (-) to start printing at a page number smaller than the actual page number.

As the following examples illustrate, you can combine the codes shown in table 12.3 with your own text to create custom headers and footers. To try these examples, type Alt,H (header) or Alt,F (footer) when the Page Setup box is displayed, and type the code line as shown. When you print or preview the document, you will see the result as shown here.

Code: &C&BUsing Excel: IBM Version &RPage &P
Result:

> Using Excel: IBM Version   Page 1

Code: &LAuthor: Karen Rose&C&F&R&D
Result:

Author: Karen Rose   FORECAST.XCL   8/12/88

Code: &L&D&CABC Investment Corp.&RMortgage Banking Div.
Result:

8/12/88   ABC Investment Corp. Mortgage Banking Div.

Headers are printed one-half inch from the top of the page, and footers one-half inch from the bottom. If text overlaps the header or footer, use File Page Setup to change the top or bottom margin.

TIP

Don't Put Column Labels in Headers

When you work with databases or large worksheets, you may be tempted to put labels in the header that align with columns of data. Don't! Instead, use Options Set Print Titles to set print titles (see this chapter's "Printing Titles" section). Print Titles automatically align with each column of data, reflect their cell contents exactly, and leave the header available for other information.

Setting the Print Range

By default, Excel prints the entire worksheet until you specify otherwise. When you need to print only a portion of the worksheet, you must define that area with Options Set Print Area. You can choose to print either one area or multiple areas.

Setting a Single Print Area

The Options Set Print Area command controls how much of the worksheet and which cell notes are printed. To define a single print area, select the range of cells you want printed, and choose **Options Set Print Area**. Notes that are within the selected range will print if you select the **Notes** or **Both** option from the **File Print** command.

After you set the print area, Excel displays dashed lines that mark the edges of the print areas. For example, figure 12.7 shows the FORCST03 worksheet created in Chapter 4, "Worksheet Quick Start." The calculated area, selected in the figure, is marked as the area to be printed when the **Options Set Print Area** is chosen. You can see in figure 12.8 the lines that mark the edges of the print area after **Options Set Print Area** has been chosen.

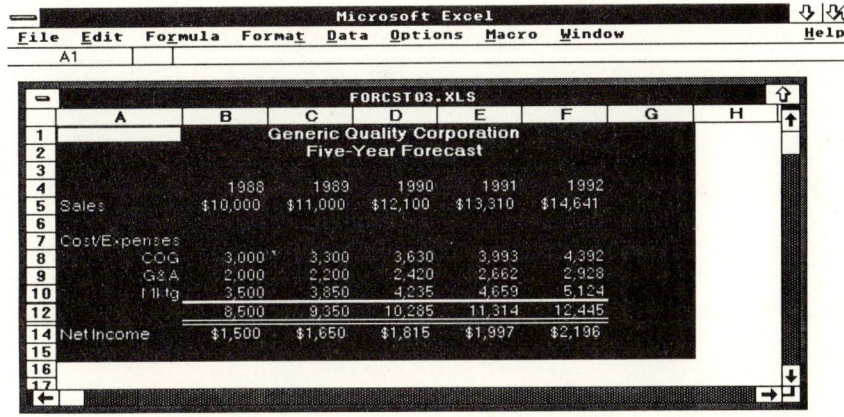

Fig. 12.7. The worksheet prior to setting the print area with Options Set Print Area.

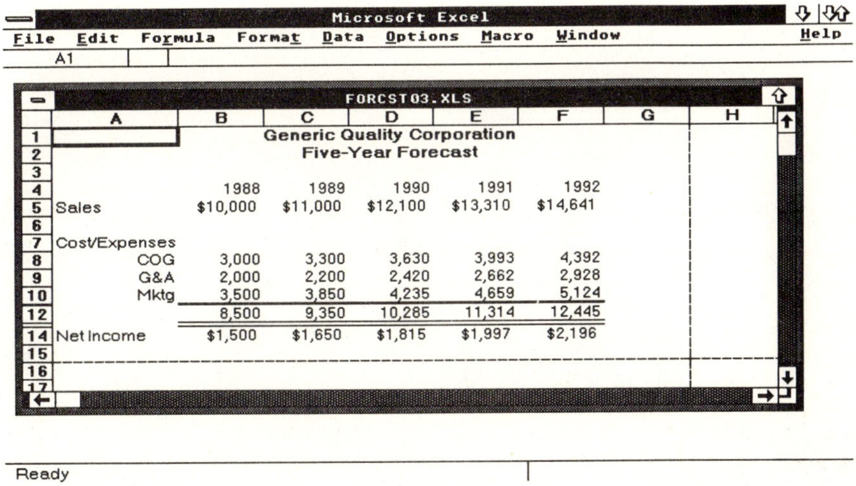

Fig. 12.8. The print area after selecting Options Set Print Area.

NOTE

Page Breaks That Don't Match the Print Area

If the dashed lines that mark the edge of the print area do not match the print area you have selected, you have selected a print area larger than a single page. Use manually inserted page breaks where you want the page to break.

Options Set Print Area creates a named range called Print_Area. You can display this range name and its cell references with the Formula **Define** Name command.

If you want to return to printing the entire worksheet, you must use Formula **Define** Name to delete the range name Print_Area. If you are going to print another portion of the worksheet, you can use Options Set Print Area again to define the next Print_Area.

Setting Multiple Print Areas

Excel can print separate areas of the worksheet as though they were adjacent on the worksheet. Select the multiple areas before you issue the Options Set Print Area command. This technique works well for creating a single printed report from different areas of a worksheet.

TIP

In What Order Do Multiple Areas Print?

Plan ahead if you are going to print multiple areas as a single print job. Each area prints in the order it was selected. Therefore, knowing the order of selection in advance is important.

TIP

Save Time When Printing Multiple Areas

If you frequently print the same multiple areas, save time by selecting the areas and giving the entire selection a name with Formula Define Name. Once named, use Formula Goto to reselect all the areas; then choose the Option Set Print Area command.

To print multiple areas of a worksheet, follow these steps:

1. Select the first area of cells you want printed.

2. Use multiple selection techniques to select the second area you want printed.

   Mouse: Hold down Ctrl as you select other areas with the mouse.

   Keyboard: Select the first area. Press Shift+F8 to enter Add mode (note the Add indicator in the lower right of the screen). Move to one corner of the next print area. Press Shift+arrow to select that area. Press Shift+F8 and move to one corner of the next area. Repeat this sequence to add another area.

3. Continue to select areas that you want printed in one long print job. The areas will print in the order selected.

4. Choose the **Options Set Print Area** command.

5. Choose the **File Print** command.

Figure 12.9 shows a small model of how printing multiple areas can be useful. With one print command, you can print the worksheet sections for assumptions; forecast; and first, second, and year-to-date sales. Each of the bordered areas on the worksheet represents a section of a full-sized worksheet. Note that Excel places a page break after each printed area.

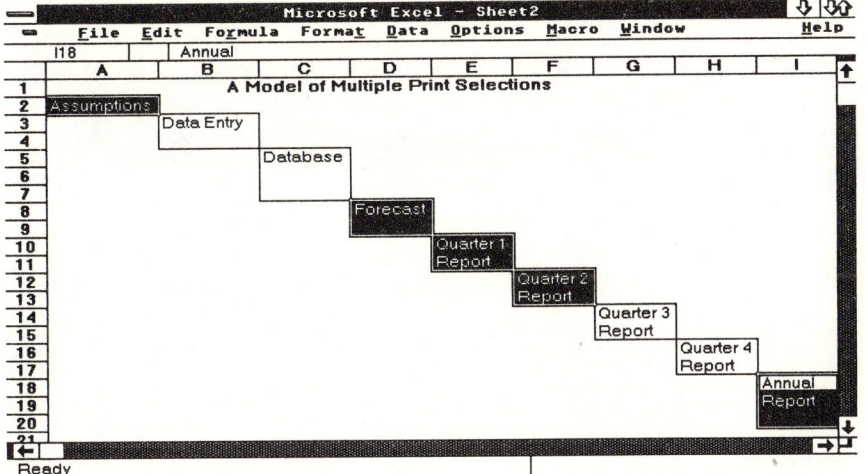

Fig. 12.9. A model of multiple worksheet areas to be printed.

Printing Titles

Repeating printed titles on each page can make large worksheet or database printouts easier to read. For example, when your worksheet is wider than one page, you can repeat row titles along the left margin of each page. You can repeat column titles at the top of each page of a database to name the data running down columns and onto following pages.

Normally, titles you include in a worksheet are printed only once. By using the Options Set Print Titles command, however, you can specify that certain titles be reprinted on each page of the printout.

To specify titles from a worksheet, follow these steps:

1. Select the entire row(s) or columns(s) of titles you want repeated, as shown in figure 12.10.

   Mouse: Click and drag over the row or column headings that contain titles.

   Keyboard: Move the active cell to the row or column to be selected. Press Shift+space bar to select the current row or Ctrl+space bar to select the current column. Press Shift+arrow in the direction of additional rows or columns that contain titles.

2. Choose Options Set Print Titles.

   If an alert box warns that the title area is invalid, check that you have selected the entire row or column and not just certain cells.

Fig. 12.10.
Selected rows of
text to be
printed as titles.

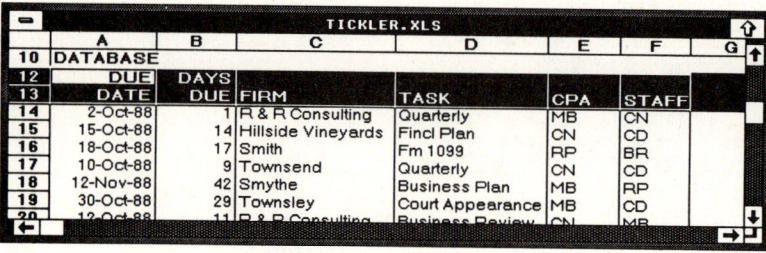

TIP

Don't Reselect Titles in the Print Range

When you select the print range with Options Set Print Area, do not reselect the rows or columns you specified with Options Set Print Titles. If you do, the titles will print twice on the page.

Options Set Print Titles creates a range named Print_Titles. To display the currently selected titles, choose Formula Goto, and then select Print_Titles. To delete Print_Titles, choose Formula Define Name, select Print_Titles from the list box, and then select the Delete button.

You can include any type of titles in the rows or columns you select. For example, you could include additional headers or page titles. You don't have to limit yourself to one row or column of titles. As long as the title rows or columns are adjacent (touching), you can include as many as you want. For example, in the title rows above a database, you might want to include the database title as well as the headings above each column.

TIP

When Titles Are Printed

Titles set with Options Set Print Titles are printed only when the selection being printed includes the same rows or columns as the Print_Titles range. For example, if the titles are in rows 3 and 4 from columns A through G, and you print data from B36 to H54, then you will have titles for only columns B through G. If you print the area from H54 to K72, you will not have any titles because the columns of the printed area are not the same columns as the titles.

Adjusting the Print Area

After you have selected a print area, you may want to make certain adjustments to it. For example, you might want to change the page breaks in order to adjust the boundaries of your printout. And you might want to change the margins or font size so that you can fit the material differently on the page.

As soon as you set a print area with Options Set Print Area, Excel displays dashed lines like those between columns G and H, and between rows 15 and 16 of the worksheet shown in figure 12.11. These automatic page-break lines define the boundaries of the print area. Automatic Page breaks are determined by the cell selection you make before you choose Options Set Print Area and by the margins you specify when you issue the File Page Setup command.

Setting Manual Page Breaks

You probably will find that automatic page breaks are not exactly where you want them. With Excel, you also have the option of entering page breaks manually.

Manual page breaks and page edges occur above and to the left of the active cell when you issue the Options Set Page Break command. Figure 12.12 shows page breaks above and to the left of the active cell, G15, after they were set

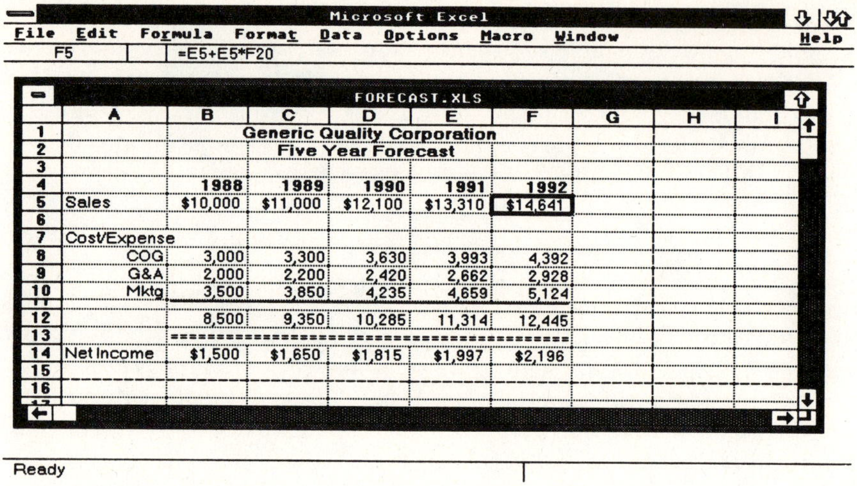

Fig. 12.11. A single dashed line indicating an automatic page break.

Fig. 12.11. A single dashed line indicating an automatic page break.

with **Options Set Page Break**. Notice that manual page breaks appear on-screen with a longer and bolder dashed line than automatic page breaks. Page breaks are easier to see on the screen when you remove gridlines with the **Options Display** command.

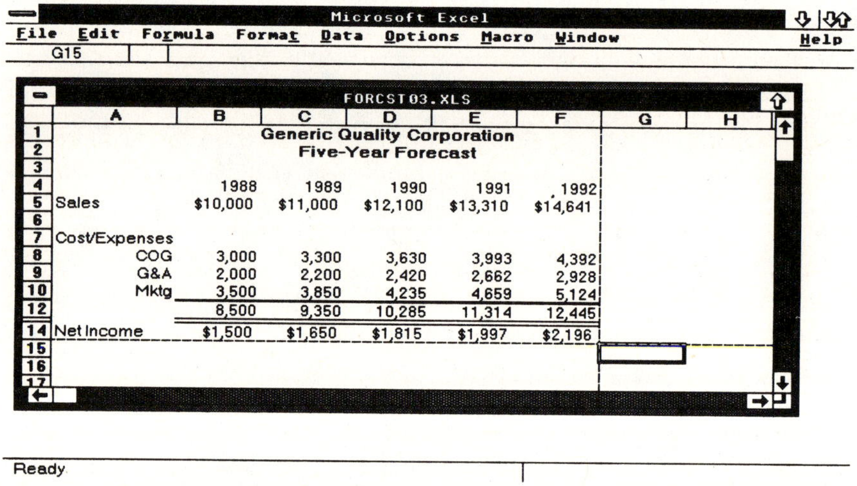

Fig. 12.12. Manual page breaks above and to the left of the active cell, G15.

Fig. 12.12. Manual page breaks above and to the left of the active cell, G15.

To insert manual page breaks, move the active cell to the cell underneath where you want the break, and then choose **Options Set Page Break**. Always start inserting manual page breaks at the top of the printing document since all changes cascade downward to affect following pages.

If you want to set only the sides of the page manually, make sure that the active cell is in row 1 before invoking **O**ptions **S**et **P**age **B**reak. The top and bottom of pages will break automatically.

If you want to set the breaks at the top and bottom of a page, move the active cell to column A, and invoke **O**ptions **S**et **P**age **B**reak. This technique does not affect the setting of page sides.

A manual page break stays at the location you set until you remove it. All automatic page breaks adjust for a manual page break. After setting a few manual page breaks, you should use the preview feature to review the location of new automatic page breaks (see this chapter's "Previewing the Page" section).

Remove manual page breaks by first moving the active cell directly below or immediately to the right of the manual page break. Then select **O**ptions **R**emove **P**age **B**reak. (This command appears on the menu only when the active cell is positioned correctly.)

NOTE

When You Can't Remove a Page Break

Be sure that you try to remove only *manual* page breaks. You can drive yourself crazy trying to remove an automatic page break you have mistaken for a manual one. Improperly adjusted contrast on your monitor may make manual and automatic page breaks look similar. Remove gridlines with the **O**ptions **D**isplay command to make page breaks easier to see. (Automatic page breaks depend on the margin settings in **F**ile **P**age **S**etup.)

Remember that the Remove Page Break command appears on the **O**ptions menu only when the active cell is immediately below or to the right of a manual break.

Adjusting the Line Width

You can fit more information on a page by decreasing the margins or by choosing a smaller font size. Use **F**ormat **F**ont to choose a smaller font size. To change row height, select the rows you want to print, choose **F**ormat **R**ow **H**eight, and select the **S**tandard Height check box. Adjust the left or right margins with **F**ile **P**age **S**etup.

The number of characters per inch on a line is a function of the font type and font size. Both are changeable through **F**ormat **F**ont. You might also be able to remove unnecessary blank areas by narrowing some columns.

Printing

With Excel, you can select the range of pages you want printed and how many copies you want. In addition, you can preview the printout on-screen before printing to paper.

Selecting Final Printing Options

After you have set the margins and print area (if you are printing a partial worksheet), then it is time to print. Choose **File Print** to display the print options in the dialog box shown in figure 12.13.

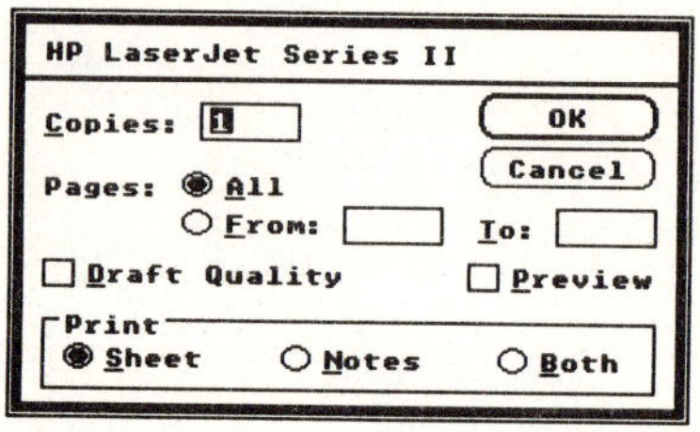

Fig. 12.13. The Print dialog box.

```
┌───────────────────────────────────────┐
│ HP LaserJet Series II                  │
│                                        │
│ Copies: [1]            ( OK )          │
│                                        │
│ Pages: ● All           ( Cancel )      │
│        ○ From: [    ]  To: [    ]      │
│ □ Draft Quality        □ Preview       │
│ ┌─Print──────────────────────────────┐ │
│ │ ● Sheet    ○ Notes    ○ Both       │ │
│ └────────────────────────────────────┘ │
└───────────────────────────────────────┘
```

In the **Copies** text box, enter the number of copies you want. Specify the number of pages to print either by selecting the **All** option for all the pages or by selecting the **From** option and entering the page numbers you want in the **From** and **To** text boxes.

When you need a quick print with lower quality characters, select the **Draft** quality check box.

Specify what you want to print by selecting either the **Sheet**, **Notes**, or **Both** button. The **Both** option prints the specified print area first and then follows it with notes that are in the print area. (To print the cell reference along with each note, make sure the **Row & Column Headings** check box is selected from the **File Page Setup** dialog box.)

Before printing, preview your print selection on-screen by selecting the **Preview** check box. To print to paper, just choose the **OK** button. Make sure that your printer is on and on-line.

Previewing the Page

Instead of doing a test print to check the appearance of your worksheet, you can view a display of the printout with miniature pages such as the one shown in figure 12.14. When you want to examine a preview page "up close," you can zoom into the area you want to see.

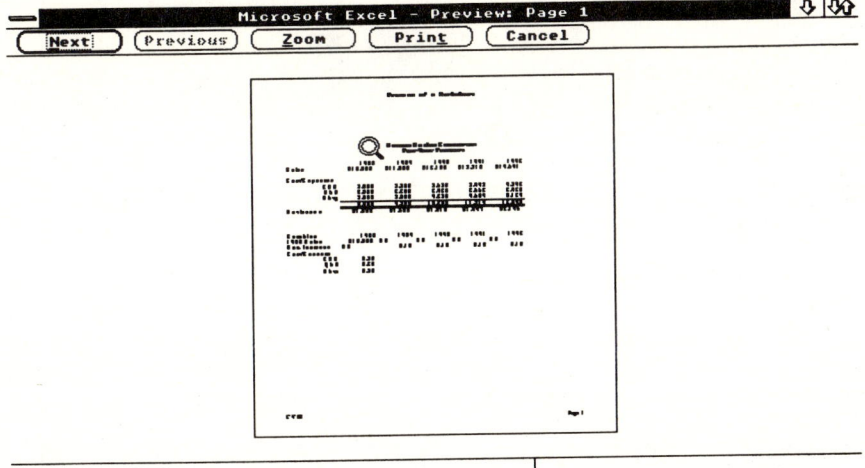

*Fig. 12.14. A
preview of a
worksheet.*

To preview pages, you select the **Preview** check box on the Print dialog box, and choose OK. A miniature of the full page displays on-screen as shown in figure 12.14. After the miniature appears, you can scroll through pages by selecting the **Next** or **Previous** buttons.

To zoom into a portion of the page, select **Zoom**. Use the cursor keys or scroll bars to move around in the "zoomed in" view. Figure 12.15 shows the "zoomed in" view of the top of the page from figure 12.14. (Figures 12.14 and 12.15 are previews of the FORCST03 worksheet created in Chapter 4. Top, left, and right margins are set at two inches, and the headings and grid-lines are turned off.) The header and footer shown in figure 12.14 were entered in the Page Setup dialog box. Select **Zoom** again to return to the miniature preview.

With the mouse, you can "zoom in" on specific areas by moving the mouse pointer, a magnifying glass, to the area you want to see, and then clicking. Click a second time to return to the miniature preview.

After you have previewed the worksheet, you can print it from the preview screen by choosing the **Print** button. If you decide to return to the worksheet instead of printing at this time, choose **Cancel**.

Controlling Print Jobs with the Spooler

Excel controls printing with the aid of a program called the Spooler. The Spooler can save you time because you can start print jobs and then return

Fig. 12.15. A zoomed-in view of a worksheet preview.

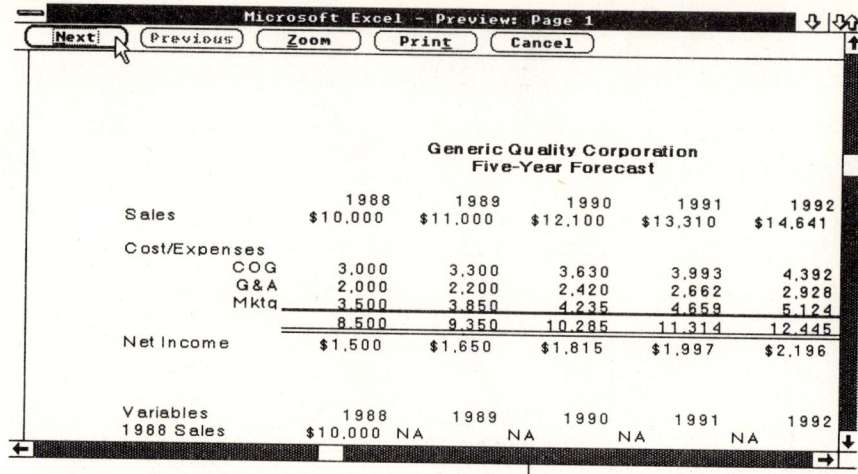

to work on the same document, a different Excel document, or even a different Windows application (if you are running Windows).

You do not have to wait for one print job to finish before starting the next with the Spooler. The Spooler keeps jobs in a queue until they are printed. The Spooler also lets you send print jobs to different printers. This capability enables you to print a number of jobs at the same time.

Whether you are running Excel under Windows or by itself, you can use the Spooler to control printer operation. With the Spooler, you also can stop a print job, and you can control the printing speed.

Printing with the Spooler

To print with the Spooler, use normal printing procedures. Your print job will be saved in a temporary file. As soon as it has been saved, you can resume work in the worksheet. The printer will print from the temporary file. Print jobs are ordered in the same order in which you choose the **File Print** command.

Stopping a Print Job

To stop a print job that is in the Spooler, follow these steps:

1. Hold down the Alt key and press Tab until you see the Spooler window appear, then release both keys.

2. Select the title of the print job you want canceled, as DATABASE.XLS has been selected in figure 12.16. Click on the title, or press the up- or down-arrow keys to select it.

   Notice that the files to be printed appear in the order they will print underneath the printer you have sent them to.

3. Choose **Queue Terminate**.

4. Press Alt, space bar, and then choose Minimize to return the Spooler to icon form.

5. Press Alt+Tab if necessary to return to Excel.

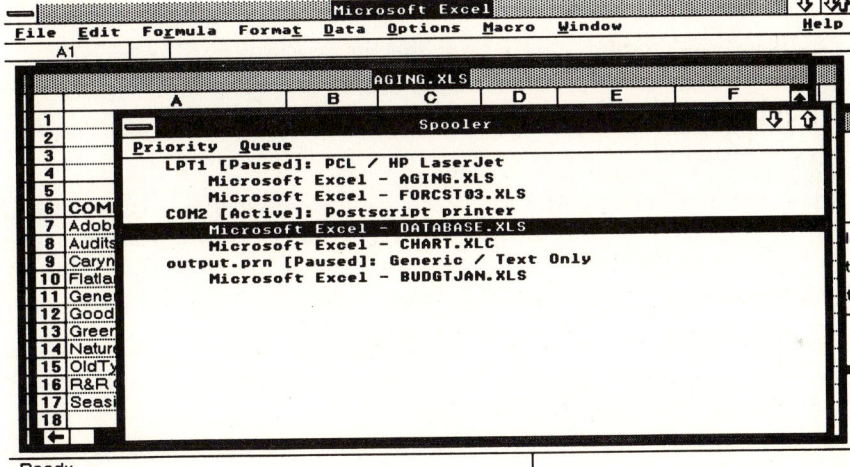

Fig. 12.16. The Spooler window.

You can have the options to pause or resume printing by choosing **Queue Pause** or **Queue Resume**, respectively. In figure 12.16, you can see that the printer on COM2 is running, whereas the printer on LPT1 has been paused.

TIP

Canceling All Print Jobs

To cancel all print jobs, close the Spooler window. Press Alt+Tab until the Spooler window is active; then press Alt, space bar for the Control Menu, and select **Close**.

Controlling the Printing Speed

To print a document and control Excel at the same time, your computer's processor must spend part of the time minding the printer and part minding the program. Normally, the Spooler is set so that most of the processor's time is spent with the Excel program. If you want the print job to go faster and the Excel operation to go slower, follow these steps:

1. Press Alt+Tab until the Spooler name appears; then release both keys.

2. Choose **Priority High**.

3. Press Alt, space bar; and then choose **Minimize** to return the Spooler to icon form.

4. Press Alt+Tab and, if necessary, the Esc key to return to Excel.

From Here . . .

Now that you know how to build, format, and print worksheets, you should begin to use Excel to improve the way you do work. As you use Excel, you may come across questions or have problems. When that happens look through the tips and notes included in the chapter that's appropriate to the topic. Also look in Chapter 13, "Troubleshooting Worksheets."

Chapter 13 explains how to improve Excel's speed, how to help Excel manage memory more efficiently, and how to find "bugs" or errors in your worksheets. It also includes a troubleshooting section that lists some of the more frequently asked questions and their answers.

TIP

Improving Excel Performance

You can make Excel run significantly faster by following the performance guidelines in Chapter 13, "Troubleshooting Worksheets," and by installing the SmartDrive software described in Appendix C.

When you have skimmed Chapter 13, you will probably want to try your hand at charting. Take 15 or 20 minutes to do the Chart Quick Start in Chapter 14. It's fun.

13

Troubleshooting Worksheets

Surveys show that 30 percent of all electronic worksheets contain errors. This is a terrifying but believable statistic when you consider that most people have been trained in command keystrokes, but not in designing or auditing worksheets. Few companies have policies for auditing or documenting worksheets. Moreover, most worksheets require an add-on software package to perform an effective audit.

Correct worksheets require careful planning and execution. You always should cross-check and review a new worksheet before using it for a critical decision. Excel has built-in commands, macros, and error values to help you discover trouble spots in your worksheets. Some worksheet design concepts were covered in Chapter 5, "Designing Worksheets." This chapter shows you how to improve the performance of your worksheets with certain hardware and with techniques for improving the operating speed of the program.

In addition, this chapter explains each of the seven error values that Excel displays. The text also tells you how to locate some common errors in formulas.

Excel includes two extra features, the Formula Select Special command and the AUDIT.XLM macro, to make troubleshooting Excel worksheets easier. This chapter shows you how to use both of these features to find errors in your worksheets.

Improving the Performance of Your Worksheets

Although Excel is designed to run on 80286- and 80386-based computers, you may find that its performance is slower than expected or that you use more memory than is available. This chapter describes some of the many ways to take care of performance problems and to gain additional memory. You can handle many of these performance problems by making minor alterations—by adding the BUFFERS line to the CONFIG.SYS file, for example. Other performance enhancements require that you add memory or that you use Microsoft's SMARTdrive disk-caching software, which is provided free of charge with Windows and Excel.

Improving Performance with Hardware

The recommended hardware for running Excel is an IBM AT or compatible computer, IBM Personal System/2 or compatible computer, or an IBM AT compatible using the Intel 80386 processor. The computer should be equipped with at least 640K of memory and 5M of free hard disk space. The graphics card must be Windows compatible.

Computers with 8088 or 8086 processors will not have enough processing speed to run Excel efficiently. Adding an accelerator card to your computer increases its speed. One such card is the Microsoft Mach 20 card that uses an 80286 processor.

In addition to processor speed, you can improve performance with additional memory or a math coprocessor. Other hardware improvements for your computer that will speed up Excel's performance are the following:

- Excel runs faster when more memory is available. In normal operation on a 640K computer with no other programs running, Excel has approximately 100K available for worksheets.

- Adding an EMS or EEMS expanded memory card to expand memory beyond 640K improves performance by storing more of the worksheet in memory. Excel automatically uses any LIM 3.2 or 4.0 expanded memory that you have installed. You can find out whether you already have expanded memory by choosing the **Help About** command. That command shows you how much conventional and expanded memory is available.

- Use your IBM PS/2™ base memory as expanded memory. Refer to the IBM PS/2 manual for more information.

- Emulate expanded memory if you use an 80386-based computer by running Excel under Windows/386.

- Math processing will be faster if you install an Intel 8087, 80287, or 80387 math coprocessor, whichever is appropriate for your computer. You do not need to change Excel in order to use the coprocessor.

Reducing Memory Requirements To Improve Speed

You can improve speed by reducing the amount of memory used by Windows or Excel. Here are some ways to reduce memory:

- Close unnecessary Excel documents. Remember, simple external references (worksheet links) can be read from worksheets that are on disk. You may not need all documents open.

- Close unnecessary applications running under Windows. (The full version of Windows allows your computer to load and use multiple Windows and DOS applications. You switch between applications by pressing Alt+Tab.)

- Limit the total number of fonts used in all Excel documents. Each worksheet can have four fonts; fonts in one worksheet may be different from those in another. If there are more than four different fonts in all the open documents, additional memory is used.

- Use small modular worksheets that are linked together rather than large cumbersome worksheets.

- Don't leave large blank areas between columns on a worksheet. Blank columns in the middle of a worksheet consume memory.

- Change similar formulas into array formulas. Formulas that are copied across rows or down columns can be entered as a single array formula to produce the same result. An array formula uses only the amount of memory used by one formula.

- Remove unnecessary device drivers. Your CONFIG.SYS may contain device drivers such as memory expanders, MOUSE.SYS, or ANSI.SYS that Windows already handles.

- If your worksheet uses expanded memory, you will be able to fit more of the worksheet in expanded memory when the worksheet does not go to the right of column FE, the 160th column.

Using Additional Performance Techniques

Your Excel worksheet will perform faster with the following changes. The CONFIG.SYS and SMARTdrive should be used when possible; other changes depend on the work you are doing.

- Make sure that your root directory (probably C:\) has a CONFIG.SYS file that includes the line:

      BUFFERS=1Ø

    This is the recommended minimum number. Chapter 1 describes how to add this line to CONFIG.SYS.

- If you are using Excel in Windows with other applications, make sure that you start the largest application first. (In many cases, this will be Excel.)

- Use SMARTdrive, the Windows-compatible disk cache program, to reduce the number of times that Windows reads information from disk. (Other disk cache programs will not work with Windows; SMARTdrive comes with Windows.) You can find information on installing SMARTdrive in Appendix C or in the book *Using Microsoft Windows*, published by Que Corporation.

- If you have a data table in your worksheet, but are not currently doing sensitivity analysis with it, choose **Options Calculation** and select Automatic except **T**ables. This technique recalculates the worksheet except for the tables. Remember to press F9 when you need to recalculate the tables.

- When entering data, you may not need to recalculate between each entry. All calculations can be performed when data entry is completed. Choose **Options Calculation** and select **M**anual. Change back to Automatic calculation or press F9 after you have entered the data.

- Turn off the **P**recision as Displayed option under **O**ptions Calculation for a slight performance increase. With this option turned off, Excel does not round off numbers.

Understanding Excel's Error Value Displays

Excel worksheets can contain two types of errors: incorrectly designed formulas and incorrectly constructed formulas. Excel cannot tell whether you are solving your problem correctly, but the program can tell you when you enter a formula or function incorrectly. Excel also shows you when formulas or functions become incorrect later.

When Excel cannot calculate a formula, the program displays an *error value* in the offending cell. Error values always begin with a pound sign (#). Excel has seven different types of error values with names that are nearly self ex-planatory (see table 13.1).

Table 13.1
Excel Error Values

Value	Meaning
#DIV/0!	The formula or macro is attempting to divide by zero.
	Check: Examine cell references for blanks or zeros. Is it possible that you accidentally deleted an area of the worksheet needed by this formula? Formulas may be written incorrectly so that the formula is attempting to divide by zero.
#N/A	The formula refers to a cell that has a #N/A entry.
	Check: You can type #N/A in mandatory data-entry cells. Then, if data is not entered to replace the #N/A, formulas that depend on that cell display #N/A. This error value warns you that not all the data has been entered.
	An array argument is the wrong size, and #N/A is returned in some cells.
	HLOOKUP, VLOOKUP, LOOKUP, or MATCH have incorrect arguments.
	You have omitted an argument from a function.
	You have referred to a linked cell that has not been updated.
#NAME?	Excel does not recognize a name.
	Check: Use Formula Define Name to see whether the name exists. Create it if necessary.
	Check the spelling of the name.
	You have used text in a formula without enclosing it in quotation marks. Excel considers the text as a name rather than as text.

Value	Meaning
	You did not replace one of the Paste Arguments names automatically pasted into a function by Formula Paste Function.
	You have mistyped an address or range so that it appears to be a name, such as the cell ABB5 or the range B12C45.
	You have referred to an incorrect or nonexistent name in a linked worksheet.
#NULL!	The formula specifies two areas that do not intersect.
	Check: The cell or range reference is entered incorrectly.
#NUM!	The formula has a problem with a number.
	Check: The numeric argument is out of the acceptable range of inputs, or the function cannot find an answer given the arguments you have entered.
	The answer is too large or too small for Excel.
#REF!	The cell reference is not correct.
	Check: Cells, rows, or columns containing a previous reference have been deleted.
	The external reference to a linked worksheet has been broken by closing the linked worksheet.
	A macro has returned a #REF! value.
	A Dynamic Data Exchange (DDE) topic is incorrectly entered or is not available. (See Chapter 28, "Using Excel with Windows Applications.")
#VALUE!	The value is not the type expected by the argument.
	Check: Verify that values used as arguments are of the type listed in Chapter 9, "Using Functions in Worksheets."

A formula also produces an error when it uses its own cell or a formula that refers back to the original cell as a reference. For example, suppose that cell B6 refers to cell C34, and C34 contains a function involving B6—the original source. Because the formula refers to itself, this error is known as a *circular error*. When this type of error occurs, Excel displays an alert box with the message

Can't resolve circular references.

When you select OK, the following message appears in the status line:

Circular: *reference*

with *reference* the address of one of the cells involved in the circular reference of formulas.

Locating Errors in Formulas

If you attempt to enter an improperly constructed formula, Excel displays an alert box telling you that a formula contains an error. Excel then tries to help you locate the error by selecting the part of the formula that may be causing the mistake. Excel also moves the cursor to where the mistake may be found.

Two of the most frequent mistakes when entering formulas are forgetting to put commas between arguments and having mismatched parentheses. You can reduce the chance of omitting commas and entering arguments incorrectly by entering functions with Formula Paste Function and selecting the Paste Arguments option.

To find mismatched parentheses in a formula, count opening parentheses by moving from left to right. Then begin at the end of the formula and count closing parentheses by moving from right to left. The number of opening and closing parentheses must match. If they do not match, begin from the outside of the formula and work inward, searching for pairs of parentheses.

If you are unable to find the mistake in a formula, delete the equal sign (=) from its front and press Enter. This technique, which enters the formula as text so that you can return to it later, saves you the time of having to delete and reenter the entire formula.

TIP

Display Formulas and Results at the Same Time

A helpful technique when troubleshooting formulas is to open a second window onto the worksheet. Choose Options Display and select the Formulas option. This procedure displays two windows on the same worksheet: one showing formulas, the other showing results.

Auditing Your Worksheet

Electronic worksheets can be like the Golem of Hebrew folklore or Frankenstein's creation. Without the proper controls, these helpmates can become monsters.

Auditing, the systematic documentation and cross-checking of worksheets prevents errors from happening. Have someone else check your ranges. Have that person use sample data sets and verify results. Write instructions that detail how the worksheet is built and explain why it runs as it does.

When a worksheet is audited, enter the name of the creator, the date the worksheet was audited, and the initials of the audit team in the footer of the printed page. Include the worksheet and version number in the footer. In this way, anyone reading the printed report can tell which version of the worksheet was used and the date of its last audit.

Excel includes two features that are the equivalent of audit programs sold separately for other major electronic worksheets: the Formula Select Special command and the AUDIT.XLM macro. These features are described in the text that follows.

Finding Errors with Formula Select Special

Finding errors such as #REF! or #N/A in your worksheet or in a range is easy. Choose Formula Select Special to display the dialog box shown in figure 13.1. Each of the options that help you find errors is described in table 13.2. Select the Formulas option and check only the associated Errors box in the dialog box. Then choose OK or press Enter. All the error values on the worksheet are selected as shown in figure 13.2. Press Tab or Shift+Tab to move the active cell between the selected errors.

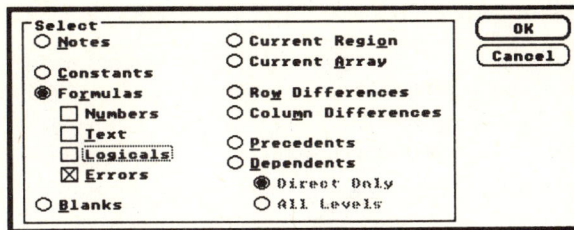

Fig. 13.1. The Select dialog box with Formulas Errors selected.

```
┌Select──────────────────────────────────────────┐   ┌─────────┐
│ ○ Notes              ○ Current Region           │   │   OK    │
│                      ○ Current Array            │   └─────────┘
│ ○ Constants                                     │   ┌─────────┐
│ ● Formulas           ○ Row Differences          │   │ Cancel  │
│    ☐ Numbers         ○ Column Differences        │   └─────────┘
│    ☐ Text                                       │
│    ☐ Logicals        ○ Precedents               │
│    ☒ Errors          ○ Dependents               │
│                         ● Direct Only           │
│ ○ Blanks                ○ All Levels            │
└─────────────────────────────────────────────────┘
```

Fig. 13.2. Error values selected.

	A	B	C	D	E	F	
			FORCST03.XLS				
1			Generic Quality Corporation				
2			Five Year Forecast				
3							
4		1988	1989	1990	1991	1992	
5	Sales	$10,000	$11,000	$12,100	#DIV/0!	#DIV/0!	
6							
7	Cost/Expense						
8	COG	3,000	3,300	3,630	#DIV/0!	#DIV/0!	
9	G&A	#VALUE!	#VALUE!	#VALUE!	#DIV/0!	#DIV/0!	
10	Mktg	3,500	3,850	4,235	#DIV/0!	#DIV/0!	
12		#VALUE!	#VALUE!	#VALUE!	#DIV/0!	#DIV/0!	
13							
14	Net Income	#VALUE!	#VALUE!	#VALUE!	#DIV/0!	#DIV/0!	
15							
16							

Table 13.2
Formula Select Special Options

Options	Action
Errors	Selects all error values
Precedents	Selects cells that support the active cell
Dependents	Selects cells that depend on the active cell
Row Differences	Selects cells in the same row that have a different reference "pattern"
Column Differences	Selects cells in the same column that have a different reference "pattern"

If you want to look in a specific range for errors, select that range before choosing Formula Select Special.

Finding Copied Formulas That Have Been Changed

You can use the Formula Select Special command with the Row Differences or Column Differences option to find copied formulas that may have been changed accidentally. The command finds changed formulas by matching the patterns of relative references in the formulas in a row or column. If one formula was copied across the row, the duplicates should use a similar pattern of relative references. For example, if you have copied one formula across the row, the formulas will have adjusted their references to the new locations. The formulas all will have the same pattern of relative references.

Both of the following formulas multiply the cell above by the cell to the left:

=C5*B6 in cell C6

=D5*C6 in cell D6

Both formulas have the same pattern of relative references. This pattern is easy to see if you switch to the R1C1 style of cell references by choosing Options Workspace and selecting the R1C1 option.

You can examine the cell contents of a row or column. To examine a row, choose Formula Select Special and select the Row Differences option. If a single cell was active, Excel selects in the active cell's row those cells that are different from the active cell. If you select a range that is one column wide before choosing the command, then the rows to the left and right of the selected cells are compared to the original active cell in the same row. The different cells are selected. If you select a range of cells, then the column of the active cell is considered the original, and the rows within the range are examined.

To examine formulas or entries that run down a column, choose Formula Select Special and select the Column Differences option. That option has three different modes of operation that act the same for columns as the Row Differences option acts for rows.

Following the Connections between Formulas

Formula Select Special enables you to see how formulas are linked to other formulas and values. The Precedents option selects the formulas and values that lead into the active formula. The Dependents option selects the formulas that depend on the results of the active formula. Figure 13.3 shows the selected cells that depend directly on B5 in the FORCST03.XLS worksheet built in Chapter 4, "Worksheet Quick Start."

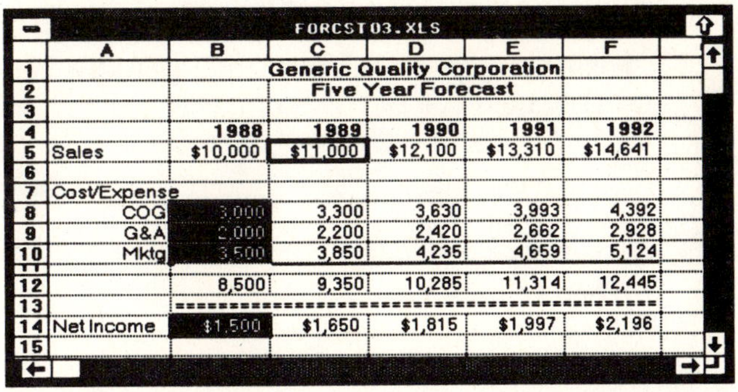

	A	B	C	D	E	F
1			Generic Quality Corporation			
2			Five Year Forecast			
3						
4		1988	1989	1990	1991	1992
5	Sales	$10,000	$11,000	$12,100	$13,310	$14,641
6						
7	Cost/Expense					
8	COG	3,000	3,300	3,630	3,993	4,392
9	G&A	2,000	2,200	2,420	2,662	2,928
10	Mktg	3,500	3,850	4,235	4,659	5,124
12		8,500	9,350	10,285	11,314	12,445
13		==========	==========	==========	==========	==========
14	Net Income	$1,500	$1,650	$1,815	$1,997	$2,196
15						

Fig. 13.3. The FORCST03.XLS worksheet with dependent cells selected.

To see which formulas depend on a single formula or value, follow these steps:

1. Select the cell containing the formula or value you want to trace.
2. Choose Formula Select Special.
3. Select the **Dependents** option.
4. Select either the Direct Only or All Levels option.

   If you choose Direct Only, only the formulas that directly refer to the active cell will be selected. If you choose All Levels, then any cell that can be linked back to the active cell (no matter how convoluted the link) will be selected.

5. Choose OK or press Enter.

All the cells that depend on the cell selected in step 1 will be selected. You can move between the dependent cells by pressing Tab.

You can select all cells that feed into a formula by selecting the formula and then choosing Formula Select Special with the **Precedents** option. You can move between the selected precedent cells by pressing Tab or Shift+Tab.

Finding Errors with the Audit Macro

Excel includes a macro (an automatic procedure) that makes your troubleshooting and documentation work much easier. This macro, AUDIT.XLM, automates many of the functions described in the previous "Finding Errors with Formula Select Special" section. When you load the AUDIT macro, it automatically runs and adds the new command, Audit, to the Formula menu.

To add the **Audit** command to the Formula menu, follow these steps:

1. Choose **File Open** and open the AUDIT.XLM file. If you installed Excel in the C:\WINDOWS directory you will find AUDIT.XLM in the C:\WINDOWS\LIBRARY directory.

2. Activate the worksheet you want to audit.

3. Choose **Formula Audit** to display the EXCEL auditor dialog box shown in figure 13.4.

Fig. 13.4. The EXCEL auditor dialog box.

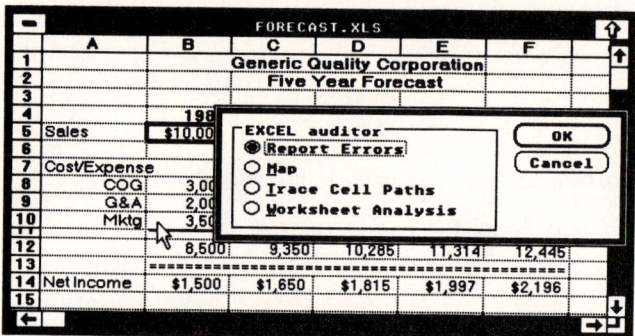

5. Select one of the four options listed in the dialog box:

Report Errors

Displays the Audit Report box shown in figure 13.5. From that box, you choose a type of error report. Each selection creates a report on a sheet that you can print.

Map

Creates a map showing your worksheet in condensed form as shown in figure 13.6. This option provides an excellent way to see which cells in your worksheet contain formulas (F), labels (A), or numbers (9). Mark your map to show where the database, data entry, and so on are located, and then file a copy with the worksheet documentation.

Trace Cell Paths

Displays the worksheet and the Info sheet for the active cell as you move forward or backward through the links that connect formulas.

Worksheet Analysis   Determines the Excel version of your worksheet, what percentage of cells are blank, and the last cell in the worksheet.

6. Choose OK or press Enter.

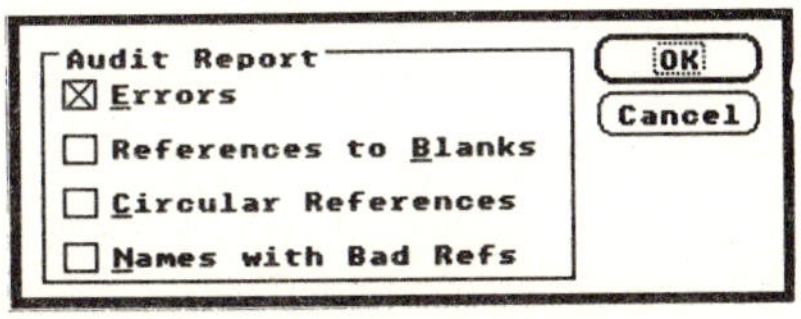

Fig. 13.5. The Audit Report box.

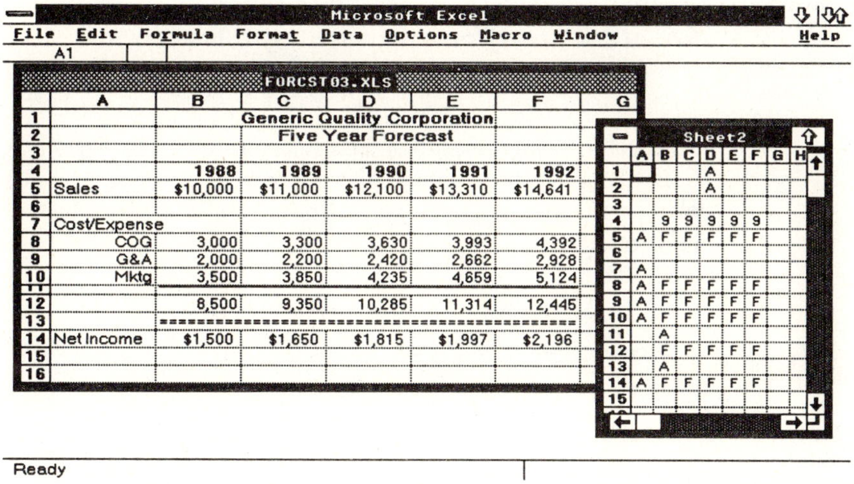

Fig. 13.6. A worksheet displayed along with its worksheet map.

When you quit Excel, do not save the AUDIT.XLM macro.

Never trust a new worksheet. Make sure that you audit it and cross-check results manually before using the worksheet for critical decisions.

Troubleshooting Tips

The following troubleshooting tips may help you solve some of the more frequent problems encountered when using Excel's worksheet.

Troubleshooting Installation Problems

Problem: The computer freezes when you first attempt to run Windows or Excel.

Solution: Check that you have connected the printer and mouse to the correct ports (COM1: and COM2:). As shown in the DOS and Windows manuals, backward installation may cause the system to lock up. Repeat the installation process using the correct ports.

Troubleshooting Worksheet Problems

Problem: Excel refuses to allow editing, inserting, or deleting of a cell.

Solution: The cell or range of cells may be protected, or it may be part of an array. If the cell or range is protected, then choose **Options Unprotect**. When the dialog box appears, enter the password if a password was used. If no password was used, press Enter.

If the cell or range is part of an array, you must edit or delete the entire array at one time. Select the array by moving the active cell into the array and pressing Ctrl-/. When the array is selected, you can edit it. To do so, press F2, edit the array, and then use Shift+Ctrl+Enter to reenter it. You also can delete a selected array.

Problem: After you delete a cell, row, or column, the #REF error value appears.

Solution: Deleting a cell, row, or column that contains values used by a formula causes that formula to display a #REF error value. Check through a row or column before deleting it. If you see the error value displayed, immediately choose **Edit Undo**.

Problem: After you copy formulas, a check for reasonable results shows that the duplicates are incorrect. An examination of the duplicate formulas reveals that some cell addresses have been changed.

Solution: Copying a formula to a new location adjusts the cell references in the formula to their new location. If you do not want a cell reference adjusted, you must make it an absolute reference by inserting dollar signs ($) in front of the row or column reference you want fixed (for example, $B$12 or C$53). For more information on absolute references, refer to Chapter 7, "Entering and Editing Worksheet Data."

Problem: An out-of-memory warning appears when you attempt to load another worksheet.

Solution: Not enough memory is available to load the additional document. Use **Help About** to see how much memory is available. Read through the alternatives described at the beginning of this chapter to learn how to increase available memory or to decrease the memory in use.

Problem: The dates from a worksheet imported from the Macintosh version of Microsoft Excel appear to be four years off.

Solution: Change to the 1904 date system by choosing **Options Calculation** and then selecting 1904 **Date** System.

Problem: When you enter a value in a cell or range, the value suddenly fills more cells than you expected.

Solution: The cell or range in which you are entering a value has been formatted with Format **Alignment Fill**. Select the affected cells and change the alignment.

Problem: After pasting a function by selecting the Paste **Arguments** option of the Formula Paste Function command, the function includes arguments like those in the following example of the PMT function:

=PMT(rate,nper,pv,fv,type)

Typing and deleting the argument placeholders is tedious. What is an easy way to replace the placeholders with the cell references?

Solution: Use the following steps to replace argument names with new cell references:

1. Select an argument placeholder name by dragging over it with Shift+arrow or Ctrl+arrow. (Don't include the separating comma.)

2. Select the cell reference you need by clicking on it or moving to it.

3. After the current reference replaces the selected argument, press F2 to get ready for the next selection. This step freezes the cell reference you just selected and lets you to move the cursor to the next spot in the formula.

4. Select the next argument and repeat step 3.

Problem: A worksheet that has been working normally begins to display #REF in a formula.

Solution: Check to see whether the formula is an external reference formula that links the cell to another worksheet. If that is the case, do the following:

1. Check the worksheets that are referred to externally to see whether they still exist on disk. They may have been moved to a different directory. Use **File Links** to redirect the links to the correct directories.

2. If the formula is a complex external reference formula, the worksheet on disk must be opened. Use **File Links** to find and open the linked worksheet.

3. Check that the externally referenced name or cell address exists or is still correct. The opened supporting worksheet may have been changed, but the dependent worksheet may not have been adjusted for the change.

Troubleshooting Calculation Problems

Problem: The displayed answer to a numeric calculation is slightly different from what a manual calculation shows as the answer.

Solution: When you format a number on Excel's screen, you format only the display, not the number used in calculations. Therefore, you might find discrepancies between the formatted numbers on the screen and the numeric result. To resolve this discrepancy, you can make the displayed number match the calculated number. For methods on making the display and calculation numbers match, refer to Chapter 8, "Formatting Worksheets," Chapter 9, "Using Functions in Worksheets," on the ROUND function and the **Options Calculation** command with **Precision as Displayed** selected.

Problem: Numbers inserted in a numeric column are not being totaled.

Solution: Check that the SUM function used to total the column includes the full column of numbers. A number inserted at the top or bottom of a totaled column may be outside the range being totaled. To avoid this problem, put a text heading at the top of the numeric column and a series of dashes (-) or equal signs (=) at the bottom of the column. Include the text heading and dashes as the beginning and end of the SUM range. With this method, inserted numbers must be between the two text boundaries and, therefore, must be within the SUM range.

Problem: After some calculations, a result that should be zero actually appears as an extremely small number.

Solution: Excel, like other electronic worksheets, stores numbers with a limited number of decimal places. Excel calculates numbers to 15 decimal places. Some numbers include an extremely small decimal portion (as small as the 15th decimal place). Ordinarily, this small portion of the number is insignificant and doesn't display. However, when two numbers subtract, this small decimal number may appear on the screen instead of the zero you expected.

If this problem occurs, use the ROUND function or **Options Calculation Precision** as Displayed to round the small decimal to zero.

Problem: An IF statement that checks for a zero condition does not work, even though the formula seems to result in zero.

Solution: Some numbers that appear to result in zero are actually small numbers near the limit of Excel's precision. When this problem occurs, replace an IF statement such as

    =IF(A12-B12=0,"TRUE","FALSE")

with a statement that works for small numbers:

    =IF(ABS(A12-B12)<.000001,"TRUE","FALSE")

Here the smallness of .000001 determines how close to zero the IF statement checks.

Problem: When entering a lookup_value for HLOOKUP or VLOOKUP, the function returns a value whether the lookup_value is in the table or not. For example, when given a part number, the HLOOKUP or VLOOKUP function returns a price even though the part number doesn't exist. Even typographical errors return results.

Solution: You need to display a warning that the lookup_value is incorrect. Use a formula such as the one that follows to tell the operator when an entry doesn't match anything in the table:

    =IF(ISNA(MATCH(lookup_value,lookup_array,
    type_of_match),"This isn't a valid Part Number",
    VLOOKUP(lookup_value,table_array,col_index))

This formula uses the MATCH function to check the lookup_array to make sure that an exact match exists for the lookup_value (Part Number) you enter. If a match doesn't exist, the warning message is displayed. If a match exists, the VLOOKUP value appears.

Problem: Array formulas and functions seem to enter, but they don't act like arrays.

Solution: Check that the formulas are enclosed in braces ({ }) to verify that they are array formulas. If they are not in braces, you may have accidentally pressed Ctrl+Enter instead of Shift+Ctrl+Enter. Pressing the Ctrl+Enter key combination fills a selected range with copies of the formula, but does not produce an array. To enter an array, hold down both the Shift and Ctrl keys, and then press Enter.

Problem: Data tables fill with a single value, fill with the wrong number, or don't work at all.

Solution: Check to be sure that your data table meets the following specifications:

- The correct cell is entered for the **Row** or **Column** Input Cell. If you have a row of data across the top of the data table, then the **Row** Input Cell is the cell in the worksheet in which you would substitute the values in the table's top row. If you have a column of data, then the **Column** Input Cell is the cell in which you would substitute the values in the table's left column.
- Data tables with a single column (or row) of input values can calculate multiple formulas. Each formula goes in the top row (or left column) of the table. The first cell in the top row of the table must be blank.
- Data tables with both a row and column of input values can calculate only one formula. That formula goes in the top left cell of the table.

Problem: A number of changes were made to worksheets that were linked together. Now the linked worksheets don't work correctly.

Solution: Update the file names or path names to the file locations with File **Links**.

Troubleshooting Printer Problems

Problem: Your printer is not listed on the screens displayed during the installation process.

Solution: Complete the Excel installation, choosing the Generic/Text Only printer. Call the Microsoft support line for an updated diskette of drivers, or contact the manufacturer of your printer or monitor. When you have the driver, choose the Excel Control menu (Alt, space bar), and choose the **Run** command. Select Control **P**anel and choose OK.

From the Control Panel's Installation menu, you will be able to add the new printer driver. Don't forget to go through the commands in the Control Panel's **S**etup command to finish the printer connection and setup.

Problem: The worksheet printed correctly earlier, but now it does not fit the page, or page breaks are at incorrect locations.

Solution: A previous user may have inserted a manual page break or changed font size. Or a different printer model (or manufacture) may have been selected, which would affect the character size and font and, therefore, the appearance of the printed spreadsheet.

A macro may have changed the page setup, font sizes, column widths, or manual page breaks without your knowledge. (A *macro* is an automatic procedure activated with Ctrl or from the Macro menu.) Go through the printing setup procedures manually and use the Preview feature to examine the results before printing. If you use any macros in a worksheet that someone else has built, ask that person to review the macros for changes to the print format or fonts.

Problem: Only part of the worksheet prints, but you want the entire worksheet printed.

Solution: When no Print_Area is defined, the entire worksheet prints. Delete the current print area by choosing Formula **D**efine Name, selecting the name Print_Area, and choosing the **D**elete button.

Problem: Titles at the top or left side of the page print twice.

Solution: Titles have been included in the print area as well as in the print titles rows or columns specified with **O**ptions Set Print Titles. Therefore, titles are printed both in the print area and in the title area. With **Options Set Print Area**, define a new print area that does not include the duplicate titles, or delete the print titles using **Formula Define Name**.

Problem: Titles continue to appear at the top or left edge of the paper even when the print area has changed.

Solution: Delete the print titles by choosing **Formula Define Name**, selecting the name Print_Titles, and choosing the **Delete** button.

Problem: Page breaks cannot be changed.

Solution: Make sure that you are attempting to remove a manual page break (they appear darker than automatic page breaks). Change automatic page breaks by adjusting the border size in **File Page Setup**. Also, note that **Options Remove Page Break** appears on the menu only when the active cell is below or directly to the right of a manual page break.

Problem: Not all the characters print across a line.

Solution: Increase the print area by making the left and right margins smaller, or select a smaller font size and decrease the column widths. Use **File Print Preview** to see the effect.

Problem: Strange characters or graphics are printed instead of or along with the correct text.

Solution: Check that the cable from your printer is firmly connected. Choose **File Printer Setup** and make sure that the correct printer model is installed. Run the Control Panel application to add the correct printer if it is not installed and designate it as the target or default printer. If your printer is not one of the choices listed during installation, then check with Microsoft for newly released printer drivers, and check with your printer manufacturer for the appropriate Window driver.

Problem: The data light on the laser printer flashes, but the printed page never ejects.

Solution: Use the Control Panel to add the correct printer, or set the correct printer connections. Check with your dealer for the connection settings such as baud rate and "handshaking" for serial printers.

Problem: The font used by the laser printer and that shown on the screen are completely different.

Solution: Your laser printer probably doesn't have a font that matches the one you used on the screen. The printer selects what it considers to be a similar font. To prevent this problem, make sure that the fonts you use on the screen match those available in your laser printer.

If you are using soft fonts, be sure to add the screen fonts to Windows or Excel through either the Control Panel Installation menu or the soft fonts installation package.

If you are using a font cartridge, be sure to indicate which cartridge you are using. To do so, choose the **File Printer Setup** command, select the printer from the list box, and then choose the **Setup** button. From the dialog box that appears, select the font cartridge you will use when you print.

Chapter 8, "Formatting Worksheets," describes how to replace one of the four worksheet fonts with the font you want. To ensure that you select only fonts available to your printer, choose the **Format Font** command, and then select the **Fonts>>** button. In the expanded dialog box, select the **Printer Fonts** check box before you make any font replacement selections from the fonts shown in the **Font** list box. When the **Printer Fonts** check box is selected, the **Font** list box shows only those fonts that your printer will print.

From Here . . .

You can reduce errors in worksheets and make them more understandable if you design them according to a few guidelines. Review Chapter 5, "Designing Worksheets," before starting your next worksheet project.

This worksheet section of the book has taken you from the simple to the complex. Having read Chapter 4, "Worksheet Quick Start"; Chapter 7, "Entering and Editing Worksheet Data"; and Chapter 8, "Formatting Worksheets," you should find Excel of immense help in solving 80 percent of the budget and forecasting problems you face. The other chapters in this section teach additional features that make the process of solving problems easier and faster or give you the power to solve problems with greater depth.

In the next section of the book, you will find that charting is fun, especially if you have a mouse. And if the bottom line is important to you, you will appreciate using Excel's charts for data analysis. When you need to present your findings and have a professional impact, you will be impressed by the "annual report quality" charts that Excel prints on a laser printer.

Part III

Excel Charts

We live in a visual world. Almost all our learning comes from what we see. People see and remember trend lines from graphs even when they do not remember the underlying numbers. Variance charts that show differences between forecast and actual budgets make problems immediately visible. Pricing errors in a database stand out when similar items are graphed. Charts increase understanding and improve communication.

One of Excel's major charting powers is its capability to graph a worksheet area quickly. You don't have to make a lot of selections. Excel makes a default selection, and you can choose one of the 44 preformatted charts. Of course, you also can customize charts and produce presentation quality graphics.

Windows enables you to copy a chart from Excel into a word-processing program such as Windows Write or Microsoft Word running with Microsoft Pageview. You can enhance Excel charts even more by using the Windows clipboard to transfer Excel's charts to professional level graphics and design programs compatible with Windows.

Excel produces six different types of charts: area, bar, column, line, pie, and scatter. Overlay charts may be used to create multiple overlapping charts in the same window.

The Chart Quick Start in the next chapter shows you how easy it is to create charts using Excel's automatic charting. You can learn a great deal by experimenting with Excel charts on your own. Excel leaves a lot of room for creativity. Have fun!

Chapter 14
Chart Quick Start

Chapter 15
Creating and Enhancing Charts

Chapter 16
Building Advanced Charts

Chapter 17
Troubleshooting Charts

14

Chart Quick Start

The Quick Start for charts, which takes approximately 15 minutes to complete, teaches you how to use a preselected format to create a basic chart and how to customize it. To be able to work through the instructions in the Quick Start, you will need to start with a worksheet that contains data. This Quick Start uses the FORCST03.XLS worksheet created in Chapter 4, "Worksheet Quick Start." If you did not complete or save that worksheet, then enter the numbers and labels as you see them in figure 14.1. You do not need to enter the formulas; entering the numbers and labels in rows 4, 5, and 12 will give you enough data to create a chart.

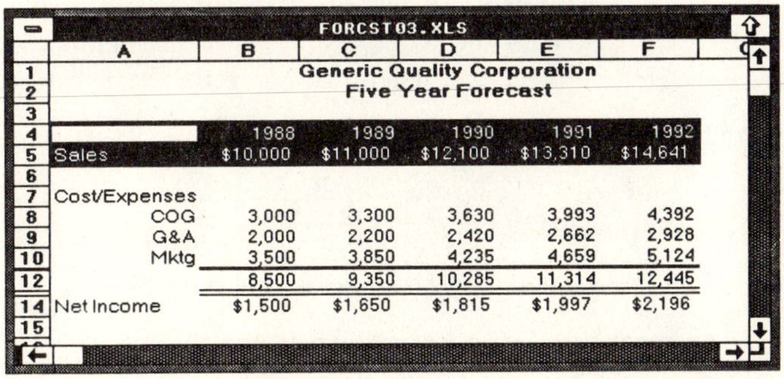
FORCST03.XLS

	A	B	C	D	E	F
1			Generic Quality Corporation			
2			Five Year Forecast			
3						
4		1988	1989	1990	1991	1992
5	Sales	$10,000	$11,000	$12,100	$13,310	$14,641
6						
7	Cost/Expenses					
8	COG	3,000	3,300	3,630	3,993	4,392
9	G&A	2,000	2,200	2,420	2,662	2,928
10	Mktg	3,500	3,850	4,235	4,659	5,124
12		8,500	9,350	10,285	11,314	12,445
14	Net Income	$1,500	$1,650	$1,815	$1,997	$2,196
15						

Fig. 14.1. The FORCST03.XLS worksheet.

To retrieve the worksheet you saved from the Worksheet Quick Start, choose **File Open**. Press Tab until a name in the list box is enclosed in dashes. Press the down arrow to scroll down and select the name of the forecast worksheet. (The name of your worksheet may be different than the name shown in the figure.) Press Enter.

Before you begin this Quick Start, choose the **Options** command and look at its menu. If the menu contains the command Full **Menus**, choose that command so that Excel displays all available menu commands. If the menu contains the command Short **Menus**, the menus already display all commands.

The Chart Quick Start gives you an overview of Excel's chart capabilities. As you use the Quick Start, remember that you can get Help information, relative to what command is selected or dialog box is displayed by pressing Shift+F1.

Creating a Basic Chart

Using preselected formats, Excel automatically creates a chart from the data you select from a worksheet. After you have created this basic chart, you can enhance it in many ways.

Here are the steps for creating a basic chart using preselected formats:

1. Select the cells to be charted, A4:F5, as shown in figure 14.1.

   Mouse: Drag the pointer from A4 to F5, and then release the mouse button.

   Keyboard: Select A4, and then hold down Shift as you move to F5.

   Because the area selected is short and wide, Excel understands that the top row will be used as the x-axis (bottom line) of the chart. The program expects the data to be located under each year listed in the worksheet. Cell A5 is included so that it can later be used as a legend to name the data in row 5.

2. Choose File New.

   Mouse: Click on the File menu heading, then click on the New command.

   Keyboard: Press Alt, then F, and then N.

3. From the dialog box shown in figure 14.2, select Chart.

4. Choose OK or press Enter.

Fig. 14.2. The New file dialog box.

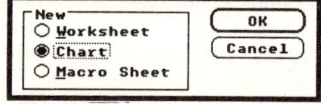

As soon as you choose the Chart option from the dialog box, Excel creates the column chart shown in figure 14.3. Also notice that because the active document is a chart sheet, the menu headings appear for chart menus and commands.

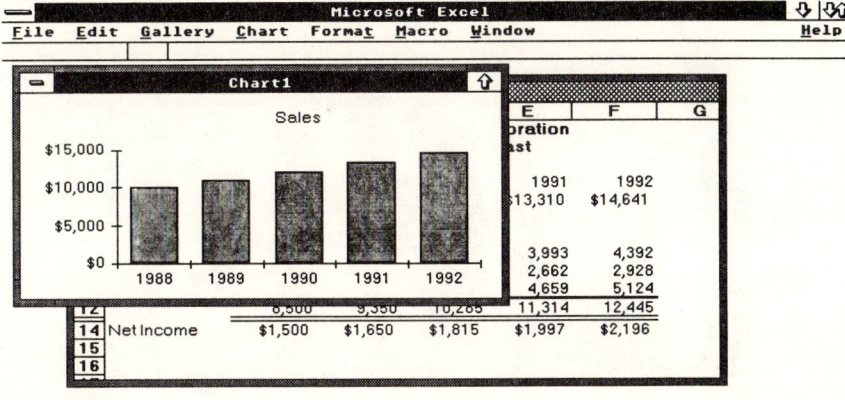

Fig. 14.3. A basic column chart created from selected data.

Because you selected only one set of data, the title of the entire chart, *Sales*, comes from cell A5. This label will be used later as a legend for the data in row 5. You also will learn how to enter custom titles and text.

Notice that Excel has automatically scaled the vertical y-axis. Also notice that the program used the same numeric format for the data along the y-axis as was used in the worksheet. The numbers along the y-axis reflect the display in the worksheet.

Selecting Chart Types from the Gallery

Excel has six different types of charts and a total of 44 predefined formats from which you can choose. The predefined formats are variations of the basic chart type. If you want to change from the preselected chart that first appears, you can pick a new format from the chart gallery.

To change the column chart to a pie chart, follow these steps:

1. Choose **Gallery** to display the menu.

   Notice the different types of charts available on the pull-down menu.

2. Select **Pie** chart.

   Figure 14.4 shows the different types of pie charts from which you can select. Pie charts plot only the first set of data you select. Therefore, if you had selected additional rows from the worksheet, only the first row would be plotted in the pie chart.

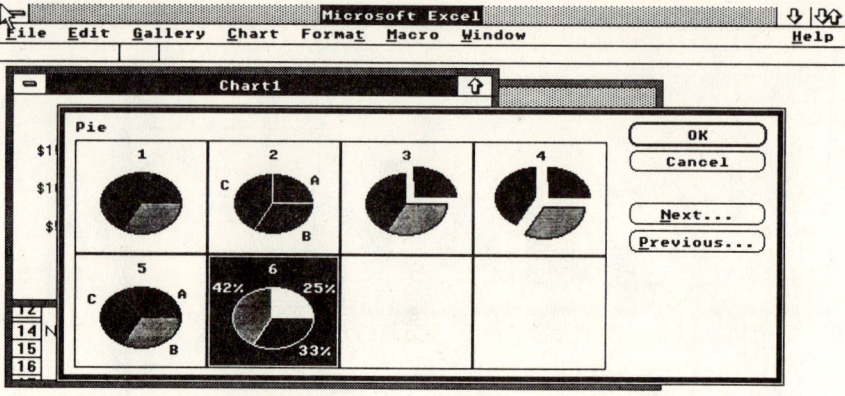

Fig. 14.4. The pie chart gallery.

3. Choose the percentage pie chart—number 6. The column chart will be replaced by a pie chart that shows the percentage for each wedge.

   Mouse: Click on the sixth chart, and then click on the OK button.

   Keyboard: Type 6, and then press Enter.

4. Maximize the pie chart to fill the screen as shown in figure 14.5.

   Mouse: Click on the maximize (up arrow) icon at the top right corner of the chart window.

   Keyboard: Press Alt and then the hyphen key, and then select Maximize.

Next, follow these steps to change the pie chart to a column chart:

1. Choose **Gallery Column** to display the available types of column charts shown in figure 14.6.

2. Choose the sixth chart type—the one that shows a horizontal grid. The chart changes to that shown in figure 14.7.

   Mouse: Double click on the square marked with 6.

   Keyboard: Type 6, and then press Enter.

Notice that the y-axis scale adjusts so that the top of the axis will have a gridline. In Chapter 15, "Creating and Enhancing Charts," you learn how to adjust scales and modify any part of a chart.

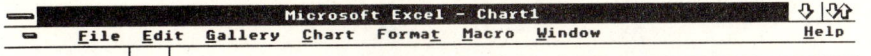

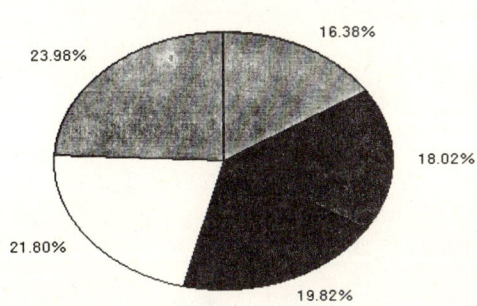

Fig. 14.5. A maximized pie chart with percentages displayed.

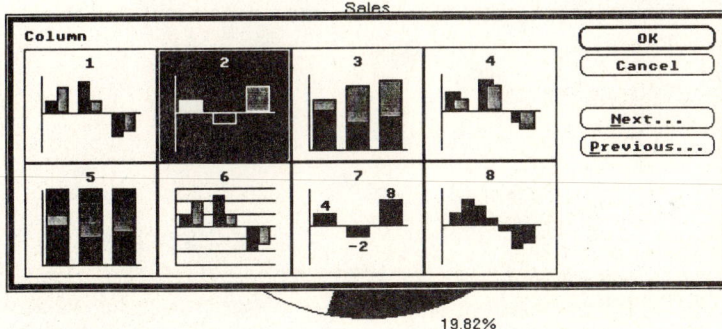

Fig. 14.6. The column chart gallery.

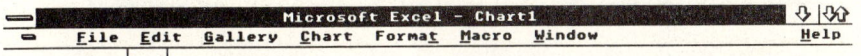

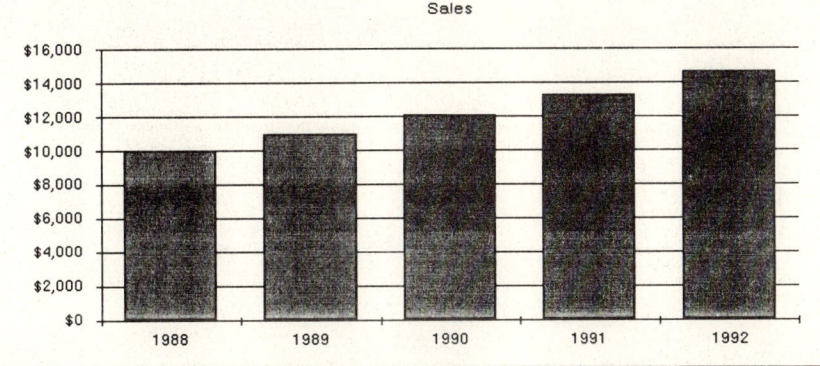

Fig. 14.7. A column chart with a horizontal grid.

Customizing a Basic Chart

In this section of the Quick Start, you learn ways to customize the basic chart you have just created. You will add additional data to the chart. Also, you will add a legend, title, text labels, and an arrow.

Adding Additional Data

Adding additional sets of data to a chart is as easy as copying from one section of the worksheet and pasting to another. The current column chart, shown in figure 14.7, displays the sales for each year. To add the total expenses to the current chart, follow these steps:

1. Restore the maximized chart to its previous size.

   Mouse: Click on the hyphen icon (at the left end of the menu bar), and then click on **Restore**.

   Keyboard: Press Alt and then the hyphen key, and then select **Restore**.

2. Activate the worksheet.

   Mouse: Click on the underlying FORCST03 worksheet.

   Keyboard: Press Ctrl+F6.

3. Select B12:F12, the data for total costs. The selection should look like figure 14.8. Notice that no label exists in A12; only data is included.

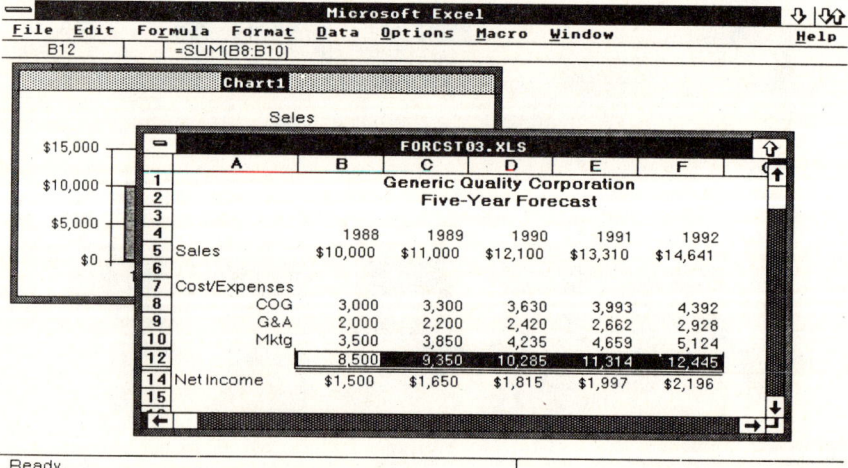

Fig. 14.8. The cells containing total costs data selected so that they can be copied to the chart.

4. Choose **Edit Copy** to copy the data in the selected cells.

5. Activate the chart.

   Mouse: Click on the underlying chart window. To see the chart window, you may need to drag the worksheet to one side by dragging on the worksheet's title bar.

   Keyboard: Press Ctrl+F6.

6. Choose **Edit Paste** to paste the total costs data into the chart.

Pasting the additional data displays the new data as a second set of columns. Figure 14.9 now shows both columns of data.

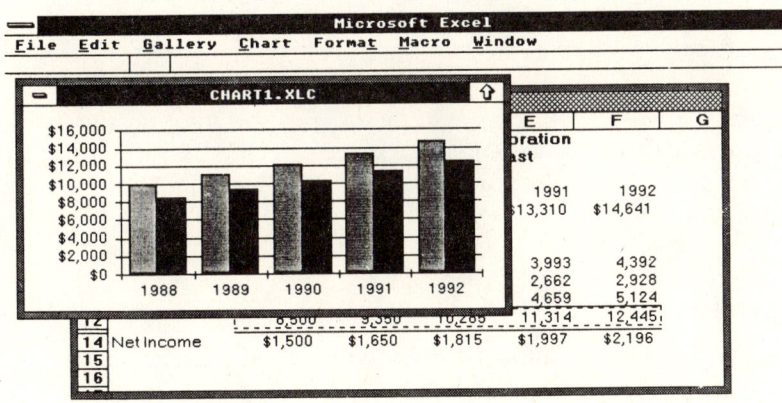

Fig. 14.9. A two-column chart with additional data pasted from the worksheet.

Adding a Legend

To add a legend to the chart, follow these steps:

1. Maximize the chart, because the rest of this section of the Quick Start involves only the chart.

   Mouse: Click on the maximize icon (the up arrow) in the upper right corner of the chart.

   Keyboard: Press Alt and then the hyphen key, and then select Maximize.

2. Choose **Chart Add Legend** to add a legend to the chart as shown in figure 14.10.

Fig. 14.10. A two-column chart with a legend added.

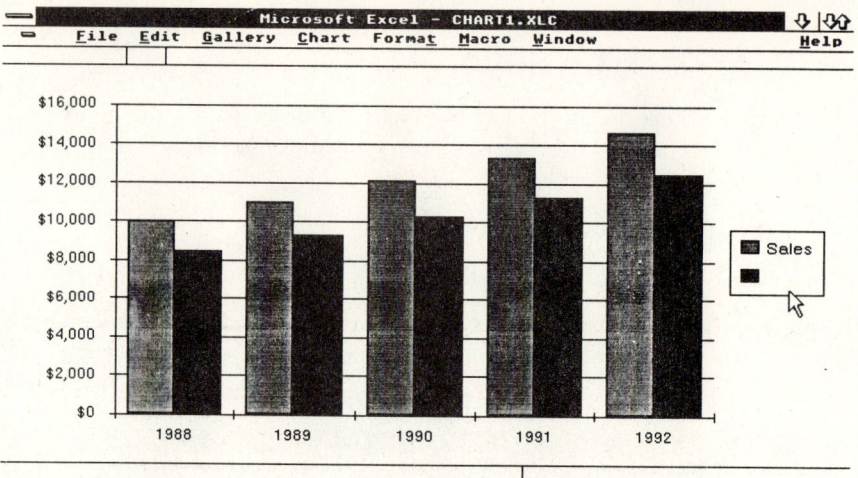

Notice that the word *Sales* appears in the legend, but *Total Cost* is not displayed in the legend because no label existed in cell A12. (Moreover, A12 wasn't included in the range that was copied.) The legend will be corrected later in the Quick Start.

Adding a Title

To add a title to the chart, follow these steps:

1. Choose **Chart Attach Text** to display the Attach Text To dialog box shown in figure 14.11.

Fig. 14.11. The Attach Text To dialog box.

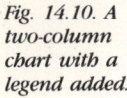

The dialog box gives you the opportunity to attach titles to the top of the chart, to either axis, or to a specific column. The Series number and Point number options are discussed in Chapter 16, "Building Advanced Charts."

2. Select the Chart Title option, and press Enter.

The word *Title* appears enclosed in white squares at the top of the chart. White squares, which enclose the currently selected chart item, indicate that you can change the font or color of this selected item, but the item cannot be moved.

3. Press F2, the Edit key, to bring the word *Title* into the formula bar to be edited. Press the backspace key to remove *Title*, then type *Generic Quality Corporation* and press Enter.

4. Choose Format Font. The Font dialog box shown in figure 14.12 gives a number of alternatives for text font, size, style, background, and color.

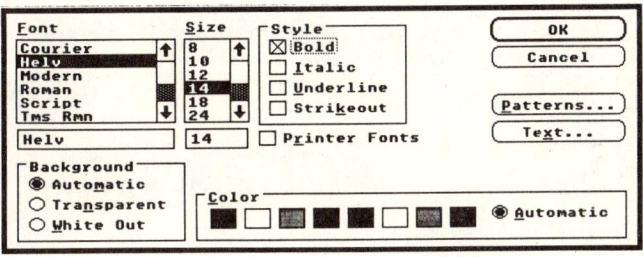

Fig. 14.12. The Font dialog box.

5. Choose the Helvetica, 14 point, **Bold** font with Automatic background and Automatic color. (If you do not have Helvetica, make another selection of 14-point type.)

6. Choose OK or press Enter.

The chart now looks like figure 14.13.

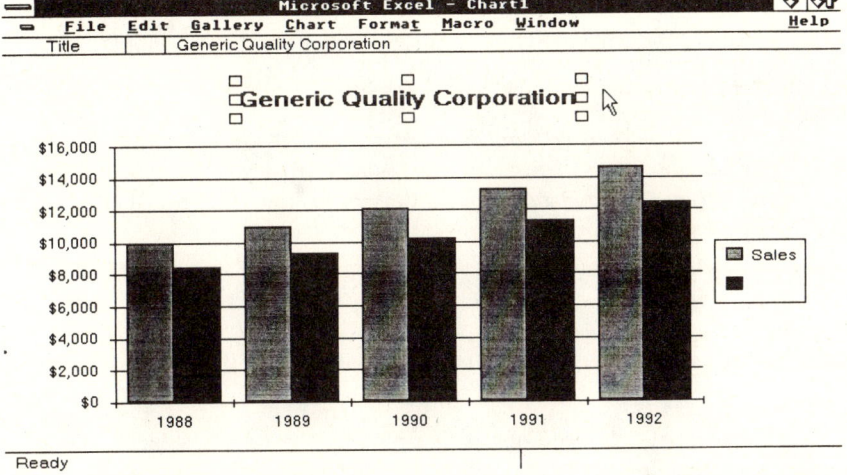

Fig. 14.13. A two-column chart with a title added.

Adding Text Labels

You can add unattached text labels anywhere on charts. These labels are useful as second titles, as identifiers for key data, or as additional information.

Be careful. Whatever text is currently selected (enclosed by black or white squares) will be replaced when you begin typing. Notice that the title is still selected. You must select some nontext object on the screen before typing the text that will become an unattached label.

To create an unattached text label, follow these steps:

1. Press the up-arrow key to move the selection to the next class of chart objects (nontext).

TIP

Selecting Objects in a Chart

Chart objects are grouped by class, such as all arrows in one class and all text in another class. With the mouse, you can click on any object to select it. With the keyboard, you press the up arrow to select the first item in the next class or press the down arrow to select the last item in the previous class.

When you have selected an item in the class you want, press the left or right arrow to select the specific item you want. Small white or black squares indicate the item currently selected.

---

2. Type the words **New Product**

3. Press Ctrl+Enter to move to a new text line in the formula bar.

4. Type the word **Release** and press Enter.

   Notice that *New Product Release* appears on the screen enclosed by black squares. These squares indicate that you can change the text font, size, and color as well as move the label to a new location.

5. Move the *New Product Release* text to the location shown in figure 14.14.

   Mouse: Drag the text to its new location, and then release the mouse button.

   Keyboard: Choose Format Move while the text is selected. The text changes to a positioning box. Use the arrow keys to move the box, then press Enter to fix it in place.

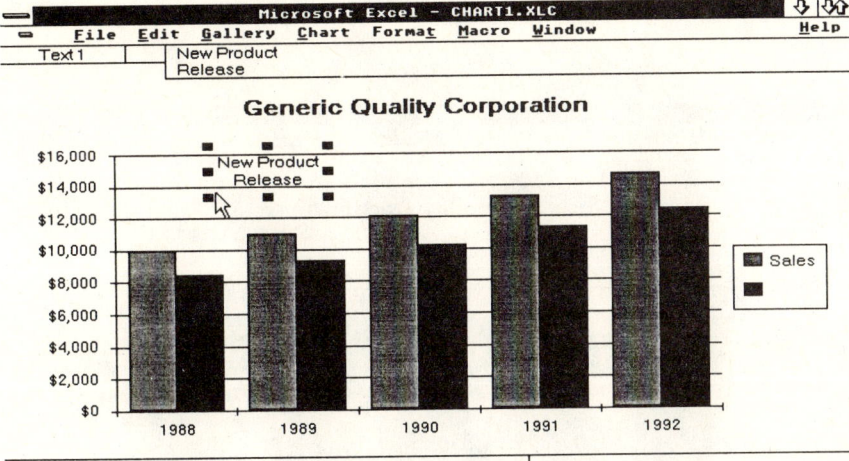

Fig. 14.14. The unattached text, New Product Release, in position.

If gridlines cut the *New Product Release* text, format the text with a white background by choosing Format **F**ont and then select **W**hite Out as the Background option. (The text still must be selected to be formatted.)

Adding an Arrow

Arrows help connect your unattached text to the specific point that the text addresses. To add an arrow to the chart, follow these steps:

1. Choose **C**hart **A**dd **A**rrow.

2. Move the arrow so that the tail is to the right of the last *e* in *Release*.

   Mouse: Drag the middle of the arrow until the tail is in position, and then release the mouse button.

   Keyboard: Choose Format Move while the arrow is selected. Press the arrow keys to move the entire arrow, and then press Enter.

3. Change the size of the arrow so that its head points to the top of the first column in 1990.

   Mouse: Drag the black box at the arrow's head to the correct position.

   Keyboard: Choose Format Size. Press the arrow keys to move the arrow's head into position, and then press Enter.

Your chart now includes the floating text and arrow that appear in figure 14.15.

Fig. 14.15. An arrow linking text to a point on the chart.

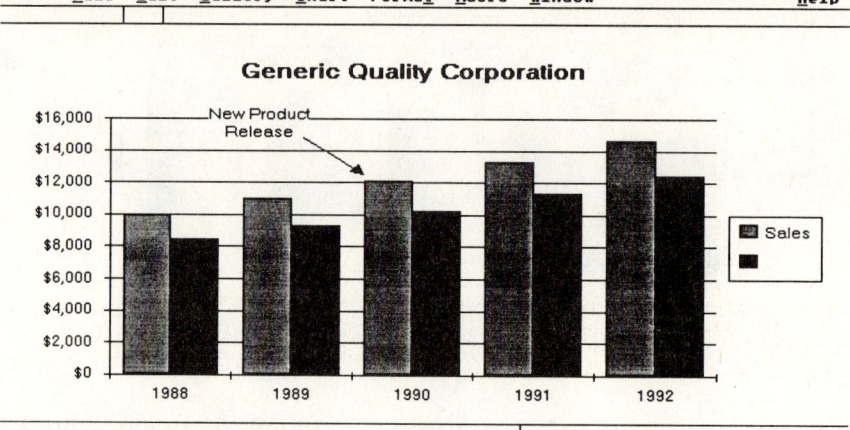

Customizing a Chart's Series Formula

The columns of a chart, known as *series markers*, are linked to worksheet data with *series formulas*. You can edit one of these formulas in the formula bar to add a name to the data series (to be used in the legend) or to change the range of the linked data. Editing the series formula is discussed more fully in Chapter 16, "Building Advanced Charts."

Complete the following steps to add text to the legend by changing the series formula of the total cost markers:

1. Select the total cost markers.

   Mouse: Click on the shortest set of total cost markers (columns).

   Keyboard: Press the up- or down-arrow key until the shortest set of total cost markers (columns) is selected.

   When the total cost markers are selected, white squares like those shown in figure 14.16 appear within a few of the markers. (White squares do not need to appear in every marker of a set.) Notice that the formula bar displays the series formula that describes the origins of the data for these markers. Because the chart data came from a worksheet, the data for the markers links to the chart via an external reference:

   FORCST03.XLS!$B$12:$F$12

The last number in the series formula, 2, indicates that this is the second data series.

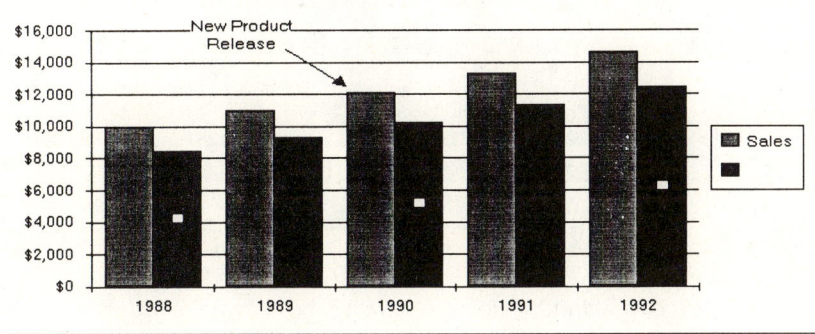

2. To add a name to this data series and simultaneously create a name in the legend, press F2 (the Edit key), and then edit the formula

   =SERIES(,,FORCST03.XLS!$B$12:$F$12,2)

   so that it appears as

   =SERIES("Total Cost",,FORCST03.XLS!$B$12:$F$12,2)

3. Press Enter.

The name you add, *Total Cost*, is text; therefore, it must be enclosed in quotation marks. Chapter 16, "Building Advanced Charts," explains how to enter into a series formula an external reference to worksheet text or to multiple sets of data.

Your finished chart now should look like figure 14.17.

Viewing Worksheet Changes in a Chart

An excellent way to take advantage of Excel's multiple window capability is to display a chart and its related worksheet in separate windows on the screen at the same time. This technique lets you perform various "what if?" calculations in your worksheet and see the results appear immediately in the chart

Fig. 14.17. A completed two-column chart.

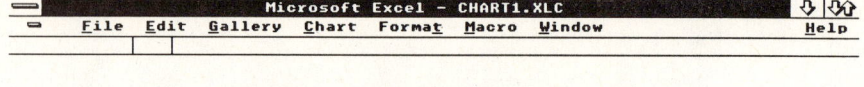

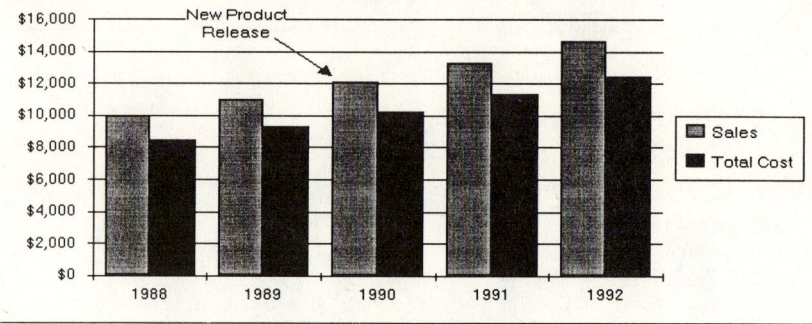

window. The chart window doesn't have to be active in order to update automatically. Figure 14.18 shows one way that you can position the worksheet and chart windows.

Fig. 14.18. Displaying the chart as you change the worksheet shows the chart changes immediately.

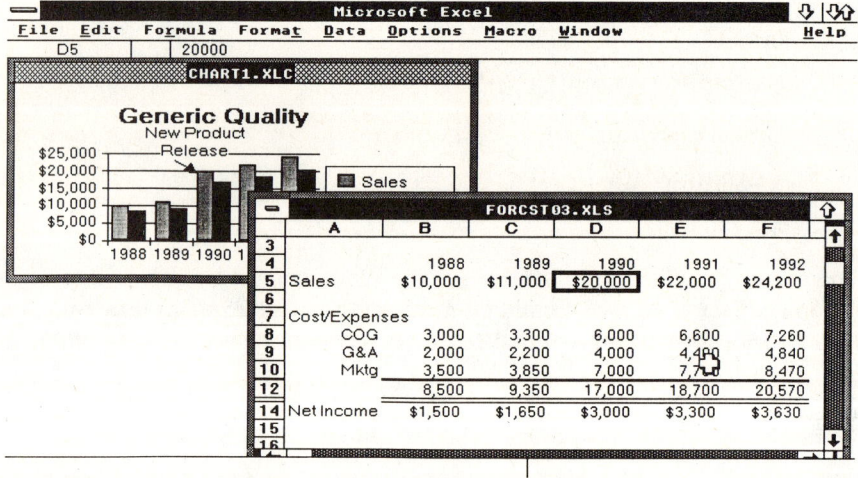

To position the chart and worksheet windows on the screen at the same time, follow these steps:

1. Restore the chart to normal window size.

   Mouse: Click on the hyphen icon (at the left edge of the menu bar), then click on **Restore**.

> **Keyboard:** Press Alt and then the hyphen key, and then select **R**elease.

2. Reposition each window so that you can see both the worksheet and chart.

> **Mouse:** Drag the title bar of each window into position, and then drag the lower right corner to resize the window.

> **Keyboard:** Press Alt and then the hyphen key, and then choose **M**ove or **S**ize to change the active window.

3. Activate the worksheet window by pressing Ctrl+F6 or clicking on it until the worksheet is on top.

Now you can change data in the lower part of the worksheet and watch the chart change.

Printing a Chart

After you have finished creating and customizing a chart, of course, you will want to print it. If your printer is already installed, follow these steps to print the chart:

1. Activate the chart window.

2. Choose **F**ile **P**rint.

3. When the Print dialog box appears, press Enter.

You can preview charts on-screen before printing, add headers and footers, or change margins just as you would when printing a worksheet.

From Here . . .

You can close the chart, save it, or leave it open. Leaving the chart open as you skim through the chapters on charting is a good idea. When you see a chart feature that looks interesting, experiment with it.

One of the best and easiest ways to learn the myriad of features available in charting is to experiment. When you run into difficulty, check the feature or command description in Chapters 15, 16, or 17.

Creating and Enhancing Charts

With Excel, you can create charts that are good enough for any boardroom presentation. When you analyze a worksheet or database, you can build any of Excel's 44 preformatted charts with just a few keystrokes, then customize it with numerous options and overlays. When you print the chart on a laser printer or plotter, the quality rivals that of an annual report.

This chapter explains the details of what you accomplished in the Chart Quick Start. You will also learn many more customizing features. After finishing this chapter, you will be able to meet the majority of business charting needs.

The chapter begins by explaining how Excel determines which text and cell contents are used as category and value labels. After looking at the 44 pre-defined chart formats in the gallery, you will find explanations showing how to customize your chart. You can customize by changing the pattern and border of any chart object, move objects such as legends, add and position arrows, and enter titles and movable text. Because Excel is so graphically oriented, you can change the type font, size, and style and see the results on-screen. Because of minor variations in printers, you will want to preview your completed chart on-screen before printing. Excel's print preview feature shows you exactly how the chart will print.

1-2-3 TIP

Improving Lotus 1-2-3 Graphs

If you have generated a graph from a 1-2-3 worksheet, you can significantly improve it with Excel. Retrieve the 1-2-3 worksheet and its current graph by choosing Excel's File Open command, changing the file name wild cards from *.XL? to *.WK? so that you can view Lotus files, and opening the 1-2-3 work-sheet in its own Excel document window. When Excel automatically translates and loads the 1-2-3 files, it also converts the active 1-2-3 graph and any named graphs into Excel charts. Now you can use Excel's charting power to change, enhance, or print the graph as you want.

> Excel does not translate Lotus 1-2-3 PrintGraph files that end with .PIC. Only graphs that are still in the worksheet are translated.

An Overview of the Charting Process

Before you begin to experiment with charts, take a few minutes to go over some of the basics. This section gives you an overview of the basic charting process, shows you a few examples of charts, and explains basic charting terms.

The Basic Steps for Creating a Chart

Usually, creating a chart consists of the steps that follow. Each of these steps, along with the specific options you can choose along the way, is described in detail later in this chapter.

1. Select the worksheet data, including the labels along the short side of the selection for each data series.

2. Choose File New, select the Chart option, and press Enter.

3. Choose Gallery, select the chart type you want, and choose one of the available formats from the selections in the dialog box.

4. Choose Chart Select Chart, and set the chart's pattern and fonts. Use a font and size that your printer can print.

5. Choose Chart Select Plot Area, and set the border and background pattern and colors.

6. Add custom objects such as titles, legends, and arrows by choosing them from the Chart menu.

7. Add and position unattached text.

8. Change the appearance or location of custom objects by selecting them and then making a choice from the Format commands.

> **NOTE**
>
> ### Changing Chart Type After You Customize
>
> When you begin customizing, changing the chart type with a Gallery command removes customization. To change the type and preserve custom enhancements, use the Format Main Chart command.

Excel Chart Examples

Figures 15.1 and 15.2 are just two examples of Excel charts you can create using Excel by itself. When coupled with other Windows software, you can enhance Excel charts even further and print them within your written reports.

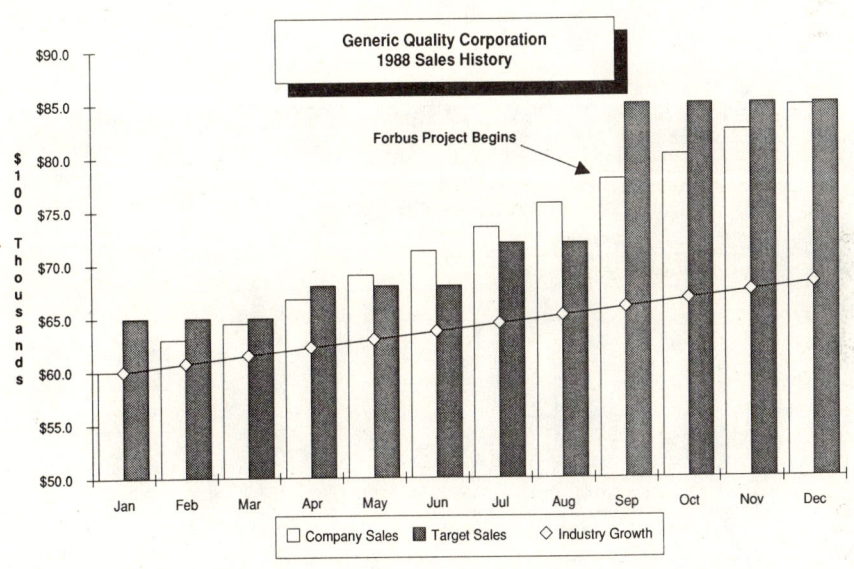

Fig. 15.1. An example of an Excel chart.

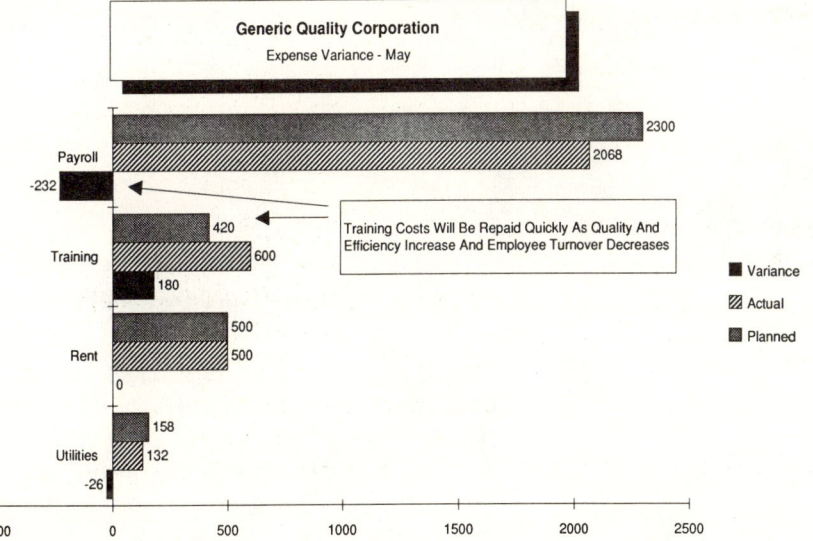

Fig. 15.2. Another example of an Excel chart.

Graphically Explicit Terms

Excel charts contain many different objects that can be selected individually and modified. Figure 15.3 shows some of these objects. Each object shown in the figure is explained in table 15.1.

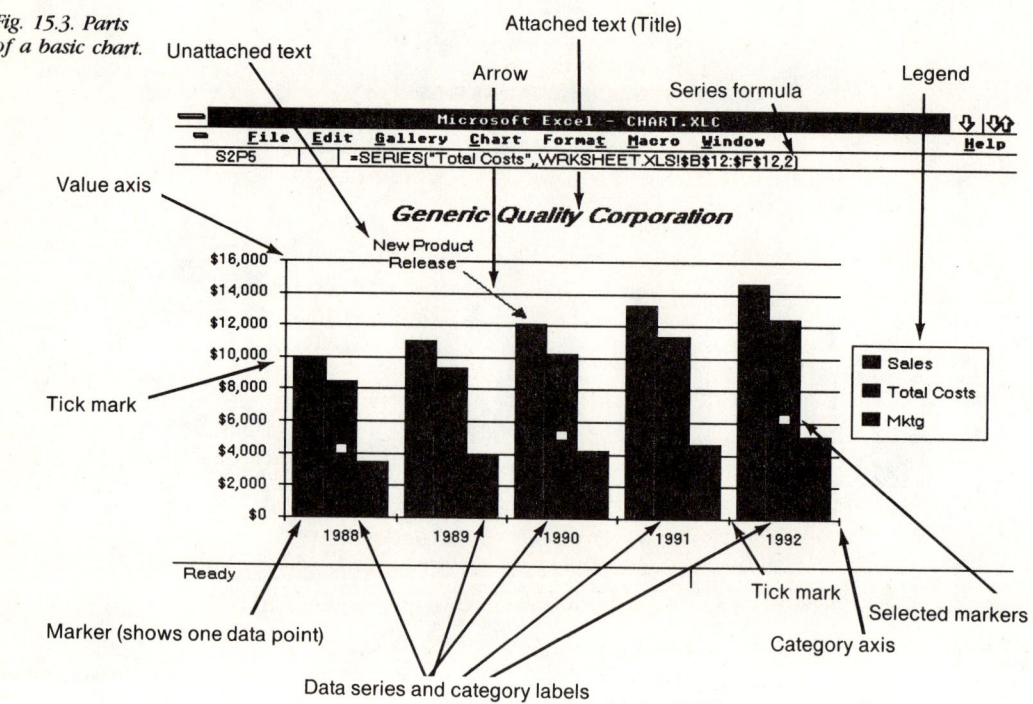

Fig. 15.3. Parts of a basic chart.

Table 15.1
Parts of an Excel Chart

Object	Description
Arrow	A movable and sizable arrow that can be formatted as an arrow or line. Charts can have multiple arrows.
Axis	The *category axis* and *value axis* form the boundaries of a chart and contain the scale against which data plots. The category axis is the horizontal or x-axis and frequently refers to time series. The value axis is the vertical or y-axis that data points are measured against.

Object	Description
	(Axes for bar charts are reversed from this. Pie charts have no axes.)
Data point	A single piece of data, such as sales for one year.
Data series	A collection of data points such as sales for the years from 1988 to 1992.
Legend	A guide that explains the symbols, patterns, or colors used to differentiate data series. The name of each data series is used as the legend title.
Marker	An object that represents a data point in a chart. Bars, pie wedges, and symbols are examples of markers. All the markers belonging to the same data series appear as the same shape, symbol, and color.
Plot area	The rectangular area bounded by the two axes. This area also exists around a pie chart. A pie chart will not exceed the plot area when wedges are extracted.
Series formula	An external reference formula that tells Excel where to look on a specific worksheet to find the data for a chart. A chart may be linked to multiple worksheets.
Text	*Attached text* such as titles or axis titles cannot be moved. Unattached text can be moved to any location on the chart and may also be used as text or blank boxes.
Tick mark	A division mark along the category or x-axis.

TIP

Bar Chart versus Column Chart

Excel uses the term *column chart* for charts using vertical columns. Excel's *bar charts* appear with horizontal bars.

Selecting Worksheet Data for Your Chart

As you discovered in Chapter 14, "Chart Quick Start," Excel finds the data series in the selected range and determines which labels in the range should be used as names for that data series. Excel examines the data and labels and then builds a chart according to the shape of the range and location of the labels in that range.

To build a chart using the default (preselected) chart type, follow these steps:

1. On the worksheet you want to chart, select the data and labels as shown in figure 15.4.

   Notice that the selected range includes more data points in a series than data series; the range has four data points in a series, but only two data series. *Data points* are the individual data items, such as Revenue for January. A *data series*, in this example, is a collection of revenues for different months.

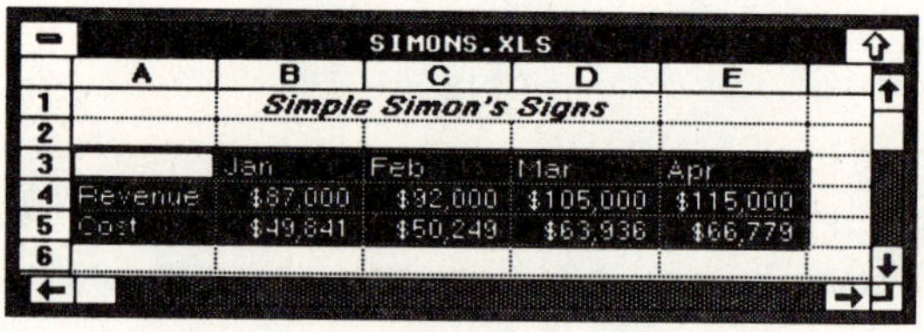

Fig. 15.4. A worksheet with two data series selected for a chart.

2. Choose **File New.**

3. Select the **Chart** option.

4. Choose **OK** or press Enter.

The data will be plotted in the default chart type—normally the column chart. Figure 15.5 shows a column chart created with these steps.

In the chart in figure 15.5, notice that the months (from the top row of the worksheet data) are used as category labels below the x-axis. What would happen if the data was listed down a column as in figure 15.6? If you select the data shown in figure 15.6 and open a new chart window, the chart in figure 15.7 appears. Notice that the chart is still drawn correctly.

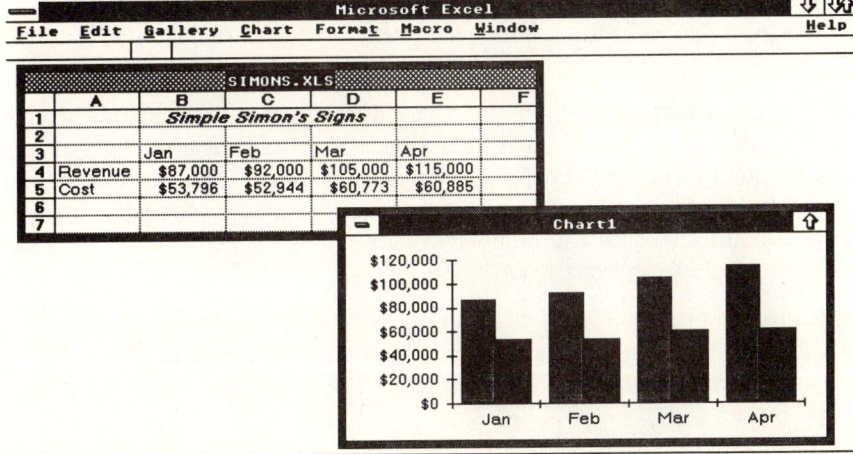

Fig. 15.5. The worksheet and the column chart created from the selected data.

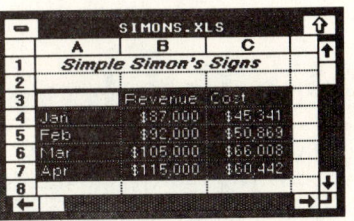

Fig. 15.6. A worksheet with a vertical data series selected.

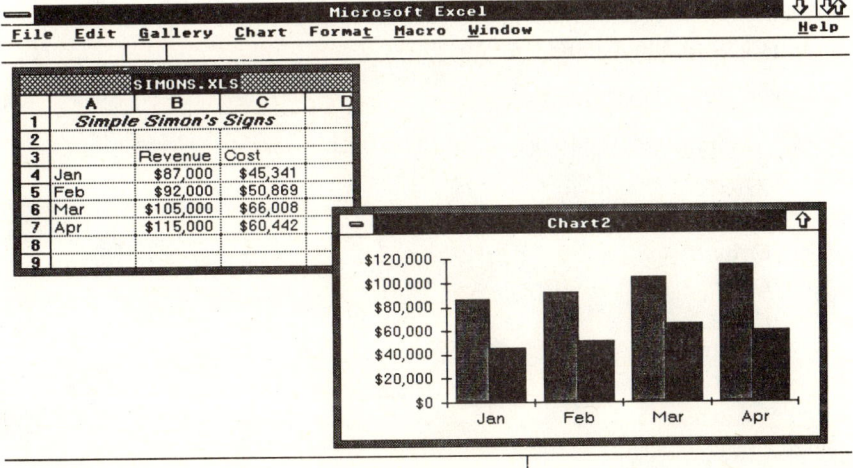

Fig. 15.7. The worksheet and the column chart created from the selected vertical data series.

In the preceding two examples, Excel drew the chart as you expected. Excel, however, can "guess" wrong about the vertical or horizontal orientation of data.

How does Excel know whether the data is horizontal or vertical and where the labels are? Excel assumes that the number of data points is always greater than the number of data series. For example, in figure 15.4, the worksheet has two series of data, Revenue and Cost; and each series has four data points, one per month. Because the number of data points exceeds the number of series, Excel draws the chart correctly.

Excel also assumes that labels along the *short* side of the data range apply to each data series. If only one data series is selected, Excel uses these labels to title the chart. If more than one data series is selected, Excel uses the labels to title the legend.

Labels along the *long* side of the data range define the category axis (x-axis). You can use numbers for the category labels, but you must make sure that the short side of the data range has text labels and has a blank cell at the upper left corner.

Using Preselected Chart Types

When Excel charts selected data, the program uses one of the 44 preformatted charts. You can change the display type of the active chart just by selecting a different type from the gallery.

1. Activate the chart you want to change.

    Mouse: Click within the chart.

    Keyboard: Press Ctrl+F6 until the chart is active or choose the chart from the **Window** menu.

2. Select the **Gallery** menu.

3. From the menu, choose one of these chart types:

    Area
    Bar
    Column
    Line
    Pie
    Scatter
    Combination

After you make your choice, a dialog box appears showing the different formats available for that chart type. Figure 15.8 shows the gallery of formats available for area charts.

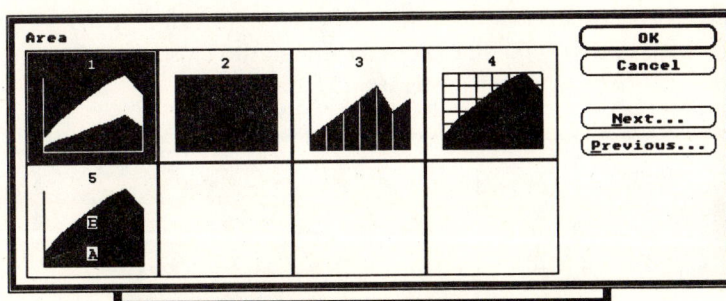

Fig. 15.8. The Area chart gallery box.

4. Select the format example you want.

   Mouse: Click on the format.

   Keyboard: Type the number of the format.

5. Choose OK or press Enter.

After seeing the formats available for that chart type, you may want to see what is available for other chart types. Instead of going back to the **Gallery** menu, choose the **Next** or **Previous** button, as shown in figure 15.8. These buttons are in each gallery box; the buttons switch to the gallery to present the chart type that is next or previous in the **Gallery** menu.

NOTE

You Lose Custom Formats When You Change the Chart Type

When you change the chart type by choosing a new type from the gallery, you lose the custom formatting on the chart. Instead of choosing from the gallery, use Format Main Chart to change types on customized charts whose customizing you want to preserve (see this chapter's "Changing Chart Types" section).

Types of Charts in the Gallery

Excel's six single chart types plus combination charts give you many options. To help you select the correct type of chart to match the data and analysis, the following pages show how each type of chart is generally used.

Line Charts

A line chart compares continuous trends. Use it in sales or stock market charts to show the trend of revenue or sales over time. In the Hi-Lo charts, numbers 7 and 8, point lines extend from the highest to the lowest value in each category. In the stock market, Hi-Lo charts show the high and low stock price on each day with the line plotted through the closing stock price. The gallery of line charts is shown in figure 15.9.

Fig. 15.9. The gallery of line charts.

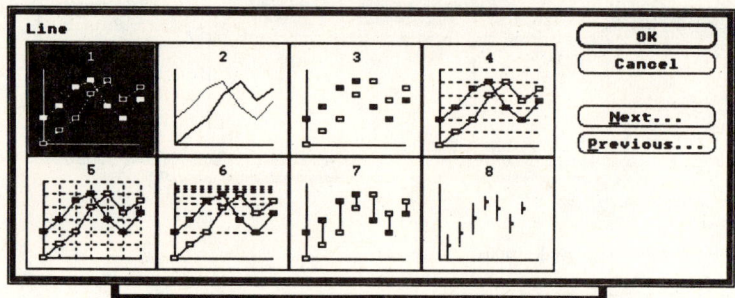

Area Charts

An area chart compares the continuous change in volume. Use this type of chart in sales and production to show how volume changes over time and to emphasize the amount or volume of change. The subjects of area charts may be similar to line charts such as units shipped per day or the volume of orders over time. The gallery of area charts is shown in figure 15.10.

Fig. 15.10. The gallery of area charts.

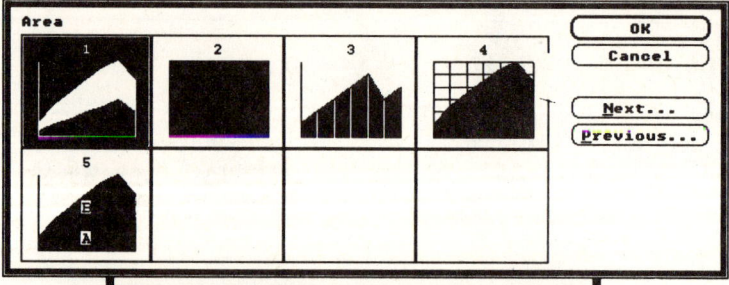

Bar Charts

A bar chart is used to compare distinct items (noncontinuous) that are not related over time. This chart type gives little impression of time, but uses horizontal bars to show positive or negative variation from a center point.

Bar charts can be used to give a "single-point-in-time" snapshot of budget variance for different items. Bars to the left of center have negative variance while those to the right have positive variance. The gallery of bar charts is shown in figure 15.11.

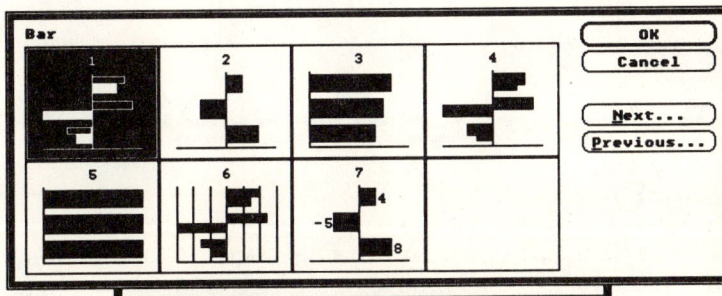

Fig. 15.11. The gallery of bar charts.

Column Charts

A column chart compares separate items (noncontinuous) as they vary over time. This chart type uses vertical columns to give the impression of distinct measurements made at different time periods. Column charts are frequently used to compare different items by placing them side by side in a column chart. For example, in the Chart Quick Start, the total sales and total costs are charted in columns by the month. The gallery of column charts is shown in figure 15.12.

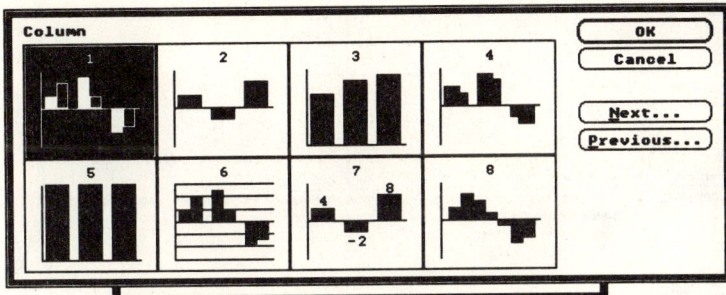

Fig. 15.12. The gallery of column charts.

Pie Charts

A pie chart compares the size of pieces that make up a whole unit. Use this type of chart when the parts total 100 percent for a single series of data. Only the first data series is plotted. Pie charts work well to show the percentage of mix in products shipped, mix in income sources, or mix in target populations. The gallery of pie charts is shown in figure 15.13.

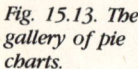

Fig. 15.13. The gallery of pie charts.

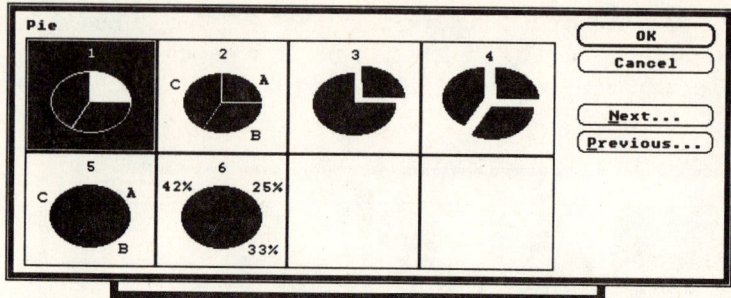

Scatter Charts

A scatter chart determines patterns from discrete X and Y data measurements. Some measurements may produce the same X value with the same or different Y values. Use scatter charts when you must plot items that aren't related over time or some other sequence. For example, survey data when plotted with response on the value axis (y-axis) and age on the category axis (x-axis) can reveal opinion clusters by age. Much scientific and engineering data is charted with scatter charts. For example, plotting hormone dosage against weight gain could reveal interesting relationships. The gallery of scatter charts is shown in figure 15.14.

Fig. 15.14. The gallery of scatter charts.

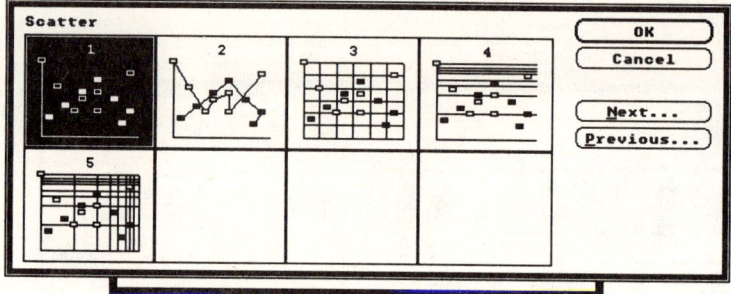

Combination Charts

A combination chart compares different chart types or different scaling systems by overlaying up to four charts. One of the many uses for combination charts is to plot raw data on a scatter chart and then overlay that with a trend line chart. Calculate the trend line from the raw data using the TREND function, then graph the trend line as an overlaid line chart. (An example TREND calculation is done in Chapter 11, "Building Advanced Worksheets.") The gallery of combination charts is shown in figure 15.15.

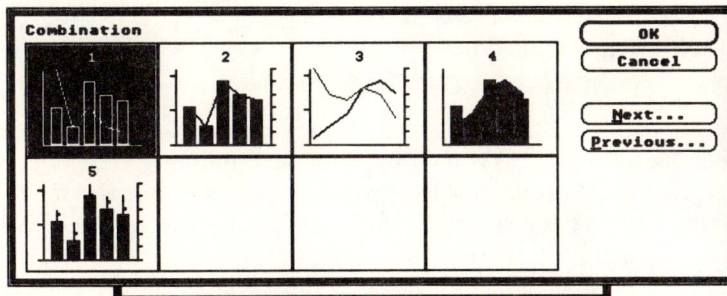

Fig. 15.15. The gallery of combination charts.

You can modify the charts available in the Combination gallery in two ways. You can add elements such as arrows, text, and legends, or you can make changes to the fundamental chart with Format Main Chart. This command, described in the "Changing Chart Types" section of this chapter, enables you to change such things as the percentage of overlap between adjacent bars, the distance between clusters, and the angle of the first wedge in a pie chart.

Choosing a Preferred Chart Format

If you deal with the same chart type and format regularly, you may want to designate that type and format as those Excel automatically uses to draw charts. To change Excel's default chart type and format, follow these steps:

1. Open a chart.

2. Choose the type chart and preformatted selection you want.

3. Customize the chart using the commands described in the "Customizing a Chart" section in this chapter.

4. Select the chart to be sure that it is active.

5. Choose **Gallery Set Preferred**.

Any new charts you open from this worksheet will use the preferred type you have set.

After you have chosen **Gallery Set Preferred**, you can continue to try different chart types and formats. Whenever you want to return to your preferred type and format, choose the **Gallery Preferred** command.

Analyzing Worksheets with Charts

With Excel, you can make changes to your worksheet and watch the chart as it immediately reflects those changes. This capability is valuable for performing "what if" types of analysis. Being able to see the effects of your work-sheet changes means that you can more easily determine emerging trends, crossover points between profit and loss, and mistakes made during data entry.

As figure 15.16 illustrates, you can set worksheet and chart windows so that they are all visible. As you change a variable in the worksheet created during Chapter 4's "Worksheet Quick Start," the Sales vs. Costs and the itemized cost charts both reflect the changes immediately. If you rearrange windows, you can see multiple analyses at the same time.

Fig. 15.16. A worksheet with two different charts.

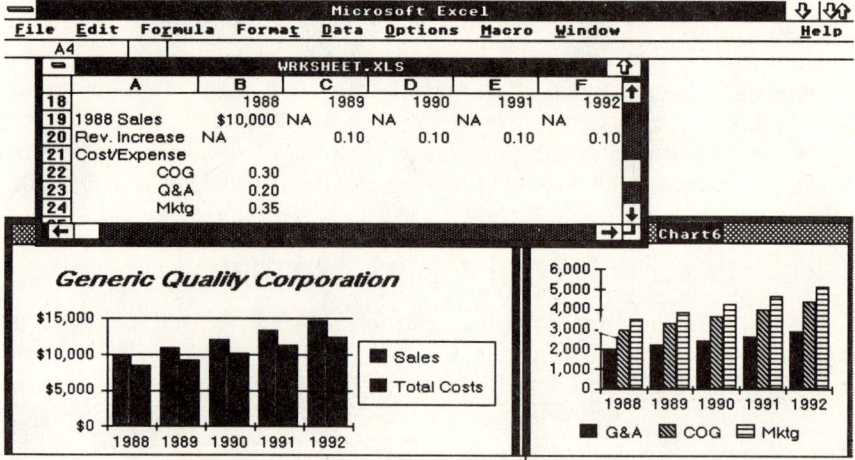

Customizing a Chart

After you decide on the basic chart format, it's time to customize your chart so that the information you want is easy to understand and the point you want to make is highlighted. Excel makes this easy to do.

Customizing uses a procedure consistent with making changes in the work-sheet. The steps to customizing are:

1. Select the graphic item you want to customize by clicking on it or by pressing an up-, down-, left-, or right-arrow key.

2. Choose the Format command to customize the selected item, or choose the **Chart** command to add or delete an item such as a legend, attached text, or arrow.

3. Select the customizing changes you want to make from the dialog box that appears.

4. Choose OK or press Enter.

This section begins by showing you how to change patterns and borders, and follows with how to add text and arrows and move them anywhere you want.

For charting that involves precision, you will learn how to format chart axes with a scale of your choice and change tick mark divisions or add gridlines to make reading charts easier.

Changing the Background Colors, Patterns, and Border

The largest areas in a chart are the chart background and the plot area. The chart background refers to the entire chart; the plot area includes only the area within the axes. You can change the colors, patterns, and boundaries of both areas. Figure 15.17 shows an area chart with patterns chosen for the chart background and plot area, and with the axes text in bold.

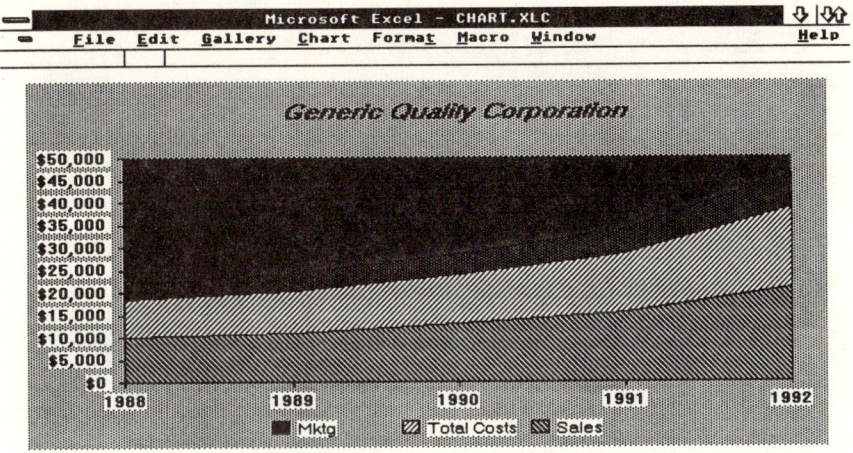

Fig. 15.17. An area chart with patterns in the chart background and plot area, and bold font in the axes text.

NOTE

Set the Chart Background before Customizing

The chart background takes priority over patterns or colors chosen for the plot area. Set the chart background first. If you later change the background, you will wipe out previous plot area settings.

To change the backgrounds of the chart and plot areas, follow these steps:

1. Activate the chart window.

   Mouse: Click on the chart.

   Keyboard: Press Ctrl+F6 until the chart appears on top.

2. Choose **Chart** Select **Chart**.

   White squares appear around the chart.

3. Choose Format **Patterns** to display the dialog box for chart patterns (see fig. 15.18).

   This dialog box has two parts. The upper part controls the color, style, and weight of the border. The lower part controls the pattern, color, style, and weight of the area.

Fig. 15.18. The dialog box for chart patterns.

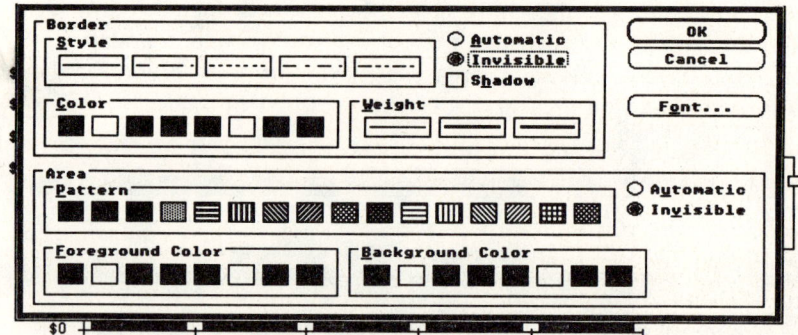

4. From the dialog box, select border and background patterns for the chart background.

   Mouse: Click on the option, color, or pattern you want.

   Keyboard: Press the underlined letter of the option you want. When the cursor appears in the option box you want, make your selection by pressing the right- or left-arrow keys.

   If you want to return the chart background to its default settings, choose the automatic options.

5. Select the Font button if you want to change the text fonts on the x- and y-axes. These fonts can also be changed by choosing Format Font when the chart is selected. Choose OK or press Enter.

6. Change the background within the plot area (the area within the axes) by choosing **Chart** Select Plot **A**rea. White squares appear at the corners of the plot area.

7. Choose Format **P**atterns and select the border and background colors, weights, and patterns for the area within the axes. The dialog box looks similar to the background pattern box; no fonts can be changed from this box.

8. Choose OK or press Enter.

Changing the Color or Pattern of a Marker

Markers are the items (bars, columns, pie wedges, or symbols) that mark a data point on a chart. You can change the color, pattern, and border of a marker by selecting the marker and choosing Format **P**atterns. (Select the marker by clicking on it with the pointer or by pressing the up- or down-arrow key until one or more of the markers you want is selected.)

Figure 15.19 shows the dialog box from Format **P**atterns that you use to change a marker. Selections from the upper boxes change the border style, weight, and color. Selections from the lower boxes change the pattern used to fill the marker. One color appears in the foreground of the pattern; the other color in the background.

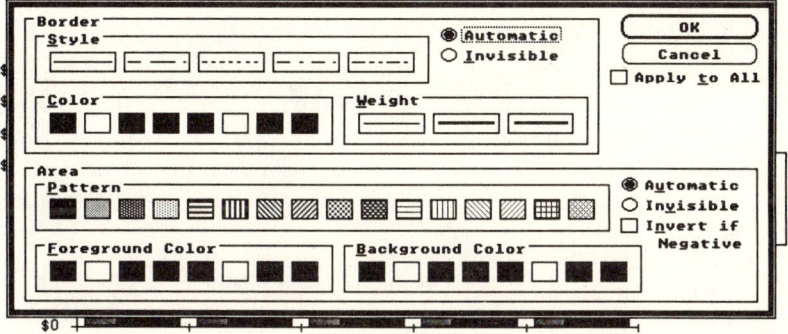

Fig. 15.19. The dialog box for marker patterns.

Make a selection from the dialog box by clicking on it with the pointer. From the keyboard, press the underlined letter of the choice. To select between colors and patterns, press the left- or right-arrow key. To return to the default, choose the automatic option.

Change Patterns and Colors Quickly

With the mouse, you can change the color or pattern of a marker, legend, or other object quickly. When you double-click on the object, the dialog box for patterns appears. When you double-click on a pattern or color, the dialog box closes, and the object changes.

Selecting, Moving, and Sizing Chart Objects

As described earlier, each chart is composed of objects such as text, markers, legends, and axes. When you customize charts, you add objects to the chart, or you select objects in the chart and change them with menu commands.

With the mouse, you select an object on the chart by clicking on that object. From the keyboard, you first select the class of object and then select the specific object from within its class. The classes of chart objects are the following:

- chart background
- axes
- legend
- arrows
- hi-lo lines

- markers
- drop lines
- plot area
- gridlines
- text

From the keyboard, select the class of objects by pressing the up- or down-arrow key to select an object in the class you want. Once you have selected a class, press the left- or right-arrow key to move between objects within that class. When you reach the first or last object in a class, the selection skips to objects in the next class.

Another way to select the two largest chart objects—the plot area and the chart background—is to select the **Chart Select Chart** or **Chart Select Plot Area** commands from the **Chart** menu. Figure 15.20 shows white squares at corners of the selected plot area, and figure 15.21 shows white squares at corners of the selected chart background.

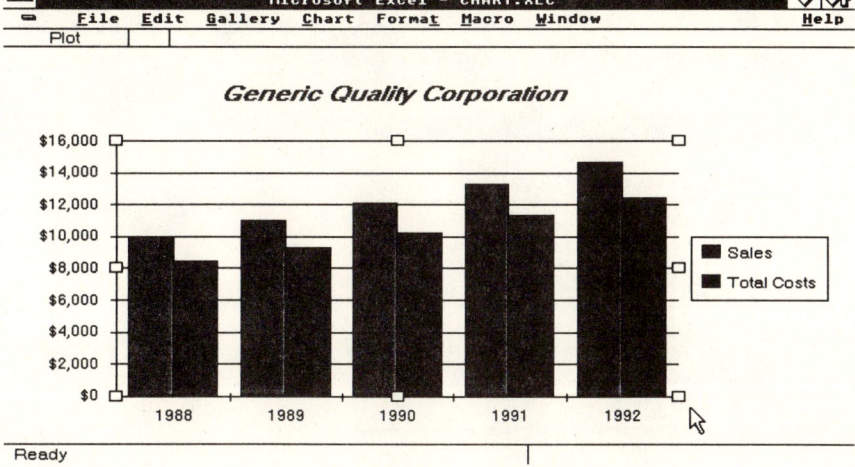

Fig. 15.20. The plot area selected.

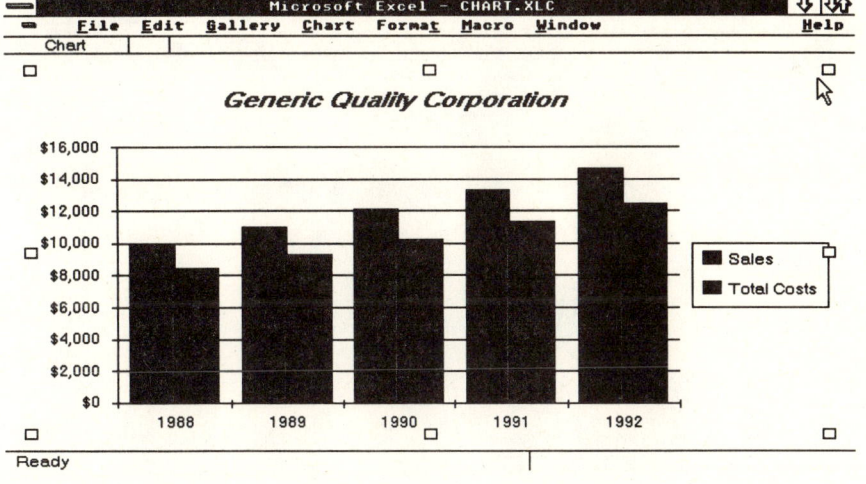

Fig. 15.21. The chart background selected.

Selected objects display white or black squares at their corners. Objects that display white squares cannot be moved or sized with the mouse or arrow keys, but those objects may have alternate locations available through the menu. For example, the legend cannot be moved by mouse or keyboard, but you can reposition the legend by selecting it and choosing Format Legend.

Objects that display black squares can be moved or sized with the mouse or keyboard. In figure 15.22, text appears with black squares enclosing it, signifying that it is selected and is movable.

Fig. 15.22. Text selected in a chart.

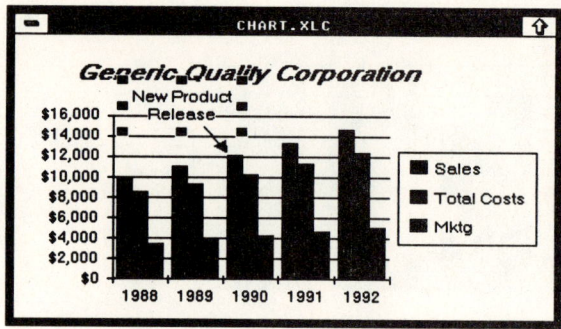

You can move or change the size of objects that display black squares when selected. Some of the movable objects are arrows, pie chart wedges, and unattached text. In figure 15.23, one wedge in the pie chart has just been moved away from the center.

Fig. 15.23. A pie chart with a wedge moved away from the center.

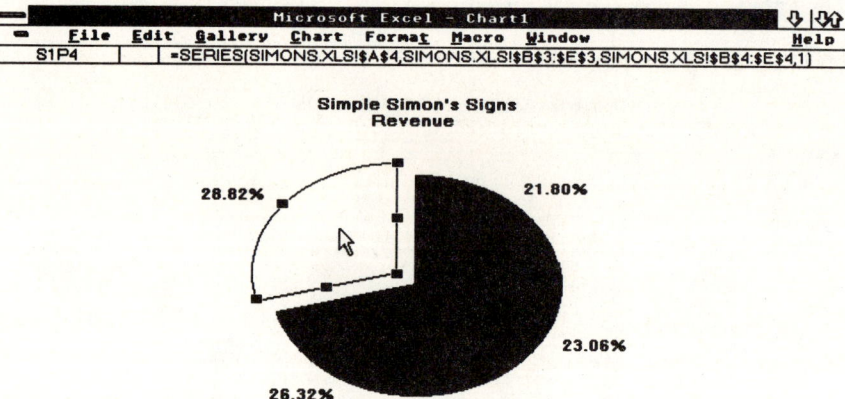

To move an object, follow these steps:

1. Select the object. (Black squares appear.)

   Mouse: Click on the object.

Keyboard: Press the up- or down-arrow key to select the class of objects. Press the left- or right-arrow key to select the specific object from the class. (Use the up- or down-arrow key alone to select markers such as bars, columns, or pie wedges.)

2. Move the object.

Mouse: Drag the object to its new location, and then release the mouse button. To move an arrow or text, drag from the center. Do not drag on a black box or you may change the size of the object. A rectangle shows the object's location as it is being moved.

Keyboard: Choose Format Move. Press the arrow keys to move the object to its new location. Press Enter when the object is positioned at the correct location. (Note: Before you press Enter, you can return the object to its original location by pressing Esc.)

To resize an object with the mouse, select the object by clicking on it, and then drag one of the black boxes in the direction you want the object resized.

To resize via the keyboard, you use a procedure similar to moving an object. Select the object. Choose Format Size, and press the arrow keys to reposition the upper left corner of the box, making it larger or smaller. You may need to move the box after resizing it.

TIP

Moving and Sizing with Precision

If the arrow keys provide movements or size changes that are too large, hold down the Ctrl key as you press the arrow keys. Each press of the arrow then makes a significantly smaller change.

Pie wedges are resized automatically when they are moved. The further they are moved from the center, the smaller the wedges become.

Using the resizing procedure on unattached text does not change the size of the text. The procedure changes only the size of the background box surrounding the text.

Entering Text

Excel charts contain three types of text. First, the chart background includes text along the category (x-axis) and value (y-axis) axes. Excel gets this text from the worksheet data. Excel's second form of text is attached to specific objects such as a title, an axis, or a data point. This text can have different fonts, colors, or patterns. The third form of text is not attached to any other object and is the most flexible of the three types of text. You can position unattached text anywhere and use different fonts, backgrounds, and colors. Unattached text is the building block for many of the tips and suggestions you will find throughout the chart chapters of this book.

Attached Text and Titles

The chart shown in figure 15.24 has text attached to the title position, value axis (y-axis) position, category axis (x-axis) position, and a data point above the third data point marker in the first series. When you first choose the location of new attached text, temporary text such as the word "Title" appears at that location surrounded by white selection squares. You then edit the temporary text to say what you want.

Fig. 15.24.
Attached text
surrounded by
white selection
squares.

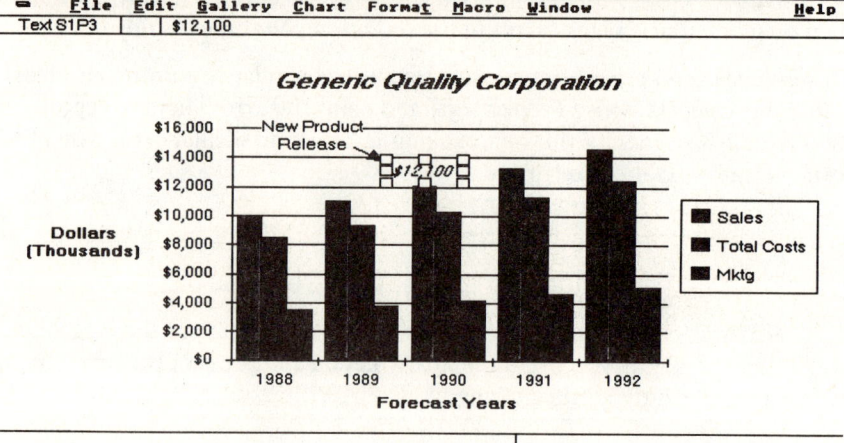

To attach text, follow these steps:

1. Choose **Chart Attach Text**.

2. Select the location for the attached text:

Object	*Location*
Chart **Title**	Centers the temporary text "Title" above the chart
Value Axis	Centers the temporary text "Y" on value (vertical) axis

Category Axis	Centers the temporary text "X" under category (horizontal) axis
Series or Data Point	Attaches label for the entire series to the last marker; or, for a data point, attaches the value of the data point to that specific marker

3. If you chose Series or Data Point, enter the number of the series in **S**eries Number and the number of the data point in **P**oint Number.

   In a column chart, the first series is the column closest to the vertical axis. In a bar chart, the first series is the bar closest to the horizontal axis. All the patterns or colors of a series are the same.

   A data point is one marker within a series. In a column chart, data points are numbered starting with the one closest to the vertical axis. In a bar chart, data point number one is closest to the horizontal axis.

4. Choose OK or press Enter.

   Temporary text is attached to the point indicated and remains selected. The surrounding white squares indicate that the text is selected but is not movable.

5. Edit the temporary text.

   Mouse: Click in the formula bar, and use normal editing procedures.

   Keyboard: Press F2 (the Edit key), and use normal editing procedures.

6. Choose OK or press Enter.

You can customize attached text further by changing its font, size, color, and background using the procedures described in the "Changing Text Appearance" section in this chapter.

> **TIP**
>
> ### Attach Text to Markers with the Mouse
>
> A quick way to attach a text value to a marker (such as the $12,100 in figure 15.24) is first to click on the marker. Then choose Chart Attach Text. The correct **S**eries Number and **P**oint Number already will be entered when you press Enter.

Unattached Text

Creating text that can be placed anywhere on a chart is easy in Excel and extremely useful. Figure 15.24 illustrates how you can add explanations linked by arrows to data points.

To add unattached text to a chart such as the "New Product Release" in figure 15.24, follow these steps:

1. Select a nontext object.

   Mouse: Click on a nontext object.

   Keyboard: Press the up arrow until a nontext object is selected.

2. Type the unattached text.

   Text appears in the formula bar, where you can edit it with normal editing procedures.

3. Press Enter or click on the check box when the text is complete.

The text appears on the chart surrounded by small black squares, which indicate that the text background can be moved and sized. The text also can be deleted or edited. Delete unattached text by selecting the unattached text, and pressing the backspace key followed by Enter.

> **TIP**
>
> ### Typing Multiple Lines of Unattached Text
>
> When you are entering unattached text and want to continue on the next text line, press Ctrl+Enter.

TIP

Editing Unattached Text

You can edit unattached text at any time by selecting it and editing it in the formula bar. Move the selected text into the formula bar by pressing F2 (the Edit key).

To move or size unattached text from the keyboard, follow these steps:

1. Select the text by pressing the up- or down-arrow key until text somewhere on-screen is selected.

2. Press the right- or left-arrow key to select the specific unattached text.

3. Choose Format Move or Format Size.

4. Move the text or change its size with the arrow keys.

5. Press Enter to fix the text's position or size. (Or, to abandon the process, press Esc.)

As you change the size of the text block, the words wrap to form new breaks, adjusting to fit the new space.

To move text with the mouse, select the text, and then drag the center of the text to its new location. Size text blocks with the mouse by selecting the text and dragging one of the black squares in the direction you want the size changed. Dragging the box does not change the size of the characters, only the size of the text background. This feature is useful when you need to insert a block of a specific size in the background to cover part of a chart.

Changing Text Appearance

After you have selected a block of unattached text, you can change its appearance with Format commands. Choosing Format Patterns displays a dialog box from which you can change the background and background border patterns (see fig. 15.25). Options you select from the dialog box affect the area between the enclosing black squares and the text.

Fig. 15.25. The dialog box for background and border patterns.

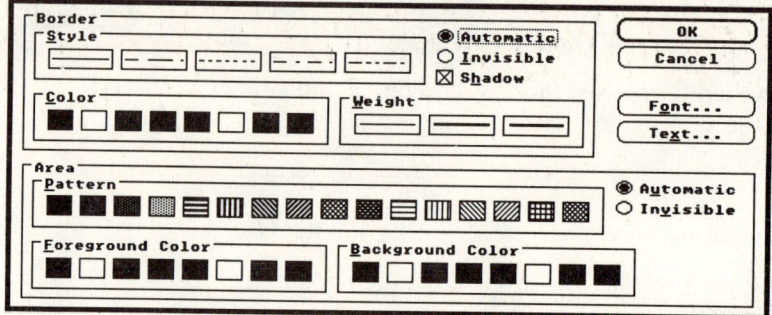

Selecting Format Font displays a dialog box from which you can change the text font, style, and color of the text in the currently selected item (see fig. 15.26). You also can change the immediate background behind the text. If you want a background color to show behind the text, choose a **White Out** background. The area behind the text will be the color selected in **Color**, (which may not be white). Choosing **Transparent** lets the background show through. **Automatic** lets Excel choose the background color.

Fig. 15.26. The Font dialog box.

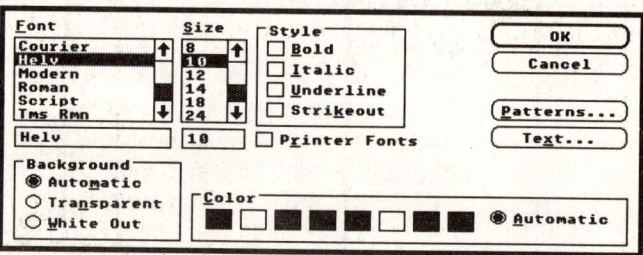

TIP

Hiding Sections of a Chart

To hide selected parts of a chart, use an empty text block with a background color that matches the chart area being covered. The procedure is similar to the one described earlier for creating unattached text. First, create an "empty" unattached text box by making an unattached text box that contains only a single space character. While the text block is still selected, choose Format **Patterns** and select a **Foreground** and **Background** color that matches the area being covered. Then use Format **Move** and Format **Size** to fit the text block over the chart area you want hidden.

Avoid Using Too Many Fonts

Be careful not to use too many fonts on a chart. Using many different fonts is confusing and wastes memory. Text is easier to read if the reader's vision doesn't have to change between more than two fonts. Use the Size and Style options from the Format Font dialog box to emphasis particular text.

The Forma**t T**ext command displays a dialog box from which you can change the text alignment and its horizontal or vertical orientation (see fig. 15.27). After choosing Vertical Text, you usually will need to resize the text block. Be sparing with your use of vertical text; this type of text is difficult to read.

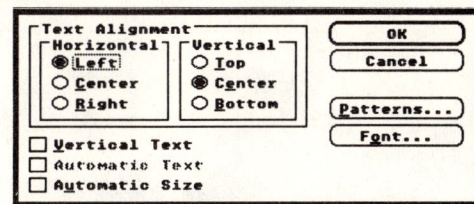

Fig. 15.27. The Text Alignment dialog box.

When a Format Patterns or Format Font dialog box is displayed, you can make your selections by clicking on your choice or by pressing the option's underlined letter. To choose between colors or patterns, press the appropriate letter, and then press the left- or right-arrow key to move between color or pattern boxes.

Unattached text is the trickster of Excel charts. You can move unattached text, color it, resize it, use it to create organizational charts or flow diagrams, and even use it to cover over parts of a chart you do not want to display.

You can add lengthy text blocks between marker clusters as shown in figure 15.28. Chapter 16, "Building Advanced Charts," explains how to insert space between specific clusters or markers.

Use an Excel Chart for Freeform Text and Drawing

You can do more than enhance charts with unattached text. As an example, create a blank chart. Select a blank cell on a worksheet, choose File New, select the Chart option, and press Enter. This procedure creates a blank chart you can use as an easel for experimenting with unattached text.

Now you can generate paragraphs of type that you can reshape to fit any column size. Enter the unattached text as explained previously. Reposition and size the text block. Choose Forma**t** **P**atterns to select invisible borders, or choose borders and backgrounds to add emphasis. You also can add arrows. To create your own diagrams, use empty text blocks that are patterned.

When you need lines, choose the no-arrowhead pattern with Forma**t** **P**atterns to change the arrowhead into a line. (See the "Making Straight Lines" tip in the following section.)

Fig. 15.28. A lengthy block of unattached text added between marker clusters.

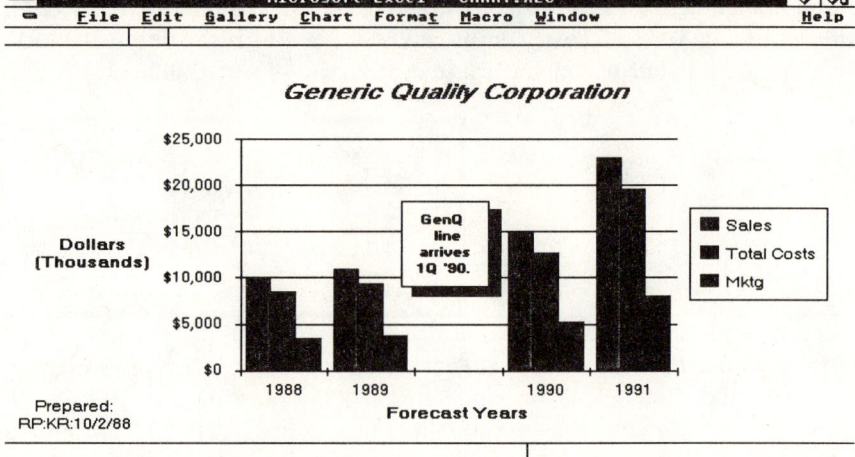

If you create programs for others to use, you can include instructions and help screens designed specifically for your programs. If you create custom menus with Excel macros, you can have these help screens appear whenever an operator makes particular selections from a custom menu. Figure 15.29 shows one such help screen.

Using a blank chart created by selecting a blank worksheet cell, you even can use unattached text to create simple organizational charts or posters such as the ones shown in figures 15.30 and 15.31.

Adding Arrows

You can really make your point with an arrow. Use arrows and unattached text to point to spots you want to identify or explain on a chart. Arrows also show direction in flow charts and organization charts. (Build flow charts and organization charts with unattached text blocks, as explained in the preceding section.) Headless arrows serve as straight lines in charts.

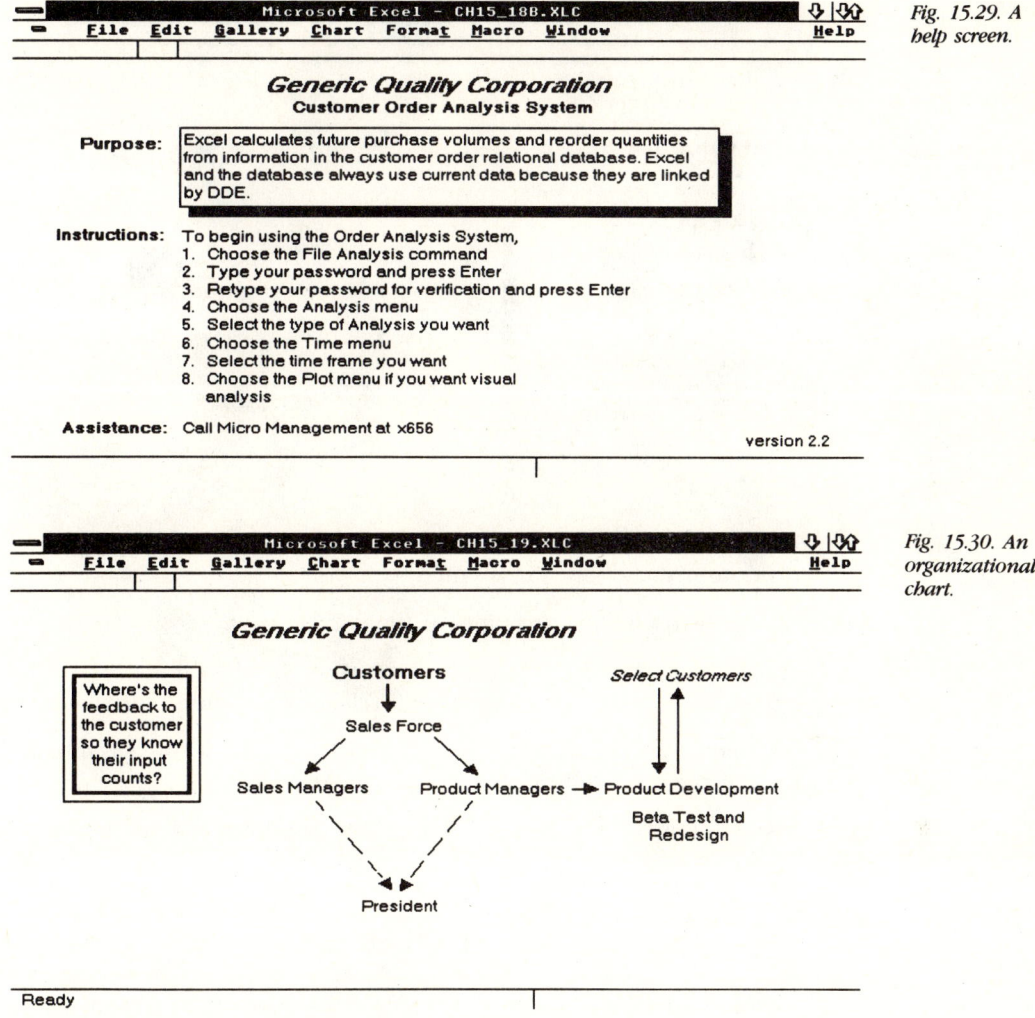

Fig. 15.29. A help screen.

Fig. 15.30. An organizational chart.

To add an arrow to an active chart, follow these steps:

1. Choose **Chart Add Arrow.**

   An arrow that points from the upper left corner to midscreen appears.

2. Move the arrow until its tail is in the correct position.

   Mouse: Drag the center of the arrow until the arrow is positioned, and then release the mouse button.

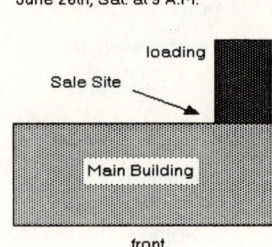

Keyboard: Choose Format Move, and then press the arrow keys to position the arrow. Press Enter.

3. Size the arrow so that it points to the correct spot.

   Mouse: Drag the black square at the arrow's head so that the head is at the correct spot, and then release the mouse button.

   Keyboard: Choose Format Size, and then press the arrow keys to position the arrow's head. Press Enter.

Move or size arrows in small increments by holding down Ctrl as you press an arrow key.

Notice that you cannot add a second arrow immediately because the **Chart Add Arrow** menu item has been replaced by **Chart Delete Arrow.** If you need additional arrows, first select a nonarrow object on the chart, and then the Add Arrow menu item reappears. (Push the up- or down-arrow key, or click on a nonarrow object to select something else.)

You can drag on the black square at either end of the arrow to change the arrow's size and position. Click anywhere on the arrow to initially select it.

Change an arrow's appearance by selecting the arrow, then choosing Format Patterns. The dialog box in figure 15.32 enables you to modify the arrow. (A shortcut to get to the pattern box with the mouse is to double-click on the arrow.)

To remove an arrow, select the arrow you want removed, then choose the Chart Delete Arrow command.

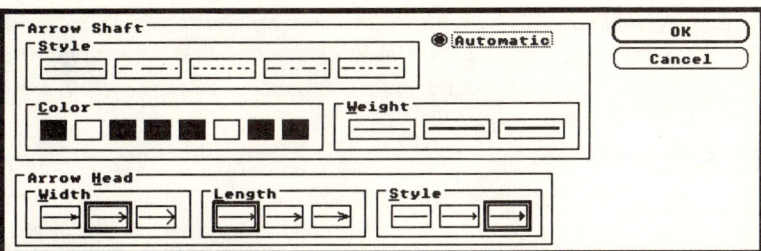

Fig. 15.32. The
dialog box for
arrow patterns.

| | TIP |

Making Straight Lines

Make straight lines from arrows that don't have arrowheads. Change an arrow
to a line by selecting the arrow, then choosing Format **P**atterns. The dialog
box shown in figure 15.32 gives you many alternatives for the color, weight,
and style of the arrow's shaft and head. To make a straight line, select the
straight line from the Arrow Head **S**tyle box at the lower right corner of the
dialog box.

Adding Legends

Legends explain the symbols used in a chart. Excel creates legends from the
labels on the short side of the worksheet data series. Figure 15.33 shows an
example of a legend for a line chart. The legend in the figure was customized
with border, pattern, and font selections.

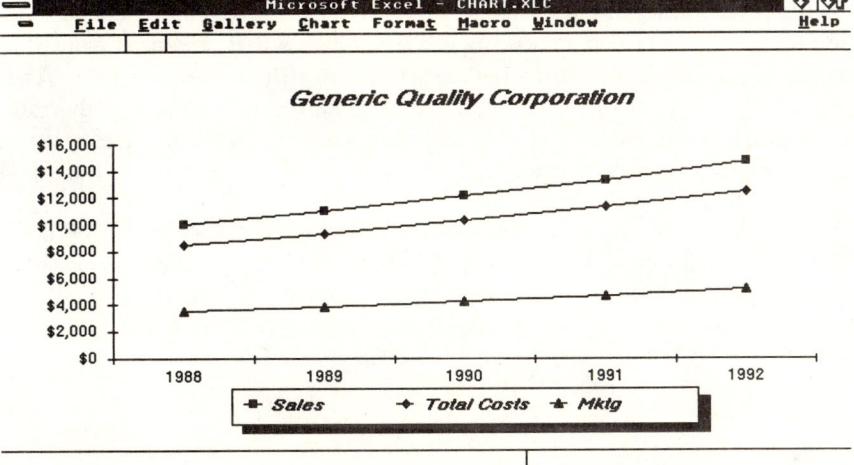

Fig. 15.33. A
line chart with
a customized
legend.

When you want to add a legend, select the chart and choose Chart Add **Legend**. The legend appears on the right side of the chart. When a legend exists on a chart, the Add Legend menu item changes to Delete Legend. You can use that option to delete a legend.

In the same way you changed display characteristics of attached and unattached text, you can change the appearance of a legend. Customize the legend by first selecting the legend so white squares appear at its corners. Then choose Format Font to change the text font, style, size, color, and text background. Use Format **P**atterns to change the border and the foreground and background colors of the area pattern. If you want the legend to blend into the chart's background so that the border and background are invisible, choose the invisible option for both Border and Area under Format **P**atterns.

You can move the legend to a new location by selecting it, and then choosing Format **L**egend. Choose a location from the dialog box shown in figure 15.34.

Fig. 15.34. The Legend dialog box.

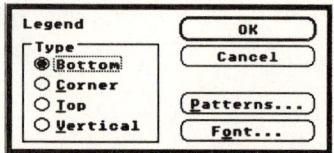

Adding Gridlines

Gridlines help viewers compare markers and read values. In charts such as pie charts, gridlines make no sense; therefore, Excel won't allow you to use them.

When you request gridlines with Chart **G**ridlines, the Gridlines dialog box (see fig. 15.35) lets you choose between gridlines that originate from the category axis (the X or horizontal axis) or from the value axis (the Y or vertical axis). You also can choose whether gridlines will originate only from major divisions on the axis shown in figure 15.35 or whether grids should also appear in between major divisions.

Too many gridlines obscure the chart. They get messy and confusing. In general, don't use gridlines if the chart will be used in an overhead projection. Use them instead in printed materials where readers will need to read charts more precisely. (If you want to display the exact value of a marker, choose Chart Attach **T**ext and select Series or **D**ata Point. This process places the value for a chart marker on that marker.)

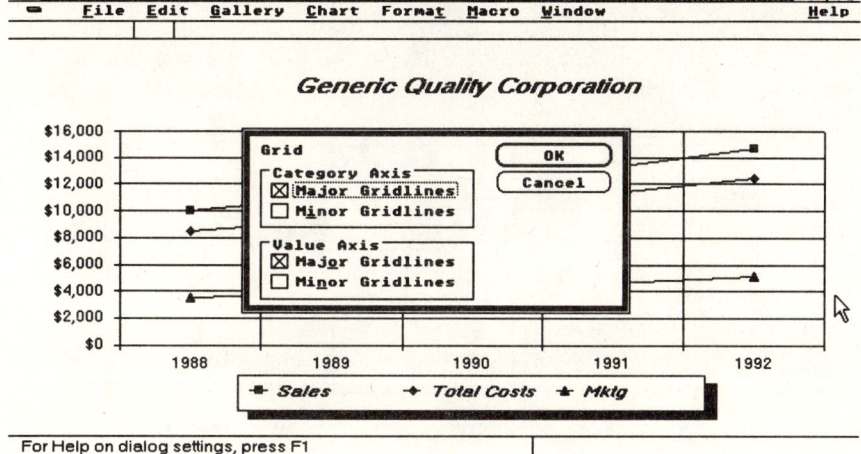

Fig. 15.35. The Gridlines dialog box.

Customizing an Axis

With the mouse or keyboard, you can alter the horizontal category axis or the vertical value axis to change its scale, tick mark placement, fonts, or colors. Follow these steps:

1. Select an axis so that white squares appear at either end.

   Mouse: Click on the axis.

   Keyboard: Press the up- or down-arrow key to select one of the axes. Press the left- or right-arrow key until the axis you want is selected.

2. Select the Format menu.

3. Choose either **Patterns** (line and tick mark styles), **Font**, or **Scale**.

   The dialog box that appears gives you buttons and boxes for the alternatives.

4. Choose the patterns, fonts, or scaling you want.

5. Choose OK or press Enter.

You can take a shortcut with the mouse. Double-click on the axis you want. The dialog box for axis patterns appears immediately. From that dialog box, select the **Font** or **Scale** buttons to make other changes.

Use the dialog box for axis patterns to customize the axis line, the tick mark type, and tick mark label (see fig. 15.36). The Automatic button returns the axis line to a standard configuration. Choose the Font button to change the font used on the axis or choose the Scale button to define a new scale.

Fig. 15.36. The dialog box for axis patterns.

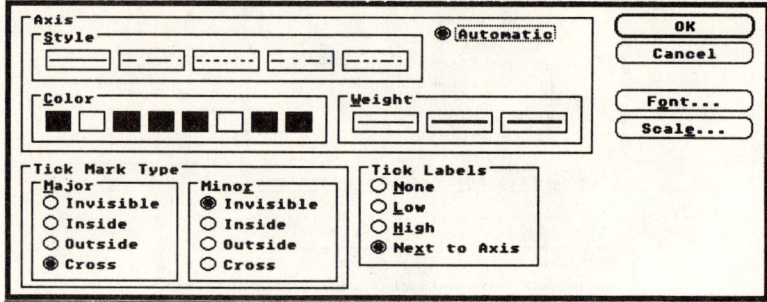

The dialog box for axis fonts gives you a choice between type styles, sizes, and colors (see fig. 15.37).

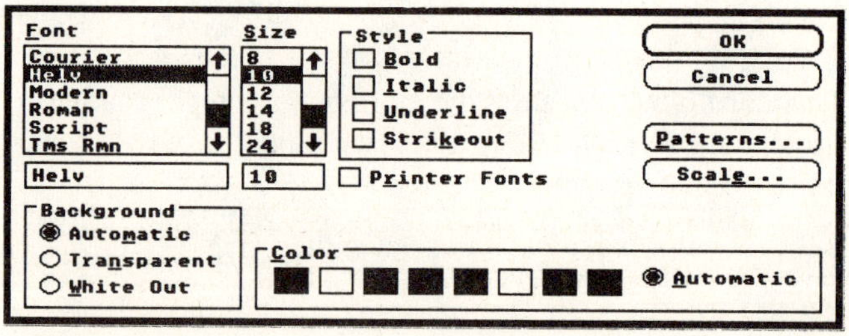

Fig. 15.37. The dialog box for axis fonts.

The dialog box for axis scale is different for the value and category axes. The Category Axis Scale dialog box, shown in figure 15.38, enables you to choose where the vertical axis will cross, how frequently to show category labels, how frequently to insert tick marks, and whether to replot categories in reverse (right to left) order.

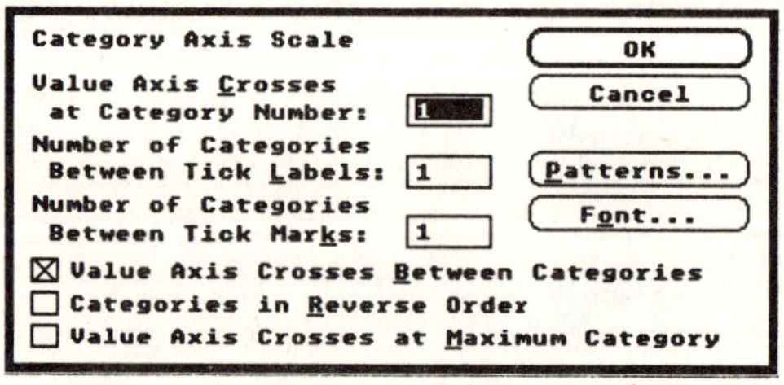

Fig. 15.38. The Category Axis Scale dialog box.

The Value Axis Scale dialog box lets you choose the units and range of the scale and the point where the category axis crosses (see fig. 15.39). You even can choose to convert the scale to logarithmic display. Choose the X boxes to return to automatic scaling.

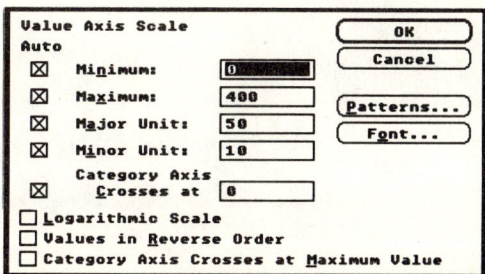

Fig. 15.39. The Value Axis Scale dialog box.

TIP

Plotting Many Points on a Chart

Charts with a large number of data points, such as stock price tracking or readings from equipment, contain so many data points that labels and tick marks crowd each other. To reduce this clutter on the bottom of the chart, select the category axis and choose Format Scale. Enter a large number into the text box for Number of Categories Between Tick Labels and the box for Number of Categories Between Tick Marks. These number entries will spread the distance between displayed labels and tick marks. The larger the numbers you enter, the more distance there will be between labels and tick marks.

TIP

Formatting and Scaling Numbers on the Value Axis

Excel assumes that you want the numbers on the value axis to appear the same as the numbers on the worksheet. If you want to change the format of the numbers along the value axis in the chart, change the numeric format in the worksheet with Format Number.

Charts such as the one shown in figure 15.40 display numbers on the value axis (the y-axis) that are difficult to read. If you scale down the numbers in the worksheet and give them a currency format, the numbers will be easier to read. For example, to scale down these numbers, divide the worksheet values by 1,000 and format the worksheet values for currency.

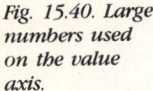

Fig. 15.40. Large
numbers used
on the value
axis.

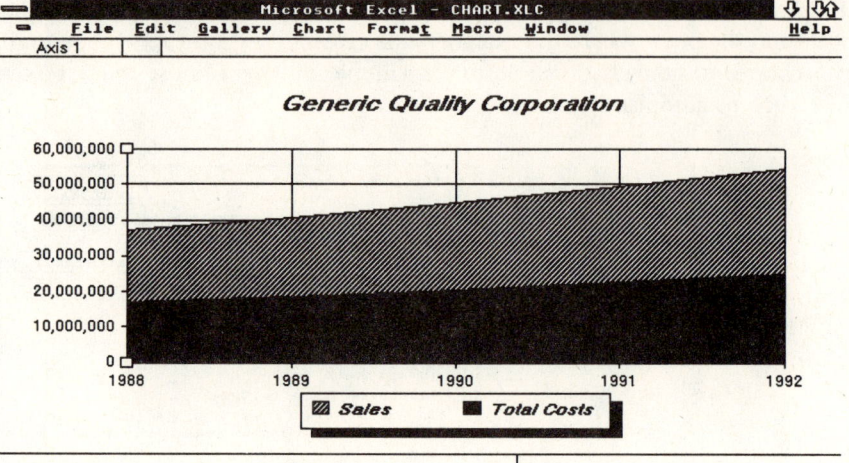

Managing Customized Charts

After you have customized your chart, there are a few things that you should be aware of. For example, did you know that choosing a new predefined format from **Gallery** completely redraws your chart and eliminates all the custom features you worked so hard to put in? The following section describes how to work around this.

Or did you know that you can copy a format from one chart and paste it onto another? That capability can save you a lot of time when you have charts that are similar. Chapter 16, "Building Advanced Charts," explains the procedure.

As a close to this chapter, you learn how to save and print your work. Because the chart is linked to a worksheet, there are a few simple rules you should abide by when saving. Printing charts is convenient because Excel prints charts directly without having to go to an outside program. What makes printing Excel charts even more convenient is the capability to preview charts on-screen so that you can see exactly how movable text is placed, where headers and footers appear, and whether page margins need to be reset.

Changing Chart Types

After you customize a chart from the gallery, use Format **Main Chart** to change chart types. For example, if you have created a customized column chart and you want to switch to a bar chart, do not use **Gallery Bar**. Choosing a new chart from the gallery will erase all the customizing you have done.

If you want to change chart types and retain your modifications, choose Format Main Chart. From the Format Main Chart dialog box (see fig. 15.41), you can choose the new type of chart. Custom formatting previously entered will be preserved if it is appropriate for the new type of chart.

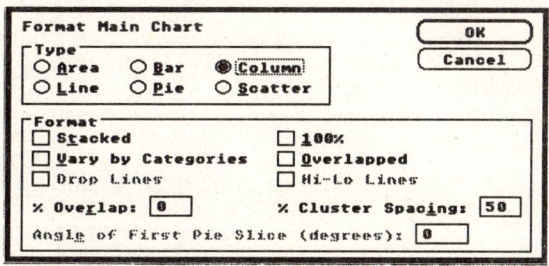

Fig. 15.41. The Format Main Chart dialog box.

You have many options in the Format Main Chart dialog box. When you choose the type of chart, different combinations of options become available. Unavailable options turn gray. Some of these options are shown in table 15.2.

Table 15.2
Main Chart Options

Option	Effect
Stacked	Stacks columns or bars on top of each other. The first data series is closest to the value axis.
Vary by Categories	When a single series is charted, produces a different color for each data point.
Drop Lines	Separates categories that might blur together with a black line.
100%	Normalizes each category to 100%. Values are shown as their percentages of the total for that category.
Overlapped	Causes bars and columns to separate when not selected and overlap when selected. The amount of overlap or separation is determined by the % Overlap option.
Hi-Lo Lines	Extends lines from the highest to the lowest value in each category. This option is used with line charts such as in stock pricing.

Option	Effect
% Overlap	Determines the amount of overlap or separation as a percentage of the bar or column. The **Overlapped** option must be selected to overlap bars and columns.
% Cluster Spacing	Determines the distance between clusters of bars or columns as a percentage of bar or column width.
Angle of First Pie Slice	Determines the angle from the vertical of the first pie wedge.

Transferring Chart Formats

If you have designed a chart with custom formats that you want to use frequently, you can paste the format from your custom chart page into other charts. This process is almost the same as cutting a numeric format from one cell on a worksheet and pasting it over another.

To transfer a chart format, follow these steps:

1. Open a new chart by selecting the worksheet data, choosing File New, and selecting Chart. Open an existing chart with **File Open**.

2. Activate the customized chart whose format you want to use.

3. Choose **Chart Select Chart**.

4. Choose **Edit Copy** to copy the active chart into the clipboard so that it can be pasted.

5. Activate the chart to receive the format.

6. Choose **Edit Paste Special**.

7. Select Formats from the Paste dialog box.

8. Choose OK or press Enter.

Clearing Custom Changes

You do not have to re-create a chart from the worksheet when you want to start over. Instead, simply clear the unwanted features from the chart using these steps:

1. Choose **Chart Select Chart**.

2. Choose **Edit Clear**.

3. Select what you want cleared:

Button	Action
All	Clears the chart
Formats	Clears the formats, but retains the data series
Formulas	Clears the data series, but retains the formats

4. Choose OK or press Enter.

Saving Custom Formats

To save a custom format and unattached text, use the procedure for clearing custom changes (see the preceding section), but clear only formulas. You can paste data from a worksheet into this seemingly blank chart to produce a formatted chart. Use normal procedures to select the data and copy it from the worksheet. Activate the chart and use **Edit Paste** to paste the data.

Saving Charts

Save a chart by activating it and then choosing **File Save As**. If you attempt to close a chart that has not been saved or that has been changed, you will be asked to confirm whether you want to save the chart.

NOTE

Charts Are Not Saved with Worksheets

Charts are not saved automatically with their associated worksheets. Each chart is separate from the worksheet and must be saved by itself.

Charts can be saved to different directories by typing the path name and file name for the chart to be saved. For example, you could type

  c:\excel\forecast\budget

This entry saves the BUDGET.XLC chart to drive C under the \EXCEL \FORECAST subdirectory. Excel adds the .XLC file extension automatically.

When you make changes to a chart, but want to retain the original version, save the new version with a different name using **File Save As**.

Saving a worksheet with a new file name may not automatically update the charts attached to the original worksheet. The next time you retrieve an attached chart, you may find that it still refers to the data in the old worksheet.

To be sure that your charts are always linked to the current worksheet, you can use any of the following techniques:

1. Make sure that all associated worksheets and charts are open when you save the worksheet under a new name. This technique automatically updates the chart's reference to the worksheet's location. Save the charts after closing the worksheets that the charts are linked to.

2. Edit the series formulas in each chart to include the new file name of the updated worksheet. This is described in more detail in Chapter 16, "Building Advanced Charts."

3. Save the updated worksheet with the same name as the original. If you use this technique, you might want to keep a backup copy of the original worksheet under a different name.

4. If your chart is no longer linked to the correct worksheet, you can reestablish links with these steps:

    1. Open the chart.

    2. Open the worksheet you want to reestablish a link with.

    3. Activate the chart.

    4. Choose the **File Links** command.

    5. Select the name of the old linked worksheet in the **Links** list box.

    6. Choose the **Change** button.

    7. Select the name of the worksheet you want to reestablish a link with from the **Files** list box.

8. Choose OK or press Enter.

9. Save the worksheet.

10. Save the chart.

Loading Charts

When you open a chart without opening its worksheet, a dialog box asks whether you want to update the chart (see fig. 15.42). If you choose Yes, the chart uses the current values stored in the worksheet file. Choose No, however, and the chart uses the last values used to draw the chart.

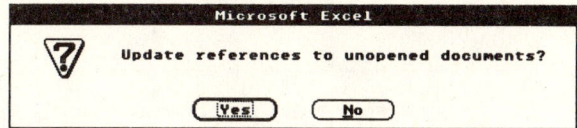

Fig. 15.42. The dialog box for updating a chart.

To see which worksheets are linked to a chart and open them if desired, choose **File Links.** If the worksheet the chart needs has been deleted or moved to another directory, a **File Open** box will appear allowing you to find the worksheet and open it. (Follow the steps in the preceding section if you need to reestablish links.)

Printing Charts

To print your presentation-quality chart, follow these steps:

1. Choose **File Pr**inter Setup, and check for the correct printer. Select the **S**etup button, and check that you have the correct font cartridge selected if you use a laser printer.

2. Choose File Page Setup, and check the page borders.

3. Enter headers, footers, page margins, and the size of the chart.

4. Choose File Print. Select the **P**review check box if you want to see on-screen how the chart will appear on paper.

5. Choose OK or press Enter.

NOTE

What's Going On When Half of a Chart Prints?

Laser printers build an image in memory of any graphics items they are going to print. If the printer does not have enough memory or some of the printer's memory is used up by downloadable soft fonts, there may not be enough memory for the entire chart to be built and printed. For example, what may occur on a Hewlett-Packard LaserJet Series II with the standard 512K of memory is that charts printed in landscape mode (sideways) at 300 dots per inch require so much memory that only half the chart prints. To get around this problem, print the chart in portrait mode (letter orientation) by selecting **Portrait** from the File **Printer** Setup command and **Setup** button. The chart will cover only half a page, but it will print in its entirety.

TIP

Using the Correct Fonts on Your Charts

To make sure you are using fonts on-screen that your printer can print, choose **Format Font** and select the **Printer Fonts** check box. Fonts other than Modern, Roman, and Script that remain in the **Font** list box are fonts that your printer will print. When you use these fonts on-screen, you will see in the print preview how the text will print on paper. Text in a font your printer does not have may print in a different position or size than the preview indicates.

From Here . . .

You can create impressive high-quality graphics with the basic charting commands described in this chapter. When you get to the point where you need to create overlapping charts, link multiple worksheets to a single chart, or do more complex charting, then be sure to go on to Chapter 16, "Building Advanced Charts."

If you have a question or run into trouble as you work with charts, remember that help information is available by pressing F1. You also may find answers to your questions in Chapter 17, "Troubleshooting Charts."

16

Building Advanced Charts

When you meet a situation that requires special charts, the techniques in this chapter will help you. Here, you learn how to overlap two different charts, how to link one chart to multiple worksheets, and how to edit the series formula to control the order of chart markers and the text used in legends. This chapter also describes how to prevent a chart from being scrambled when the worksheet is rearranged.

Creating Combination Charts

Combination charts present two or more series of data on the same chart, using two different chart types. The first chart type applies to the first half of the data series, and the second chart type applies to the second half of the data series. Combination charts work well to compare trends in two different types of data or to look for possible interactions between two sets of data.

Figure 16.1 shows a combination column chart and line chart created by adding a third data series to the final chart created in Chapter 14, "Chart Quick Start," and then choosing the Chart Add Overlay command. In the figure, marketing expenses were pasted into the chart so that it contains three series of data. This third series of data appears as the line.

You can create a combination chart in either of two ways. The method you choose depends on whether you are creating a new chart or customizing an existing one.

If you are creating a new chart or are working with a chart that does not contain a title or other custom features, you can create a combination chart by choosing Gallery Combination. You can choose from five different combination formats. Issuing this command removes any custom formatting such as arrows or unattached text.

If your chart has custom features that you don't want to lose or if you want a combination different from one of the five gallery combinations, choose

Fig. 16.1. A column chart with a line chart overlay.

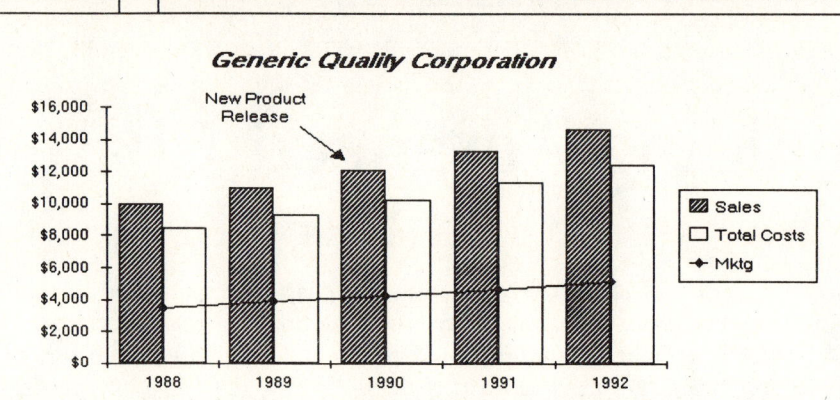

Chart Add Overlay to create a combination chart. You can alter the type of overlay by choosing Format Overlay as described in this chapter's "Changing the Overlay Chart Format" section.

In combination charts, the chart in back is called the *main chart*, and the one in the foreground is the *overlay*. Choosing Chart Add Overlay divides the data series evenly, giving the first half of the data series to the main chart and the second half of the data series to the overlay chart. If an odd number of data series exists, then the main chart receives the extra series. When an overlay chart already exists in the current chart, the menu command becomes Chart Delete Overlay.

TIP

Moving a Data Series between the Main Chart and Overlay Chart

To move a data series from the main chart to the overlay chart or vice versa, edit the series formula for that data so that the formula's *marker_order_number* moves nearer the first data series if you want it in the main chart, or nearer the end of the data series if you want it in the overlay. For example, if January's cluster contains seven columns, then changing the *marker_order_number* of the sixth data series from 6 to 1, 2, 3, or 4 will move the data series from the overlay chart into the main chart. You will learn how to edit the series formula in this chapter's "Customizing with Series Formulas" section.

Changing the Main Chart Format

The main chart contains the primary data series you are analyzing. You may find it necessary to change the main chart during analysis. For example, you might change it from a **Line** to a **Column** and then to an **Area** to see if the different graphics representations reveal something unique. While switching between these chart types with the Format **Main** Chart, you can customize the chart with features such as hi-lo lines or overlapping columns.

To change the main chart (the one behind the overlay), follow these steps:

1. Choose Format **Main** Chart.

2. Select the options you want to use for the main (background) chart in the combination.

   Figure 16.2 shows the selections available for the main chart. The list of options available depends on the type of main chart you select. These options are described in Chapter 15's "Changing Chart Types" section.

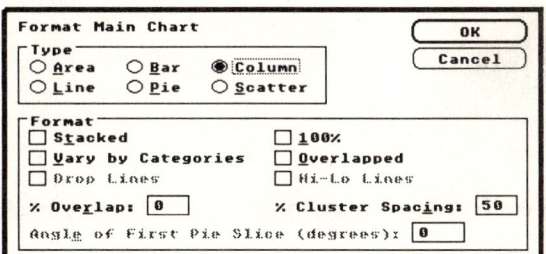

Fig. 16.2. The Format Main Chart dialog box.

3. Choose OK or press Enter.

Changing the Overlay Chart Format

As you work with your graphs, you may find that a different chart type lets you compare data better between a main chart and an overlay chart. For example, you could overlay a line chart of a calculated trend line onto a main **Scatter** chart of raw data. Choosing the hi-lo lines option would allow you to show a margin of error bracketing the line.

To change the type of overlay chart, choose Format **Overlay** and select the options appropriate to the type of overlay chart you select. Figure 16.3 shows the selections available in the Format Overlay Chart dialog box. Selections vary depending on the type of overlay chart you select. The selections shown in figure 16.3 are for a line chart.

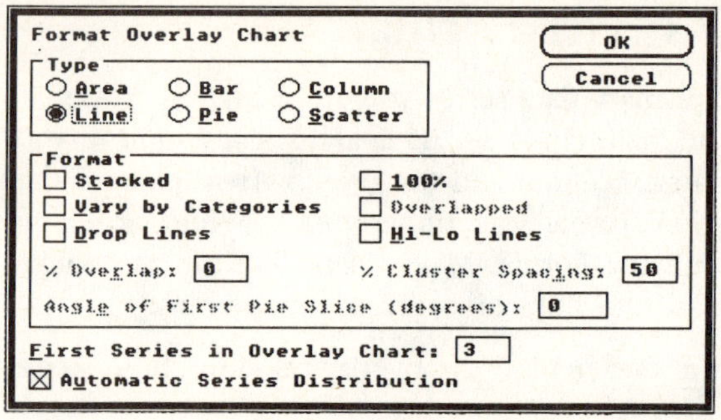

Fig. 16.3. The Format Overlay Chart dialog box.

```
┌─────────────────────────────────────────────┐
│ Format Overlay Chart              ┌────────┐ │
│ ┌─Type────────────────────────┐   │   OK   │ │
│ │ ○ Area   ○ Bar    ○ Column  │   └────────┘ │
│ │ ◉ Line   ○ Pie    ○ Scatter │   ┌────────┐ │
│ └─────────────────────────────┘   │ Cancel │ │
│ ┌─Format──────────────────────────┘└────────┘│
│ │ □ Stacked            □ 100%                 │
│ │ □ Vary by Categories □ Overlapped           │
│ │ □ Drop Lines         □ Hi-Lo Lines          │
│ │ % Overlap: 0      % Cluster Spacing: 50      │
│ │ Angle of First Pie Slice (degrees): 0       │
│ └────────────────────────────────────────────┘
│ First Series in Overlay Chart: 3             │
│ ⊠ Automatic Series Distribution              │
└─────────────────────────────────────────────┘
```

Whenever a chart with an overlay is active, the **Chart** menu displays the command Delete Overlay. Choosing Delete **O**verlay removes the overlay chart so that all data series appear on the main chart.

Creating Hi-Lo Line Charts

Figure 16.4 is an example of a simple hi-lo line chart along with the worksheet from which it was created. Hi-lo charts require three series of data to describe the high, median, and low point at each position. Although you can create hi-lo charts by selecting them from the line gallery, the method described here will give you much more flexibility and control. This method permits you to create multiple hi-lo lines and to decide which points to connect with those lines.

Fig. 16.4. A hi-lo line chart and the worksheet from which it was created.

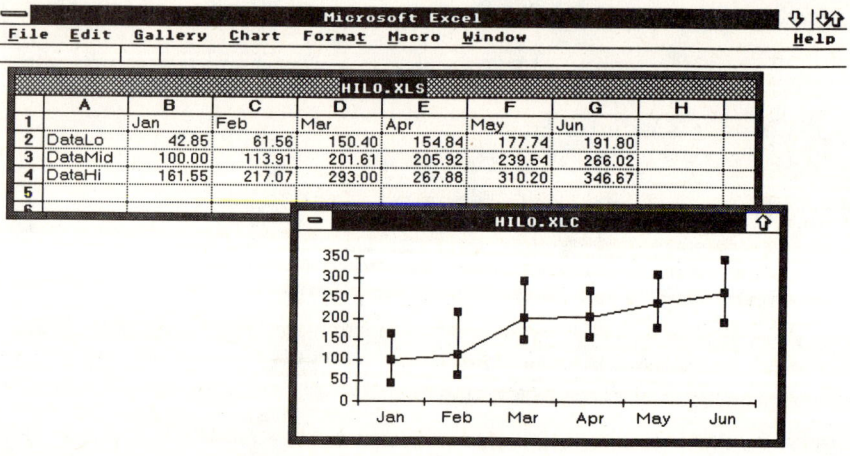

To produce the hi-lo chart shown in figure 16.4, follow these steps:

1. Select the worksheet area to be charted.

   In the HILO worksheet of figure 16.4, the selected area is A1:G4. The chart appears in your current preferred chart type. If you have not set a preferred type, the chart appears as a column chart type with three columns per cluster.

2. Choose Format Main Chart.

3. Select **Line** as the chart type.

4. Select **Hi-lo** Lines.

5. Choose OK or press Enter.

   The chart appears as in figure 16.5. This chart contains three lines with each data point connected by vertical hi-lo lines.

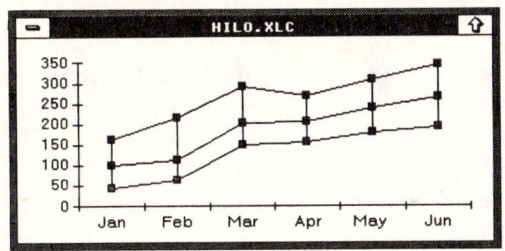

Fig. 16.5. A hi-lo line chart with data points connected by three lines.

To eliminate the unneeded top and bottom lines, continue with these steps.

6. Select the top line.

   Mouse: Click on the top line.

   Keyboard: Press the up-arrow key until the top line is selected.

7. Choose Format **Patterns**.

8. Select the Invisible line style.

9. Choose OK or press Enter.

10. Select the bottom line and repeat Steps 7-9.

This method gives you the flexibility to choose the data points to be connected by lines and enables you to create multiple hi-lo lines on the same chart.

If you want to put a hi-lo line over the top of another chart type, use **Chart Add Overlay** to add an overlay. Use **Format Overlay** to format the overlay as a line chart with hi-lo lines. Again, you must choose which lines will be invisible.

Inserting Blank Areas in Bar and Column Charts

Sometimes adding space between a chart's bars or columns, or between the clusters of bars or columns, can be visually appealing. You can introduce large spaces between clusters of bars or columns to allow room for inserting un-attached text labels. You can give charts this extra room in a couple of ways.

To insert space between bar or column clusters, choose **Format Main Chart**, and then enter a number such as 200 in the % Cluster Spacing text box. This number is the distance between clusters measured as a percentage of one bar or column width.

For more room between individual bars or columns, choose **Format Main Chart**, unselect the **Overlapped** option, and enter a number in the % Overlap text box. This number controls the distance between individual markers as a percentage of bar or column width. Make sure that **Overlapped** is unselected; otherwise, the bars or columns will overlap.

When the **Overlapped** box is checked, the % Overlap number measures the amount markers overlap. If the **Overlapped** box is not checked the % Overlap number measures the distance between individual markers.

To get extra room in the middle of a chart, insert a blank column in the worksheet at the point in the data series where you need blank space rather than marker clusters. Figure 16.6 shows how a column inserted in the work-sheet results in a chart with a blank column. The extra room appears in the same location of the chart as data clusters would for that data location.

Combining Chart Formats and Data

You can copy all of one chart and paste it into another chart, combining the data of the two charts or replacing the original format with the format of the pasted chart.

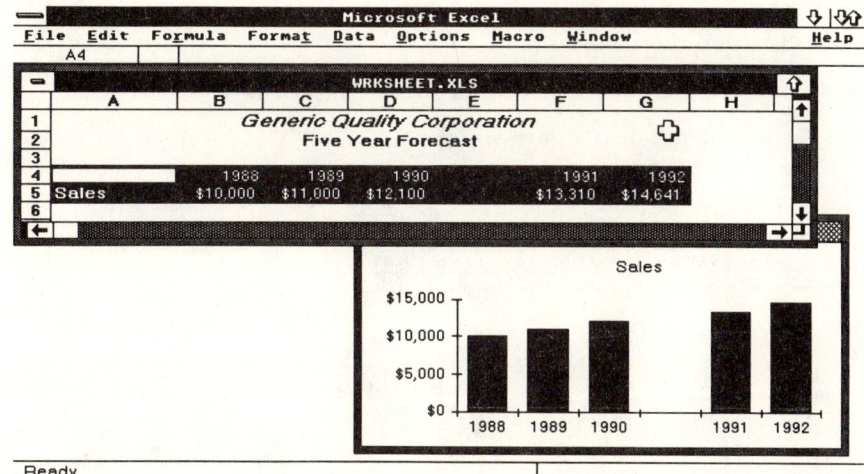

Fig. 16.6. An inserted blank column in a worksheet and the resulting added space in the chart.

When you want to transfer the data or the format from one chart to another, follow these steps:

1. Activate the chart containing the data or format you want to transfer.

2. Choose the **Chart Select Chart** command to select the entire chart.

   Figure 16.7 shows a line chart selected for copying. Notice the white squares at the chart's perimeter.

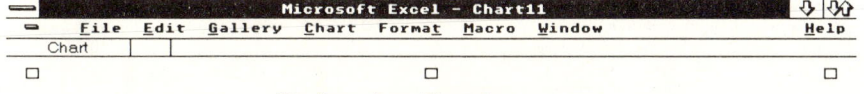

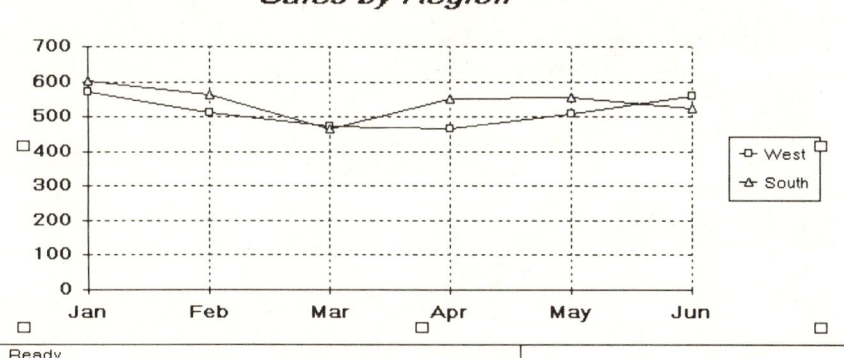

Fig. 16.7. A line chart selected for copying.

3. Choose the **Edit Copy** command to copy the chart's format and data into the clipboard.

4. Activate the chart that will receive the format or data.

   The column chart shown in figure 16.8 will receive the format and/or data from the line chart.

Fig. 16.8. The column chart that will receive the format and data from the line chart.

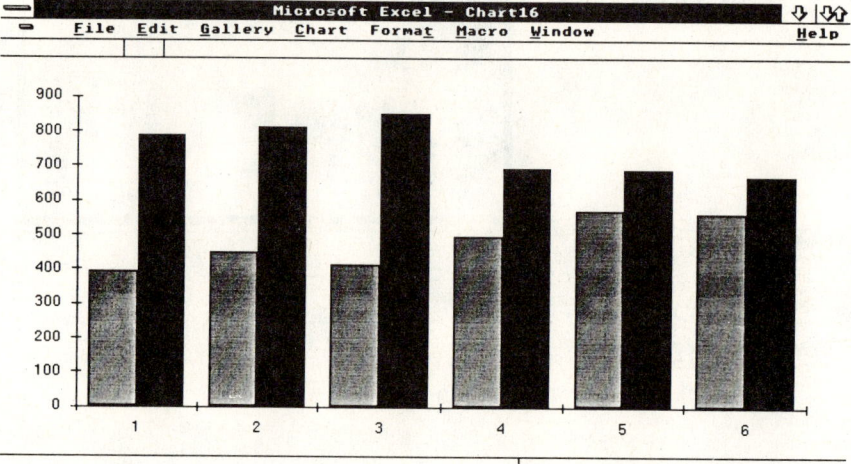

5. Choose **Edit Paste Special**.

6. Select the information you want to transfer to the active chart:

All	Transfers data and formats
Formats	Transfers chart format, but not data
Formulas	Transfers data, but not chart format

7. Choose **OK** or press Enter.

The chart shown in figure 16.9 was created by selecting **All**, which combined both series of data and pasted the line chart's type and custom formatting onto the finished chart.

Linking a Chart to Multiple Data Selections and Worksheets

Linking the data from separate locations on a worksheet or from multiple worksheets into a chart is also a process of copying and pasting. If you can link worksheets, you can link multiple worksheets to a single chart.

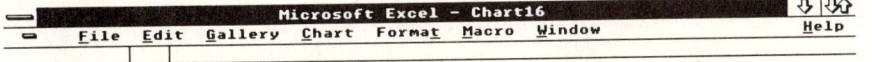

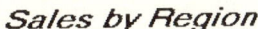

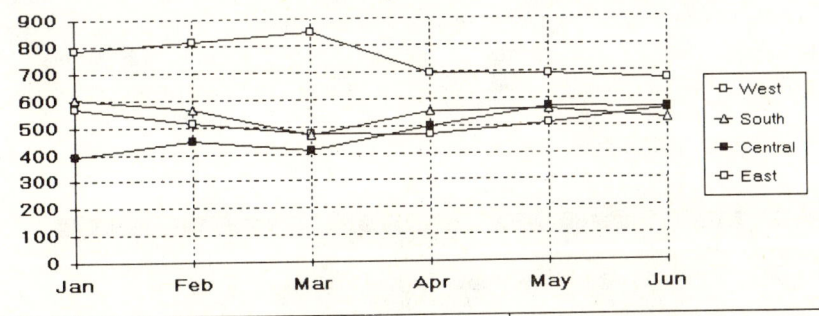

Fig. 16.9. A line chart with combined data.

Charting Data in Nonadjacent Cells

Worksheet data does not have to be in adjacent rows or columns to create a chart. You can create an original chart with nonadjacent data series by selecting multiple nonadjacent ranges before choosing File New and selecting Chart. Make sure that each data series has the same number of data points. Figure 16.10 shows a worksheet where three nonadjacent rows have been selected to create a new chart.

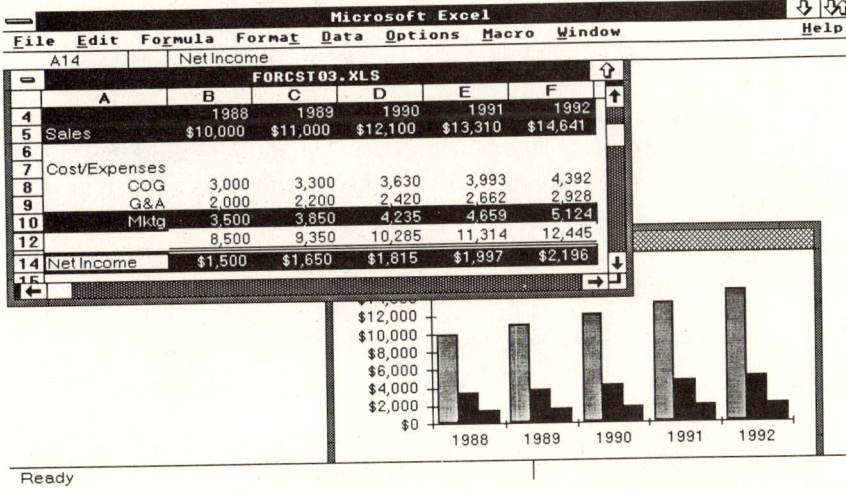

Fig. 16.10. Four nonadjacent rows selected from a worksheet to create a new chart.

Adding a Data Series to a Chart

You can add data series to existing charts. The finished chart from the Chart Quick Start was created originally by selecting the adjacent cells A4:F5. To add the nonadjacent data series A14:F14 to the existing chart, select the data in cells A14:F14, as shown in the worksheet in figure 16.11, and then choose Edit Copy. This procedure copies the data into the clipboard. Activate the receiving chart and select the Edit Paste command. This procedure pastes the data into the chart. Both the original markers and the markers for the pasted data in the chart will appear.

Fig. 16.11. A worksheet data series about to be pasted into the chart.

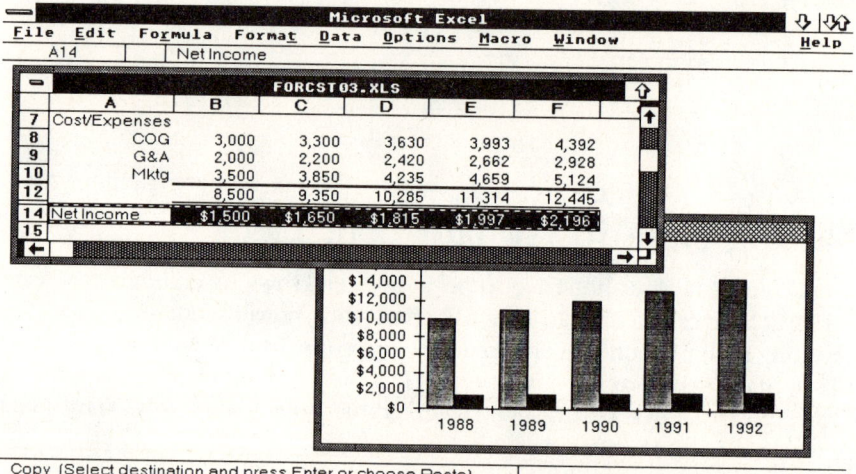

Adding Data from Multiple Worksheets

Now that you know how to paste a data series into a chart, you will find that you can just as easily create a chart using data from multiple worksheets. You can create one chart, for example, that reflects data from four different quarters, even though each quarter is on a different worksheet.

Add data from multiple worksheets by copying the data from each worksheet and pasting it into the chart. Follow these steps:

1. Create a chart from the worksheet data you want as the first series in the chart.

2. Activate a different worksheet.

3. Select a data series with the same number of data points as contained in the chart. Do not include labels.

4. Choose **Edit Copy.**

5. Activate the chart.

6. Choose **Edit Paste.**

Pasting Data Using Paste Special

Another method of pasting data from a worksheet into a chart gives you more control over how you want the data added to the chart. You use the same process as that just described. Instead of choosing the Edit Paste command, however, choose the Edit Paste Special command.

When you choose the Edit Paste Special command the dialog box in figure 16.12 appears. Depending upon the shape of the selected area in the worksheet, Excel guesses at whether a series of data is oriented along rows or columns. The two options are

Rows   Each row in the selected worksheet area contains a
                    data series

Columns   Each column in the selected worksheet area contains
                    a data series

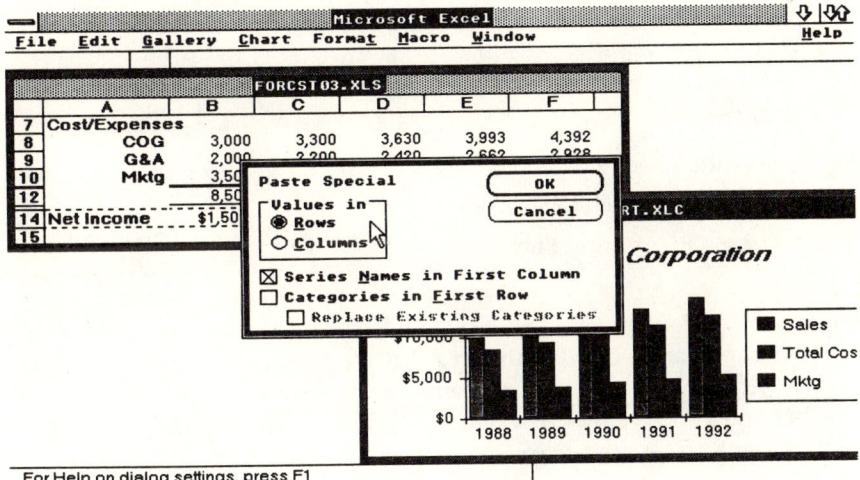

Fig. 16.12. The Edit Paste Special command lets you choose how you want to paste data into a chart.

TIP

Changing Excel's Automatic Selection of Data for Charts

Excel automatically assumes that a chart's data series runs along the longest direction of a selected worksheet range. For example, if you chart a worksheet area two cells high and six cells wide, then Excel assumes that all the data in a series runs the long direction, along the row. When you want to create a chart with the data oriented on the chart different from Excel's automatic assumption, then follow this process:

1. Create a blank chart by selecting a single blank cell on the worksheet, then choosing **File New**, selecting the Chart option, and pressing Enter.

2. Activate the worksheet containing the data you want to chart.

3. Select the data you want to chart including relevant labels along the left side or top of the data.

4. Choose the **Edit Copy** command.

5. Activate the blank chart.

6. Choose the **Edit Paste Special** command.

7. Select either the **Rows** or **Columns** option to determine which values Excel charts together as a series.

   Since you are probably using this method because Excel hasn't produce a chart with data oriented as you want, you will probably select the option opposite of what automatically appears in the Paste Special box. For example, if the **Rows** option appears, then you will want to select **Columns**.

8. Select the check boxes that describe where the series name is located and where the category names are located.

9. Choose OK or press Enter.

The Paste Special box also lets you tell Excel where the series name and category names are located in the area that you are pasting. The check boxes for the series name or category name locations change depending upon whether you choose **Rows** or **Columns**. If the area you are pasting does not contain labels to be used as series or category names, then do not select any check boxes.

If you are using the **Edit Paste Special** command to paste data into an existing chart, then you can replace the category names in the existing chart with the category names of the pasted data by selecting the Replace Existing Categories check box.

Customizing with Series Formulas

When you create a chart or add a data series to a chart, Excel links the data on the worksheet to the chart. The program creates this link with a series formula.

A *series formula* tells the program where the worksheet is located on the disk or network, which worksheet to use, and which cells in that worksheet contain the data to be charted. One series formula exists for each data series. You can display a series formula for a series of data by selecting one of the markers in that series. As figure 16.13 shows, selecting a data marker displays its series formula in the formula bar. The formula in figure 16.13 belongs to the first data series (shown with white squares inside the markers). The worksheet corresponding to the chart appears behind the chart.

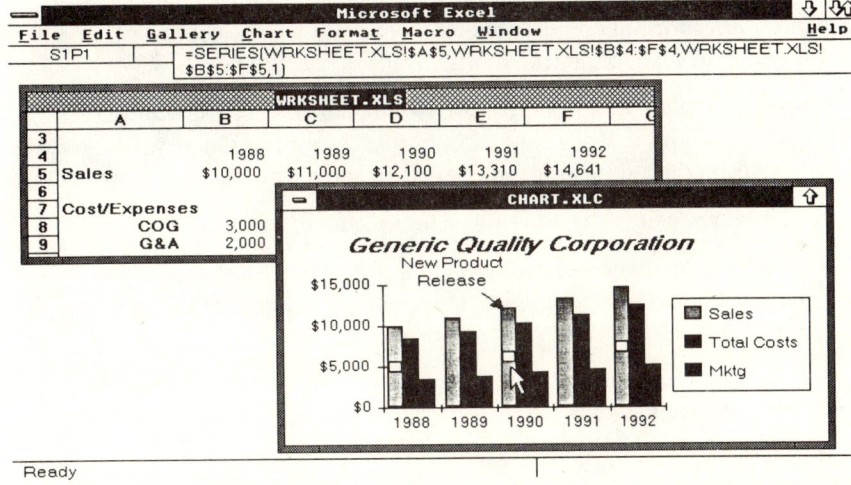

Fig. 16.13. A data marker selected in the chart, and the corresponding series formula displayed in the worksheet.

Whether Excel enters the series formula automatically or you type it, all series formulas follow the same pattern. When you examine both the worksheet and the resulting chart, you can see how the formula works. All series formulas are constructed on this pattern:

=SERIES("series_name",worksheet_name!category_reference,
   worksheet_name!values_reference,marker_order_number)

The *"series_name"* is either text (in quotation marks) or an external reference to the cell containing the label for the data series. An external reference to a text label in a cell is not enclosed in quotation marks. The *series_name* is used in the legend.

The *worksheet_name!category_reference* is an absolute external reference specifying the cells that contain the labels for the category axis. The *worksheet_name!values_reference* specifies which cells in a worksheet contain the values for the data series.

The *marker_order_number* dictates the order in which the data series display. In the example in figure 16.13, the *marker_order_number* is 1; therefore, the markers for this data series appear before any other columns. A *marker_order_number* of 2 would cause this data series to be the second series of markers.

Editing a Series Formula

Although Excel automatically enters the series formula for pasted data, you can edit it or manually type an additional series formula. To edit a series formula, use the same editing procedures you use to edit formulas. You can make the series formula refer to specific cells and worksheets, displaying data in the order and way that you want.

If you want to take full advantage of customizing your charts with Excel, you will need to know a few rules about series formulas. Once you know the rules, you can edit a series formula as you would a formula from a worksheet.

- The series name (legend) must be in quotation marks if it is text.

- Enter external references by opening the worksheet and then typing the external reference (without quotation marks) into the series formula.

- Commas must separate arguments inside the parentheses, even when an argument is blank.

- Cell references must be absolute.

- Absolute reference names can be used.

- The *marker_order_number* must be an integer number.

- The series formula with *marker_order_number* 1 dictates the *category_reference* and *series_name* used in the chart.

To edit a series formula, you first must select the markers in the chart that belong to the series formula you want to change. With the mouse, select markers by clicking on any marker in the series. From the keyboard, press the up- or down-arrow key until the marker series you want is selected. A white square appears in some of the markers of series when they are selected.

Now you can edit the series formula with the same procedures you use to edit worksheet formulas. After you have selected the marker, the series formula for that series appears in the formula bar, as shown in figure 16.13. With the mouse, you can click in the formula bar at the point where you want the cursor to appear. From the keyboard, press F2 (the Edit key) to enter the formula bar.

You can type new characters, or select characters and delete them. You can copy part of one series formula to another formula with **Edit Copy** and **Edit Paste**. Just be sure to follow the rules for series formulas listed earlier in this section.

Normally, Excel recalculates the worksheet and updates the chart as soon as you enter your edited series formula. This recalculation and update won't happen, however, if recalculation has been turned off. If calculation has been set to manual, select **Chart Calculate Now** to recalculate the worksheet manually and to redraw the chart with the new series formula.

Changing a Chart's Data Series

Editing a series formula enables you to delete data, add data from other areas of a worksheet, or add data from different worksheets. When you want to change only a few series of data, this technique is much more convenient than creating an entire new chart. To change an external reference to an existing worksheet, edit the cell reference to refer to the cells you want. Don't refer to more cells than there are data points on the category axis.

To enter a series formula to an existing chart manually, open the worksheet containing the data. Activate the chart. Click in the formula bar, or press F2 to move the cursor to the formula bar. Type in the series formula that references the opened worksheet. Do not put quotation marks around external references. You do not need to type the worksheet's full path name in the series formula. Type only the worksheet's name as it appears in the title bar. Follow the worksheet's name with an exclamation point (!) and the absolute reference of the cells you want. Save the worksheet before saving the chart so that the chart will know where the worksheet is located.

Deleting Data from a Chart

You can delete markers from a chart by deleting the series formula from the formula bar. Deleting a series formula from a chart deletes the bars, symbols, and other markers associated with that data.

To delete a data series, such as the selected line shown in figure 16.14, follow these steps:

Fig. 16.14. A
line overlay
chart with the
line selected.

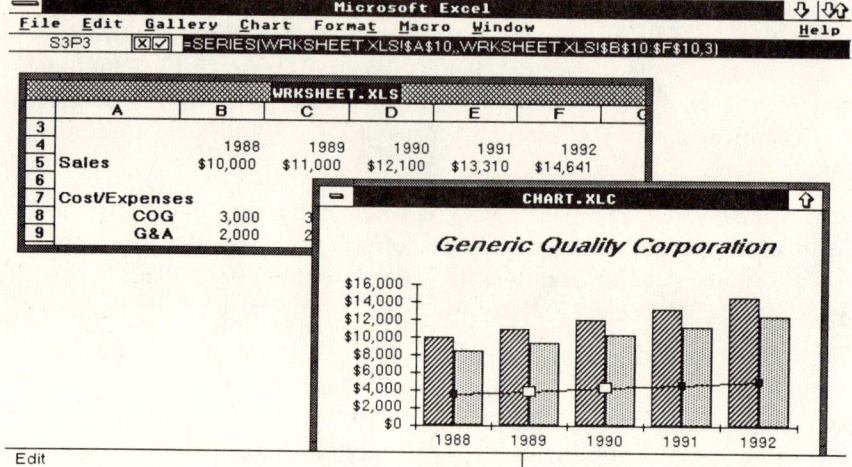

1. Select the markers for the data series you want to remove. Some of the selected markers will have white squares when selected.

   Mouse: Click on one of the markers you want to remove.

   Keyboard: Press the up- or down-arrow key until any marker belonging to the series you want to delete is selected.

2. Activate the formula bar.

   Mouse: Click in the formula bar.

   Keyboard: Press F2 (the Edit key).

3. Select the entire formula in the formula bar (as shown in fig. 16.14).

   Mouse: Drag from before the equal sign (=) to the end of the formula.

   Keyboard: Move to before the equal sign (=) by pressing Home, and then press Shift+arrow until the entire formula is selected.

4. Press Del to delete the data series formula.

5. Click on the check mark or press Enter.

Deleting the data series formula from the formula bar deletes the corresponding markers from the chart.

Changing the Names Used in Legends

You can change the names used in the legend by editing the *series_name* within a series formula. To do this, select the markers you want to change. Click in the formula bar or press F2 to edit the series formula.

Delete the old external reference to a label or delete the series name from between the quotation marks, and type the new external reference or the text name you want to appear in the legend. Make sure that a new text name is enclosed in quotation marks. Press Enter to enter the edited series formula. A series formula with a text series name of Expenses would appear in a series formula similar to

=SERIES("Expenses",,WORKSHEET.XLS!$B$10:$F$10,3)

Changing the Order of Chart Markers

You do not have to move rows or columns of worksheet data to change the order in which chart markers appear. You can change the order of bars, symbols, or pie wedges with a simple edit of the series formula.

Figure 16.15 shows a chart with three data series. Notice that the first data series has the tallest columns.

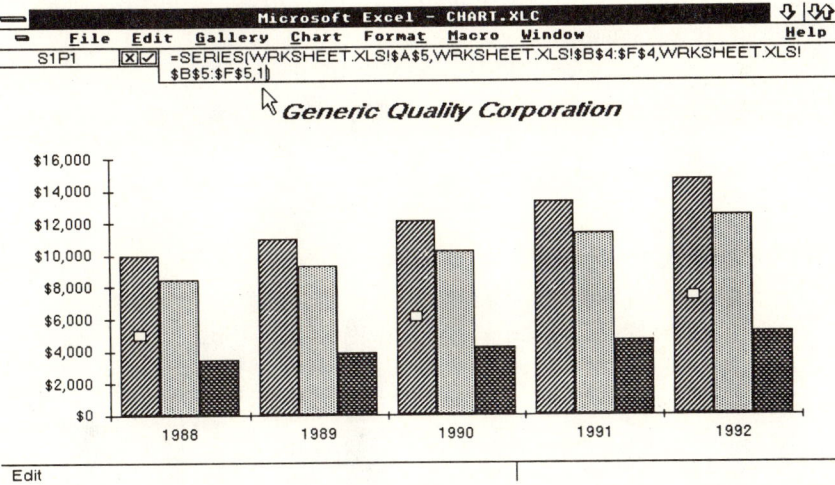

Fig. 16.15. A column chart with the first data series, the highest markers, selected and its series formula.

In the steps that follow, you will edit the first series formula—the tallest markers—so that they become the third series of markers. You will edit the first series formula so that the *marker_order_number* for the chart is changed from 1 to 3. This change moves the series with the highest columns from the first position to the third. Other data series automatically adjust their *marker_order_numbers*.

1. Select the data series you want to change. In figure 16.15, the first series has been selected.

2. Activate the formula bar.

   Mouse: Click the pointer before the closing parenthesis in the series formula.

   Keyboard: Press F2 (the Edit key), and then move the cursor so that it is before the closing parenthesis in the series formula.

3. Delete *marker_order_number* 1 by pressing the backspace key.

4. Type a 3 for the *marker_order_number* so that it appears as the last argument in the series formula.

5. Press Enter.

The chart should be redrawn with the tall markers last. If the chart is not redrawn, Excel may have been set for manual recalculation. In that case, choose the Chart Calculate Now command.

The new chart, shown in figure 16.16, displays the data series with the tallest bars as the third series. Compare figures 16.15 and 16.16, and you can see that the order has changed.

Fig. 16.16. The same column chart with the highest markers now displayed as the third data series.

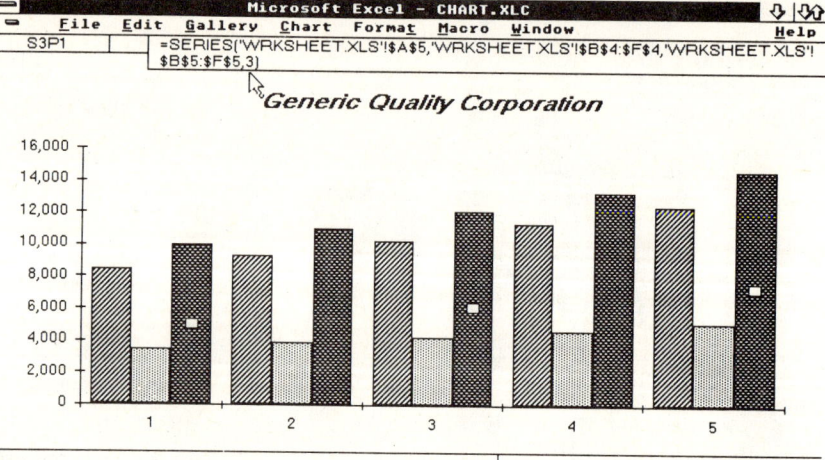

TIP

Prevent Worksheet Changes from Scrambling Charts

Inserting, deleting, and moving worksheet cells can destroy a chart if the chart uses absolute external references to refer to cells in the worksheet. When you change a worksheet, a chart does not update series formulas automatically. As a result, the chart may refer to the wrong cells.

To prevent your charts from being scrambled, edit series formulas so that they contain named ranges instead of absolute references. Editing these names into the series formulas keeps the chart intact when you move chart-related data. For example, figure 16.15 uses the following formula to refer to its first data series:

```
=SERIES(WRKSHEET.XLS!$A$5,WRKSHEET.XLS!$B$4:$F$4,
    WRKSHEET.XLS!$B$5:$F$5,1)
```

If the cells in B5:F5 are given the range name SALES with Formula Define Name or Formula Create Names, the series formula can be rewritten as follows:

```
=SERIES(WRKSHEET.XLS!$A$5,WRKSHEET.XLS!$B$4:$F$4,
    WRKSHEET.XLS!SALES,1)
```

A chart using range names as in the preceding formula will not become scrambled if the data in B5:F5 is moved. The chart will look for the range of cells carrying the name SALES, regardless of the location of the range.

From Here . . .

Keep in mind that Excel charts have a wide variety of uses. You can create them quickly and use them for data analysis. Yet all your charts can have the quality of professionally created graphics.

If you run into problems using Excel charts, refer to Chapter 17, "Trouble-shooting Charts." You may also find help in the tips and notes scattered throughout the other chart chapters of this book.

To use your charts inside other Windows programs and some standard DOS applications, refer to Chapter 28, "Using Excel with Windows Applications," and Chapter 29, "Using Excel with Standard DOS Applications." In those chapters, you will learn how to meld Excel charts into your word-processing documents and how to paste charts into more advanced graphics packages for further enhancements.

17

Troubleshooting Charts

The charts created from your worksheets can be enlightening and almost fun. But even Excel's charts can sometimes produce unusual results when you do something outside normal chart operations. The troubleshooting tips in this chapter reveal some of the ways charts may produce a different result than what you expected. The tips also suggest ways that you can solve common problems.

Problem: The chart is not updated or redrawn after you change data on the worksheet or after you edit one of the chart-related series formulas.

Solution: The worksheet may be set for manual recalculation. To redraw the chart using new worksheet data or to update the chart to the new series formula, choose **Chart Calculate Now.**

Problem: The numbers along the value axis are too large and do not have a format that looks good with the rest of the chart. Which command formats the values along the value axis?

Solution: Excel does not have a command to format values along the values axis. Values in Excel charts reflect the values and formats in the worksheet. If you need to scale down the numbers on the axis, divide them by 100, 1000, or some other appropriate number in the worksheet. You may want to create a special data row or column in the worksheet for these scaled numbers. Format the worksheet numbers as you want them to appear in the chart. Be sure to use unattached text to denote that the data is scaled and to indicate the units of measure.

Problem: All the category labels that were 1988, 1989, and so on, have changed to numbers, such as 1, 2, 3, and 4. This change occurred after you edited a series formula so that a specific data series would be the first cluster.

Solution: Excel takes its category labels from the second item in the series formula of the first data series. If this formula does not contain a reference to cells containing category labels, Excel creates its own numeric category labels. This usually happens when you copy a data selection from a worksheet and paste it into an existing chart. If you later make that pasted series the first series, you end up with this problem. Edit the external reference of the cells containing the category labels into the series formula. See Chapter 16, "Building Advanced Charts," for more information on the series formula and numerous examples of external cell references that refer to text used as the category.

Problem: When plotting a large amount of data in a line chart, the category labels and tick marks squeeze together too closely. How can their appearance be improved?

Solution: To "thin out" the labels or tick marks along the category axis but still keep all the data, first select the category axis (a white square should appear at either end). Choose Format Scale, and then select either or both text boxes labeled Number of Categories Between Tick Labels and Number of Categories Between Tick Marks. Enter a number larger than the one displayed in the box, and then choose OK or press Enter. If the labels or tick marks still have not been thinned enough, repeat the process using a larger number.

Problem: Excel won't display negative numbers as area charts.

Solution: You're right!

Problem: The legend always appears in the same spot. How can it be moved to another location?

Solution: Select the legend by clicking on it or by pressing the up- or down-arrow key until the legend is enclosed by white boxes. Then choose Format Legend. Excel offers four options for legend position.

Problem: Some combinations of colors and patterns on charts are aesthetically offensive (ugly)! How can the colors be returned to their original selections and patterns?

Solution: You can return to the default colors and patterns by selecting the chart object you want changed, and then choosing Format Patterns and selecting the automatic options.

Problem: Pie chart labels overlap each other.

Solution: Refer to the tips in Chapter 15, "Creating and Enhancing Charts," to learn how to use unattached text to cover and hide portions of a chart. After covering the overlapped labels, create your own unattached text to replace the labels and position them as you want.

Problem: Color charts appear fine on the screen; but when printed, some of the gray-scale shades can't be distinguished. How can charts be printed to show the shading differences more clearly?

Solution: To show a major difference between the colors and patterns, begin by making a printed copy of the current chart. Using this copy as a guide, select the markers (rows, columns, or wedges). Choose Format **P**atterns, select a black foreground color and white background color, and then pick patterns that will show better on a black-and-white printer.

Problem: The printed copies of the chart don't look the same as the chart that appears in the window. Why does this difference exist, and what can be done about it?

Solution: Excel attempts to fit data into the screen window even when that window is not large enough. To get a true feeling for how your chart will look when printed, choose File **P**rint, select the **P**review check box, then press Enter or choose OK. Because the printer makes a difference in how a graph prints, make sure you have the correct printer selected in the File **P**rinter Setup command.

Problem: One font was used on-screen, but a different font prints. In addition, not all of the font sizes shown on-screen print on the laser printer.

Solution: Excel's graphs use graphic mode on the laser printer, but characters are created from the softfonts, font cartridges, or internal fonts used with your laser printer. The printer only prints with the fonts and sizes it has available. If the correct size font is not available, the text may appear out of position.

To reduce the chance of this happening, check the File **P**rinter Setup command to ensure that the correct printer and cartridge are selected. Use the Format **F**onts command with the **P**rinter Fonts check box selected to limit fonts to ones that Windows thinks your printer has. Finally, use the

Preview option after choosing **File Print** to see what you're going to get.

Make sure you install the display fonts that come on a diskette with the cartridges. To install fonts use the Control menu (Alt, space bar). **Run** the Control **P**anel command to start the Control Panel application. Then choose the **I**nstallation Add New Font command.

(A versatile cartridge for the Hewlett-Packard® LaserJet™ family and Windows is the "Z" cartridge or Microsoft 1. It contains both Times Roman and Helvetica.)

Problem: After customizing a chart, the chart type cannot be changed with the **G**allery commands without losing the custom objects.

Solution: When you want to change the chart type of a modified chart, choose **Format Main Chart.** The dialog box enables you to switch chart types while preserving custom features that are appropriate to the new chart type. (For example, gridlines would not be appropriate for a pie chart and therefore would not be preserved.)

Problem: The printer prints only black and white. Is there any way to produce color prints for transparencies?

Solution: There are two ways. One takes money; the other takes time. First, you could buy a color plotter. Check with the Microsoft support line and the plotter's manufacturer to determine whether Windows supports the color option on the printer or plotter you select.

Second, you can hand-color your transparencies with press-on overlays. To do this, use **Format Patterns** on your chart to remove the color and pattern from inside markers such as bars, columns, and wedges. Print the chart and create a transparency. Cut the color overlay to fit the marker and rub the overlay into place on a transparency of the black-and-white chart. Wear thin white photo-developer's gloves to keep the oil from your hands from staining the transparency over time. Most art supply stores carry transparent overlays and gloves.

Problem: The year numbers that should appear along the category axis (x-axis) become part of the data.

Solution: Make sure that year numbers are along the long side of the data range. The short side of the data range must have text labels. The upper left corner of the data range must be blank. If you still have problems, change numeric years to text with formulas such as the following:

=″1989″

Problem: After moving either a chart or its supporting worksheets to a different directory, the chart loses its link because the chart doesn't know where the worksheet is located. How can the chart be relinked to its worksheet?

Solution: Activate the chart that needs to be relinked. The worksheet being relinked must be open, so use the **File Open** command to find that worksheet and open it.

Reactivate the chart so that it is on top. Choose **File Links** and select the name of the worksheet that was the original link. Choose the **Change** button, and a new dialog box appears. From this dialog box, select the replacement link's drive, directory, and file name from the list boxes. Choose OK or press Enter. The old directory and file name of the supporting worksheet in the chart's series formula is replaced by the directory and file name you choose from the list boxes. Save your updated chart.

Problem: Blank areas appear in the chart, either between markers or between groups of markers.

Solution: Blank cells have been included in the data series. Check the cell ranges used in your chart for blank cells, or for inserted rows or columns. You can find which cells are used by selecting the markers and reading the series formula. For more information, refer to Chapter 16's "Customizing with Series Formulas" section.

Blank areas between markers or between clusters of markers may also be caused by too large a setting in the % Overlap in the Format **M**ain Chart command or in the Format **O**verlay command.

Problem: The chart becomes scrambled after you rearrange some areas of the worksheet. Some data markers are missing, and others are in the wrong location or are the wrong color.

Solution: Charts use external cell references that do not automatically update when you make changes to the supporting worksheet. When you move cells, or insert or delete rows and columns, the chart does not reflect the changes. As a consequence, the chart may refer to cells that no longer contain data or that contain the wrong data.

Prevent this problem by naming the cell ranges in worksheets that are used for creating charts. Use Formula Define Name or Formula Create Names to name the cells. Edit these names into the series formulas in the chart. Then, even if an area of a worksheet is changed, the chart can find the named area. This technique is explained further in a tip in Chapter 16, "Building Advanced Charts."

From Here . . .

Now that you are using charts with your worksheets, look for ways that charts can reduce your workload or improve your efficiency. Charts can be used for much more than adding flash to presentations. If you find that you use a similar chart format frequently, you may want to learn how to create macros that automate the process. Chapter 25 contains a Macro Quick Start.

You can transfer your Excel worksheet results and charts to a word-processing program in order to produce reports that really stand out. Chapter 28, "Using Excel with Windows Applications," and Chapter 29, "Using Excel with Standard DOS Applications," show you how to print your charts inside some word-processing reports and how to include Excel worksheets in nearly all word-processing reports.

Part IV

Excel Databases

An Excel database stores information so that you can sort it, search it, extract from it, and analyze it. At its simplest, an Excel database might be thought of as an automated Rolodex that can store and retrieve names, phone numbers, and addresses. But Excel databases can serve far broader and more flexible functions than that.

You can sort Excel database information in alphabetical and numerical order. And you aren't limited when you sort. You can sort by rows or columns, and you can sort by as many headings as you want. You can find data that meets conditions you specify, such as finding all accounts that are more than 30 days overdue. You even can use an extract command to withdraw specific information and prepare it for a printed report. Database statistical functions let you quickly analyze a database's contents to find information, such as the amount expended in June for project code 1025.

You will find Excel's database easier to use than other worksheet and database combinations. For example, you can use Excel's database in the same ways you might use a Lotus 1-2-3 database. But with Excel, you have the option of using a much easier method. You can use a form that Excel creates automatically. You can use that form for data entry, editing, and searching. Using the form allows you to enter, edit, find, and delete data effortlessly.

You can link database information to worksheet calculations. You can even create a relational database by linking databases located on different sheets. Unlike programs that are databases only, the Excel database is an integral part of the worksheet. This feature makes it easy to link database contents to worksheet calculations, or vice versa. You will find this feature particularly important when you want to use database information in worksheet calculations or use worksheet calculations to control database contents.

You can put your database in one worksheet and your calculations in another worksheet. By linking the two, you conserve memory and allow for a larger database. You can link worksheets and databases, for example, when you calculate future business trends from a database of company history, when you use a database of parts and prices to estimate project costs, or when you use prices in a database to provide information for a worksheet's calculations.

Chapter 18
Database Quick Start

Chapter 19
Designing Databases

Chapter 20
Entering and Sorting Data

Chapter 21
Finding and Editing Data

Chapter 22
Extracting and Maintaining Data

Chapter 23
Building Advanced Databases

Chapter 24
Troubleshooting Databases

18

Database Quick Start

An Excel database helps you store, sort, find, extract, and analyze data. In this Quick Start, you learn how to use the database capabilities that are an integral part of Excel.

Microsoft has made the Excel database easy to use by including a data-entry form that is generated automatically as soon as you define the database range. From that form, you can add, delete, edit, and find data in the database. More involved data manipulation, such as finding records that satisfy multiple conditions or extracting data from reports, uses a criteria range to hold the specifications of what you want to match. Excel's criteria range is similar to the one used in Lotus 1-2-3.

Before you begin this Database Quick Start, you need to know how to enter and edit data in Excel and how to choose from Excel menus and dialog boxes. If you are not familiar with these techniques, review Chapter 2, "Windows Quick Start," and Chapter 4, "Worksheet Quick Start."

Setting Up the Database Example

In order to work through the exercises in the Database Quick Start, you first will need to enter the sample database information shown in figure 18.1. Notice that related information is kept in a *record* that occupies a single row. All the information of the same type is stored in the same *field*—a column. A *field name* above each column describes the type of information in that field. Field names must be text or a text formula and can occupy only one row—row 12 in the example. Although figure 18.1 shows two rows of headings, rows 11 and 12, Excel recognizes only the headings in the row immediately above the database columns. This means that each heading in row 12 must be unique.

Fig. 18.1. The sample database for the Database Quick Start.

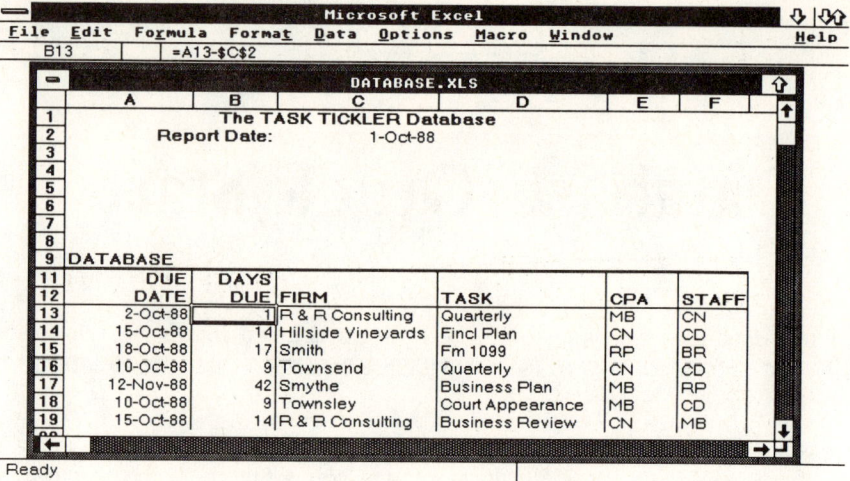

To prepare the sample database, follow these steps:

1. Type the data shown in figure 18.1. Be careful to enter the data in the same rows and columns as shown in the figure.

   Row 10 has been outlined using Format **B**order, and its height has been reduced to 1 with Format **R**ow Height. This technique creates a solid underline. You can use Format **B**order to enter lines and boxes around the data. These do not affect database operation.

   To ensure that the exercises in the Quick Start work correctly, use the dates shown in the figure rather than current dates. Use Format **N**umber to format the dates so that they appear as shown.

2. In cell B13, enter the formula

   =A13-$C$2

   This formula takes the date in row 13 and subtracts from it the Report Date in C2 to calculate the Days Due.

3. Copy the formula from B13 into the range B14:B19 so that the DAYS DUE values appear as in the figure.

NOTE

Use Absolute References To Refer to Cells outside the Database

Formulas within a database must use relative cell references, such as A13, to refer to cells in the same row. Formulas in the database that reference a cell outside the database, such as the Report Date in cell C2, must use absolute cell references, such as $C$2.

Sorting Data

Excel has a sort command that enables you to sort information, whether or not it is part of a database. You can use the sort command to reorder work such as lists, forecasting worksheets, or expense account databases. The **Data Sort** command sorts either by row or by column, allowing you to reorder a worksheet either vertically or horizontally.

To sort the rows of data in the sample database by date and then by firm name, follow these steps:

1. Select the data cells you want to sort, as shown in figure 18.2.

   Always make sure that you have included the full width of the rows to be sorted.

   Labels are not included in the sort selection. Including the labels in the sort selection might move them from their column heading position.

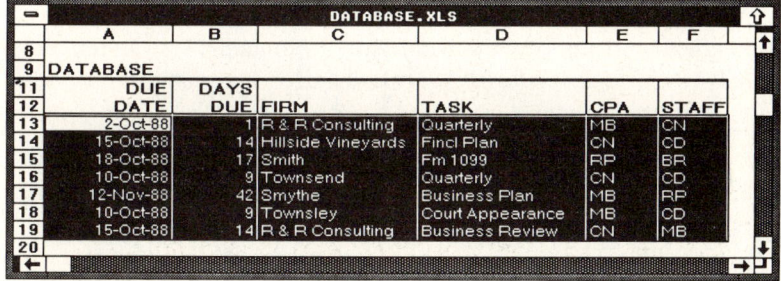

Fig. 18.2. Data selected for the sort operation.

2. Choose **Data Sort.**

3. Move the Sort dialog box so that you can see the top row of the selected range. Your screen should look similar to figure 18.3.

   Mouse: Drag the title bar of the Sort dialog box.

   Keyboard: Press Alt and then the space bar, and then choose Move and press the arrow keys.

4. Check to make sure that the **R**ows option is selected.

   You want to keep each row together during the sort.

Fig. 18.3. The Sort dialog box.

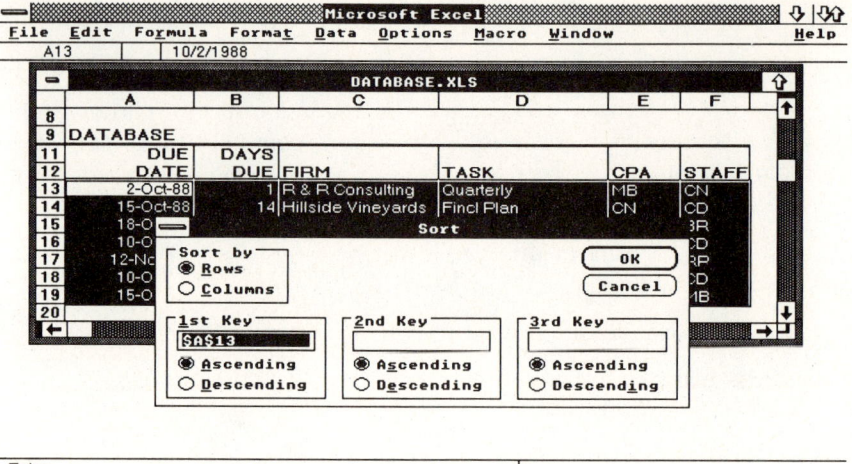

5. Enter the **1st Key** as $A$13.

   Mouse: Make sure that the **1st Key** text box is selected completely. If the box does not already contain $A$13, click on cell A13. The absolute reference is entered automatically.

   Keyboard: Make sure that the **1st Key** text box is selected completely. If the box does not already contain $A$13, press the arrow keys to move the active cell to A13. The absolute reference is entered automatically.

   The first field on which you are sorting is Due Date in column A. The top cell in the selected range of this column is $A$13. The Due Date will be the first sort item just as the last name is the first sort item in a phone book.

6. Verify that **Ascending** order is selected so that dates will be sorted from earliest to most recent.

   Mouse: Click on **Ascending** to select it.

   Keyboard: Press Alt+A to select Ascending sort order.

7. Enter the **2nd Key** as $C$13.

   Mouse: Click in the **2nd Key** box, and then click on cell C13.

   Keyboard: Press Alt+2, and then move the active cell to C13.

8. Select **Ascending** order for the 2nd key.

   The Sort dialog box now should look like figure 18.4.

9. Choose OK or press Enter.

The data will be sorted by rows as shown in figure 18.5. Rows that contained the same Due Date, such as 10-Oct-88 and 15-Oct-88, are sorted further by Firm name.

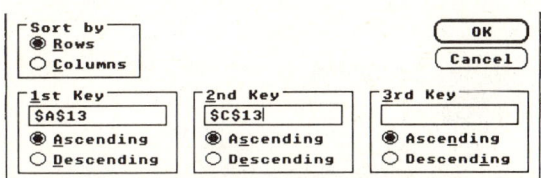

Fig. 18.4. Two sort keys specified in the Sort dialog box.

Fig. 18.5. Database rows sorted by date and then by firm name.

	A	B	C	D	E	F
8						
9	DATABASE					
11	DUE	DAYS				
12	DATE	DUE	FIRM	TASK	CPA	STAFF
13	2-Oct-88	1	R & R Consulting	Quarterly	MB	CN
14	10-Oct-88	9	Townsend	Quarterly	CN	CD
15	10-Oct-88	9	Townsley	Court Appearance	MB	CD
16	15-Oct-88	14	Hillside Vineyards	Fincl Plan	CN	BR
17	15-Oct-88	14	R & R Consulting	Business Review	CN	MB
18	18-Oct-88	17	Smith	Fm 1099	RP	BR
19	12-Nov-88	42	Smythe	Business Plan	MB	RP

Ready

Setting the Database Range

Before you can use database commands that find or extract information, you must let Excel know where the database is located. To set the database range, follow these steps:

1. Select the database range. Make sure that you include the full width of the rows and the single row of field headings above the data.

   Figure 18.6 shows how the field-name row next to the data is included in the selection.

2. Choose **Data Set Database.**

   The **Data Set Database** command assigns the range name DATABASE to the selected range. Excel looks for field headings in the top row of this range.

You can view the current DATABASE range by choosing Formula Define Name and selecting DATABASE from the list box.

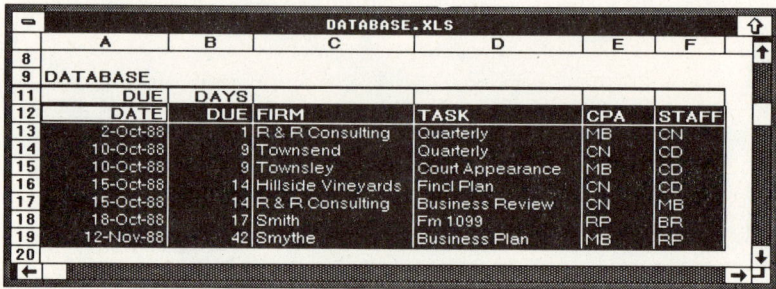

Using the Database Form

After you have defined the location of the database with Data Set Database, Excel automatically creates a database form. This form is useful for viewing, adding, deleting, editing, and finding data.

Display the database form by choosing Data Form. The form appears in its own window, as shown in figure 18.7.

The form uses the names from the top of the DATABASE range to label each field. The field names appear on the left side of the form. Most fields have an underlined letter in the field name. The data from one record (row) appears in the text boxes to the right of the field names.

The top right corner of the form shows *1 of 7* to indicate that this is the first of seven records.

The right side of the form contains buttons used to add, delete, ask a question (Criteria), and find data.

Select fields or buttons by pressing Alt and the underlined letter or by clicking the mouse on the field text or button. The Tab key moves forward through fields and buttons, while Shift+Tab moves backward. Notice that when all letters have been used for underlining, one heading, CPA, may not have an underlined letter. When this happens, use Tab or Shift+Tab to select that field.

Viewing Records

To view the records in the database from the database form, follow these steps:

1. Scroll through the records using the database form.

   Mouse: Click on the arrow in the form's scroll bar or drag the "thumb" box on the scroll bar.

   Keyboard: Press the up- or down-arrow key to move to the same field of the next or previous record. Press Enter or Shift+Enter to move to the first field of the next or previous record.

2. Choose the Find **Prev** button repeatedly until the first record is displayed.

Additional ways of moving between records are described in Chapter 20, "Entering and Sorting Data."

Finding Records

You can find particular records in the database by specifying a certain description that records must match. The description of what you want to find is known as *criteria*.

In the sample database, follow these steps to find those records where the Due Date is 10-Oct-88:

1. From the database form, select the **Criteria** button.

   The buttons on the form change, and the text box for each field clears so that you can enter the criteria that describe the records you want to match.

2. Select the DATE text box.

   Mouse: Click in the DATE text box.

   Keyboard: Press Alt+A or Tab until the text box is selected.

3. Type the following criteria:

   10/10/88

   The form now should appear as shown in figure 18.8.

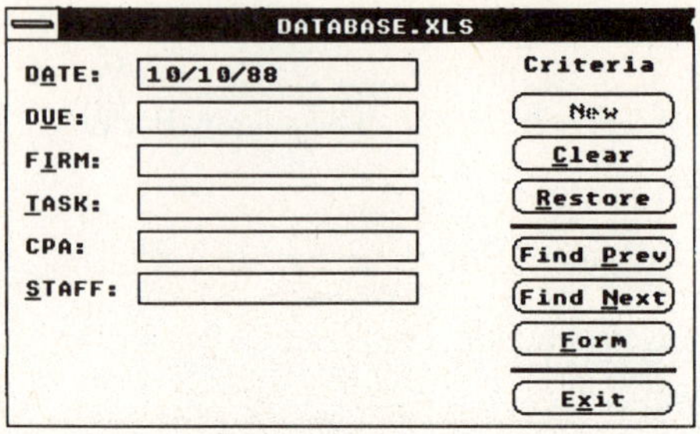

Fig. 18.8. The database form with criteria for finding certain records specified.

4. Choose Find Next.

   Because you started from the first record, Excel begins there and searches for the next record containing a Date Due of 10/10/88. The record appears in the form as shown in figure 18.9. (On your first search in the database, you may want to make sure you start at the first record.)

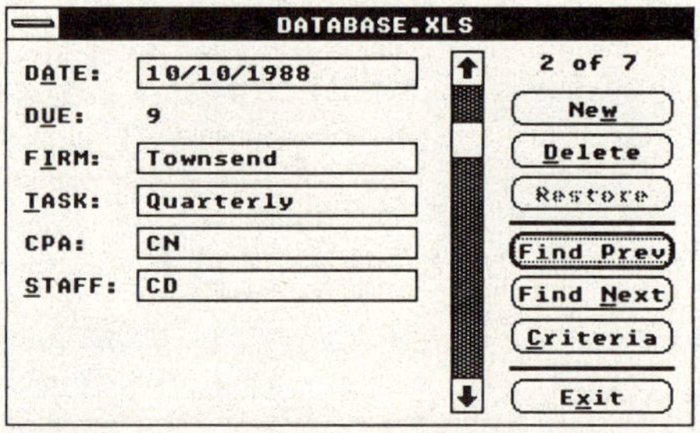

Fig. 18.9. The database form with the first record that matches the criteria displayed.

Note that when you conduct this type of search, you can enter criteria in more than one field text box of the database form.

Editing Records

You can edit records from the database form. The current record, for Townsend (see fig. 18.9), can be changed now that it is has been found.

To change the initials CD to BR in the Staff field, follow these steps:

1. Select the **STAFF** text box.

   Mouse: Click in the box.

   Keyboard: Press Tab repeatedly or press Alt-S.

2. Use normal editing techniques to change the initials CD to BR, then press Enter.

Adding Records

Adding new records to the database is as easy as selecting the New button. Follow these steps to add a new record to the sample database:

1. Choose the New button.

    The cursor positions itself in the text box of the first field.

2. Type a new record using the data in the fields shown in figure 18.10.

    Mouse: Click in a box, type the information, and then click in the next box.

    Keyboard: Type in a box, then press Tab to move to the next box. (Pressing Enter moves you to the next record.)

    Notice that you cannot enter information in or edit the DUE field. This is a calculated field that cannot be changed or entered within the database form.

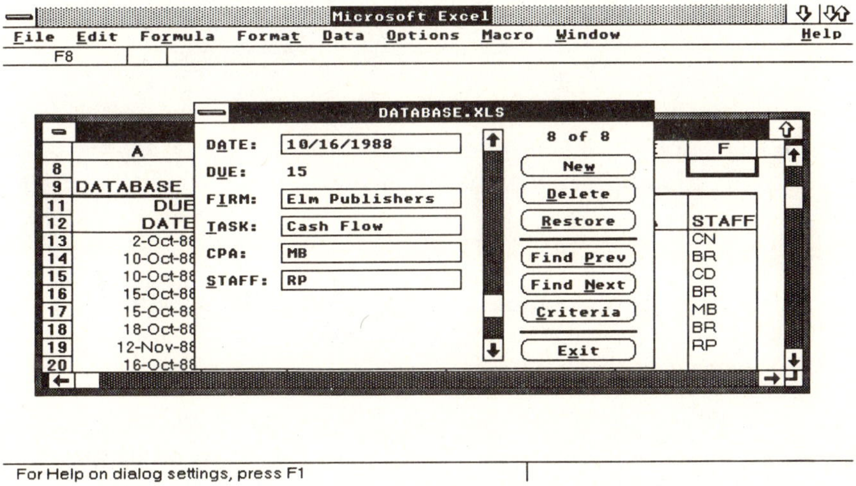

Fig. 18.10. A new record added through the database form.

3. Choose the Exit button to leave the form and retain all the changes and additions to the database.

    If you want to close the window without saving your additions and changes, you can double-click on the control icon at the upper left corner of the form; or press Alt and then the space bar, and then choose Close. Additions and changes will not be kept if you Close directly after adding or deleting.

Figure 18.11 shows the result of your changes in the database. The added record has been inserted in a row below the original database range. Excel automatically has expanded the range to include the added row. You can view the new database range by choosing Formula Goto and selecting DATABASE from the list box.

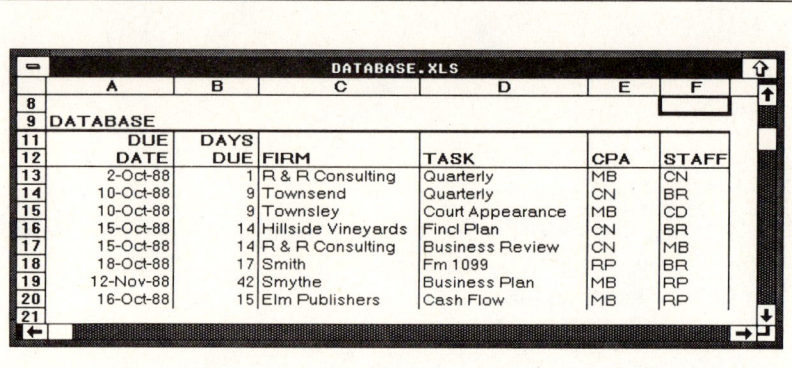

When you add data using the database form, Excel extends the database range as long as there is room below the database. You will not be allowed to add data if room is not available to extend the range.

Deleting Records

You can use the database form to delete records just as you use it to add records. Follow these steps to delete the record for Elm Publishers from the sample database:

1. Choose **Data Form** to reopen the database form.

2. Scroll through the records until you reach the added record for Elm Publishers.

3. Select the **Delete** button.

   The alert box shown in figure 18.12 appears, warning that you are about to delete this record permanently.

4. Choose OK or press Enter.

5. Select the **Exit** button to save your changes and to return to the database.

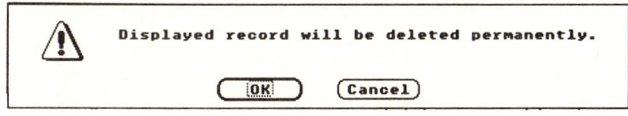

Fig. 18.12. An alert box that warns you that you are about to delete a record permanently.

Setting the Criteria Range

To conduct complex searches and extract records, you must enter a criteria range on the worksheet. The criteria range contains two rows. The top row contains field names that *exactly* match the field names at the top of the database. You do not have to use all the field names, but the ones you use must be the same as they appear in the database. In the second row of the criteria range (below the field names), you enter information describing the records for which you want to search.

Although the criteria range does not need to have borders around it, including borders creates a more attractive appearance and reduces the chance for entry errors.

Use the following steps to create the criteria range for the sample database, as shown in figure 18.13:

1. Enter the word **CRITERIA** in cell A4 and make it bold.

2. Select cells A5:F5, use Format **B**order to outline the cells, and then change the row height to 1 with Format **R**ow Height. This step creates a solid line in row 5.

3. Copy the field names from row 12 to row 6 by selecting cells A12:F12 and choosing the **E**dit **C**opy command. Move the active cell to A6 and press Enter.

4. Select cells A7:F7; choose Format **B**order; and select **L**eft, **R**ight, and **B**ottom. Then choose OK.

You have just created a criteria range that is easy to see. By copying the field names from the database you ensure that they are exactly the same. You now must tell Excel where that criteria range is located.

1. Select cells A6:F7.

2. Choose **D**ata **S**et Criteria.

The selected range shown in figure 18.14 has been given the range name CRITERIA. You can view or delete this range name with Fo**r**mula **D**efine Name.

Fig. 18.13. A criteria range added to the sample database.

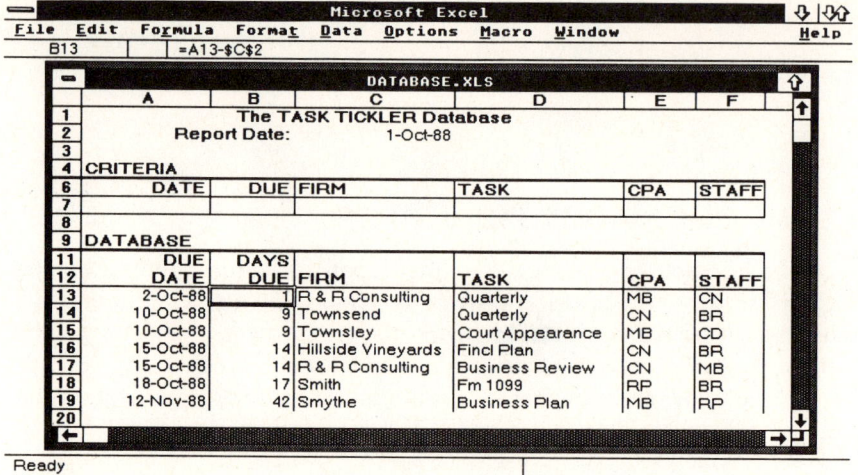

Fig. 18.14. The CRITERIA range selected.

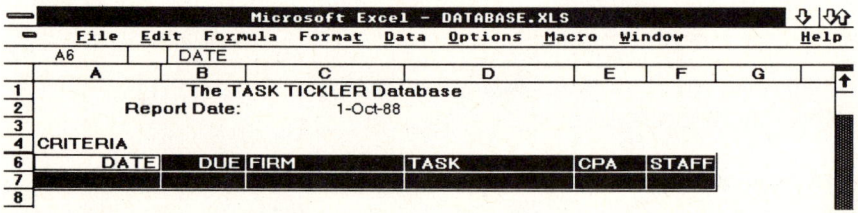

Finding Records with the Criteria Range

After a criteria range has been selected, you can enter criteria just as you entered criteria in the database form. Using a criteria range enables you to enter complex criteria that you could not enter in the database form. This Quick Start shows you some examples of simple criteria you can enter in the criteria range. More complex criteria are discussed in Chapter 22, "Extracting and Maintaining Data."

One simple type of criteria uses *wild cards* to check for close as well as exact matches in text data. (Wild cards also can be used in a data form.) For example, suppose that you know that a name begins with *Sm* and has *th* in it. The asterisk (*) wild card will accept any number and type of characters as a match at the same location as the asterisk. In the following example, the asterisk (*) will be between *Sm* and *th*.

In the sample database, use the following steps to enter criteria in row 7 (just as you entered them in the database form) and to find the records that match that criteria:

1. In cell C7, directly under the FIRM heading, enter

    Sm*th

    Your screen will look like figure 18.15.

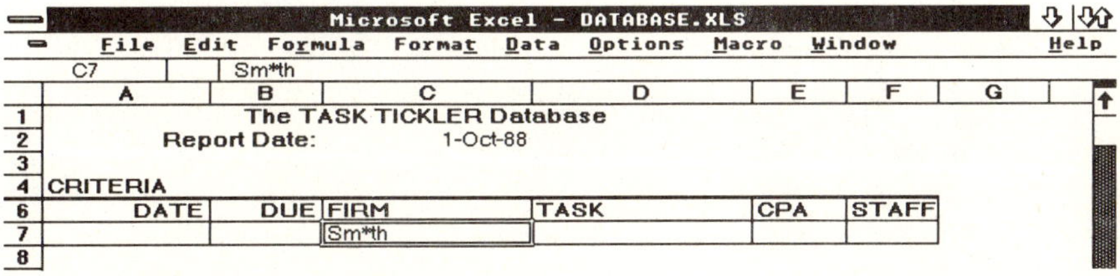

Fig. 18.15. Criteria that uses a wild card entered.

2. Choose **Data Find.**

    The database immediately shifts on the screen and selects the first record matching the pattern in the criteria range (see fig. 18.16). The scroll bars change to a new pattern, and a message appears in the status bar to show that the Find command is active.

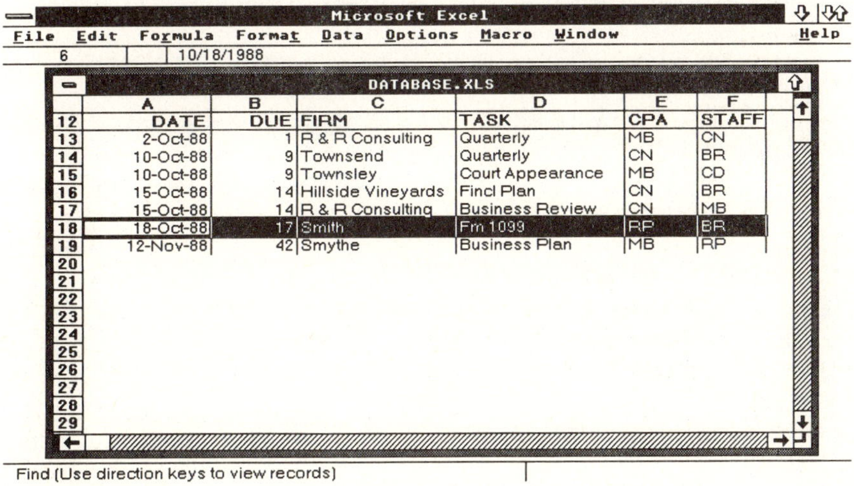

Fig. 18.16. Row 18 selected based on criteria entered in the criteria range.

The record containing *Smith* is highlighted.

3. Scroll down to the next matching record.

    Mouse: Click on the down arrow in the scroll bar.

Keyboard: Press the down-arrow key.

The seventh record in the database contains the FIRM name of Smythe. *Smythe* also matches the pattern of *Sm*th* because the asterisk (*) matches the *y* and because Excel disregards any characters following the criteria. That is, Excel accepts the *e* in Smythe. Notice that the record number appears to the left of the formula bar.

4. Delete the old criteria from C7 by selecting C7, pressing Del and then enter. (You are deleting this criteria in preparation for a later example.)

To exit from the Find command, choose **Data Exit Find**, select a cell outside the database range, or press Esc.

Extracting Records for a Report

Using the criteria range you have just created, you can command Excel to extract information from the database, copy it to another area, and paste it in. You then can print this extract as a report.

Before you can extract information, you must create an extract range. This range shows Excel the field names of the data you are interested in and where you want the copy of extracted data placed.

To prepare your extract range, you must use field headings that *exactly* match the field names in the database. If the headings don't match, Excel will not be able to match the correct columns.

NOTE

The Extract Range Is Different from the Criteria Range

The extract range and criteria range are different and separate. The criteria range is where you indicate what you are looking for. The extract range is where you want that information copied to.

Use the following steps to create an extract range in the sample database:

1. Enter the word **EXTRACT** in cell A24 and make it bold.

2. Select cells A25:F25, use Format **B**order to outline the cells, and then change the row height to 1 with Format **R**ow Height. This step creates a solid line in row 25.

3. Copy the field names from row A12:F12 to row A26:F26. If you want, use Format **B**order to remove the borders around the field names.

The extract headings should appear similar to those shown in figure 18.17. Make sure that the names are the same as those in the database headings.

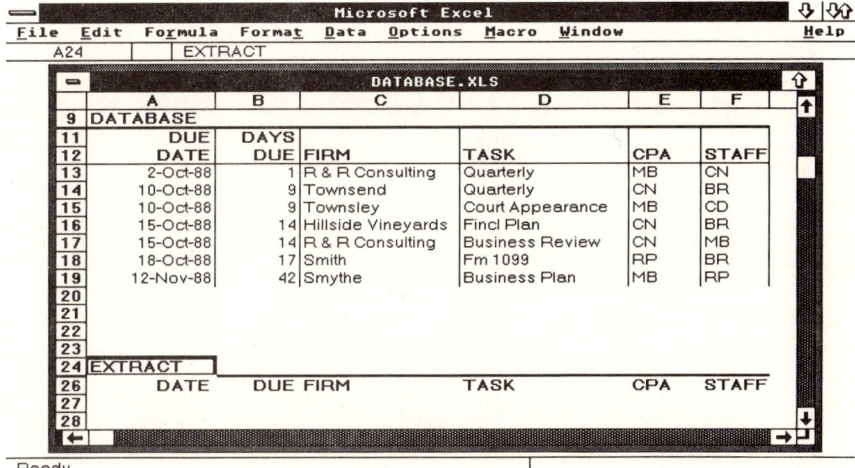

Fig. 18.17. The sample database with extract headings added.

Although the field names in the extract range must match the database field names exactly, the names do not have to be in the same order, nor does the extract range have to include every field name.

Using the sample database, follow these steps to extract records that contain information due in _less than_ 15 days:

1. In cell B7 of the criteria range, directly underneath the DUE heading, enter <**15**.

    Note that < is the symbol for _less than_. Chapter 21, "Finding and Editing Data," lists other symbols that help you search for ranges of numbers.

2. Select cells A26:F26, as shown in figure 18.18, so that Excel will know where the extract headings are located. These selected headings tell Excel which columns from the database you want selected. You don't have to have all field names listed or selected.

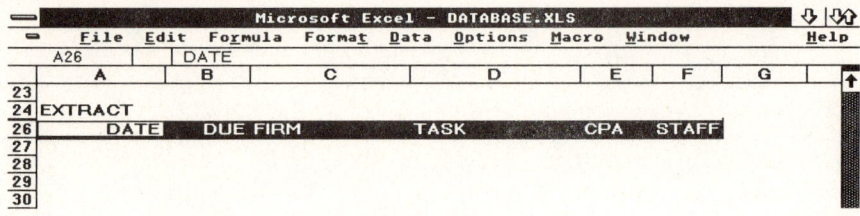

Fig. 18.18. The
extract headings
selected.

3. Choose **Data Extract** to display the Extract dialog box.

4. Choose OK or press Enter.

Figure 18.19 shows that the records with less than 15 days until due have
been copied from the database to the rows below the extract headings. The
extract range is ready for you to format and print.

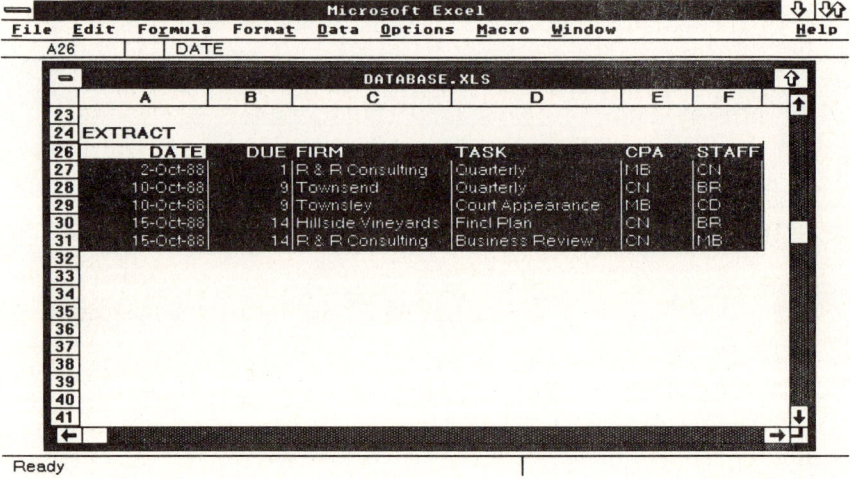

Fig. 18.19. The
extract range
after Data
Extract.

NOTE

Do Not Put Anything below an Unlimited Extract Range

Excel can extract data to a limited area or unlimited area. When you highlight
only the extract headings, you tell Excel to erase all the cells below the extract
headings and use as many cells below as necessary (unlimited area). This
technique is convenient when you don't know how many rows of data will
be extracted. The practice is hazardous, however, if you have anything below
the extract range. Chapter 22, "Extracting and Maintaining Data," describes
how to create a limited extract range.

From Here . . .

The simplest and quickest way to add, delete, edit, and find database information is with the database form. In the chapters that follow, you will learn how to use the database form to perform the functions you want.

When you want to perform complex searches, such as finding all records with dates between January 15 and February 15 with amounts due of more than $500, then you will want to learn how to use a criteria range to enter your query. Chapter 22, "Extracting and Maintaining Data," discusses these criteria and shows you how to extract information from the database in order to create reports.

When you understand the fundamentals of Excel's database, make sure that you review the more advanced database techniques described in Chapter 23, "Building Advanced Databases." That chapter has a number of techniques that can save you considerable amounts of work and time. For example, the text discusses how to use database statistics functions such as DSUM, a function that can be used to find the total amount due for records with a specific account code. Combining the DSUM function with the **Data Table** command enables you to total the amount due for each account code in your database. This one procedure can turn an eight-hour job into just a few minutes.

Because many database operations are repetitive, you may find that using macros in your database operations can be helpful. For information about macros, see Chapter 25, "Macro Quick Start." That chapter demonstrates how easily you can reduce repetitive functions to a single keystroke.

19

Designing Databases

If you understand how your database relates to the rest of the worksheet, and you draw a sketch of the worksheet arrangement, you will need to make fewer changes after you build the database worksheet. This chapter helps you design databases. The chapter describes what a database is, explains the parts of a database, advises how to choose the contents for a database, and shows you how to lay out a database on the worksheet.

What Is a Database?

The first example of a database that most office workers encounter is the familiar Rolodex card file (see fig. 19.1). You can quickly flip through a Rolodex to find information such as a client's address, phone number, or favorite restaurant. A Rolodex is easy to use as long as the cards are kept in alphabetical order according to a single key word, such as the client's name. A Rolodex can present problems, however, when you want to do anything other than finding a client by the firm's name. For example, if you wanted to review your Rolodex for all the financial analysts in San Francisco, using a Rolodex could take considerable time.

```
Turnigan, Kathleen          (415) 579-2650

Financial Analyst

Brown, James & Assoc.
213 California St.
San Francisco, CA 94003

Background:       Interned w/ Peterman & Assoc., new MBA, Stanford

Expertise/Interest:     Bond portfolio analysis

Computer experience:    Excel aficionado
```

Fig. 19.1. A Rolodex file.

Excel's database quickly and easily handles functions such as finding information on file cards. It also handles complex jobs just as well. But before reading about all you can do with Excel's database, take the time to read through the terms that describe an Excel database.

An Excel database, like most databases, is built from *records* and *fields*. Each record is a row of related information. Within the row, individual items are stored in fields (cells). Each column of a database must be named with a *field name*.

The file card for Kathleen Turnigan contains a group of related information. In a computer database, that information is a record. All the information from one file card goes into one database record. In Excel, a database is set up on a worksheet grid. All the information in a record must be in the same row.

Each different piece of data in the database record (row) must be entered in a separate cell in that row. For example, Kathleen's first name goes in one cell (a field), last name in another, firm name in a third, and so on. To keep all the information for different records organized, each field of information is assigned to a specific column. For example, first names belong only in column A, last names belong in column B, and so on. Figure 19.2 shows how part of Kathleen's Rolodex card would be entered in row 12 of an Excel database. The specific types of information, separated by columns, are the database fields.

Fig. 19.2. An Excel database with field names as column headings.

	A	B	C	D	E
11	First Name	Last Name	Firm	Phone	Address
12	Kathleen	Turnigan	Brown, James & Assoc.	(415) 579-2650	213 California St.
13	Bob	Flindt	Pacific Bank Systems	(408) 623-5043	411 Coral Ave.
14	Karen	Brace	CPA Marketing	(415) 332-5469	12 Redwood Highw
15	Jerry	Thompson	Sanduskey Mortgages	(617) 879-3987	8900 Tillman Way
16	Roger	Karnley	Harvard Construction	(617) 554-6203	980 Industrial Blvd.
17	Kevin	Pearson	Elm Management	(408) 953-7809	31 El Camino Real
18	Ellen	Robinson	Health Systems, Inc.	(707) 432-0909	233 Maple Dr.

A database actually will have many rows of information (or records), each row containing the information that would have been on one card and each column containing one field of information. But something more is needed.

When you ask Excel for the records of everyone in San Francisco, you must tell it what field (column) to search in. To do this, you must give it the exact field name for that column. In this case the field name is City. Field names must be text or text formulas. Figure 19.2 shows how the field names and data are arranged within an Excel worksheet.

In figure 19.2, you can also see that the collection of information from the card in figure 19.1 now appears in a single record (row) of the database. Each record in the database contains information that would have gone on a different file card. Each cell in the row contains a different field of data. From the field names at the top of each database column, you can easily tell what data each field contains.

What Are the Parts of a Database?

Each part of an Excel database is a range of cells. An Excel database can contain as many as three parts:

Range	Description
Database	Contains the information in rows with a unique text field name at the top of each column
Criteria	Contains field names and the specification of what information is being searched for or extracted
Extract	Contains field names and may contain a selected area of blank cells where extracted information is copied

Before you can use Excel's powerful database features, you need to tell the program where the database range is located on the worksheet. Excel needs to know the range containing both the data and the field names. To use most functions in the database, you need to specify only the database range. If you want to ask complex questions or extract information for reports, then you also must use the criteria and extract ranges.

Tell Excel the location of the database range by selecting the field names and data, as shown in figure 19.3, and then choosing Data Set Database. This command gives the database and its field names the range name DATABASE. Remember, field names should only occupy a single row.

After the database range is named, you can begin to add, delete, edit, and find information. Choosing Data Form automatically creates a database form with buttons to make your work easy. Figure 19.4 shows the form created for figure 19.3 by choosing Data Form. Notice that the form shows fields that were not immediately visible in this part of the worksheet.

Fig. 19.3. The database range selected.

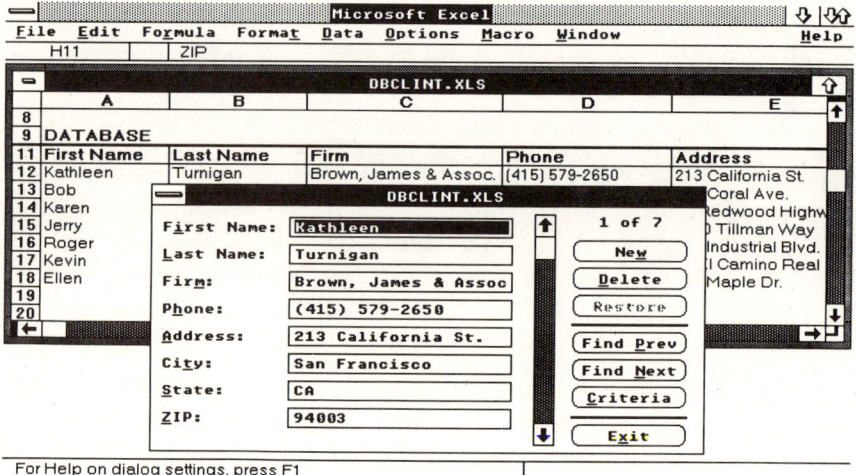

	A	B	C	D	E
8					
9	DATABASE				
11	First Name	Last Name	Firm	Phone	Address
12	Kathleen	Turnigan	Brown, James & Assoc.	(415) 579-2650	213 California St.
13	Bob	Flindt	Pacific Bank Systems	(408) 623-5043	411 Coral Ave.
14	Karen	Brace	CPA Marketing	(415) 332-5469	12 Redwood Highw
15	Jerry	Thompson	Sanduskey Mortgages	(617) 879-3987	8900 Tillman Way
16	Roger	Karnley	Harvard Construction	(617) 554-6203	980 Industrial Blvd.
17	Kevin	Pearson	Elm Management	(408) 953-7809	31 El Camino Real
18	Ellen	Robinson	Health Systems, Inc.	(707) 432-0909	233 Maple Dr.
19					

If you want to do complex searches or extract information from the database, then Excel needs to know the range containing the information you are looking for. This is the criteria range. The criteria range must contain the field names on top and at least one blank row underneath. The blank row is where you enter the criteria that specifies what you are searching for. Selecting the criteria range and then choosing **Data Set Criteria** names this area CRITERIA. Figure 19.5 shows the criteria range selected. (You do not have to place borders around the criteria range.)

Fig. 19.4. A form created by the database.

For Help on dialog settings, press F1

The last database area you need to know is the extract range. If you want to copy information that matches a specific criteria from the database to another part of the worksheet, you must tell Excel where you want that data placed. The top row of the extract range must contain the field names of the information you want extracted. Without the field names, Excel would not know which columns of information you wanted extracted.

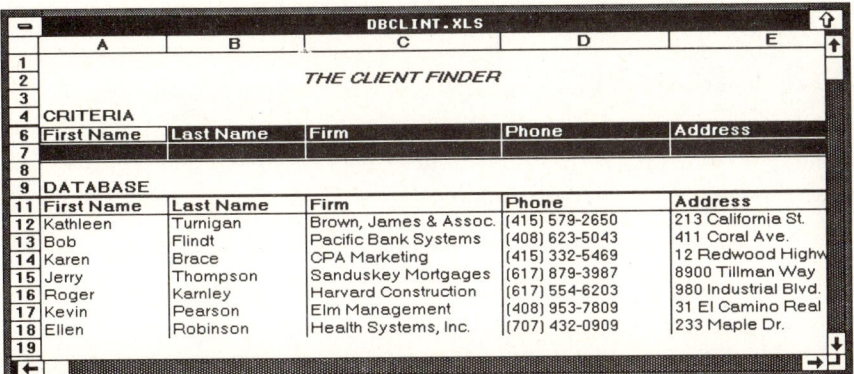

*Fig. 19.5. The
criteria range
selected.*

One danger exists when you extract data. If you do not limit the length of the range in which extracted data will be placed, Excel erases all the cells below the field names in order to allow for the extract range. Excel does this to prevent old and new extracted data from appearing together. When you lay out your database, keep in mind that this erasure can happen. Figure 19.6 shows a single row of headings selected in preparation for choosing **Data Extract**. Because only a single row of headings has been selected, all cells below the selected extract headings will be cleared before the extracted data is copied down.

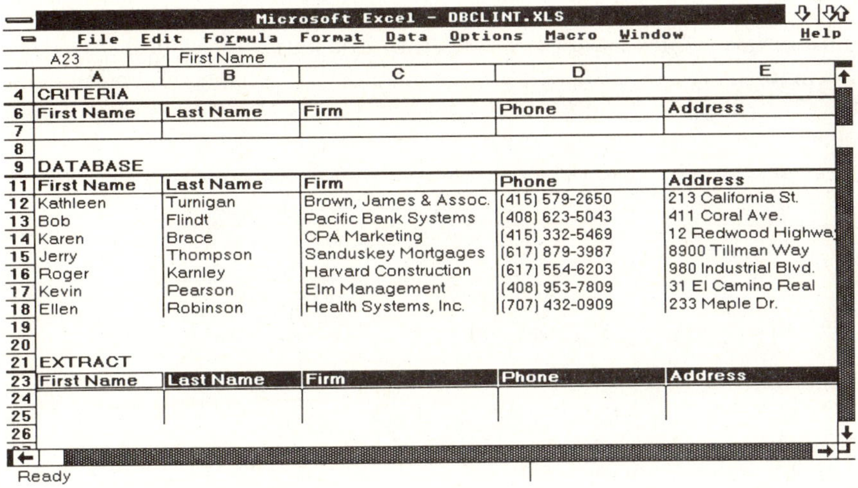

*Fig. 19.6. A
database with
an extract row
selected.*

How Do You Choose the Contents for a Database?

You can save yourself time and trouble by planning your database before building it. As a simple checklist for what data to include in a database and how to name it, consider these points:

- List the groups of data you want in each record—for example, Name.

- Break these groups of data into the smallest elements possible. For example, Name might be divided into separate fields such as First Name, Last Name, and Title. This technique makes searching the database easier and enables you to reorder data in new combinations.

- Delete fields you probably will never use.

- Delete fields that can be calculated in a report. (Why waste memory storing information that can be calculated?)

- Create short field names having no more characters than the longest piece of data.

- Use only text or text formulas in field names. Do not use numeric values.

Choose fields that are small and contain the most usable part of the data. For example, instead of using Name as a single field containing an entire name, use three fields: Title, First_Name, and Last_Name. This technique gives you the option of reordering the data in many different combinations. For example, suppose that your data looks like the following:

Title	First_Name	Last_Name
Ms.	Kathleen	Turnigan

From this data, you can create any of the following combinations:

Ms. Turnigan
Kathleen
Ms. Kathleen Turnigan
Kathleen Turnigan

You also should keep ZIP codes as a separate field. Never include the ZIP code in the city and state fields. Demographic and market data may be tied to the ZIP code. In addition, you can reduce postage rates by sorting mailings by ZIP code. If you include the ZIP code within the city and state data, searching and sorting by ZIP code only is difficult.

Be on the lean side when including data fields. Many business information systems lie unused because some well-meaning person wanted the database to contain too much information. The result is a database that is expensive, time-consuming, and tedious to maintain. When a database isn't maintained, it isn't used. Include only data you can evaluate and keep up-to-date.

How Do You Lay Out a Database on the Worksheet?

Before building your database, consider how it fits with the rest of the worksheet and how to coordinate it with other worksheets and databases for your business. Remember: Excel databases and worksheets in different files can be linked together. Here are some additional points to consider:

- Draw diagrams of other databases and worksheets in your business and notice where the data is stored twice. Can linked worksheets prevent this wasted data entry time and wasted memory?

- Consider linking databases or worksheets to reduce memory requirements, reduce data-entry time, and reduce data-entry errors. This is described in Chapter 10, "Using Multiple Windows and Linking Worksheets," and in Chapter 23, "Building Advanced Databases."

- Be sure that nothing lies below the extract range. An unlimited extract range clears all cells below it.

- Position the database so that room is available for it to expand downward. If you use Data Form to add records (rows) to your database, rows are added without pushing down the information below the database. If not enough room is available to insert cells for the new database, the database form will not let you add a new record.

- If you want to insert rows to add records to the middle of a database, make sure that no worksheet calculations exist on either side of the database. Inserting a row through a database also inserts a row through anything on the sides of the database.

• Conserve memory by beginning the database in column A.

In summary, make a thumbnail sketch or map of how the worksheet is laid out so that you can see whether database expansion will be limited, whether the extract area will erase data below it, and whether rows inserted through the database will insert through other worksheet sections. A sketch of the database layout as compared to other parts of the worksheet lets you see where conflicts might exist.

From Here . . .

The quickest way to learn the basics of Excel databases is to work through Chapter 18, "Database Quick Start." The Quick Start requires a little data entry in order to get set up; but once you have entered that data, the Quick Start goes quickly.

To get started with your database, read Chapter 20, "Entering and Sorting Data," and Chapter 21, "Finding and Editing Data." Those chapters will help you use the automatic database form to add, delete, edit, and find data quickly and easily.

If you need to perform complex queries or extract information from the database so that you can create a report, refer to Chapter 22, "Extracting and Maintaining Data." Chapter 23, "Building Advanced Databases," shows you how to link databases that are on separate documents and how to analyze database contents.

20

Entering and Sorting Data

This and the following chapters describe how to build and use a database that resides on an Excel worksheet. Although Excel is primarily a worksheet, it does have database capability that can help you analyze stock market trends, store expense accounts, and monitor sales figures.

Excel gives you two methods of working with its database. When the cells that comprise the database have been defined with the Data Set Database command, you can use Excel's automatically generated data form. The form makes it easy to enter, edit, delete, and search for data.

The second method of working with data uses a method similar to that used in 1-2-3. The database is specified in one range of the worksheet, and another range is used for criteria or questions. This method is used for complex searches or when you need to extract information from the database.

While Excel's database is powerful for analyzing and storing a few thousand items of information, it does have limitations. Excel's database, because it is on a worksheet, must reside within memory at all times. That means that a large database may run out of computer memory before it runs out of rows on the worksheet. This also means that an Excel database should be used for storing, tracking, and analyzing information that can be held in a few thousand rows of the database. Such jobs range from a simple name and address file, to a job cost tracking system, to a stock analysis system that contains a few years' worth of data.

TIP

When You Need an Extremely Large Database

If you have an extremely large amount of data to store, such as a piece parts inventory for a manufacturing business, you should use a disk-based database such as Paradox or dBASE III Plus. When you need to analyze data held in these databases, store a subset of the full database as a dBASE file from dBASE III or as a 1-2-3 file from Paradox. Excel will then be able to load this file into a worksheet with the File Open command.

In this chapter, you learn how to build a database and enter information into that database. If you are interested in entering just a few records of information, the discussion on the automatic database form will be of interest. When you want to enter information in a list (more like the worksheet appears), you will find the additional methods valuable.

After creating your database, you will want to keep it sorted for better presentation in reports. Excel's sorting command will let you sort your data in ascending or descending order over as many fields as you want.

In general, you use the following steps to create a database. Each of these steps is described in detail later in this chapter.

1. Enter field names above each data column.

2. Enter the initial data in columns.

3. Select the database range including a single row of field names.

4. Choose **Data** Set Data**base**.

5. Choose **Data** **Form**.

6. Add, delete, or edit existing data.

Entering the Field Names and Initial Data

Your database must have unique field names in a single row across the top of the database. These field names identify each column of data. Enter the initial data directly below the field names.

Figure 20.1 shows the database created in Chapter 18, "Database Quick Start." Not all this information was necessary for the database. Figure 20.2 shows the mandatory parts of a database: the single row of field headings and the data. The extra formatting and text in figure 20.1 serve to enhance the database's appearance and to reduce errors.

Fig. 20.1. The database created in the Quick Start.

	A	B	C	D	E	F
8						
9	DATABASE					
11	DUE	DAYS				
12	DATE	DUE	FIRM	TASK	CPA	STAFF
13	2-Oct-88	1	R & R Consulting	Quarterly	MB	CN
14	10-Oct-88	9	Townsend	Quarterly	CN	CD
15	10-Oct-88	9	Townsley	Court Appearance	MB	CD
16	15-Oct-88	14	Hillside Vineyards	Fincl Plan	CN	BR
17	15-Oct-88	14	R & R Consulting	Business Review	CN	MB
18	18-Oct-88	17	Smith	Fm 1099	RP	BR
19	12-Nov-88	42	Smythe	Business Plan	MB	RP
20						
21						

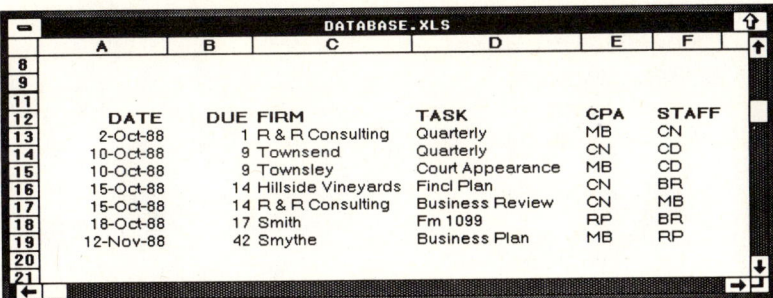

Fig. 20.2. The essential parts of a database: the field headings and data.

Field names entered across the top of the database must follow these rules:

- Field names must be text or text formulas such as ="9540".

- Field names can be up to 255 characters long, but short names are easier to use.

- Only the names in the row directly above the data are used as field names. A second row, above the field names, can be added; but that row is for appearance only.

- Names must be unique.

- Be careful not to enter leading blanks in a field name.

Now that the field names are created, you will need to add a row or two of data before building the rest of the database. Add one or two rows with normal worksheet entry techniques. When the database is created, there are more convenient methods of entering data.

Setting the Database Range

After creating field names and with at least one row of data, you can set the database range. This lets Excel know where the database is located on the worksheet. Setting the database range gives the database the range name DATABASE.

The database range contains the field names in the top row and the data below. Figure 20.3 shows a database range selected. Notice that only the row of field names directly above the data has been selected.

To define the location of the database, follow these steps:

1. Select the row of field names and records underneath the field names.

2. Choose **D**ata Set Data**b**ase.

Fig. 20.3. The database range selected.

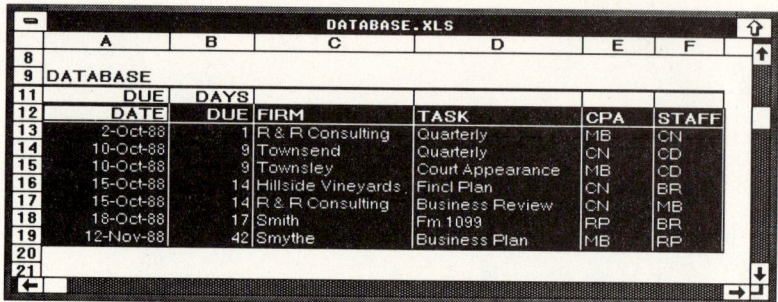

	A	B	C	D	E	F
8						
9	DATABASE					
11	DUE	DAYS				
12	DATE	DUE	FIRM	TASK	CPA	STAFF
13	2-Oct-88	1	R & R Consulting	Quarterly	MB	CN
14	10-Oct-88	9	Townsend	Quarterly	CN	CD
15	10-Oct-88	9	Townsley	Court Appearance	MB	CD
16	15-Oct-88	14	Hillside Vineyards	Fincl Plan	CN	BR
17	15-Oct-88	14	R & R Consulting	Business Review	CN	MB
18	18-Oct-88	17	Smith	Fm 1099	RP	BR
19	12-Nov-88	42	Smythe	Business Plan	MB	RP
20						
21						

This procedure creates a named range called DATABASE. You can view the currently selected database range at any time by choosing Formula Goto and selecting DATABASE from the list box.

To delete the current database choose Formula Define Name, select the name DATABASE from the list box, and then select Delete.

Only one database at a time can be defined with Data Set Database. To use a different database, you need to name the new database range by selecting it and again choosing Data Set Database. The following tip explains a fast way to do this.

TIP

Changing Databases Quickly

You can quickly change between different databases by giving each database a range name with Formula Define Name. Using names such as DB_AR, DB_CLIENT, and DB_SALES will make the databases easier to find and remember. After each range is named, you can switch quickly between databases by following these steps:

1. Choose the Formula Goto command.

2. Select the name of the database you want to use, such as DB_AR, and then press Enter.

3. Choose the Data Set Database command.

You don't need to move the cursor in order to select the database range. The Goto command selects the new range for you.

To speed this process even more, create a command macro and assign it to a Ctrl+key combination. Include a pause in the macro that waits for you to choose the new database from the Goto list box. Chapter 25, "Macro Quick Start," and Chapter 26, "Building Command and Function Macros," explain how to create macros.

TIP

Selecting a Range of Data Quickly

Databases or any range of filled cells can be selected quickly and easily by using shortcut keys. To select a range of filled cells, follow these steps:

1. Move to the leftmost cell in the field name row.

2. Press Ctrl+Shift+right arrow (hold down Ctrl and Shift while you next press the right arrow).

   This step moves the selected cells across the row until a blank cell is encountered. Figure 20.4 shows the row selected with this technique.

3. Press Ctrl+Shift+down arrow once.

   This step moves the selected row down until the active cell reaches a blank cell, as shown in figure 20.5.

The Ctrl+arrow key makes the active cell move across filled cells until a blank cell is reached. If the active cell starts on a blank cell, then the active cell moves until a filled cell is reached. The Shift key selects cells as the active cell moves.

Caution: Make sure that the active cell is not stopped prematurely by a blank cell as it travels. After the entire range is selected, hold down the Shift key and move down and right a few cells to verify that the entire range of the database is selected.

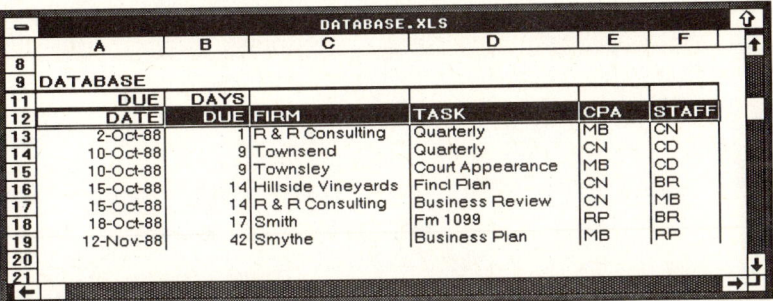

Fig. 20.4. The field names row selected with the shortcut key method.

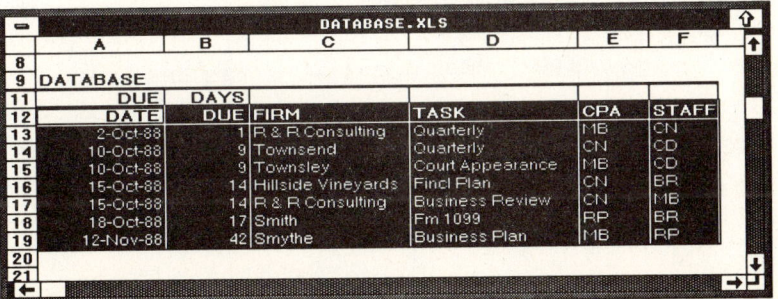

Fig. 20.5. The database range selected with the shortcut key method.

Entering Data

Now that you have entered the field headings and initial data and have selected the database range, you can use one of four different methods for entering data.

- Enter data with Excel's automatic database form. This is the quickest and easiest method of entering data.

- Enter data directly into a selected range of blank rows inserted in the database.

- Enter data in a protected database. You can use this method to insert data, protect certain data, and skip over formulas.

- Use a macro to automate any of the above methods. Part V of this book explains how to create and use macros.

Any of these methods can include checks to make sure that the data is entered correctly.

Entering Data with the Database Form

The easiest method of entering data is with Excel's automatically generated database form. After you have set the database range with **Data Set Database**, you can use the form to enter data by following these steps:

1. Choose the **D**ata **F**orm command.

    A database form similar to the one shown in figure 20.6 will appear on top of the worksheet.

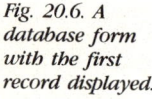

Fig. 20.6. A database form with the first record displayed.

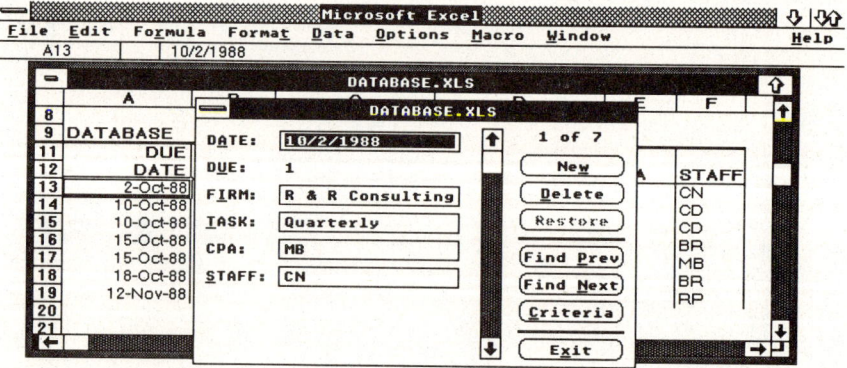

2. Select the New button.

3. Enter data in each field's text box, pressing Tab or Shift+Tab to travel forward or backward between fields. You can also click in a text box if you use a mouse.

4. Continue to select New, or press Enter for each new record you want to add.

5. Select New after the final record you add.

6. Select Exit to quit the form and return to the worksheet.

Selecting the New button or pressing Enter takes the new record you have typed in the form and puts it in the database. After selecting Exit, you will need to save the database with File Save As to record these additions on disk.

The records added with the form are added below the last row of the database. The database range is extended automatically to include the added records.

TIP

Leaving Enough Room To Add to Your Database

The data form will not let you add new records if there are not enough blank rows below the current database range. When you create your database, put it where there will be room to expand.

You can change the data in the record you are adding up until you select New or Exit to add the record to the database. After you add a record to the database, you must use the editing techniques described in Chapter 21, "Finding and Editing Data," to make changes.

TIP

Viewing the Corners of a Large Database Range

Use the Formula Goto command to select the database range, then press Ctrl+. (period) to move the active cell so that you can see each corner.

Entering Data Directly into the Worksheet

A second method for entering data is in list format, as the records appear on the worksheet. Entering data directly on the worksheet can be the easiest method when you want to create forms and data-entry checking formulas that work under macro control.

Before you use this data-entry method, you must make room in the database range for new records (rows). To preserve the existing database range and to copy formats automatically, insert new rows or cells between the existing records.

NOTE

Insert New Rows or Cells between Existing Database Records

To preserve your database range, insert new rows or cells between existing database records (rows). If you insert new rows or cells below the last record of the database, they will not be included in the database range. If you insert new rows or cells directly underneath the field headings, the format for the record will not be copied.

If you add new records below the existing database, you must select the new database range and use **Data Set Database** to rename the database range so that it includes the new records.

Inserting entire *rows* through the database will move down everything below that point across the entire worksheet. To move down only the cells directly below the database, then insert *cells* in the database. Insert cells in the database when you don't want to disturb areas to the right or left of the database.

In figure 20.7, the cells of the middle two records have been selected so that they can be moved down to allow for the addition of two more records. Cells outside the database are not selected. Notice the markers in column G; these indicate the cell locations outside the selected cells.

Fig. 20.7. Cells selected and the dialog box for inserting blank database records.

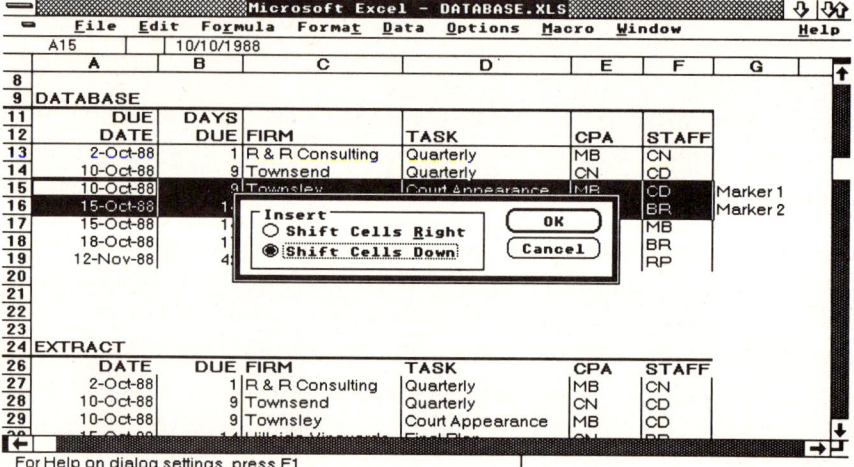

Choose the **Edit Insert** command to display the dialog box for inserting cells (see fig. 20.7). In this box, you specify whether the cells should be moved down or right. Choosing OK moves down everything below the selected cells, as shown in figure 20.8. The markers in column G have not moved.

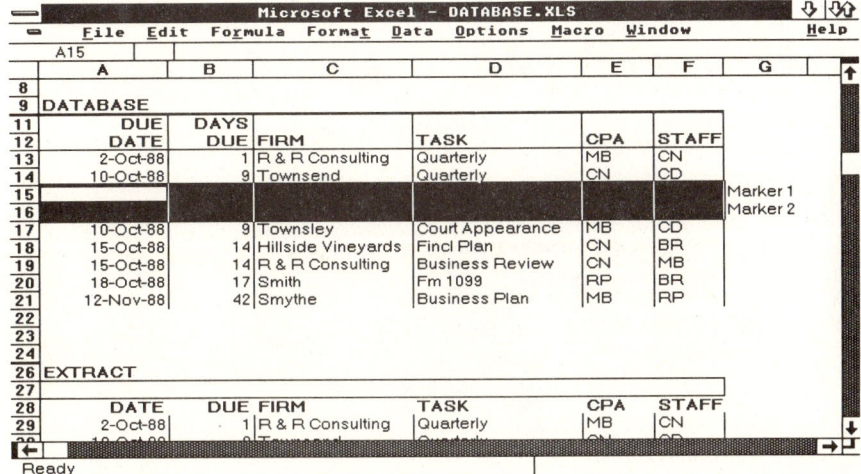

Fig. 20.8. Blank cells inserted into the database.

When you enter data directly into the worksheet, the active cell moves across every cell in the inserted range. When you use this method, you must be careful that you don't accidentally enter data over a formula. To avoid this problem, see this chapter's "Entering Data in a Protected Database" section.

Using certain data-entry keys allows you to move in any direction over the selected area. Being able to move in any direction lets you skip over cells that contain formulas.

To enter data in the blank cells that have been inserted in the database, follow these steps:

1. Select the cells to receive data.

2. Type data into the active cell.

3. Press one of the keys shown in table 20.1 to enter the data and move the active cell. Be sure to skip over the cells that contain formulas.

4. After the data is entered, press an arrow key to unselect the range.

5. Format the columns of data if necessary.

6. Create and copy formulas down the appropriate columns.

Table 20.1
Data-Entry Keys

Key	Action
Tab	Enter data and move right
Shift+Tab	Enter data and move left
Enter	Enter data and move down
Shift+Enter	Enter data and move up

While you are working within a selected data-entry range, the active cell will remain within the data-entry area. The active cell automatically wraps from one edge of the selected range to the next edge.

Excel has five shortcut key combinations that can speed your data-entry work. The key combinations are shown in table 20.2.

Table 20.2
Shortcut Keys for Data Entry

Key combination	Action
Ctrl+; (semicolon)	Enters computer's current time
Ctrl+: (colon)	Enters computer's current date
Ctrl+' (apostrophe)	Copies formula from cell above without adjusting cell references
Ctrl+" (double quotation marks)	Copies value from cell above
Ctrl+arrow	Moves over filled cells to first blank cell, or moves over blank cells to first filled cell

TIP

When You Copy a Formula

If you want to copy a formula from the cell above with its cell references adjusted to the new location, create a command macro (see Chapter 25, "Building Command and Function Macros,") and assign a Ctrl+key combination to the function. Make sure that you create the macro using **Macro Relative Record** so that the macro will work anywhere.

Entering Data in a Protected Database

The third method of entering data uses the Forma**t** Cell **P**rotection and **O**p-tions **P**rotect Document commands to restrict the active cell to unprotected cells. This method prevents you from accidentally making entries in formula cells.

Before you can use this method, you must prepare the worksheet and database for cell protection by marking the changeable cells. Begin by selecting cells that you allow to be changed. In the sample database, these cells are in the record areas—column A, C, D, E, and F. Next, choose Forma**t** Cell **P**rotection and unselect the **L**ocked option as shown in figure 20.9. Then choose OK or press Enter. This procedure marks the cells you selected as being unlocked and therefore changeable.

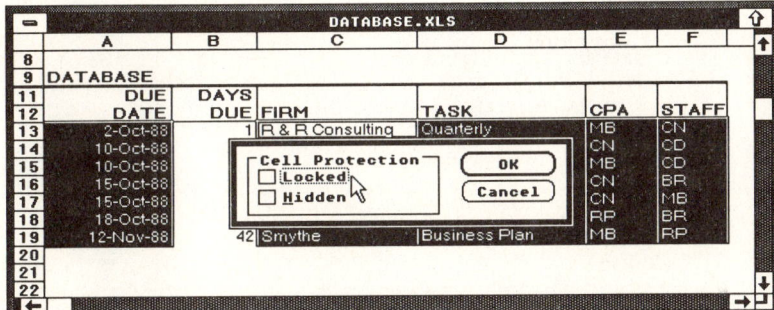

Fig. 20.9.
Changeable cells
selected in the
database and
cell protection
unlocked.

Now, protect all other cells in the worksheet from change by choosing **O**ptions **P**rotect Document. Make sure that the **C**ontents option is selected in the dialog box. You may want to enter a password. Choose OK or press Enter. This procedure protects from change all cells that you have not "unlocked" in the preceding procedure. Unprotected cells will appear underlined like those shown in figure 20.10. Notice that some menu commands are una-vailable while the worksheet (document) is protected. For example, you will not be able to insert blanks with protection on.

Fig. 20.10.
Unprotected cells
underlined
automatically
when document
protection is on.

	DATABASE.XLS					
	A	B	C	D	E	F
8						
9	DATABASE					
11	DUE	DAYS				
12	DATE	DUE	FIRM	TASK	CPA	STAFF
13	2-Oct-88	1	R & R Consulting	Quarterly	MB	CN
14	10-Oct-88	9	Townsend	Quarterly	CN	CD
15	10-Oct-88	9	Townsley	Court Appearance	MB	CD
16	15-Oct-88	14	Hillside Vineyards	Fincl Plan	CN	BR
17	15-Oct-88	14	R & R Consulting	Business Review	CN	MB
18	18-Oct-88	17	Smith	Fm 1099	RP	BR
19	12-Nov-88	42	Smythe	Business Plan	MB	RP
20						
21						

You can use the Tab and Shift+Tab keys to move the active cell between unprotected cells. The arrow keys move the active cell between any cell, but changes can be made only to the unlocked cells.

To add data to your protected database, follow these steps:

1. Choose **Options Unprotect Document**. Enter the password, if required. Choose OK or press Enter.

2. Select the full record width, and select down for as many records as you need to insert. Choose **Edit Insert**, and insert cells to make room for new data.

3. Copy formulas down into the appropriate cells.

4. Move to the first cell in the inserted cells.

5. Protect the database again with **Options Protect Document**.

6. Type data for the current cell.

7. Press Tab to enter the data and move to the next field. Press Shift+Tab to enter and move to the previous field.

While in protected mode, you can make changes only to those fields that are unlocked with **Format Cell Protection**.

TIP

Quick Database Preparation

Figure 20.11 illustrates how you can save steps by creating above your database a blank row that contains the formulas and formats used in a row of the database. Instead of copying formulas down columns in the database, you can copy the entire prepared row into one of the blank rows you insert.

In the figure, the row A7:F7 contains formulas and formats. When you copy row 7 into rows 15 and 16, those rows receive those formulas and formats. To make data entry even faster and easier, set up a macro that automatically inserts a blank row through the middle of the database and copies the pre-configured row down. Operate the macro with a Ctrl+key combination for fast use.

When entering data, guard against misspelling words or typing blanks before an entry. These mistakes make finding data difficult. If you enter data with frequently used names, prices, and codes, then you should study the automated data-entry technique described in Chapter 23, "Building Advanced Databases." Automated entries work by using a preceding entry, such as a part code, to

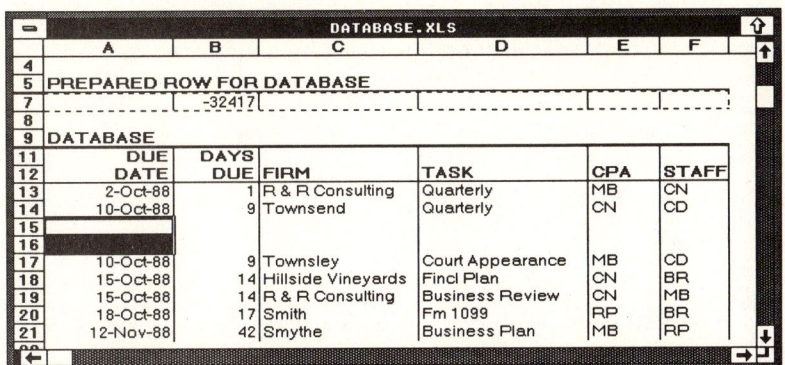

Fig. 20.11. Row 7 prepared with formulas and formats, and blank rows 15 and 16 inserted and ready to receive copies.

look up related data from elsewhere on the same or different worksheet and enter it in the database. This technique can save you from repetitious typing and reduce the possibility of typing errors.

Speeding Up Data Entry

Excel calculates fast because it only recalculates formulas that depend on the changed cells. But in large databases that contain numerous calculations, constant recalculation can slow cursor movement during data entry.

To speed data entry, turn off automatic recalculation by choosing **Options Calculation**, selecting the **Manual** option, and pressing Enter. While Excel is in manual calculation mode, the program will not update the formulas as you enter data. Watch the bottom of the screen for a *Calculate* signal that indicates when formulas are not correct because they have not been recalculated. Whenever you see *Calculate* at the bottom of the screen, do not trust the formula results.

When you need to recalculate all open worksheets, but stay in manual calculation mode, choose **Options Calculate Now** or press F9. If you want to recalculate only the active document, press Shift+F9.

After making your database entries, you can return to automatic calculation by choosing **Options Calculation** again and selecting **Automatic**.

Sorting Data

Sorting is a method of organizing your data or worksheets to put everything in ascending or descending alphabetical and numeric order. Excel can sort the rows of a database or the columns of a worksheet.

Excel can sort thousands of rows or columns in the time it would take you to sort a few, and it can sort on three fields at a time. In fact, by using multiple sorts, you can sort on as many fields as you want.

When you select **Data Sort**, Excel displays the Sort dialog box (see fig. 20.12). Some of the unique terms in that box are *Key* and the choices *Ascending* and *Descending*.

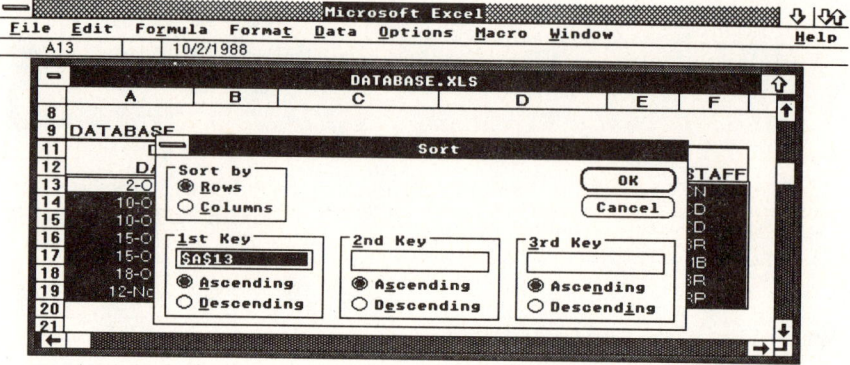

The key indicates which field Excel sorts on. For example, in a telephone book, the first key is *last name*, and the second key is *first name*. In the database shown in figure 20.13, the first sort key will be in column A, the second key will be in column E, and the third key will be in column F. Notice that the key is an absolute cell reference that can be anywhere in the column you want to sort.

The Ascending and Descending options beneath each key tell Excel to sort in A to Z or Z to A order, respectively. Excel sorts in ascending order from top to bottom for rows, or left to right for columns. The Descending option reverses this order. In addition, the program uses this order of priority:

Numbers from negative to positive

Text

FALSE results

TRUE results

Error values

Blanks

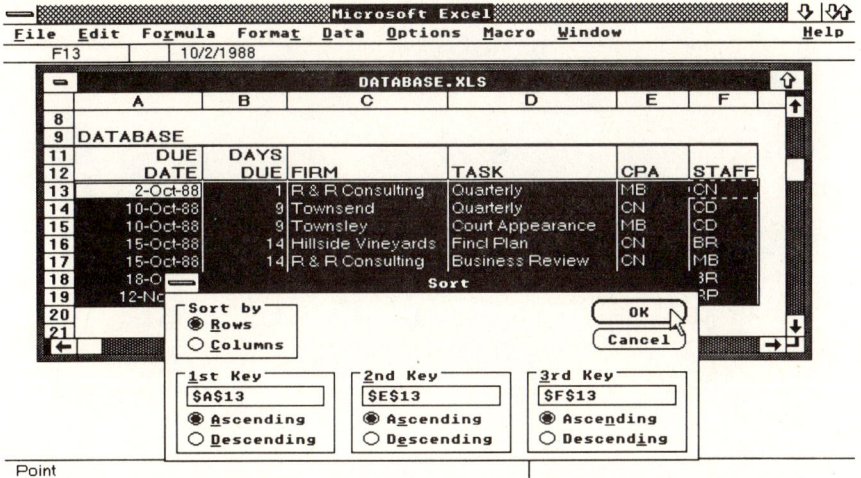

Fig. 20.13. Three keys specified for sorting the database.

Excel ignores the difference between upper- and lowercase, and does not recognize international accent marks. This feature makes finding entries easier.

1-2-3
TIP

Sorting with Blank Rows

In Excel, blanks remain at the bottom of sorted rows. In Lotus 1-2-3, blank rows "float" to the top.

When using **D**ata **S**ort to resequence your database entries, choose the **R**ows option to keep rows together during sorting or the **C**olumns option to keep columns together.

Rearranging Database Columns

Excel gives you the power to sort sideways as well as up and down. This capability provides an excellent way to rearrange the columns in your database without doing a lot of cutting and pasting.

Figure 20.14 shows the sample database about to be re-sorted with a new column order. A blank row inserted at row 11 now contains numbers indicating the desired new column order. Notice that the Days Due column must remain directly to the right of Due Date in order for the formula to calculate correctly after sorting. The Sort dialog box shows that the sort will be by columns and that you want to sort on row 11, the row containing the new column order.

Fig. 20.14. A database prepared for sorting by columns and the related Sort dialog box.

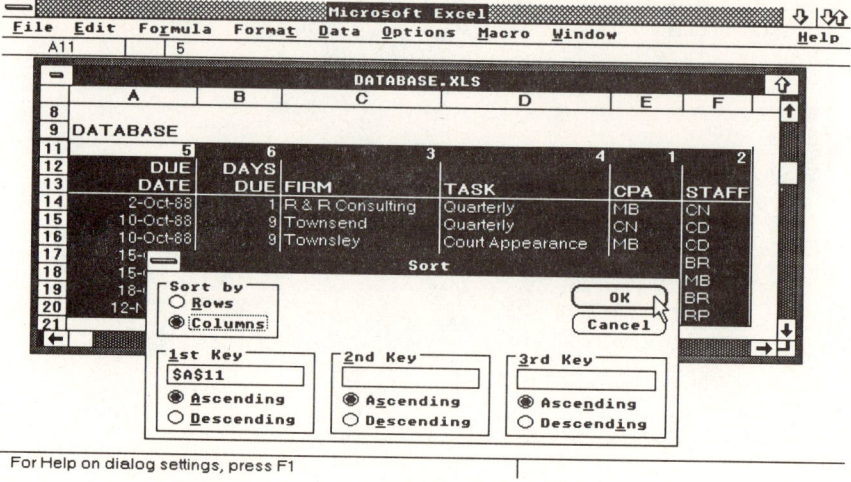

Figure 20.15 shows the database after the columns have been re-sorted in the order specified in row 11. If the Days Due column had not stayed directly to the right of the Due Date column, the formulas would now display the error #VALUE!. Note that you may have to widen columns after you reorder a database in order to get rid of the #### narrow column warning.

Fig. 20.15. The database sorted to the order specified in row 11.

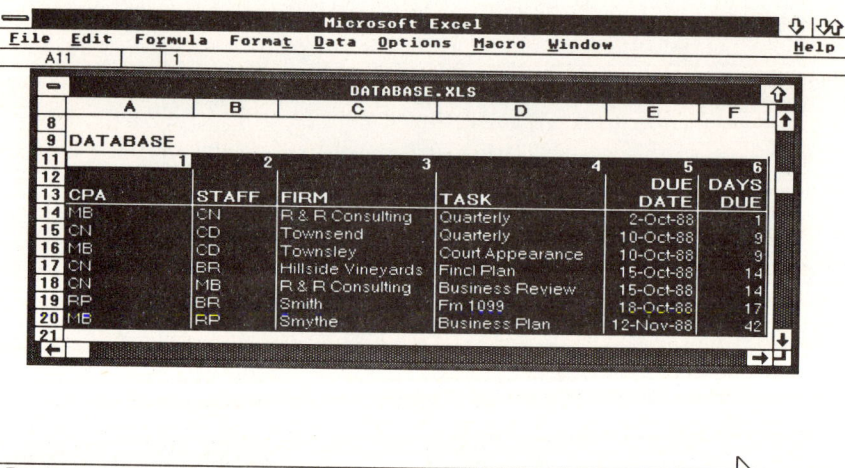

Be careful when you perform a column sort on a worksheet such as the one in the example. Formulas still refer to the same relative addresses (for example, two cells left) or refer to an absolute address. When you shift worksheet columns around, the appropriate cell may no longer be where it is expected. This creates a #VALUE! error.

Performing the Sort Operation

Sorting incorrectly can scramble your worksheet by splitting it into pieces that cannot be recombined correctly. One way to prevent this problem is to save the worksheet before you sort it. Use a file name you will not use again so that you can retrieve the file if you find that your sort has scrambled the data.

To prevent sorting problems, select the full width of the sorted rows before sorting (or full column length when sorting by column). Scrambled records can occur when the left part of a row is sorted in a different order than the right part of a row. This problem occurs most frequently when a database extends past the right of the screen, and the operator selects only the cells visible on-screen. If you immediately recognize that the sort has created a problem, choose **Edit Undo Sort**.

To sort a database or worksheet, follow these steps:

1. Choose **File Save As**, and save the worksheet to a temporary file for safekeeping.

2. Select the data to be sorted.

   Do not select field names at the top of databases. Including the field names in the sort area may move the field names down into the data area.

   Select the full width of the rows if sorting by **R**ows or the full height of the columns if sorting by **C**olumns.

3. Choose **Data Sort**.

4. Enter the **1**st Key.

   Mouse: Click anywhere in the column by which you want to sort when sorting rows, or click in the row by which you want to sort when sorting columns.

   Keyboard: Move the active cell into the column by which you want to sort when sorting rows, or move the active cell into the row by which you want to sort when sorting columns.

5. Select **A**scending or **D**escending sort order on the **1**st Key.

6. Move to the **2**nd or **3**rd Key, and repeat the procedures in Steps 4 and 5.

7. Select **R**ows to keep rows together when sorting databases or **C**olumns to keep columns together when sorting worksheets.

8. Choose OK or press Enter.

You may sort databases or database extracts that have field names at the top of columns. Do not include these field names in the selected sort range. Selecting the field names will sort them down into the data.

Returning a Sort to Its Original Order

When you need to sort a database but later return it to its original order, you need to add a record index to your database. A record index assigns a number to each record in accordance with its position, date of entry, or some other ordinal criteria you decide upon. Figure 20.16 shows an index in column A for the database. You can insert a column or cells to make room for an index.

Fig. 20.16. A record index in column A to allow returning to the original order.

	A	B	C	D	E	F	G
8							
9	DATABASE						
11	RECORD	DUE	DAYS				
12	INDEX	DATE	DUE	FIRM	TASK	CPA	STAFF
13	1	2-Oct-88	1	R & R Consulting	Quarterly	MB	CN
14	2	10-Oct-88	9	Townsend	Quarterly	CN	CD
15	3	10-Oct-88	9	Townsley	Court Appearance	MB	CD
16	4	15-Oct-88	14	Hillside Vineyards	Fincl Plan	CN	BR
17	5	15-Oct-88	14	R & R Consulting	Business Review	CN	MB
18	6	18-Oct-88	17	Smith	Fm 1099	RP	BR
19	7	12-Nov-88	42	Smythe	Business Plan	MB	RP
20							
21							

DATABASE.XLS

To index your database records so that they can be returned to their original order, follow these steps:

1. Insert a column on one side of the database.

2. Choose **D**ata Series, and fill the side column with numbers in increasing order. These are the index numbers.

Select the range of data to be sorted, and include the column of index numbers. Sort as many times as you want in any order.

When you want to return to the original database order, sort by **R**ows with the column of index numbers as the **1**st key. Make sure that the Ascending option is selected.

Sorting by Date

Excel sorts date fields by the serial number that lies hidden beneath the date format displayed on the screen. Sorting works correctly only on dates entered with the correct date procedure or on dates created with date functions.

If your dates appear to be sorted by text order rather than date sequence, you will need to change them to serial date entries. Change text dates to serial date numbers with a command macro that edits each field or with the DATEVALUE function. The DATEVALUE function is described in Chapter 9, "Using Functions in Worksheets."

Sorting Account Codes, Service Codes, or Part Numbers

Sorting account codes, service codes, and part numbers can be confusing at first because they may contain a prefix, body, and suffix. For example, your business may use codes such as the following:

AE-576-12

02-88022-09

PRE-56983-LBL

When single codes are entered in individual cells, those codes become difficult to sort. Sorting may be difficult because numbers may appear in the same character positions as letters, and different sections of a code may have different numbers of characters for different items, as in AE-576-12 and AE-2576-12.

You can solve this problem by making sure that all codes begin with text and that each section has exactly the same number of characters. For example, you could enter the previous examples as AE-0576-12 and AE-2576-12.

Another way to solve this problem puts each section of the code in its own column. Narrow the column widths so that they are just wide enough for the necessary characters.

You can designate certain sections to contain only number entries. If a section has a mixture of cells containing numbers, text, and both text and numbers, then make all your entries as text with a consistent number of characters. Table 20.3 demonstrates different entry methods. Pick a method and use it consistently.

Table 20.3
Entry Methods for Sorted Fields

Number	Entry	Text Display
576	="0576"	0576
57	="0057"	0057
A57	0A57	0A57
576	'0576	'0576
57	'0057	'0057
A57	'0A57	'0A57

You can create a macro that accepts your code, formats it to the correct style, and enters it in the database.

Sorting on More than Three Fields

With Excel's **D**ata **S**ort command, you can sort on as many fields as you want. You are not limited to just three keys when you sort; you can re-sort on additional fields as many times as you want. The guideline for sorting on more than three keys is to sort the lowest levels first, then the higher levels, working your way up to the major keys.

For example, if you want to sort column A as the 1st Key, column B as the 2nd Key, column C as the 3rd Key, and so on for six keys, you would need a sort like this one:

Key	1	2	3	4	5	6
Column	A	B	C	D	E	F

Even though Excel has only three sort keys, you still can sort by the six columns needed. Your first sort will use the lowest level columns:

Key	1	2	3
Column	D	E	F

A second sort will sort the higher level columns with these keys:

Key	1	2	3
Column	A	B	C

Using Functions To Sort Data

You are not confined to sorting on the contents of a given cell. You have the option of adding to your database or worksheet a column that contains a function for "pulling out" your sort characteristics.

In figure 20.17, column F contains the function

   =RIGHT(E13,5)

This function extracts the ZIP code from column E. This technique enables you to sort on the column containing the extracted ZIP code.

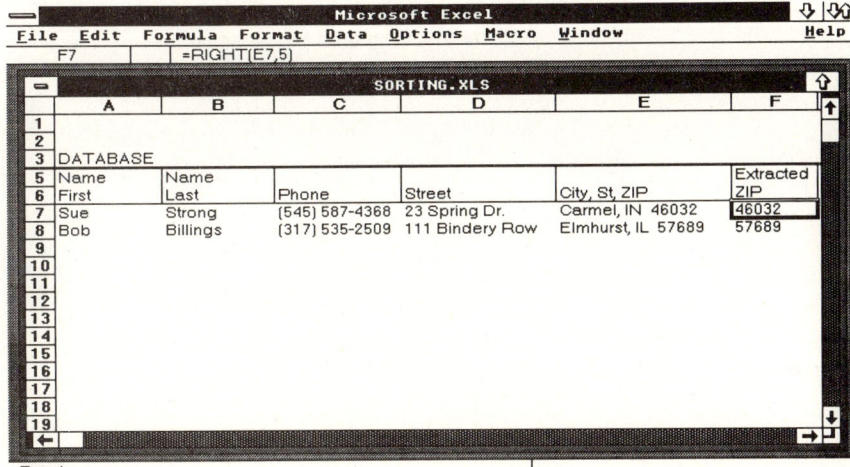

Fig. 20.17. The RIGHT function used to extract ZIP codes.

From Here . . .

When you have your database set up and data entered, you will want to find records that match the criteria you set. Chapter 21, "Finding and Editing Data," shows you how to search the database for records. You should read Chapter 21 and understand what a criteria is before you go on to Chapter 22, "Extracting and Maintaining Data." Chapter 22 describes how to extract information from the database in order to create a second database or a report.

If you have problems entering data or operating your database, consult Chapter 24, "Troubleshooting Databases." You also can look for help in the Notes and Tips displayed in this book's other database chapters.

Finding and Editing Data

Your most frequent database activity will be finding records. You will want to look up information, cross-check criteria before extracting data, and locate records you want to edit. How can you find records most efficiently?

Excel's **Data Form** command, which displays the automatic database form, enables you to find data quickly and easily using simple search criteria. If you need to use more complex search criteria, you must establish a criteria range and issue the **Data Find** command. With the information in this chapter, you will be able to find and edit any type of data in your database.

Finding Data—the Basic Procedure

Finding data in your database is a process that consists of four general steps:

1. Decide what you want to find.

2. Define a "pattern" you want the records you find to match. This pattern is known as criteria.

3. Enter that pattern in the database form or criteria range.

4. Invoke the **Data Find** command, or choose Find Next on the database form.

The patterns describing what you want to find are known as *criteria*. The simplest of criteria are exact matches. For example, if you want to find someone named Smith, you enter **Smith** as the criteria under the Last Name field. Criteria can specify text, dates, numbers, numeric ranges, or logical values (TRUE or FALSE). Criteria can be simple, specifying a search for a single item, or complex, specifying a search for several items and multiple ranges of numbers.

You can find records in two ways. The easiest method uses the **Data Form** command's database form, which accepts simple criteria. The second method of finding information uses a *criteria range*. After you enter simple or complex criteria in the criteria range, you use the **Data Find** command to search the database for matching records.

Both the **Data Form** and **Data Find** methods of finding records are described in this chapter. The text begins by showing you how the methods work with simple criteria. Later in the chapter, examples of more complex criteria are given so that you can learn to find any type of data.

Finding Data with the Database Form

Using Excel's database form is an excellent method for finding records that meet simple criteria. You enter your criteria in a blank form and request the next or previous record that matches the criteria. The database form displays the next or previous record matching your criteria.

To search for records using the database form, follow these steps:

1. Select the database range, and choose **Data Set Database** if you have not already done so.

2. Choose **Data Form** to display the database form.

3. Select the **Criteria** button.

   Selecting **Criteria** changes the buttons on the database form and clears the text box next to each field. Figure 21.1 shows the form ready to accept criteria.

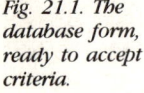

Fig. 21.1. The database form, ready to accept criteria.

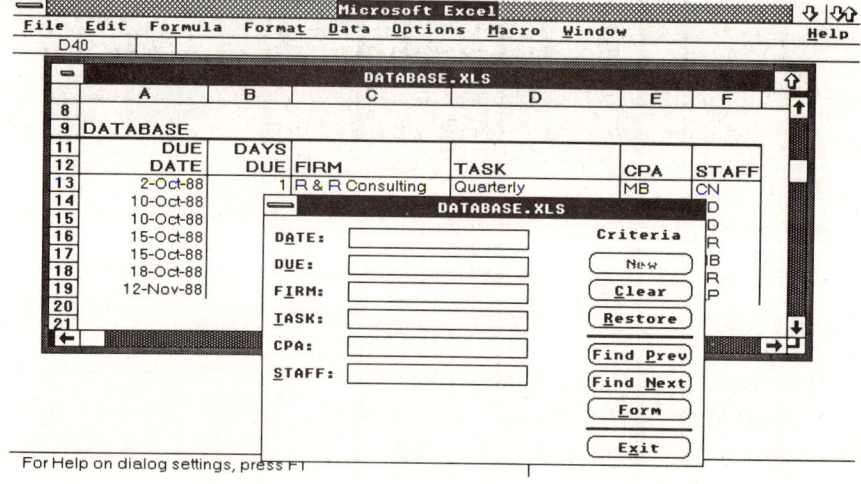

4. Select the text box next to the field you want to search. Press Tab for the next box, Shift+Tab for the previous box, or the Alt+key combination for a particular field.

5. Type the criteria, but do not press the Enter key.

6. Press Tab to move to the next box.

7. Choose Find **Next** or Find **Prev** to move from the current record to the record meeting the criteria entered.

Figure 21.2 shows a database form with criteria entered that will match records where the CPA has the initials *MB*. In figure 21.3, the criteria in the DUE field indicates that items with less than 15 days will be found. You even can find records that must satisfy criteria in more than one field. For example, the criteria in figure 21.4 specifies a search for records with a CPA who has initials *CN*, the DAYS DUE is *less than 15* days, and the FIRM name starts with *H*.

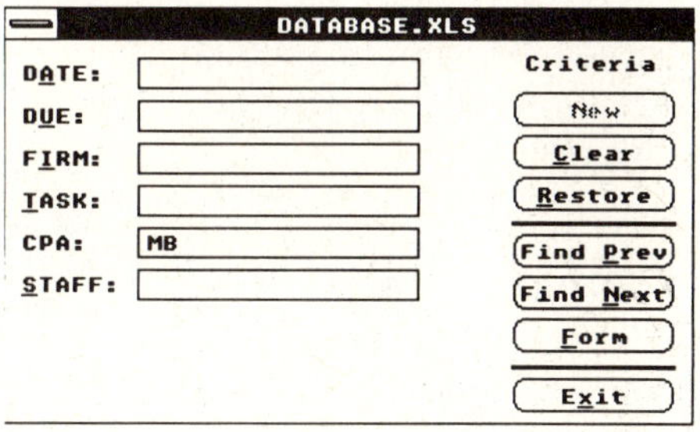

Fig. 21.2. A database form with the CPA's initials of MB specified as criteria.

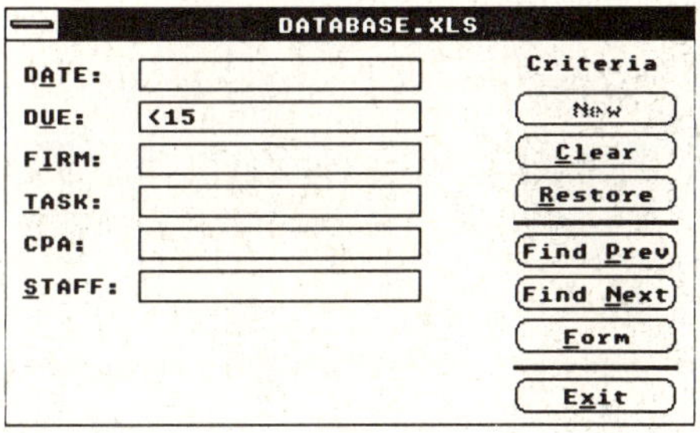

Fig. 21.3. A database form with DAYS DUE of less than 15 days specified as criteria.

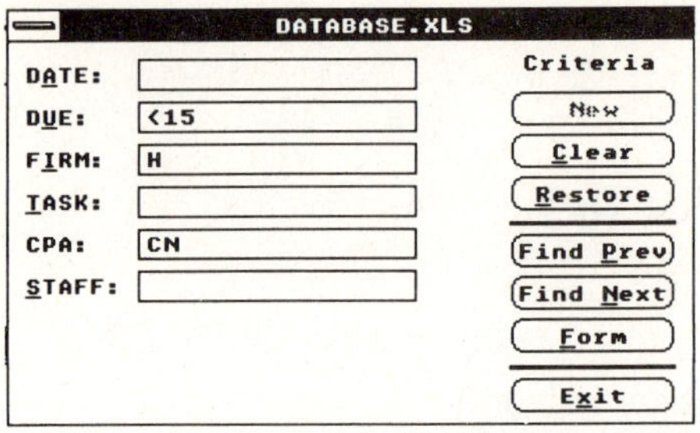

Fig. 21.4. Multiple criteria specified on a database form.

The database form is easy enough to use that you will be able to search for data after only a few minutes of practice. If you want to search for complex or calculated criteria, use the **D**ata **F**ind command.

Setting the Criteria Range for Data Find

Although using the **D**ata **F**ind command involves more work than using the database form, the command allows you to search for data with complex or calculated criteria. In addition, setting a criteria range and using **D**ata **F**ind lets you extract records from a database and copy them to another area of the worksheet.

Defining the Criteria Range

After defining the database range, you create and define a criteria range, in which you enter complex criteria. The top row of the criteria range contains field names that are the same as those above the database. Excel uses the row of field names to determine which criteria apply to each data column. The criteria range also includes at least one blank row below the field names. The criteria are entered in this row. Figure 21.5 shows a selected criteria range. In this example, Forma**t** **B**order was used to outline selected cells.

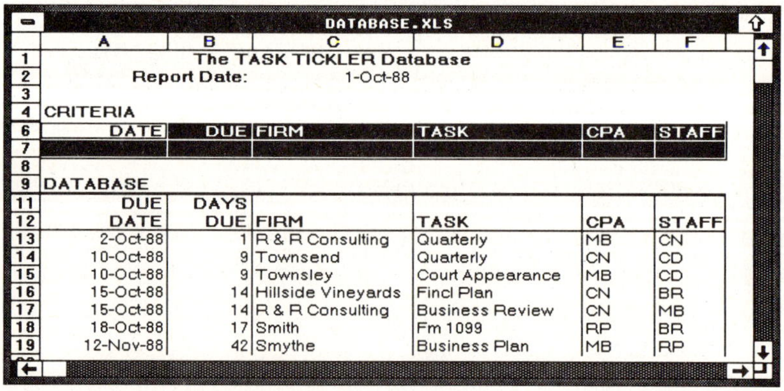
DATABASE.XLS

	A	B	C	D	E	F
1			The TASK TICKLER Database			
2		Report Date:	1-Oct-88			
3						
4	CRITERIA					
6	DATE	DUE	FIRM	TASK	CPA	STAFF
7						
8						
9	DATABASE					
11	DUE	DAYS				
12	DATE	DUE	FIRM	TASK	CPA	STAFF
13	2-Oct-88	1	R & R Consulting	Quarterly	MB	CN
14	10-Oct-88	9	Townsend	Quarterly	CN	CD
15	10-Oct-88	9	Townsley	Court Appearance	MB	CD
16	15-Oct-88	14	Hillside Vineyards	Fincl Plan	CN	BR
17	15-Oct-88	14	R & R Consulting	Business Review	CN	MB
18	18-Oct-88	17	Smith	Fm 1099	RP	BR
19	12-Nov-88	42	Smythe	Business Plan	MB	RP

Fig. 21.5. A selected criteria range.

The criteria range is defined in much the same way that you set the database range. Follow these steps to define a criteria range:

1. Copy the field names from the top of the database range to the top row of the criteria range. Copying the field names reduces the chance of mistakes from retyping.

2. Select all the field names and one blank row underneath the field names.

3. Choose **D**ata **S**et **C**riteria.

Choosing **D**ata **S**et **C**riteria names the selected range CRITERIA. Use **F**ormula **D**efine Name to see or delete the range name CRITERIA.

If the field names in the CRITERIA range do not match those in the database, the **D**ata **F**ind command will not work. Make sure that your criteria field names exactly match the database field names by copying them from the database with the **E**dit **C**opy and **E**dit **P**aste commands. You need not include every field name in the criteria range, and you can include the names in any order you want as long as you make sure that the ones you use match the field names used in the database. The field names in the criteria range must be either text or a formula that produces text.

NOTE

Do Not Leave an Extra Blank Row in the Criteria Range

Excel will find or extract all the records in the database if you include an extra blank row in the criteria range. The extra blank row is sometimes created when you have used more than one criteria row and then return to using a single row. The unused blank row as a criteria matches against all records. Solve this problem by redefining the criteria range.

Although you can have only one named criteria range at a time, you can quickly switch between criteria ranges. Chapter 20, "Entering and Sorting Data," contains a tip, "Changing Databases Quickly," that can also apply to changing criteria ranges.

Entering Criteria and Invoking the Data Find Command

After you set the database and criteria ranges, you are ready to search for records in the database. Follow these steps to enter the criteria and invoke the search:

1. Enter criteria in the criteria range.

The criteria range can contain simple criteria such as *Smith* under the FIRM heading. Simple criteria are described in this chapter's "Using Simple Text Criteria" section. The criteria range also can contain complex and calculated criteria that match ranges of numbers and contain TRUE/FALSE comparisons. Complex and calculated criteria are described in this chapter's "Using Complex Criteria" section.

2. Move the active cell outside the database in order to begin the search at the first database record. Or move the active cell inside the database in order to begin the search with the records following the active cell.

3. Choose **D**ata **F**ind. (Hold down Shift while choosing **D**ata **F**ind if you want to search backward through the database.)

When Excel encounters a record that meets the criteria you specified, a number of things happen. The database moves into the document window if the database was not visible before. The status line displays the word *Find*, and the number of the found record appears to the left of the formula bar. The scroll bars become striped, and the found record appears selected in the window as shown in figure 21.6. If no records meet the criteria, Excel instead beeps and displays a dialog box.

Fig. 21.6. A "found" record that matches the criteria.

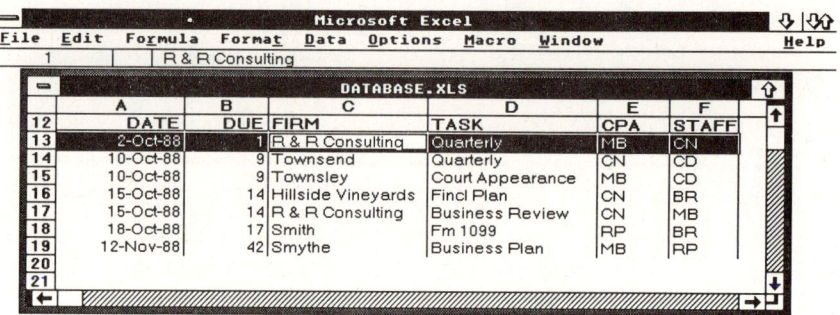

4. Press the up- or down-arrow keys or click on the scroll arrows to move to the next or previous matching record.

5. Choose **D**ata **E**xit **F**ind, press Esc, or click on a cell outside the database range to exit Find mode.

While in Find mode, you can scroll through the records meeting the criteria. Use the commands listed in table 21.1 to scroll the database.

Table 21.1
Scrolling a Database

Action	Result
Mouse	
Click on up scroll arrow	Move to previous matching record
Click on down scroll arrow	Move to next matching record
Click in scroll bar	Jump to match at least one page (screen length) away
Keyboard	
Down arrow or F7	Move to next matching record
Up arrow or Shift+F7	Move to previous matching record
Right arrow	Move active cell right
Left arrow	Move active cell left
PgUp	Move to previous matching record at least one window away
PgDn	Move to next matching record at least one window away

You cannot scroll outside the database either vertically or horizontally while in Find mode. Although you can move outside the database area with arrow keys, doing so cancels the **D**ata **F**ind command.

When you are ready to exit from **D**ata **F**ind, choose **D**ata **E**xit Find or press Esc.

TIP

View More Matching Records at Once

To view more matching records at one time, first sort the database by the fields on which you are searching. Then invoke the **D**ata **F**ind command.

TIP

View the Criteria and Database Ranges Simultaneously

As you scroll down through your database, you will lose sight of the criteria range as it scrolls off the screen. To enter the next criteria, you would have to scroll through the worksheet to find that range again.

A much simpler method is to split the database window so that you can see both the criteria and database ranges at the same time. You can jump back and forth between the split windows by pressing F6. Using the mouse, split the window by dragging the split bar down from the top arrow. From the keyboard, press Alt and then the hyphen key, and then choose Split. Use the down-arrow key to position the split, and then press Enter.

You should verify your criteria with the **Data Find** command before extracting data or using **Data Delete** to remove records. If you do not find what you expected, your criteria were not correct.

Using Simple Text Criteria

Simple criteria are those that do not involve mathematical calculations or the use of AND or OR logical operators. You can use these simple criteria in the database form and in the criteria range. If you need to use a complex or calculated criteria, you must use a criteria range in conjunction with the **Data Find**, **Extract**, or **Delete** commands (see this chapter's "Using Complex Criteria" section).

The simplest and easiest criteria match records against text criteria. These criteria work in both the database form and in the criteria range. Figures 21.7 and 21.8 show how a simple text criteria for the name *Smith* is entered in both the database form and in the criteria row of the criteria range. You can see that the criteria is typed exactly as you expect it to be entered in the database.

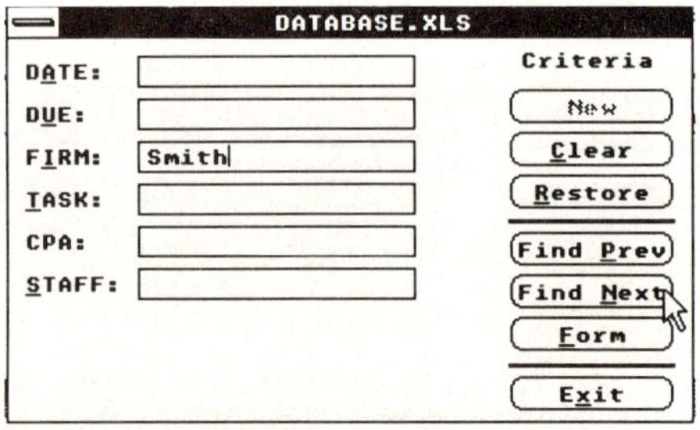

Fig. 21.7. Simple criteria entered in the database form.

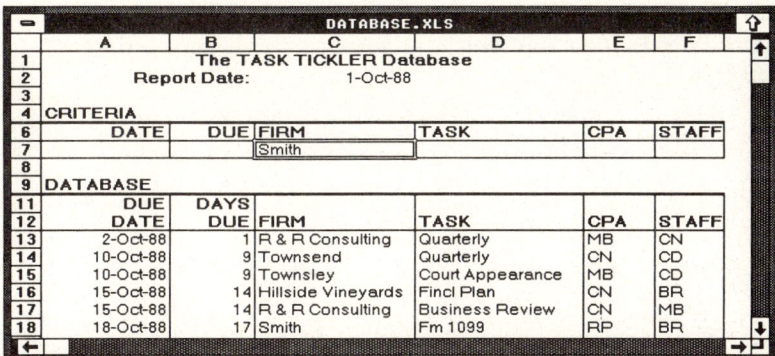

Fig. 21.8. Simple criteria entered in the criteria range.

Selecting **Data** **F**ind or Find **N**ext at this point would find records containing any of the following:

Smith
Smithely
Smithington

Notice that Excel matches more words than just *Smith*. Excel matches the text you enter and accepts any spaces or text after the last character in the criteria. This feature helps you to find records in which a blank space was accidentally typed after the last character.

If you want to find records that contain exactly the word *Smith* and no other variations, then enter the criteria in the criteria range as follows:

="=Smith"

Make sure that you enclose the text in quotation marks. In the criteria range, you may include a wild card such as the following (see fig. 21.9):

="=Sm?th"

	Microsoft Excel					⇩⇩⇩
File	**E**dit	For**m**ula	Forma**t**	**D**ata	**O**ptions	**M**acro	**W**indow	**H**elp

C7 | ="=Sm?th"

Fig. 21.9. A wild-card character in a text formula criteria.

	DATABASE.XLS					⇧
	A	B	C	D	E	F
3						
4	CRITERIA					
6	DATE	DUE	FIRM	TASK	CPA	STAFF
7			=Sm?th			
8						
9	DATABASE					
11	DUE	DAYS				
12	DATE	DUE	FIRM	TASK	CPA	STAFF
13	2-Oct-88	1	R & R Consulting	Quarterly	MB	CN
14	10-Oct-88	9	Townsend	Quarterly	CN	CD
15	10-Oct-88	9	Townsley	Court Appearance	MB	CD
16	15-Oct-88	14	Hillside Vineyards	Fincl Plan	CN	BR
17	15-Oct-88	14	R & R Consulting	Business Review	CN	MB
18	18-Oct-88	17	Smith	Fm 1099	RP	BR
19	12-Nov-88	42	Smythe	Business Plan	MB	RP
20						

Ready

See this chapter's "Finding Near Matches with Text Wild Cards" section for more information about wild cards.

Clearing the Criteria Range Correctly

One of the most frequent causes of database problems is incorrectly cleared criteria. If old criteria are not cleared from the criteria range, Excel will try to find records that match both the old and new criteria.

To clear the criteria row correctly, use Edit Clear, or select the old criteria, press Del, and then press Enter.

Do not clear cells by pressing the space bar and then pressing Enter. That procedure enters a blank character in the criteria row. In that case, Excel would attempt to find records that contain a blank character in that field.

Finding Near Matches with Text Wild Cards

If you are not sure of the spelling of a word in the database, or you need to find records containing similar but not identical text, you will need a couple of extra cards up your sleeve. In Excel, these are called *wild cards*, and they are part of the game.

The two wild cards used with text criteria are the asterisk (∗) and the question mark (?). They represent characters as follows:

?   Any single character in the same position

∗   Any group of characters in the same position

The question mark (?) is useful if you are uncertain how the word you want to match is spelled. For example, if a name in the Last Name field could be either *Smith* or *Smythe*, then you would enter your criteria as follows:

sm?th

The ? matches any single letter between the *m* and *t*. Excel accepts the *e* in *Smythe* because the program accepts any letters following the end of the criteria word. Because Excel does not distinguish between upper- and lowercase when matching, the program also matches the lowercase *s* in the criteria with the capital S.

The asterisk (*) matches groups of characters and can be used at any location in the text criteria—beginning, middle, or end. You therefore can use criteria such as the following to locate data in the Gallon field:

   * paint

This criteria will find matches such as the following:

   blue paint

   red paint

   yellow paint

If you need to find the symbols * or ? in a database, then precede the * or ? with a tilde (~). The tilde lets Excel know that you are not using the * or ? as a wild card.

1-2-3 TIP

Position the * Wild Card Anywhere in a Text Search

Excel lets you use the asterisk (*) wild card at the beginning, middle, or end of text criteria. In 1-2-3, you can use this wild card only at the end of text criteria.

Making Simple Numeric Comparisons

To make simple numeric comparisons, you set criteria for an exact numeric match. Enter the number in the criteria row directly under the field name, just as the name *Smith* was entered under Last Name in the criteria range or in the database form.

If you want to find numbers greater than or less than a number, enter comparison criteria, such as shown in figures 21.3 and 21.4. In that case, the expression <*15* tells Excel to look in the DUE field (column) for database values that are less than 15. Other comparison operators you can use in numeric criteria of the criteria range or database form are illustrated in table 21.2.

Table 21.2
Comparison Operators

Operator	Meaning	Criteria	Explanation
=	Equal	=200	Is record equal to 200?
=	Equal	=	Is record blank?
>	Greater than	>200	Is record greater than 200?
>=	Greater than or equal to	>=200	Is record greater than or equal to 200?
<	Less than	<200	Is record less than 200?
<=	Less than or equal to	<=200	Is record less than or equal to 200?
<>	Not equal to	<>200	Is record not equal to 200?
<>	Not equal to	<>	Is record not blank?

Comparing Dates in Criteria

Using dates in criteria is simpler in Excel than it is in other programs. You do not enter functions the same way you do in other computerized worksheets. For example, to search the Date field in the database shown in figure 21.9 for dates greater than October 14, 1988, you would enter the following criteria:

>10/14/88

You can use a date in the criteria that is in any of Excel's predefined date formats, such as >14 OCT 88. You can search dates with the other comparison operators (see table 21.2) in the same way you search for number ranges.

Using Multiple Simple Criteria

The examples given in previous sections all are considered simple criteria. By combining simple criteria as a group of criteria, however, you can ask some powerful questions.

You can define multiple criteria in the database form by entering each criteria in the appropriate field of the criteria range of database form. This technique tells Excel that criteria 1 AND criteria 2 AND criteria 3 and so forth, all must be true in order for a record to be found. Excel finds only those records satisfying all the criteria at once. For example, figure 21.10 finds records that have a DATE DUE greater than 14 and have a CPA's initials of CN.

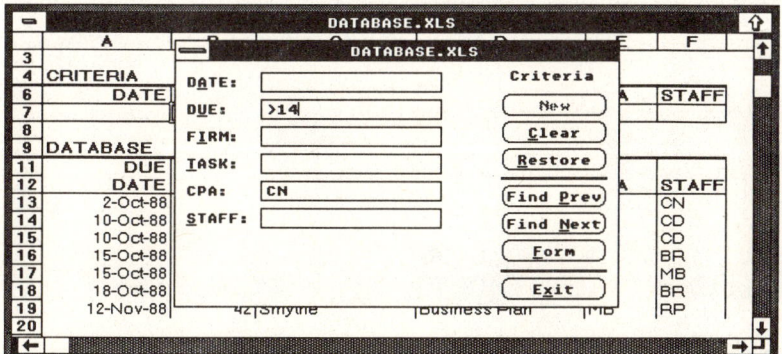

Fig. 21.10. Multiple criteria defined in the database form.

When using **Data Find**, you can link criteria by entering them on the same criteria row. When multiple criteria are entered on the same criteria row, then *all* the criteria must be met in order for a record to qualify as a match. Figure 21.11 shows the criteria range where DAYS DUE must be greater than 14 AND CPA must be CN. Because both of these criteria are in the same row, a database record must meet both criteria.

	A	B	C	D	E	F	
			DATABASE.XLS				
	A	B	C	D	E	F	
1			The TASK TICKLER Database				
2		Report Date:		1-Oct-88			
3							
4	CRITERIA						
6	DATE	DUE	FIRM	TASK	CPA	STAFF	
7		>14			CN		
8							
9	DATABASE						
11	DUE	DAYS					
12	DATE	DUE	FIRM	TASK	CPA	STAFF	
13	2-Oct-88		R & R Consulting	Quarterly	MB	CN	
14	10-Oct-88		Townsend	Quarterly	CN	CD	
15	10-Oct-88	9	Townsley	Court Appearance	MB	CD	
16	15-Oct-88	14	Hillside Vineyards	Fincl Plan	CN	BR	
17	15-Oct-88	14	R & R Consulting	Business Review	CN	MB	
18	18-Oct-88	17	Smith	Fm 1099	RP	BR	
19	12-Nov-88	42	Smythe	Business Plan	MB	RP	
20							

Fig. 21.11. Two criteria defined in the same row of the criteria range.

To find records where one OR the other criteria is met, use the criteria range and **Data Find**. Insert a second or third row in the criteria range to hold the criteria to be linked with OR. Figure 21.12 shows a criteria range with two rows for criteria. (Separate rows in the criteria range are linked with the logical OR.) The criteria entries shown in the figure find records where the CPA is MB OR the CPA is CN.

	A	B	C	D	E	F
			The TASK TICKLER Database			
1						
2		Report Date:	1-Oct-88			
3						
4	CRITERIA					
6		DATE	DUE	FIRM	TASK	CPA	STAFF
7						MB	
8						CN	
9							
10	DATABASE					
12		DUE	DAYS				
13		DATE	DUE	FIRM	TASK	CPA	STAFF
14	2-Oct-88			R & R Consulting	Quarterly	MB	CN
15	10-Oct-88			Townsend	Quarterly	CN	CD
16	10-Oct-88		9	Townsley	Court Appearance	MB	CD
17	15-Oct-88		14	Hillside Vineyards	Fincl Plan	CN	BR
18	15-Oct-88		14	R & R Consulting	Business Review	CN	MB
19	18-Oct-88		17	Smith	Fm 1099	RP	BR
20	12-Nov-88		42	Smythe	Business Plan	MB	RP

NOTE

Blank Criteria Rows Are Dangerous

Be careful when you use two or more rows in the criteria range. A blank cell in the criteria range tells Excel to find all values in that field. A blank row tells Excel to find all values in every field. Leaving a row blank in the criteria range, therefore, causes Excel to find, extract, or delete all data in the database.

To insert rows in the criteria range, first select the criteria row beneath the field names. Then choose Edit Insert. Use Formula Goto to check when you are not sure whether the criteria range is still defined correctly.

1-2-3 TIP

Inserting and Deleting in Excel Ranges

In 1-2-3, accidentally deleting the top or bottom row of a range such as the criteria range destroys the range name. If you delete the top or bottom criteria range row in Excel, the range automatically adjusts to the new size without destroying the range name.

Figure 21.13 shows how you can combine simple criteria to ask complex questions of your database. The criteria range uses two rows so that you can find records matching either one value or the other. All the criteria within either row must be true in order for a record to be found. Here is the English equivalent of this criteria range:

The DAYS DUE are less than 15 AND the CPA is CN

OR

the DUE DATE is 18-Oct-88 AND the FIRM name begins with S.

Excel finds the records that meet these criteria in rows 15, 17, 18, and 19.

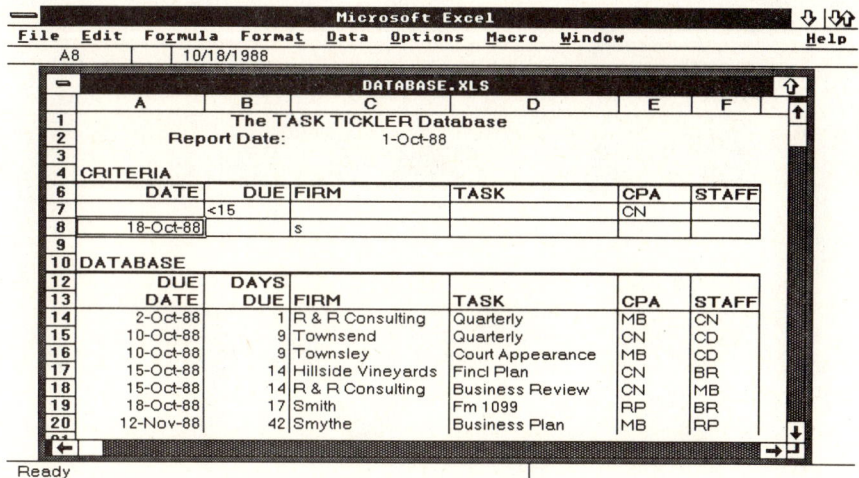

Fig. 21.13.
Multiple criteria specifying AND in the same rows and specifying OR between rows.

Using Complex Criteria

Using the criteria range to set up your database queries adds a few more steps to the process, but also lets you search for records according to more complex requirements. For example, using complex criteria, you can perform calculations that test whether a record fits your criteria. You also can specify compound criteria which finds records that meet AND, OR, and NOT conditions.

Using Calculated Criteria

You can select records according to any calculation that results in a TRUE or FALSE logical value as a criteria. Calculated criteria are needed, for example, when you want to find records where stock quantities are less than the reorder quantity, where two records contain the same data, or where a record contains the letter B as its fifth character.

Figure 21.14 shows an example of calculated criteria that finds Parts that were sold for less than 90 percent of Retail price. Notice that calculated criteria must be entered in the criteria range beneath a name that *does not* exist in the database. In this example, the name CALC was inserted in the middle of the criteria range. As you can see in the figure, the field name above the calculated criteria does not exist as a field name in the database. You can use any descriptive name above the calculated criteria.

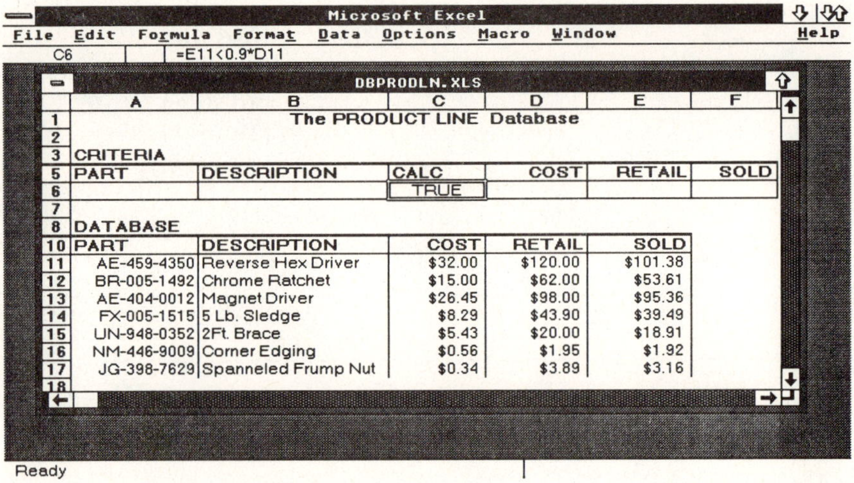

Fig. 21.14.
Calculated criteria must use a new field name in the criteria range.

<table>
<tr><td colspan="6">Microsoft Excel</td><td></td></tr>
<tr><td colspan="7">File   Edit   Formula   Format   Data   Options   Macro   Window   Help</td></tr>
</table>

	A	B	C	D	E	F
	C6		=E11<0.9*D11			
			DBPRODLN.XLS			
1		The PRODUCT LINE Database				
2						
3	CRITERIA					
5	PART	DESCRIPTION	CALC	COST	RETAIL	SOLD
6			TRUE			
7						
8	DATABASE					
10	PART	DESCRIPTION	COST	RETAIL	SOLD	
11	AE-459-4350	Reverse Hex Driver	$32.00	$120.00	$101.38	
12	BR-005-1492	Chrome Ratchet	$15.00	$62.00	$53.61	
13	AE-404-0012	Magnet Driver	$26.45	$98.00	$95.36	
14	FX-005-1515	5 Lb. Sledge	$8.29	$43.90	$39.49	
15	UN-948-0352	2Ft. Brace	$5.43	$20.00	$18.91	
16	NM-446-9009	Corner Edging	$0.56	$1.95	$1.92	
17	JG-398-7629	Spanneled Frump Nut	$0.34	$3.89	$3.16	
18						

Ready

NOTE

Where To Enter Calculated Criteria

Calculated criteria must be entered in the criteria range under names that do not exist as field names in the database.

In your calculated criteria formula, use cell references to cells in the top row of the database. You nearly always will use relative reference addresses (without $ signs). Use absolute cell references for any cell that is outside the database.

Calculated criteria can involve multiple fields and equations, but the result must produce a TRUE or FALSE condition. The Excel database commands select those records that produce a TRUE result. Some simple calculated criteria, where the first data row is row 36, are illustrated in table 21.3.

Table 21.3
Simple Calculated Criteria

Criteria	Explanation
=B36=G36	Compares the values of fields in the same database row. Selects the record when the value in column B equals the value in column G.
=B36<G36/2	Compares the value in B36 to one half the value in G36. Both cells are in the same record. Selects the record when the value in column B is less than half of the value in column G.
=B36-G36>10	Compares two values in the same database record. Selects the record when a value in column B minus a value in column G is greater than 10.

TIP

Check Your Calculated Criteria Formula

If you use the correct syntax when you enter a calculated criteria formula, Excel displays a TRUE or FALSE in the cell after you enter the formula. This TRUE or FALSE applies to the specific cells you used in the formula. Check to see whether the TRUE or FALSE response is the one you wanted.

More complex, but extremely useful calculated criteria include comparisons between values in one record with other records or with values outside the database. These types of criteria are useful when you want to compare records or use criteria calculated elsewhere in the worksheet. Table 21.4 shows some examples of these types of criteria where the first data row is again row 36.

Table 21.4
Complex Calculated Criteria

Criteria	Explanation
=B36-G35>10	Compares two values in different database records. Selects the record when a value in column B minus a value in column G of the previous row is greater than 10.
=B36=$C$24	Compares database values with a cell outside the database. Selects the record when the value in column B equals the value in $C$24, where C24 is a cell outside the database.

As you can see from the table, calculated criteria can involve cell references that are outside the database. However, you must use an absolute reference to refer to any location outside the database range.

The first example in table 21.4, which compares fields from two different rows, provides an excellent way to search for duplicate data in your database (see the Tip that follows). You also can use this type of criteria to locate data that increases by a specific amount between adjacent records.

TIP

Finding Duplicates in Your Database

Finding duplicate records in a database can be time-consuming, but it needs to be done occasionally if you are managing a mailing list or parts inventory. If you want to create a totally new collection of nonduplicate records, you can use **Data Extract** and select the Unique Records Only option. If you want to find records that match only on selected cells instead, follow these steps:

1. Sort the database in ascending order on the field you will use for comparison. This puts records with the same fields adjacent to each other.

2. In the criteria range, insert a field name for the calculated criteria. Use a name that does *not* exist in the database or criteria ranges. This prepares the criteria range to accept calculated criteria.

3. Enter a calculated criteria formula that compares the values in the first and second rows of the search field. This compares your selected field in one row with the same field in an adjacent row.

4. Choose **Data Find**.

Excel will find those records where the two adjacent field values are equal. This lets you press the up- or down-arrow key to jump between pairs of records that have a matching field.

In figure 21.15, for example, the criteria in the formula bar is

=B14=B13

This criteria compares the current cell of the DAYS DUE field to the next cell of the same field. If the two are the same, Excel finds the current cell.

Using Compound Criteria

You can use Excel's AND, OR, and NOT functions to create complex compound criteria. This method is useful for specifying complex queries that cannot be handled by inserting additional rows in the criteria range.

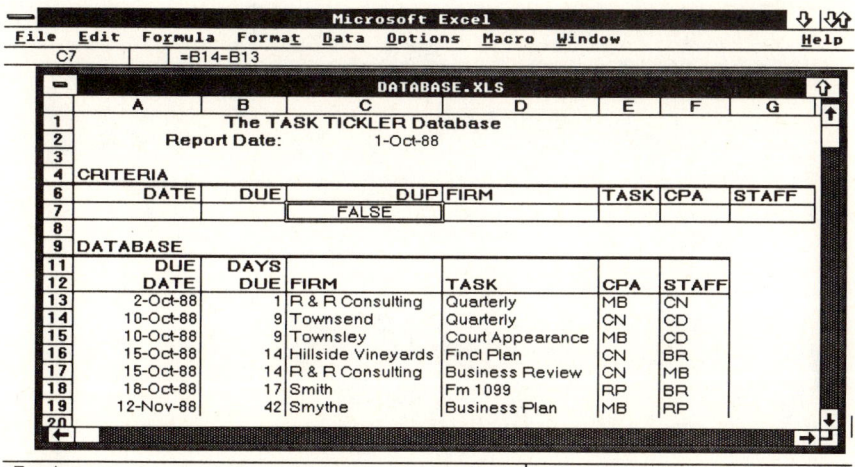

*Fig. 21.15.
Criteria for
finding
duplicate fields
in adjacent cells.*

You can use any of the following functions in your compound criteria. In order for a record to be selected by a **Data** command, the function must return the TRUE or FALSE value as follows:

AND   All conditions must be TRUE.

OR   One condition or the other or both must be TRUE.

NOT   The condition is reversed. TRUE changes to FALSE; FALSE changes to TRUE.

Just as you can enter calculated criteria that results in a TRUE or FALSE, you can enter AND, OR, and NOT functions that evaluate to TRUE or FALSE. For example, consider the database in figure 21.16. For each of the following queries, stated in English syntax, the associated compound criteria formula is presented, and the resulting records found are listed.

English statement:	The CPA is CN AND the STAFF is BR.
Compound criteria:	=AND(E13="CN",F13="BR")
Result:	Finds the record in row 16.
English statement:	The FIRM is Townsley OR the FIRM is Smith.
Compound criteria:	=OR(C13="Townsley",C13="Smith")
Result:	Finds the records in rows 15 and 18.
English statement:	The FIRM is NOT Townsley AND the DAYS DUE is 9.
Compound criteria:	=AND(NOT(C13="Townsley"),B13=9)
Result:	Finds the record in row 14.

*Fig. 21.16. A
sample database
with associated
criteria range.*

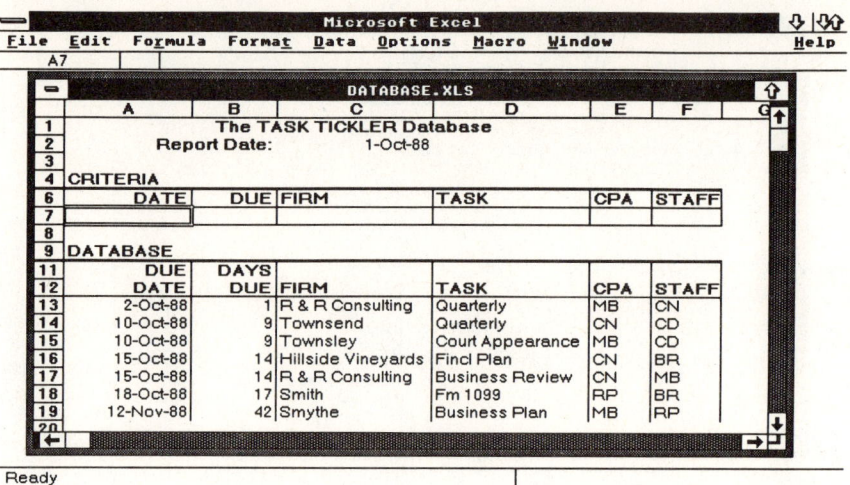

Microsoft Excel						
File	**Edit**	**Formula**	**Format**	**Data** **Options**	**Macro**	**Window**	**Help**

A7

DATABASE.XLS

	A	B	C	D	E	F	G
1			The TASK TICKLER Database				
2		Report Date:	1-Oct-88				
3							
4	CRITERIA						
6	DATE	DUE	FIRM	TASK	CPA	STAFF	
7							
8							
9	DATABASE						
11	DUE	DAYS					
12	DATE	DUE	FIRM	TASK	CPA	STAFF	
13	2-Oct-88	1	R & R Consulting	Quarterly	MB	CN	
14	10-Oct-88	9	Townsend	Quarterly	CN	CD	
15	10-Oct-88	9	Townsley	Court Appearance	MB	CD	
16	15-Oct-88	14	Hillside Vineyards	Fincl Plan	CN	BR	
17	15-Oct-88	14	R & R Consulting	Business Review	CN	MB	
18	18-Oct-88	17	Smith	Fm 1099	RP	BR	
19	12-Nov-88	42	Smythe	Business Plan	MB	RP	
20							

Ready

NOTE

The AND and OR Functions Are Easy To Confuse

If you are searching a single field for two different text entries, for example *Smith* and *Jones*, use the OR function. An OR function specifies that one name OR the other can be found (TRUE). An AND function specifies that *Smith* AND *Jones* must be in the field at the same time—something that will not happen.

Editing Data

A database is only as good as it is up-to-date. Keeping a database current involves two basic functions: ongoing updating of individual records and periodic "scrubbing" to get rid of old records. The balance of this chapter describes how to edit records. The next chapter describes how to maintain the overall database.

The following descriptions cover two methods of editing the database: editing in the database form and editing directly in the worksheet. In cases where you will be editing one or two unique records, the database form may be preferable. However, when you have to do reformatting or edit many adjacent records, you will want to edit directly in the worksheet.

TIP

Jumping to the First Database Cell

To get to the top of the database or criteria range quickly, no matter where the active cell is positioned, choose Formula Goto, select the name of either the database or criteria range, and then choose OK or press Enter. Press an arrow key to unselect the range and leave the active cell at the top.

Editing Data with the Database Form

The easiest way to edit individual records is with the database form. If you can find the record using the simple criteria available in the database form, then use the same form to do your editing.

Begin by defining the database range with **Data Set Database**. After you have defined the range, follow these steps to find the records you want and edit them:

1. Choose **Data Form**.

2. Select the **Criteria** button.

   Mouse: Click on **Criteria**.

   Keyboard: Press Alt+C.

3. To define the records you want to edit, type the criteria. Press Tab or Shift+Tab to move between fields.

4. Select the Find **Next** button to find the next record matching the criteria and to display that record in the form.

   Mouse: Click on Find **Next**.

   Keyboard: Press Alt+N.

5. Edit the field contents using normal mouse or keyboard techniques. Press the appropriate Alt+key combination to select a text box or press the Tab key to move between them. Figure 21.17 shows the **TASK** text box selected after pressing Alt+T.

6. Select Find **Next** to save the changes and move to the next record, or select **Exit** to save the changes and return to the worksheet.

If you need to delete a record you have found with the form, then choose the **Delete** button on the form. An alert message will warn that you are about to delete the current record (see fig. 21.18). Choose OK or press Enter to complete the deletion. Keep in mind that deleted records cannot be recovered.

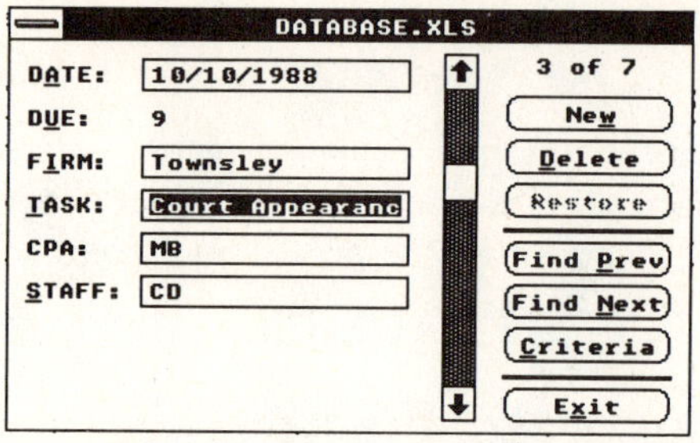

Fig. 21.17. The TASK text box selected in the database form.

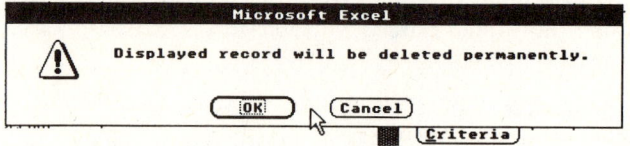

Fig. 21.18. The delete record alert box.

Editing Data Directly in the Worksheet

Some of the records you want to edit may require a calculated or compound criteria to find. In other cases, you may want to edit or format adjacent rows all at once. You can enter the criteria in the criteria range, use **Data Find** to find the records, and make your changes directly in the worksheet.

To find the appropriate records with the help of the **Data Find** command and edit data directly in the worksheet, follow these steps:

1. Enter the criteria in the criteria range for the records you want to edit.

2. Choose **Data Find**.

3. Move to the record you want to edit.

    Mouse: Click on the scroll bar arrows.

    Keyboard: Press the down arrow or PgDn key to scroll to the appropriate record.

4. Select the cell you want to edit.

    Mouse: Click on the cell you want to edit.

    Keyboard: Press the Tab or Shift+Tab keys to position the cursor on the cell you want to edit.

5. Edit the cell contents.

   Mouse: Click in the formula bar, and then edit.

   Keyboard: Press F2 (the Edit key) and make your changes.

   Going into Edit mode throws Excel out of Find mode. You are now back to editing in a normal worksheet.

6. Press Enter to complete the change.

TIP

Making Changes to Multiple Records

Usually, you will have to make changes to multiple records that all meet the same search criteria. However, as soon as you begin to edit a found record, Excel puts you back into the normal worksheet. To conduct the next edit, you again must choose **Data Find**. You therefore may want to create a simple command macro that replaces the three keystrokes needed to choose **Data Find** with a single Ctrl+key combination. Using a macro, you can keep your cursor in the same record you edited and have Excel find the next record. Work through the "Macro Quick Start" (Chapter 25), and you will learn how to create simple but useful macros such as this one.

If you want to delete a record directly from the worksheet, follow these steps:

1. Press Esc to return to normal worksheet mode.

2. Select the row or cells you want to delete. If you select cells, be sure to select the full width of the record.

3. Choose **Edit Delete**.

   If you are deleting cells, the Delete dialog box asks whether you want to shift the remaining cells up or left. Select the Shift Cells Up option from the dialog box.

4. Choose OK or press Enter.

TIP

Quickly Selecting a Row of Cells in the Database

To select a row of cells in the database without selecting the entire row, use these shortcut keys:

Home	Move to the left edge of the row.
Shift+Home	Select from the current cell to the start of the row.

| End | Move to the last filled cell in the row. |
| Shift+End | Select from the current cell to the last filled cell in the row. |

NOTE

Deleting Rows in a Database Can Be Hazardous to Your Worksheet

Deleting the entire row may delete parts of the worksheet on either side of the database. Using the preceding steps to delete only the cells within the appropriate database row is a safer technique.

From Here . . .

Two important database topics have not yet been discussed in this text: extracting information for reports and maintaining a database. These topics are covered in Chapter 22, "Extracting and Maintaining Data."

Even if you are just starting to use Excel's database, you also should read Chapter 23, "Building Advanced Databases," to discover the types of applications you can perform. An important topic discussed in that chapter concerns the database functions that total or average records in the database.

22

Extracting and Maintaining Data

This chapter shows you how to create database reports and maintain your database. You will use the **Data Extract** command and what you already have learned about criteria to pull information from the database and copy it to a new worksheet location. You also will learn how to copy old data into a new file for safekeeping and how to delete groups of old records from your database. These procedures keep your current database trim.

Extracting Data

The **Data Extract** command makes a copy of data meeting the criteria in the criteria range. The copy, which is placed in a separate section of the worksheet from the original database, is useful for creating special reports, for making subsets of the original database, and for preparing data to be transferred to other programs. A special option of the **Extract** command copies only those records that are unique. The original database remains intact after you have extracted the data.

Like **Data Find**, **Data Extract** needs to have the database and criteria ranges specified before it will work. In addition, **Data Extract** needs to know where to put the copied information and how to arrange the columns of data.

The location of a third set of field names—similar to those in the database and criteria ranges—tells Excel which data you want extracted and how you want it arranged. Figure 22.1 shows a small database containing the three parts important to extracting: the criteria range in A6:F7, the database range in A12:F19, and the selected field names in the extract range in A23:F23. In figure 22.2, the data meeting the criteria have been extracted from the database range and copied below the field names in the extract range. Notice that in figure 22.2 the two extracted records in rows 24 and 25 each have 14 days due. This matches the criterion set in row 7.

Fig. 22.1.
Database,
criteria, and
extract ranges.

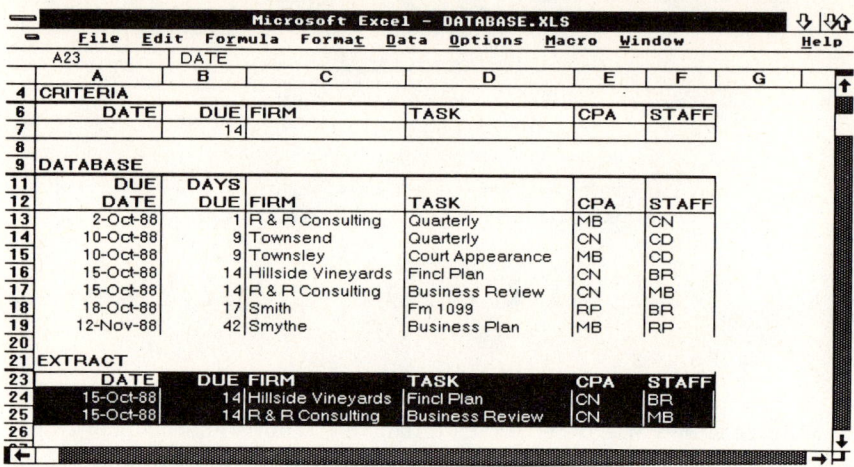

Fig. 22.2.
Extracted data
displayed below
the field names
in the extract
range.

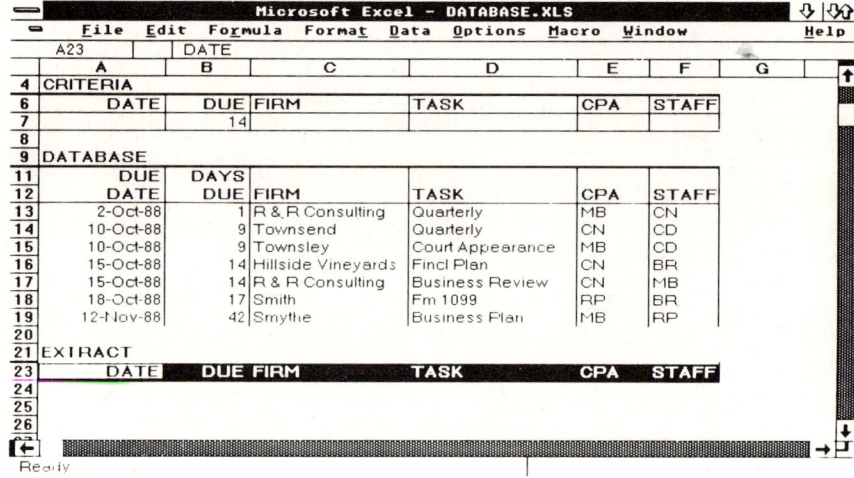

Keep the Extract Range Separate from the Criteria Range

The extract range is a separate range from the criteria and database ranges. In figures 22.1 and 22.2, notice that three ranges are used. The field names selected when you choose **Data Extract** define where the data will be copied. The row of field names selected for **Data Extract** must be separate from the row of field names that head the database and criteria range.

When Excel extracts the data meeting the criteria, the program extracts only values. If the database contains formulas, the extract range contains only the values that are the result of those formulas.

Recalculate Before Extracting Data

If Excel is set to recalculate formulas manually, and the worksheet needs to be recalculated, the word *Calculate* will appear at the bottom of the screen. To ensure that all calculations are current, press the F9 key before executing the **Extract** command.

The field names at the top of the extract range must be identical to the field names used at the top of the database range. The best way to prepare your extract range is by copying the field names you want from the top of the database.

As figures 22.3 and 22.4 illustrate, you don't have to use all the field names in the extract range, nor do the field names have to be in the same order as they appear in the database range. You can create reports with the information you need and in the order you want it by using selected field names and reordering them according to how you want to display the data.

Extracting Data—the Basic Procedure

Use the following basic procedure to extract from the database the information you want. Note that each of these steps is described in greater detail in the text that follows.

1. Create an extract range by copying the single row of field names from the top of the database range and arranging the field names at the top of the area in which the extracted data will be displayed.

2. Enter the criteria in the criteria row.

3. Select the extract range.

   For an unlimited extract area, select only the field names. To fill a limited area, select the field names and as many cells below as you expect to fill with extracted data.

4. Choose the **Data Extract** command.

5. Select the **Unique Records Only** option if you do not want records (rows) of data that are duplicates.

6. Choose OK or press Enter.

Fig. 22.3. The extract range, containing only some of the field names from the database.

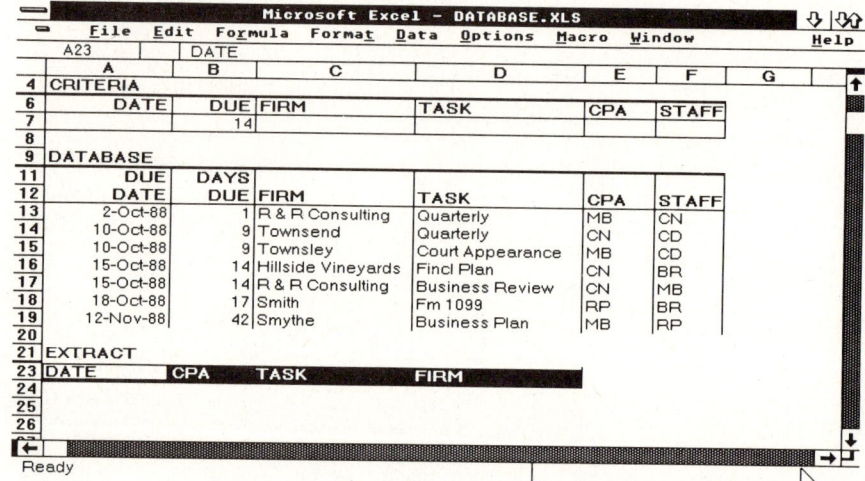

Fig. 22.4. Extracted data arranged according to the order of the selected field names.

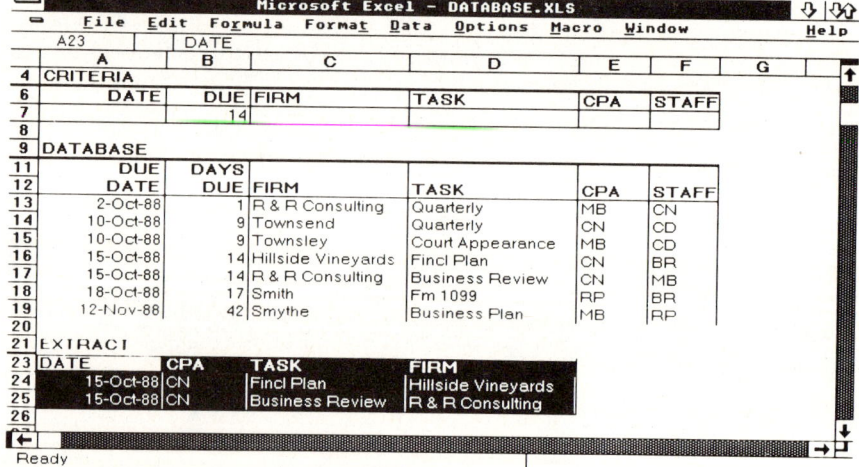

Excel Specifies the Extract Range Differently

In 1-2-3, you use the Data Query Output command to specify the extract range. In Excel, you do not specify an extract range with a command. Instead, the extract range is considered to be the cells currently selected when you choose the **Data Extract** command.

Selecting the Extract Range

In Excel, you can extract data into two sizes of extract range. An unlimited extract range allows you to extract an unlimited number of records. (Actually, there may be a limit if your computer runs out of memory.) This type of extract works well when you don't know how many records will be extracted.

The second type of extract range limits the area that will hold extracted records. This type of extract works best in a crowded worksheet with limited space.

Extracting a Limited Amount of Data

To extract a limited amount of data, you must define the extract range before you choose **Data Extract**. Select the extract row containing the field names, and then select as many rows below that as you need to hold the data being extracted. Figure 22.5 shows an extract range with the field names selected and room for four rows of extracted data.

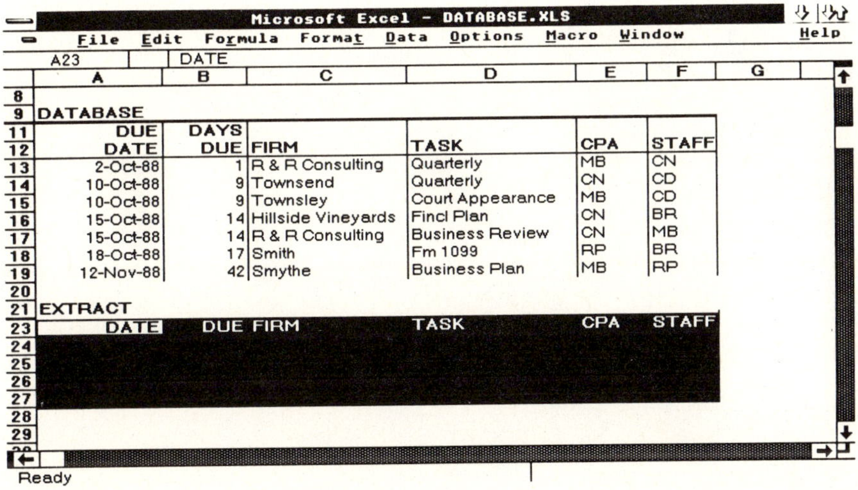

Fig. 22.5. A limited range selected to hold extracted data.

Excel clears the extract range before copying the extracted data into the range. In this way, the program prevents old and new extract data from mixing.

If Excel attempts to extract more rows of data than will fit in the range you selected, an alert box appears telling you that the extract range is full (see fig. 22.6). This message indicates that still more data could be extracted.

Fig. 22.6. An alert box warning that the extract range is full.

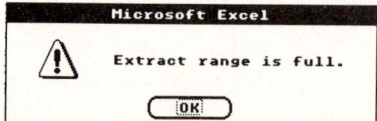

When you see the alert box, you have four options: accept the limited amount of data extracted, choose a larger extract range, make your criteria more limiting, or use the technique described in the following section to create an unlimited extract range.

Extracting Unlimited Rows of Data

You probably will want to use an unlimited extract range when you are not sure how much data will be extracted or when the amount of data varies widely. In those cases, select only the field names of the extract range, as shown in figure 22.7. Excel extracts all the appropriate data, regardless of how much exists, and displays it below the extract field names.

Fig. 22.7. The extract field names selected to create an unlimited extract range.

	A	B	C	D	E	F	G
3							
4	CRITERIA						
6	DATE	DUE	FIRM	TASK	CPA	STAFF	
7							
8							
9	DATABASE						
11	DUE	DAYS					
12	DATE	DUE	FIRM	TASK	CPA	STAFF	
13	2-Oct-88	1	R & R Consulting	Quarterly	MB	CN	
14	10-Oct-88	9	Townsend	Quarterly	CN	CD	
15	10-Oct-88	9	Townsley	Court Appearance	MB	CD	
16	15-Oct-88	14	Hillside Vineyards	Fincl Plan	CN	BR	
17	15-Oct-88	14	R & R Consulting	Business Review	CN	MB	
18	18-Oct-88	17	Smith	Fm 1099	RP	BR	
19	12-Nov-88	42	Smythe	Business Plan	MB	RP	
20							
21	EXTRACT						
23	DATE	DUE	FIRM	TASK	CPA	STAFF	
24							
25							

Microsoft Excel – DATABASE.XLS

File   Edit   Formula   Format   Data   Options   Macro   Window   Help

A23   DATE

Ready

Be careful when designing a worksheet with an unlimited extract range. During the extraction process, Excel clears the cells in all columns below the extract field names to prevent mixing old and new data. During the extraction process, any old data in the extract range is cleared. Never put anything below an unlimited extract range!

Figures 22.8 and 22.9 illustrate the process of extracted data to an unlimited range. In figure 22.8, markers are displayed beneath and to the side of the extract range. Figure 22.9 shows the result of the **Data Extract** command; the markers underneath the extract range are cleared to make room for the extracted data. Notice that the markers on the side are still intact.

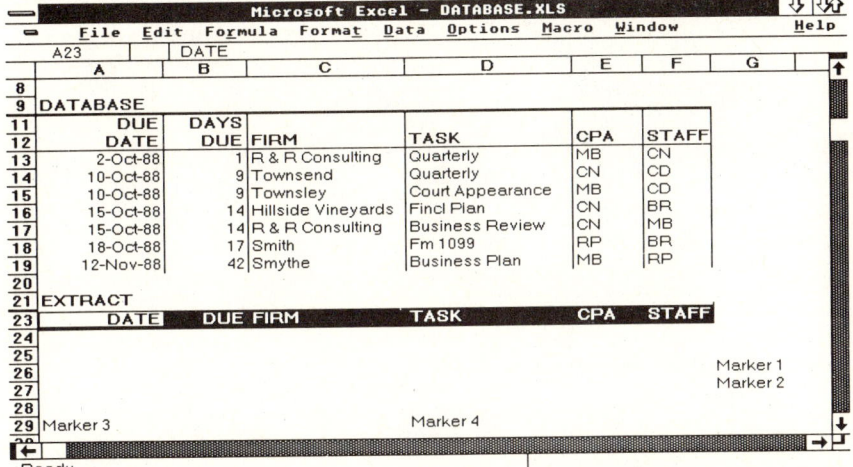

Fig. 22.8. An extract range before an extraction; markers below and to the right of the range.

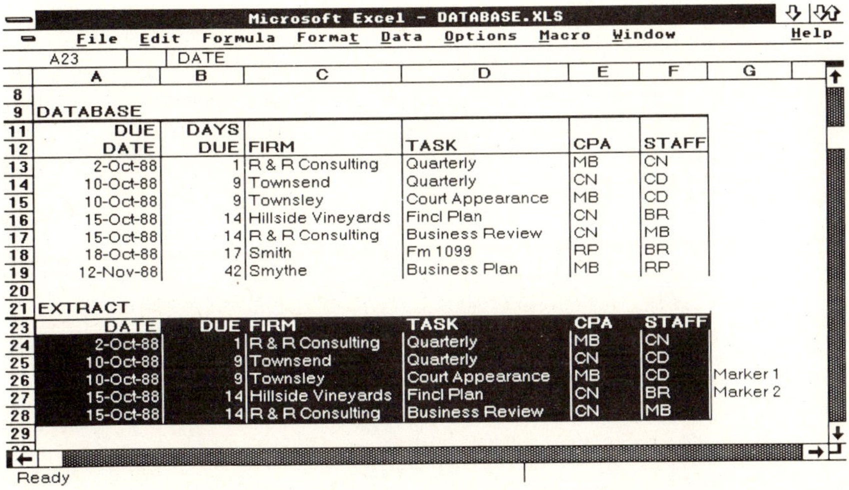

Fig. 22.9. An extract range after an extraction; markers below the extract range deleted.

> **TIP**
>
> ## Use Extraction To Prepare Data for Other Programs
>
> Extracting data from your worksheet is an excellent way of selecting and preparing the data you need to transfer to other programs or to other Excel worksheets.
>
> To prepare a database for transfer, first extract the records and fields you want transferred. Then cut the extracted data out of the extract range and paste it into a new, blank worksheet. Format each column as you want it for the next program and set the column widths so that they are wide enough to display all the data. Finally, save the extracted data with text, 1-2-3, or dBASE format, or use the data as the core of a new Excel database.

Extracting Unique Records

After you choose **D**ata Extract, Excel displays the Extract dialog box (see fig. 22.10). If you do not want to display duplicate data, select the **U**nique Records Only option. Selecting Unique Records Only prevents duplicate records from being displayed in the finished extract range.

Fig. 22.10. The Extract dialog box.

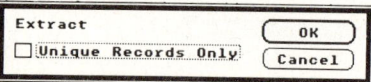

In figure 22.11, for example, the records in rows 16 and 17 are almost the same but have one field different. If you extract with *all* field headings and the Unique Records Only option, both records appear in the extract range.

Fig. 22.11. Unique records extracted using all fields.

Microsoft Excel – DATABASE.XLS						⇩⊗
File **E**dit Fo**r**mula Forma**t** **D**ata **O**ptions **M**acro **W**indow						Help
A23		DATE				
A	**B**	**C**	**D**	**E**	**F**	**G**
8						
9 DATABASE						
11 DUE	DAYS					
12 DATE	DUE	FIRM	TASK	CPA	STAFF	
13 2-Oct-88	1	R & R Consulting	Quarterly	MB	CN	
14 10-Oct-88	9	Townsend	Quarterly	CN	CD	
15 10-Oct-88	9	Townsley	Court Appearance	MB	CD	
16 15-Oct-88	14	Hillside Vineyards	Fincl Plan	CN	BR	
17 15-Oct-88	14	Hillside Vineyards	Business Review	CN	BR	
18 18-Oct-88	17	Smith	Fm 1099	RP	BR	
19 12-Nov-88	42	Smythe	Business Plan	MB	RP	
20						
21 EXTRACT						
23 DATE	DUE	FIRM	TASK	CPA	STAFF	
24 2-Oct-88	1	R & R Consulting	Quarterly	MB	CN	
25 10-Oct-88	9	Townsend	Quarterly	CN	CD	
26 10-Oct-88	9	Townsley	Court Appearance	MB	CD	
27 15-Oct-88	14	Hillside Vineyards	Fincl Plan	CN	BR	
28 15-Oct-88	14	Hillside Vineyards	Business Review	CN	BR	
29						
Ready						

If, however, the TASK field is left out of the extract range, only one record will be extracted. Without considering the data in the TASK field, the two records are duplicates. Figure 22.12 shows the result of an extraction without the TASK field.

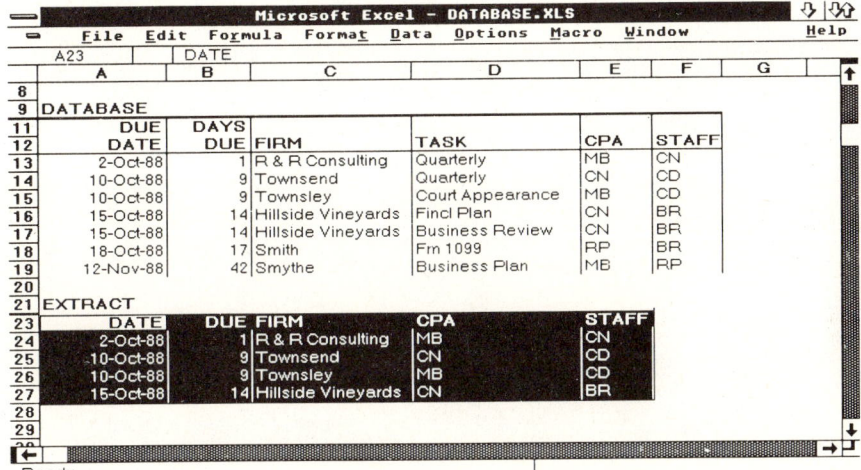

Fig. 22.12.
Unique records
extracted
without the
TASK field.

TIP

Use a Unique Extract as a Database Spelling Checker

One trick you can use a unique extract for is in cross-checking databases for typographical errors. Suppose, for example, that you have entered a list of part names into a database. You may have entered 16 different part names into a total of 320 records. To cross-check for misspelled part names, you can extract unique records using only the field containing the part names. Each of the 16 correctly spelled part names will appear once in the extract range. Any misspelled part name will appear in the extract range as an additional row. Use **Data Form**, **Data Find**, or **Formula Find** to locate the misspelled part name within the database or use **Formula Replace** to search for and replace the mistake.

Extracting from a Database on Another Worksheet

You can extract data to one worksheet from a database that is on another worksheet. In the following example, all items with a Quantity field greater than 10 will be extracted from the database on the FLIMINV.XLS worksheet and put in the extract range on the CORPINV.XLS worksheet.

Figure 22.13 shows the two worksheets. The FLIMINV.XLS worksheet contains a database in the range A5:C14 that has been named Database with the **Data Set Database** command.

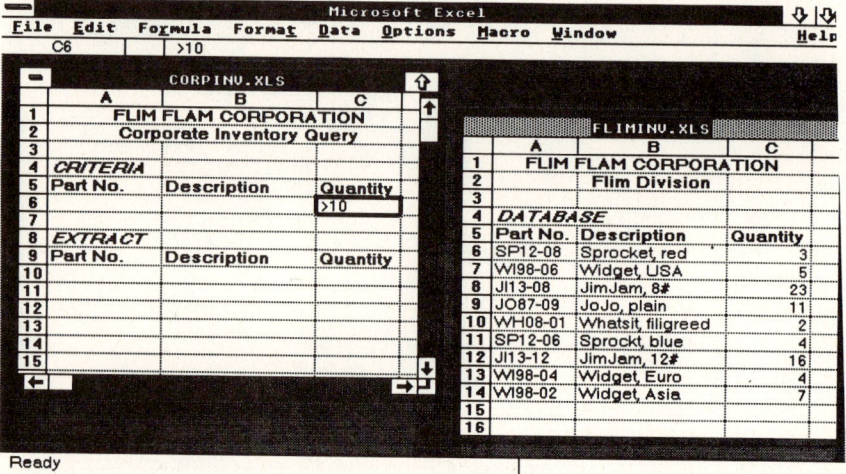

The CORPINV.XLS worksheet contains a criteria and extract range. The criteria range of A5:C6 was set with the **Data Set Criteria** command. The field names that will act as headings for the extract in CORPINV.XLS are in cells A9:C9.

Choosing the **Data Extract** command makes Excel attempt to extract data from the range named Database. In this case however, the desired Database range is on another worksheet. It is up to you to let Excel know what worksheet to look on for the Database range.

To do this, you use the Formula Define Name command. First, activate the receiving worksheet; CORPINV.XLS is the active sheet in figure 22.14. Choose the Formula Define Name command. It is in the Define Name dialog box shown in figure 22.14 where you will tell Excel that the range name Database should be interpreted as the external reference =FLIMINV.XLS!Database. The figure shows that the **Name** text box has the name Database typed in. The external reference for the FLIMINV.XLS database is typed into the **Refers to** text box. The external reference is

=FLIMINV.XLS!Database

(Don't forget that the FLIMINV.XLS worksheet had its database range set previously with the **Data Set Database** command.) This process has defined the Database range on CORPINV.XLS as an external reference to the FLIMINV.XLS worksheet.

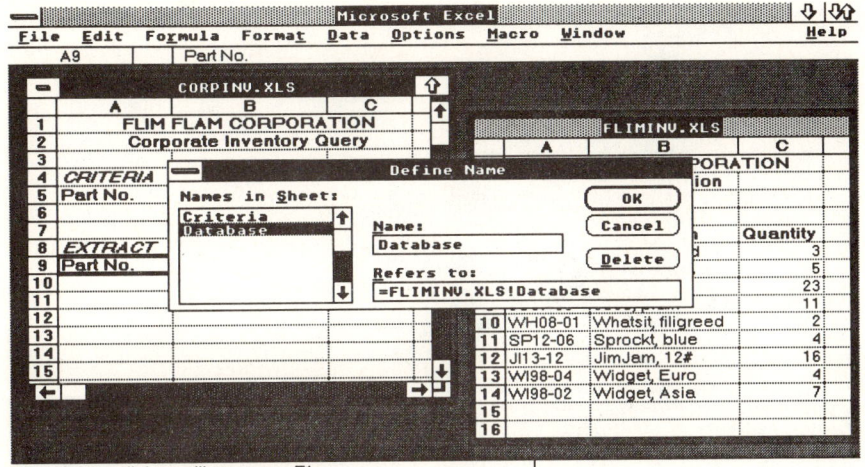

Fig. 22.14. Use the *Formula Define Name* command to define a database on another worksheet.

Now you can use normal extract procedures on the CORPINV.XLS worksheet to extract data. For example, figure 22.15 shows the extract field names selected in A9:C9 and the **D**ata **E**xtract command about to be chosen. The criteria in cell C6 (hidden) is >10, so extracted records must have a quantity greater than 10. Figure 22.16 shows the resulting extracting from the FLIMINV.XLS database to the CORPINV.XLS extract range.

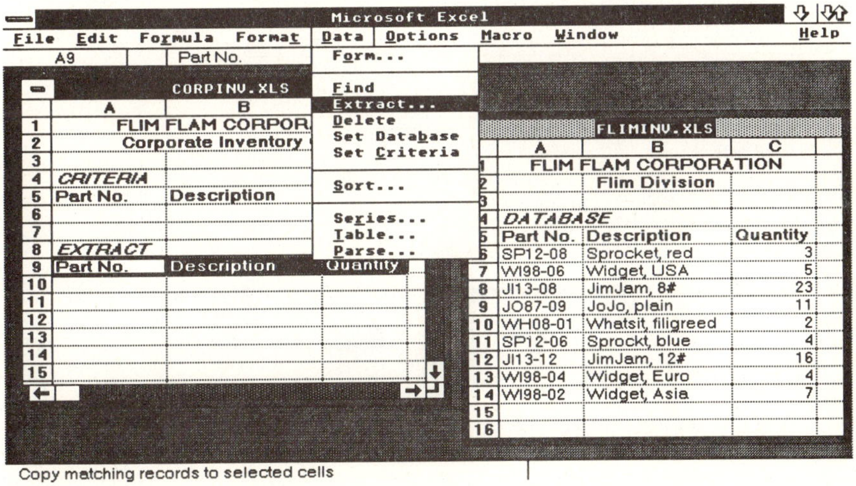

Fig. 22.15. An extract command from another worksheet about to be completed.

Fig. 22.16. A
completed Data
Extract from
another
worksheet.

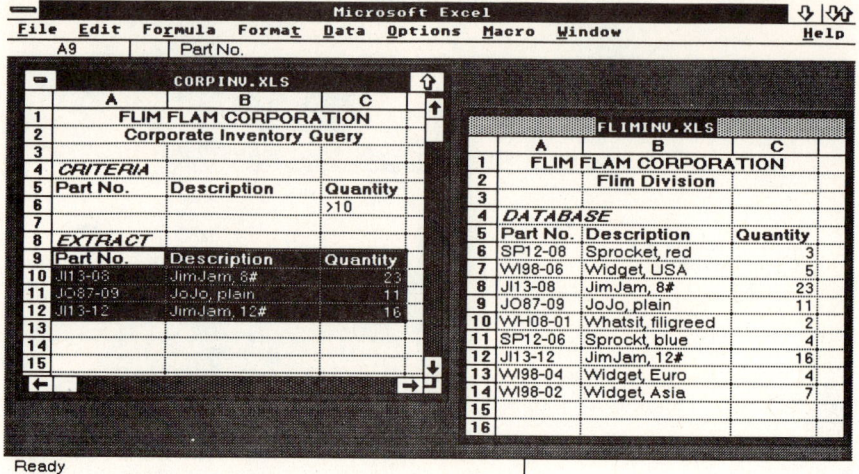

Creating Special Report Formats

As figure 22.17 illustrates, you can display extracted columns of data in any order you want. Change the column order of extracted data by changing the order of the field names in the extract range. Keep in mind that you can extract the data you want by using only the field names you need. Make sure that the field names you use are identical to those used in the database.

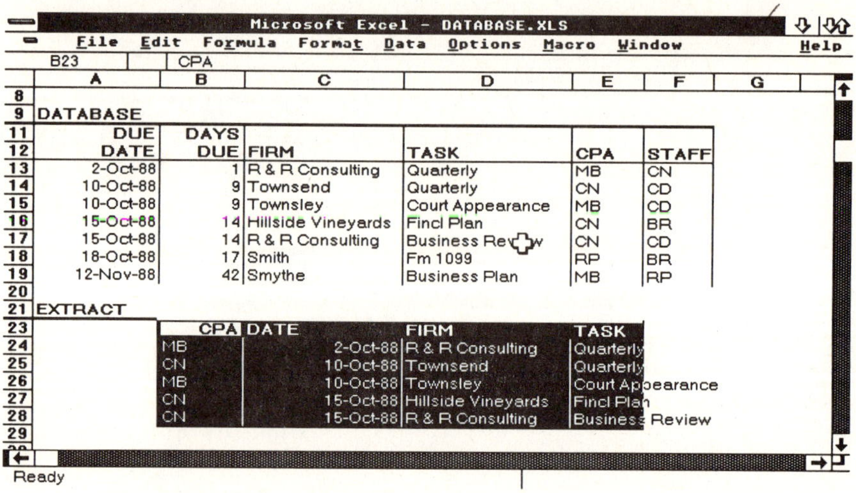

Fig. 22.17.
Extracted data
columns
displayed in a
different order
from the
database.

> **TIP**
>
> ### Confidential Reports
>
> Reports for different people may contain data that reflects different levels of security or relevance. A report being sent to sales managers may contain the commissions earned by each salesperson. However, the same report printed for the salespersons should not contain that private information.
>
> For information on hiding specific elements of the worksheet, see the "Controlling the Worksheet Display" section in Chapter 8, "Formatting Worksheets." That chapter explains how you can do the following when you prepare confidential reports:
>
> - Hide columns of information in a report by reducing the width of the column to zero.
>
> - Hide selected rows of information by reducing the row height to zero.
>
> - Return hidden rows or columns to normal.

Maintaining Data

Databases have a tendency to grow and grow. There comes a time when memory and speed limitations dictate that you should clean house. As part of this process, you will need to make backup copies of the old information and remove it from the working database.

Backing Up Work As You Go

A unpleasant surprise awaits you if you continually save your database to the same file name. When you choose **File Save**, the current Excel file replaces the original file on disk. That practice is fine as long as you never make a mistake. But what if you accidentally delete the wrong records, make a number of incorrect edits, or add some incorrect data? If you save garbage over the good data, you are left with trash.

> **TIP**
>
> ### Save Only the Old Data
>
> A good policy is to save a printed copy and a disk file of the old data before deleting it from your working database. Suppose, for example, that you want to delete all of April's records. Use **Data Extract** to create a printed report of the April records. Then cut out the April extract report and paste it into a new document. Save this new document as a file containing only the records that will be deleted.

If you prefer a little more job security in your life, save the database you are editing every 15 to 30 minutes using **File Save As**. Each time you save with **File Save As**, edit the file name so that it is different than the previous name. For example, you might want to use a sequence of file names such as the following:

ACCTS_01
ACCTS_02
ACCTS_03

The last two characters indicate the file's version number. This technique lets you return to an older file in order to recover previous data. When files get so old that you know you will not need them again, erase them from the disk with **File Delete** or return to the Windows MS-DOS Executive and erase multiple files all at once.

Keep more than one copy of your important database files. In addition, do not keep the backup copy in the same building as the original. Take the backup files to a different building or bank vault. If your building burns or a thief takes the computers and disks, you still will have your data.

Deleting a Group of Records

Your database is of little use unless someone maintains it. While editing, adding, and deleting single records requires manual work, Excel can help you delete groups of records. You delete a group of records in the much the same way as you extract a group of specific records. You use the **Data Delete** command to delete from the database all records that meet the criteria you specify and thereby remove old data from the database. However, because you cannot undo deleted records, a good practice is to adhere to the safety procedures outlined in the following steps:

1. Choose **File Save As**, and save your worksheet with a unique file name.

2. Enter the criteria for the records you want to delete.

3. Choose **Data Find** to see whether the criteria you enter selects the records you want deleted.

4. Choose **Data Delete** to delete records matching the criteria.

   Excel displays the alert box shown in figure 22.18.

5. Select the OK button or press Enter.

6. Choose **File Save As**, and save the resulting worksheet with a name different from the original file name.

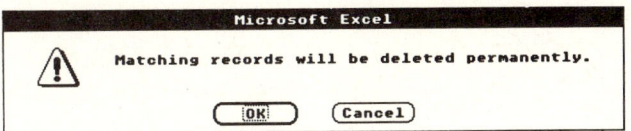

Fig. 22.18. An alert box warning that records will be deleted permanently.

> **NOTE**
>
> ### Deleting Is Forever!
>
> **Data Delete** cannot be undone. Follow the safety procedures outlined in the preceding steps to make backup files and cross-check the criteria before deleting. Save your database with a new file name before deleting, and cross-check the criteria with **Data Find** before choosing **Data Delete**.

Data Delete shifts records up to fill the gaps left by deleted records. The command also automatically redefines the database range. The rest of the worksheet remains unchanged. Figure 22.19 shows the sample database with a new Report Date of 16-Oct-88. The criteria range is set to select records where the date is past (the Days Due field is negative). In figure 22.20, records matching the criterion have been deleted, and the database has closed up to fill the gaps.

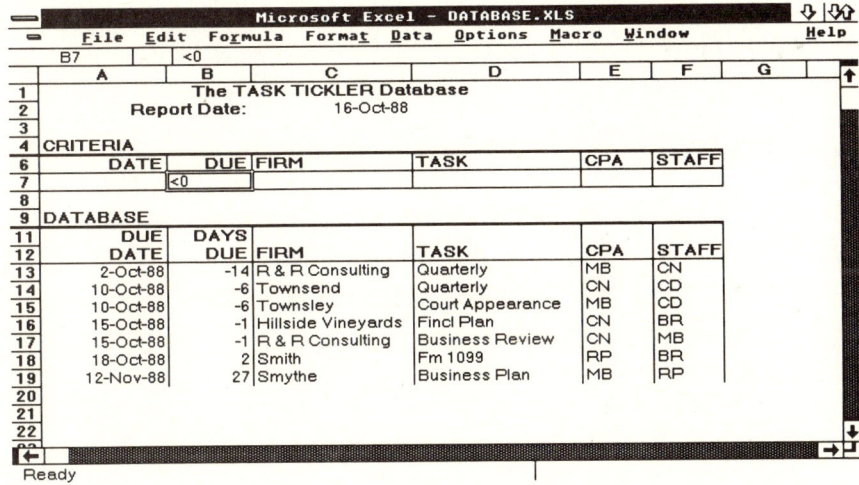

Fig. 22.19. The sample database before records are deleted; the criterion for deletion entered.

If you have only a few records to delete—records that might be difficult to describe with criteria—you may want to delete them manually. Use **Data Form** to find the records, and then select the Delete button on the form to delete the current record. If you use **Data Find** and delete rows or cells manually, other parts of the worksheet will move up. In this case, you must make sure that you adjust the worksheet as needed after you make the deletion.

Fig. 22.20. The sample database after records specified in the criteria range have been deleted.

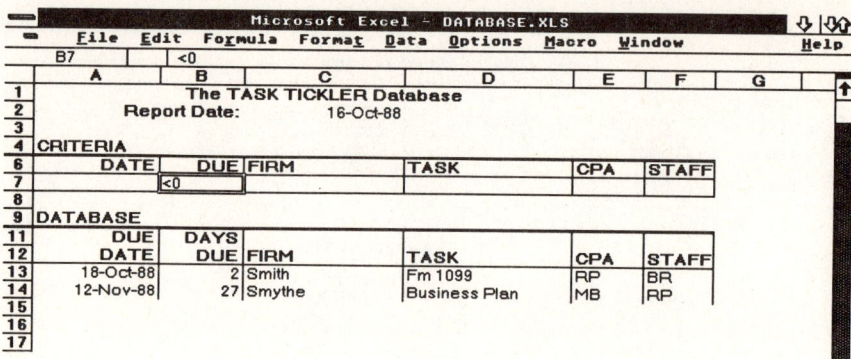

From Here . . .

Chapter 23, "Building Advanced Databases," shows you a number of ways to combine worksheet commands and techniques with the database. Even if you do not plan to use these techniques now, you should skim through that chapter to learn ideas that might help you in your future work.

Don't forget Chapter 24, "Troubleshooting Databases," if you run into trouble with your database. That chapter contains answers to some of the more common questions about operating an Excel database.

23

Building Advanced Databases

You can use Excel's database as no more than an electronic filing system. But what a waste! There's so much more you can do.

All you need or want for many business applications is a good, quick database. But because Excel's database is an integral part of the worksheet, you can do much more. You can use database results within worksheet calculations, analyze database contents with worksheet functions, and link databases together so that separate databases share common information.

The collection of techniques and tips presented in this chapter add power to Excel's database by combining the database with one or two other worksheet functions. Look through this chapter with an eye to areas that will save you time. Here are some of the techniques you will learn in this chapter:

- How to reduce errors in worksheets and databases by cross-checking data as it is entered

- How to use database functions such as DSUM and DCOUNT to analyze your database and extract summary information that matches the criteria you set

- How to combine the database functions with the **Data Table** command to produce multiple summaries from the database

- How to combine the INDEX and MATCH functions so that Excel automatically looks up and enters data for you

- How to create simple relational databases by linking fields between databases on different worksheets. This technique does away with redundant typing, reduces the size of each database involved, and lets you build reports involving data from multiple databases.

Cross-Checking Data Entries Automatically

Whether you are entering data in a database form you have created on a worksheet or making entries directly into the cells of a worksheet, you can prevent accidental errors with formulas that automatically cross-check the data as you enter it. Figure 23.1 shows an example of a data-entry form that uses formulas to cross-check entered data.

Fig. 23.1. A data-entry form with tables of allowed inputs.

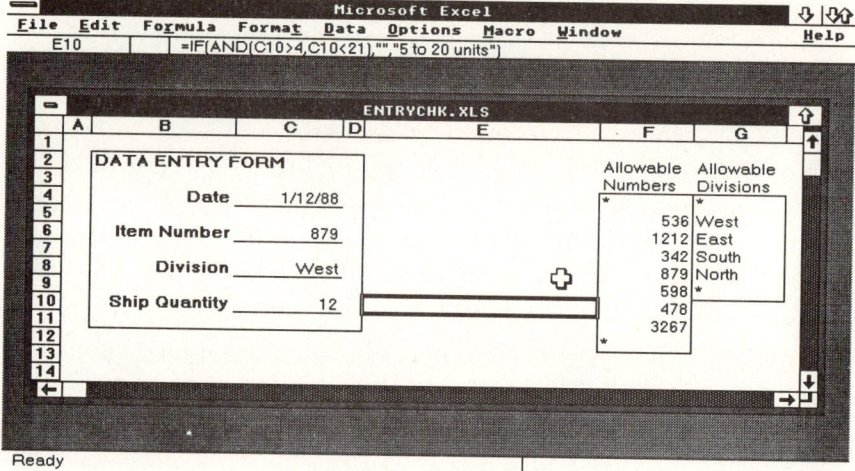

Figure 23.2 shows the same form with incorrect data entered. Notice the warnings that appear to the side of the data-entry cells. The formulas used in those cells are given in table 23.1.

Fig. 23.2. The data-entry form with warnings indicating that incorrect entries have been made.

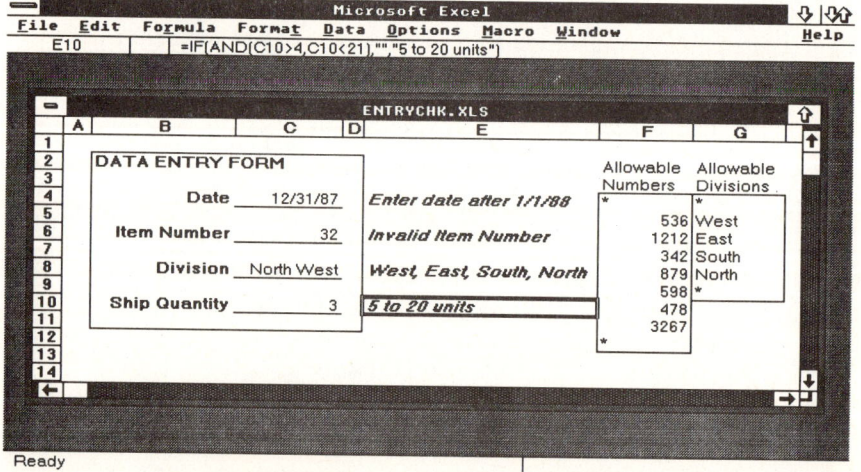

Table 23.1
Formulas in Figure 23.2 Cells

Cell	Cross-check	Formula
E4	Date after 1/1/88	=IF(C4>=DATEVALUE("1/1/1988"),"", "Enter date after 1/1/88")
E6	Item number in list	=IF(ISNA(MATCH(C6,F4:F12,0)), "Invalid Item Number","")
E8	Division name in list	=IF(ISNA(MATCH(C8,G4:G9,0)), "West,East,South,North","")
E10	Range of quantities	=IF(AND(C10>4,C10<21),"", "5 to 20 Units")

In each of these formulas, an IF function combined with a conditional test decides whether the entry in column C is correct. The formula in cell E4 checks whether the date serial number from C4 is greater than the date serial number inside the DATEVALUE function. If the serial number is greater, then blank text, "", is displayed. If the value in C4 is not greater, the prompting text is displayed.

In cell E6, the MATCH function looks through the values in F4:F12 to find an exact match with the contents of C6. The 0 tells MATCH to look for an exact match. When an exact match is not found, an error value (#N/A!) is returned. The ISNA function detects #N/A! values when a match is not found and displays the text warning. When a match is found, "" (nothing) is displayed on the screen. Notice that when you use MATCH, the items in the list do not have to be sorted as they do with the LOOKUP functions.

Cell E8 uses the same MATCH method to check the division name against acceptable spellings. This formula demonstrates that you should try to show the operator what the acceptable values are, either as part of the form or as part of the error message.

The value of Ship Quantity must be 5 to 20 units. Therefore, the formula in E10 uses an AND statement to check that the number in C10 is greater than 4 *and* less than 21. When both checks are true, nothing is displayed. If the number is out of the range, the message "5 to 20 Units" is displayed.

Analyzing Database Contents

If you work with accounting or job-costing databases, you probably have had to wade through files and reports counting how many items of a specific type were included or totaling amounts for certain types of records. You don't have to go through that drudgery if you keep your data in Excel. Excel can search your database for you and find totals, counts, and even statistical results for records that meet the criteria you specify.

You can use Excel to count the number of client contacts by sales representative, to total the amount for specific account codes by month, or to find how repairs are distributed through the vehicles in your fleet by type of repair and by type of vehicle. Excel's database functions combined with data tables can literally turn a 10-hour job into a few minutes of work.

Using Basic Database Functions

Database functions can perform operations such as counting or totaling the values in a database field for those records that meet the criteria you specify. Two database functions used frequently for these purposes are DSUM and DCOUNT. These functions are similar to SUM and COUNT. DSUM totals items in a database; DCOUNT counts items in a database.

When you use database functions, you need to specify three arguments: the range where the database is located, the column on which the function will act in the database range, and the range where the criteria is located. The format for database functions is

D*function*(database,field,criteria)

The *database* and *criteria* ranges can be the same as or totally different from the ranges you use with **Data Find**, **Form**, or **Extract**. You may use the same database range as that set with **Data Set Database**, while using a totally different criteria range.

The *field* argument in the function can be either the column number in the database (the first column in the database is 1) or the field name at the top of the database. If you use a field name, such as CODE, make sure that you enclose it in quotation marks (").

1-2-3 TIP

Excel's *Field* Number Is One Different in Dfunctions

1-2-3 begins counting the columns in a database for the *field* argument starting with the first column or field as zero. Excel begins counting with the first column or field as one.

In figure 23.3, the DSUM formula in cell E28 totals the AMOUNT column for all records having an EXP CODE of 12. The formula in E28 is

=DSUM(A13:E23,"AMOUNT",B27:B28)

The range A13:E23 is the database, including the field names. The range B27:B28 is the criteria used by just this function. The column being summed is "AMOUNT". This argument also could have been specified as the fifth column—5.

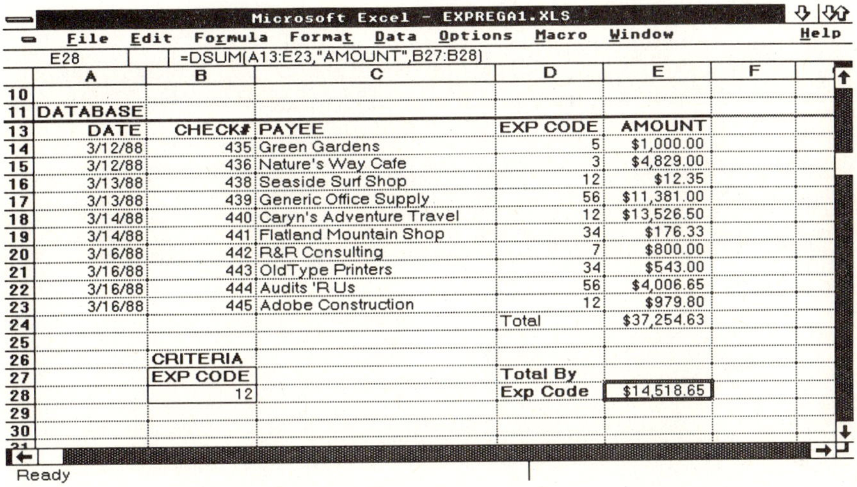

Fig. 23.3. A DSUM formula in cell E28 that totals the AMOUNT column for all records having an EXP CODE of 12.

In figure 23.4, the criteria range has been extended to A27:B28, and the field name DATE has been added to the criteria range. Now, only records with an EXP CODE of 12 and a DATE of 3/16/87 are totaled.

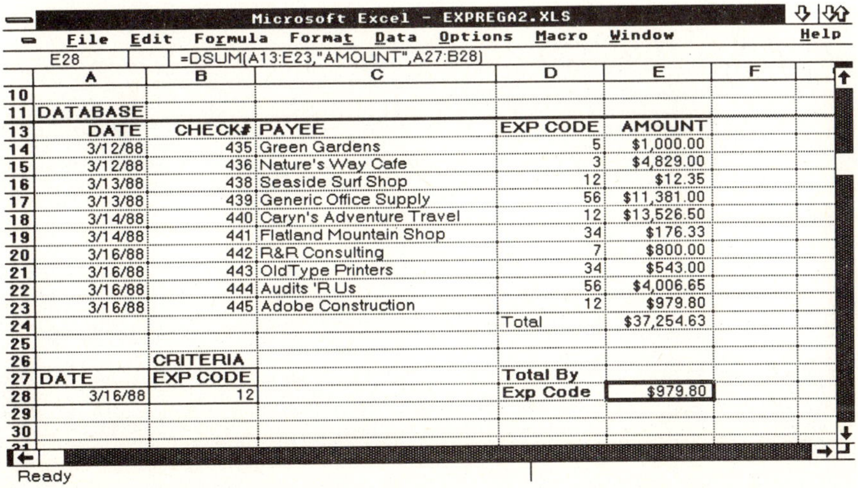

Fig. 23.4. The criteria range extended to total the AMOUNT column for records that have an EXP CODE of 12 and a DATE of 3/16/87.

Combining Database Functions with Data Tables

Although database functions are quite useful, using them to analyze a database with a large number of items still requires a lot of time. By combining the database functions with the **Data Table** command, however, you can perform repetitive analysis more quickly.

If you were to manually analyze the database in figure 23.5 for each total by expense code, it would take a few minutes. On a large database, it could take hours. By combining the DSUM function, described in the previous section, with the **Data Table** command, described in Chapter 11, "Building Advanced Worksheets," Excel will do the expense code totals in 1/100th of the time.

Fig. 23.5. A data table that lists expense codes and totals.

Microsoft Excel – EXPREGA3.XLS						
File **Edit** **Formula** **Format** **Data** **Options** **Macro** **Window**						**Help**
E25	=DSUM(A13:E21,"AMOUNT",B25:B26)					
	A	**B**	**C**	**D**	**E**	**F**
11	DATABASE					
13	DATE	CHECK#	PAYEE	EXP CODE	AMOUNT	
14	3/12/88	435	Green Gardens	5	$1,000.00	
15	3/12/88	436	Nature's Way Cafe	3	$4,829.00	
16	3/14/88	440	Caryn's Adventure Travel	12	$13,526.50	
17	3/14/88	441	Flatland Mountain Shop	34	$176.33	
18	3/16/88	442	R&R Consulting	7	$800.00	
19	3/16/88	443	OldType Printers	34	$543.00	
20	3/16/88	444	Audits 'R Us	56	$4,006.65	
21	3/16/88	445	Adobe Construction	12	$979.80	
22						
23						
24		CRITERIA			AMOUNT BY EXP CODE	
25		EXP CODE			$14,506.30	
26		12		3	$4,829.00	
27				5	$1,000.00	
28				7	$800.00	
29				12	$14,506.30	
30				34	$719.33	
31				56	$4,006.65	

Ready

The **Data Table** command is used along with the DSUM function in E25 to take the expense codes in D26:D31 and produce the total amounts for each expense code shown in E26:E31. **Data Table** takes each code from column D and inserts it into the criteria. The DSUM result from that criteria is then placed under the DSUM formula in the cell next to the appropriate expense code.

In figure 23.5, the DSUM function combined with a data table produces a table of expense codes and their totals. The table is in cells D25:E31, and the DSUM formula is in cell E25. The left column lists each expense code, while the right column lists the resulting total amount for each expense code to its left.

The DSUM formula in cell E25 is

=DSUM(A13:E21,"AMOUNT",B25:B26)

This is the same type of formula used in previous examples. The criteria range, B25:B26, again holds the criteria for the EXP CODE field. Because the current criteria in B25:B26 says that the EXP CODE must be 12, the total of the "AMOUNT" field is $14,506.30 for the formula in E25.

See Chapter 11, "Building Advanced Worksheets," for a step-by-step description of the process used to create data tables.

TIP

Data Tables That Are Updated with New Data

If you use DATABASE as a named range for the database used by both the **D**ata **T**able command and the database functions, then adding a new record with **D**ata **F**orm expands the database range to include the new record. Because the table uses the same range name, the data table also expands automatically. Therefore, new records will be included in any results shown in the data table.

If the data table refers to the database range by cell reference or with a name other than DATABASE, records added with **D**ata **F**orm are not reflected in the data table.

If figure 23.5 contained 537 different expense codes, the process of entering them in column D when you built the table would be quite time-consuming. Instead, use **D**ata **E**xtract to enter the expense codes for you. Use the **E**xtract command to extract each unique expense code from the database, just as though you were creating a report.

Use **D**ata **S**et Data**b**ase and **D**ata **S**et **C**riteria to assign the DATABASE and CRITERIA names to the ranges used by the database function. Because you want to extract all expense codes, do not enter criteria.

Now copy the field heading EXP CODE to the cell above where you want the new column of expense codes (in this case, cell D25). Then select EXP CODE in cell D25, as shown in figure 23.6, and choose **D**ata **E**xtract. Select the Unique Records Only option, and click OK or press Enter.

The result, shown in figure 23.7, illustrates that **D**ata **E**xtract used the heading EXP CODE as an extract range. Because the Unique Records Only option was selected, only one of each expense code was extracted. Now you can use the **D**ata **S**ort command to rearrange the expense codes.

Fig. 23.6. The EXP CODE field heading copied and selected in preparation for extracting expense codes.

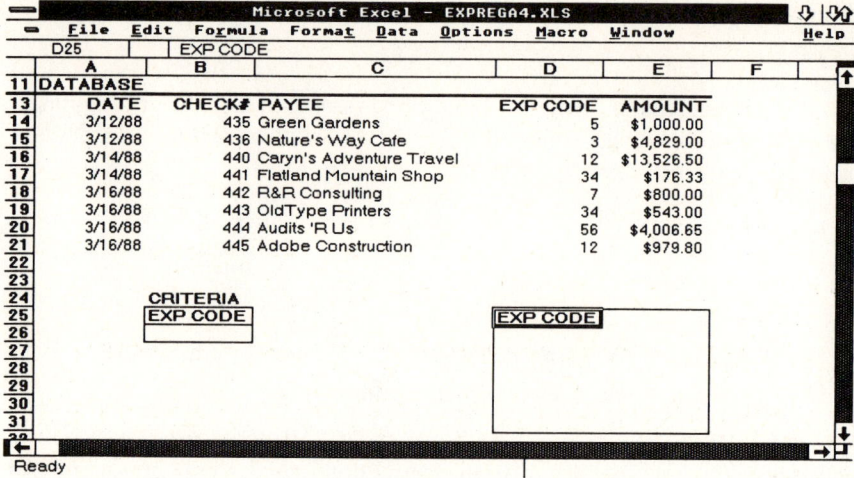

Fig. 23.7. Extracted expense codes.

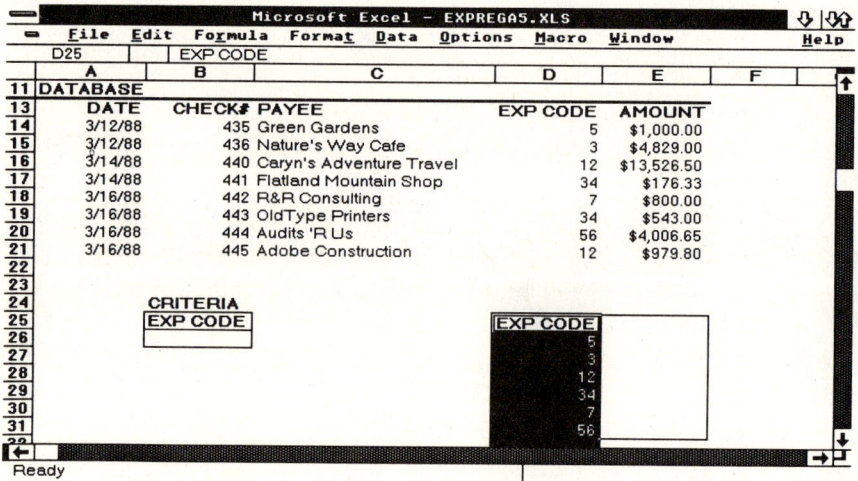

Beware! The **Data Extract** command erases all cells below the extract heading. You may want to move the extract heading to a safe area of the worksheet before you extract numbers. Then you can cut and paste the data to the appropriate place on your worksheet after the extraction.

Entering Data Automatically

One way to prevent data-entry errors is to have Excel enter some of the data for you. For example, suppose that an operator must enter an item code and an item description that belongs to that code. Having the operator enter the item description could introduce errors. A better arrangement is to have the operator enter only the item code and to let Excel look up the description. This technique not only reduces typing, but cross-checks the item code by displaying either the description or an error message that the item code is incorrect.

In figure 23.8, Excel automatically enters the item description as soon as the item code is entered. If the item code is nonexistent, the worksheet displays #N/A in the Description cell (C8).

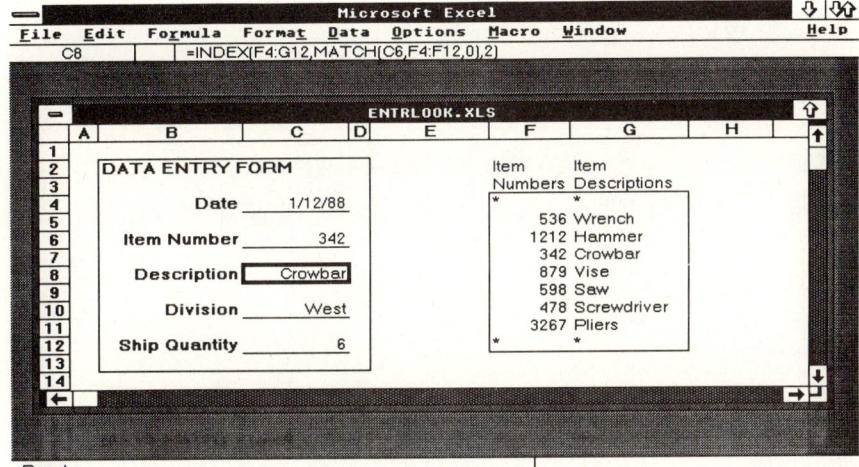

Fig. 23.8. An item description looked up and entered automatically by Excel.

The following formula, in cell C8, looks up the description and enters it:

=INDEX(F4:G12,MATCH(C6,F4:F12,0),2)

The INDEX function looks in the range F4:G12 and returns the contents of the cell located at the intersection of the row specified by the MATCH function and column 2.

The MATCH function looks through the range F4:F12 until it finds the exact match for the contents of cell C6. The last argument in MATCH, 0, specifies that the match must be exact. When it finds an exact match, the MATCH function returns the position of the match—in this case, row 4 of the specified range. Notice that the MATCH function finds the first match in the range. The contents of the range F4:F12 do not have to be in alphabetical order.

The table of item numbers and descriptions is outlined in order to identify visually the table as a single entity. The asterisks (*) at the top and bottom of the table mark the corners of the ranges. The function continues to work correctly as long as you insert any new data item codes and descriptions between the asterisks.

Linking Databases

Excel not only can link fields between databases on the same worksheet, but it also can link databases in separate documents. You therefore can create a rudimentary relational database or generate reports containing data from multiple databases.

Figure 23.9, for example, shows three separate databases that are linked together to create a fourth summary report and database. The databases shown in the figure are described in table 23.2.

Fig. 23.9. Four linked databases.

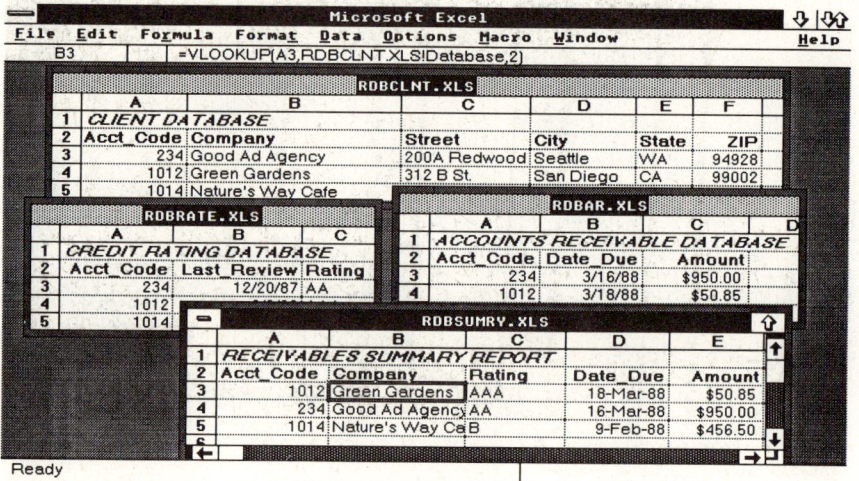

Table 23.2
Linked Databases Shown in Figure 23.9

Worksheet	Database
RDBCLNT	Client Database containing the client's address. Supports RDBSUMRY.
RDBAR	Accounts Receivable Database containing the amounts owed and dates owed. Supports RDBSUMRY.

Worksheet	Database
RDBRATE	Credit Rating Database containing each client's credit rating and when it was last reviewed. Supports RDBSUMRY.
RDBSUMRY	Receivables Summary Report containing selected information from the other three databases.

The Receivables Summary Report, also a database, can be sorted on any field. You can use the **Data** commands, such as Find, Form, and Extract, to manipulate the data.

TIP

Extracting Data from a Linked Database

Information extracted from a linked database with **Data Extract** is converted to its values. Because formulas are not extracted, changes made in the other databases will not update the extracted data. This feature can work to your advantage. You can manipulate the extracted data without affecting the linked formulas or the other databases.

For databases to link together, they must have a common field. In figure 23.9, the Acct_Code is the common field. A unique Acct_Code is used to prevent duplicate or incorrectly typed client names. The formulas that link the databases use the Acct_Code to find the appropriate record or row in other databases.

Note that each of the worksheet databases has been named with **Data Set Database** on its individual worksheet. If the database has not been named with the **Data Set Database** command, you will not be able to extract from it.

You can link databases in two different ways. The first method uses the VLOOKUP function to find information in a supporting database, such as RDBCLNT. Although using VLOOKUP is the faster of the two techniques, it has some inherent problems. The supporting database must be sorted in ascending order on the common field. Furthermore, VLOOKUP may produce incorrect results. Using VLOOKUP is a good method for linking databases when the supporting database is always sorted and when little possibility for entry errors exists.

In the figure, the formula in cell B3 of the RDBSUMRY.XLS database is

=VLOOKUP(A3,RDBCLNT.XLS!Database,2)

The parts of this formula are as follows:

=VLOOKUP(lookup_value,table_array,col_index)

The formula takes the value of Acct_Code from cell A3 and looks down the left column of the database range in the RDBCLNT worksheet. When the formula finds an Acct_Code that is equal to or less than the value in A3, the formula looks across to column 2 and finds the name *Green Gardens*.

A slightly slower way to link databases, but one that is accurate and does not require sorting, uses the INDEX and MATCH functions. MATCH searches the supporting database for the row that contains an *exact* match for the Acct_Code. After the MATCH function locates the row, the INDEX function looks up the company name.

The MATCH and INDEX formula for cell B3 is

=INDEX(RDBCLNT.XLS!Database,MATCH(A3,
RDBCLNT.XLS!Acct_Code,0),2)

The two functions used in this formula following this syntax:

=INDEX(array,row_num,column_num)
=MATCH(lookup_value,lookup_array,type_of_match)

The MATCH function searches the range Acct_Code on the RDBCLNT worksheet until it finds an exact match for the contents of cell A3. (The 0 argument specifies an exact match.) When it finds an exact match, the function returns the row number. If no exact match is found, the function returns #N/A.

After the MATCH function finds the row number, the INDEX function takes over. The INDEX function looks in the database range on the RDBCLNT worksheet at the intersection of the found row number and column 2, and then returns the value found there. The value is *Green Gardens*.

Two problems inherent in the VLOOKUP method are solved by the MATCH and INDEX method. If the RDBCLNT database is not sorted by Acct_Code, or if an incorrect Acct_Code is entered, the VLOOKUP formula returns the wrong company name. The result could be incorrect billing or a bad rating for a good account. Using the MATCH and INDEX method, however, avoids both these problems. The database does not need to sorted; and if an incorrect entry is made, the MATCH function returns #N/A.

Creating a Custom Database Form

Excel's automatic database form is easy to use and convenient, but in some cases, it is not adequate. You can modify Excel's data form to add instructions, remove some fields from the form, or arrange fields as they appear on paper.

A custom database form uses the same two elements as Excel's automatic database form: text as labels and text boxes for data entry. As in the automatic database form, protected or calculated fields in a custom form are displayed without a text box and cannot be changed.

Using the database DATABASE.XLS from the "Database Quick Start," the database form in figure 23.10 appears automatically. The following text explains how to rearrange this form so that it appears like figure 23.11.

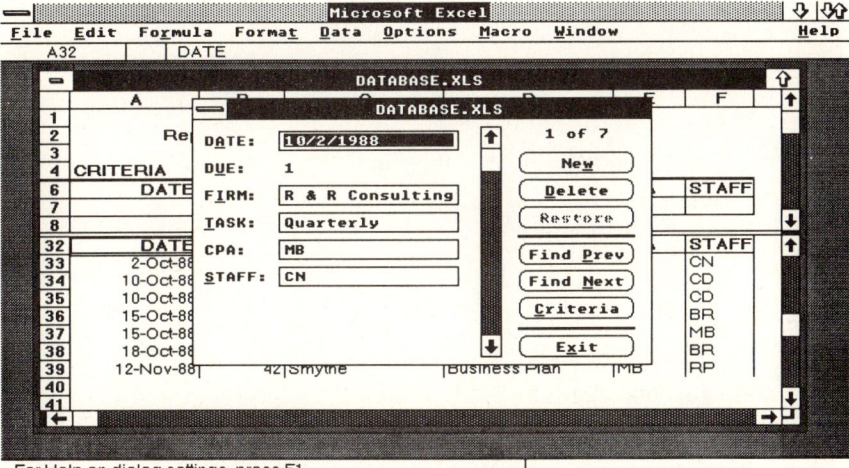

Fig. 23.10. The automatic database form created from the database in the "Database Quick Start."

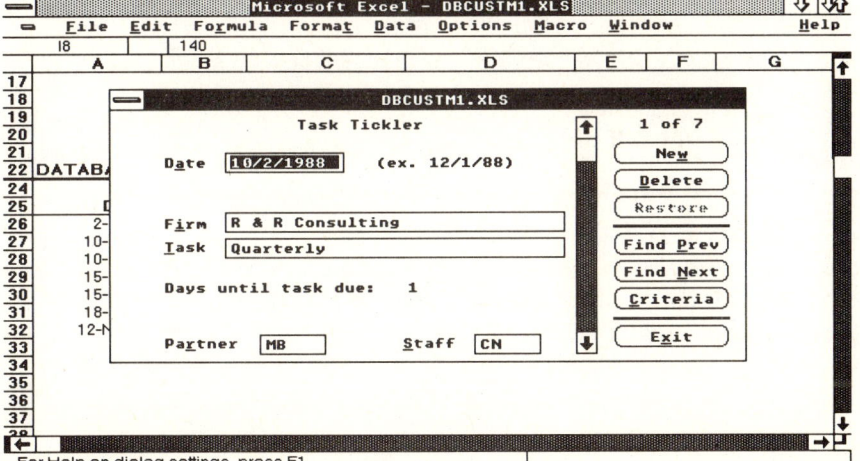

Fig. 23.11. A custom database form.

To create a custom database form, begin by making a list that describes how you want the form to appear. Figure 23.12 shows the list that was used to create figure 23.11. After you have entered the list, name the range H7:N20 with the name Data_Form using the Formula Define Name command. The labels in row 6 are not part of the Data_Form range. The labels are included only to make the following description easier to understand.

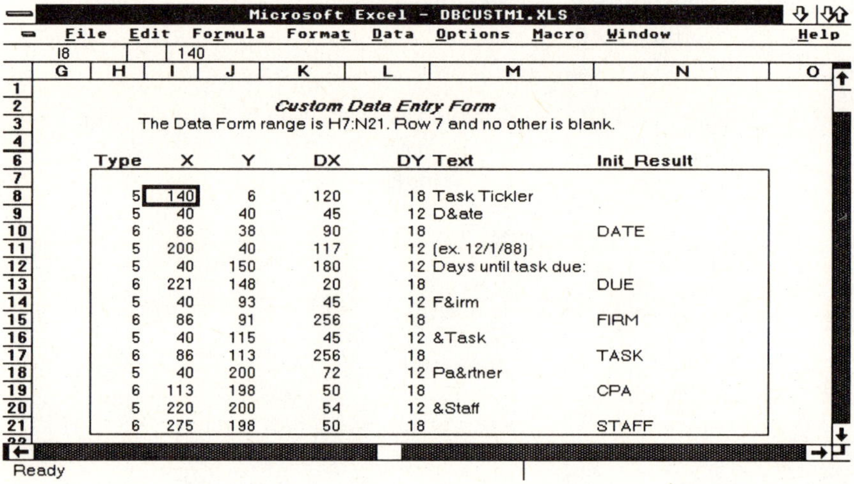

Microsoft Excel - DBCUSTM1.XLS

File Edit Formula Format Data Options Macro Window Help

I8 140

Custom Data Entry Form

The Data Form range is H7:N21. Row 7 and no other is blank.

Row	Type	X	Y	DX	DY	Text	Init_Result
7							
8	5	140	6	120	18	Task Tickler	
9	5	40	40	45	12	D&ate	
10	6	86	38	90	18		DATE
11	5	200	40	117	12	(ex. 12/1/88)	
12	5	40	150	180	12	Days until task due:	
13	6	221	148	20	18		DUE
14	5	40	93	45	12	F&irm	
15	6	86	91	256	18		FIRM
16	5	40	115	45	12	&Task	
17	6	86	113	256	18		TASK
18	5	40	200	72	12	Pa&rtner	
19	6	113	198	50	18		CPA
20	5	220	200	54	12	&Staff	
21	6	275	198	50	18		STAFF

Ready

Fig. 23.12. The Data_Form range that generated the form in figure 23.11.

The description of the custom data form is in the range H7:N20. This range must be named Data_Form in order for the **Data Form** command to find and use it. The top row must be blank, and no other blank rows can be included. Each row in this range describes the type, location, and contents of an object on the data form.

Column H, *Type*, contains a 5 or 6. The number 5 indicates a test label. The number 6 is a field name that will receive data from the Init_Result field.

Columns I and J give the X and Y coordinates for the upper left corner of the label text or text box. Columns K and L give the coordinates for the lower right corner of the label text or text box. The upper left corner of the database form has the coordinates 0,0. The outside edge of the form changes shape automatically to accept the label text or text boxes you enter.

Column M, *Text*, contains the text used as labels in the form. Any letter preceded by an ampersand (&) is the letter underlined on the screen and used in combination with the Alt key. Column N, *Init_Result*, lists the names of the fields in which data will be entered. You need to be sure that you position the text box for the correct field next to its label.

To build a custom database form, follow these steps:

1. Write down the field headings and underlined letters used in the automatic database form.

2. Move the active cell to a clear area of the worksheet where rows and columns will not be inserted accidentally.

3. Enter the headings, as shown in row 6, as a guide.

4. Leave a blank row under the headings. This is the first row of the Data_Form range.

5. Enter a title for the form, if you want, as shown in cell M8 of row 8. Use a Type of 5 for label text.

6. Enter data for two or three rows.

7. Select the data form range so that the top row is blank but includes the data rows below the top row.

8. Choose Formula **D**efine Name.

9. Name the range Data_Form.

10. Choose **D**ata Form. (Remember: You must have assigned the name DATABASE to a corresponding database previously.)

11. Examine your custom form.

12. Exit the form.

13. Edit the form description data in the Data_Form range.

14. Add additional data to the form description.

15. Choose Formula **D**efine Name and expand the Data_Form range to include the new data.

16. Choose **D**ata Form and examine the information you have added.

Continue adding to the description, renaming the range, and checking the form until the custom form is satisfactory. If you enter too many incorrect descriptions without checking the appearance, you may end up with a garbled form that is difficult to correct.

> **TIP**
>
> ### Add Data-Entry Aids and Titles
>
> Customize your database form by adding helpful instructions and examples of proper entry formats. The added text and titles will help operators complete the form more accurately. Add titles and instructions using a row like row 8 in figure 23.12.

From Here . . .

After reviewing this and previous chapters, you should be familiar with Excel's worksheet and database capabilities. Now you can work through Chapter 25, "Macro Quick Start," to improve your skills and knowledge even more. You soon will see how easily you can automate database and report creation.

Then, to build up your proficiency even further, sit in front of an Excel screen as you scan through the "Excel Function Dictionary" in Chapter 9. When you think of a way to use a function or to combine multiple functions and commands, go ahead and experiment. That's how new ideas are generated.

24

Troubleshooting Databases

In this chapter, you find ways to make your database more efficient. You also find answers to some common database questions.

Conserving Memory

Databases usually take a lot of room on the worksheet and a lot of memory in your computer. You can make your worksheets and databases more memory-efficient by properly storing values, by building separate worksheets and linking them together, and by correctly positioning databases on the worksheet. This not only lets you build larger systems that run more quickly and are more understandable, but also it can save you money because you may not have to buy expansion memory.

Storing Values To Conserve Memory

Excel stores different types of values in different ways. Choosing the correct format for values can save memory and increase performance. Empty, formatted cells, for example, use memory.

When possible, use integer numbers rather than numbers with decimal fractions. Integers take less memory.

You can save memory in a database by converting formulas to constant values. When you transfer data from a data-entry area into a database, copy the data with **Edit Copy**, then use **Edit Paste Special**, and select **Values** to paste only the values.

If you have a large worksheet or table area that uses similar formulas, then create the formulas as an array. Array formulas take less memory.

Using Worksheet Modules
To Conserve Memory

There is no need to fit a large business model and database on a single work-sheet. Building everything on one worksheet takes too much memory and leads to slow recalculations. Instead, link worksheets, databases, and tables with the methods described in Chapter 11, "Building Advanced Worksheets," and Chapter 23, "Building Advanced Databases." Don't forget you can extract from a database on another worksheet using the technique described in Chapter 22, "Extracting and Maintaining Data."

Positioning Data To Conserve Memory

Excel reserves memory for blocks of worksheet cells. The way calculations and databases are positioned in the worksheet changes the number and type of cell blocks reserved. This affects the amount of memory used to store the worksheet.

These blocks of cells are each 32 rows deep; if your computer has expanded memory, they are 16 rows deep. For example, in a computer with expanded memory, cell blocks will be from rows 1 to 16, 17 to 32, and so on. To preserve memory, you should arrange your worksheet to keep as much data as possible within existing cell blocks. Letting a few cells "leak" into a new cell block wastes memory.

Within a cell block, Excel reserves memory for rows that contain a filled cell. You can make better use of memory by filling rows as completely as possible. (There is a tradeoff here, because you must also consider worksheet appearance and the ability to make changes and reorganize contents.)

Excel keeps track of the cells at the left and right edges of each cell block. Blocks that are more than 160 columns wide are handled differently if the computer has expanded memory. If you use expanded memory, then you can conserve memory and improve performance by keeping cell blocks narrower than 160 columns.

Retrieving Memory As You Work

As you edit or build your worksheet, Excel tracks the old worksheet and how the new changes fit into the old worksheet. All this tracking takes up memory. You can regain the memory used in tracking changes by saving your worksheet and reopening it.

Troubleshooting Tips

Problem: The database doesn't work.

Solution: Use the following checklist to help you find the problem:

1. Choose Formula Goto, and select the database range and the criteria range. Check that they each include a single row of field names at the top of the selected range. The criteria range should contain at least one row in addition to field names.

2. Select the rows under the field names in the criteria range, and use Edit Clear to remove any hidden blanks in the criteria range.

3. Make sure that field names in the criteria and extract ranges are spelled exactly the same as they are in the database range. Use only text names or formulas that produce text names.

4. Field names cannot be numeric. If you must use a numeric field name at the top of a database column, then change it into text with a formula such as

    ="9540"

5. Make sure a third set of field names is used for the extract range headings. The extract range with field names at the top of the range must be selected when you choose the Data Extract command.

Problem: Some of the database commands listed in the book do not appear in the menus.

Solution: Choose Options Full Menus.

Problem: Computed criteria does not produce a find or extract result.

Solution: Computed criteria must be entered in the criteria range beneath a heading that is *not* a field name. Replace an existing field name in the criteria range, or increase the size of the range to accommodate the new heading. Make a new descriptive heading that is different from the database field names.

Problem:	Formulas in the database that refer to values outside the database return incorrect results.
Solution:	Database formulas must refer to cells or names outside the database using absolute reference.
Problem:	The database and worksheet calculations are on the same worksheet. But now the database is so large that there isn't enough memory, and calculations take too long.
Solution:	Separate the worksheet calculations and database into different documents. Review the sections on linking worksheets and linking databases to learn how to pass data between the documents.
Problem:	During data entry, there is a long pause after Enter is pressed before the next cell can be entered. This pause drastically slows data-entry time.
Solution:	Choose Options Calculation, select the Manual button, and choose OK. This prevents Excel from recalculating the entire worksheet after each entry. Make sure that you recalculate after entering all data by pressing F9 or by switching back to automatic calculation.
Problem:	The Data Find, Extract, and Delete commands act on the entire database and ignore the criteria.
Solution:	Choose Formula Goto, select the Criteria name, and choose the OK button. This selects the criteria range so that you can see it on-screen. Make sure that there are no blank rows included in the criteria range.
Problem:	The Data Find, Extract, and Delete commands do not act on records that obviously satisfy the criteria.
Solution:	Complete the following steps:

1. Check that the field names at the top of the criteria rows are exactly the same as the field names that head each database column. Use Edit Copy and Edit Paste to duplicate field names.

2. Use Formula Goto to verify that the database and criteria ranges are correct.

3. Use Edit Clear to erase all "blank" cells in the criteria range. Cells may appear blank, even when they contain blank characters entered with the space bar. Excel tries to find fields that match these blank characters.

Problem: An exact text search such as ="Smith" finds only a few of the records known to contain Smith.

Solution: Incorrectly spelled words and blank spaces can prevent what appears to be an exact match. Here are some ways to find near matches:

1. Instead of entering ="Smith", type **Smith**, without quotation marks or equal signs. This finds words beginning with *Smith*, even where the name may be followed by blanks or additional characters.

2. Use wild cards to find misspelled words. For example, enter **sm?th** to find *Smith* or *Smythe*. Search with **?smith** if a leading blank space may have been accidentally entered.

3. Check some of the other database problems that cause partial database operation.

Problem: A complex criteria using AND and OR does not work as expected.

Solution: AND statements must satisfy the first condition "and" the second condition simultaneously. OR statements can satisfy either one "or" the other condition or both conditions. For example:

$$=AND(A15>500,A15<750)$$

This finds records where the data in column A is between 500 and 750. Those are the only values where both conditions are true. Remember, if you are searching for values between two points, use AND.

Problem: The database does not work correctly with dates.

Solution: Make sure that dates have been entered with a method producing a serial date number. Without a serial date number, database functions treat your date entry as text or a number. For more information, read the sections on entering dates in Chapter 7, "Entering and Editing Worksheet Data."

Problem: Part of the worksheet disappears whenever **Data Extract** is used.

Solution: When you select only the field names in the extract range and then use the **Data Extract** command, Excel assumes that you are extracting an unlimited amount of data. Excel then clears the area below the field names in the selected extract range to ensure extracted data is not mixed with previously extracted data. To prevent this, review Chapter 22, "Extracting and Maintaining Data," where you learned how to extract limited amounts of data.

Problem: Data at the bottom of the database is not found or extracted.

Solution: Use Formula Goto to check that the bottom rows are included in the database range. Use **D**ata Form to add data and preserve the database, or insert new rows through the middle of the database range.

Problem: Data on the left side of the records does not match data on the right side.

Solution: The database may have been "torn" in half and scrambled by sorting without including all columns. There is no way to repair the problem. Use a previously saved version.

Problem: The *custom* database form does not work. An alert box appears with an error, and no form shows.

Solution: Because the custom database form depends on a number of previous steps being completed correctly, you may have one or more of the following problems:

1. The area of the worksheet containing the form description must have the range name Data_Form.

2. The top row of the Data_Form range must be blank.

3. Descriptive information must be entered in the order described in Chapter 23, "Building Advanced Databases."

4. The names used in the Init_Result column must be spelled exactly the same as the field names in the

5. There cannot be any blank rows in the database form description except the top row.

6. The database range, including the field names, must be assigned a name with **D**ata Set Database.

7. The Type for labels in the form should be five. For a field name that receives data, it should be six.

From Here . . .

If you skipped over Chapter 23, "Building Advanced Databases," because it had the word *Advanced* in the title, you should reconsider. Even if you don't read or work through the advanced chapters, take three minutes to skim through the topic headings, figures, and tips. You may find ideas that later can save you many hours of work. Some of the topics covered include data-entry checking, using data tables with databases to extract accounting information, linking databases together, and more.

The next section describes macros. Macros are automatic procedures that you create and assign to a name. Whenever you want the procedure repeated, you can press a Ctrl+key combination or choose the macro's name from a list. With the automatic macro recorder, macros are easy to make. Try 'em; you'll like 'em!

Part V

Excel Macros

In the first 10 to 20 hours of using Excel, you should be automatically recording macros to decrease your work, while increasing your production and quality. A macro is a string of instructions that Excel runs automatically when you request it. There are two types of macros: command macros and function macros.

Command macros give you the power to automate frequent tasks such as printing reports with a single keystroke, checking data as it is being entered, and reducing repetitious formatting commands to a single keystroke. Those are simple macros that you can create at the beginning level. More advanced command macros produce custom dialog boxes, create new menu bars and commands, control other Windows applications, and even link data from other applications directly to Excel worksheets. Because command macros are on their own macro sheet, you can use a macro with any worksheet, not just the worksheet it was originally created for.

The second type of macro is the function macro. With function macros, you can create your own worksheet functions. For example, if you have specific formulas or equations that you wish were part of Excel, you can design them yourself as function macros. By writing these equations on a macro sheet, you can use your custom worksheet functions with any worksheet. You can even paste them into cells using the Formula Paste Function command.

To begin learning macros, start Excel and run through the Macro Quick Start in Chapter 25. The first portion of the Quick Start teaches you how to record a macro and customize it with a few simple edits. The second portion of the Quick Start demonstrates how to create your own worksheet functions using a function macro.

More in-depth explanation is provided in Chapter 26, "Building Command and Function Macros." And if you have a question about a macro that isn't working correctly, then you can refer to Chapter 27, "Troubleshooting Macros."

Don't miss Appendix B, "Macro Directory." This is a directory of Excel's 355 different macro functions. The first portion of the directory lists macro functions according to the menu command they perform, the action that they produce, or the decision process they make. The second portion of the directory gives the arguments for all Excel's macro functions. Explanations on the use of most of the macro functions are included, but due to the large number of macro functions, not all functions are explained in depth.

Chapter 25
Macro Quick Start

Chapter 26
Building Command and Function Macros

Chapter 27
Troubleshooting Macros

25

Macro Quick Start

Whenever you perform a repetitive action, whenever you want a procedure done by an inexperienced operator, or whenever you customize Excel, you should be using a macro.

Excel has two types of macros: command macros and function macros. Command macros enable you to replace sequences of keystrokes and command choices with a Ctrl+key combination or with a name selected from a list box. Function macros enable you to create your own numeric or text functions.

Excel command macros are easy to create and use. You create the macro by turning on a recorder, doing the sequence of keystrokes or command choices, and then turning off the recorder. Excel writes the command macro code for you. If you decide to edit your recorded macro or write one by hand, you will find the majority of macro codes are easy to understand. For example, the macro code equivalent to Format Font is FORMAT.FONT.

Excel function macros work just like Excel's built-in functions. For example, if the built-in PMT function does not calculate the types of loans you work with, you can write your own function to do the calculations the way you want.

The Macro Quick Start has two macro examples. The first example shows how to record keystrokes and commands with the recorder and then go back and modify the recording. The second example demonstrates how easy it is to write your own functions to complement Excel's numerous built-in functions.

Creating Command Macros

Command macros duplicate menu commands and actions on the worksheet. Command macros can be as simple as replacing a few command sequences with a Ctrl+key combination. On the other hand, command macros can be as complex as any programming language. In fact, the Excel command language gives you the capability to create custom applications with dialog boxes, menus, and links to other Windows programs.

Macros are created on a special macro sheet. A macro sheet looks like a worksheet. Columns are set wider in a macro sheet, however, and formulas are displayed. Commands and actions are replaced with easy-to-understand code words.

There are a number of advantages to macros created this way. Most of the edit and command features you learned for worksheets operate the same on macro sheets. A major advantage to having macro sheets separate from worksheets is that you can use a macro sheet with any worksheet.

This Quick Start guides you through the creation of a command macro that centers the contents of a worksheet's cell, changes the font to bold italic, and increases the row height.

1. Choose **File New**, select the **Worksheet** option, and choose OK or press Enter.

2. Move the worksheet so that columns A through E show on the right side of the screen as shown in figure 25.1.

   Mouse: Drag the title bar to the right.

   Keyboard: Press Alt+hyphen. Choose Move and press the right-arrow key. Press Enter when the worksheet is positioned as shown.

Fig. 25.1. The worksheet where the formatting macro will be used.

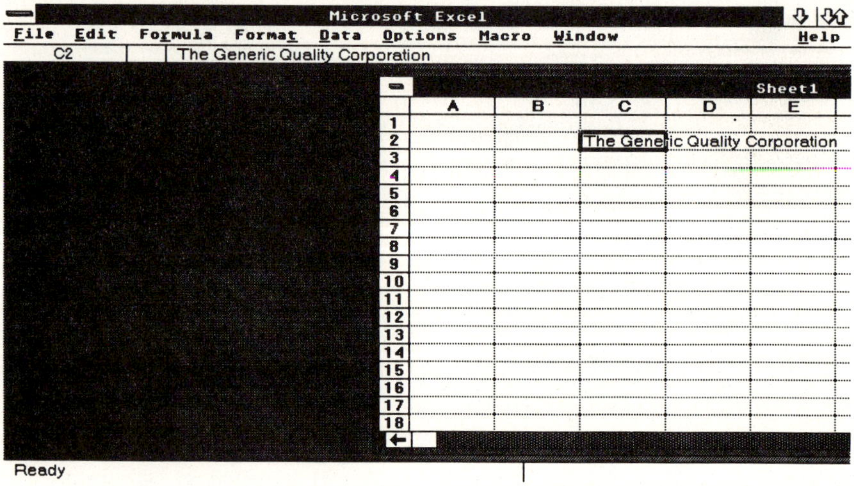

3. Enter **The Generic Quality Corporation** in cell C2. Keep cell
    C2 selected because this is where you will want to use your new
    macro.

Make sure that all menu commands are visible before continuing with the
rest of this Quick Start. If you see only two commands under **Macro**, then
choose **Options Full Menus** so that all commands are visible.

You are now ready to create a macro that can format this title or other titles.
Before you can create a macro, you need to open the macro sheet that stores
the macro code.

1. Choose **File New**, select **Macro Sheet**, and choose OK or press
    Enter. The macro sheet appears on top of the worksheet.

2. Type the macro name **Heading** into cell A1.

3. Select cell A2, and choose **Macro Set Recorder**.

    This marks cell A2 as the first cell to receive macro code. As
    you type and select commands, Excel automatically enters
    corresponding macro code beginning at cell A2 and moving
    down to other cells in the column.

4. Activate the worksheet window so that it appears on top.

    Mouse: Click on the worksheet if it is visible.

    Keyboard: Choose **W**indow and select the worksheet.

The macro sheet should now be underneath and to the left of the worksheet.
This will let you see macro code as it is entered. Now you are ready to begin
recording the macro.

1. Choose **Macro Start Recorder**.

    At this point Excel starts recording any *completed* command or
    actions. Commands in which you choose Cancel from the dialog
    box or press Esc are not recorded.

2. Choose **Macro Relative Record**.

    If **Macro Absolute Record** appears on the menu instead of
    Relative Record, then **Macro Relative Record** has already been
    chosen. The Relative Record command records all movements of
    the active cell relative to its position when you started recording
    the macro. **Macro Absolute Record** records the *exact* location
    of the cells selected when the macro was recorded.

3. Choose **Format Font**, select 4 (Helv 10, Bold Italic), and press
    Enter.

Figure 25.2 shows macro code in cell A2 of the macro sheet. In many cases the code, such as FORMAT.FONT, duplicates the command chosen from the menu.

Fig. 25.2. Macro code is recorded in cell A2.

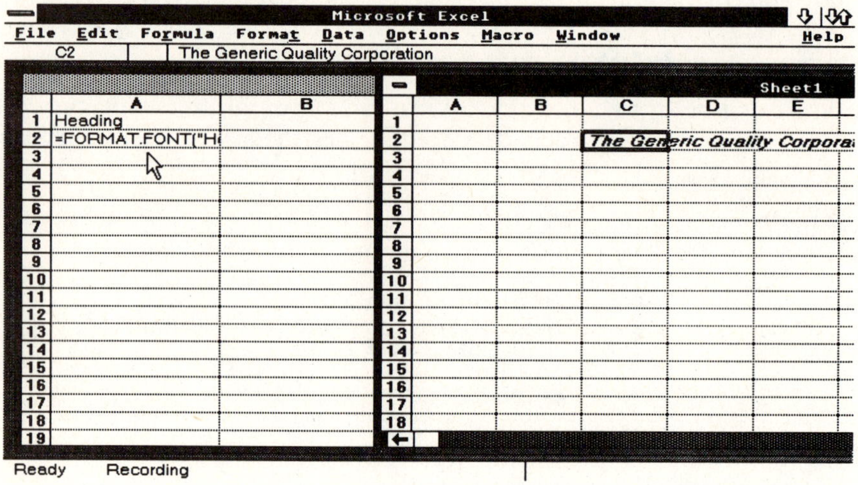

4. Choose Format Alignment, select Center, and press Enter.

   The code ALIGNMENT appears in A3, the next cell down on the macro sheet.

5. Choose Format Column Width, type 20 in the Column Width box, and press Enter.

   The code COLUMN.WIDTH appears in A4 of the macro sheet.

6. Choose Format Row Height, type 26 in the Row Height box, and press Enter.

   The code ROW.HEIGHT appears in A5 of the macro sheet.

7. Choose Macro Stop Recorder.

   The Stop Recorder command inserts a RETURN macro formula at the end of the macro recording, marking the end of the macro. The macro sheet should now appear like the one in figure 25.3. Each command or action appears in sequence, one macro code per cell, down the column.

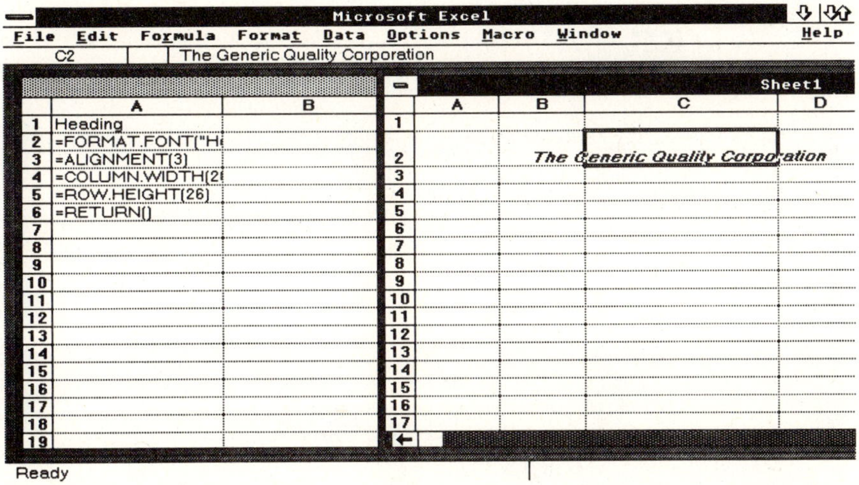

Fig. 25.3. Completed macro from recording.

Next, you must name the macro to tell Excel where it is located on the macro sheet. Unnamed macros do not work.

1. Activate the macro window. Select cell A1, which contains the macro title, Heading.

2. Choose Formula Define Name.

   Formula Define Name displays a dialog box used to name macros. Generally, you name the macro whatever is in the first cell of the column of macro code. This will tell Excel not only the name of the macro but also its location on the sheet. In the dialog box, you will specify whether the macro is a command or function macro. If it is a command macro, you can assign a Ctrl+key combination in the dialog box.

3. Select the Command button.

   Macros that record menu commands or keyboard and mouse actions are always command macros.

4. Select the Key text box and type **h**.

   The letter *h* is easy to remember for the Heading macro. You can use a number, an uppercase letter, or a lowercase letter in combination with the Ctrl key.

   The Define Name dialog box should now appear as shown in figure 25.4.

Fig. 25.4. Dialog box for naming macros.

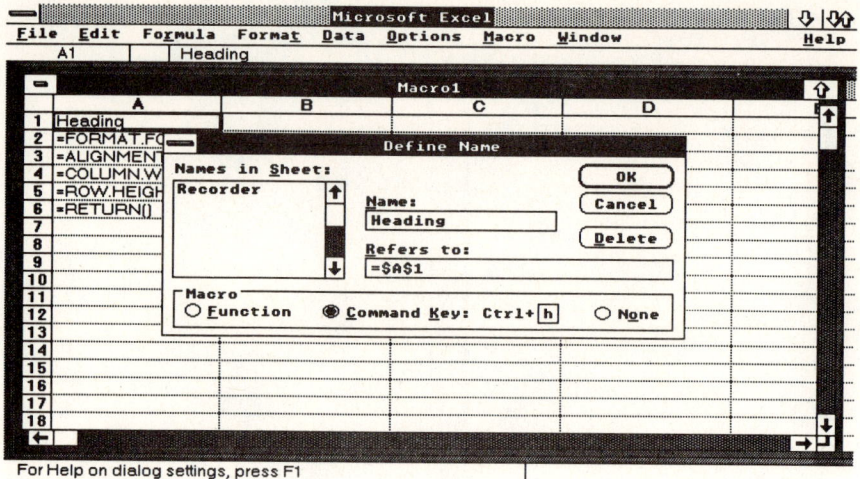

5. Choose OK or press Enter.

1-2-3 TIP

Excel Command Macros

In addition to recording macros for you, Excel command macros differentiate between Ctrl+key combinations using number keys, uppercase letters, and lowercase letters. (Excel automatically translates Lotus 1-2-3 macros. For more information, see Chapter 30, "Making the Switch from 1-2-3 to Excel.")

Testing the Command Macro

Now you can test your macro.

1. Activate the worksheet, and enter **North Division** in cell A5.

2. With A5 still selected, choose **Macro Run**.

    The dialog box in figure 25.5 appears, showing you a list of all available macros. Notice that the title of the macro sheet precedes the name of the macro. You can have multiple macro sheets open. The left side of the list shows each macro's associated Ctrl+key combination.

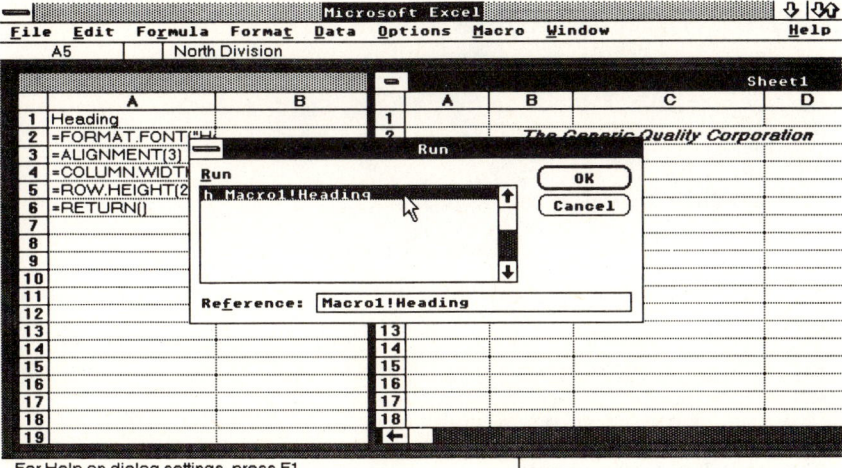

Fig. 25.5. List of available macros.

3. Select the Heading macro from the list box; press Enter, or choose the OK button.

   The macro immediately repeats all the keystrokes you recorded and changes cell A5 to appear as shown in figure 25.6.

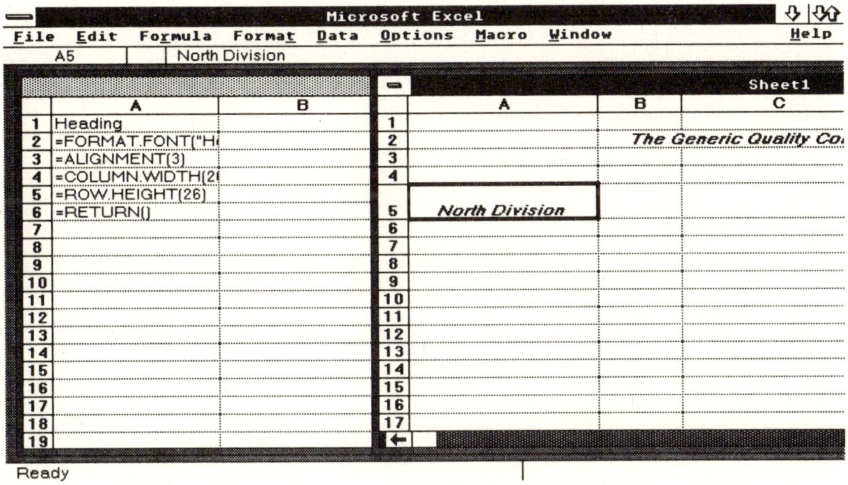

Fig. 25.6. Cell A5 has been altered by the Heading macro.

Editing the Command Macro

When you see the results of your macro, you realize that the macro would be more versatile if it did the following:

- asked the operator to enter the text title

- left the columns at the original width

- gave the operator the chance to select the font

To make these changes, you need not re-create the macro; merely edit the contents of the macro just as you would edit the contents of a worksheet.

To read the macro before editing:

1. Select the macro document.

   Mouse: Click on the macro window so that it appears on top.

   Keyboard: Choose Window and select the macro sheet.

2. Widen column A so that you can read the macro code (see fig. 25.7).

Fig. 25.7. Widen the column on a macro sheet to read the code.

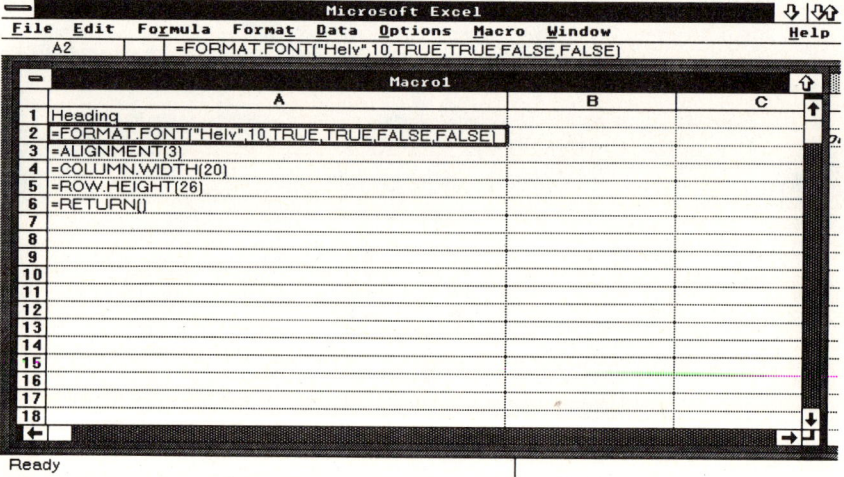

Before you make any changes, read the macro code. Macro commands closely mimic the menu command names or actions, so they are easy to read. Table 25.1 shows the code for your Heading macro.

Table 25.1
Codes for Heading Macro

Code	Result
FORMAT.FONT("Helv",10, TRUE,TRUE,FALSE,FALSE)	formats the font with 10-point Helvetica in bold and italic
ALIGNMENT(3)	uses the third alignment selection, Center
COLUMN.WIDTH(20)	changes column width to 20
ROW.HEIGHT(26)	changes row height to 26
RETURN()	ends the macro

Each argument in a macro formula reflects the option selected or text entered in the equivalent dialog box. Using the macro directory in Appendix B, you can quickly understand what most macro code does and how to change it.

Edit your macro as you would edit a worksheet; select cells, and use edit commands or the formula bar to change them. For example, if you decide you do not want the column width to change, you can delete that command.

1. Select cell A4, which contains the COLUMN.WIDTH command.

2. Choose Edit Delete. Then select the Shift Cells Up option as shown in figure 25.8, and press Enter.

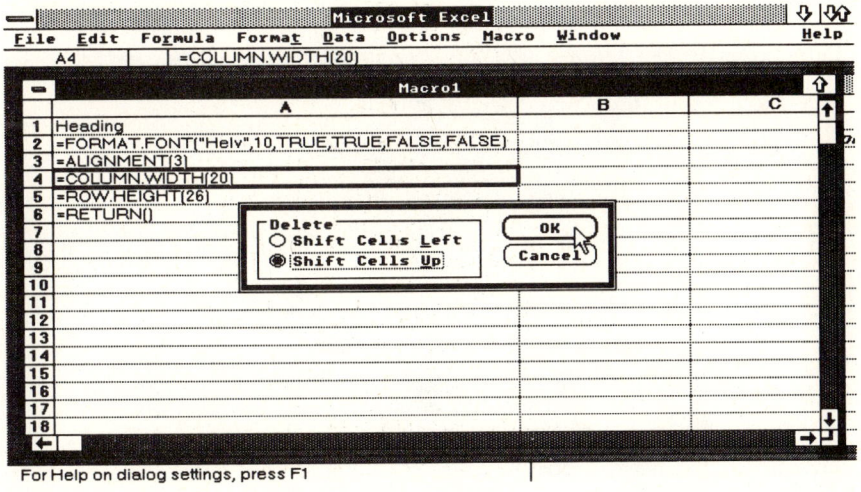

Fig. 25.8. The Delete dialog box.

Deleting the COLUMN.WIDTH code from the column removes that command from macro operation. The code in cells below A4 moves up just as it would in a worksheet.

Inserting a cell and adding a macro formula give you room to add a macro code that cannot be selected from the menu bar during the recording process. The following steps add a dialog box that asks the operator to enter the title.

1. Select cell A2, and choose **Edit Insert**. Select the Shift Cells **Down** option, and press Enter.

2. In the blank cell at A2, enter this macro formula:

    =FORMULA(INPUT("Enter the title",2))

The FORMULA(INPUT( )) combination stops the macro, displays a dialog box, and prompts the operator to enter data. The data is then displayed in the active cell. The INPUT macro formula uses the text enclosed in quotation marks as text in a dialog box. The *2* argument tells Excel that you are entering text data. The FORMULA macro enters the data entered into INPUT in the active cell on the worksheet.

Another way you can customize your recorded macro is to change the entries made in dialog boxes during the recording or to make the dialog box reappear when the macro runs. For example, you can change the FORMAT.FONT code so that the macro stops, displays the Fonts dialog box, and waits for your selections. After you make selections, the macro continues.

Using the macro directory in Appendix B, you find that the FORMAT.FONT code takes the following forms and arguments:

    FORMAT.FONT(name_text,size_num,bold,italic,underline,strike)
    FORMAT.FONT?(*name_text,size_num,bold,italic,underline,strike*)

The recorded code in cell A3 now appears:

    FORMAT.FONT("Helv",10,TRUE,TRUE,FALSE,FALSE)

This translates into the Helvetica font type (notice the quotation marks around text words), 10-point size, bold, and italic. The underline and strike arguments are FALSE, so they are not selected.

The question mark (?) in the second form of FORMAT.FONT causes a dialog box to appear. (Not all commands have associated dialog boxes.) When the macro reaches the question mark, it stops, displays the dialog box for that command, and waits for you to make selections. The italicized arguments in the second form of FORMAT.FONT indicate optional entries. Making an entry here creates a default entry for that argument in the dialog box.

Now, add a dialog box to the FORMAT.FONT code.

1. Select cell A3 so that the FORMAT.FONT code appears in the formula bar.

2. Select the formula bar by clicking on it or pressing F2.

3. Enter a question mark after FORMAT.FONT and before the first parenthesis; then enter the formula.

   The question mark makes the Fonts dialog box appear at this point in the code. The macro sheet should now look like figure 25.9.

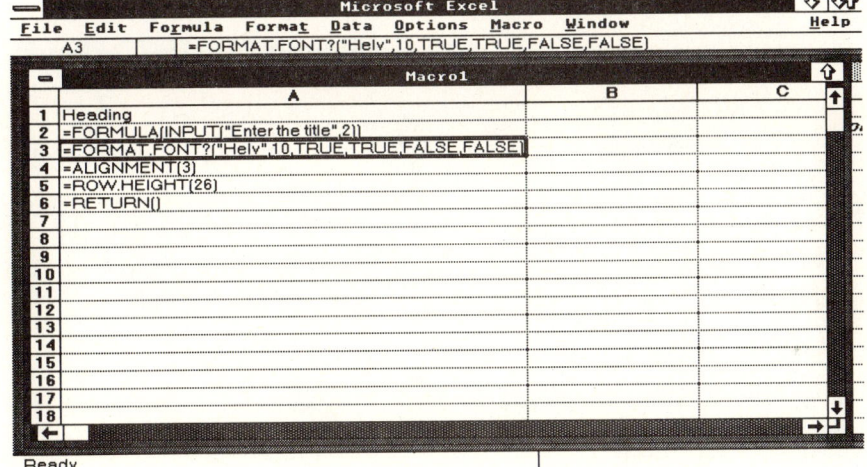

Fig. 25.9. Macro sheet after editing.

Display the original worksheet, and try your edited macro.

1. Choose **Window**, and select the worksheet you want. Select cell B6.

2. Activate the macro with the Ctrl+h key combination. (The previous method started the macro with **Macro Run**.) A dialog box like the one shown in figure 25.10 appears so that you can "Enter the title."

3. Enter the word **Sales** in the text box, and press Enter.

   The Fonts dialog box appears and indicates 10-point Helvetica bold and italic type (see fig. 25.11).

4. Select **2**. Helv 10; Bold, and press Enter. (You couldn't make this selection in the original macro.)

Fig. 25.10. The data-entry dialog box created by your macro.

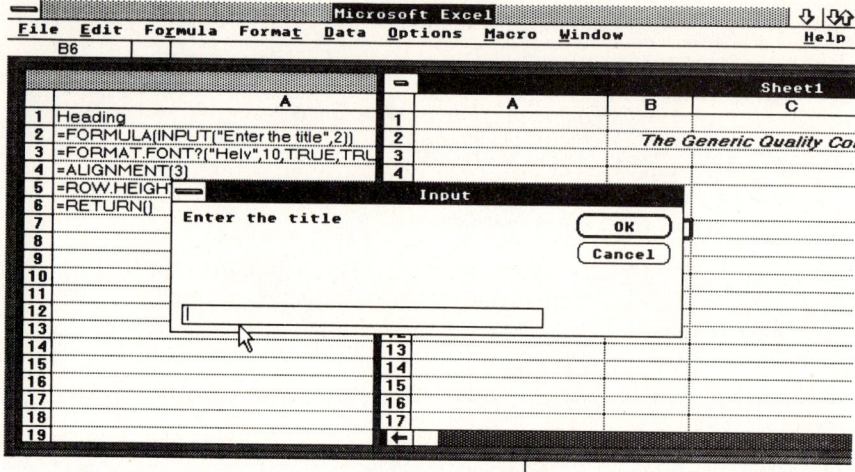

Fig. 25.11. Fonts dialog box with default values.

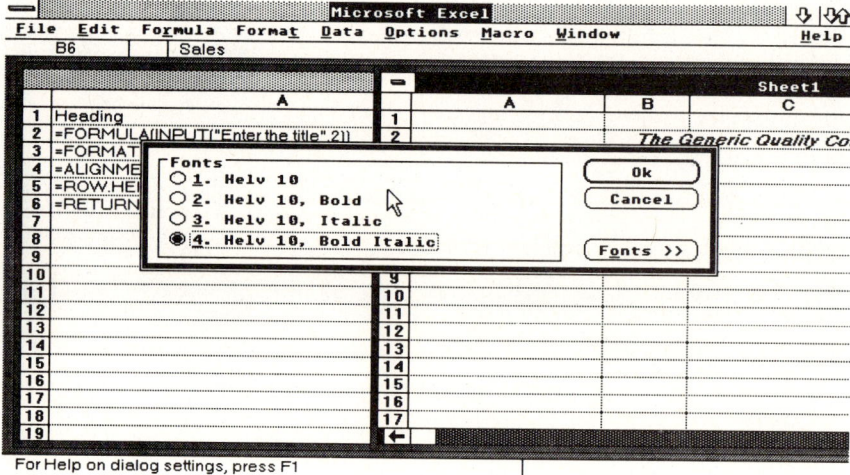

The rest of the macro continues to run, aligning the text and changing the row height. The worksheet results and macro appear as in figure 25.12. Notice that the column width did not change, because you deleted that code from the macro.

The next Quick Start example demonstrates how to create a function macro and how to add a macro to an existing macro sheet. At this point, you can either save the macro you have just created and come back at a later time, or you can continue and build the function macro.

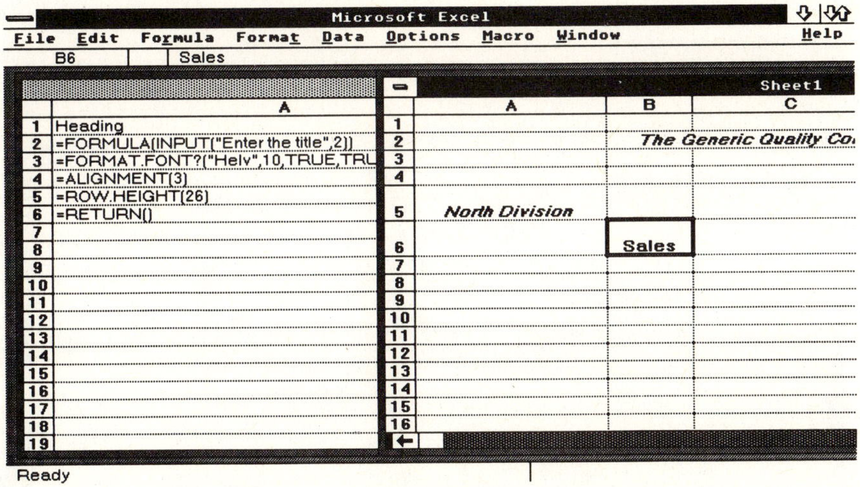

*Fig. 25.12.
Completed
macro and
worksheet.*

Save a macro sheet the same way you save a worksheet.

1. Activate the macro window, and choose File Save **As**.

2. Give the sheet the name QSMACRO. Excel will add the file
   extension .XLM.

3. Choose OK or press Enter.

You can add macros to this sheet as the next example shows. To use a macro,
you must have the macro sheet open, but it is not necessary for it to be the
top or second sheet on your screen. Open macro sheets the same way you
open a worksheet—with the File Open command.

Creating Function Macros

Excel contains 141 functions, ranging from simple ones, such as SUM, to
complex financial ones, such as MIRR. There may be functions, however, that
you need but that Excel does not have. The following steps demonstrate how
to create your own function using a function macro, and how to add a macro
to an existing macro sheet.

Because function macros use worksheet functions or formulas rather than
menu commands or actions, you cannot record a function macro. Instead,
you paste or type macro functions into function macros. The completed function macro uses arguments you specify just the same as the arguments used
by built-in Excel functions.

In this example, you create a function macro that calculates profit margin from the following formula:

=(Sales-Cost)/Sales

When you are finished, you can use the function macro you create just as though it were a built-in Excel macro of the form PMARGIN(Sales,Costs). Figure 25.13 shows the completed function macro.

Fig. 25.13.
Completed
function macro.

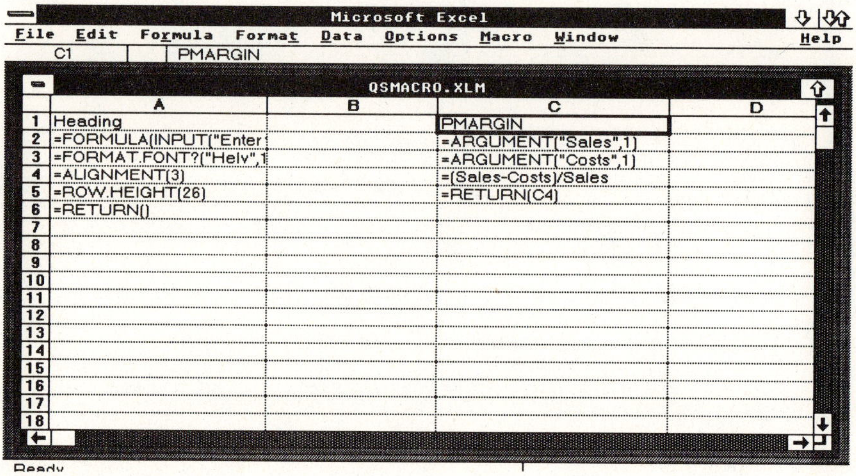

First, open and activate a macro sheet.

1. If you are continuing from the command macro, and its macro sheet is still open, go to step 4.

2. If you saved the command macro sheet created earlier in the chapter, choose File Open and open the macro sheet named QSMACRO (macro sheets end with .XLM).

3. If you did not go through the command macro Quick Start, then open a new, blank macro sheet with File New. Select Macro Sheet.

4. Activate the macro sheet.

Next, construct your function macro:

1. Select cell C1, and enter the name of the macro function, PMARGIN.

2. Select cell C2. Choose Formula Paste Function, and select the Paste Arguments check box to paste arguments into the macro sheet along with the function.

3. Select ARGUMENT( ) from the list box. Choose OK or press Enter.

4. Select the argument type,

    name_text,data_type_num

    from the scroll box. Choose OK or press Enter.

    This puts the function and arguments,

    =ARGUMENT(name_text,data_type_num)

    in the formula bar as shown in figure 25.14. The *name_text* argument is the text name, in quotation marks, for one of your PMARGIN function's variables.

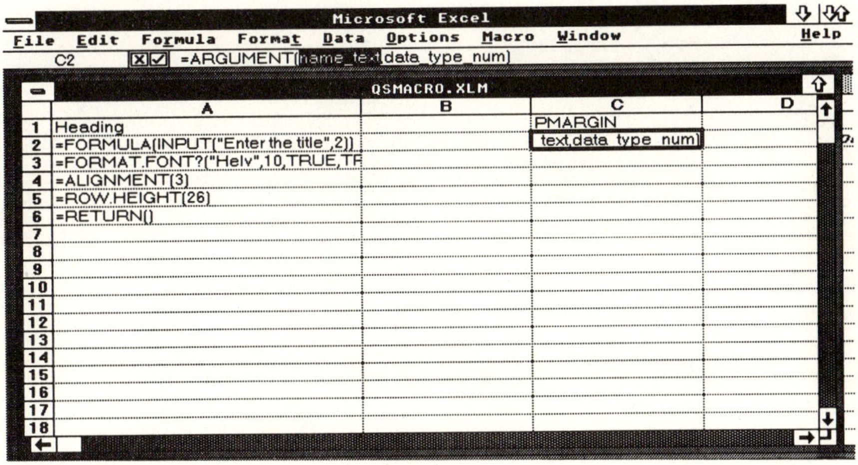

Fig. 25.14.
Creating arguments for the function macro.

5. Edit the formula to match the following:

    =ARGUMENT("Sales",1)

    and enter the edited formula in cell C2.

    Sales is the first argument to appear between parentheses in PMARGIN(Sales,Costs). Sales is also used to create the formula that defines what PMARGIN does. The second argument, the number 1, says that Sales accepts only numbers.

6. In cell C3, enter or paste the following formula:

    =ARGUMENT("Costs",1)

Costs, a numeric argument, is the second variable used in PMARGIN.

7. Using the text names for variables, enter the following formula to calculate the profit margin in cell C4:

=(Sales-Costs)/Sales

8. Enter the following RETURN code in cell C5:

=RETURN(C4)

The RETURN code does two things. It ends the PMARGIN macro, and it returns the value in C4 on the macro sheet to the location of the PMARGIN( ) function in the worksheet.

Now you must name the macro function so that Excel knows where it is. Follow these steps:

1. Select cell C1.

2. Choose Formula **Define** Name.

   Notice that the function's name *PMARGIN* is already in the **Name** text box and =$C$1 shows in the **Refers to** box.

3. Select the **Function** option.

   When you select Function, the capability to choose a Ctrl+key combination disappears. You cannot use a Ctrl+key to execute a function macro.

4. Choose OK or press Enter.

   You have created and named the function macro PMARGIN shown in figure 25.15.

Fig. 25.15. The PMARGIN function macro.

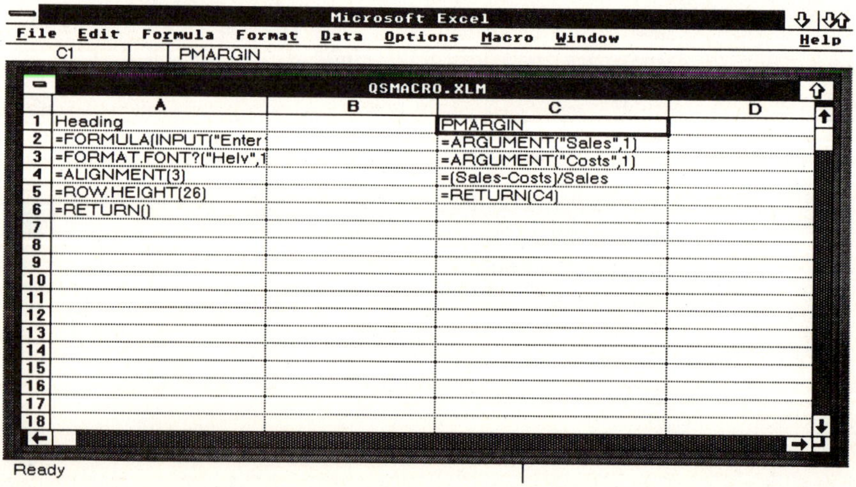

To check that your function macro works correctly, do the following:

1. Choose **File New** and select **Worksheet**. Choose OK or press Enter to open a new worksheet.

2. Use the Ctrl+h macro, which is on the QSMACRO sheet also, to help you enter the labels and numbers shown in figure 25.16.

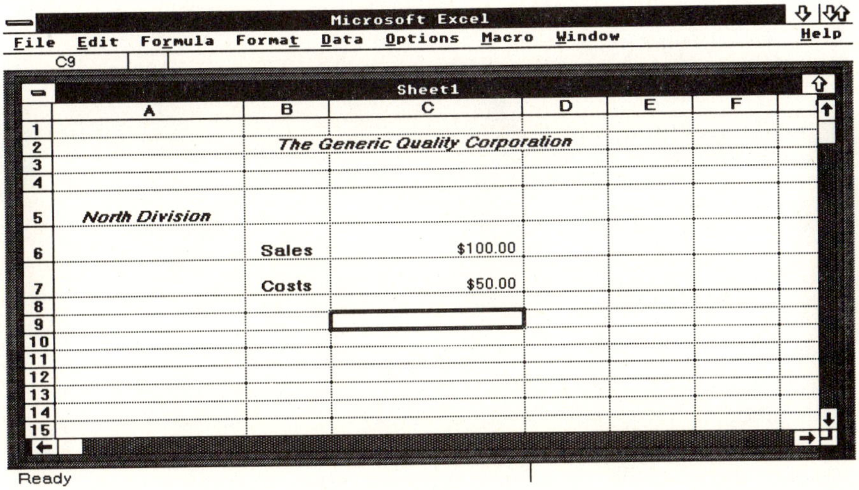

Fig. 25.16.
Worksheet with
labels and
numbers.

3. Select cell C8, and choose **Formula Paste Function**. Press the End key to go to the bottom of the list, and select the function you have created:

   =QSMACRO.XLM!PMARGIN( )

   Because the function is on a sheet external to the worksheet, its name must refer to that sheet. Your macro sheet may have a different name than QSMACRO.XLM.

4. Choose OK or press Enter. Edit the PMARGIN function in the formula bar to look like the following:

   =QSMACRO.XLM!PMARGIN(C6,C7).

5. Enter the function. The answer, 0.5 or 50%, appears as shown in figure 25.17.

Notice that you had to enter the argument values, C6 and C7, in the same order that the ARGUMENT terms appeared in the column of code. The Sales argument was first, and Costs was second.

Fig. 25.17.
Worksheet
showing result
of PMARGIN
macro.

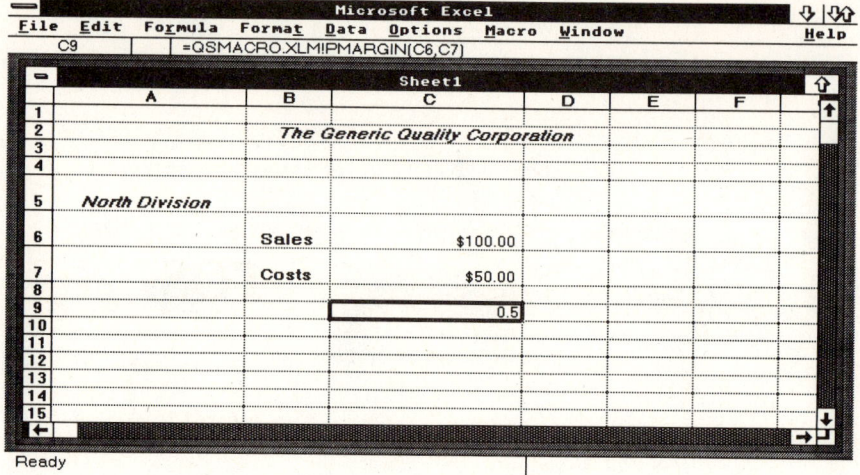

If you want to preserve this sheet of macros to use again, you must save it. Make sure you save the macro sheet first with File Save **As**, then save the worksheet. Saving in this order updates the external reference names used in the function macros (names like QSMACRO.XLM). That way, the worksheet knows which macro sheet contains the macro. The macro worksheet must be open for the macro functions on the worksheet to work.

From Here . . .

Excel's macro recorder makes it easy to record macros that save you a lot of time. Eventually, however, you will want to modify recorded macros and write macros from scratch. When you reach that point, read Chapter 26, "Building Command and Function Macros," then look through the commands available for macros in Appendix B, "Macro Directory."

The large number of macro codes available may intimidate you at first. As you work with macros, you will find you can solve most problems by recording the macro first and then making changes to it. Functions can be pasted into the macro with visible arguments to help you see exactly what you are doing. Of course, as with any endeavor, practice improves your confidence.

26

Building Command and Function Macros

Macros are sequences of commands and functions that automatically run Excel operations for you. You can create macros to replace simple repetitive keystrokes, such as setting a numeric format and selecting a font. On the other hand, you can create macros that turn Excel into a specialized program designed to perform specific, complex tasks, such as medical accounting or inventory analysis.

Macros are composed of functions similar to worksheet functions. Each function is the equivalent of a command, action, or worksheet function. Most macro functions are easy to understand. For example, FORMAT.FONT does the same as the Format Font command. Macros can also use worksheet functions to make calculations.

A macro contains its sequence of functions on a macro sheet, which looks like a worksheet with wide columns. Functions are displayed instead of results in a macro sheet. Most menu commands, such as Edit Copy or Formula Paste Function, work the same on a macro sheet as they do in a worksheet. Everything you have already learned about editing worksheets can be applied to macros.

Macro functions run down a column in the macro sheet, one function to a cell. Each macro function performs some command or action according to arguments found within its parentheses, much the same as a worksheet function. These arguments define what options are selected, such as which font and style is selected by the FORMAT.FONT function. Appendix B, "Macro Directory," contains listings of the macro functions and their arguments.

When you run a macro, its functions are calculated one cell at a time from the top of the macro to the bottom. If a macro crosses multiple columns, the macro continues calculation to the next column. A macro stops when it reaches a macro function such as RETURN or HALT. You can manually stop some macros by pressing Esc.

There are two types of macros: command macros and function macros. Command macros store action sequences containing commands from the menu, as well as keystrokes and mouse actions. These macros can also contain additional Excel commands not available from the menu. Command macros are activated by pressing a Ctrl+key combination that you define or by choosing the macro name from a list box.

TIP

Try Excel Macros: They Are Easy To Create

In spreadsheets that do not have a macro recorder, you must learn the macro language and write "grammatically correct" code in order to make a macro work. This can be a learning hurdle for many users.

In Excel the macro recorder will create a macro for you by recording your actions. The recorder is a quick and easy way to become more efficient. Run through Chapter 25, "Macro Quick Start," to give Excel macros a try.

Command macros can range from the simple, such as formatting a range, to the complex, such as industry-specific applications with custom menus, custom help files, and custom dialog boxes. Excel macros can even invoke other Windows programs. Possible uses for command macros include:

- formatting a preselected range with bold and currency
- printing a frequently used report
- preparing data entry rows
- cross-checking data entry values
- creating custom menus, help files, and alert and dialog boxes
- linking and controlling other Windows applications
- calling procedures from Microsoft Windows' dynamic library
- building custom applications

1-2-3 TIP

1-2-3 Macro Translator

If you have 1-2-3 worksheets that contain macros you want to use in Excel, the Macro Translator program will translate them into Excel macros. The Translator is described in Chapter 30, "Making the Switch from 1-2-3 to Excel."

Function macros contain custom worksheet functions, which can be used in worksheets the same way as built-in Excel functions like SUM and MIRR. Function macros cannot be recorded; you must type or paste them into the macro sheet.

Running and Stopping Command Macros

If you have inherited files from someone else, have purchased an Excel "template," or have run through the Quick Start, you may already have macros. To run an existing macro, you must first load it.

Loading Macro Sheets

Before you can use a macro, its macro sheet must be open.

1. Choose **File Open.**

2. Look in the list box for files with the extension .XLM or change the name in the file name box to *.XLM. This file name pattern masks out nonmacro files.

3. Press Enter to display the macro file names. Select the macro sheet you want, then choose OK or press Enter.

If you have more than one macro sheet open, you can tell the macros apart because the name of each macro sheet precedes the macro name in the list box of the **Macro Run** command. Figure 26.1 shows this list box. Note that macros on the macro sheet do not show their sheet name.

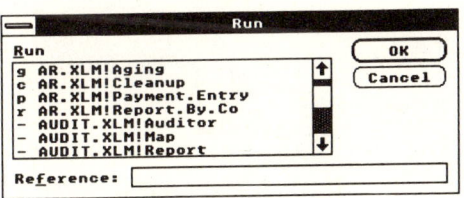

Fig. 26.1. The Run list box.

You will want to load many of your macros with the worksheets they control. One way to load multiple documents is with the **File Save Workspace** command. Open and arrange on the screen all the worksheets, charts, and macro sheets you want to load together. Choose **File Save Workspace,** and then name the file. When you next want all these documents loaded together, choose

File **Open** and select that workspace file. (Workspace file names end with .XLW.) All the documents must be available on disk and must still use the same names.

Running Macros

When the macro sheet is open (but not necessarily visible), you can run one of the macros it contains in three different ways. You can execute a macro by pressing its shortcut key combination—holding down the Ctrl key and pressing the macro's associated character. (Only command macros can be assigned a Ctrl+key combination.) Second, you can activate a macro by choosing the **Macro Run** command, selecting the macro name from the list box (see fig. 26.1), and pressing Enter. Finally, you can run a macro that runs another macro.

The shortcut key, a Ctrl+key combination, can be assigned to the macro when it is built. If you forget the key combination for a macro, choose **Macro Run**, and look at the letter or number on the left side of the list box. You can also see the shortcut key at the bottom of the **Formula Define** Name dialog box after you select a macro.

NOTE

Macros with the Same Shortcut Key

When two macros have the same shortcut key, the macro appearing first in the list box of the **Macro Run** command is the one that will be activated. You cannot give the same name to two macros on the same sheet because the act of naming the second macro reassigns the name away from the first macro.

1-2-3 TIP

More Keys Are Available To Start Macros

Excel discriminates between macros named with upper- and lowercase letters. This means that you have more than twice as many key combinations available for starting macros as are available in 1-2-3.

Excel records macros in either relative or absolute reference mode. A macro recorded in relative reference mode refers to the cells it acts on relative to the position of the last active cell. Macros using absolute reference mode move the active cell to the absolute cell address stored in the macro.

Stopping Macros

You can stop most macros by pressing Esc. Pressing Esc stops the macro and displays an alert box such as the one shown in figure 26.2. The box shows the cell on which the macro stopped and gives you a chance to Halt, single Step through the macro, or Continue. (If a macro is displaying a dialog box with a Cancel button, the Esc key selects the Cancel button and does not stop the macro.)

Fig. 26.2. An alert box for a stopped macro.

Many macros that create custom menus also add an Exit or Quit Macro command to the available menu commands. These macros may use a macro function that prevents the Esc key from stopping the macro. If this is the situation with a macro you are using, you must use the menu command to stop the macro.

Building Command Macros

There are three ways Excel users create and modify macros: recording macros automatically, recording followed by modifying the macro manually, and typing the entire macro by hand.

In the first method (recording the entire macro), the macro replays exactly as you recorded it, selecting the same menu items and options. This works well for simple jobs such as preparing cells with a frequently used format, font, and border.

The second method of creating macros is most effective for the majority of Excel users. You build the main structure of the macro with the recorder, then edit this structure to add features. For example, you can use the macro recorder to open and format new rows in a database. You can then manually add INPUT, FORMULA, and IF macro functions that request the data for entry and cross-check the data before entering it in a database.

The third method of building macros treats the Excel macro language as the complete programming language it is. With its programming power, Excel can read and write disk-based sequential records or text files, build custom menus and help files, link and control other Microsoft Windows applications, and build custom application programs. In these more complex applications, most of the macro must be written manually.

Recording a Command Macro

Even the newest Excel user can learn to record command macros. Command macros save time and work, yet are easy to create and use.

When you build a command macro, Excel records all your menu choices, mouse actions, and keyboard entries as functions on a macro sheet. A macro sheet looks the same as a worksheet with some of the commands in the menu bar disabled when the macro sheet is active; the **Options Display** command is preset to display functions, not their results. Columns in macro sheets are wider than in worksheets so that you can see the macro functions more easily.

Macro functions that relate to commands and actions will seem familiar. For example, the macro equivalent of the Forma**t** Font command is FORMAT.FONT. The equivalent of selecting a range of cells is SELECT. Figure 26.3 shows one such simple macro that was recorded automatically. The explanations in the adjacent cells in column B describe what each of the macro functions in column A does. (The macro recorder enters only the functions in column A; the explanations in column B were added manually afterward.)

Fig. 26.3. An automatically recorded macro.

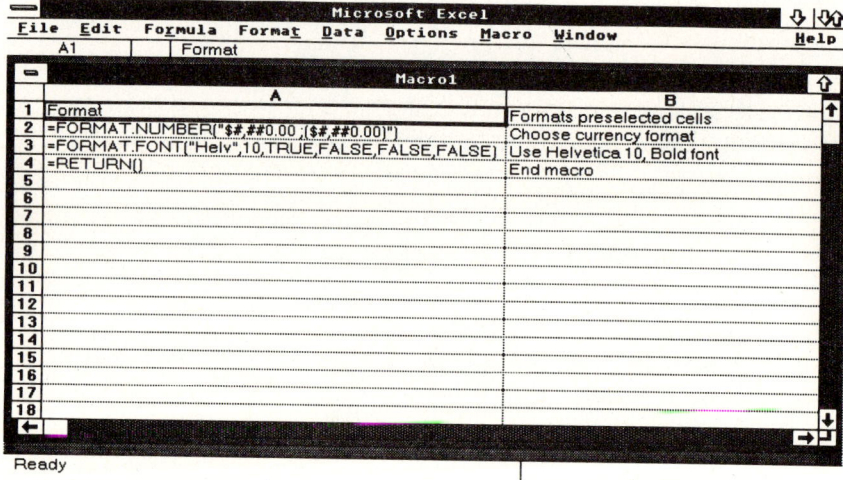

There are two methods you can use when recording a macro. The **Macro Record** method works best when a macro sheet is not open and you want to record on a new macro sheet. The **Macro Record** command steps you through the process of creating the first macro on the sheet. The command opens a new, blank macro sheet, positions the active cell at A1, asks you for the name and type of macro, and turns on the recorder.

The second method of recording macros requires that you do more manual work, but it gives you flexibility in positioning new macros on sheets of existing macros. This method (illustrated in Chapter 25, "Macro Quick Start") uses the **Macro Set Recorder** and **Macro Start Recorder** commands. **Macro Set Recorder** tells Excel to put the top of the column of macro functions at the active cell in the macro sheet. After setting the macro's starting location with **Macro Set Recorder**, you turn on the recorder with the **Macro Start Recorder** command. You have to name the macro manually with **Formula Define Name**.

Recording a Command Macro on a Blank Macro Sheet

To open a macro sheet and record a new macro, do the following:

1. Activate the worksheet on which you want to use the macro. If you plan to select cells or chart objects before you activate the macro, you should select a similar cell or chart object before starting the macro recorder.

2. Choose the **Macro Record** command.

    This does two things. First, if a macro sheet is not already open, the command opens a blank macro sheet and asks you to name the macro. Second, this command turns on the macro recorder to record your actions.

    The Record Macro dialog box appears after you choose the **Macro Record** command (see fig. 26.4).

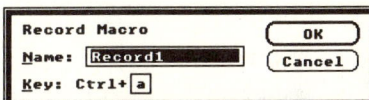

Fig. 26.4. The Record Macro dialog box.

3. Type the **Name** of the macro in the Record Macro dialog box.

    The name you type becomes the name of this macro. The name must conform to Excel's rules for names. The macro will begin with the macro name in cell A1 of the macro sheet.

4. Select the **Key** text box and type a single character for use in the Ctrl+key combination. (This step is optional; you do not have to assign a command macro a key combination.) Choose OK or press Enter.

The macro name and the Ctrl+key combination give you two ways of activating your macro. You will later be able to start the macro by choosing the macro name from the **Macro Run** command's list box or by typing the Ctrl+key combination. For example, Ctrl+C might format preselected cells with your own custom currency format.

The key character can be an upper- or lowercase letter or a number. Because Excel can distinguish between upper- and lowercase letters, you can have up to 62 different Ctrl+key combinations. Do not choose a character that has been used already.

NOTE

Macro Name and Ctrl+Key Combination Conflicts

Excel lets you name macros on the same sheet with the same name or the same Ctrl+key combination as an existing macro. When a duplicate name occurs, the existing name transfers to the newly named macro, leaving the old macro unusable. Macros can have duplicate Ctrl+key combinations, but pressing the Ctrl+key combination activates only the macro listed first in the **Macro Run** command's list box. Macros on separate macro sheets can have the same name. Macros are differentiated by the name of the worksheet they are on. (A later topic in this chapter describes how to rename macros.)

Notice that the word *Recording* appears in the status bar at the bottom of the screen. From this point on, Excel records your menu choices and mouse or keyboard actions.

5. Make the menu choices and keyboard or mouse actions that you want recorded. With each menu command chosen or action taken, the recorder adds another macro function to the column. Figure 26.5 shows macro functions extending down the column. Complete macros end with a RETURN function.

The recorder records absolute references to cell and range addresses. If you want to switch to relative references during or before the recording, choose **Macro Relative Record**. When you want to return to absolute addresses, choose **Macro Absolute Record**.

Excel ignores menu selections you make from dialog boxes when you select the Cancel button or press Esc.

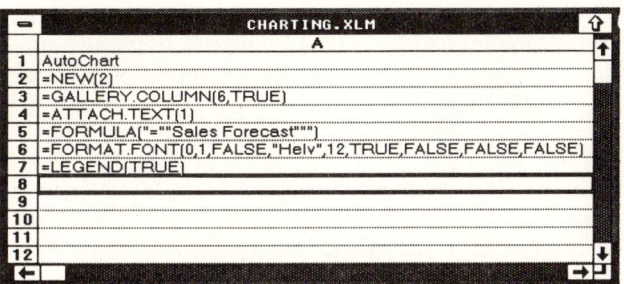

Fig. 26.5. A partially completed macro.

If you make a mistake while you are recording the macro, you can remove the incorrect macro function after you stop the recorder. Use the **Edit** commands to make the correction. Do not try to remove a macro function with the UNDO macro command while you are recording. With the recorder on, choosing **Edit Undo** enters the UNDO function into the macro.

6. Choose **Macro Stop Recorder** when you are finished with the task you want recorded. Choosing the stop command inserts a RETURN macro function at the end of the macro as shown in figure 26.6. This marks the end of the macro. It also means your macro is now usable.

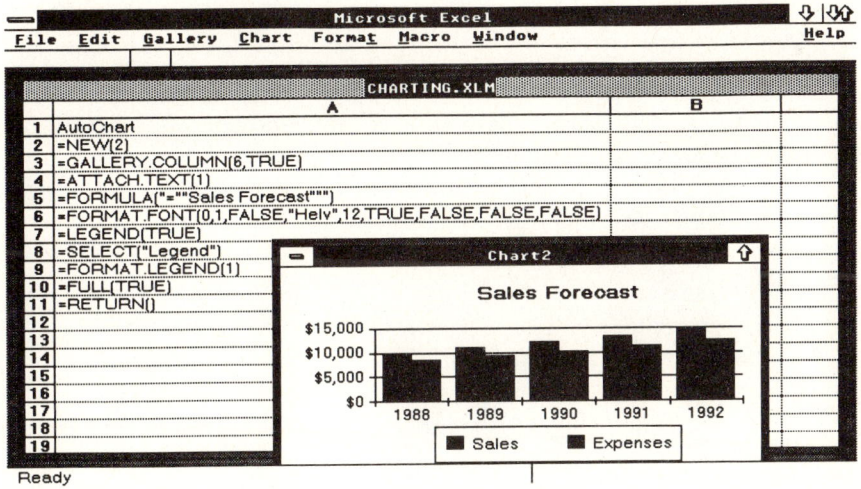

Fig. 26.6. Completed macro with RETURN.

7. Choose **File Save As** to name and save the macro sheet. Macro sheets are saved with the .XLM file extension.

Use the techniques in the next section to add macros to an existing macro sheet. Don't forget to add documentation in the columns adjacent to the macro that describes how the macro works. Documentation makes a macro's operation and functions easier to remember.

You can see the macro you have created by activating the macro sheet with the **Window #** command, where # is the number of the macro sheet.

Recording a Command Macro on an Existing Macro Sheet

To add a macro to an existing macro sheet, do the following:

1. To record on an existing macro sheet that is not open, choose **File Open** and open the macro sheet you want. Remember, macro sheets use the file extension .XLM.

   Or, if the macro sheet is open, choose the **Window #** command to activate the macro sheet you want.

2. Enter the new macro name in the first cell of the area where you want the macro to appear. Select the cell(s) you want to contain the macro. The cell containing the name must be the first cell in the upper left corner of the selection.

   The following figures show different types of cell selections used to specify how macro functions fill in the macro sheet. The same automated charting macro is used in all the examples.

   When recording begins, the first macro function goes in the first blank cell below the name. Selecting a single cell, as in figure 26.7, marks the beginning point of a macro. Functions can be added down the column as shown in figure 26.8. If a macro reaches the bottom of the column, it wraps to the top of the next column.

   Selecting a range of cells, as shown in figure 26.9, starts the macro recording below the name and fills the range with macro functions, snaking between columns as it has in figure 26.10. When the range is full, an alert box displays the message

   Recorder range is full.

   and the recorder is turned off.

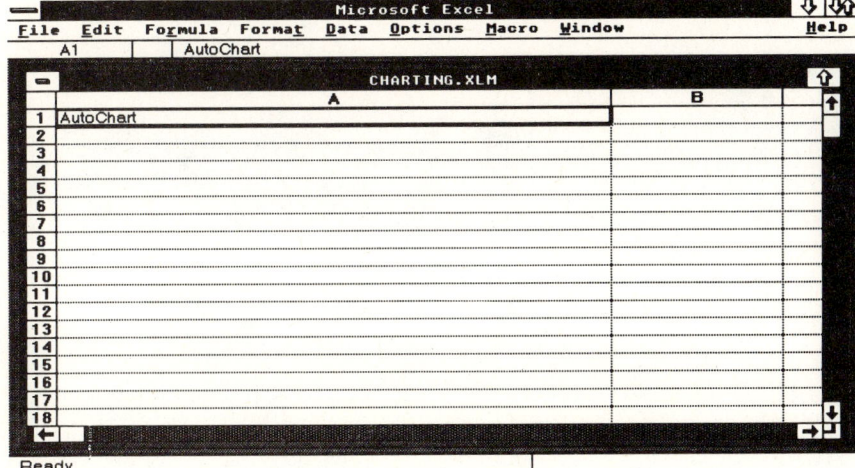

Fig. 26.7. A single cell selected containing the macro name.

```
┌─────────────────────────────────────────────────────────────┐
│ ═               Microsoft Excel                    ⇩ |⇗⇘      │
│ File  Edit  Formula  Format  Data  Options  Macro  Window   Help │
│ A1              AutoChart                                     │
│ ┌─ ═               CHARTING.XLM                    ⇧ │        │
│ │                       A                    │    B    │ ⇧    │
│ │ 1  AutoChart                               │         │      │
│ │ 2                                          │         │      │
│ │ 3                                          │         │      │
│ │ 4                                          │         │      │
│ │ 5                                          │         │      │
│ │ 6                                          │         │      │
│ │ 7                                          │         │      │
│ │ 8                                          │         │      │
│ │ 9                                          │         │      │
│ │10                                          │         │      │
│ │11                                          │         │      │
│ │12                                          │         │      │
│ │13                                          │         │      │
│ │14                                          │         │      │
│ │15                                          │         │      │
│ │16                                          │         │      │
│ │17                                          │         │      │
│ │18                                          │         │ ⇩    │
│ │ ←                                          │      →  │      │
│ Ready                                                         │
└─────────────────────────────────────────────────────────────┘
```

Fig. 26.8. Functions fill down the column when a single cell is set.

```
┌─────────────────────────────────────────────────────────────┐
│ ═               Microsoft Excel                    ⇩ |⇗⇘      │
│ File  Edit  Formula  Format  Data  Options  Macro  Window   Help │
│ A11             =RETURN()                                     │
│ ┌─ ═               CHARTING.XLM                    ⇧ │        │
│ │                       A                    │    B    │ ⇧    │
│ │ 1  AutoChart                                              │
│ │ 2  =NEW(2)                                                │
│ │ 3  =GALLERY.COLUMN(6,TRUE)                                │
│ │ 4  =ATTACH.TEXT(1)                                        │
│ │ 5  =FORMULA("=""Sales Forecast""")                        │
│ │ 6  =FORMAT.FONT(0,1,FALSE,"Helv",12,TRUE,FALSE,FALSE,FALSE)│
│ │ 7  =LEGEND(TRUE)                                          │
│ │ 8  =SELECT("Legend")                                      │
│ │ 9  =FORMAT.LEGEND(1)                                      │
│ │10  =FULL(TRUE)                                            │
│ │11  =RETURN()                                             │
│ │12                                                        │
│ │13                                                        │
│ │14                                                        │
│ │15                                                        │
│ │16                                                        │
│ │17                                                        │
│ │18                                                       ⇩ │
│ │ ←                                                     →   │
│ Ready                                                         │
└─────────────────────────────────────────────────────────────┘
```

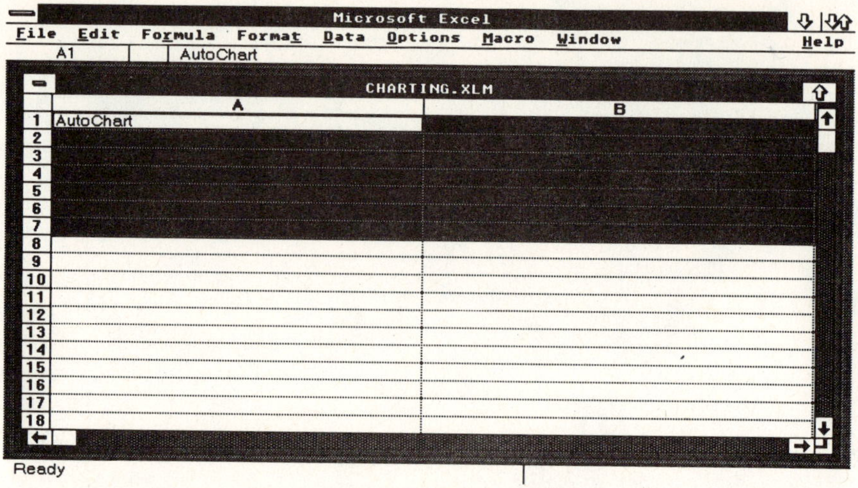

Fig. 26.9. Macro sheet with range selected.

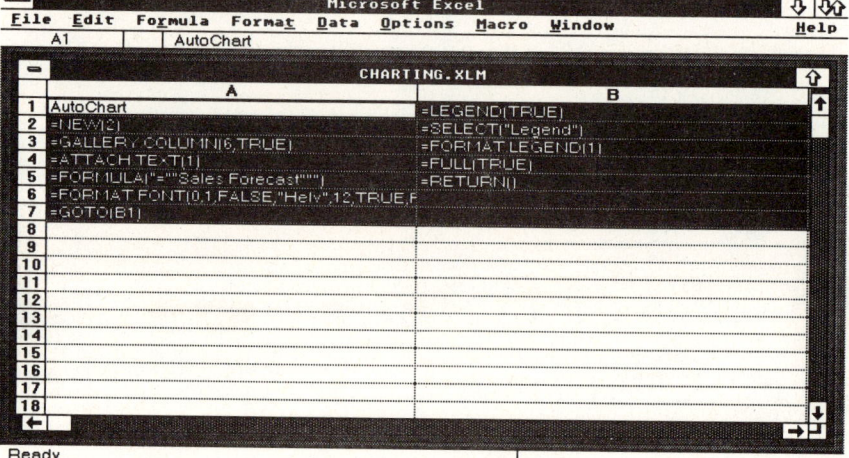

Fig. 26.10. Functions wrap from the bottom of one column to the top of the next.

3. Choose Macro Set Recorder to define the selected area as the macro area. Activate your worksheet and choose Macro Start Recorder.

4. Choose Macro Relative Record or Macro Absolute Record if necessary.

   The menu command changes between Absolute and Relative depending on the current mode of the recording. Absolute reference records the exact cell locations. Relative reference records locations relative to the active cell at the time when Relative Record is chosen.

5. Make the menu choices and keyboard or mouse actions you want recorded. Choose **Macro Stop Recorder** when you are finished with the task.

   Choosing the **Macro Stop Recorder** command inserts a RETURN macro function at the end of the macro. This function marks the end of the macro.

RETURN Marks the End of a Macro

Excel macros end with a RETURN or HALT macro function, not with a blank space. This lets you separate sections of macro functions with blank spaces or insert normal text as remarks that help explain or segment the macro. Only cell contents that begin with an equal sign (=) or that are in a named cell are used by the macro.

---

6. Activate the macro window to see the complete macro like that of figures 26.8 or 26.10. The name or macro area you selected in step 2 should still be selected. If it is not, select the name again.

7. Choose **Formula Define Name**. A Define Name dialog box appears bearing the macro's name in the Name text box (see fig. 26.11).

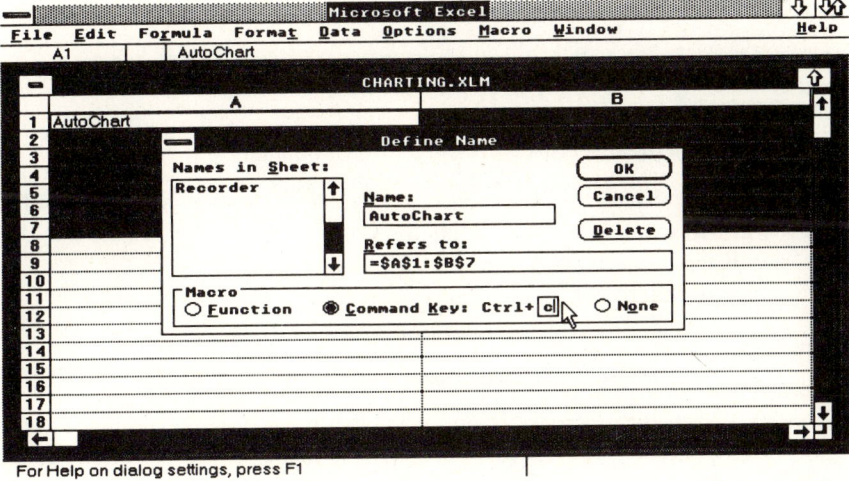

*Fig. 26.11.
Define Name
dialog box with
name and key
character
entered.*

You are about to use the Formula Define Name command to name the first cell in the macro using the name at the top of the macro. This does a number of things. First, it tells Excel the name of the macro. Second, it tells Excel where the macro with that name begins. Third, it lets you specify whether the macro is a command or function macro. Lastly, if it is a command macro, you get a chance to enter your choice of Ctrl+key combinations.

8. Select the Command button. Because this is a command macro, select the Key button, and type an uppercase or lowercase letter to use with the Ctrl key. Choose OK or press Enter.

9. Choose File Save As, and save the macro sheet. You can now repeat the keystrokes and menu commands you entered with this macro.

Customizing Recorded Macros

The easiest way to produce custom macros is to use the recorder to create a foundation automatically, then modify this foundation by adding dialog boxes, warning boxes, and data entry checking functions. You can enter the additional macro functions required to do this with the same editing commands you learned to use in the worksheet—the Edit Insert and Formula Paste Function commands. Chapter 25, "Macro Quick Start," demonstrates how to change the arguments within a recorded macro function, how to delete a macro function, and how to insert a macro function.

In the macro sheet, you can use the editing procedures you learned to use in the worksheet. Select the cell to edit, then press F2 or click in the formula bar to edit the macro function argument. To copy or clear parts of a macro and to insert or delete cells, use the Edit commands.

Inserting rows through one macro may insert a blank row through other macros in the same row. This affects the appearance of the macro, but does not stop it from running.

NOTE

Enclose Text Arguments in Quotation Marks

Some arguments for macro functions are expected to be text. These arguments usually have the word *text* in the argument name, such as name_*text* or format_*text*.

NOTE

Make Sure the Macro Recorder Is Off before Editing a Macro

Be sure that the macro recorder is off before editing a macro, or your Edit commands and actions will appear as macro functions in the macro being recorded.

TIP

Let Excel Check Your Macro Spelling for You

Type your macro functions and names in lowercase characters. Then when you press Enter, functions that are correctly typed convert to uppercase, while range names and misspelled functions remain lowercase.

The two macros shown in figure 26.12 are examples of how a simple recorded macro can have additional power added to it. These charting macros create a chart from the selected worksheet area. The macro on the left is the original recorded macro that centers and bolds the active cell for use as a title. The macro on the right is the same macro with some additions: an input box to accept text for the chart title and the option to choose from dialog boxes. Note the changes made in cells B3, B5, B6, and B9.

```
                Microsoft Excel - CHARTIN2.XLM
   File  Edit  Formula  Format  Data  Options  Macro  Window           Help
   B5           =FORMULA(INPUT("Enter the title",2,"Chart Title"))
                A                              B
 1  AutoChart                      Chart with Input
 2  =NEW(2)                        =NEW(2)
 3  =GALLERY.COLUMN(6,TRUE)        =GALLERY.COLUMN?(6,TRUE)
 4  =ATTACH.TEXT(1)                =ATTACH.TEXT(1)
 5  =FORMULA("=""Sales Forecast""")  =FORMULA(INPUT("Enter the title",2,"Chart Title"))
 6  =FORMAT.FONT(0,1,FALSE,"Helv",12,TRUE,FALS  =FORMAT.FONT?(0,1,FALSE,"Helv",12,TRUE,FAl
 7  =LEGEND(TRUE)                  =LEGEND(TRUE)
 8  =SELECT("Legend")              =SELECT("Legend")
 9  =FORMAT.LEGEND(1)              =FORMAT.LEGEND?(1)
10  =FULL(TRUE)                    =FULL(TRUE)
11  =RETURN()                      =RETURN()
12
13
14
15
16
17
18
19
20
21
Ready
```

Fig. 26.12. Original and modified macros.

Finding the Right Macro Function

Excel has a large number of macro functions available that you can add to existing macros or use to write new macros. The list of functions is as extensive as most programming languages. The list of results and commands shown in table 26.1 simplifies finding what you need. Appendix B, "Macro Directory," contains the full list of commands and descriptions.

Table 26.1
Common Macro Functions

When you want to:	*Use this function:*
Choose from a dialog box	Add a ? before the ( ) in the macro function.
Select a cell or range, or move the active cell	SELECT
Enter a value from the keyboard	INPUT, FORMULA
Cross-check data entry	IF, TYPE, INPUT
Display a message or warning	ALERT, MESSAGE
Control macros by time	WAIT, ON.TIME
Activate on a key	ON.KEY
Change the direction of program flow in a macro	GOTO, subroutine
Make a decision	IF
Format	FORMAT.*command*
End or stop a macro	HALT, RETURN
Repeat a procedure	FOR, WHILE, NEXT, BREAK
Return the value from a cell in the macro sheet to the active cell in the worksheet	RETURN
Retrieve information about references, formulas, windows, documents, or notes	GET.*command*

Adding Dialog Boxes to Recorded Macros

Normally, when you run a prerecorded macro, you do not get a chance to make any changes to the dialog box selections. The macro runs as recorded without letting you select different options. One easy and useful change you can make to your recorded macros makes dialog boxes wait for your selections.

Identify the dialog boxes you want displayed by inserting a question mark (?) after the corresponding macro function and before its opening parenthesis. Figure 26.12 shows formatting functions with question marks inserted. When the macro reaches these functions, it stops, displays the appropriate dialog box, and waits for your input. Note that the arguments (between parentheses) entered in the macro functions are the default selections when the box appears. With the box displayed, you can make changes to the selections and choose OK or press Enter to continue with the macro.

The macro directory in Appendix B shows the format and arguments for each command that accepts a question mark. Some macro functions that display dialog boxes accept default values for arguments. For example, PAGE.SETUP has four forms listed in Appendix B. The first two forms work with worksheets or macro sheets, and the second two forms work with charts. The italicized items are optional.

PAGE.SETUP(head,foot,left,right,top,bot,heading,grid)

PAGE.SETUP?(*head,foot,left,right,top,bot,heading,grid*)

PAGE.SETUP(head,foot,left,right,top,bot,size)

PAGE.SETUP?(*head,foot,left,right,top,bot,size*)

Enter the macro function, for example, as follows:

=PAGE.SETUP?("My Title",,,2,2,,FALSE,TRUE)

This function stops the macro and displays a Page Setup dialog box with the defaults selected. Notice that FALSE in the macro function turns off a check box, and TRUE turns it on.

Displaying Custom Messages

Use the ALERT and MESSAGE macros to generate custom messages and warnings. ALERT displays a dialog box containing a message. The user must choose the OK or Cancel buttons to put away the box and continue. Figure 26.13 shows an alert box that was added to a recorded macro by adding the following macro function:

=ALERT("The value entered is outside the acceptable range",3)

*Fig. 26.13. Alert
box generated
from a macro.*

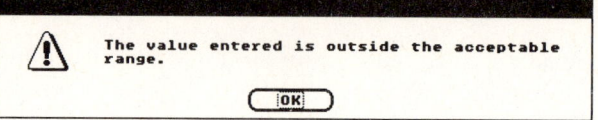

<table>
<tr><td>⚠</td><td>The value entered is outside the acceptable range.</td></tr>
</table>

`OK`

> **TIP**
>
> ### Checking Whether OK or Cancel Is Chosen
>
> Macro functions that display a box with OK or Cancel will hold the result TRUE if OK is chosen or FALSE if Cancel is chosen. Use an IF macro function to check whether a macro function returns TRUE or FALSE.

The MESSAGE macro is more subtle. The message appears in the status bar at the bottom of the screen and stays there until the macro tells it to go away. MESSAGE works well for letting the operator know what type of function the macro is performing, such as a FIND or Calculation.

To display messages, use the form:

=MESSAGE(TRUE,*"message"*)

To return the status bar to normal, use the form:

=MESSAGE(FALSE)

To keep the status bar completely clear, use the form:

=MESSAGE(TRUE,"")

Changing Cell References in Macros

Recorded macros store cell addresses in R1C1 style as text within quotation marks. Function arguments that contain the word *text* need to have arguments within quotation marks. If an argument is a reference and text, such as *ref_text*, then use R1C1 style and put quotation marks (") around the cell reference.

A1 style references also can be used in macros, but the references must be entered manually. A1 style references are not entered within quotation marks. A1 style references must be preceded by an exclamation point (!) to indicate that they are addresses for the currently active worksheet.

You can manually enter cell references in a macro and use either the R1C1 or A1 style, but the reference style used must match the current display format of the worksheet. External references can be used to address worksheets other than the active worksheet. Relative reference addresses can be used unless indicated otherwise by the macro directory for that specific function.

Some macro functions, such as FORMULA(formula_text,*ref*), can specify that their actions affect the reference indicated by *ref*. Other functions, such as FORMAT.NUMBER(format_text), affect whatever cell or range is currently selected. To choose the cells you want affected by this type of function, use the SELECT function to select the cell or range before the macro reaches the function.

Use Names Instead of Cell References within Macros

Moving cells or inserting and deleting rows and columns on a worksheet does not adjust the cell references that are in a macro sheet. Rearranging the worksheet creates extra work and errors, and requires that you cross-check the cell addresses in the macros designed for that worksheet.

To prevent this problem, use macro names for macro references that are the names of areas on the worksheet. Adjustments to the worksheet then will not require that you edit the macros.

Another advantage to using names in macros is that you can use one macro with many different worksheets. For example, even if each worksheet has the final report area in a different location, using the name, such as Final_Report, in a print macro allows that macro to work with all the worksheets.

For Easier-To-Understand Recorded Macros, Switch to R1C1 Style

To make cell references in your worksheet easier to compare to cell references in a recorded macro, activate the worksheet, choose **O**ptions **W**orkspace, select the **R1C1** option, and press Enter. (Recorded macros use R1C1 style regardless of the worksheet style.)

By switching the worksheet into R1C1 style, you also ensure that edits you make to macro cell references appear in R1C1 style.

Cell references added to macros after they are recorded can refer to the worksheet by name just as linked worksheets refer to each other by name. Using an external cell reference that includes the document name makes the macro work with only the named document (worksheet, chart, or macro sheet). For example, to make a cell selection specific to the ACCTRCV.XLS worksheet, write the SELECT function as follows:

    =SELECT("ACCTRCV.XLS!R2C5:R2C10")

The ACCTRCV.XLS worksheet must be active before the cells on it can be selected.

To make the macro work with whatever sheet is currently active, precede the reference with an exclamation point (!). For example, to select the range D15:E20 on the currently active worksheet and to make cell D15 the active cell in the range, use the formula

=SELECT(!D15:E20,!D15)

(This is the same as external reference formulas that link multiple worksheets, described in Chapter 10, "Using Multiple Windows and Linking Worksheets.")

Select multiple noncontiguous ranges on a worksheet by separating the ranges or range names with commas. For example:

=SELECT("R5C2:R8C2,R7C3:R10C3","R7C3")

As figure 26.14 shows, the SELECT statement describes two noncontiguous ranges. The last address, "R7C3", describes the active cell.

Fig. 26.14. The SELECT statement.

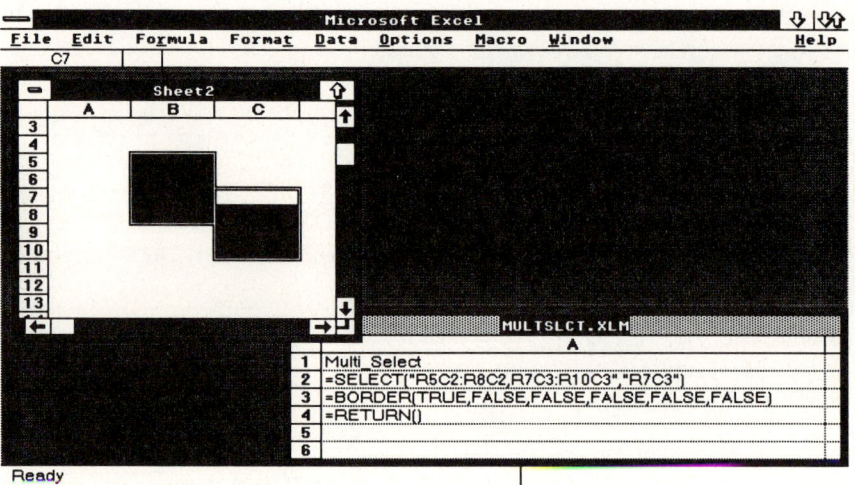

Cell B14 in figure 26.15 shows an example of mathematically calculating the location of the next active cell.

Moving the Active Cell in a Macro

When you need to move the active cell in a macro, use the relative reference form with R1C1 style inside a SELECT formula. Remember to put the R1C1 reference in quotation marks. Make the movement relative to the current

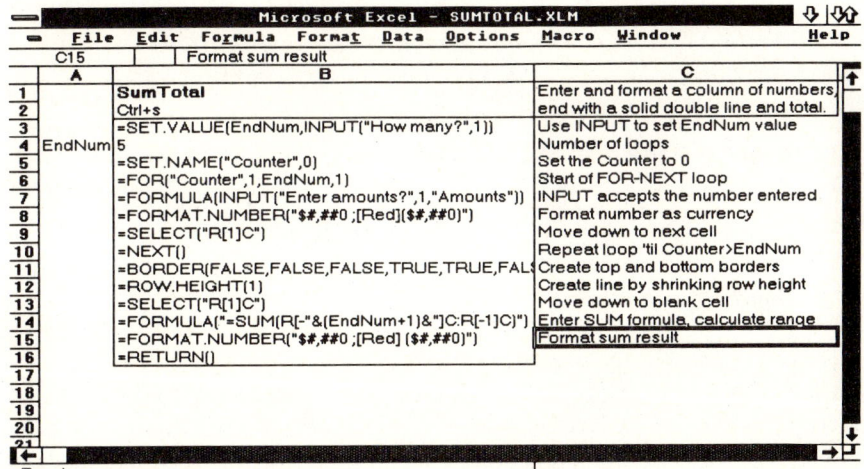

Fig. 26.15.
Mathematical
calculation in
B14 of range
for SUM.

location by enclosing the number of cell position changes in square brackets. For example, if you want the active cell to move down three rows and right two columns, enter the following:

=SELECT("R[3]C[2]")

To move up two rows in the same column, use the following:

=SELECT("R[-2]C")

Entering Worksheet Values through a Macro

You can enter macro formulas and values as though you typed them into a cell. You can also enter macro formulas and values through a dialog box.

The form for the FORMULA function is

=FORMULA(formula_text,*ref*)

where formula_text is the formula being entered enclosed in quotation marks. Because *formula_text* is text, it must be enclosed in quotation marks, and any cell references must use R1C1 style. *ref* is an optional reference to the location of the result. If *ref* is not used, the formula puts the result in the currently active cell. Use the SELECT macro function to specify the active cell before the FORMULA function operates. A simple example is

=SELECT("R3C2")
=FORMULA("=R1C2*R2C2")

The macro formulas in figure 26.15 use an INPUT command nested inside FORMULA in cell B7. The command accepts data from an INPUT dialog box and then enters the amount typed into the active cell. In this macro, the active cell moves down after each entry.

In cell B14, the FORMULA function enters a SUM formula into the active cell. The SUM formula has within it a calculated cell reference. The top row of the column is calculated by the result of *(EndNum+1)*.

Values entered with FORMULA do not need to be enclosed in quotation marks. For example:

=FORMULA(345)

But formulas being entered must be enclosed in quotation marks, and cell references must be in R1C1 format. If the formula being entered contains text in quotation marks, then use two quotation marks for each quotation mark surrounding the text.

Use the INPUT function to request data in a dialog box and to test the entry type. INPUT displays a simple dialog box that requests information. INPUT also can check for the type of data being entered. Use the FORMULA function to put the entered value into the worksheet.

INPUT takes the following form:

=INPUT(*"message",type*)

The *type* argument is a number specifying whether allowable inputs are formula, text, name, and so on. Refer to the macro directory in Appendix B for a list of types. If you enter data of the wrong type, Excel displays an alert box, then displays the dialog box again so that you can edit your entry. If you choose Cancel in the INPUT dialog box, then INPUT returns the value FALSE to the cell containing FORMULA.

Naming Macro Cells for Better Understanding

Assigning names to macro cells has two advantages: not only does it make understanding macros easier, but also cell references in the macro remain correct if you move, insert, or delete in the macro sheet. Figure 26.16 shows the DATACHK.XLM macro. The names in column A refer to the adjacent cell in column B. This enables the macro to look at cell contents within its own macro sheet.

To create all the names in column A at one time, do the following:

1. Enter names down the left column. Select the range of the macro to include the names and the adjacent macro formulas as shown in figure 26.16.

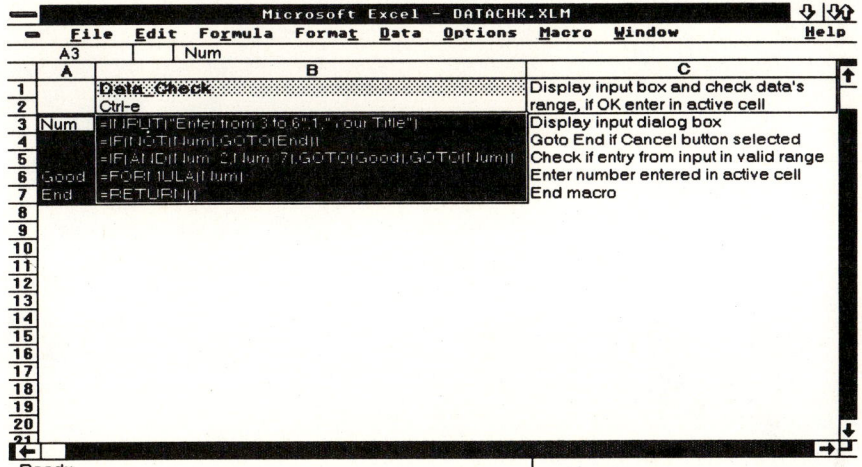

Fig. 26.16. The DATACHK.XLM macro as names are about to be created.

2. Choose Formula Create Names, and select the **Left Column** option to use the names in the left column.

3. Choose the OK button or press Enter. You can now use the names in place of cell references.

Reading Values

You can read values from both worksheets and macro sheet and use them in controlling results.

The macro sheet appears to contain only functions, but these functions return results, just as in a worksheet. A result can be a number, text, or logical value (TRUE/FALSE). You can see the results from macro functions by activating the macro window, selecting **Options Display**, and unchecking the **Formula** box. Figure 26.17 shows the DATACHK macro in two windows. The left window shows macro functions; the right window displays the values returned by each function. Notice that after the Cancel button is chosen, cell B3 holds a FALSE result.

The value a macro function returns is useful when calculating results, making decisions, and controlling macro operation.

Many macros listed in Appendix B, "Macro Directory," return values from different parts of the macro sheet or worksheet. You can find the names of worksheets, directories, contents of cells, formats of cells, and much more.

Fig. 26.17.
Macro displayed
with functions
or results.

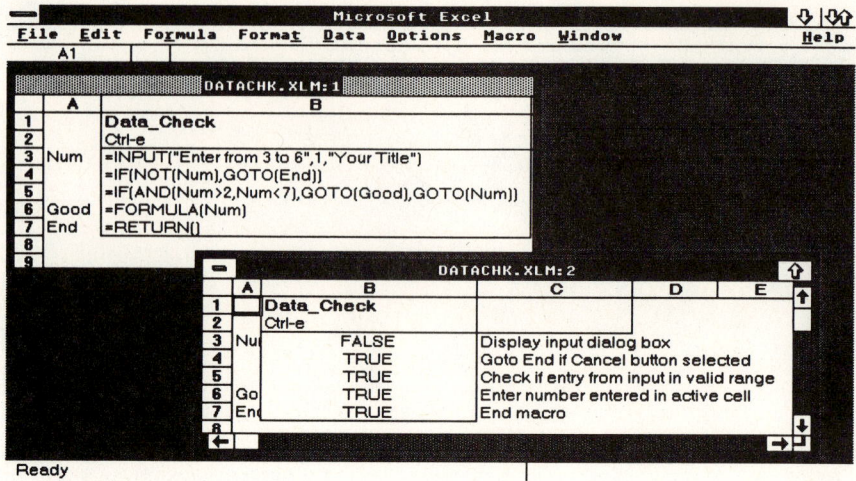

Some of the useful macros are

- ACTIVE.CELL

- GET.DOCUMENT

- GET.CELL

- GET.NAME

- GET.WINDOW

- GET.FORMULA

- SET.VALUE

- DIRECTORY

You can also bring values into an area of the macro worksheet by pasting them into the macro sheet or by linking the macro sheet and the worksheet with an external reference.

Decision Making and Condition Testing

The IF function is the great decision maker in Excel. Use it to decide how a macro reacts based on comparisons of values in a worksheet or in a macro. IF works well for checking data entry values and for branching the macro to new operations.

IF takes the following form:

=IF(logical_test,value_if_true, *value_if_false*)

When the comparison or logical condition you enter in *logical_test* is true, then the value or formula in *value_if_true* executes. If the comparison or logical condition is not met, then the value or formula in *value_if_false* executes.

Figure 26.17 shows the DATACHK.XLM macro. The macro uses two IF functions. The IF function in B4 checks to see whether the Cancel button was selected from the input box. The IF function in B5 checks to see whether the data is within limits; if the data is not within limits, the macro returns macro operation to the INPUT function in B3.

Renaming Macros and Their Ctrl Keys

You may want to rename a macro or change its Ctrl+key combination when you edit the macro for new capabilities or when its name or Ctrl+key conflicts with that of another macro. Follow these steps to rename your macro:

1. Activate the macro sheet containing the macro you want to change. Choose Formula Define Name.

2. Select from the list box the macro name to be changed, and then select the Name box to edit the name. Figure 26.18 shows the name of an existing macro being edited.

3. Select Command Key, and edit the Ctrl+key character.

4. Finally, choose OK or press Enter.

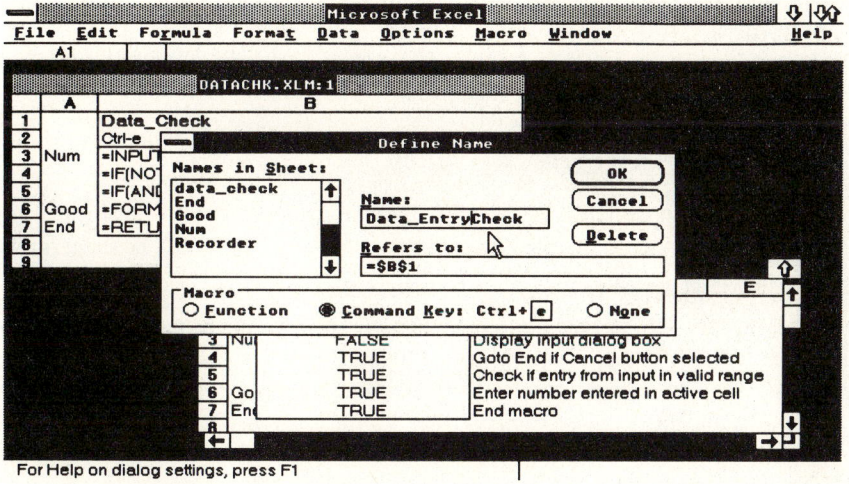

Fig. 26.18.
Renaming a
macro.

Copying and Deleting Macros

You probably will create macros that you want to use with several worksheets. Rather than opening multiple macro sheets, you can use **Edit Copy** and **Edit Paste** to copy the macros you need onto one sheet. Rename them with **For**-mula **Define Name**. Make sure that any cell references refer to either the active sheet (showing just "R1C1" or !A1 style reference) or use external references to refer to the new worksheet (such as "FORCAST.XLS!R1C1" or FORCAST.XLS!A1).

Clearing the macro functions from the macro sheet is not enough to get rid of a macro. You must also delete the macro name. After you clear all the functions from the macro sheet, use **Formula Define Name** to select and delete the macro names you want to get rid of.

Manually Programming Macros

You can manually enter all or part of the macro functions that create a macro. The macro functions and structure of the sequence can be likened to programming in an interpretive language such as BASIC. For most procedures, you will want to record sequences of commands and actions and then make small editing changes to them. But for complex programming needs, you will need to write the macro or macro subroutines manually.

If you are familiar with programming, you know how important planning and documentation are. Any time you write macros manually, you can save time by designing the macro before you begin. The most important point to remember is to write your macro in subroutines and have a main macro that controls when and how each subroutine runs.

Designing the Macro

Before you begin building the macro, you should organize what you want the macro to do. Write down the steps and tasks to be done. Break these tasks into small subroutines.

Macros are easier to test and troubleshoot if you can isolate problems in subroutines. Use sample data to test each subroutine; then paste together the subroutines into a larger macro, or link them to a master control macro that tells each subroutine when to run. (The "Using Subroutines for Specific Tasks" section of this chapter describes how to link subroutines to a main macro.)

Another advantage of programming macros from a collection of subroutines is that you can create a library of subroutines that handle frequently needed tasks. This library can be useful to many worksheets.

Macros are easier to understand if you break up sections with text headings. Format the headings with italic or bold so that they are easy to see. (Excel does not read text or blanks in macros.)

> **TIP**
>
> **Hide Macro Sheets from Inexperienced Operators**
>
> If the operators of your worksheets are inexperienced, you may want to protect and hide your macro sheets with **Window Hide** and **Options Protect Document**. The HIDE macro function also hides the active worksheet or macro sheet.

Documenting the Macro

Documenting macros is rather like backing up files on your hard disk. Many people fail to do it until they have caused themselves a lot of work and job insecurity. With macros, it is easy to create macros and use them immediately, leaving documentation for later. Then weeks or months later, when you or someone else must modify the macro, you have forgotten how it works.

Even if you are a novice Excel user who does not understand many of the macro functions, you should put an explanation of what the macro does in the column to the right of the macro. You can also attach a note of instructions to the cell with the macro name by selecting the cell containing the macro name and choosing Formula Note.

The sample macro in figure 26.19 shows one of the best methods for documenting macros. This method makes macros easier to read, edit, and understand. The method titles the top cells in a macro so that the macro is more organized. Borders and shading are used to separate distinct parts. The layout of the macro is

A1:A7   Cell names
B1   Macro name
B2   Ctrl+key combination
C1:C2   Explanation of macro
B3:B7   Macro functions
C3:C7   Explanations of each function

Fig. 26.19. A
well-documented
macro.

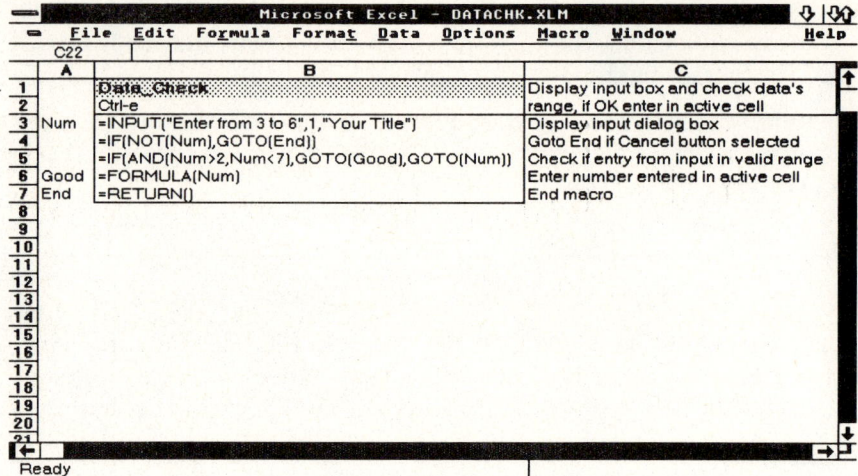

The actual macro begins with the macro name in the second column, cell B1. Formula **Define Name** named this cell as the first cell in the command macro.

You can separate segments of one continuous macro by including text and blank cells as dividers in this central column. The text and blank cells do not affect macro operation but do help to show where separate tasks begin and end within a large macro. Because Excel macros ignore text and blank cells, you can enter remarks or segment headers by typing them as text. You may want to format these remarks with italic or bold so that they stand out.

Another way of making your macros easier to read is to use Format **Border** to outline the column containing macro functions or the column containing documentation.

NOTE

Excel Macros Ignore Text That Does Not Begin with an Equal Sign

Do not use an equal sign (=) to begin text in the macro function column. It confuses Excel into thinking that you are trying to enter a formula.

Excel macros ignore text like that in cell B2 of a macro (see fig. 26.19). Use text titles or blank cells to divide long macros into readable sections.

The first column of the macro contains names that identify the adjacent cell containing a macro function. Naming macro cells makes it easy for later formulas to refer to the result of a previous function. For example, the macro function in cell B4 of figure 26.19 uses the name Num instead of the cell reference B3. Remembering that Num represents the number entered in the input box is easier than remembering what B3 represents.

The third column of the macro contains explanations of what each macro function does. This makes it easy to decipher what different segments of the macro do.

Changing the Order of Macro Operation

Macro functions execute in the order they are listed down the column. However, you can change this flow of execution in a number of ways. A GOTO command or a subroutine call can reroute the macro to a different section of the macro. The IF function is an excellent method of controlling when branching takes place.

GOTO(*ref*) permanently branches macro operation to the cell location specified by *ref*. The macro in figure 26.19 gives an example of a GOTO function. If the Cancel button from the input box displayed by cell B3 is selected, the input box returns a FALSE value to B3. The IF function in B4 reads the value in Num (B3) and reroutes the macro's flow to the cell named End (B7).

Be careful when using GOTO because it makes the flow of logic and operation difficult to unravel and understand. You can end up with macros that GOTO other macros that GOTO other macros that GOTO the original. Trying to correct problems in situations like this can be a nightmare.

Using Subroutines for Specific Tasks

To prevent snarls of GOTO commands, it is often better to use subroutines. Subroutines are small subtasks that are used to do specific and frequently repeated tasks. When a main macro needs one of these small tasks performed, it transfers macro operation to a subroutine. When the subroutine is finished, control returns to the original macro and continues from where it left. Not only are subroutines easier to understand and write than GOTO statements, but also you can often share subroutines between macros or paste subroutines onto other macro sheets.

Subroutines are nothing more than macros that perform a specific task for the main macro. They act like efficient subcontractors who are designed to do a special and repetitive job. For example, you may have a subroutine that sets the page layout and displays dialog boxes requesting header and footer information. This same subroutine can be used by different macros. Another example is a data extract subroutine used by different databases on the same worksheet.

Subroutine macros end with RETURN just like normal macros. When a subroutine macro reaches RETURN, it returns to the macro function following the one that called the subroutine.

The best way to write macros using subroutines is to write one main control macro that acts as a script. This script tells the different subroutines when to run. The control macro should do little work itself; it should check results and coordinate which subroutine runs.

To get a subroutine to run, "call" it by name, where *macroname* is the cell reference or name at the beginning of the macro. Use the following form:

    =macroname( )

If the subroutine is on another macro sheet (perhaps a sheet containing a whole library of subroutines), then include an external reference call to the macro. Use the following form:

    =worksheet!macroname( )

Macros that are used only as subroutines can include arguments specified within the parentheses. If you use a subroutine macro as a normal macro, then don't set it up to accept arguments.

Repeating Tasks by Looping

When you need a macro that repeats a task numerous times, use a loop. One type of loop uses FOR-NEXT functions. It repeats the macro segment between the FOR and NEXT macro functions "for" the number of times specified by a counter.

Another type of loop, WHILE-NEXT, continues to repeat a loop "while" a condition is met. When the condition is not satisfied, the loop breaks and the macro continues. A special command, BREAK, can be used to break out of either type of loop under special conditions that you define.

FOR-NEXT loops use a counter stored in a macro cell to track how many times a loop repeats. The cell storing the counter must be named with Formula Define Name. The change in the counter after each loop is governed by the *step_number*, which adds to the counter after each loop. The *end_number* tells the loop when it has repeated enough times. The format of the FOR function is

    =FOR(counter_name_text,start_number,end_number,*step_number*)

Use the FOR-NEXT loop as a method for repeating data entry movements or formatting across rows. You can reduce the size of your recorded programs by replacing long sequences of repeated macro functions with shorter FOR-NEXT loops that repeat a process.

Figure 26.20 shows a FOR-NEXT loop that repeats the sequence between B6 and B10. The SumTotal macro asks how many numbers you want to enter, asks you for each number, enters the number in the column, and then repeats the process as many times as you request. When the loop is done, the macro enters a solid line at the bottom and puts in a SUM function. Each element of the FOR-NEXT loop is described in Appendix B, "Macro Directory."

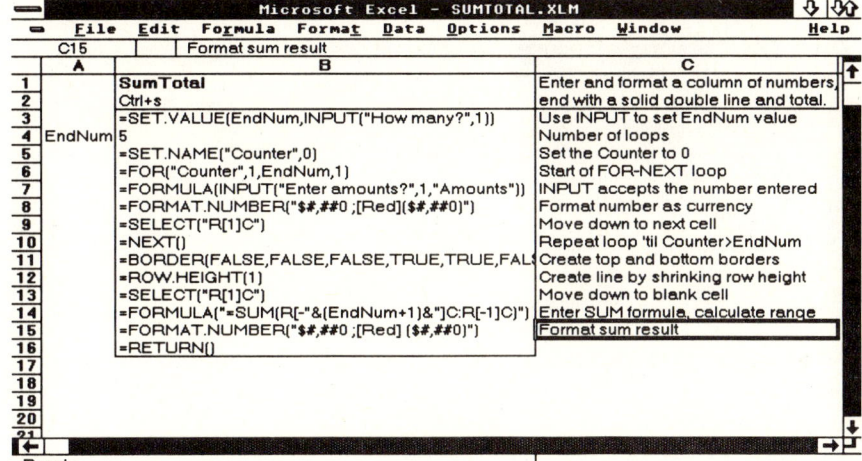

Fig. 26.20. The SumTotal macro.

NOTE

The Counter in FOR Must Be in Quotation Marks

Enter the Counter name in quotation marks as shown in figure 26.20. Excel uses this name to hold a count of how many loops have been completed. You do not have to name a cell as Counter, and you can use different names than Counter.

The WHILE-NEXT loop is easier to enter than FOR-NEXT. The WHILE-NEXT loop begins with the following macro function:

=WHILE(logical_test)

In this function, logical_test is a conditional or comparative equation that results in TRUE or FALSE. The macro functions being repeated follow underneath the WHILE cell until ended by the NEXT macro function.

WHILE-NEXT loops operate by repeating the macro segment between the WHILE and the NEXT until the logical_test within WHILE turns FALSE. The macro then drops out of the loop when it reaches NEXT. If you want to set a special condition that causes looping to stop, then refer to the discussion of the BREAK macro function in the macro directory.

Figure 26.21 shows a WHILE-NEXT loop that continues until the Cancel button is selected from the GOTO dialog box. The macro then continues until it reaches NEXT and then exits the loop.

Fig. 26.21. PrintRequest macro with WHILE-NEXT loop.

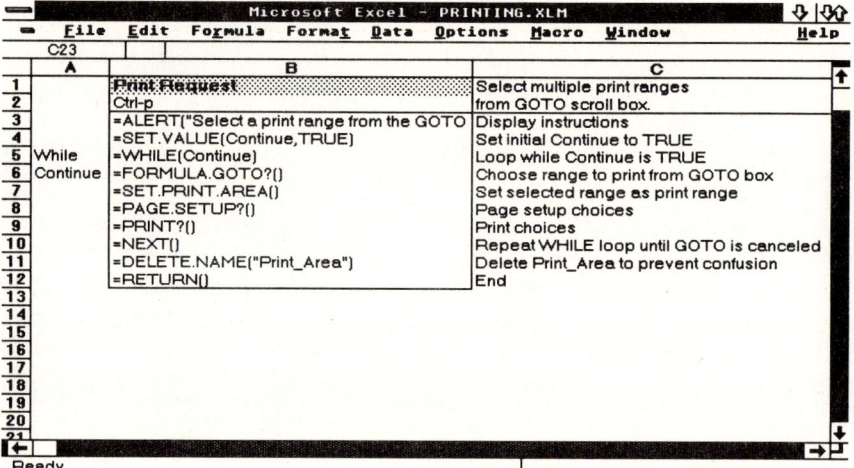

Sample Command Macros

The following macros show how simple macros can be, yet how they can save you time and work. These macros were created by recording a macro and then modifying it. Don't forget to name the top cell in the macro using the Formula Define Name command and to select the Command macro option.

Data Checking Macro

The macro shown in figure 26.19 cross-checks data entered by less experienced operators. You can use it to cross-check data being entered into a database row or into entry areas of a worksheet. The IF function in B4 checks for the Cancel button selection from the input box. The IF function in B5 checks to make sure that the value entered in the input box—stored in cell B3 (Num)—is greater than 2 and less than 7.

Multiple Printing Macro

When you have a lot of print jobs to do, the macro shown in figure 26.21 cuts through the keystrokes. It shows you how to use the FORMULA.GOTO macro function to select named ranges or to type in ranges you want changed. The result is as though you had programmed your own scrolling list box. The WHILE-NEXT loop lets you continue to select named ranges or typed cell ranges until you choose the Cancel button on the GOTO box. Choose Cancel on the Page Setup and Print boxes after you have made your last selection.

Column Totaling Macro

SumTotal is just the macro you need when you have a long column of numbers to total. It also demonstrates how to set up a FOR-NEXT loop for repetitive processes. This macro is set up so that you can use it in any worksheet location.

To use the macro shown in figure 26.20, move the active cell to where you want the first number in the column, and then run the macro. You will be asked how many numbers you want to enter. This number is stored in B4 and is used by the FOR function in B6 as the *end_number* to stop the data entry loop. A FOR-NEXT loop from B6 to B10 asks for each number. FORMULA(INPUT()) in B7 enters each number, and the FORMAT.NUMBER function formats it. The SELECT("R[1]C") function in B9 moves the active cell down one row in the same column. The loop then repeats until Counter equals EndNum. At that point the cells from B11 to B15 enter a solid total line, and the function in B14 enters a SUM function. The value in EndNum is used in B14 to calculate how many cells will be included in the SUM.

Chart Titling Macro

The macro shown in figure 26.22 demonstrates that you can use macros to control charts as well as worksheets. To operate the macro, select the worksheet range you want charted, then press Ctrl+C.

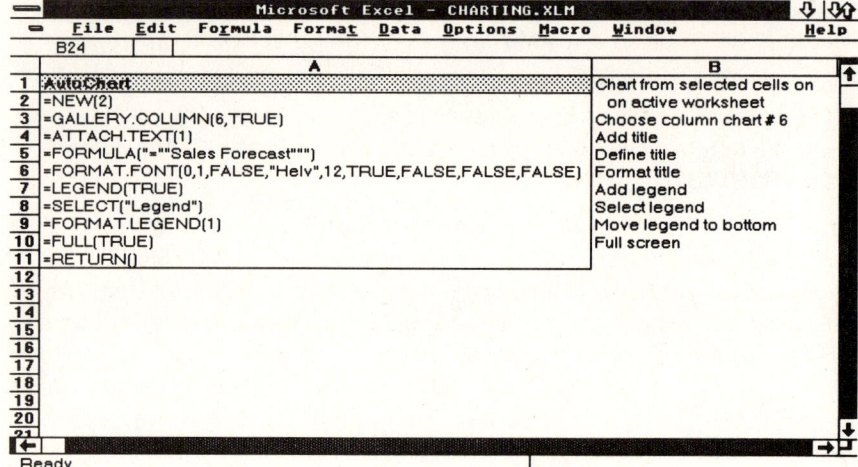

Building Function Macros

Excel has a wide selection of built-in math, financial, logical, and text functions. But you may find yourself wishing for functions specific to your business. Imagine the time and frustration saved if the formulas you frequently use were built-in functions.

Excel gives you the power to make that happen. You can create custom function macros that work just like Excel's built-in functions such as SUM or LOOKUP. If you went through Chapter 25, "Macro Quick Start," you created a function macro that calculated profit margin.

The difference between function macros and built-in functions is that you define how the function macros work. After you have defined a function macro on a macro sheet, you can use it the same as you would any built-in function. Function macros are custom-built functions.

Building your own functions increases the accuracy of your formulas, reduces repetitive typing, hides complex formulas from novices, presents a cleaner and clearer worksheet, and ensures that the formulas used are those approved by management or an audit team.

Function Macro Structure

Function macros, like command macros, reside on a macro sheet. Unlike command macros, function macros never take actions or choose commands. Function macros accept arguments just as normal worksheet functions do. Function macros return a value or answer to the same cell that contains the macro.

Creating a function macro is similar to manually typing a command macro although function macros are limited to using certain macro worksheet functions. Function macros cannot be recorded because they cannot contain action or menu commands. Macro and worksheet functions can be entered in function macros by typing them or by pasting them into cells from the Formula Paste Function list box.

Function macros must be built in a specific order. The macro in figure 26.23 is an example. After you open a new or existing macro sheet, the order of entries as you work down a column on the macro sheet is as follows:

1. Enter a name for the function macro in the first cell of the function macro range.

2. Enter a RESULT function to specify the type of result returned to the worksheet. (1 specifies numeric result; 2 specifies text. Others are listed in the macro directory.)

3. Enter ARGUMENT functions down the column in the same order they will appear between parentheses in the function macro.

4. Enter the equation or formulas that the function macro uses to calculate its result.

5. Enter the RETURN function.

6. Select the cell containing the macro name.

7. Choose Formula Define Name and select the Function option.

8. Choose OK or press Enter.

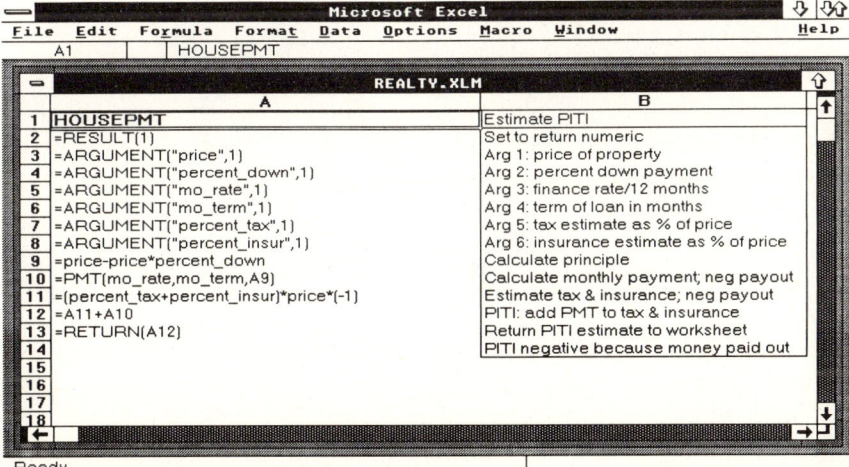

Fig. 26.23. The HOUSEPMT function macro.

Enter one ARGUMENT function to define each variable used in the calculation. A function can have up to 14 arguments. The order the arguments are entered in the macro sheets dictates the order you must enter variable values between parentheses that follow the function. For example, in the Quick Start function macro, PMARGIN(Sales,Costs), Sales is the first argument, and Costs is the second.

There are two forms for the ARGUMENT function. The first form is as follows:

=ARGUMENT(name_text,*data_type_num*)

In this form, name_text is a text name in quotation marks that describes that argument—for example, ARGUMENT("Sales").

The second form of the ARGUMENT function is as follows:

=ARGUMENT(*name_text,data_type_num*,ref)

This form names the cell address *ref* with the name of *name_text*. The value associated with *name_text* is entered in the *ref* cell. *ref* is a cell on the macro sheet.

For both of the forms, *data_type_num* is a number specifying the type of data, such as text or numeric. If no number is specified, then the argument assumes text, number, or logical value as the type. If the argument is the incorrect type, the #VALUE! error value is returned.

The RETURN function must reference the cell containing the final result of the equations in step 4. For example, RETURN(C4) returns to the worksheet the contents of cell C4 from the macro sheet. (Remember, functions in the macro sheet *do* produce results. The macro sheet is just formatted to show the functions and not the results. Reformat the macro sheet with **Options Display Formula** to see the results.)

Using Function Macros

Function macros work only when their macro sheet is open. Use **File Open** to open any macro sheet containing the function macro(s) you want. Remember that macro sheet names end with .XLM.

Once the macro sheet is open, you can paste the name of a function macro into a worksheet cell or macro sheet cell with **Formula Paste Function** just as you paste built-in worksheet functions. Of course, you also can type in the function macro and its arguments.

To use the appropriate macros in your worksheet, you must have the correct macro sheet open. Two ways of opening worksheets and macro sheets together are by saving them as a workspace or by creating a macro that automatically loads the function sheet.

You can edit function macros the same way you edit worksheet cells and formulas. You can copy and paste cell and formula contents. You can also use the Formula Paste Function command to enter macro formulas.

Sample Function Macros

The HOUSEPMT function macro shown in figure 26.23 calculates the approximate cost of house payments for purchasing a home. The macro uses Excel's built-in PMT function to calculate the loan payment and then adds the approximate cost of insurance and taxes.

Before using this function in a worksheet, make sure that the macro sheet containing HOUSEPMT is open. Then enter a formula with arguments like the following:

=REALTY.XLM!HOUSEPMT(price,percent_down,mo_rate,mo_term,percent_tax,percent_insur)

where each argument is on a monthly basis. For example:

=REALTY.XLM!HOUSEPMT(225000,.2,.095/12,360,0.01/12,0.0075/12)

This formula returns the amount –$1841.66. The amount is negative because you are paying it out. Notice that you must enter the name of the macro sheet that contains the function REALTY.XLM. This is a major reason for using the Formula Paste Function command to enter macro functions.

TIP

Getting to the Bottom of the Paste Functions List

It takes a long time to scroll to the bottom of the Paste Functions list where all the macro functions are displayed. To get there quickly, press End. You will zoom to the bottom of the list.

If you have tables of taxes, depreciation schedules, or shipping rates, you will appreciate the macro shown in figure 26.24. Instead of putting a table on each worksheet, you can create one macro function to look up values from a table. That macro can be used by any worksheet. This keeps your worksheets uncluttered because they contain only a function, not a large table.

Fig. 26.24. The SHIPCOSTS function macro.

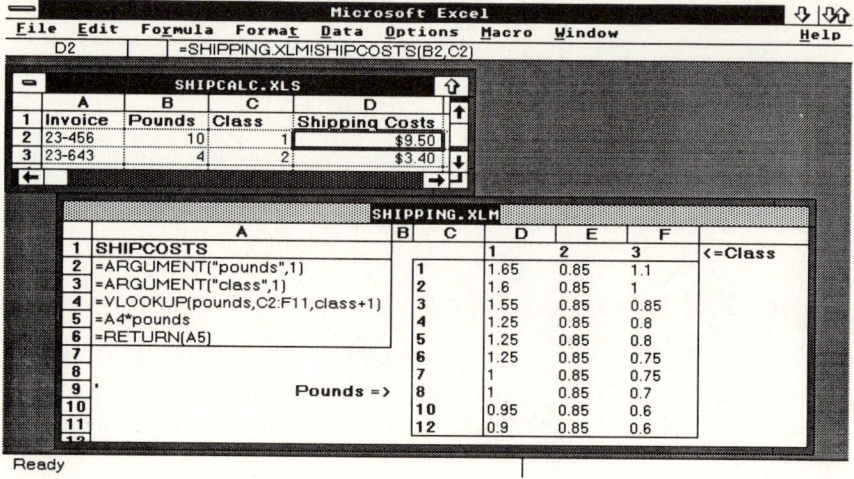

The format for the function in a worksheet is

=SHIPCOSTS(Lbs,Type)

For example:

=SHIPCOSTS(10,1)

This function returns the amount $9.50. The value of Lbs is used to look down the left column of the table in C2:F12. Once an amount equal to Lbs or the next lesser amount is found, the VLOOKUP function looks across the table to find the shipping rate in the column specified by (Type+1).

From Here . . .

Recording macros is easy, but you soon will want to modify them. In the process of customizing macros, it is not unusual to run into obstacles. When that happens, take a look at Chapter 27, "Troubleshooting Macros."

As you alter your macros, you will probably find yourself wishing there was a macro function that does something special. There probably is, and you can find it in Appendix B, "Macro Directory." As you look through the directory, realize that each macro function is a small building block.

You can learn a great deal about writing your own macros by reading and dissecting macros written by others. Look in magazines, books, and the \LIBRARY directory of your hard disk for sample macros.

27

Troubleshooting Macros

Macros save a great deal of time and work. When you customize recorded macros by making small modifications, they become even more valuable. But when you begin to make significant changes, or when you begin to type macros directly onto the macro sheet, the probability of errors increases—especially when you are first learning.

This chapter includes some tips on how to troubleshoot macros and how to deal with some of the more common difficulties. Two of the most important tips are to keep your macros short and simple and to plan what they will do. If you need to accomplish more than what a short and simple macro can handle, use subroutines to join together small macros into a larger macro. You can plan what a macro will do by writing a script of what will be done.

TIP

Enhancing Macro Performance

You can make your macros run faster by turning off the screen updating until the macro is complete. Because the screen is not redrawn until the macro is complete, longer macros run faster.

Insert the macro function

=ECHO(FALSE)

at the point in the macro where you want screen refreshing turned off. To turn screen refreshing back on in the middle of a macro, insert

=ECHO(TRUE)

Screen refreshing is always turned back on when the macro is finished.

You can spend a lot of time troubleshooting macros that do not work correctly. With the right approach, you can prevent many errors from ever happening.

Preventing Macro Problems

Reduce the chance of making errors by recording the foundation for your macro whenever possible. You can then use **Edit Insert** or **Delete** to make room for typed functions or to remove functions. You know you are starting from a valid base if your original macro worked.

Give your macro a different version number in the name each time you save it, and save frequently. For example, save versions as AUTOCH01, AUTOCH02, and so on. This lets you return to a previous version that worked correctly if you go down the wrong development path. You can always delete the unneeded versions with **File Delete**.

When you save the macro sheet with a new name, don't forget to change any references to the macro sheet's name. Use the **Formula Replace** command to make these changes quickly and accurately.

Type macro functions and worksheet functions using lowercase letters, for example:

    =formula(input("Enter a number",1))

If your typing is correct, Excel will automatically convert the lowercase letters to uppercase. Range names remain in lowercase.

To reduce the chance of entering macro functions and their arguments incorrectly, use **Formula Paste Function** with the Paste **Arguments** box selected.

Build macros in small segments, and test each segment separately. Then cut and paste the segments together, or link them as subroutines controlled by a master macro.

Finding the Cause of a Problem

Excel tries to catch errors when it runs the macros. For example, errors in macro syntax cause an alert box to be displayed on the screen. The alert box tells you which cell in the macro has a problem (see fig. 27.1).

In addition, you can monitor the values that macro functions produce. These values tell you the results of button selections, results of calculations, and show error values. Figure 27.2 shows two windows on the same macro sheet. The window on the right has **Options Display** set with **Formula** unselected so that you can see the values from a macro as the macro runs. After running, the macro functions return values based upon their calculations and operation during the run. In most cases macro functions return TRUE when they run correctly.

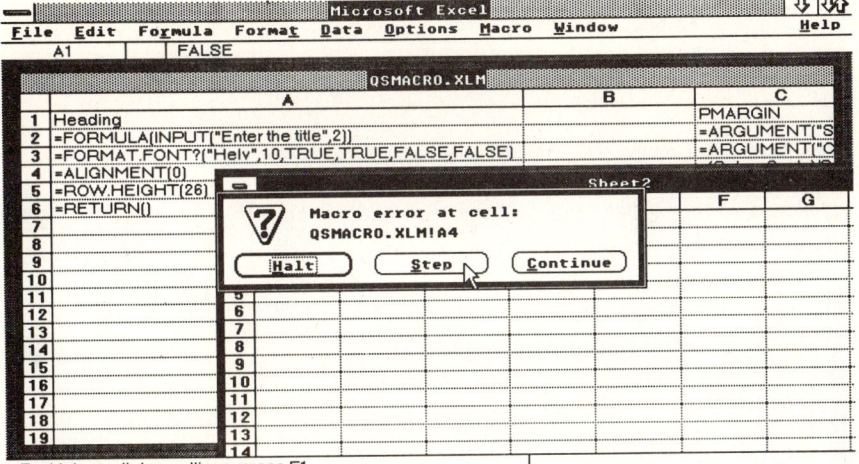

Fig. 27.1. Macro error alert box.

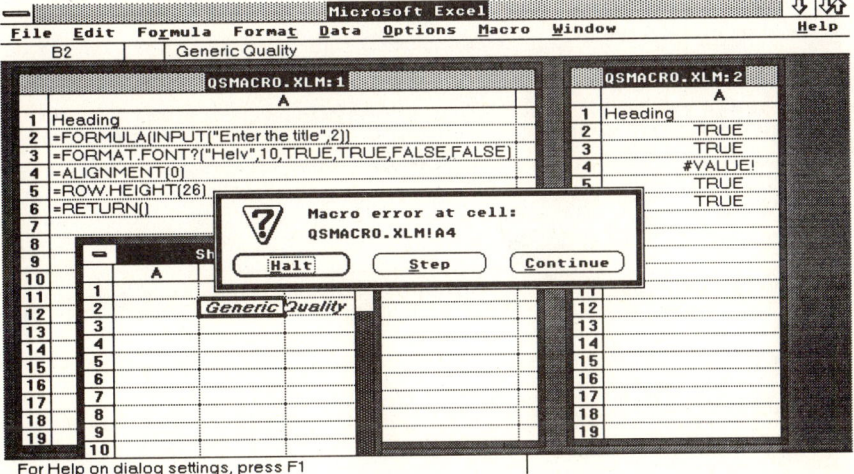

Fig. 27.2. Macro displayed in two windows: as a function and as a result.

See Appendix B, "Macro Directory," to see the values returned by different macro functions. Selecting a Cancel button in a dialog box, for example, results in a FALSE value in the cell that activates the dialog box.

A great aid in correcting errors in macros is the STEP formula. You can put as many STEP formulas as you want in your macro. Whenever Excel comes across the STEP formula, it presents a dialog box with three options (see fig. 27.3):

1. **Step**—Take a single step to the next macro cell, and stop again.

2. Halt—Exit the macro, and return to the active document.

3. Continue—Return to normal macro operation until another STEP formula is met.

Fig. 27.3. Step dialog box created by the STEP function in cell A2.

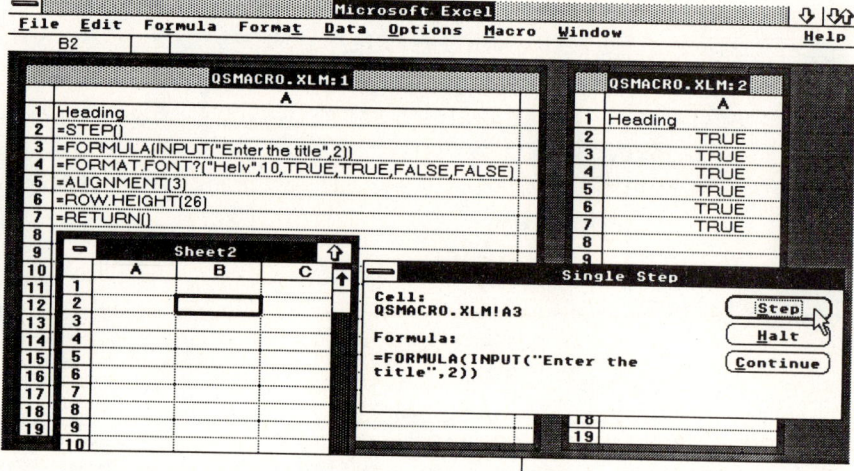

Whenever you have a possible macro problem, insert a STEP formula before the suspected macro problem with the following procedure:

1. Select a macro function cell before the problem, and choose Edit Insert.

2. Select the Shift Cells **D**own option, then choose the OK button or press Enter.

3. Enter =STEP( ) into the blank cell (see fig. 27.3).

4. Print a copy of the macro sheet for the suspected cells following the STEP formulas.

5. Arrange the worksheet and macro sheet so that you can see the active worksheet area and the suspect macro area, and activate the macro.

Now, when you run the macro, it stops when it reaches the first STEP function. The dialog box shows you what cell is about to execute and what function is in that cell. The printed copy of the suspected macro functions can help you if you cannot see all of the macro on the screen. Select the **STEP** button to step through the macro one macro function at a time. To exit the macro, select the **H**alt button, or select **C**ontinue to continue at normal macro speed. You can move the Single Step dialog box wherever you want so that you can see the rest of the screen.

Press Esc to enter single-step operation during normal macro operation. You need not enter STEP formulas to do this. When you press Esc, an alert box shows you what macro cell you stopped on. The Single Step box then lets you **S**tep through the macro, **H**alt the macro, or **C**ontinue normal operation.

Excel comes with a macro that helps you troubleshoot (debug) your macros. The macro, named DEBUG.XLM, automates troubleshooting features such as entering STEP formulas, setting break points, and switching the macro sheet between formula display and results display.

To run the DEBUG macro, do the following:

1. Open the worksheets and macro sheets you want to troubleshoot.

2. Choose **F**ile **O**pen, select the \EXCEL\LIBRARY subdirectory, and open the DEBUG.XLM macro.

    DEBUG.XLM is an automatic macro that runs as soon as it is loaded. It hides itself from the screen and adds the command **D**ebug to the **M**acro menu.

3. Activate the macro sheet containing the macro you want to troubleshoot, and choose **M**acro **D**ebug. The menu bar changes to display **D**ebug, **F**ormula, and **D**isplay.

    Debug allows you to easily set and remove STEP and breakpoints. **F**ormula displays a macro function, even when the sheet shows results. You can also search out cells on the macro sheet containing STEP functions or containing error values. **D**isplay lets you quickly switch between showing macro functions and showing their results. You can also see all the information about a macro cell and its preceding and depending functions by selecting **D**isplay **S**how Info.

4. Select any macro function where you want to begin troubleshooting. Choose **D**ebug Set **T**race Point to wrap STEP functions around the selected existing macro function, or choose **D**ebug Set **B**reakpoint to wrap an alert box around the existing macro function. The alert box is similar to the STEP function, but lets you insert a message.

5. Activate the worksheet that the macro controls. Choose **D**ebug **R**un Macro, select the macro you want, and press Enter.

The macro begins running, stopping at the STEP and breakpoints you have set and displaying boxes that enable you to check macro operation.

6. If the macro suddenly begins to work incorrectly, choose the Halt button from a STEP box or breakpoint alert box. Notice the macro cell and the function displayed. These are for the next macro function. The problem has occurred *prior* to this.

When the macro is finished running, or when you choose Halt from a STEP or breakpoint, you can check the macro sheet to see the results of macro functions and to check for error values. Follow these steps:

1. Activate the macro sheet, and choose the Formula Select Errors command to find any error values that have occurred. Alternatively, choose Display Formulas/Values to display results on the macro sheet.

   When results are displayed, check for incorrect values in response to Formulas Errors option, INPUT formulas, TRUE or FALSE values resulting from IF statements, and error values such as #N/A or #NAME!.

2. Remove STEP formulas and breakpoints by finding them with Formula Select Debug Points and removing them with Debug Erase Debug Point.

3. Return to normal operation by choosing Debug Exit Debug.

Troubleshooting Tips

The following problems and some of the possible solutions may save you time when you are faced with macros that do not work.

Troubleshooting Approaches

Problem: The macro doesn't work at all.

Solution: Go through the following steps to filter out the most common problems for a macro not working.

1. Choose Formula Define Name or Formula Goto, and verify that the top cell of the macro is named and that it is selected as the appropriate type of macro (with an optional Ctrl+key combination if it is a command macro).

2. Choose **Options Display**, and unselect the **Formula** option. If you see error values displayed in macro function cells, check them out. For example, #NAME? means that the macro function cannot find one of the names used. Macro functions generally display TRUE or a value when they perform correctly.

3. Check that the macro is not starting and then being sent to the end of the macro by an incorrect macro function.

4. Insert a STEP function as the first cell in the macro.

Problem: The macro works, but not correctly.

Solution: Go through the following checklist in order:

1. If an alert box appears, check the cell listed for the correct syntax (grammar). Common syntax errors are missing commas, leaving out mandatory arguments, and forgetting quotation marks around text items.

2. Choose **Options Display**, and unselect the **Formula** option. If you see error values displayed in macro function cells, check them out. For example, #NAME? means that the macro function can't find one of the cell reference names used. This is frequently a spelling or typographical problem. Macro functions generally display a value of TRUE if the macro function performs correctly.

3. Insert STEP functions prior to sections of the macro where you suspect a problem. Watch the worksheet results and the macro values simultaneously in separate windows as you step.

Problem: After a reasonable amount of searching and fruitless corrections, the macro still does not work correctly.

Solution: Try these escalating approaches to inscrutable macros:

1. Leave the problem alone for awhile, and let your subconscious work on it.

2. Try "breaking" the macro into sections and testing the operation of each section separately. This may isolate a section that does not work correctly.

You can temporarily stop the macro at an early stage by inserting a RETURN formula where you want it to stop. Move the RETURN down the macro as you work your way through.

Another method is to separate sections of the macro. When the sections work correctly, join them together by pasting them, using GOTO formulas or subroutines. Retest the operation as you add each section to the whole.

3. Start over! On difficult bugs, you may save time by starting again from scratch, but rethink, replan, and approach the macro with a different solution. Build your new macro in small sections that can each be tested independently. Link these sections together.

Problem: A message appears from a macro problem.

Solution: Press F1 for Help in deciphering what the message means.

Troubleshooting Macros That Are Missing

Problem: The name of the function macro does not show up in the Formula Paste Function list box.

Solution: Ensure that the macro sheet is open. If it is, then name the macro with Formula **D**efine Name.

Problem: You open the macro sheet and go through the recording steps, but no macro functions appear in the macro sheet.

Solution: When you return to the worksheet and position the cursor (if necessary), you must turn on the recorder with **M**acro **S**tart Recorder before any recording occurs.

Problem: The macro is recorded, but the code appears at the end of another macro.

Solution: Make sure you reposition the starting point of the macro recorder by using the **M**acro **S**et Recorder command.

Problem: Inexperienced operators enter values or make selections that "bomb" the macro.

Solution: Use alert boxes that display instructions and error-trapping formulas to prevent errors by those unfamiliar with the program. The DATACHK macro in Chapter 26, "Building Command and Function Macros," illustrates how to check for the Cancel button being selected and how to check for correct entry values.

Troubleshooting Cell Reference and Active Cell Problems

Problem: Typed macros do not move the active cell.

Solution: Move the active cell by using R1C1 style with the SELECT formula and relative reference. For example, if you want the active cell to move down one row, enter

=SELECT("R[1]C")

To move up two rows and left two rows, use

=SELECT("R[-2]C[-2]")

Problem: The active cell in the macro keeps jumping back to the same cell location used when the macro was originally recorded. The macro is unusable in different worksheets and different locations.

Solution: This problem occurs when the macro is recorded in absolute reference mode. The macro replays exactly the same cell selections as the ones selected during recording.

Use relative addressing. This allows the macro to work on cell locations that are in the same relative location but have different physical addresses. To record with relative addressing, choose **Macro Relative Record**. You can alternate between Relative Record and **Absolute Record** as you record the macro.

Problem: As macro cells are inserted and deleted, the cell names and documentation in the adjacent column are sometimes left in their old location. The cell names need to be relocated so that they are adjacent to the correct cell.

Solution: Use **Formula Goto** to pinpoint the actual cell given a particular name. Either cut and paste the name in the left column or insert and delete cells to move all the names up and down the column.

Troubleshooting Macro Formula Problems

Problem: There is an error somewhere in a macro function, but after five minutes of searching, you still cannot find it.

Solution: Put the function on hold, and take a break or work on something different. To put the function on hold, delete the equal sign (=) in front of it. This changes the macro function to text, which is ignored. You can return later to fix the problem.

Problem: A worksheet function doesn't seem to work correctly in the macro.

Solution: Check the worksheet function's syntax and behavior as listed in Chapter 9, "Using Functions in Worksheets."

Problem: Unselecting Options Display Formula reveals the values that result from macro functions. Most of these values are TRUE or FALSE, but some produce numeric and text results. Incorrect macro functions produce error values.

Solution: If a macro function shows the error value #N/A, suspect that an argument has been left out of the macro function. If #NAME! appears, then you have forgotten to give a name to some cell reference, you have misspelled a name, or you have forgotten to enclose a text value in quotation marks.

Troubleshooting Incorrect Macro Results

Problem: The command or function macro does not work, even though the macro code is visible on the macro sheet.

Solution: You may have forgotten to give the macro a name, or you may have named an incorrect cell.

Activate the macro sheet, then choose Formula Goto. If your macro's name is not in the list box, the macro has not been named. If your macro's name is in the list box, select the macro and press Enter. See if the first cell in the macro range is the first cell of your macro. If not, you need to rename your macro with the correct location. Refer to the beginning of Chapter 26, "Building Command and Function Macros," and the command Formula Define Name to learn how to name a macro.

Problem:	The macro produces the wrong results and appears to have additional unnecessary macro functions attached to the end of the original macro.
Solution:	Recording a second macro without resetting the recorder to a new location adds the new recording to the end of the last macro recorded. Cut out the unwanted macro functions, paste them into a new location, and use Formula Define Name to name the beginning of this new macro. You may be able to use them for their original purpose. Make sure you end the original macro with a RETURN( ).
Problem:	The macro acts as though it has other macros attached to it. The first macro works, then others work that have not been requested.
Solution:	Check that your first macro ends with a RETURN( ) or HALT( ). A blank cell does not stop a macro. It continues going down the column looking for more macro functions. If it runs into another macro, it begins to execute that macro.

From Here . . .

Macros can be tremendous time-savers, but poorly constructed macros can be tremendous time-wasters. Remember to plan your macro, build it in small segments, test each segment separately, and then link the segments together. Use the STEP macro function and the DEBUG macro from the \LIBRARY directory to help you find problems.

One of the best ways to learn macros is by "reading" and modifying macros that others have built. There are many sample macros and worksheets in which to run them located in the \LIBRARY directory. These macros and the directory were loaded on your hard disk when you installed Excel. You can get more free macros from magazines, newsletters, and PC users groups.

There are many powerful things about the Windows environment; and one of those is it give you the ability to use Windows applications with other Windows and standard DOS applications. The following, and final, section of *Using Excel: IBM Version* explains how to share data between Excel and Windows or standard DOS applications.

Part VI

Advanced Techniques

E xcel gains power from its synergy with other applications. Excel reads
and writes files from major applications without you even knowing a file
conversion has taken place. With Windows and Presentation Manager
applications, Excel can exchange data with applications through Dynamic Data
Exchange. The applications act as though they were designed to work together—which they were! Excel macros can even control other Windows
applications. All of these factors add together to produce an electronic spreadsheet that works in concert with other Windows, Presentation Manager, and
MS-DOS applications.

In Chapter 28, "Using Excel with Windows Applications," you learn how easy
it is to move data or charts between Excel and other Windows applications.
For example, you can copy a portion of your Excel worksheet with Excel's
Edit Copy command, switch to a Windows or Presentation Manager word-
processing program, and use its **Edit Paste** command to paste what you have
copied into a report. You can even copy and paste charts. Chapter 28 also
explains how to customize Excel through the Control Panel application.

Chapter 29, "Using Excel with Standard DOS Applications," shows you how
to use Excel, Windows, and standard DOS applications together. Excel reads
and writes many major DOS application files, such as 1-2-3, dBASE II, dBASE
III, dBASE III Plus, two types of text files, and more. You don't have to translate
files; you just open them, work with them, and save them. Translations and
conversions are all done invisibly. Excel even saves files in the original format
unless you tell it otherwise. Chapter 29 describes how you can copy and paste
screen data between Excel and standard DOS applications such as Word-
Perfect, 1-2-3, and accounting applications.

Those of you familiar with 1-2-3 may first want to turn to Chapter 30, "Making
the Switch from 1-2-3 to Excel." It explains how to get up and running by
using your knowledge of 1-2-3 as a base. The chapter includes tips on learning
Excel quickly and explains how to use Excel's built-in help features for
1-2-3 users. It also includes descriptions of Excel's differences from 1-2-3 and

Excel's enhanced features and benefits. Even if your business environment demands a slow transition from 1-2-3 to Excel, you will want to use at least one Excel copy immediately so that you can take advantage of Excel's enhanced printing of 1-2-3 worksheets, databases, and graphs.

Chapter 28
Using Excel with Windows Applications

Chapter 29
Using Excel with Standard DOS Applications

Chapter 30
Making the Switch from 1-2-3 to Excel

28

Using Excel with Windows Applications

Excel is one of the new generation of software taking advantage of greater processor power and the new Windows and Presentation Manager software environments. These environments have three big advantages:

1. the capability to transfer learning between Windows applications

2. the capability to run multiple applications

3. the capability to cut and paste "static" information between Windows applications

4. the capability to create "hot links" for passing live data between certain Windows or Presentation Manager applications

Customizing Excel with the Control Panel

You can customize Excel features and appearance with the Control Panel application. The Control Panel runs from Excel or from the Windows MS-DOS Executive. In the Control Panel, you can set the computer's date and time, install or delete printers and fonts, change Windows colors, select international date and currency formats, and more. (You can do more extensive customizing by manually editing the WIN.INI file. See Appendix C, "Technical Tips.")

To start the Control Panel from Windows, do the following:

1. Activate the MS-DOS Executive by pressing Alt+Tab until the MS-DOS Executive appears on the screen, then release Alt.

2. Change to the \WINDOWS directory.

3. Select CONTROL.EXE by pressing the down arrow or the C key, then press Enter.

With the mouse, just double-click on the file name CONTROL.EXE.

To start the Control Panel from Excel, do the following:

1. Activate the Excel control menu by pressing Alt+space bar.

2. Press U to choose the Run command. The Run Application dialog box appears, as shown in figure 28.1.

Fig. 28.1. The Run Application dialog box.

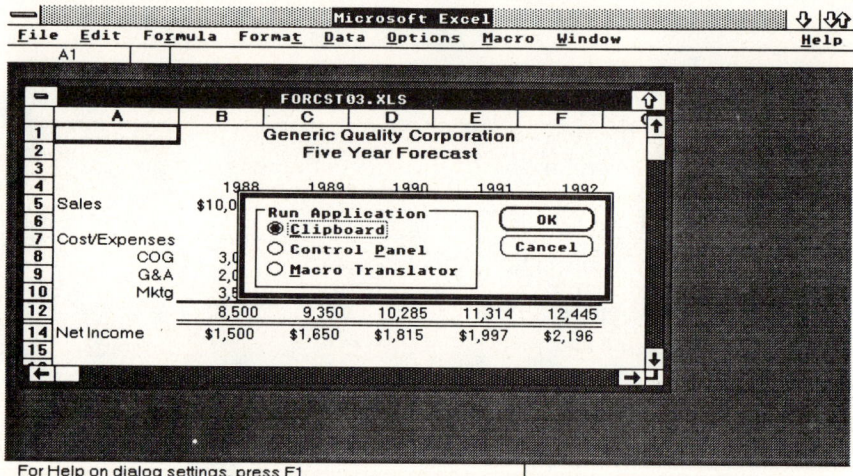

3. Press Alt+P to select Control Panel; then choose OK or press Enter. The Control Panel window is displayed (see fig. 28.2).

Fig. 28.2. The Control Panel window.

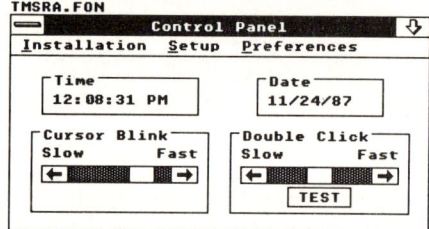

Changing Date, Time, and Cursor

To change the computer's date, time, cursor blink rate, or speed required for a double-click, select what you want to change by pressing the Tab key until the item you want to change is selected or by clicking on the item with the mouse.

Figure 28.2 shows the panel with the Time area in the upper left quadrant. Press Tab to move to this area. Move between hours, minutes, and seconds and between months, days, and years by pressing the left- or right-arrow key. Increase or decrease the setting by pressing the up- or down-arrow key.

To change the cursor blink rate or the speed required for a mouse double-click, press Tab until the square "thumb" in a horizontal scroll bar flashes gray. Press the left- or right-arrow key to increase or decrease the setting.

Press Alt to go into the menu to exit the panel or to make further changes.

Changing the Screen Appearance

You can change the color or gray scale for most portions of the Excel screen. Choose **Preferences Screen Colors** to display the Screen Colors dialog box in figure 28.3. This box has three parts. The scroll box at top left lets you choose the screen area being changed. The slide bars on the lower left change the hue, brightness, and color for that area. The results of changes appear in the Sample window on the right.

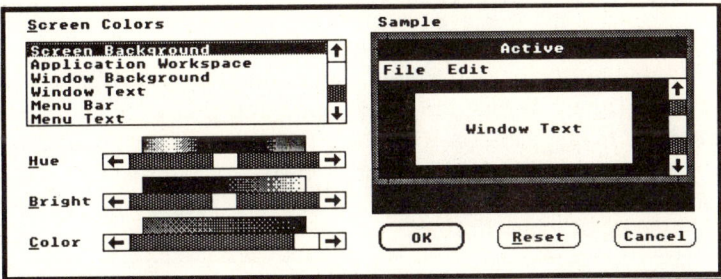

Fig. 28.3. The Screen Colors dialog box.

To test a new color combination, choose the part of the Sample screen you want to change from the **S**creen Colors dialog box (Alt+S, then up or down arrow). Choose the appropriate slide bar (**H**ue, **B**right, or **C**olor) with the mouse or with the Tab key. Major color changes are easiest if you set all three slide bars to the middle and then adjust hue first, color second, and then brightness. Some sample screen areas show only as pure colors and do not appear shaded.

While you are in the **Screen Colors** dialog box, you can return to the original setting by selecting **Reset**. When you choose OK, the Control Panel records the color settings and forgets the original settings. Screen colors change as soon as you exit the **Screen Colors** dialog box.

NOTE

Returning to Your Original Color

You can reset the screen color settings to their original values as long as you remain in the **Screen Colors** dialog box, but when you choose OK, the original settings are gone forever. If you have any doubt about how colors will look, draw a sketch of where the Hue, Bright, and Color settings were before you reset the settings.

Changing Mouse Speed and Button Selection

Only one button on the mouse works. This is normally the left button. If you are left-handed and want the right button to work instead, choose the **Preference Mouse** command. Select Swap left/right mouse buttons.

To adjust the rate at which a movement of the mouse moves the pointer on the screen, choose **none**, **medium**, or **high** from the Mouse Acceleration area. Experiment to find which mouse movement rate you prefer.

Changing International Character Sets

One advantage to Windows applications is the capability to switch between different international character sets, time and date displays, and numeric formats. These international settings are available within Excel. Choose **Preferences Country Settings** to display the Country Settings dialog box shown in figure 28.4. After making your country selection and closing the Control Panel, exit and restart Excel to use the new country formats.

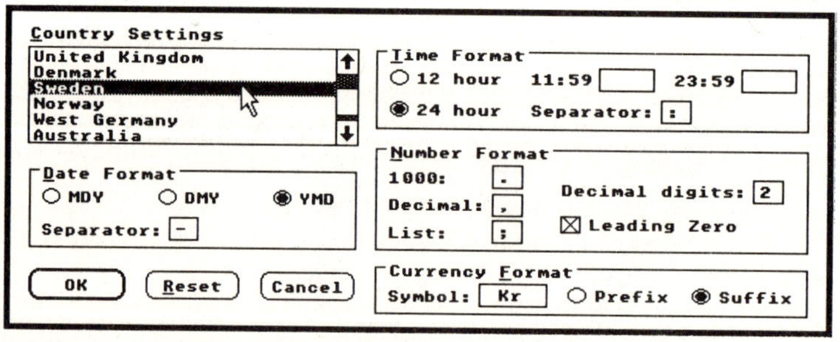

Fig. 28.4. The Country Settings dialog box.

You will rarely have to select anything more than the country from the **Country Settings** list box. Select a country, and all the parameters change. These changes will be reflected in Excel the next time you start Windows or Excel. For example, figure 28.5 shows part of the Format **Number** list box after the country setting was changed to Sweden and the application restarted. Notice that the FORCAST03.XLS worksheet from the Worksheet Quick Start is reformatted for Swedish Kronor.

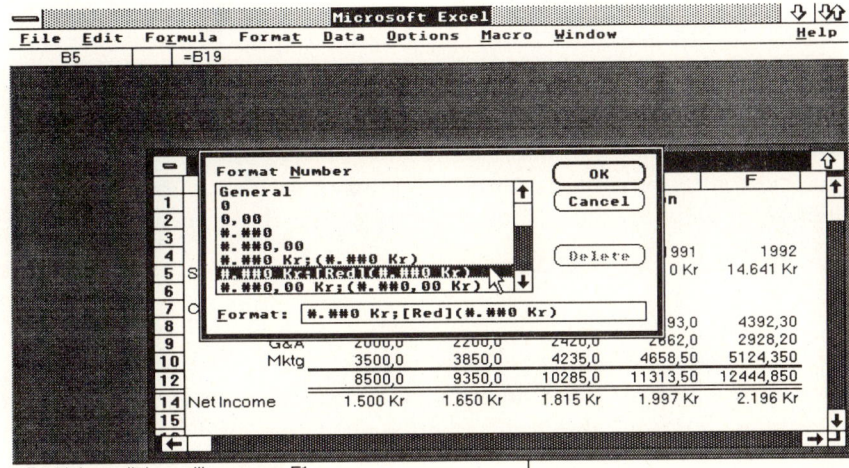

Fig. 28.5. The Format Number list box with Swedish formats.

TIP

Defining Other Country Settings

If you need country settings that are not shown, select Other Country from the list box, and make changes to all the options throughout the dialog box manually.

Changing the Installed Printers and Fonts

To add a new printer, follow these steps:

1. Choose **Installation Add New Printer.** Insert the disk containing the printer driver files, type the disk drive for this disk, and press Enter.

2. Select from the list box the name of the printer you want to add.

3. Choose the Add button, and type the drive or directory where you want the printer driver copied. This should be the same directory as Windows. Choose the Yes button.

4. Set the printer connection and communication port as described in the "Setting Printer Connections and the Communications Port" section.

TIP

Where Do You Get Printer Files?

Excel comes with disks that contain definitions and appropriate fonts for most printers. If your printer is not on the disk, call the Microsoft telephone support line and your printer manufacturer. Both should maintain a library of printer definitions and font files for more printers than those enclosed with the package.

To remove a printer from Windows, choose Installation Delete Printer, select the printer you want to delete, and press Enter.

When you add printers or plotters to your system, you may need different fonts than were installed during Excel setup. To add fonts, do the following:

1. Choose Installation Add New Font. Insert the disk containing the font sets, type the disk drive for this disk, and press Enter.

2. Select the font you want to add from the list box, then choose the Add button.

3. Enter the drive and directory for Windows. Choose the Yes button.

Not all fonts are available for every printer. Stroke fonts are used for plotters; raster fonts are used for dot-matrix printers. A few guidelines are given in table 28.1.

Table 28.1
Font Guidelines for Excel

Font set	*Description*
set #1	stroke fonts for any device
set #2	raster fonts, 640×200, CGA
set #3	raster fonts, 640×350, EGA and Hercules
set #4	raster fonts, 60 dpi (Okidata, Epson®, IBM)
set #5	raster fonts, 120 dpi (Okidata, Epson, IBM, Star® Micronics)
set #6	raster fonts, 640×480

For more information on fonts and printers, refer to *Using Microsoft Windows*, published by Que Corporation.

Setting Printer Connections and the Communications Port

After adding a new printer, you should go through the following steps:

1. Set the printer connection with the **Setup Connections** command.

2. Set the target printer and default printer settings with the **Setup Printer** command.

3. Set the printer communications port with the **Setup Communications Port** command.

You can choose these commands in any order, but if you have multiple printers connected to different ports, the setup can be confusing if you do the setup in an order that is different than the preceding one.

After you have added a printer or changed the port to which a printer is attached, you need to tell Excel where the printer is connected. Follow these steps:

1. Choose **Setup Connections**, and select the printer and its connection from the list boxes.

2. Choose OK or press Enter.

If you use one printer more than others, you will want to choose it as the default printer and set its default print settings. Do the following:

1. Choose **Setup Printer**.

2. Select the printer that you want to be the default printer.

3. Cross-check that the printer you select is connected to the correct physical connection. If it is not, use the previous procedure to connect the printer and connection.

4. Choose the OK button or press Enter.

   A new dialog box appears (see fig. 28.6). This dialog box lets you choose default print settings such as paper size, font cartridge, and print orientation.

Fig. 28.6. The Printer setting boxes for HP LaserJet printers.

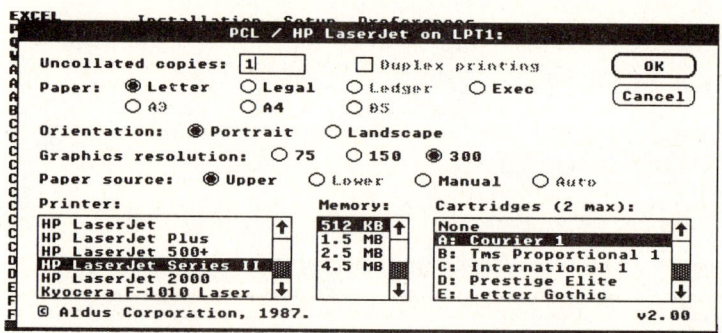

5. Select the most frequent paper size and the orientation in which you print most pages (Portrait for vertical, Landscape for horizontal). Choose OK or press Enter.

Windows must understand which physical connection to send printer information to and how to send that information. You must set up the printer once either during initial setup or with the Control application. You can change the settings at any time.

If you have a printer that uses a serial connection (usually a letter quality or laser printer), then you must set the serial communications port as follows:

1. Choose **Setup Communications Port**. The Communications Port dialog box appears (see fig. 28.7).

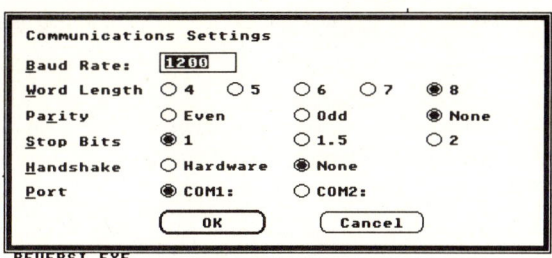

Fig. 28.7. The Communications Settings dialog box.

2. Select the communication settings required for each printer. First, select the **P**ort (COM1: or COM2:) to which your serial printer is connected. Then select the rest of the settings. Frequently used settings include the following:

Baud Rate: 1200 (letter quality wheel or thimble)
      9600 (laser printer)

Word Length: 8

Pa**r**ity: None

Stop Bits: 1

Handshake: Hardware

3. Choose the OK button, or press Enter to save these settings to disk.

If you print to the Apple LaserWriter® or LaserWriter Plus, and have initialized the LaserWriter or LaserWriter Plus for hardware handshaking, you will need to select hardware handshaking. (Initializing the LaserWriter needs to be done only once. Check your original Windows disks for a README file containing this information.)

Transferring Information through the Windows Clipboard

Using Excel in the Windows or Presentation Manager environment is like having a large integrated software system, even if the applications come from different vendors. With the Windows clipboard, you can copy or cut information from one Windows application and paste it into another Windows application. (Chapter 29, "Using Excel with Standard DOS Applications," explains how to copy and paste between Excel and standard DOS applications.)

Copying and Pasting Text between Windows Applications

To copy or cut text information from Excel and paste it into another Windows application such as Write, the Windows word-processing application, follow these steps:

1. Select the range of cells you want to transfer, and choose **Edit Copy** or **Edit Cut**.

2. Activate the Windows application into which you want to paste the information by pressing Alt+Tab until the application appears. Then release Alt.

3. Move the insertion point to where you want the information inserted.

4. Choose **Edit Paste** for the receiving Windows application.

When Excel reads the data from the Excel screen, it creates a long text row of each screen line with a carriage return at the end of each row. You can edit this text just as though it had been typed into the receiving application. (Pasting a picture of a worksheet, as described in the next topic, preserves the worksheet appearance, but the copied worksheet cannot be edited in the receiving application.)

Use the same process to transfer data into Excel by cutting from another Windows application and pasting the data into a selected cell in Excel.

NOTE

Some Standard DOS Applications Aren't What They Seem

Some standard DOS applications appear to display text but actually display text using the graphics mode. One such application is Reflex. Windows can capture a graphics "picture" of such application screens with Alt+PrtSc, but Windows cannot read text from the screen into the clipboard. This prevents you from copying text off the Reflex screen and pasting it into a Windows application.

Transferring an Excel Chart to Another Windows Application

You can capture an entire Excel chart or a "picture" of the worksheet and paste it into applications such as Aldus PageMaker, the Windows word-processing application Microsoft Windows Write, or Microsoft Word 4.0 running with Microsoft Pageview. To do this, start with the desired Excel chart or worksheet on the screen, and follow these steps:

1. Hold down the Shift key, and choose the Edit Copy Picture command. The Edit menu contains the Edit Copy Picture command when you hold down Shift while selecting Edit.

   Depending upon whether you are copying a chart or worksheet as a picture, you will see one of two dialog boxes. You can choose whether the picture will be what you see on the screen or as it appears when printed with the currently selected printer. If you are copying a worksheet, you can also choose either the size shown on screen or the size of the printed worksheet for the copied picture.

2. Select the Appearance and the Size; choose OK or press Enter.

3. Activate the other Windows application.

4. Use that application's Edit commands to paste in the picture.

The Edit Copy Picture command puts a copy of the chart or worksheet into the clipboard in *metafile* format. Most Windows applications can then paste the metafile format from the clipboard. The metafile format is a programming description of the graphics image; the format is not limited by the screen's resolution (fineness). That means you can copy and paste between applications that support metafile and maintain the highest quality graphics image.

TIP

Windows Applications That Don't Accept Metafile Pictures

If your application will not accept the metafile format from the clipboard, the Edit Paste command will be gray in the receiving application. But you can still paste a picture in bitmap format. However, bitmapped pictures require more memory and, depending upon the output device, may not print correctly or with as fine a resolution as the picture in metafile format.

If you want to copy the bitmapped picture into the clipboard, hold down the Shift key when you choose OK to confirm your selections of appearance and size (step two in the preceding procedure).

Linking Data between Applications with DDE

Windows applications can communicate with each other via Dynamic Data Exchange (DDE). With DDE, a Windows application can get or give data to another Windows application and can start and control another Windows application. (This applies to Windows/386 and Windows 2.0 or higher.)

DDE takes place in two ways: linking Excel to other applications using a remote reference formula (much as you link Excel worksheets and charts together using external references) or using macros to control DDE.

In DDE, there are *clients* and *servers*. A client receives the data given by a server. Excel can act as both a client and a server and can handle multiple clients and multiple servers.

Linking Excel to Other Windows Applications

Excel can receive data from other Windows applications through "hot links" created by DDE between Excel and other Windows applications. As data in the server application changes, the data in Excel (the client) is updated automatically. Applications where this is important could include tracking prices in stock transactions, updating inventory analysis, and analyzing real-time laboratory data. These applications require Excel to be linked to communications applications, to a relational database, or to instrumentation monitors.

When linking Excel to other Windows applications, you can use a remote reference formula similar to that used to link worksheets. A remote reference formula that links an Excel cell to a value in a Windows application appears in the following form:

    =App|Topic!Item

where *App* is a legal Excel name for the application being linked to. This name will be in the documentation for the Windows application if it is capable of DDE. App must be enclosed in single quotation marks if App is not a legal Excel name. Precede App with an equal sign and follow it with a vertical bar, created by pressing Shift+\ (Shift+backslash).

Topic is the legal Excel name for the document or "topic" within the application. The application manual should explain whether to use a document or Topic name. A Topic is similar to an Excel worksheet name. If Topic is not a legal Excel name, then enclose it in single quotation marks. Topic must be followed by an exclamation point (!).

Item is the legal Excel name for the cell, range, value, or data field within the topic. Item specifies the exact point within the Topic that produces the data being transferred. (If the Item name resembles a cell reference that could be confusing to Excel, then enclose the Item name in single quotation marks.) The Item name will be dependent on the server application. The Item name could be a field name from a database or a cell address or range name from a worksheet.

An example remote reference formula that links Excel to a custom script in a communications package might appear as

=CommApp|ServerScript!Request1

Linking Excel worksheets to other Windows applications should be no more difficult than linking two worksheets together. Follow these steps to link Excel to another application:

1. Open both Excel and the other Windows application. Activate the Windows application passing data to Excel.

2. Select the cell, range, value, or data fields you want linked. Choose **Edit Copy** or its equivalent from the Windows application.

3. Activate Excel by pressing Alt+Tab until Excel appears, then release the Alt key. Press Ctrl+F6 until the worksheet to which you want to link appears.

4. Select the cell or range where you want to paste the remote reference. Choose **Edit Paste Link** from the Excel menu.

Just as with external cell references and external reference formulas, you can either paste a link as just described, or you can type in the remote reference formula. Excel displays a warning message if you type in a remote reference formula for an application or topic that is not open.

To type in a remote reference, follow these steps:

1. Select a range of cells on an Excel worksheet large enough to hold the data from DDE.

2. Type the remote reference formula in the active cell of the range. It might look like

=CommApp|ServerScript!Request1

3. Hold down the Ctrl and Shift keys as you press Enter to enter the remote reference as an array formula in the selected range.

TIP

Remote References Pasted in Multiple Cells Are Array Formulas

Remote references in an Excel cell or range are array formulas. If you want to edit them, you must either clear the entire range and paste again or use array editing procedures.

NOTE

It's a Gray Day in the Paste Link Menu

When the Paste Link command is not available (grayed) after you have cut data from another Windows application, it means that the application from which you copied does not support DDE; the data cannot be pasted into Excel.

Linking Other Windows Applications to Excel

You can link other Windows applications to Excel so that Excel acts as the server. To do this, use *Excel* as the App name, the worksheet and path as the Topic name, and the cell reference or range name as the Item. For charts the only legal Item is the name *Chart*.

Starting Worksheets Linked to Windows Applications

Starting worksheets with remote references is the same as starting worksheets linked to other worksheets. If the supporting applications are already open when the linked Excel worksheet opens, you will see no difference in operation.

If you open an Excel worksheet linked to applications that are closed, Excel displays a message asking if you want to establish links. Choose OK to establish the link; choose Cancel, and the last value in the worksheet is used again.

If you choose OK, Excel will ask you if you want the application started. If the application cannot be started or the document cannot be found, an error appears in the appropriate cell in the Excel worksheet.

Turning Excel DDE Links On and Off

When you want the active Excel worksheet to use the last worksheet value and not request remote reference updates from other applications, choose

Options Calculation in Excel. Unselect the Update **R**emote References option, and press Enter. (You can put the remote reference links back in effect by selecting the Update **R**emote Reference option.)

Excel can respond to DDE information requests from other Windows applications just as well as initiating information requests. By default, Excel responds to DDE requests from other Windows applications. However, you can turn off Excel's capability to pass data to other applications by choosing **O**ptions **W**orkspace, then selecting the **I**gnore Remote Requests option. To enable remote requests and allow information to pass out of Excel, unselect the **I**gnore Remote Requests option.

Controlling DDE and Applications with Macros

You can control other Windows applications and DDE with Excel macros. Use the following macro formulas to control DDE in Windows applications:

- INITIATE("App","Topic") initiates a DDE channel and returns the Channel_Id in this cell. The App name and a description of Topics will be specified in the application manual. (Note that the App and Topic names are enclosed in double quotation marks.)

- REQUEST(Channel_Id,"Item") returns an array of data beginning at the macro sheet cell containing REQUEST. The Item is a reference specified by the serving application that could be a name, a cell reference, a number, or other reference. Channel_Id is a cell reference to the INITIATE macro function that opened the DDE channel.

- POKE(Channel_Id,"Item","Data_reference") sends information to the application assigned to Channel_Id and the Item within the application. The data sent is from the address "Data_reference" on the active Excel worksheet.

- EXECUTE(Channel_Id,"Execute_text") executes a string of keystrokes in the application assigned to Channel_Id just as though those keystrokes were entered manually.

- TERMINATE(Channel_Id) closes DDE channel at the end of the macro. Some applications have a limited number of channels, so they should be closed when you are finished.

An example of an Excel macro and comments appears in figure 28.8.

Fig. 28.8. An
Example of an
Excel macro to
control DDE.

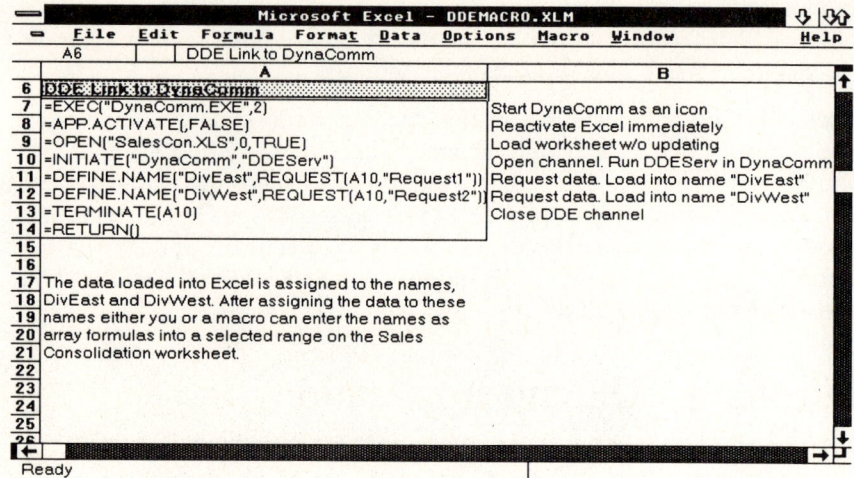

```
                    Microsoft Excel - DDEMACRO.XLM
  =    File   Edit   Formula   Format   Data   Options   Macro   Window              Help
       A6              DDE Link to DynaComm
                                   A                                       B
  6  DDE Link to DynaComm
  7  =EXEC("DynaComm.EXE",2)                          Start DynaComm as an icon
  8  =APP.ACTIVATE(,FALSE)                            Reactivate Excel immediately
  9  =OPEN("SalesCon.XLS",0,TRUE)                     Load worksheet w/o updating
 10  =INITIATE("DynaComm","DDEServ")                  Open channel. Run DDEServ in DynaComm
 11  =DEFINE.NAME("DivEast",REQUEST(A10,"Request1"))  Request data. Load into name "DivEast"
 12  =DEFINE.NAME("DivWest",REQUEST(A10,"Request2"))  Request data. Load into name "DivWest"
 13  =TERMINATE(A10)                                  Close DDE channel
 14  =RETURN()
 15
 16
 17  The data loaded into Excel is assigned to the names,
 18  DivEast and DivWest. After assigning the data to these
 19  names either you or a macro can enter the names as
 20  array formulas into a selected range on the Sales
 21  Consolidation worksheet.
 22
 23
 24
 25
Ready
```

TIP

Use DEFINE.NAME To Store Requested DDE Data

As the example in figure 28.8 shows, you can put REQUEST within
DEFINE.NAME. This assigns the array of data received by DDE to a name(s)
you specify—in this case, WESTSALES and EASTSALES. These two names can
then be entered (using Ctrl+Shift+Enter) as array formulas into the worksheet
that was active during the DDE request. The result will be a range(s) of data
in the worksheet.

Retrieving Data from Non-DDE Windows Applications

For those Windows applications that do not have DDE capability, you can
write a macro that cuts and pastes static data between applications just as
though you had cut and pasted them from the keyboard. This macro must
start the other Windows application, select the appropriate target items, run
the copy command in that application, activate Excel, and finally paste the
data into Excel.

Use the EXEC macro formula to start another Windows application or the
APP.ACTIVATE macro formula to activate an open application. Use the
SEND.KEYS macro to send the key sequences that control the active Windows
application.

From Here . . .

Without Windows, you lack the ability to easily integrate applications. In addition, the Windows desktop applications and word-processing application, Write, operate with the consistent commands and dialog boxes you've learned in Excel. For the small cost of Windows and a small investment in learning, you will get a substantial and profitable return.

29

Using Excel with Standard DOS Applications

If you use standard DOS applications such as dBASE II, dBASE III, Paradox™, Lotus 1-2-3, Multiplan, WordPerfect®, or Microsoft® Word, you will find it easy to share information with Excel. Excel loads and saves standard file formats such as dBASE, 1-2-3, and Multiplan. Also, Excel loads or creates text files for information transfer with applications that do not use one of the formats Excel understands. (1-2-3 compatibility and data exchange are discussed in Chapter 30, "Making the Switch from 1-2-3 to Excel.")

There are multiple methods of transferring data between Excel and other applications. In most cases large amounts of data are best transferred through the use of a file format Excel understands. If you want to retrieve a dBASE III Plus file, for example, you only have to open the file. Excel automatically converts it.

Even if you are using a program that does not have an "understood" format, you are probably in for an easy conversion. For example, Excel does not understand Paradox database files, but Paradox can save its files in 1-2-3 format, which Excel can then read. Similarly, data can be returned from Excel to Paradox using 1-2-3 files as the intermediary.

Information that displays on a single screen can be copied from the screen of one application and pasted into another. This works well for moving important numbers from an accounting program into Excel for analysis. You can even use this method between two standard DOS applications or between a DOS application and a Windows application.

When neither of the previous methods works, it's time to use a text file format to transfer data. Nearly all applications have a method of saving data to a text format and reading it from a text format. Excel reads information in three different text formats. As you will learn in the chapter, Excel automatically separates (parses) data into individual cells when the text file is in the comma-separated values (CSV) text format or when it uses tab-separated values (Text) format. If the text contains continuous lines of text without comma or tab separators, then you can use Excel's **Data Parse** command to separate the data into separate cells.

Copying and Pasting between DOS Applications and Excel

To copy from Excel to a standard DOS application, follow these steps:

1. Load the DOS application in Windows, and reduce it to an icon.

2. Run Excel and display it on the screen.

3. Select the cells in the worksheet to be copied, and choose the **Edit Copy** command.

4. Press Alt+space bar, select Minimize, or close Excel for more available memory.

5. Press Alt+Tab to select the standard DOS application icon. Continue to hold the Alt key until the correct application is selected. Release the Alt key when the correct application's name appears. The DOS application will be restored on-screen.

6. Move the DOS application cursor to where you want to paste data.

7. Press Alt+space bar to display the Windows control menu for DOS applications. Figure 29.1 shows the control menu displayed. WordPerfect is ready to receive a posted table of text and numbers copied from the Excel screen.

8. Select Paste.

The data cut from Excel is pasted into the DOS application as long text strings with a carriage return at the end of each screen line. If you paste into a database entry field or into a 1-2-3 worksheet field, you may see that all lines will paste but only the last one is left on the screen. Each pasted line is replaced by the following line.

Copy and paste individual cells when transferring from Excel into a worksheet, database, or accounting entry field. If you have more data to transfer, you may want to use methods described later in this chapter.

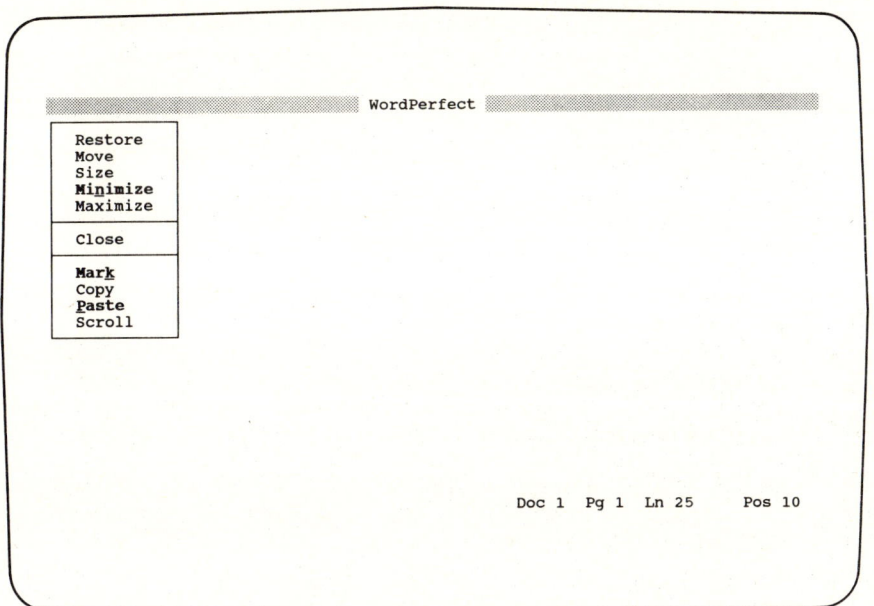

Fig. 29.1.
Control menu
for WordPerfect.

TIP

Cutting and Pasting between Large Applications

Applications do not have to remain open after you copy from them. If there is enough memory for both applications, copy from the first one, close it, run the second application, and paste to it.

To copy from a standard DOS application to Excel when the DOS application and Excel are running under Windows, follow these steps:

1. Activate the DOS application.

2. Press Alt+space bar to display the Control menu. Choose Mark.

3. Move the cursor to the upper left corner of where you want to copy. Hold Shift, and press the arrow keys to select (mark) the area you want to copy.

4. Press Alt+space bar to display the Control menu. Choose Copy to copy the "marked" data into the Windows Clipboard.

5. Press Alt+space bar, and choose Minimize to freeze the DOS application as an icon or quit the application using normal application procedures. (Quit if your computer has memory limitations.)

6. Open or start Excel.

7. Move to the upper left cell, where you want the data to appear, and choose Edit Paste. Each row of data pastes into its own cell.

To segment a row of data into multiple cells, use the **Data Parse** command described later in this chapter.

TIP

Converting Columns of Data into Cells in Excel

When you use Windows to copy data from a standard application into Excel, the data comes across as solid lines of text (and numbers) with a carriage return at the end of each line. When you paste this into Excel, each line goes into a single cell. Multiple lines fill down a column. As a result, multiple columns of data copied from 1-2-3 or an accounting screen fill a single column in Excel, with one line of original data in each cell.

You may need to place each piece of data in a row into its own cell, in which case you must tell Excel to segment each line and to put the contents into individual cells. Use the **Data Parse** command to show Excel how to divide the line. The next set of sections describes the **Data Parse** command.

Importing or Loading Data from Standard DOS Applications

Excel senses what type of file you are loading and automatically translates that file as necessary. All you need to do is open the file with **File Open**. There is no need for a special translation program. Excel saves files in the same format as the original unless you specify otherwise.

To change the format of a previously saved file, choose **File Save As** and select the **Options** >> button. You will see a list of available formats (covered in detail later in this chapter).

Importing or Loading Common File Types

Excel automatically recognizes a number of file types and translates the files automatically when the file loads. Excel recognizes normal Excel formats as well as ASCII text, comma-separated values (CSV), SYLK, WKS, WK1, DIF, DBF 2, or DBF 3. This means you can load files from programs such as 1-2-3 Release 1A or 2, Multiplan, dBASE II, dBASE III, or text files just as if you were loading a normal Excel worksheet.

To see non-Excel files in the File Open dialog box, you need to change the file extension in the File Name text box from *.XL* to *.*, and then press Enter.

When Excel loads a non-Excel file, it sets the File Save As options to reflect the original file type. That way when you save the file back to disk, the file is automatically saved back in the same format as the original. Select the Options >> button from the File Save As dialog box, and make a file type selection if you want to save the file in a format different from the original. (Remember, Normal is the Excel format.)

TIP

Excel As a File Translator

Excel makes loading and translating files easier than most applications. You can use its loading and saving options and the Data Parse command as an easier file translator than the one that comes with many other applications.

Importing ASCII Text Files into Excel

An ASCII text file is a medium for passing data between applications that do not understand each other's format. For example, you may want to load data into Excel from applications from which Excel is unable to use File Open to place the data in individual cells. Such applications might include: accounting programs, a non-dBASE database, or columnar data from a word-processing program.

Most applications can either print their files as ASCII text to a disk file (similar to printing to paper), or they have a file export facility that generates an ASCII text output. (For information on how to do this, check the index of your program's manual under the words *ASCII* or *text file*.)

TIP

Check Your Application for CSV Export

Check your application to see if it can export using comma-separated values (CSV). If so, export with CSV, and load the data into Excel. You may find that it saves you more work than using an ASCII text file as the intermediary. Before loading, change the file name extension to .CSV.

If you use a file export facility, check first to see if CSV is supported. If it is not supported, then select column-delimited ASCII as the export file type. To create a column-delimited ASCII file in an accounting or word-processing program, locate the data in nonoverlapping columns with data either left or right aligned. In a column-delimited file, each field is always located within the same character positions. For example, First Names may be assigned to character locations 12 through 24. (For information on creating an ASCII file, look in your application manual's index under *export*, *ASCII*, *text file*, or *column-delimited file*.)

You can see, edit, print, and save ASCII text files by opening them with the Windows Notepad as long as they are less than 16K in size. To see the file, from DOS use the following command:

TYPE *filename.ext*

If you have a parallel printer, you can print the file with

TYPE *filename.ext*>LPT1:

To import a text file into Excel, follow these steps:

1. Use **File Open** to switch to the correct directory.

2. Change the File Name text box pattern to *.*, and press Enter so that you can see all the file names.

3. Select the text file you want to import, and press Enter. Text files usually end with .PRN, .TXT, or .DOC. (Microsoft Word and MultiMate® files also end with .DOC.)

4. Choose OK or press Enter.

   A new Excel worksheet opens and lines of text fill the cells down column A. The screen may show what appears to be data in multiple cells across each row, but an examination of the formula bar shows that each line of text is stored in one cell in column A.

   Figure 29.2 shows a small ASCII text file that has just been imported. Notice the formula bar that reflects the contents of cell A1. Before proceeding, save the imported file as an Excel worksheet.

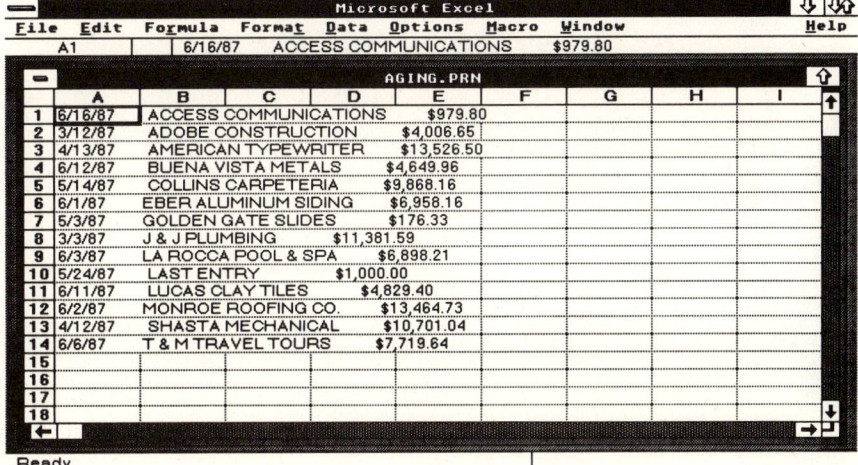

*Fig. 29.2.
Imported text
enters into a
new worksheet.*

5. Choose **File Save As**, select **Options** >>, select the **Normal** file
   format button, and press Enter (see fig. 29.3).

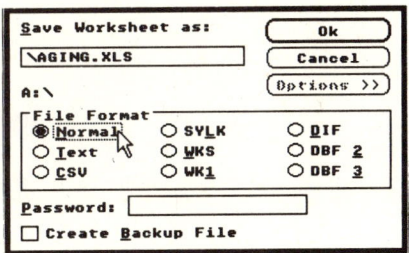

*Fig. 29.3. Save
Worksheet as
dialog box with
Options
extended.*

Notice that the text in figure 29.2 does not appear to be in the
column-delimited format (columns of data aligned by position).
This is because font 1 in Excel is usually a proportional font
where different characters have different widths.

You do not have to switch to a nonproportionally spaced font,
but it makes what you are doing much more apparent. Figure
29.4 shows how the imported data appears after changing to
Courier, an evenly spaced font.

6. Select the entire column A, and use **Format Font Fonts** >> to
   change the font to a nonproportionally spaced font, such as
   Courier if it is available. You may want to resave the file with this
   font.

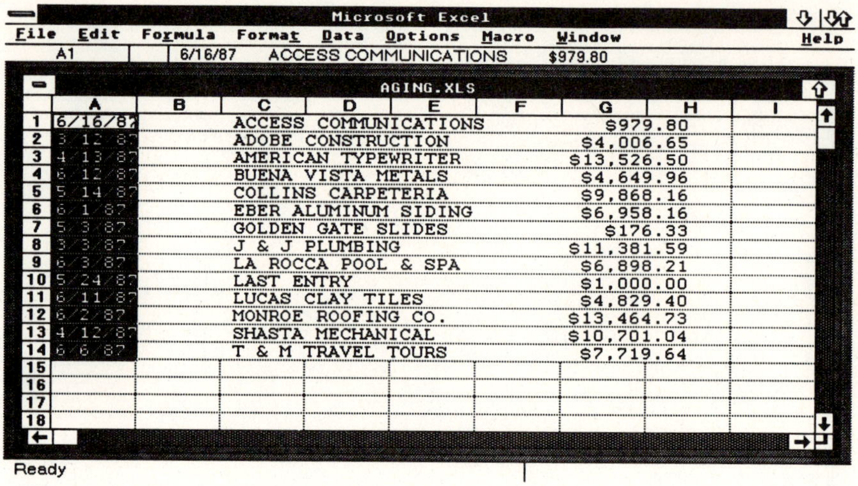

Fig. 29.4.
Imported text
converted to a
Courier font.

At this point, the text file has been imported into Excel, but each row of data is in a single cell in column A. The next section describes how to divide each row's contents into separate cells.

Parsing Long Text Lines into Cells

Imported text files appear as one row per cell in column A of a new worksheet. To be usable, you must *parse* or divide up the contents of each long line into segments. These segments must then be put into individual cells. To parse the column of text shown in figure 29.4, follow these steps:

1. Select the column of cells containing data.

   You are about to parse (divide into components) the single long line of text. This will put each part of the long line into an individual cell.

   Make sure the first cell in the selected range is a representative model for character spacing of the lines that follow it. If you have lines with different character spacing, you may have to parse each different line separately.

   Lines that have overlapping data from different columns will not parse correctly. Use the space bar to realign the lines so that they do not overlap, or re-create the original text file with spacing that does not overlap.

2. Choose **Data Parse**. The **Parse** Line dialog box displays the first selected row and shows a ruler of character locations (see fig. 29.5).

Fig. 29.5. Parse Line dialog box.

3. Select the **Guess** button. Excel attempts to put square brackets around the data you want parsed (divided into segments).

4. Enter or edit square brackets ([]) where necessary to enclose the data you want in the row.

The square brackets define the left and right edges of what will be placed in separate cells. Use the left and right arrows, left and right square bracket keys, Del, and Backspace to edit the **Parse** Line. Make sure the brackets are wide enough to include the full width of all characters in a field. For example, after selecting the **Guess** button, brackets appear around the first dollar amount as [$979.80]. Leaving this field with only seven characters between the brackets will leave out the leading parts of large numbers such as $13,526.50. The brackets must be edited to allow for three more leading spaces as shown in figure 29.6.

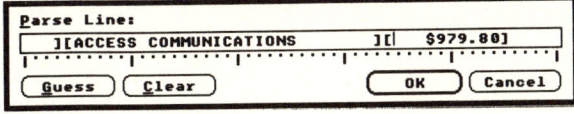

Fig. 29.6. The brackets have been edited to allow enough space in the field.

Figure 29.6 shows the right portion of the **Parse** Line dialog box set for a correct parse. Notice how the brackets are placed back-to-back (][) to ensure that all data is included. You can skip data by not including its character positions within brackets. Move to the extreme right in the parse box to see the full line of data.

5. Choose OK or press Enter.

Figure 29.7 shows the results of the parse in the selected range. The data in each line has been segmented between individual cells. Columns may need to be widened after parsing to show the full cell's content.

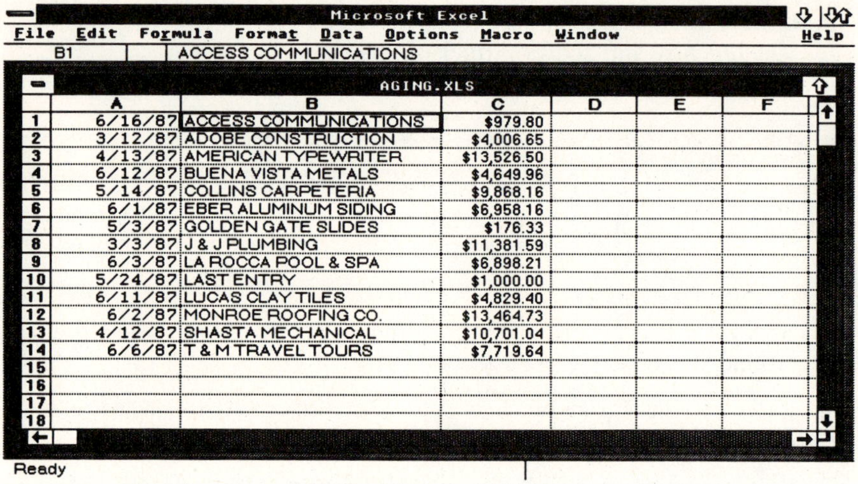
Microsoft Excel
File Edit Formula Format Data Options Macro Window Help
B1 ACCESS COMMUNICATIONS
AGING.XLS
A B C D E F
1 6/16/87 ACCESS COMMUNICATIONS $979.80
2 3/12/87 ADOBE CONSTRUCTION $4,006.65
3 4/13/87 AMERICAN TYPEWRITER $13,526.50
4 6/12/87 BUENA VISTA METALS $4,649.96
5 5/14/87 COLLINS CARPETERIA $9,868.16
6 6/1/87 EBER ALUMINUM SIDING $6,958.16
7 5/3/87 GOLDEN GATE SLIDES $176.33
8 3/3/87 J & J PLUMBING $11,381.59
9 6/3/87 LA ROCCA POOL & SPA $6,898.21
10 5/24/87 LAST ENTRY $1,000.00
11 6/11/87 LUCAS CLAY TILES $4,829.40
12 6/2/87 MONROE ROOFING CO. $13,464.73
13 4/12/87 SHASTA MECHANICAL $10,701.04
14 6/6/87 T & M TRAVEL TOURS $7,719.64
15
16
17
18
Ready

Fig. 29.7. Selected range with cells filled.

Widen the columns to see all the data in a cell. Always cross-check the serial date numbers between different applications; applications may use different starting dates in the century. (Use the Format Number General format to change a date into the serial date number.)

TIP

Parse Pasted Text To Get the Text in Individual Cells

Use the **Data Parse** command to parse lines of data pasted into Excel from other applications. When it is pasted, use the command to separate the data into individual cells.

Exporting Data

You can export data easily to the majority of applications using one of Excel's eight DOS application file formats. Most standard DOS applications can then translate from one of these formats into their own format.

Exporting or Saving in Non-Excel Format

To save Excel worksheets in a format for another application, follow these steps:

1. Choose **File Save As**. Type the file name in the text box. Do not add a file extension.

2. Select the **Options** button. The dialog box expands to display different file saving formats (see fig. 29.3).

3. Select the File Format button you want as the saved file's format.

4. Choose OK or press Enter.

The file formats Excel can load or save are shown in table 29.1. Many other applications use one of these eight formats as a translation medium.

Table 29.1
Excel File Formats

Type	Applications
Text	Most applications, especially word-processing programs or databases. Saves text and data as it appears on-screen. Columns are separated by tabs, and rows are separated by carriage returns. Cells containing commas or tabs are enclosed in double quotation marks.
CSV	Comma-Separated Values; databases. Same as text; however, columns are separated by commas. Cells containing commas are enclosed in double quotation marks. Save and retrieve CSV files with a .CSV file extension.
DIF	Data interchange format; common low-level worksheet media
SYLK	Multiplan, Microsoft Works
WKS	1-2-3 Release 1A, Microsoft Works
WK1	1-2-3 Release 2
DBF 2	dBASE II
DBF 3	dBASE III

NOTE

CSV File Retrieval

Comma-Separated Value files must have a .CSV extension, or Excel retrieves them as text files.

Exporting Text Files for Word-Processing and Database Programs

Text files are standard media for importing new information in word-processing and database programs. Saving an Excel worksheet as a text file allows you to retrieve the worksheet in your word-processing program so that it can be included in a report. Using a text file to pass a worksheet to a word-processing program allows you to pass multiple pages. (Copying and pasting as described at the beginning of this chapter is limited to what is on-screen.)

When you save in a text format for retrieval by another application, consider these tips:

- Set worksheet column widths wide enough to show all data in the widest column.

- If you are exporting to a database, format Excel dates to General number format, or put the month, day, and year in separate columns. Be aware that the database may use a different base for calculating serial dates. For a word-processing program, select the Excel date format to appear the way you want.

TIP

Exporting Dates

Some databases may have trouble reading dates in a text format. For these databases, use the MINUTE, HOUR, DAY, MONTH, and YEAR functions to break out pieces of the date into separate cells. Use a two-digit format, such as mm, dd, or hh, to format each cell.

TIP

Exporting to a Word-Processing Program

When you save an Excel file with the Text option, it inserts tabs between columns and quotation marks around anything containing a comma. This is designed to help databases; but when you know how, it can also help you align columns in word processing. To use the tabs to your advantage, follow these steps:

1. Save the data you want from Excel using the Text option.

2. Switch to Windows Write or your word-processing program.

3. Retrieve the text file created in step 1. (Your word-processing program may use a special command to retrieve text.)

4. When the document appears, column spacing will probably be incorrect. To fix this, set new tab settings to align the columns. Use decimal tabs to align numeric columns.

5. Remove unwanted quotation marks with your word-processing program's search-and-replace command. Search for a double quotation mark ("), and replace with nothing. The tabs will keep columns aligned even though you are deleting characters.

Macintosh Excel

Microsoft Excel with Windows and Macintosh Excel 1.04 and lower can transfer files using the SYLK format. This method transfers cell contents, names, calculation settings, and display settings. Some other settings do not transfer. Open the SYLK file using the importing and loading techniques described earlier in this chapter.

Later versions of Macintosh Excel are expected to have direct file compatibility with Excel for Windows.

If, after importing the Macintosh Excel worksheet, the dates are four years off, change Excel's date system with **Options Calculation**, and select 1904 **Date System**.

To transfer files between the Macintosh and your MS-DOS computer, use a null modem serial cable with serial adapters on either end for the PC serial port and the Macintosh modem (printer) port. (A null modem serial cable has wires from pins 2 and 3 on the Macintosh end connected in reverse order to pins 3 and 2 on the PC end. A standard serial cable does not work. Most computer shops can have them made up for under $30.)

You will also need PC and Macintosh communications software. Some of the following communications applications translate numerous file types between the PC and Macintosh:

MacLink Plus
DataViz
16 Windfield St.
Norwalk, CT 06855

PC to Mac and Back!
PC Quik-Art
394 S. Milledge Ave., Ste 200
Athens, GA 30606

Dayna FT100
Dayna Communications Inc.
50 S. Main St., Ste 530
Salt Lake City, UT 84144

30

Making the Switch from 1-2-3 to Excel

If you use 1-2-3, you can make the transition to Excel smoothly and continue to work in a 1-2-3 office. Excel automatically loads and saves 1-2-3 worksheets, translates 1-2-3 macros, and provides a help file for 1-2-3 users.

Excel and 1-2-3

If you are already familiar with 1-2-3, you will find Excel easy to learn for a number of reasons:

- Worksheet concepts such as menu selection, cell addressing, range selection, formula entry, and database operation are the same for both Excel and 1-2-3.

- Excel reads and writes 1-2-3 Release 1A and 2 files. Graphs in 1-2-3 worksheets are converted, but Excel charts are not converted to Lotus graphs. (1-2-3 .PIC files are not "loadable.")

- Excel has 1-2-3 help facilities on-line. Type a 1-2-3 command, and the help facility shows you how to do the same thing in Excel.

- Excel translates the majority of 1-2-3 macros with the 1-2-3 Macro Translator. Excel's macro recorder makes new macros easy to create.

- Both Excel and 1-2-3 use eight function keys in the same way.

- Excel has an undo command for typing and editing mistakes.

- Excel menus are easier to browse through and have more understandable titles.

- Excel's pop-up dialog boxes show current defaults and selection options. You do not have to remember arcane codes, such as printer control codes.

- Excel automatically generates a database form for entering, editing, deleting, and searching data.

- All Excel functions, names, and macro formulas can be selected from a scrolling list and pasted (with prompts for arguments) into formulas.

If you are already familiar with 1-2-3, the quickest way to learn Excel is to work through the Quick Starts at the beginning of each section of the book. The Quick Starts help you gain proficiency and learn the most important concepts quickly. You should also watch for 1-2-3 Tip boxes throughout the book. These explain how Excel has solved a problem that plagued 1-2-3 users, a different way of doing things, or a significant performance improvement.

Excel Help for 1-2-3 Users

Excel helps you translate 1-2-3 commands into their Excel equivalents. To use this 1-2-3-to-Excel help facility, follow these steps:

1. Choose the Help Lotus 1-2-3 command. A 1-2-3 Help box appears (see fig. 30.1).

   Mouse: Move the pointer to the Help menu item, and click the mouse button. Move the pointer to the Help command in the pull-down menu, and click the mouse button again. (The left mouse button is the default button.)

   Keyboard: Press Alt to activate the menu bar, then press H, the underlined letter in Help. When the pull-down menu appears, press L, the underlined letter in Lotus 1-2-3. (You don't have to wait for the menu to appear if you know what you want.)

Fig. 30.1. Lotus 1-2-3 Help box.

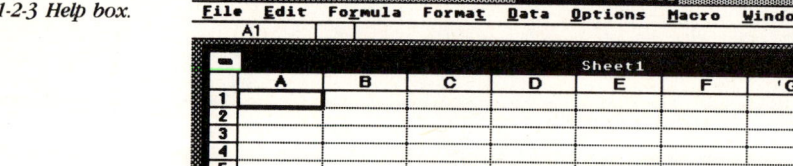

For Help on dialog settings, press F1

2. Type the 1-2-3 command keystrokes, such as /fs, in the text box.

3. Choose the OK button or press Enter.

Excel displays a help window like that shown in figure 30.2 that gives information about the equivalent command in Excel. Press the up- or down-arrow keys or PgUp and PgDn to move through the help window. Click on the scroll bar to scroll with the mouse. Press Esc to close the help window.

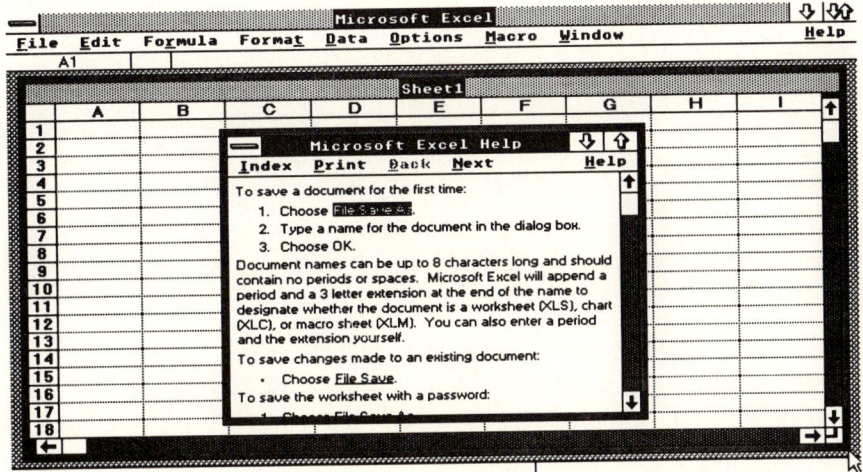

Fig. 30.2. Help window for Excel command corresponding to Lotus 1-2-3 command /fs.

If you type just the first word from a 1-2-3 command, such as *file*, you will be taken to the appropriate area of the Help menu. Use the Tab and Enter keys to select the exact command from the menu. Press Esc to return to the worksheet.

Tips on Learning Excel for 1-2-3 Users

You can operate Excel almost any way you want. It is not a mouse-only application. You can select from an Excel menu with the arrow keys, by touch typing, by pointing and clicking with a mouse pointer, or by pressing Ctrl+key combinations. In addition, you can record macros and assign Ctrl+key combinations to them. Excel has a mode of operation suited for everyone from the newest beginner to the most expert computer user.

The following overview of Excel contains tips for using the keyboard. If you are using a mouse, you should run through Chapter 4, "Worksheet Quick Start," to cover the same information.

Following Excel Procedures

Excel follows a standard procedure for changing a worksheet, chart, or macro. Use these same steps for nearly all commands:

1. Select the cell, range, or chart object to be selected.

2. Choose a command from a pull-down menu, or press a shortcut key.

3. Respond to any dialog box that asks you to select options.

Moving and Selecting Cells and Ranges

To move the active cell, use the arrow keys, page keys, or Ctrl+arrow. An alternate method is to press the Goto key, F5, enter a location, and press Enter.

For commands such as formatting, editing, entering data, or setting ranges, you must select the cell or range of cells to be affected. Follow these steps:

1. Move to one corner of the rectangular range you want selected.

2. Hold down the Shift key, and move to the opposite corner of the range; or click the pointer at the opposite corner of the range.

3. Make your menu selection.

You can select multiple ranges simultaneously with the ADD key, Shift+F8.

Selecting Commands from Menus

Excel commands are found on menus you pull down from the menu bar at the top of the screen. The lower left corner of the screen is the status bar where explanations of commands or prompts for actions appear.

In the menu bar and pull-down menus, some letters are underlined. These underlined letters can be used to select that menu or command. Some commands are followed by an ellipsis (. . .) to indicate that when you choose the command, a dialog box appears, requesting more information.

Activate the menu bar by pressing either the slash key (/) or the Alt key. Deactivate the menu or dialog box by pressing Esc. The Alt key is the standard menu activation key in Windows applications. Excel also accepts the slash key to make the transition for 1-2-3 users easier.

To choose a command:

1. Press / or Alt to activate the menu.

2. Press the underlined letter to select a menu item.

3. Press the underlined letter of the command you want, or press the up- or down-arrow keys until you have highlighted the correct command, and press Enter (see fig. 30.3).

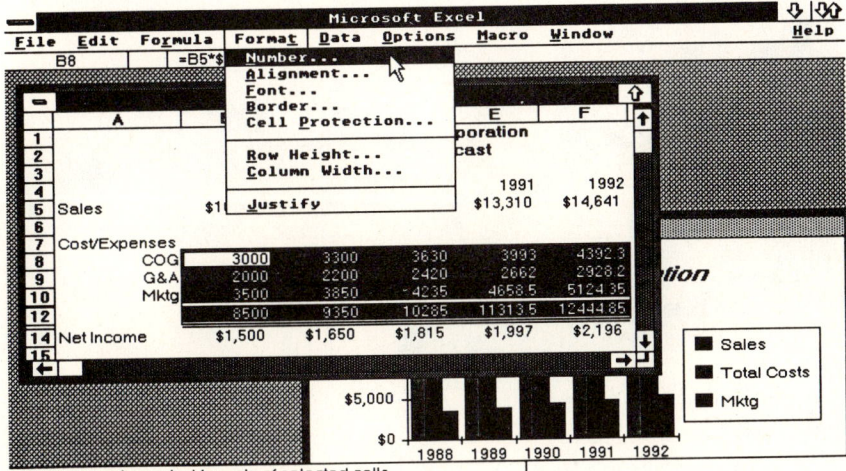

Fig. 30.3. Pull-down menu with highlighted command.

To help learn what each command does, use the arrow keys to highlight a menu heading or command, then check the message in the Status bar at the bottom left of the screen.

1-2-3 TIP

A Learning Tip: 1-2-3 to Excel

If you have used 1-2-3 for a considerable length of time, your mind is programmed for certain keystroke sequences. As you unlearn 1-2-3 keystrokes and learn Excel keystrokes, you may experience some frustration when 1-2-3 keystrokes creep back into use.

One of the best ways to avoid falling back to the old keystroke sequences is to avoid "triggers" that cause the old sequences to start. In this case, the trigger is the slash key (/), which can be used to activate Excel menus. Your mind associates the slash key as the lead key into all the 1-2-3 sequences. Prevent this association by using Alt to activate the Excel menu. (The Alt key is used throughout the book.)

Selecting from Dialog Boxes

Some Excel commands need additional information. Rather than use up to five layers of menus to gather this additional information, Excel displays a single dialog box (see fig. 30.4). The dialog box lets you immediately see all the default settings and your available options. You can change just what you need to change.

Fig. 30.4. Dialog box for saving files in different formats.

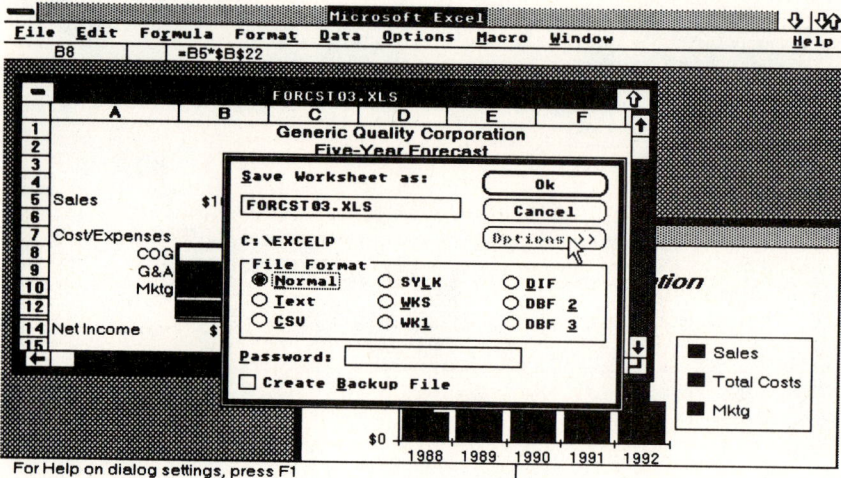

Press Alt+underlined letter to select the option or text entry you want to change. Click the mouse pointer on an option or text entry location to select it.

You can turn multiple square check boxes on or off by selecting the ones you want to change. You can only select one option from among a group of round option buttons.

Complete a dialog box by clicking OK or pressing Enter. Click on Cancel or press Esc to back out of the command.

Using Formulas

Begin formulas with a plus sign (+) or an equal sign (=).

Do not type @ before functions. Paste functions and their arguments by choosing Formula Paste Function and selecting the Argument box. Use the down-arrow key or press the first letter of the function to scroll to the function in the list box, then press Enter.

Press the Edit key, F2, to edit the formula in the active cell. Point to enter cell references the same way you would in 1-2-3.

Press the Absolute reference key, F4, to cycle between absolute and relative references while entering or editing a cell reference.

Using the Function Keys

Many of the Excel function keys are the same as those in 1-2-3. Excel has additional function keys and shortcut keys created by holding down Shift, Ctrl, or Alt as you press the function key. Some of the Excel function keys appear in table 30.1. More Ctrl and Alt key combinations are listed in the Quick Reference Card.

Table 30.1
A Partial List of Excel and 1-2-3 Function Keys

Function key	1-2-3	Excel
F1	Help	Help
Shift+F1		Context Help
F2	Edit	Edit Formula Bar
Shift+F2		Edit Cell Note
F3	Name	Paste Name
Shift+F3		Paste Function (Excel displays file names and range names in a scrolling window.)
F4	Absolute	Absolute Reference (cycles)
F5	Goto	Goto
Shift+F5		Formula Find (find cell with specified contents)
F6	Window	Next Pane
Shift+F6		Previous Pane (Excel uses next and previous because Excel can have up to four window panes.)
F7	Query	Formula Find Next

Function key	1-2-3	Excel
Shift+F7		Formula Find Previous (Formula Find searches worksheet values and formulas to find your request.)
F8	Table	Extend selected cells
Shift+F8		Add selected cells (Select multiple, noncontiguous ranges.)
F9	Calc	Calculate Now (all worksheets)
Shift+F9		Calculate Document (active worksheet only.)
F10	Graph	Activates menu bar.
F11		New Chart
Shift+F11		New Worksheet
F12		File Save As
Shift+F12		File Save

F8 and F10 differ from 1-2-3. Excel recalculates tables automatically, so there is no need for the F8 key to calculate tables. (Automatic table calculation can be toggled on or off through the menu. Excel's F8 enables you to select multiple ranges at the same time.) The Graph key, F10, is unnecessary in Excel because you can display graphs simultaneously with their supporting worksheets.

Creating Macros

Another feature that speeds learning Excel and increases proficiency is the macro recorder. Whether or not you learned 1-2-3 macros, you can quickly record your own macros in Excel. Excel records your keystrokes on a separate macro sheet. You can play this "macro recording" back exactly as created, or you can edit it.

Of course, you can also write macros manually. Excel makes this easy by allowing you to choose macro commands and their argument names from lists. You don't have to memorize commands and arguments. Excel's macro language has over 355 commands. Macros also allow custom menu and dialog boxes.

In Excel, you also can write function macros that work the same as built-in worksheet functions. You can use these function macros just as though they came with Excel.

Excel macros occupy their own sheets, so you can use them with any worksheet, chart, or database.

Additional Excel Features

The following list shows some of the additional features and functions available in Excel.

1. Data Entry

   - The cursor automatically wraps around in selected entry area.

   - Excel automatically formats a cell to match the format used when you type a date. For example:

     8/8/88

   - Numbers can be entered for automatic formatting. For example:

     $4,500.36

   - Data is automatically formatted using typed formats that match one of Excel's recognized formats.

2. Editing Formulas or Text

   - Enter cell references by pointing even during editing.

   - Functions and their arguments can be pasted into formulas, so you do not have to remember the correct syntax.

   - You can paste names into formulas.

   - You can undo typing, editing mistakes, and many commands with Edit Undo.

   - You can search and replace terms in formulas with Formula Replace.

3. Debugging and Documenting

   - "Pop-up" notes can be tagged onto cells with Formula Note.

- Formulas, terms, or errors can be found with Formula Find or Formula Select Special.

- You can find dependent and precedent cells to a formula with Formula Select Special.

- Excel displays error values beyond 1-2-3's NA and ERR:

  #N/A
  #VALUE!
  #DIV/0!
  #NAME?
  #NULL!
  #NUM!
  #REF!

4. Formatting

- You can format each cell with a unique font, size, style, and color.

- Up to four character fonts can be used per worksheet.

- You can change row heights as well as column widths. (You can change multiple rows or columns simultaneously.)

- You can hide worksheets, rows, columns, or cells.

- Custom number and date formats can be created in addition to 22 predefined number and date formats.

- You can align numbers, dates, or text.

- You can switch number, currency, and date formats to many international styles.

5. Printing

- You can preview documents on-screen to see exactly how they will appear on paper.

- You can print vertically or horizontally.

- With Excel, you can print "annual report quality" output.

- You can create presentation quality graphics.

- Charts and worksheets can be merged into other Windows programs.

- Print spooling enables you to continue work as multiple jobs print.

6. Worksheet Functions

   - Excel has 131 built-in functions.

   - You can use advanced functions such as WEEKDAY, MIRR (Modified Internal Rate of Return), and many array and text functions.

   - Formulas and values can be named so that you can use them by name.

   - You can create custom macro functions that work the same as built-in functions.

7. Database

   - Data Form can automatically generate a data entry, edit, and search form.

   - Formats automatically copy into inserted database rows.

   - You do not "blow up" a range when a row at the end of a database range is deleted.

   - You can create relational database links with the LOOKUP function and linked databases.

8. Charts

   - You select from 44 predefined chart formats.

   - Charts can be customized with features such as patterns, shading, fonts, overlay charts, hi-lo points, floating text, scaling, arrows, and more.

   - You print directly from screen without switching to another program.

9. Linking and Consolidating Worksheets

   - You can create data links between worksheets, databases, and charts.

   - You can use simple data links to worksheets even when the linked worksheet is not open on the screen but is a file on disk or in the network.

   - You can use complex data links between open worksheets.

   - You can link data to other Windows applications via Dynamic Data Exchange (DDE).

10. Calculation

   - Worksheets can be recalculated faster because only formulas dependent on the change are recalculated.

   - Tables can be recalculated automatically when desired.

   - Worksheets can calculate in the background as you continue to work.

   - You can use iterative calculation to find solutions within limits you set.

11. Windowing

   - Four panes are available on one window.

   - Multiple windows can be open on any worksheet.

   - Multiple worksheets or charts can be open and visible at the same time.

   - Data between multiple worksheets and charts can be linked.

12. Macros

   - The macro recorder records keystrokes and menu selections.

   - Custom worksheet functions can be created with macros.

   - You can use 355 macro commands for writing extensive macros.

   - Macros are on separate sheets, so the macros are usable by any worksheet or chart.

   - With macros, you can create custom menus and dialog boxes.

   - The extensive macro language can communicate with and control other Windows applications.

13. Windows Environment

   - You can cut and paste text and numbers to and from standard DOS applications.

   - You can cut and paste text, numbers, or graphics to and from other Windows applications.

   - You can use "real time" data links with other Windows applications.

Using Excel in a 1-2-3 Workplace

Excel coexists with 1-2-3 in many workplaces. Excel reads and writes Release 1A and Release 2 files and translates the majority of macros, so you can read files from coworkers, enter new data, or make changes and save them back to disk in 1-2-3 format.

TIP

Use Excel To Make 1-2-3 Output Appear More Professional

If your office has older equipment such as 8088- and 8086-based computers that are unable to run Excel, you may want to continue some work with 1-2-3. Use Excel to do the printing for these 1-2-3 files when you need finished worksheets that appear professionally formatted and even typeset. Because Excel also reads the 1-2-3 graphs attached to a worksheet, it is an easy matter to use Excel's chart customizing features to create and print high quality, professional-appearing charts that are impossible to create in 1-2-3 Releases 1A and 2 alone.

Loading and Saving 1-2-3 Files

Loading and saving 1-2-3 files is easy. There are differences between the applications, however, that can cause an alert box to be displayed that describes the discrepancy.

Loading 1-2-3 Worksheet Files

To load a 1-2-3 worksheet file, follow these steps:

1. Choose the **File Open** command.

2. Select the text box, and edit the file pattern to appear as *.WK?.

Figure 30.5 shows the Open File dialog box with the text box edited to list files ending with either .WK1 or .WKS. The *.WK? file pattern displays either Release 1A or Release 2 files.

3. Choose the **Open** button, or press Enter to list the files you want.

4. Select the **Files** list box by pressing Alt+F. Press the up- or down-arrow key to highlight the file name of the file you want opened.

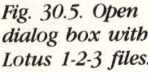

Fig. 30.5. Open dialog box with Lotus 1-2-3 files.

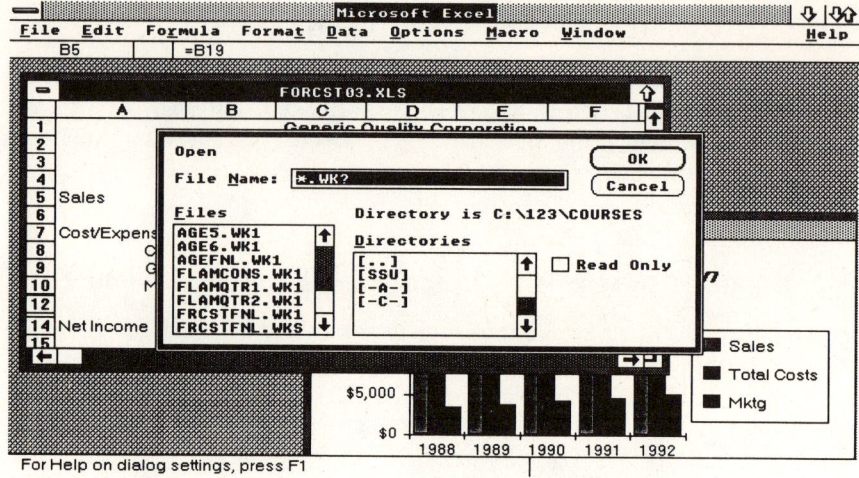

5. Choose the **O**pen button or press Enter.

   The Lotus file you selected is retrieved and automatically translated. If this file contains macros, you need to refer to the 1-2-3 macro translation section later in this chapter. If Excel encounters a formula it cannot translate, Excel displays a box containing the reference for that formula.

Saving Excel Worksheets As 1-2-3 Files

To save Excel worksheets as 1-2-3 files, follow these steps:

1. Choose **F**ile Save **A**s, and type the file name in the text box. Do not add a file extension.

2. Select the **O**ptions button. The dialog box expands as shown in figure 30.6 to display different file saving formats.

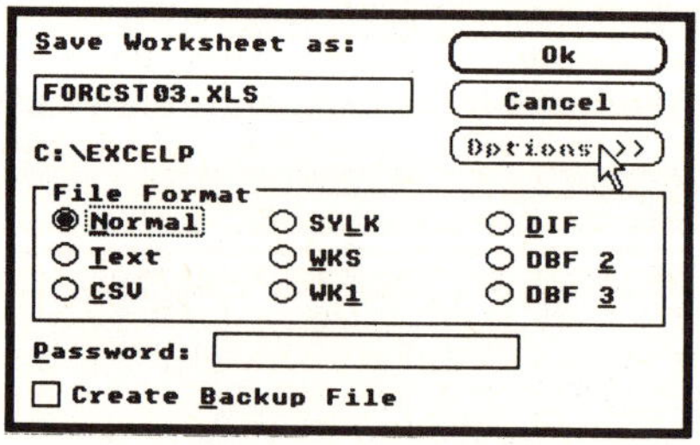

Fig. 30.6. File Save As with dialog box expanded to show file formats used when saving.

3. Select the **WKS** button for 1-2-3 Release 1A, or the **WK1** button for 1-2-3 Release 2.

   If you retrieved the worksheet from a Lotus file, either the WKS or WK1 buttons will have already been selected. Excel automatically saves a file back to disk in the same format as the original.

4. Choose OK or press Enter.

If your worksheet used functions that cannot be converted, then Excel displays an alert box when that cell is converted and uses only the value produced by the formula in the target worksheet.

Translation Differences: Excel to 1-2-3 and Back

Excel automatically converts 1-2-3 worksheets into Excel and saves them back in 1-2-3 format. A few 1-2-3 worksheet characteristics do not convert. When converting from an original Excel worksheet into 1-2-3, be sure to remember that Excel has more capabilities than 1-2-3. Those extra features and functions cannot be converted to 1-2-3.

Excel does a good job of converting formats, cell protection, formulas, names, and 1-2-3 graphs. However, some characteristics, such as windowing, cannot be converted because of their major differences.

If any 1-2-3 function or formula does not translate into Excel, a dialog box appears showing the cell location of the errant formula. Choose the Yes button if you want to continue seeing these messages. Choose the No button if you want to convert the 1-2-3 worksheet without the messages. Cells containing formulas that do not convert will contain the value of the original formula.

Data tables do not translate between either application. Formulas and values in the left column and top row of the tables remain in their original cells, but the Data Table commands for both applications must be reissued. Excel data tables constantly recalculate and are actually formulas, whereas 1-2-3 tables are generated with the /Data Table command and must be recalculated by pressing a key. (The 1-2-3 database extract range does not convert to Excel. Excel uses the currently selected range as the extract range.)

Hidden cells in Excel will be shown when converted to 1-2-3. Excel's seven error values translate into ERR and NA values in 1-2-3 as appropriate.

Excel worksheets can be much larger than 1-2-3, so Excel rows beyond 2,048 and 8,192 do not translate to 1-2-3 Releases 1A or 2, respectively. 1-2-3 Releases 1A and 2 cannot handle references to other worksheets, so external references (links) to other worksheets do not translate. 1-2-3 cannot handle multiple simultaneous ranges, range operators (intersect, range, and union), or array formulas, so these features are not converted from Excel.

Excel loads 1-2-3 graphs that are active in the worksheet or are named with the /Graph Name command. Each named graph appears in its own window. Excel does not save Excel charts as Lotus 1-2-3 graphs because Excel's charts have more features and formats. Excel cannot read or translate Lotus PrintGraph files, .PIC files that have been saved for printing with PGRAPH.

Translating 1-2-3 Macros

Excel's Macro Translation Assistant converts the majority of 1-2-3 macros into Excel macros. Those 1-2-3 macro items that do not translate can be shown so that you can manually make adjustments.

To get help about translating a 1-2-3 macro, choose the Help Index command. When the index of topics appears, press Tab until Macro Translation Assistant is selected, then press Enter. Press F1 (Help) or Esc to return to the sheet.

The Macro Translation Assistant help file includes information on setting aside 128K of expanded memory for use by the Macro Translator. (You must edit the WIN.INI text file to change *Emm Reserved = 0* to *Emm Reserved = 128* or some higher number. Do this only if your computer has expanded memory.)

TIP

Use Excel's Macro Recorder To Create New Macros

In some cases, you can create better macros quickly by using Excel's macro recorder instead of translating 1-2-3 macros.

Run through Chapter 25, "Macro Quick Start," to learn how easy it is to create macros in Excel.

To translate a 1-2-3 macro into Excel, follow these steps:

1. Choose File Open, and open the 1-2-3 worksheet containing the macros. Use a file extension of *.WK? to see Lotus files in the Files box.

2. Select the Control menu by pressing Alt+space bar. Choose Run by pressing U.

3. Select the Macro Translator, and choose OK or press Enter.

4. Choose the Translate Lotus 1-2-3 command. Select the document containing the macros from the dialog box, and choose OK or press Enter.

5. Select one or more macros to be translated from the list box in the dialog box. Unselect the Verbose box if you do not want the original Lotus macro displayed next to the translation.

6. Choose OK or press Enter.

1-2-3 macros are translated from the Excel worksheet and put on their own macro sheet. With the Verbose check box selected, the 1-2-3 macro is placed above the converted equivalent and appears in italics.

Excel places comments adjacent to the macro cell being described when a translation is not exact. The meaning of comments such as

Inexact Translation: Sets All Column Widths

is explained in **Help Index Macro Translation Assistant Translation Comments.**

Press Esc to stop translation. Errors are displayed in an alert box during translation. When translation is complete, you are asked if you want to close the translation assistant. Choose Yes, and you are given a chance to run the translated macro.

> **NOTE**
>
> ### Macros Translate into Excel but Not into 1-2-3
>
> Excel's macro language is much more extensive than the 1-2-3 language. It is the equivalent of a programming language such as BASIC. Because of all this extra capability, Excel macros cannot be reduced to the commands available in 1-2-3.

The Macro Translation Assistant requires a lot of memory, so it is best to close Help windows and unnecessary documents while running it. If you are running in Windows and have other applications open, you may want to close those applications to release more memory. Large 1-2-3 macros may require expanded memory.

For information on translating 1-2-3 macros, choose **Help Index**, and select **Macro Translation Assistant.**

From Here . . .

After we ... ...ficult to return to using Lo... ...and dialog boxes, extensiv... ...ddictive. What you will see ... ...users who switch to Exce... ...user. Intermediate 1-2-3 u... ...rt 1-2-3 user's pro-ductivi... ...Excel will be able to do t... ...ustom applications, links t... ...ndows applications. Of cou... ...earning how to use softwa...

If you... ...little strange to use at firs... ...ople is that they first dislike... ...for selecting ranges, enhar... ...don't have to leave the ke... ...ow-key control, touch typin... ...is most efficient for the job.

If you have read this chapter before other chapters in the book, you should go back to Chapter 2, "Windows Quick Start," and learn the fundamental concepts that control all applications running under Windows. Then take the half-hour or so for the hands-on Worksheet Quick Start in Chapter 4. This Quick Start guides you through building a forecasting worksheet. As you go through the Quick Starts, remember to use the Help Lotus 1-2-3 command for additional information.

One last caution about minds in transition. When you learn new patterns (as in Excel keystrokes) that are similar to old patterns (as in Lotus 1-2-3 key-strokes), your fingers may get confused. If you can touch type your way through all the 1-2-3 menus, you may have more "finger confusion" during the learning process than a beginning 1-2-3 user. To help reduce this confusion, press the Alt key to activate the menu bar rather than the slash key (/), which also activates the menu bar. In addition, read the command and option names as you look for the underlined letter to press. This not only reduces your keystroke errors but also helps you learn where different commands are located. In a few hours, you should be comfortable with Excel; and in two weeks, you will be doing far more with Excel than you could ever do with Lotus 1-2-3.

A

Table of Tips, Notes, and 1-2-3 Tips

689

6   Operating Worksheets

7 Entering and Editing Worksheet Data

8 Formatting Worksheets

9 Using Functions in Worksheets

Notes

1-2-3 Tips

10 Using Multiple Windows and Linking Worksheets

Tips

11   Building Advanced Worksheets

12   Printing Worksheets

Notes

13 Troubleshooting Worksheets

Tips

Part III
Excel Charts

14 Chart Quick Start

Tips

15 Creating and Enhancing Charts

Tips

16 Building Advanced Charts

Part IV
Excel Databases

18 Database Quick Start

20 Entering and Sorting Data

21 Finding and Editing Data

22   Extracting and Maintaining Data

23   Building Advanced Databases

Part V
Excel Macros

25 Macro Quick Start

26 Building Command and Function Macros

Notes

B

Macro Directory

This appendix has two sections. The first section organizes and lists all Excel macros by type. The second section gives the syntax (grammar), the menu command if there is an equivalent, and the action the macro performs or the result it returns.

The Excel macro language is so extensive that not all the macro functions can be covered in depth in *Using Excel: IBM Version*. This appendix describes important macro functions that can give you the most productivity with the least amount of programming knowledge. All Excel commands have been listed so that you can see the full power available.

Many macro functions are the equivalent of Excel menu commands or worksheet functions. To learn the most about these macros, read the menu command and worksheet descriptions as well as the macro function descriptions.

When you use a macro function, pay particular attention to its syntax or structure. You must follow the syntax exactly to get the desired results. Commas are especially important in separating arguments. Use periods to separate parts of a macro name, such as FILE.DELETE; and enclose in quotation marks text arguments, such as window names, R1C1 references, and messages.

Macro Functions Listed by Type

There are two fundamental types of macros: command macros, which take actions, and function macros, which make calculations but do not take action.

Command macros can use any type of macro function except ARGUMENT and RESULT. Command macros can take actions, do calculations, and make decisions. Function macros are limited to macros that do not perform actions. Both types of macros can include worksheet functions.

Before jumping into the macro function descriptions, you may want to read through the lists that group macro functions by the type of tasks they perform. The lists may help you keep the functions organized in your mind. You may also refer to the lists when you know what you want to do, but do not know which macro function to use.

Menu Equivalent Commands

Some macro functions perform the same commands as the commands you choose from menus. These functions appear frequently in macros you record.

Some Excel commands prompt you for more information by displaying a dialog box that the user fills in. The equivalent macro function gets that information in two ways. The macro can receive the information from the macro arguments (variables inside parentheses), or the macro can display the dialog box and let the user select options and enter values.

An example of this is the Format Border command. The macro equivalent of this command is

   BORDER(*outline,left,right,top,bottom,shade*)

With this macro function, you identify the options that are selected in the dialog box by entering TRUE for the appropriate arguments. A FALSE entry turns off an option's selection. For example:

   BORDER(FALSE,TRUE,TRUE,FALSE,TRUE,TRUE)

creates borders on the left, right, and bottom sides of the selected range, and shades the cells. Arguments in some macro functions accept cell references, formulas, logical values, numbers, or text in quotation marks.

The following lists of commands and their associated macro functions can help you locate the correct macro functions for nearly any use. After finding the function name, refer to the directory description and syntax.

Excel Control Commands

These macro functions execute the commands found on the Application Control menu (Alt+space bar).

Maximize	APP.MAXIMIZE
Minimize	APP.MINIMIZE
Move	APP.MOVE
Restore	APP.RESTORE
Run	none
Size	APP.SIZE
Close	QUIT

Document Control Commands

These macro functions execute the same commands you execute from the Document Control menu (Alt+hyphen).

Close	CLOSE
Maximize	FULL(TRUE)
Move	MOVE
Restore	FULL(FALSE)
Size	SIZE
Split	SPLIT

File Menu Commands

These macro functions execute the same commands you execute from the File menu.

File Close	FILE.CLOSE
File Delete	FILE.DELETE
File Exit	QUIT
File Links	OPEN.LINKS
File New	NEW
File Open	OPEN
File Page Setup	PAGE.SETUP
File Print	PRINT
File Printer Setup	PRINTER.SETUP
File Save	SAVE
File Save As	SAVE.AS
File Save Workspace	SAVE.WORKSPACE

Edit Menu Commands

These macro functions execute the same commands you execute from the Edit menu.

Edit Clear	CLEAR
Edit Copy	COPY
Edit Copy Picture	COPY.PICTURE
Edit Cut	CUT
Edit Delete	EDIT.DELETE
Edit Fill Down	FILL.DOWN
Edit Fill Up (w)	FILL.UP
Edit Fill Right	FILL.RIGHT
Edit Fill Left (h)	FILL.LEFT

Edit Insert	INSERT
Edit Paste	PASTE
Edit Paste Link	PASTE.LINK
Edit Paste Special	PASTE.SPECIAL
Edit Undo	UNDO

Formula Menu Commands

These macro functions execute the commands found on the Formula menu.

Formula Apply Names	APPLY.NAMES
Formula Create Names	CREATE.NAMES
Formula Define Names	DEFINE.NAME
Formula Delete Names	DELETE.NAME
Formula Find	FORMULA.FIND
Formula Goto	FORMULA.GOTO
Formula Note	NOTE
Formula Paste Name	LIST.NAMES
Formula Replace	FORMULA.REPLACE
Formula Select Special	SELECT.SPECIAL
Formula Note	NOTE

Format Menu Commands

These macro functions execute the commands found on the Format menu.

Format Alignment	ALIGNMENT
Format Border	BORDER
Format Cell Protection	CELL.PROTECTION
Format Column Width	COLUMN.WIDTH
Format Font	FORMAT.FONT
Format Font	REPLACE.FONT
Format Justify	JUSTIFY
Format Legend	FORMAT.LEGEND
Format Main Chart	MAIN.CHART
Format Move	FORMAT.MOVE
Format Number	FORMAT.NUMBER
Format Overlay	OVERLAY
Format Patterns	PATTERNS
Format Row Height	ROW.HEIGHT
Format Scale	SCALE
Format Size	FORMAT.SIZE
Format Text	FORMAT.TEXT

Data Menu Commands

These macro functions execute the commands found on the Data menu.

Data Delete	DATA.DELETE
Data Exit Find	DATA.FIND
Data Extract	EXTRACT
Data Find	DATA.FIND
Data Form	DATA.FORM
Data Parse	PARSE
Data Series	DATA.SERIES
Data Set Criteria	SET.CRITERIA
Data Set Database	SET.DATABASE
Data Sort	SORT
Data Table	TABLE

Options Menu Commands

These macro functions execute the commands found on the Options menu.

Options Calculate Now	CALCULATE.NOW
Options Calculation	CALCULATION
Options Display	DISPLAY
Options Freeze Display	FREEZE.PANES
Options Full Menus	SHORT.MENUS
Options Protect Document	PROTECT.DOCUMENT
Options Remove Page Break	REMOVE.PAGE.BREAK
Options Set Page Break	SET.PAGE.BREAK
Options Set Print Area	SET.PRINT.AREA
Options Set Print Titles	SET.PRINT.TITLES
Options Short Menus	SHORT.MENUS
Options Unfreeze Panes	FREEZE.PANES
Options Unprotect Document	PROTECT.DOCUMENT
Options Workspace	WORKSPACE

Window Menu Commands

These macro functions execute the commands found on the Window menu.

Window #document	ACTIVATE
Window Arrange All	ARRANGE.ALL
Window Hide	HIDE
Window New Window	NEW.WINDOW
Window Show Info/Document	SHOW.INFO
Window Unhide	UNHIDE

Chart Menu Commands

These macro functions execute the commands found on the Chart menu.

Chart Add Arrow	ADD.ARROW
Chart Add Overlay	ADD.OVERLAY
Chart Add Legend	LEGEND
Chart Attach Text	ATTACH.TEXT
Chart Axes	AXES
Chart Calculate Document	CALCULATE.DOCUMENT
Chart Calculate Now	CALCULATE.NOW
Chart Delete Arrow	DELETE.ARROW
Chart Delete Legend	DELETE.LEGEND
Chart Delete Overlay	DELETE.OVERLAY
Chart Gridlines	GRIDLINES
Chart Protect Document	PROTECT.DOCUMENT
Chart Select Chart	SELECT
Chart Select Plot Area	SELECT.PLOT.AREA

Gallery and Chart Format Commands

These macro functions execute the commands found on the Gallery and Chart Format menus.

Gallery Area	GALLERY.AREA
Gallery Bar	GALLERY.BAR
Gallery Column	GALLERY.COLUMN
Gallery Combination	COMBINATION
Gallery Line	GALLERY.LINE
Gallery Pie	GALLERY.PIE
Gallery Preferred	PREFERRED
Gallery Scatter	GALLERY.SCATTER
Gallery Set Preferred	SET.PREFERRED
Format Font	FORMAT.FONT
Format Legend	FORMAT.LEGEND
Format Main Chart	MAIN.CHART.TYPE
Format Move	FORMAT.MOVE
Format Overlay	OVERLAY
Format Patterns	PATTERNS
Format Size	FORMAT.SIZE
Format Text	FORMAT.TEXT

Macro Menu Commands

This macro function executes the **Macro Run** command from the Macro menu.

Macro Run   RUN

Action Commands

The action macros repeat mouse and keyboard actions such as scrolling with the mouse or pressing function keys.

A1.R1C1	HLINE
ACTIVATE	HPAGE
ACTIVATE.NEXT	HSCROLL
ACTIVATE.PREV	SELECT
CANCEL.COPY	SELECT.END
COPY.CHART	SELECT.LAST.CELL
DATA.FIND.NEXT	SHOW.ACTIVE.CELL
DATA.FIND.PREV	SHOW.CLIPBOARD
DELETE.FORMAT	STYLE
DIRECTORY	UNLOCKED.NEXT
FORMULA	UNLOCKED.PREV
FORMULA.ARRAY	VLINE
FORMULA.FILL	VPAGE
FORMULA.FIND.NEXT	VSCROLL
FORMULA.FIND.PREV	

Macro Functions for Customizing Excel

These macro functions modify Excel to give it the screen appearance, menus, dialog boxes, and help files you need. This group also includes macro functions that read and write data to disk and help you in cross-checking macro operation.

ADD.BAR	DELETE.COMMAND
ADD.COMMAND	DELETE.MENU
ADD.MENU	DIALOG.BOX
ALERT	DISABLE.INPUT
APP.ACTIVATE	ECHO
BEEP	ENABLE.COMMAND
CALL	ERROR
CANCEL.KEY	EXEC
CHECK.COMMAND	EXECUTE
DELETE.BAR	FCLOSE

FOPEN	ON.TIME
FPOS	ON.WINDOW
FREAD	POKE
FREADLN	REGISTER
FSIZE	RENAME.COMMAND
FWRITE	REQUEST
FWRITELN	SEND.KEYS
HELP	SET.NAME
INITIATE	SET.VALUE
INPUT	SHOW.BAR
MESSAGE	STEP
ON.DATA	TERMINATE
ON.KEY	WAIT

Control Macro Functions

These macro functions can start, stop, or redirect the flow of macro operation. Excel also runs subroutine macros that act as subcontractors to a main macro. Functions such as FOR, WHILE, and NEXT enable you to repeat parts of macros by looping.

ARGUMENT	RESTART
BREAK	RESULT
FOR	RETURN
GOTO	WHILE
HALT	*subroutine*
NEXT	

Macro Functions That Return Values

These macro functions return information about the worksheet environment. Information such as the name of windows, locations, or names of linked worksheets is returned in the cell containing the macro function. To see the returned value on the macro sheet, select Options Display and unselect the Formulas option.

ABSREF	GET.CHART.ITEM
ACTIVE CELL	GET.DEF
CALLER	GET.DOCUMENT
DEREF	GET.FORMULA
DOCUMENTS	GET.KEY
FILES	GET.NAME
GET.BAR	GET.NOTE
GET.CELL	GET.WINDOW

GET.WORKSPACE	RELREF
LINKS	SELECTION
NAMES	TEXTREF
OFFSET	WINDOWS
REFTEXT	

Worksheet Macro Functions

You can use the worksheet functions within command or function macros. Use the ARGUMENT macro function to assign values to the arguments used in a worksheet function. Function macros return a value to the worksheet cell containing the function macro you create. Chapter 25, "Macro Quick Start," demonstrates how to create a function macro and how to use ARGUMENT.

Macro Descriptions

The majority of macro functions have English command names and are easy to remember. Macros that duplicate commands from the menu frequently use the menu command word, a period, then the command, such as FORMAT.FONT. In the following descriptions of macro functions, menu command equivalents appear immediately following the function definition.

Macro functions receive information from the arguments listed between parentheses. These arguments can be values, cell references, or range references, and they must be separated by commas. Arguments that define position or movement measure locations in *points*. There are 72 points per inch. (Points are the same units used to measure the height of fonts.)

Here are some rules for entering and using arguments in macro functions:

- *Italicized* arguments in the following descriptions are optional.

- You do not have to enter an optional argument, but you must include the appropriate comma as a placeholder.

- Arguments must be entered in the order shown and separated by appropriate commas.

- Text arguments and arguments that include the word "text" in their argument name must be enclosed in double quotation marks (").

- Options in dialog boxes are turned on or off in response to a TRUE or FALSE value for that argument. If you enter TRUE as an argument, the option will be selected (turned on), while FALSE will unselect (turn off) the option.

To make macro functions and their arguments easier to remember, use the Formula Paste Formula command with the Paste Arguments option selected. This pastes in the macro function and puts a named description of the arguments within parentheses. For example, choosing PMT( ) from the list box when Paste Arguments is selected produces the following entry in the formula bar:

=PMT(rate,nper,pv,fv,type)

TIP

Use Pasted Argument Names as Range Names

The argument names that are pasted, such as *rate* and *nper*, can be left in the macro functions and used as range names. Beware of duplicate names, because some functions use arguments with the same name.

Some macro functions produce results that duplicate the worksheet function with the same name, such as ABS( ). For these macro functions, please see the description of the worksheet function for more information.

You can make your own choice about options for those macro functions that duplicate menu commands and produce a dialog box. To make the dialog box appear under macro control, insert a question mark (?) between the macro function name and the first parenthesis of the arguments. For example:

=DATA.SERIES?(*row_col,type,date,step,stop*)

acts the same as the **Data Series** command by displaying the Series dialog box. Any argument you enter in the macro function will be the default argument for the box.

NOTE

About the Macro Function Descriptions

The names of arguments in the function syntax are printed in roman type if the argument is mandatory, in italic type if the argument is optional. Arguments within a description, however, always appear in italics for easy identification. The use of italic type within a description, therefore, does not mean that the argument is optional. All compound argument names are joined by underscore marks.

Some macro functions duplicate commands, functions from the worksheet, or key and mouse actions. To learn more, please check the index for additional information under the name of the command, worksheet function, or action.

Learning About Macro Functions

You can learn the syntax and understand how to use macro functions together by recording a short macro that uses the functions you are interested in. Compare the commands and actions you issued with the resulting macro.

A1.R1C1(r1c1)

Replicates **O**ptions **W**orkspace R1C1. Switches between A1 and R1C1 style cell references.

Argument	Use
r1c1	TRUE results in A1 reference style. FALSE results in R1C1 reference style.

ABS(number)

Replicates ABS worksheet function.

ABSREF(ref_text,ref)

Returns the new absolute cell reference or range that is the result of the original cell or range location, *ref*, and the relative change *ref_text* given in R1C1 style. The reference *ref_text* must be in R1C1 format and enclosed in quotation marks. The reference moves with respect to its upper left corner if it is a range. If *ref_text* is a range, a range is returned. (Also see the description of the RELREF macro function.)

For example:

    =ABSREF("R[−1]C[−1]",QTR.XLS!C2)

is $B$1 on the QTR worksheet.

    =SELECT(ABSREF("R[2]C[1]",!$A$7))

selects $B$9 on the active worksheet.

ACOS(number)

Replicates ACOS worksheet function.

ACTIVATE(*window_text, pane_num*)

Replicates F6. Activates a pane in a window. Put *window_text* (the window name) in quotation marks; for example, "QRTR1" or "QTR1:2". If a document has more than one window open and you do not specify a window in

window_text, then the first window is affected. Omitting *window_text* specifies the current document.

Argument	Use	
pane_num	1	Top, left, top left, or only pane
	2	Right or top right pane
	3	Bottom or bottom left pane
	4	Bottom right

ACTIVATE.NEXT( )

Replicates Ctrl+F6. Activates next window.

ACTIVATE.PREV( )

Replicates Shift+Ctrl+F6. Activates previous window.

ACTIVE.CELL( )

Returns the active cell reference in external reference format. Because Excel
automatically evaluates this cell reference for its contents, you will actually
receive the value in that active cell. If you want a text string of the actual
cell reference, use the REFTEXT function. For example:

    =ACTIVE.CELL( )

in cell A2 of the macro sheet results in 5 in cell A2 if the active cell of the
worksheet contains 5. Within another macro function, ACTIVE.CELL acts like
an address. For example:

    =SELECT(!A1:ACTIVE.CELL( ))

selects the range on the active worksheet from A1 to the active cell.

ADD.ARROW( )

Replicates Chart Add Arrow. Adds an arrow; takes no argument.

ADD.BAR( )

Adds an empty menu bar and returns its ID number if successful. Up to 15
bars can be created. SHOW.BAR displays the menu bar. Excel has 6 resident
menu bars:

Bar number	Menu bar and menu size
1	Worksheet and macro, full menu
2	Chart, full menu
3	Nil menu, file only when no documents are open

4	Info window
5	Worksheet and macro, short menu
6	Chart, short menu

ADD.COMMAND(bar_num,menu_position,menu_ref)

Adds the command found in *menu_ref* area to the menu defined by *bar_num*. Returns the command position of the command last added.

ADD.MENU(bar_num,menu_ref)

Adds the menu defined in *menu_ref* area to the menu bar *bar_num*. Menu is added to the right of existing menus on the bar with the ID *bar_num*. Returns the position number for the new menu.

ADD.OVERLAY()

Replicates Chart Add Overlay. Adds overlay to chart. If overlay already exists, then TRUE is returned. No arguments.

ALERT(message_text,type_num)

The ALERT function is excellent for asking for verification or for warning about data entry errors. ALERT displays your message in an alert box and waits for the operator to select a button. ALERT returns TRUE when OK is chosen, FALSE when Cancel is chosen. Enclose message in quotation marks.

Argument	*Use*	*Type of Alert Box*
type_num	1	User selects button. OK button results in TRUE. Cancel button results in FALSE.
	2	Information only
	3	Error warning with no operator choice

For example:

=ALERT("Choose OK to delete data",1)

=ALERT("The number must be between 1 and 12",3)

ALIGNMENT(type_number)

ALIGNMENT?(*type_number*)

Replicates Format Alignment. Changes the alignment of text. Select first the text you want to align.

Argument	*Alignment*	
type_number	1	General
	2	Left
	3	Center
	4	Right
	5	Fill

For example:

```
=SELECT("Titles")
=ALIGNMENT(3)
```

centers the contents of the range Titles.

AND(logical1,*logical2*, . . .)

Replicates AND worksheet function.

APP.ACTIVATE(*title_text,wait_log*)

Activates the application with a title bar of *title_text*. If no *title_text* is shown, then Excel activates. If *wait_log* is TRUE or omitted, you must activate Excel before the application activates. If FALSE, the application activates immediately. Make sure that the *title_text* exactly matches the title bar.

APP.MAXIMIZE( )

Replicates Application Control Maximize.

APP.MINIMIZE( )

Replicates Application Control Minimize.

APP.MOVE(x_num,y_num)

APP.MOVE?(*x_num,y_num*)

Replicates Application Control Move. Moves the application window, Excel, to a new location on the screen. The value of *x_num* specifies the horizontal position from the left edge of the window in points (72 points per inch on paper); *y_num* specifies the vertical position in points measured from the top of the screen down. Using the ? form enables you to position by keyboard or mouse.

APP.RESTORE( )

Replicates Application Control Restore. Restores Excel window to previous size and location.

APP.SIZE(x_num,y_num)

APP.SIZE?(*x_num,y_num*)

Replicates Application Control Size. Changes the size of the Excel application window. *x_num* and *y_num* are the horizontal and vertical size, respectively, in points (72 points per inch on paper). Using a ? lets you size the window by keyboard or mouse.

APPLY.NAMES(name_array,ignore,use_rowcol,omit_col,omit_row, name_order,append)

APPLY.NAMES?(*name_array,ignore,use_rowcol,omit_col,omit_row, name_order,append***)**

Replicates Formula Apply Names. Works the same as the Formula Apply Names command.

Argument	Description
name_array	The name or names to apply as text elements of an array
name_order	1 = Row Column 2 = Column Row

Other arguments are TRUE or FALSE to select or unselect options in the Apply Names dialog box.

AREAS(reference)

Finds the number of areas in *reference*.

ARGUMENT?(name_text,data_type_num)

ARGUMENT(name_text,*data_type_num*)

Every function macro must use at least one ARGUMENT to pass values to the function macro. Chapter 26, "Building Command and Function Macros," describes how to use ARGUMENT.

Argument	Use
name_text	Name of the argument enclosed in quotation marks
data_type_num	Type of argument 1 Number 2 Text 4 Logical 8 Reference 16 Error 64 Array

ref	The referenced cells in the macro sheet where arguments will be stored

For *data_type_num*, except 8 and 64, you can add the numbers together. For example, 3 indicates a text or numeric entry is acceptable. (See the function macros in Chapters 25 and 26.)

ARRANGE.ALL( )

Replicates Window Arrange All.

ASIN(number)

Replicates ASIN worksheet function.

ATAN(number)

Replicates ATAN worksheet function.

ATAN2(x_number,y_number)

Replicates ATAN2 worksheet function.

ATTACH.TEXT(attach_to_num,*series_num,point_num*)

ATTACH.TEXT?(*attach_to_num,series_num,point_num*)

Replicates Chart Attach Text. Attaches text in charts. See the command description for more information.

Argument	*Use*
attach_to_number	Where text will attach
	1 Chart title
	2 Value axis
	3 Category axis
	4 Series or data points
series_num	
point_num	Use *series_num* or *point_num* to indicate which series number or point number the text will attach to. For more information, see the chart reference functions.

AVERAGE(number1,*number2, . . .*)

Replicates AVERAGE worksheet function.

AXES(*main cat,main value,over cat,overvalue*)

AXES?(*main_cat,main_value,over_cat,overvalue***)**

Replicates Chart Axes. Selects the axis display in the current chart. Arguments correspond to dialog box options. TRUE enables an option; FALSE disables it. See the command description for more information.

BEEP(*number***)**

Produces a tone depending on *number*. Numbers can be 1, 2, 3, or 4.

BORDER(outline,left,right,top,bottom,shade)

BORDER?(*outline,left,right,top,bottom,shade***)**

Replicates Format Border. Arguments correspond to options. TRUE enables an option; FALSE disables it. See the command description for more information.

BREAK( )

Stops a FOR-NEXT or WHILE-NEXT loop in a macro. Use an IF macro function to break when a condition is met. BREAK exits the loop. The macro continues after the NEXT statement.

CALCULATE.DOCUMENT( )

Replicates Options Calculate Document and Chart Calculate Document. Calculates the active document only.

CALCULATE.NOW( )

Replicates Options/Chart Calculate Now. Calculates all open documents.

CALCULATION(type_num, *iter,max_num,*
*max_change,update, precision,date_1904***)**

CALCULATION?(*type_num,iter,max_num,*
*max_change,update, precision,date_1904***)**

Replicates Options Calculation. Sets the Calculation dialog box. TRUE enables options; FALSE disables them. See the command description for more information.

Argument	*Use*
type_num	Type of calculation:
	1 Automatic
	2 Automatic except Tables
	3 Manual
iter	Iteration check box

max_num	Maximum number of iterations
max_change	Maximum change
update	Update Remote References check box
precision	Precision as Displayed check box
date_1904	1904 Date System check box

CALL(call_text,*argument1*, . . .)

Calls procedures from the Microsoft Windows dynamic library. Only knowledgeable programmers should use this macro function. If used incorrectly, this function can stop computer operation.

CALLER( )

Results in the reference of the cell containing the function that called the currently running function macro. If the currently running macro is a command macro, the returned value is #REF!. The function can return a range from array formulas.

CANCEL.COPY( )

Replicates Esc. Eliminates the marquee (dashed line) surrounding a cut or copied area.

CANCEL.KEY(enable,macro_ref)

Prevents macros from being stopped or tells which macro to transfer control to after interruption.

Argument	Use
enable	TRUE reactivates Esc if *macro_ref* is not given.
	TRUE transfers control to *macro_ref* if the current macro is interrupted by Esc.
	FALSE or omitted prevents macro interruption by the Esc key.
macro_ref	The reference that specifies where macro control will transfer to

CELL(type_of_info,*reference*)

Replicates CELL worksheet function.

CELL.PROTECTION(*locked,hidden*)

CELL.PROTECTION?(*locked,hidden*)

Replicates Format Cell Protection. TRUE enables an option; FALSE disables it. See the command description for more information.

CHANGE.LINKS(old_link,new_link)

CHANGE.LINKS?(*old_link,new_link*)

Replicates File Links. The arguments *old_link* and *new_link* must be linked files enclosed in quotation marks. See the command description for more information.

CHAR(number)

Replicates CHAR worksheet function.

CHECK.COMMAND(bar_num,menu_pos,command_pos,check)

Adds and removes check marks alongside commands in a menu.

CHOOSE(index_number,value1,*value2*, . . .)

Replicates CHOOSE worksheet function. Chooses from the list of values depending on the *index_number*. See the function description for more information.

CLEAN(text)

Replicates CLEAN worksheet function. Deletes all control characters from *text*.

CLEAR(*number*)

CLEAR?(*number*)

Replicates Edit Clear. Sets the Clear dialog box. See the command description for more information.

Argument	*Use*	
number	1	All
	2	Formats
	3	Formulas (the default if *number* is not entered
	4	Notes

CLOSE(*save_logical*)

Replicates Document Control Close. Closes the active window.

Argument	Use
save_logical	TRUE—document is saved
	FALSE—document is not saved and not entered. A message appears asking whether you want to save. Running ERROR(FALSE) prevents the document from saving.
	Omitted—a message displays asking whether you want to save the document.

CLOSE.ALL( )

Replicates File Close All command displayed by Shift+File.

CODE(text)

Replicates CODE worksheet function. Produces the ASCII decimal code of the first character in *text*.

COLUMN(*reference*)

Replicates COLUMN worksheet function. Produces the number of columns in *reference*.

COLUMN.WIDTH(width_num,*ref*)

COLUMN.WIDTH?(*width_num,ref*)

Replicates Format Column Width. Changes the columns in *ref* to the width of *width_num*. See the command description for more information.

Argument	Use
width_num	Width measured as the width of one character in the first font of the Format Font dialog box
ref	Don't specify for the current selection. Use an external reference if you enter *ref*.

For example:

=COLUMN.WIDTH(12)

changes the columns of the currently selected cells to widths of 12.

   =COLUMN.WIDTH(0,!$B:$E)

hides columns B through E in the active worksheet.

COLUMNS(array)

Replicates COLUMNS worksheet function. Returns the number of columns in *array*.

COMBINATION(number)

COMBINATION?(*number*)

Replicates Gallery Combination. Selects a combination chart format. The value of *number* must be one of the available formats.

COPY( )

Replicates Edit Copy. Copies the current selection.

COPY.CHART(number)

COPY.CHART?(*number*)

This is the Macintosh Excel equivalent of COPY.PICTURE. The function is included for macro compatibility.

COPY.PICTURE(appearance,size)

Replicates Shift+Edit Copy Picture. Copies the selected worksheet or picture to the Clipboard to be pasted later to another picture or different Windows application.

Argument	*Use*
appearance	1—as shown on-screen 2—as shown when printed
size	Only available if you are copying a chart 1—as shown on-screen 2—as shown when printed

COS(radians)

Replicates COS worksheet function.

COUNT(value1,*value2*, . . .)

Replicates COUNT worksheet function.

COUNTA(value1,*value2*, . . .)

Replicates COUNTA worksheet function.

CREATE.NAMES(*top,left,bottom,right*)

CREATE.NAMES?(*top,left,bottom,right*)

Replicates Formula Create Names. Sets the Create Names dialog box. TRUE enables an option; FALSE disables the option.

CUT( )

Replicates Edit Cut. Cuts the current selection.

DATA.DELETE( )

DATA.DELETE?( )

Replicates Data Delete. The form with a question mark displays a dialog box with warning; the other macro function immediately executes the **Data Delete** command on the database.

NOTE

Beware of DATA.DELETE

Make sure that you test DATA.DELETE with a sample database. Use the COUNTA function to test for criteria in the Criteria range; if no criteria are specified, all records will be deleted.

DATA.FIND(logical)

Replicates Data Find. TRUE executes the find; FALSE stops the find.

DATA.FIND.NEXT( )

DATA.FIND.PREV( )

These are the same as pressing up- or down-arrow keys, respectively, to move to the next or previous found record. You must first execute DATA.FIND. These functions produce FALSE if nothing is found.

DATA.FORM( )

Replicates Data Form. Same as the **Data Form** command. The database range must be set.

DATA.SERIES(row_col,type,date,step,stop)

DATA.SERIES?(*row col,type,date,step,stop*)

Replicates Data Series. Sets the Series dialog box.

Argument	*Entry*
row_col	1—Rows 2—Columns
type	1—Linear 2—Growth 3—Date
date	1—Day 2—Weekday 3—Month 4—Year
step	Incremental number
stop	Stopping value

DATE(year,month,day)

Replicates DATE worksheet function.

DATEVALUE(date_text)

Replicates DATEVALUE worksheet function.

DAVERAGE(database,*field*,criteria)

Replicates DAVERAGE worksheet function.

DAY(serial_number)

Replicates DAY worksheet function.

DCOUNT(database,*field*,criteria)

Replicates DCOUNT worksheet function.

DCOUNTA(database,*field*,criteria)

Replicates DCOUNTA worksheet function.

DDB(cost,salvage,life,period)

Replicates DDB worksheet function.

DEFINE.NAME(name_text,refers_to,*macro_type,shortcut_text*)

DEFINE.NAME?(*name_text,refers_to,macro_type,shortcut_text*)

Replicates Formula Define Name. Defines the name of *name_text* on the active worksheet.

If refers_to is	Then name_text is
Value	That value
External reference	Cells on external worksheet
Formula	The formula
Omitted	The current cell selections

If the active document for DEFINE.NAME is a macro sheet:

macro_type	Result
1	Function macro
2	Command macro
3	Default, not a macro
shortcut_text	The Ctrl+key combination for a command macro

DELETE.ARROW( )

Replicates Chart Delete Arrow. Deletes the selected arrow. Produces FALSE if the selection is not an arrow.

DELETE.BAR(bar_num)

Deletes the custom menu bar that has the number *bar_num*.

DELETE.COMMAND(bar_number,menu_pos,command_pos)

Deletes the commands in *command_pos* on the *menu_pos* from within the bar with the ID *bar_num*. *bar_num* can be an original or added Excel menu bar. If the command to be deleted does not exist, #VALUE! is returned. After deleting a command, all remaining *command_pos* numbers decrease by one.

NOTE

Enclose Text Items in Quotation Marks

When an argument name is ???_text, or the description specifies text, the argument must be enclosed in quotation marks or refer to a cell or range containing text.

DELETE.FORMAT(format_text)

Replicates Format Number. Deletes the custom numeric format specified by *format_text*. The text *format_text* must be enclosed in quotation marks and be the same as an existing custom format in the list box. You cannot delete default numeric formats.

DELETE.MENU(bar_num,menu_pos)

Deletes the menu specified by *menu_pos* in the bar specified by *bar_num*.

DELETE.NAME(name_text)

Replicates Formula Define Names. This function does the same thing as deleting a name with the Formula Define Names command. Enclose the text in quotation marks.

DELETE.OVERLAY( )

Replicates Chart Delete Overlay. If the overlay chart is already deleted, then TRUE is returned.

DEREF(reference)

Returns the values in the location referenced. The returned values correspond to the referenced area. A single reference returns a single value, a referenced range returns an array of values. If *reference* refers to the active sheet, then it must be an absolute reference. See SET.NAME for an example.

DIALOG.BOX(dialog_ref)

Displays the custom dialog box you describe in the range *dialog_ref*. DIALOG.BOX returns the item number of the button pressed. Choosing Cancel return FALSE.

DIRECTORY(*path_text*)

Changes the drive and directory to the path name specified. The function results in the name of the set directory as text. You can refer back to this macro cell to find the current directory. If you do not enter *path_text*, the macro returns the current directory. For example:

   =DIRECTORY( )

returns "C:\EXCEL\FORECAST" if the current drive and directory are C:\EXCEL\FORECAST

   =DIRECTORY("C:\BUDGET")

changes the active drive and directory to C:\BUDGET.

DISABLE.INPUT(logical)

Stops input from the keyboard or mouse when *logical* is TRUE. Enables input when *logical* is FALSE.

DISPLAY(*formula,gridline,heading,zero,color*)

DISPLAY(*cell, formula, value, format, protect, names,*
*precedents, dependents, note, levels***)**

The first form replicates Options Display and sets options in the Display dialog box. TRUE enables options, and FALSE disables them. Colors are numbered from one to eight as shown in the box. Zero is the Automatic button.

The second form replicates Window Show Info and sets the Info menu. Use TRUE and FALSE to enable or disable options. *levels* applies to *precedents* and *dependents*. For *levels*, use 1 for Direct Only and 2 for All Levels.

DMAX(database,field,criteria)

Replicates DMAX worksheet function.

DMIN(database,field,criteria)

Replicates DMIN worksheet function.

DOCUMENTS( )

Returns an array of text names listing all the open documents in alphabetical order. Use this with the MATCH and INDEX functions to find document names for use by other macros.

DOLLAR(number, *decimal***)**

Replicates DOLLAR worksheet function.

DPRODUCT(database,field,criteria)

Replicates DPRODUCT worksheet function.

DSTDEV(database,field,criteria)

Replicates DSTDEV worksheet function.

DSTDEVP(database,field,criteria)

Replicates DSTDEVP worksheet function.

DSUM(database,field,criteria)

Replicates DSUM worksheet function.

DVAR(database,field,criteria)

Replicates DVAR worksheet function.

DVARP(database,field,criteria)

Replicates DVARP worksheet function.

ECHO(*logical***)**

TRUE or no entry leaves screen updating on. FALSE turns updating off. Use TRUE during troubleshooting. Use FALSE to increase macro speed.

EDIT.DELETE(num)

EDIT.DELETE?(*num*)

Replicates **Edit Delete.** Sets the Delete cells dialog box.

Argument	*Check box*
num	1—Shift Cells Left
	2—Shift Cells Up

ENABLE.COMMAND(bar_num,menu_pos,command_pos,enable)

Enables or disables the command in *command_pos* position for the *menu_pos* in the menu bar with the ID *menu_bar*. TRUE as the *enable* value enables the command. If the command being disabled is a built-in Excel command or does not exist, then #VALUE! is returned.

ERROR(enable,*macro_ref*)

Tells Excel what to do about errors that occur during macro operation. (During normal macro operation, an error displays a dialog box from which you can choose to stop the macro, single-step through it, or continue operation.)

Argument	*Use*
enable	TRUE—with a *macro_ref*, it transfers macro control to the error-handling routine in the macro located at *macro_ref*.
	TRUE—without a *macro_ref*, normal error checking is turned on.
	FALSE—error checking is disabled. Excel continues to run regardless of errors.

ERROR(TRUE) is the only condition that will give you error conditions. In ERROR(TRUE,macro_ref), you must build in your own error-trapping and message routines.

EXACT(text1,text2)

Replicates EXACT worksheet function.

EXEC(program_text,*window_number*)

Starts the program named program_text in a window with a size specified by *window_number* as 1—Normal, 2—Minimized, or 3—Maximized. Use the full file name with extension. Any program arguments, such as /S or /R, can be included in *program_text*. This works only under Windows 2.0. Specify *program_text* the same as you would in Windows 2.0 for the **File Run** command.

EXECUTE(channel_num,execute_text)

Used in conjunction with the INITIATE macro function to communicate with another application through the DDE channel. The *channel_num* should be a reference to the macro cell containing the INITIATE macro function.

EXP(number)

Replicates EXP worksheet function.

EXTRACT(unique_log)

EXTRACT?(*unique_log*)

Replicates **Data Extract**. Same as the **Data Extract** command. Use TRUE for the *unique_log* value to check the Unique option. FALSE disables the option.

FACT(number)

Replicates FACT worksheet function to calculate factorials of *number*.

FALSE( )

Replicates FALSE worksheet function.

FCLOSE(file_number)

Closes the disk file identified as *file_number*. This file must be opened by FOPEN. *file_number* is the value returned by the FOPEN function.

FILE.CLOSE( )

Replicates **File Close**. Closes the active document.

FILE.DELETE(name_text)

FILE.DELETE?(*name_text*)

Replicates **File Delete**. Enter the drive, path, and file name as text. You can use the asterisk (✱) and question mark (?) wild cards. If a matching file name is not found, then a dialog box appears requesting that you insert the appropriate disk.

FILES(*directory_text*)

Produces a horizontal array of up to 256 file names found in the directory you specify. You can use the asterisk (✱) and question mark (?) wild cards to specify file name patterns.

To read file names, enter

=FILES( )

as an array formula across a row for as many cells as you want names. Cells that exceed the array size return #N/A!. You also can use the INDEX function to read a specific file, for example,

=INDEX(FILES( ),1,1)

FILL.DOWN( )

Replicates Edit Fill Down.

FILL.LEFT( )

Replicates Edit Fill Left.

FILL.RIGHT( )

Replicates Edit Fill Right.

FILL.UP( )

Replicates Edit Fill Up. Corresponds to the Edit Fill commands.

FIND(find_text,within_text,*start_at_num*)

Replicates FIND worksheet function.

TIP

Macro Functions That Duplicate Commands and Functions

If a macro function is shown as a duplicate of a menu command or worksheet function, refer to the command or function description for more information.

FIXED(number,*decimals*)

Replicates FIXED worksheet function.

FOPEN(file_text,access_number)

Opens a text file on disk by the name *file_text*. *access_number* controls the read/write access. A *file_number* results in the formula cell. Close the file with FCLOSE.

Argument	*Type of access*
access_number	1—Read/Write access
	2—Read-only access
	3—Create a new file (Read/Write access)

FOR(counter_name,start_num,end_num,*step_num*)

Controls a FOR-NEXT loop to repeat macro procedures. Step number is 1 if omitted. Use the BREAK macro with a conditional macro like IF to interrupt a FOR-NEXT loop before it is complete. See Chapter 26, "Building Command and Function Macros," for examples.

FORMAT.FONT(name_text,size_num,bold,italic,underline,strike)

FORMAT.FONT?(*name_text,size_num,bold,italic,underline,strike*)

FORMAT.FONT(color,backgd,apply,name_text,size,bold,italic,underline,strike)

FORMAT.FONT?(*color,backgd,apply,name_text,size,bold,italic,underline,strike*)

Replicates Format Font. Applies one of the four available fonts as appropriate for the Font dialog box under a worksheet or chart. The first two forms are used for worksheets or macro sheets; the second two forms are used for charts.

Argument	Use
name_text	Use the name of the font as it appears in the list box, enclosed in quotation marks. For example: "TmsRmn".
size	Font size in points
size_num	Font size in points
bold	TRUE for bold
italic	TRUE for italic
underline	TRUE for underlined
strike	TRUE for strikeout
color	Colors: 1–8, 9 automatic
backgd	1—Automatic 2—Transparent 3—White Out
apply	Apply to All check box

FORMAT.LEGEND(position_num)

Replicates Format Legend. Same as the dialog box that positions a chart legend.

Argument	*Description*
position_num	Legend position
1	Bottom
2	Corner
3	Top
4	Vertical

FORMAT.MOVE(x_pos,y_pos)

Replicates Format Move.

FORMAT.MOVE?(*x_pos,y_pos*)

Moves the lower left corner of a selected chart object to the *x_pos, y_pos* location. (The position indicates the butt end of an arrow and the point of a pie wedge.)

FORMAT.NUMBER(format_text)

FORMAT.NUMBER?(format text)

Replicates Format Number. Use a text string enclosed in quotation marks that is the equivalent of an existing number or date format in the Numbers list box. For example:

   =FORMAT.NUMBER("d-mmm-yy")

FORMAT.SIZE(width,height)

FORMAT.SIZE?(*width, height*)

Replicates Format Size. Sizes a selected chart object. Sizes are measured in points with measurements starting at the lower left corner of text rectangles or the butt end of arrows. Pie charts cannot be sized.

FORMAT.TEXT(x_align,y_align,vert_text,auto_text,auto_size, *show_key,show_value*)

Replicates Format Text. Same as the dialog box for the Format Text command. Arguments are equivalent to the dialog box options and are selected by TRUE and unselected by FALSE.

Argument	Description
x_align	Horizontal alignment
	1—Left
	2—Center
	3—Right
y_align	Vertical alignment
	1—Top
	2—Center
	3—Bottom

FORMULA(formula_text,*ref*)

Enters a formula in the *ref* cell of the active worksheet. Omitting *ref* enters the formula in the active cell. For example:

=FORMULA("=R2C3*3")

enters the formula

=$C$2*3

into the active cell. (See Chapters 25 and 26 for additional examples.)

FORMULA.ARRAY(formula_text,*ref*)

Enters an array formula just as if you pressed Shift+Ctrl while entering. Specify the range with *ref* or with the currently selected range.

FORMULA.FILL(formula_text,*ref*)

Fills the selected range or *ref* with the formula upon entry, just as though Shift were pressed while entering a formula.

FORMULA.FIND(text,in_num,at_num,by_num)

FORMULA.FIND?(*text,in_num,at_num,by_num*)

Replicates Formula Find. Sets the Formula Find dialog box. The text you want to find, *text*, must be in quotation marks.

Argument	Use for dialog box options
in_num	1—Formulas
	2—Values
	3—Notes
at_num	1—Whole
	2—Part
by_num	1—Rows
	2—Columns

FORMULA.FIND.NEXT( )

FORMULA.FIND.PREV( )

Replicates F7 or Shift+F7, respectively. Finds the next or previous cell in the worksheet as specified in the Formula Find dialog box. These functions return FALSE if no cell is found.

FORMULA.GOTO(reference)

FORMULA.GOTO?(*reference*)

Replicates Formula Goto. The *reference* argument should refer to a cell in the macro sheet, an R1C1 style reference as text, or an external reference to a worksheet. For example:

    =FORMULA.GOTO(!$B$3)

goes to $B$3 on the active worksheet, while

    =FORMULA.GOTO("R5C3")

goes to C5 on the active worksheet. With named ranges, use formats similar to the following:

    =FORMULA.GOTO(!Sales)
    =FORMULA.GOTO("Sales")

FORMULA.REPLACE(find_text,replace_text,*look_at,look_by,current_cell*)

FORMULA.REPLACE?(*find_text,replace_text,look_at,look_by,current_cell*)

Replicates Formula Replace. Enclose *find_text* and *replace_text* in quotation marks or use a cell reference. The asterisk (∗) and question mark (?) wild cards can be used in *find_text*.

Argument	Use
find_text	Searches for the text enclosed in quotation marks
replace_text	Replaces the text enclosed in quotation marks
look_at	1—Whole 2—Part
look_by	1—By rows 2—By columns
current_cell	TRUE—Replaces in current cell only FALSE—Replaces in selection or entire document

FPOS(file_number,*position_number*)

Positions the file in preparation for reading or writing. The first position is 1. Another function, FOPEN, opens the file and returns the *file_number*. FPOS returns #VALUE! if the *file_number* is not valid.

FREAD(file_number,num_chars)

Reads the specified number of characters from the file, beginning at the current location in the file.

FREADLN(file_number)

Reads the current position in the file to the end of the line. *file_number* is returned by FOPEN when the file was opened.

FREEZE.PANES(logical)

Replicates Options Freeze Display. TRUE freezes the panes; FALSE thaws them.

FSIZE(file_number)

Returns the number of characters in the file specified by *file_number*.

FULL(logical)

Replicates Document Control Maximize/Restore. TRUE expands the active window to maximum size. FALSE restores the original size.

FV(rate,nper,pmt, *pv,type*)

Replicates FV worksheet function.

TIP

Learning about Functions

To learn more about a macro function, such as FV, read the description of the same worksheet function.

FWRITE(file_number,text)

Writes the text string to the file specified by *file_number*, beginning at the current position in the file. FWRITE returns #N/A! if the function is unable to write to the document.

FWRITELN(file_number,text)

Starts at the current position in the text file and writes the specified *text*, followed by a carriage return and line feed.

NOTE

About GALLERY Functions

In GALLERY macro functions, the delete_overlay item can be TRUE, FALSE, or absent. TRUE in *delete_overlay* deletes the overlay, if present, and applies the new format to the main chart. Using FALSE or omitting the *delete_overlay* value applies the new format to the chart that contains the currently selected chart item.

These commands choose the type of chart by the number associated with that type when the gallery displays on-screen.

GALLERY.AREA(number,*delete_overlay*)

GALLERY.AREA?(*number,delete_overlay*)

Replicates Gallery Area.

GALLERY.BAR(number,*delete_overlay*)

GALLERY.BAR?(*number,delete_overlay*)

Replicates Gallery Bar.

GALLERY.COLUMN(number,*delete_overlay*)

GALLERY.COLUMN?(*number,delete_overlay*)

Replicates Gallery Column.

GALLERY.LINE(number,*delete_overlay*)

GALLERY.LINE?(*number,delete_overlay*)

Replicates Gallery Line.

GALLERY.PIE(number,*delete_overlay*)

GALLERY.PIE?(*number,delete_overlay*)

Replicates Gallery Pie.

GALLERY.SCATTER(number,*delete_overlay*)

GALLERY.SCATTER?(*number,delete_overlay*)

Replicates Gallery Scatter.

GET.BAR( )

Returns the number of the active menu bar.

GET.CELL(type_of_info,*reference*)

This is a valuable function that finds characteristics such as formatting, location, or contents of a cell or area. The *type_of_info* argument specifies the type of cell information returned.

type_of_info	Returned value
1	Top left cell of *reference* as text
2	Row of top cell in *reference*
3	Column of left most cell in *reference*
4	Same as TYPE(reference)
5	Contents of *reference*
6	Formula in *reference* as text
7	Format of cell as text
8	Number equaling cell's alignment, numbers as in ALIGNMENT( )
9	TRUE if cell has left border
10	TRUE if cell has right border
11	TRUE if cell has top border
12	TRUE if cell has bottom border
13	TRUE if cell shaded
14	TRUE if cell locked
15	TRUE if cell hidden
16	Column width in font 1 characters
17	Row height in points
18	Name of font as text
19	Size of font in points
20	TRUE if cell is bold
21	TRUE if cell is italic
22	TRUE if cell is underlined
23	TRUE if cell is struck over

GET.CHART.ITEM(x_y_index,*point_index*,*item_text*)

Returns the vertical or horizontal location of a point on a selected chart item.

Argument	Description
x_y_index	1—Request horizontal coordinate
	2—Request vertical coordinate
point_index	1—Point, lower left point of line, or upper left of object
	2—Upper right point of line or upper middle of object
	3—Upper right of object
	4—Right middle of object

5—Lower right of object
6—Lower middle of object
7—Lower left of object
8—Left middle of object

For an arrow,

1—The base
2—The head

For a pie slice,

1—Outermost counter-clockwise point
2—Outer center point
3—Outermost clockwise point
4—Midpoint of the most clockwise radius
5—Center point
6—Midpoint of the most counter-clockwise
    radius

item_text   If omitted, this is the currently selected chart
                     item. *item_text* options are listed in the chart
                     version of SELECT( ).

GET.DEF(*def_text,document*)

Returns the range name corresponding to the reference, *def_text*, in *document*. *def_text* is a reference in R1C1 style in quotation marks. If multiple names are at the address *def_text*, only the first is returned.

GET.DOCUMENT(type_of_info,*name_text*)

Returns information about the document defined by *name_text*. There are 26 *type_of_info* results.

type_of_info	*Returned value*
1	Name of document as text
2	Pathname corresponding to *name_text* if document has been saved
3	1 if worksheet, 2 if chart, 3 if macro, 4 if Info window
4	TRUE if changes have been made since last save
5	TRUE if read-only
6	TRUE if file is protected
7	TRUE if document contents are protected
8	TRUE if document windows are protected

9	Number of first row used in worksheet or macro. 0 returned if document is blank.
10	Number of last row used in worksheet or macro. 0 returned if document is blank.
11	Number of first column used. 0 if sheet is blank.
12	Number of last column used. 0 if sheet is blank.
13	Number of windows
14	Calculation mode where 1 is Automatic, 2 is Automatic Except Tables, 3 is Manual
15	TRUE if iteration is enabled
16	Maximum number of iterations
17	Maximum change between iterations
18	TRUE if remote references update
19	TRUE if Precision as Displayed is enabled
20	TRUE if 1904 date numbering is enabled
21	A text array four cells wide of the names of the four fonts
22	A numeric array four cells wide of the four fonts
23	A logical array four cells wide showing which of the four fonts are bold
24	A logical array four cells wide showing which of the four fonts are italic
25	A logical array four cells wide showing which of the four fonts are underlined
26	A logical array four cells wide showing which of the four fonts are struck over

For charts use the following results for *type_of_info* 9 through 12:

9	The type of main chart, where 1 is Area, 2 is Bar, 3 is Column, 4 is Line, 5 is Pie, 6 is Scatter
10	The type of overlay chart using the same numbering scheme as when *type_of_info* equals 9. #N/A! is returned if there is no overlay.
11	Number of series in main chart
12	Number of series in overlay chart

HALT( )

Stops a macro from running. Use with an IF macro function to stop a macro when a condition is met.

HELP(*help_ref*)

Replicates Help. Displays help for the topic *help_ref*. HELP without a *help_ref* displays the main Help index. The *help_ref* argument must refer to a valid Help topic. This function is used to call custom help topics if *help_ref* is of the form

   filename!topic_number

HIDE( )

Replicates **Window Hide.** Increase macro speed by hiding windows you are working on. Show the hidden windows with the ACTIVATE macro function.

HLINE(number_cols)

Horizontally scrolls the active window by the number of columns specified by *number_cols*.

HLOOKUP(lookup_value,table_array,row_index_num)

Replicates HLOOKUP worksheet function.

HOUR(serial_number)

Replicates HOUR worksheet function.

HPAGE(number_windows)

Scrolls the active windows one window width to the right or left. A positive *number_windows* scrolls right; a negative scrolls left.

HSCROLL(scroll,col_log)

Scrolls the active window horizontally. When *col_log* is TRUE, the window scrolls to the column specified by scroll. When *col_log* is FALSE, the window scrolls by the fraction of a window width specified by scroll. To scroll to a specific column, use a format such as

   HSCROLL(n,TRUE)

where *n* is the column you want.

IF(logical_test,value_if_true,*value_if_false*)

Replicates IF worksheet function. See Chapter 26, "Building Command and Function Macros," for examples on using the IF macro function.

INDEX(ref,row_num,column_num,*area_num*)

INDEX(array,row_num,column_num)

Replicates INDEX worksheet function. Indicates a location in *ref* or *array* by index number.

INDIRECT(ref,*type_of_ref*)

Replicates INDIRECT worksheet function.

INITIATE(app_text,topic_text)

Opens and initiates communication with another Windows application through the DDE channel. The *app_text* argument is the DDE name of the application you are accessing as specified in the application manual. INITIATE returns the channel Id number for DDE communication with the application specified in *app_text*. Refer to Chapter 28, "Using Excel with Windows Applications," for more information on DDE.

INPUT(prompt,type,*title*, *default*,*x_pos*, *y_pos*)

Creates a dialog box and returns the information entered into it. *prompt*, *title*, and *default* are text, and must be enclosed in quotation marks. Other arguments are numbers. Choosing OK from the box or pressing Enter returns the entry in the box to the macro function cell. Choosing Cancel returns FALSE. Chapter 26, "Building Command and Function Macros," illustrates how to use this function for data entry.

Argument type	Data type
0	Formula, returned as R1C1 in text
1	Number
2	Text
4	Logical
8	Absolute reference
16	Error
64	Array

You can add together *type* numbers. For example, a *type* with the value 3 indicates that the function will accept number or text entries.

INSERT(shift_num)

INSERT?(*shift_num*)

Replicates Edit Insert. Use 1 to shift cells right, 2 to shift cells down the same as in the **Edit Insert** command.

INT(number)

Replicates INT worksheet function.

IPMT(rate,per,nper,pv,*fv*,*type*)

Replicates IPMT worksheet function.

IRR(values,*guess*)

Replicates IRR worksheet function.

NOTE

About IS Functions

The IS functions work the same as their worksheet function counterparts. Each returns a TRUE value when its argument test is valid.

ISBLANK(value)

Replicates ISBLANK worksheet function.

ISERR(value)

Replicates ISERR worksheet function.

ISERROR(value)

Replicates ISERROR worksheet function.

ISLOGICAL(value)

Replicates ISLOGICAL worksheet function.

ISNA(value)

Replicates ISNA worksheet function.

ISNONTEXT(value)

Replicates ISNONTEXT worksheet function.

ISNUMBER(value)

Replicates ISNUMBER worksheet function.

ISREF(value)

Replicates ISREF worksheet function.

ISTEXT(value)

Replicates ISTEXT worksheet function.

JUSTIFY( )

Replicates Format Justify.

LEFT(text,*number_of_characters*)

Replicates LEFT worksheet function.

LEGEND(*logical*)

Replicates **Chart Add Legend**. Adds a legend if *logical* is TRUE or omitted. Deletes the legend when *logical* is FALSE.

LEN(text)

Replicates LEN worksheet function.

LINEST(known_y's,*known_x's*)

Replicates LINEST worksheet function.

LINKS(*doc_text*)

Returns a horizontal array of all worksheets linked to the document specified by *doc_text*. The default is the name of the active document. If there are no links, the returned value is #N/A! To open all links to the worksheet FORCAST.XLS, for example, use

    =OPEN.LINKS(LINKS("FORCAST.XLS"))

LIST.NAMES( )

Replicates the Formula **P**aste Name command with the Paste List button.

LN(number)

Replicates LN worksheet function.

LOG(number,*base*)

Replicates LOG worksheet function.

LOG10(number)

Replicates LOG10 worksheet function.

LOGEST(known_y's,*knows_x's*)

Replicates LOGEST worksheet function.

LOOKUP(lookup_value,lookup_vector,result_vector)

LOOKUP(lookup_value,array)

Replicates LOOKUP worksheet function.

LOWER(text)

Replicates LOWER worksheet function.

MAIN.CHART(type,stack,10,vary,overlap,drop,hilo,overlap%,cluster,angle)

Replicates Format Main Chart. All arguments are options in the Main Chart dialog box. Enable an option with TRUE; disable with FALSE.

Argument type	Chart
1	Area
2	Bar
3	Column
4	Line
5	Pie
6	Scatter

MAIN.CHART.TYPE(type)

Macro function included for compatibility with Macintosh Excel.

MATCH(lookup_value,lookup_array,*type_of_match*)

Replicates MATCH worksheet function.

MAX(number1,*number2, . . .*)

Replicates MAX worksheet function.

MDETERM(array)

Replicates MDETERM worksheet function.

MESSAGE(logical,*text*)

Displays messages in status bar. When *logical* is TRUE, *text* is displayed. FALSE removes messages and returns status bar to normal. Only one message displays at a time.

MID(text,start_number,number_of_characters)

Replicates MID worksheet function.

MIN(number1,*number2, . . .*)

Replicates MIN worksheet function.

MINUTE(serial_number)

Replicates MINUTE worksheet function.

MINVERSE(array)

Replicates MINVERSE worksheet function.

MIRR(values,finance_rate,reinvest_rate)

Replicates MIRR worksheet function.

MMULT(array1,array2)

Replicates MMULT worksheet function.

MOD(number,divisor_number)

Replicates MOD worksheet function.

MONTH(serial_number)

Replicates MONTH worksheet function.

MOVE(x_ pos,y_ pos,*window_text*)

Replicates **Window Move.** Moves the entire window by repositioning the upper left corner. The active window moves if *window_text* does not specify a different window.

N(value)

Replicates N worksheet function.

NA( )

Replicates NA worksheet function.

NAMES(*doc_text*)

Returns a horizontal array of all names in the document defined by *doc_text*. The default is the active document.

NEW(type_number)

NEW?(*type_number*)

Replicates **File New.** Use *type_number* of 1 for worksheet, 2 for chart, or 3 for macro sheet.

NEW.WINDOW( )

Replicates **Window New Window.** Creates a new window.

NEXT( )

Ends a FOR-NEXT or WHILE-NEXT loop. See Chapter 26, "Building Command and Function Macros," for examples.

NOT(logical)

Replicates NOT worksheet function.

NOTE(*add_text,cell_ref,start_char,count_char*)

In a note attached to *cell_ref*, the *add_text* value replaces the text, beginning at *start_char* and continuing for *count_char*. The default for *cell_ref* is the active cell. The text added (*add_text*) must be less than 255 characters. NOTE( ) deletes the note attached to the active cell.

NOW( )

Replicates NOW worksheet function.

NPER(rate,pmt,pv,*fv,type*)

Replicates NPER worksheet function.

NPV(rate,value1,*value2, . . .*)

Replicates NPV worksheet function.

OFFSET(ref,rows,cols,*height,width*)

Determines a cell reference or range that is offset from *ref*. The upper left cell in the returned reference is *rows* down and *cols* right of *ref*. The returned reference is *height* tall and *width* wide. For example:

    =OFFSET(D4,–1,1,1,1)

is E3.

ON.DATA(document_text,macro_text)

Runs the *macro_text* macro when an application sends data to the document named *document_text*. Omit *macro_text* to turn off the ON.DATA macro function.

ON.KEY(key_text,macro_text)

Runs the *macro_text* macro when the key specified by *key_text* is pressed. The *key_text* argument can indicate single keys or combination keys such as Shift+Ctrl+right arrow. Use a set of double quotation marks (″) as the *macro_text* for no response to a keystroke. Omit *macro_text* to return a key to normal operation.

The value of *key_text* can be composed of the following codes:

Key	*Code*
Backspace	{Backspace}
Break	{Break}
CapsLock	{Capslock}
Clear	{Clear}
Delete	{Delete}
Down	{Down}
End	{End}
Enter	{Enter}
Escape	{Escape}
Help	{Help}
Home	{Home}
Insert	{Insert}
Left	{Left}
NumLock	{NumLock}
PgDn	{PgDn}
PgUp	{PgUp}
PrtSc	{PrtSc}
Right	{Right}
Tab	{Tab}
Up	{Up}
F1	{F1}
F2	{F2}
F3	{F3}
F4	{F4}
F5	{F5}
F6	{F6}
F7	{F7}
F8	{F8}
F9	{F9}
F10	{F10}
F11	{F11}
F12	{F12}
F13	{F13}
F14	{F14}
F15	{F15}
F16	{F16}

Combine keys with Shift, Ctrl, and Alt.

Combine with	*Precede key with*
Shift	+
Ctrl	^
Alt	%

For example:

   =ON.KEY("+%{F1}","MONTHEND.XLM!Extract")

runs the macro Extract on the macro sheet MONTHEND.XLM when Shift+Alt+F1 is pressed.

   =ON.KEY("+%{F1}")

returns the Shift+Alt+F1 key to its normal use.

ON.TIME(time,macro_text,*tolerance,insert_log*)

When *insert_log* is TRUE or omitted, Excel will run the macro named *macro_text* at the time specified by *time*. *macro_text* must be a text reference in R1C1 style. The *time* can indicate a time only so that the macro runs every day, or *time* can also include the date.

ON.WINDOW(*window_text,macro_text*)

Starts the macro named *macro_text* when the window named *window_text* is activated. Turn off ON.WINDOW for a window by giving the macro function again without a *macro_text*.

OPEN(file_text,update_ext,read_only_rem)

OPEN?(file_text,update_links,read_only)

Replicates File Open. Opens *file_text* as though selected manually to open a file. TRUE in any position selects the option in the appropriate dialog box. The *update_links* argument can have values of 0 to update neither external nor remote references, 1 to update external references only, 2 to update remote references only, and 3 to update both. If you use the OPEN? form, you can use the asterisk (*) and question mark (?) wild cards in the *file_text* name.

OPEN.LINKS(doc_text1,*doc_text2*, . . . ,*read_only_log*)

OPEN.LINKS?(*doc_text1,doc_text2*, . . . ,*read_only_log*)

Replicates File Links. Opens files necessary for links to other documents.

Argument	Use
doc_text	Up to 13 document names
read_only_log	TRUE enables Read Only

For example, to open the links to the active worksheet, use the following:

=OPEN.LINKS(LINKS())

OR(logical1,*logical2, . . .*)

Replicates OR worksheet function.

OVERLAY(type,stack,100,vary,overlap,drop,hilo,overlap%, cluster,angle,series,auto)

Replicates Format Overlay. Use the same argument values as used in MAIN.CHART. *series* is the number of the first series in the overlay. *auto* represents the Automatic Series Distribution option.

OVERLAY.CHART.TYPE(type)

This macro function is included for compatibility with Macintosh Excel.

PAGE.SETUP(head,foot,left,right,top,bot,heading,grid)

PAGE.SETUP?(*head,foot,left,right,top,bot,heading,grid*)

PAGE.SETUP(head,foot,left,right,top,bot,size)

PAGE.SETUP?(*head,foot,left,right,top,bot,size*)

Replicates File Page Setup. Use the first two forms to set the page for worksheets or macro sheets. Use the second two forms for charts.

Argument	Use
head	Header as text in quotation marks
foot	Footer as text in quotation marks
left	Left margin number
right	Right margin number
top	Top margin number
bottom	Bottom margin number
heading	TRUE to check Row & Column Headings box

grid	TRUE to check Gridlines box
size	1—Screen Size
	2—Fit to Page
	3—Full Page

PARSE(parse_text)

Replicates Data Parse. The *parse_text* argument is the parse line in the dialog box in text form. Use the recorder to create this function within your macro.

PASTE( )

Replicates Edit Paste.

PASTE.LINK( )

Replicates Edit Paste Link.

PASTE.SPECIAL(paste_what,operation,skip_blanks,transpose)

PASTE.SPECIAL?(*paste_what,operation,skip_blanks,transpose*)

Replicates Edit Paste Special. Equivalent to the Paste Special dialog box when pasting into a worksheet or macro sheet. Use TRUE to select *skip_blanks* and transpose options.

Value	*paste_what*	*Operation*
1	All	None
2	Formulas	Add
3	Values	Subtract
4	Formats	Multiply
5	Notes	Divide

PASTE.SPECIAL(row_col,series,categories,apply)

PASTE.SPECIAL?(*row_col,series,categories,apply*)

Replicates Edit Paste Special. Equivalent to the Paste Special dialog box when pasting from a worksheet into a chart. Use a value of 1 for *row_col* to be Rows, and 2 for Columns. For other arguments use TRUE to enable the option.

PASTE.SPECIAL(paste_what)

PASTE.SPECIAL?(*paste_what*)

Replicates Edit Paste Special. Equivalent to the Paste Special dialog box when pasting from a chart into another chart.

Value	*paste_what*
1	All
2	Formats
3	Formulas

PATTERNS( )

Replicates Format Patterns. The PATTERNS macro function has five forms depending on what has been selected. In general, review the dialog box for each type of selection. Then use numbers as argument values where the numbers begin with one for the first option and increase to the right or down. For example, line weights range from one to three as the options go from right to left. To see the available arguments, paste the macro function into your macro sheet with the **Arguments** option selected.

PI( )

Replicates PI worksheet function.

PMT(rate,nper,pv,*fv,type*)

Replicates PMT worksheet function.

POKE(channel_num,item_text,data_ref)

Uses the DDE channel specified by *channel_num* to send DDE data to *item_text* from the *data_ref*. Use INITIATE to open a channel to another WINDOWS 2.0 application. INITIATE returns the *channel_num*.

PPMT(rate,per,nper,pv,*fv,type*)

Replicates PPMT worksheet function.

PRECISION(logical)

Replicates **O**ptions **C**alculation **P**recision as Displayed. TRUE enables Precision as Displayed.

PREFERRED( )

Replicates **G**allery **P**referred.

PRINT(range,from,to,copies,draft,preview,parts)

PRINT?(*range,from,to,copies,draft,preview,parts*)

Replicates **F**ile **P**rint. Use the PRINT macro function to print the selected area.

Argument	*Use*
range	Page range 1—Print all 2—Print specified range
from	First page if 2 chosen in *range*
to	Last page if 2 chosen in *range*
copies	Number of copies
draft	TRUE selects Draft Quality
preview	TRUE previews the print
parts	Indicates what should be printed 1—Sheet 2—Notes 3—Both

PRINTER.SETUP(printer_text)

PRINTER.SETUP?(*printer_text*)

Replicates **File Printer** Setup. Use the name of the printer (enclosed in quotation marks) as you see it in the Printer Setup dialog box.

PRODUCT(number1,*number2*, . . .)

Replicates PRODUCT worksheet function.

PROPER(text)

Replicates PROPER worksheet function.

PROTECT.DOCUMENT(*contents,windows*)

PROTECT.DOCUMENT?(*contents,windows*)

Replicates **Options Chart Protect** Document. Use TRUE and FALSE to enable or disable the options.

PV(rate,nper,pmt,*fv,type*)

Replicates PV worksheet function.

QUIT( )

Quits Excel and displays a dialog box asking whether documents that have changed should be saved.

RAND( )

Replicates RAND worksheet function.

RATE(nper,pmt,pv,*fv,type,guess*)

Replicates RATE worksheet function.

REFTEXT(ref,*a1*)

Converts the reference in *ref* to an absolute reference in text form. Set *a1* to TRUE for an A1 style reference. FALSE returns an R1C1 style.

REGISTER(module_text,procedure_text,argument_text)

Use with the CALL function. Because REGISTER can cause system errors, it should be used only by experienced programmers.

RELREF(ref,rel_to_ref)

Returns the relative location of *ref* with respect to *rel_to_ref*. The relative location is specified as text in R1C1 style, such as "R[-2]C[3]".

REMOVE.PAGE.BREAK( )

Replicates Options Remove Page Break. No action is taken if the active cell is incorrectly positioned.

RENAME.COMMAND(bar_num,menu_pos,command_pos,name_text)

Renames the command in *command_pos* with the name *name_text* on the menu *menu_pos* in the menu bar number *bar_num*.

REPLACE(old_text,start_num,num_chars,new_text)

Replicates REPLACE worksheet function.

REPLACE.FONT(font,name_text,size_num,bold,italic,underline,strike)

Replicates Format Font. Arguments are the same as the Font dialog box options. *font* must be the number of the font you want replaced, 1 to 4. Use a *name_text* that matches an available font, such as "Courier".

REPT(text,number_times)

Replicates REPT worksheet function.

REQUEST(channel_num,item_text)

Requests data associated with *item_text* over DDE link from the application specified by *channel_num*. REQUEST receives data as a data array.

RESTART(*level_number*)

Removes *level_number* return addresses from stack. This prevents a subroutine from returning to its original macro.

RESULT(type_number)

Used with a function macro to specify the type of data the macro returns to the worksheet.

type_number	Data type
1	Number
2	Text
4	Logical
8	Reference
16	Error
64	Array

The *type_number* can be the sum of other type numbers.

RETURN(*value*)

Stops execution of the macro. Control returns to whatever initiated the macro: another macro or the keyboard if the user activated the macro. *value* is the value or reference to a value that a function macro returns to the worksheet. See Chapter 26, "Building Command and Function Macros," for examples.

RIGHT(text,*number_of_chars*)

Replicates RIGHT worksheet function.

ROUND(number,number_of_digits)

Replicates ROUND worksheet function.

ROW(*reference*)

Replicates ROW worksheet function.

ROW.HEIGHT(height_num,*ref,standard_height*)

ROW.HEIGHT?(*height_num,ref,standard_height*)

Replicates Format Row Height. Rows specified by *ref* are changed to the height in points as indicated by *height_num*. Omitting *ref* uses the rows of the active cells. Return to standard height rows by using a TRUE value for *standard_height*.

ROWS(array)

Replicates ROWS worksheet function.

RUN(reference)

RUN?(*reference*)

Replicates Macro Run. The *reference* must be either an external reference to a macro or an R1C1 style reference in text form.

SAVE( )

Replicates File Save. Saves the active document under the last file name used.

SAVE.AS(name_text,type_num,passwd_text,backup)

SAVE.AS?(*name_text,type_num,passwd_text,backup*)

Replicates File Save As. Save the active document under a new name or in a different format.

Argument	Use
name_text	Drive, path, and file name in quotation marks. For example: "C:\EXCEL\FORCAST.XLS"
type_num	Specify the saving format: 1—Normal Excel format 2—SYLK 3—Text 4—WKS 5—WK1 6—CSV 7—DBF2 8—DBF3 9—DIF
passwd_text	Password in quotation marks
backup	TRUE for a backup file

SAVE.WORKSPACE(*name_text*)

SAVE.WORKSPACE?(*name_text*)

Replicates File Save Workspace. Use a name in quotation marks for the workspace. Omitting the *name_text* saves the workspace as RESUME.XLW or the name of the last workspace document from the current session.

SCALE(cross,cat_labels,cat_marks,between,max,reverse)

Replicates Format Scale. Use this when the category axis is selected and the chart is not a scatter chart. *cross* is the number of the category where the value axis should cross. *cat_labels* and *cat_marks* specify the number of categories between labels and marks, respectively. Use TRUE to enable options for the last three arguments.

SCALE(min,max,major,minor,cross,logarithmic,reverse,max)

Replicates Format Scale. Use this function when the value axis is selected or for scatter charts. For the first five arguments, use TRUE to select the automatic option or enter a number. For the last three arguments, use TRUE to enable the option.

SEARCH(find_text,within_text,*start_at_num*)

Replicates SEARCH worksheet function.

SECOND(serial_number)

Replicates SECOND worksheet function.

SELECT(selection,active_cell)

Use this function with worksheets or macro sheets to select cells or change the active cell. The *selection* argument specifies the cells selected, and *active_cell* specifies which of those cells is active.

The *selection* should be either a reference to the active worksheet, such as !B3:C12, or an R1C1 style reference, such as "R[3]C:R[5]C[4]". For example:

    =SELECT(,"RC[1]")

moves the active cell to the right, while

    =SELECT(!A1:ACTIVE.CELL())

selects the range on the active worksheet from A1 to the active cell. See Chapter 26 for more examples.

SELECT(item_text)

This form of SELECT selects named items on a chart. An *item_text* must be enclosed in quotation marks.

The text values understood for *item_text* are

    Chart
    Plot
    Legend
    Axis 1
    Axis 2
    Axis 3
    Axis 4
    Title

Text Axis 1
Text Axis 2
Text *n* (nth floating text)
Arrow *n* (nth arrow)
Gridline 1
Gridline 2
Gridline 3
Gridline 4
Dropline 1
Dropline 2
Hiloline 1
Hiloline 2
S*n*P*m* (marker for point *m* in series *n*)
Text S*n*P*m* (text attached to point *m* in series *n*)
Text S*n* (series title for series *n*)

SELECT.CHART( )

This macro function is included for compatibility with Macintosh Excel.

SELECT.END(direction_num)

Moves the active cell in the direction indicated to the edge of the block. Similar to Ctrl+arrow.

direction_num	Direction
1	Left
2	Right
3	Up
4	Down

SELECT.LAST.CELL( )

Selects the cell at the lower right corner of the worksheet or macro sheet that is used or referred to.

SELECT.PLOT.AREA( )

Replicates Chart Select Plot Area. You can also use the SELECT("Plot") macro function.

SELECT.SPECIAL(type_number,*value_types*,*levels*)

Replicates Formula Select Special. Use the following *type_number* values for SELECT.SPECIAL:

type_number	Description
1	Notes
2	Constants
3	Formulas
4	Blanks
5	Current region
6	Current array
7	Rowwise equivalents
8	Columnwise equivalents
9	Precedents
10	Dependents

If you specify a *type_number* of 2 or 3, you must also indicate the *value_type* as 1 for numbers, 2 for text, 4 for logicals, or 16 for error values. When you specify a *type_number* of 9 or 10, select *levels* of 1 for Direct Only or 2 for All Levels.

SELECTION( )

Returns an external reference of the current selection. Most macro functions use this reference as the value contained within the reference. If you want to work with the actual reference, use the REFTEXT function to convert the SELECTION reference to text.

SEND.KEYS(key_text,*wait_log*)

Transmits the keystrokes in *key_text* to the active Windows 2.0 application, just as though the keys were typed from the keyboard. The function enables you to control other Windows 2.0 applications. Sends character keys such as "fas". Use the key codes in ON.KEY for additional codes.

SET.CRITERIA( )

Replicates Data Set Criteria.

SET.DATABASE( )

Replicates Data Set Database.

SET.NAME(name_text,*value*)

Defines the *name_text* on the macro sheet as *value*. Omitting *value* deletes the name. Use SET.NAME to store values during macro operation. For example:

    =SET.NAME("Rate",.12)

sets the name Rate equal to .12

    =SET.NAME("Print",B42:F54)

sets the name Print equal to the range B42:F54, and

=SET.NAME("Contents",DEREF(B16))

sets the name Contents equal to the value in cell B16.

SET.PAGE.BREAK( )

Replicates Option Set Page Break.

SET.PREFERRED( )

Replicates Gallery Set Preferred.

SET.PRINT.AREA( )

Replicates Option Set Print Area.

SET.PRINT.TITLES( )

Replicates Options Set Print Titles.

SET.VALUE(ref,values)

Changes the contents of the cells referred to by *ref* to *values*. If the cells contain formulas, they are not changed. Using this function is a good way of setting up worksheets or data forms with initial values. For example:

=SET.VALUE(B3,6)

puts the value 6 in B3. Worksheet ranges can be filled from arrays such as the following:

=SET.VALUE(!A3:B5{2,3;4,5;6,7})

SHORT.MENUS(logical)

Replicates Options Short Menus.

SHOW.ACTIVE.CELL( )

Replicates Ctrl+Backspace. Moves the window to show the active cell.

SHOW.BAR(bar_num)

Displays the menu bar indicated by the ID *bar_num*. *bar_num* can be the ID of one of Excel's menu bars or the ID of a custom bar. A custom bar's ID is returned by the ADD.BAR macro function.

SHOW.CLIPBOARD( )

This function is included for compatibility with Macintosh Excel.

SHOW.INFO(enable_log)

Replicates **W**indow **S**how Info/Document. TRUE for *enable_log* displays the Info window. If the Info window is already displayed, then FALSE for *enable_log* activates the document for that Info window.

SIGN(number)

Replicates SIGN worksheet function.

SIN(radians)

Replicates SIN worksheet function.

SIZE(width,height,*window_text*)

Replicates Document Control Size. The upper left corner of *window_text* stays fixed as the lower right corner adjusts to the requested *width* and *height*. The *width* and *height* are in points. Omitting *window_text* changes the size of the active window.

SLN(cost,salvage,life)

Replicates SLN worksheet function.

SORT(sort_by,key1,order1,*key2,order2,key3,order3*)

SORT?(*sort_by,key1,order1,key2,order2,key3,order3*)

Replicates **D**ata **S**ort. Use a *sort_by* of 1 to sort by rows, or 2 to sort by columns. Define the keys with either an external reference in either style, with R1C1 style enclosed in quotation marks, or with a name enclosed in quotation marks. Enter 1 for ascending order or 2 for descending order.

SPLIT(col_split,row_split)

Replicates **W**indow **S**plit. The function puts a split through the window on the column or row indicated. The *col_split* argument splits the window into left and right, while *row_split* splits it into top and bottom. Enter a zero for the split you want removed.

SQRT(number)

Replicates SQRT worksheet function.

STDEV(number1,*number2*, . . .)

Replicates STDEV worksheet function.

STDEVP(number1,*number2*, . . .)

Replicates STDEVP worksheet function.

STEP( )

Begins single-step operation through a macro that is helpful for troubleshooting. You can manually start single-stepping during macro operation by pressing the Esc key. Refer to Chapter 27, "Troubleshooting Macros," for more information and examples.

STYLE(bold,italic)

STYLE?(*bold,italic*)

This function is included for compatibility with Macintosh Excel. Use TRUE and FALSE to enable or disable the style on selected cells.

Subroutines

ref(*arg1,arg2*, . . .)

Subroutines act as subcontractors to perform tasks for the main macro. When a main macro reaches *ref*, it branches to the new macro at *ref* and begins operation at the upper left corner of *ref*. The argument *ref* can be either a cell reference or a name, and you can use external references for *ref*. When the subroutine macro is complete, a RETURN( ) macro function at the end of it sends control back to the original macro. Subroutines can be either command or function macros. Command macros and function macros that are used solely as subroutines can accept arguments. Subroutines can have up to 14 arguments. See Chapter 26, "Building Command and Function Macros," for more information.

SUBSTITUTE(text,old_text,new_text,*instance_number*)

Replicates SUBSTITUTE worksheet function.

SUM(number1,*number2*, . . .)

Replicates SUM worksheet function.

SYD(cost,salvage,life,per)

Replicates SYD worksheet function.

T(value)

Replicates T worksheet function. Translates a *value* into text.

TABLE(row_ref,column_ref)

TABLE?(*row_ref,column_ref*)

Replicates **Data Table**. *row_ref* specifies the row input, and *column_ref* specifies the column input. The references should be either external references, such as !$B$3 or QTR.XLS!$C$5, or R1C1 style references in quotation marks. You must select the table area before using the TABLE macro function.

TAN(radians)

Replicates TAN worksheet function.

TERMINATE(channel_num)

Closes DDE channels opened with the INITIATE macro function. Because some applications have a limited number of channels, you should close channels that are not in use. The *channel_num* is returned by INITIATE.

TEXT(value,format_text)

Replicates TEXT worksheet function.

TEXTREF(text,*a1*)

Changes the argument *text* into a reference. Use TRUE for *a1* for an A1 style reference. FALSE or an omitted *a1* argument produces R1C1 style.

TIME(hour,minute,second)

Replicates TIME worksheet function.

TIMEVALUE(time_text)

Replicates TIMEVALUE worksheet function.

TRANSPOSE(array)

Replicates TRANSPOSE worksheet function.

TREND(known_y's,*known_x's*,*new_x's*)

Replicates TREND worksheet function.

TRIM(text)

Replicates TRIM worksheet function.

TRUE( )

Replicates TRUE worksheet function.

TRUNC(number)

Replicates TRUNC worksheet function.

TYPE(value)

Replicates TYPE worksheet function.

UNDO( )

Replicates Edit Undo.

UNHIDE(window_text)

Replicates Window Unhide. The *window_text* argument names the window to be displayed.

UNLOCKED.NEXT( )

UNLOCKED.PREV( )

Replicates Tab or Shift+Tab, respectively. Moves active cell to the next or previous unlocked cell on a protected worksheet.

UPPER(text)

Replicates UPPER worksheet function.

VALUE(text)

Replicates VALUE worksheet function.

VAR(number1,*number2, . . .*)

Replicates VAR worksheet function.

VARP(number1,*number2, . . .*)

Replicates VARP worksheet function.

VLINE(number_rows)

Scrolls the active window by rows. A positive *number_rows* scrolls down; a negative scrolls up.

VLOOKUP(lookup_value,table_array,col_index)

Replicates VLOOKUP worksheet function.

VPAGE(number_windows)

Scrolls the active window vertically by the number of full screens specified by *number_windows*. A positive *number_windows* scrolls the window down; a negative scrolls the window up.

VSCROLL(scroll,row_log)

Scrolls the active window vertically. When *row_log* is TRUE, then the window scrolls to the row scroll. When *row_log* is FALSE, then the window scrolls a percentage of the entire window as indicated by the *scroll* argument. For example:

    VSCROLL(50,TRUE)

scrolls to row 50;

    =VSCROLL(.5)

scrolls to row 8192.

WAIT(serial_number)

Puts macro operation on hold until the time specified by *serial_number*. You can interrupt the WAIT by pressing Esc.

WEEKDAY(serial_number)

Replicates WEEKDAY worksheet function.

WHILE(logical_test)

Begins a WHILE-NEXT loop. These loops are described in Chapter 26, "Building Command and Function Macros."

WINDOWS( )

Returns the names of all windows as a horizontal array of text values. The names are given in the order of the level on-screen.

WORKSPACE(fixed,decimals,r1c1,scroll,formula,status,menu,remote)

WORKSPACE?(*fixed,decimals,r1c1,scroll,formula,status,menu,remote*)

Replicates **O**ptions **W**orkspace. Arguments corresponding to options in the Workspace dialog box are enabled with TRUE and disabled by FALSE.

YEAR(serial_number)

Replicates YEAR worksheet function.

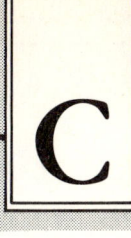

Technical Tips

In this appendix, you will see how to increase the performance of Windows applications with the use of extended or expanded memory and the SMART-drive utility that comes on the Windows disks.

Changing the WIN.INI File To Increase Performance

The WIN.INI file is an ASCII text file that contains information Windows reads when it starts. This information governs such characteristics as Windows colors, character sets, and automatic loading of applications.

You can change much of the information in the WIN.INI file with the Control Panel, which is the easiest way to modify the file. When you want to make changes to WIN.INI like those described in this appendix, you must edit WIN.INI.

Because WIN.INI is a text file, you can edit it with any text editor. The Notepad desktop application that comes with Windows is an excellent editor to use for making changes.

NOTE

Always Make a Backup Copy of WIN.INI Before Making Changes

WIN.INI contains information important to the operation of Windows. Always copy WIN.INI before changing it. Name your copy WIN.SAV. Then if your modifications don't work the way you want, you can copy the backup file over the modified one by copying WIN.SAV back to the name WIN.INI.

What Are You Looking for in WIN.INI?

You can see and edit the WIN.INI file by choosing the file from the MS-DOS Executive or by starting Notepad and then opening WIN.INI. Figure C.1 shows the beginning of the WIN.INI file displayed in Notepad.

*Fig. C.1.
Beginning of
WIN.INI file
displayed in
Notepad.*

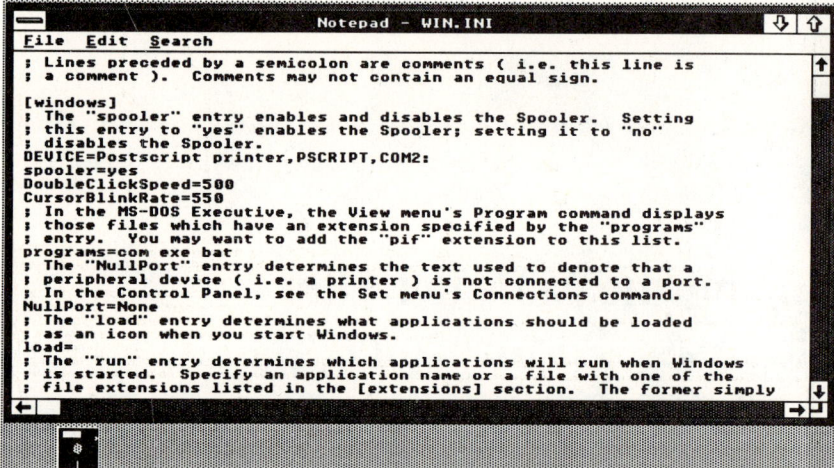

In the figure, you can see that some lines begin with a semicolon (;). These are comment lines. They are invisible to Windows when WIN.INI is read on start-up. Comment lines must not contain equal signs (=).

WIN.INI contains sections of parameters that control different aspects of Windows and applications. Some section titles are

- [windows]   window characteristics
- [extensions]   file name extensions
- [colors]   window colors
- [pif]   memory sizes for non-pif standard applications
- [intl]   international character controls
- [ports]   printer ports
- [devices]   which printer are attached to each port
- [fonts]   font specifications

When you run Windows applications, they are added to WIN.INI with section names like [Microsoft Excel].

Inside each section, you will see settings containing equal signs (=), which specify certain parameters that Windows will use the next time it starts. For example,

> beep=yes

tells Windows to turn on the beep.

TIP

Manual Changes to WIN.INI Do Not Take Effect Until You Restart

Because Windows reads WIN.INI on starting, the changes you make from Notepad do not take effect until you restart Windows.

Making Changes to WIN.INI with Notepad

You can make changes within WIN.INI using normal Notepad editing functions, or you can use any text editor or word-processing program to make changes. When you save the edited file, however, make sure you save in text format (ASCII). Notepad does this automatically. Usually, word-processing programs require a special command for saving in text format.

Normally, you will be able to choose the WIN.INI file from MS-DOS Executive, and the Notepad will automatically start and load WIN.INI. If this does not happen (because someone has changed the [extensions] section of WIN.INI), then start Notepad and load WIN.INI.

Specifying Which Files Start
Which Applications

The [extensions] section of WIN.INI tells Windows which application to start when you choose a data file. For example, from the MS-DOS Executive, you normally can choose the file FORCAST.XLS, and Excel will start and load the file FORCAST.XLS. This is because the [extensions] section contains settings like the following:

```
[extensions]
cal=calendar.exe ^.cal
crd=cardfile.exe ^.crd
txt=notepad.exe ^.txt
```

```
wri=write.exe ^.wri
xls=excel.exe ^.xls
xlc=excel.exe ^.xlw
xlw=excel.exe ^.xlm
```

If the [extensions] section has two file extensions that are the same, it will run the application closest to the top of the list. For example, from the following lines, choosing a .TXT file would start Write:

```
txt=write.exe ^.txt
txt=notepad.exe ^.txt
```

TIP

Automatic Starting of Excel with 1-2-3 Files

If you use Microsoft Excel but have associates or clients who use 1-2-3, you can modify WIN.INI so that choosing a 1-2-3 file from the MS-DOS Executive will start Excel and load the file. For 1-2-3 Releases 1A and 2, add these lines:

```
wks=excel.exe ^.wks
wk1=excel.exe ^.wk1
```

Increasing Performance by Swapping to Expanded Memory

Normally, Windows swaps portions of applications from RAM memory to disk when additional space is needed in memory. Applications swapped to disk can be recalled to memory when they are needed.

By changing the swapdisk and swapsize settings at the beginning of the [pif] section of WIN.INI, you can increase the performance of Windows. For example, if you have two different hard disks, you can tell Windows to use the faster one for swapping. You also can tell Windows to use expanded memory for swapping. Because data can be stored and retrieved much faster with expanded memory than with a disk, the result is that switching time becomes unnoticeable, and you can have nearly instant access to multiple applications.

Within WIN.INI look for

```
swapdisk=?
```

The default settings are

```
swapdisk=?
swapsize=0
```

Here are some examples of different settings:

- swapdisk=?

  Windows swaps to the directory indicated by the DOS command SET TEMP in the AUTOEXEC.BAT file. If a temporary directory is not set, then Windows swaps to the root directory ($\backslash$) of the first hard disk in the system. This is the default.

- swapdisk=? /e

  Windows swaps to expanded memory when it is available. When expanded memory is not available, swapping is to the directory specified by the SET TEMP command in the AUTOEXEC.BAT file.

- swapdisk=C: /e

  Windows swaps to expanded memory when it is available. This speeds up performance. When expanded memory is not available, Windows swaps to the directory on drive C set by the DOS command SET TEMP. If SET TEMP is not used, then Windows swaps to the root directory, C:$\backslash$.

- swapdisk=0

  This setting disables swapping completely. This setting limits the number of applications you can load and run.

- swapsize=0

  This setting sets the swap size on the hard disk in relation to the first application that is run and that can be swapped. When swapsize=0, Windows runs faster if the first application run is large because more hard disk is reserved for swapping. This is the default.

- swapsize=258

  This setting reserves 256K of expanded memory for use as swapping space and reserves an additional 2K of expanded memory for swapping information used by Windows. This amount is the minimum that will be used for swapping. This reserved expanded memory will not be available for applications that normally access expanded memory.

> **TIP**
>
> **To Get the Best Performance When You Don't Change WIN.INI**
>
> If you leave swapsize=0 in WIN.INI, then it is important to start the largest application first when running Windows.

Increasing Performance with Extended or Expanded Memory

If you have extended or expanded memory and are running Windows with a hard disk, then you really should add the SMARTdrive software to get increased Windows performance.

SMARTdrive is a disk-caching application. When Windows swaps data and applications from memory to disk it takes time. Disk-caching replaces these slow swaps to disk with fast swaps of important data kept in a reserved part of memory, known as the "cache." SMARTdrive tries to keep in memory those pieces of data that it calculates will be needed again in the near future.

> **NOTE**
>
> **Do Not Use SMARTdrive with Other Cache Software**
>
> SMARTdrive is designed specifically to work with Windows and major extended and expanded memory boards such as the INTEL Above Board™, the AST Rampage®, and the AST® Premium. Do not use other disk-caching software simultaneously with SMARTdrive.
>
> SMARTdrive takes the place of other disk-caching programs like CACHE.EXE. Make sure you remove any commands in the CONFIG.SYS file that install other disk-caching programs. Check the program's manual to find the appropriate commands to be removed from CONFIG.SYS, and use Notepad to remove them.

Should You Use Extended Memory or Expanded Memory?

SMARTdrive is a disk-cache program for either extended or expanded memory boards. If you have a board that can be extended or expanded, then set it up as expanded memory.

If you have both types of memory boards in the computer, use SMARTdrive with the extended memory board, and save the expanded memory for memory use by large applications.

Your Windows or Excel installation disks contain a READMEEM.TXT file describing how to best take advantage of expanded memory. Use the DOS TYPE command or the Write word processor in Windows to read the READMEEM.TXT file.

Installing SMARTdrive For Disk Caching

Before installing SMARTdrive, you must install the expanded or extended memory board in your computer and follow the manufacturer's procedure for installing the expanded memory management software.

To install SMARTdrive, follow these steps:

1. Use the MS-DOS Executive to find the original Windows disk containing the file SMARTDRV.SYS. Normally, this will be one of the utility disks.

2. Start Notepad.

3. Open the CONFIG.SYS file in the root directory.

   If your computer does not have a CONFIG.SYS file, you can create one with Notepad. CONFIG.SYS is described in DOS manuals.

4. Add or change the buffers line to at least BUFFERS=10.

   Some applications require a higher setting than 10. Don't set BUFFERS higher than 10 if it is unnecessary.

5. Enter the SMARTdrive command line in the CONFIG.SYS file—for example:

   DEVICE=C:\WINDOWS\SMARTDRV.SYS 512 /A

   If you are using expanded memory, then the SMARTdrive command must be after the expanded memory manager command line. The expanded memory manager command usually appears with a command similar to REMM.SYS or CEMM.SYS. The SMARTdrive command line must also be after the ENHDISK.SYS listed in the CONFIG.SYS file for COMPAQ Deskpro computers. Include the full path name of the directory containing SMARTDRV.SYS if SMARTDRV.SYS is not in the same directory as COMMAND.COM.

6. Check to make sure other disk-caching programs have been removed from CONFIG.SYS.

7. Save CONFIG.SYS in the root directory (\ ).

    If you are using a word-processing program, make sure you save CONFIG.SYS as a text file and not a word-processing file. The NOTEPAD application automatically saves files in text format.

8. Insert the disk containing SMARTDRV.SYS in drive A.

9. Choose **File Copy** from the MS-DOS Executive, and copy the file SMARTDRV.SYS into the Windows directory (\WINDOWS).

10. Quit Windows and press Ctrl+Alt+Del to restart your computer. (The CONFIG.SYS file is read only on start-up.)

    Your computer will now use SMARTdrive for virtual disk and disk-caching with standard applications as well as with Windows.

TIP

Don't Change WIN.INI

You don't have to make any changes to WIN.INI when you install SMARTdrive.

Setting the SMARTdrive Configuration

The command line you typed into CONFIG.SYS in step 5 above controls what operations SMARTdrive performs and how much memory it uses for those operations.

The command line you type in CONFIG.SYS should have the following form:

DEVICE=C:\WINDOWS\SMARTDRV.SYS size /A

If SMARTDRV.SYS is not in the root directory, you must enter the path name. The name of the SMARTdrive file is SMARTDRV.SYS.

The *size* specifies how much memory is used for cache. If you don't specify a size, then SMARTdrive uses 256K in extended memory or all available expanded memory. If you are running applications that use expanded memory (such as Excel or 1-2-3, Release 2), then you may want to save some expanded memory for the application's use. You can also conserve extended memory for application use. Enter the size as the number of K, but enter only the number.

You must add the parameter /A if you have expanded memory and want to use expanded memory.

Installing a Virtual Disk with Windows

Windows includes a virtual disk named RAMDRIVE.SYS on the original installation disks. A virtual disk is a section of RAM memory set aside to act as a fast disk drive.

Instructions for installing RAMDRIVE for use with extended memory are included in the file RAMDRIVE.TXT found on your original installation disks. RAMDRIVE.TXT can be read from Notepad or a word-processing program that imports text files.

Virtual disks appear at the top of the MS-DOS Executive as icons just as though they were actual disks.

NOTE

Virtual Disks Lose Everything When the Power Fails

Unlike a real physical disk, a virtual disk loses everything it contains when the power fails or the computer freezes. Remember to save frequently data you are working on to a real disk.

Installing Expanded Memory for Use by Windows 2.0

Windows 2.0 uses expanded memory that meets the Lotus/Intel/Microsoft 4.0 specification. Some of the memory boards that meet these requirements are the INTEL Above Board, the AST Rampage, and the IBM PS/2 Expanded Memory Option. The memory managers for these three board types are located on the Windows utilities disks in files EMM.SYS, REMM.SYS, and PS2EMM.SYS respectively.

The instructions for installing these memory managers are also on the original installation disks in files EMM.TXT, REMM.TXT, and PS2EMM.TXT. You can read or print these files from the Windows Notepad or Write.

Improving Windows/386 Performance

Windows/386 automatically takes advantage of extended memory. If you have an expanded memory board, then it must be reconfigured as extended memory for it to be used by Windows/386. In most cases reconfiguring your expanded memory board from expanded to extended memory requires changing switch settings on the board in accordance with the manual.

Computers with 80386 processors do not use expanded memory, but you can install SMARTdrive so that it uses extended memory for disk caching. This means you will not use the /A option when you enter the SMARTdrive device line in the CONFIG.SYS file.

Windows operating parameters are stored in the WIN.INI text file found in the directory in which you installed Windows/386. Two of the settings in the WIN.INI file control Windows/386 operation and are found under the [win386] heading.

Virtual machines in Windows/386 start with 640K of memory allocated to each application. If you want to change the amount of default memory allocated for each virtual machine, change the WINDOWMEMSIZE= line in WIN.INI to a smaller memory size. For example:

    WINDOWMEMSIZE=384

Windows/386 uses its own expanded memory manager to use extended memory for applications requiring expanded memory. Windows/386 can specify as much as half of the available memory as expanded memory. To specify exactly how much should be allocated for expanded memory, use EMMSIZE= to set expanded memory in multiples of 16K. For example:

    EMMSIZE=512

To disable expanded memory use this setting:

    EMMSIZE=0

Setting EMMSIZE=0 to prevent expanded memory use by standard DOS applications may also inhibit the performance of some Windows 2.0 applications.

Running Excel and Windows on a Network

Load network drivers before starting Windows. When you run Windows, the network appears in the MS-DOS Executive as a drive with its own directories.

If the network has its own print spooler, then turn the Windows Spooler off by changing the WIN.INI setting to

    spooler=no

Windows 2.0 and Windows/386 are compatible with the following networks:

- IBM PC Network
- IBM Token Ring Network
- AT&T STARLAN
- Ungermann-Bass/One
- 3Com 3+
- 3Com EtherSeries
- Novell Netware

D

Using Microsoft Excel for OS/2

If you know Excel on one computer system, you know it on another. Excel works nearly the same on Macintosh, Windows, and the OS/2 Presentation Manager. The files and macros you create on one computer system are usable on another. This appendix covers advancements in Excel on the OS/2 Presentation Manager. These new features, not yet available in the Windows and Macintosh versions of Excel, include the following:

- the use of up to 256 fonts on a worksheet
- the consolidation of values across multiple worksheets

Installing and Running Excel on OS/2

To use Excel for OS/2, you must have the following equipment:

- an IBM PC, AT, PS/2, or compatible computer with at at least 2.5M of memory; a hard disk with at least 5M of space; and an EGA-or-better screen resolution
- OS/2 Presentation Manager, version 1.1 or better, already installed and operating

To install Excel for OS/2 by using the keyboard, do the following:

1. Put the Setup disk in drive A.

2. Return to the OS/2 command prompt.

3. Type **A:SETUP** and press Enter.

4. Follow the on-screen instructions.

To install Excel for OS/2 from within the Presentation Manager, complete the following steps:

1. Put the Setup disk in drive A.

2. Select the A-drive icon.

3. Double-click on SETUP.EXE.

4. Follow the on-screen instructions.

To start Excel from the File System, complete the following steps:

1. Open the File System application.

2. Select the drive and directory in which Excel was installed.

3. Start the EXCEL.EXE file.

   Mouse: Double-click on EXCEL.EXE.

   Keyboard: Select EXCEL.EXE; then press Enter.

To start Excel for OS/2 from the Start Programs window, do the following:

1. From the Group menu, select the group in which Excel was installed.

2. Start Microsoft Excel.

   Mouse: Double-click on Microsoft Excel.

   Keyboard: Select Microsoft Excel; then press Enter.

Quit Excel as you would in Windows Excel.

Using Fonts in OS/2 Excel

With up to 256 fonts available in OS/2 Excel, the formatting capabilities are nearly unlimited. If you use Excel on the Macintosh, you are already familiar with these capabilities. OS/2 Excel uses two types of fonts. *Bit-mapped fonts* display faster, use less memory, and are most useful for text of normal size. *Outline fonts*, useful for text larger than 20 points, display slower and require more memory.

The bit-mapped fonts in OS/2 Excel consist of the following types and sizes:

- Courier in 8, 10, and 12 points

- Helv in 8, 10, 12, 14, 18, and 20 points

- Tms Rmn in 8, 10, 12, 14, 18, and 20 points

- System Proportional in 12 points

Other fonts are outline fonts.

Setting a Default Worksheet Font

When Excel worksheets open, they use the Helvetica (Helv) 10-point normal font. This font, called the standard font, is used throughout a new worksheet. The standard font is then used for all cell contents that are not reformatted with the Format Font command.

You may change the standard font by completing the following steps:

1. Choose the Options Standard Font command.

2. Select the font, its size, and its style or color from the scrolling list boxes.

3. Choose OK or press Enter.

Choosing a new standard font changes the font used in all cells that have not been formatted with the Format Font command. Changing the standard font also changes the column widths and size of header and footer fonts, because these are based on the standard font.

Formatting Fonts in Cells

You may use up to 256 fonts to format the text or numbers in cells. (Keep in mind, though, that each additional font uses additional memory.) The fonts, sizes, and styles available depend on which printers and fonts you have installed. To change the font, size, or style used in a cell or range of cells, complete the following steps:

1. Select the cell(s).

2. Choose the Format Font command.

3. Select the Printer Fonts check box to ensure that the fonts on-screen match the fonts available at the printer.

4. Select the Standard Font check box to change the current selections to the standard font.

5. Select other options such as Font, Size, Style, or Color.

6. Choose OK or press Enter.

> **TIP**
>
> ### Use Fonts that Are Available on the Target Printer
>
> You may use different fonts in the worksheet, but many of them may not be available in the current printer. You can format a worksheet by using fonts available on a different printer, but to do so may cause confusion. For example, you may create a worksheet that the printer is unable to print correctly. If the printer does not have the correct fonts or sizes, it substitutes other fonts and smaller sizes.
>
> To ensure that you use fonts and sizes that are available only in the current printer, choose the Format Font command and select the Printer Fonts check box. When this check box is selected, the Font and Size lists show those fonts available only in the current printer. Unselect the Printer Fonts check box to see all fonts available in the current configuration (all the installed printers and fonts).

Formatting Fonts with Shortcut Keys

In Excel for OS/2, the shortcut keys that format fonts do not work the same as in Excel for Windows because of the large number of fonts available.

To format selected cells quickly, use the following shortcut keys:

Press...	to...
Ctrl+1	apply the standard font
Ctrl+2	turn bold on or off
Ctrl+3	turn italic on or off
Ctrl+4	turn underline on or off
Ctrl+5	turn strikeout on or off

Consolidating Data across Multiple Sheets

Excel for OS/2 summarizes data across multiple worksheets by using the Data Consolidate command. Data summarization is especially useful when you need to consolidate information coming from many different worksheets. The information may come from multiple product lines, multiple regional offices, or multiple divisions of your company. How the information is consolidated is up to you. You may use 11 different functions in the consolidation, such as AVERAGE, COUNT, and SUM.

When you consolidate information, you have a *consolidation area*, which will contain the results, and multiple *source reference areas*. Consolidation results are constant values, not linked references. The consolidation area does not update automatically when you change a source area; rerun **Data Consolidate** to get updated results.

The data being consolidated comes from the source reference areas. Usually, multiple sources span multiple worksheets. The source information may be values or formulas. Figure D.1 shows a consolidation worksheet and two source worksheets.

Consolidations may summarize information according to the physical layout of the cells or according to the top row or left column text headings. In figure D.1, the physical layout of the consolidation worksheet and the two sources are the same, so the physical-layout method may be used. Because the top row and left column headings are the same on all the worksheets, "categories" may be used as an alternative.

Fig. D.1. You may consolidate according to a worksheet's physical layout or according to the top row or left column headings.

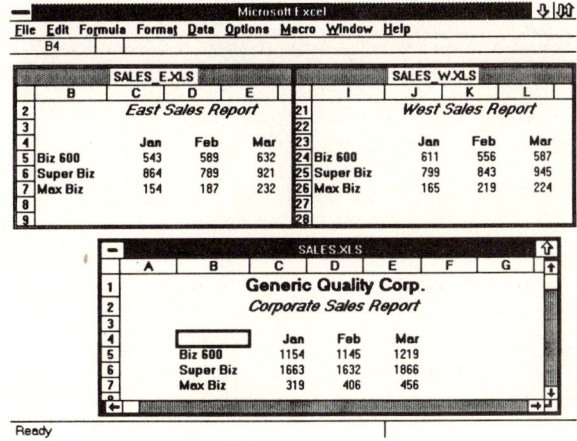

Selecting Destination Areas

To specify the consolidation area, do one of the following:

- Use **Formula Define Name** to name the consolidation area.

- Select a cell or range of cells before choosing **Data Consolidate**. This process works only when the name of the consolidation area does not already exist. If the name already exists, you must delete it with **Formula Define Name** before using a selected range.

The consolidation area's size affects how much data is consolidated. If the area is a single cell, the consolidated area expands downward and to the right to accept all the consolidated information from the sources.

If the consolidation area occupies cells in a single row—for example, B12 through E12—then Excel automatically expands downward to include as much area as necessary to contain all the rows from the sources. The width of the area, columns B to E, stays the same as that of the original selection.

If the consolidation area occupies cells in a single column—for example, D10 through D20—then Excel automatically expands to the right to include as wide an area as necessary to contain all the columns from the sources. The height of the area, rows 10 to 20, stays the same as that of the original selection.

If the consolidation area includes more than a single row and more than a single column, then Excel fills the area with as much information as possible but does not expand the area. You may get a warning that some information has not been consolidated.

The Data Consolidation command replaces constant text or numeric values in the consolidation area but does not replace formulas. Numeric formats are replaced.

Selecting Source Areas

Excel may consolidate up to 255 source areas. A *source area* is the range on a worksheet that supplies information to the consolidation. Only worksheets that have been saved can be consolidated.

You choose a source area by entering the area's reference into the **Reference** text box of the **Data Consolidate** dialog box. The dialog box is shown in figure D.2. The source area must be specified completely. Worksheets containing source areas must have been previously saved to disk.

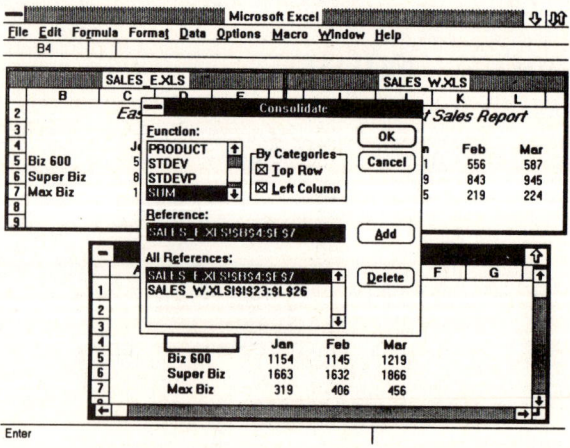

Fig. D.2. The Data Consolidate dialog box enables you to consolidate information from numerous worksheets by using one of 11 functions.

You may enter the source area into the **R**eference text box by typing the information or by using the mouse to activate a worksheet and selecting the source area. The reference must include the full path name, file name, and cell range. Otherwise, each of the source worksheets must be open in order to be used in the consolidation.

Once you enter a source area reference into the **R**eference text box, add that reference to the list of all sources by choosing the **A**dd key. The list of all sources being consolidated appears in the **A**ll References list box.

TIP

Use Wild Cards for Fast Consolidation across Many Worksheets

If you are consolidating information from 10 divisions, you do not have to enter the source area reference for each of the 10 worksheets. Instead, ask contributors to use a file name convention you define for worksheets that they send to you. You also may rename the files yourself. For example, a consolidation of sales results for four regions may use the files SALES_W.XLS, SALES_E.XLS, SALES_N.XLS, and SALES_S.XLS. These files are for results from the West, East, North, and South. You may consolidate the files by entering this in **R**eference:

   C:\EXCEL\MKTG\SALES*.XLS!$A$12:$F$56

The asterisk in SALES*.XLS consolidates all worksheets that begin with SALES. Be sure that you do not have inappropriate worksheets in the C:\EXCEL\MKTG directory that begin with SALES.

Understanding the Consolidation Functions

You may consolidate by using one of 11 functions: AVERAGE, COUNT, COUNTA, MAX, MIN, PRODUCT, STDEV, STDEVP, SUM, VAR, and VARP. After choosing the **D**ata Co**n**solidate command, you select from the Function list box the type of consolidation function you want. For descriptions of these functions, see Chapter 9, "Using Functions in Worksheets."

Consolidating by Position

Consolidating by position is the easiest method to use. You may use this method if all worksheets being consolidated have the same physical arrangement. To consolidate by position, do not select either option from the By Categories group. When you use this method, Excel consolidates each cell according to its location relative to the top left corner of the area. For example, if the function chosen is SUM, then all cells at the top left corner are summed and placed at the top left corner of the destination area; all cells one cell to the right of the top left corner are summed and placed one cell to the right of the top left corner in the destination area; and so on.

Consolidating by Categories

You want to consolidate by category when some of the source worksheets have different layouts. Consolidation by category uses the names in the top row or left column of the source areas to define which cells consolidate.

If you select the By Categories Top Row option, then Excel consolidates columns from the source area according to the text name in the top row of the source area. The names may be in any order. The first cell under a name consolidates with the first cell under the same name in other worksheets.

If you select the By Categories Left Column option, then Excel consolidates rows from the source area according to the text name in the left column of the source area. The names may be in any order. The first cell to the right of a name consolidates with the first cell to the right of the same name in other worksheets.

If you select both the By Categories Top Row and Left Column options, then Excel consolidates those cells whose text names in the top row and left column match.

TIP

Use Wild Cards When Category Names May Not Match

If the source areas have category names that are not exactly the same, you may still be able to consolidate by name. Suppose that you consolidate division profit reports for two divisions, one division using the text PROFIT in the top row of the source area, and the other division using PROFITS. To handle the difference in names, type **PROFIT*** in the top row of the consolidation area and select the By Category Top Row option when consolidating. The * matches against any group of letters, so that PROFIT* consolidates other columns with headings such as PROFIT, PROFITS, and PROFITABLE.

Using the Data Consolidate Command

Long before you need to consolidate worksheets, you should plan how worksheets are to be laid out. In your planning, you should follow one of these two design restrictions to make consolidation easier: lay out each source area with the same physical arrangement, or use the same names in row and column headings in source areas. To prepare the worksheets for consolidation, complete the following steps:

1. If possible, rename the files containing source areas so that one name using a wild card may refer to multiple files.

2. Open the files you want to consolidate. Write down the full path name and cell references of worksheets too large to be opened.

3. Check whether the source areas have the same physical layout or the same row and column headings.

4. Open the destination worksheet that receives the consolidation and create either an exact image of the source layout or a destination area by using the same row or column headings.

Now consolidate the information by doing the following:

1. Activate the destination worksheet.

2. Specify the consolidation area by using Formula **D**efine Name or by selecting the area with the mouse or keyboard. If the name of the consolidation area already exists, you must delete the name with the Formula **D**efine Name command before using this method.

3. Choose the **D**ata Co**n**solidate command.

4. Select from the **F**unction list how you want source areas consolidated.

5. Select the By Categories options in the following manner:

Select...	*to consolidate data...*
Top Row	if the text in the top row of the source areas matches
Left Column	if the text in the left column of the source areas matches
Both	if the text in both the top row and left column of the source areas matches

6. Select the **R**eference text box.

7. Type or select a source reference.

8. Choose the **A**dd key to add the reference to the **A**ll References list.

9. Repeat Steps 7 and 8 until all source areas are entered.

10. Choose OK or press Enter to save the list of source areas and to consolidate, or choose Cancel or press Esc to save the list of source areas and not consolidate.

If you are consolidating with the By Categories method, you may control the arrangement of consolidation results in the consolidation area. You achieve control by typing the appropriate consolidation text names, in the order you want, along the top row or left column of the destination area. Excel then consolidates information from the source areas and places the result into the appropriate cell of the destination area. If neither of the By Categories options is selected, the category names you type into the consolidation area are overwritten.

TIP

Create a Macro for Multiple Consolidations or for Frequent Consolidations

You may have only one consolidation area on a worksheet at a time. With only one area, you cannot complete multiple consolidations simultaneously. Each must be done individually. If you want multiple consolidations on a worksheet, and you update them frequently, use the macro recorder to record the consolidations.

Deleting Sources from a Consolidation

You may need to remove a source from the consolidation when your company sells a division, merges two sales regions, or combines product lines. Remove a source from the list of source areas by doing the following:

1. Open or activate the consolidation worksheet.

2. Choose the **Data** Consolidate command.

3. Select the **All** References list box.

4. Select the source area you want to delete.

5. Choose the **Delete** key.

6. Repeat Steps 4 and 5 to remove additional source areas.

7. Choose Cancel.

E

Using Excel with Word for Windows

Word for Windows is one of the most powerful word processors available. Word combines the features of a robust word processor with many of the capabilities of a desktop publishing program. You may run Excel and Word together, copying data and charts between them and even creating linked data and charts so that changes in one application produce changes in the other application.

Word for Windows's powerful features include these:

- pull-down menus, commands, and dialog boxes familiar to Excel users

- screen displays for speed typing, outlining, and layout

- full editing and typing in page-layout view

- ribbon and ruler icons for direct formatting with the mouse so that you do not have to go through menus

- the importing and integrating of text, graphics, and numerical data from other applications such as Microsoft Excel, Lotus 1-2-3, Autodesk AutoCad, WordPerfect, and Windows applications

- the linking of data with automatic updating with Windows applications that have Dynamic Data Exchange

- a table feature for spreadsheet-like tables that makes lists, parallel text columns, and page layouts easy to create and change

- style sheets to save you time and increase consistency in formatting

- glossaries of reusable text that make "boilerplate" documents easy to update

- macros that may be recorded or written with all the power of a high-level language such as Microsoft QuickBASIC. Macros may be assigned to specific keys or to menus through a Macro menu command.

- document templates that link together formatting, macros, glossaries, and custom menus that are used on a specific job

- the automatic reading and writing of files from major word processors and graphics applications

- desktop publishing features such as text or graphics assigned to a fixed position; borders and page breaks that adjust when the mouse is dragged; text-wrap around figures, multiple columns, lines, and borders; and an editing screen that looks the same as the printed document

- field codes that calculate results such as page numbers and dates; import files; request data from the operator; or mark entries for indexes and tables of contents

- hypertext fields that enable users to jump between locations or start a macro by clicking on a "hot spot"

- extensive keyboard merge and mail merge capabilities to automate tasks

In addition to these features, Word for Windows includes everything you may expect from the most powerful word processors, such as a 130,000-word dictionary, a 70,000-word thesaurus, sorting, math, headers/footers, footnotes/endnotes, automatic line numbering, and more.

Working with Excel and Word for Windows

The following example demonstrates two types of linking. The first link transfers the cost of goods as a percentage from within the Word document to a cell in an Excel worksheet. The second link transfers a financial forecast and chart from Excel to the Word document. Thus when the Word operator changes the cost-of-goods percentage in Word, Excel recalculates the forecast and chart, which automatically updates the forecast and chart in the document. A sample document appears in figure E.1.

Linking between Excel and Word for Windows can increase your business productivity by making the following possible:

- linking Excel and database tables and charts into management, marketing, financial, production, medical, and technical reports produced in Word (as conditions change, printed reports or on-screen reviews through Word are always up to date)

- linking Word to mailing lists stored in Excel or Q+E (dBASE files)

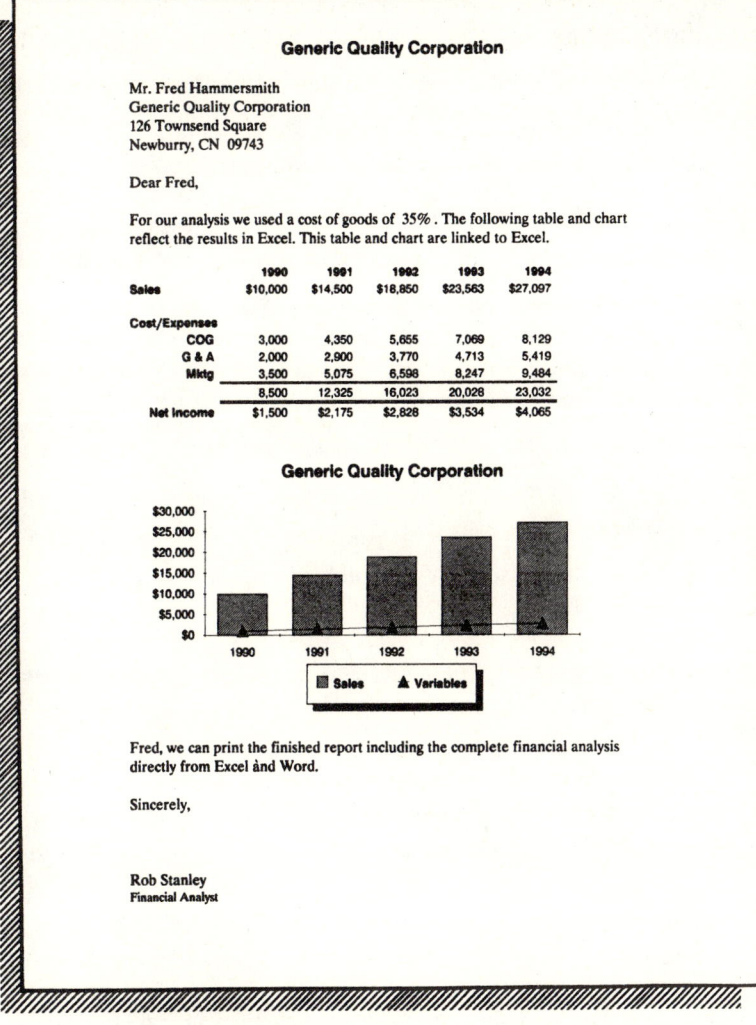

Fig. E.1. By using Edit Copy and Edit Paste Link, you may create automatically updated links that pass data between Excel and Word for Windows.

- linking invoices in Word to accounts receivable stored in Excel or Q+E (dBASE files)

- linking production lists, bills of materials, or customer orders in Word to databases in Excel or Q+E (dBASE files)

Linking from Word into Excel

Linking data in Word to a cell in the Excel worksheet is as simple as linking cells between two Excel worksheets.

To prepare for linking between Excel and Word for Windows, complete the following steps:

1. Start both applications with their documents and worksheets.

2. Save the Excel worksheet and Word document by using the names that are used after the link is complete.

3. Activate the Word document.

Now create the link from Word to Excel by completing the following steps:

1. Select the number or text in the Word document that you want linked to Excel. Include the space around the number or text and any numeric formatting, such as % or $. Do not include a sentence period after the number.

2. Choose the **Edit Copy** command in Word.

3. Press Alt+Tab until the Excel title bar appears; then release the keys to activate Excel.

4. Select the Excel cell in which you want the link.

5. Choose the **Edit Paste Link** command in Excel.

6. Save the Excel worksheet and Word document with their original file names.

These steps create a bookmark with the name DDE_LINK for the selected text in Word. A bookmark in Word is the equivalent of a range name in Excel. A document with multiple links has automatically assigned bookmarks such as DDE_LINK, DDE_LINK2, DDE_LINK3, and so on.

When you select a number or date in Step 1, include a blank space on either side of the number. Include the numeric formatting, but do not include the period if the number is at the end of a sentence. The sentence period causes Excel to misinterpret the number, and you get an error the same as if you had mistyped a numeric entry in Excel.

Including the extra spaces or % that enclose the number or date enables you to type a new number over the current number without destroying the ends of the bookmark. If you replace the number and the number's surrounding spaces, the bookmark and the bookmark's associated link disappear.

The linked cell in Excel now contains an external reference formula with the form

    =WinWord| 'C:\WINWORD\BOOK\FORECAST.DOC'!DDE_LINK

To change the cost-of-goods percentage in the document and have the new number transfer to Excel, complete the following steps:

1. In Word, select the number without selecting the space or % that encloses the number.

2. Type a new number to replace the original.

3. The new number transfers to Excel when you are finished typing.

Linking from Excel into Word

Bringing the resulting forecast and chart from Excel back into Word is just as easy as linking the cost-of-goods percentage. You have used this same copy-and-paste link process before.

To prepare the documents and applications, complete the following steps:

1. Make sure that both applications and their documents and worksheets are running.

2. If the Excel worksheet and Word document use new names after the link, save the worksheet and document with those new names now.

3. Activate the Excel worksheet.

Now link the Excel forecast to Word by completing the following steps:

1. Select the cells containing the forecast.

2. Choose the Edit Copy command in Excel.

3. Press Alt+Tab until Word is active.

4. Move the insertion point in Word to where you want the forecast to appear.

5. Choose the Edit Paste Link command in Word.

6. Select Auto Update from the dialog box that appears.

7. Choose OK or press Enter.

The Excel table appears in Word. You may use Word's table ruler to change the column widths of any cell in the table (cells may have different widths in Word). You also may type over data in the table and format the data by using any of Word's formatting capabilities. If you have typed over data in the forecast table, the table reverts to Excel's numbers the next time the table is updated.

To link the Excel chart to Word, complete the following steps:

1. Press Alt+Tab to activate Excel.

2. Press Ctrl+F6 until the chart is active.

3. Choose the Chart Select Chart command.

4. Choose the Edit Copy command.

5. Press Alt+Tab to activate Word.

6. Position the insertion point where you want the chart to appear.

7. Choose the Edit Paste Link command.

8. Select Auto Update from the dialog box that appears.

9. Choose OK or press Enter.

The chart appears in the document, which is similar to figure E.2. When the Excel chart changes, the chart in the document changes. Also, when table data is changed in Excel, table data changes in the Word document.

Fig. E.2.
Microsoft Word
for Windows
links data and
charts to other
applications,
such as Excel.

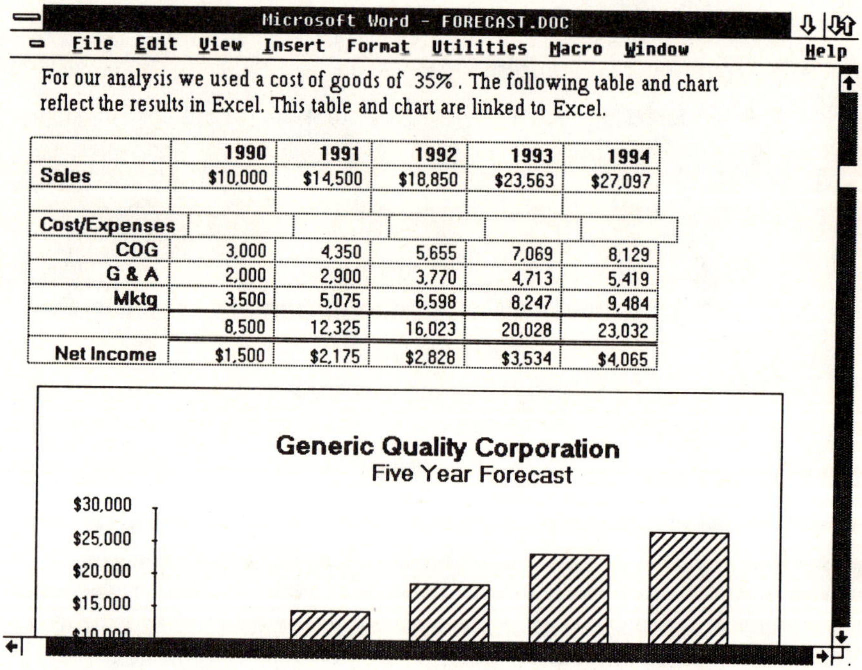

Microsoft Word - FORECAST.DOC

| File | Edit | View | Insert | Format | Utilities | Macro | Window | Help |

For our analysis we used a cost of goods of 35%. The following table and chart reflect the results in Excel. This table and chart are linked to Excel.

	1990	1991	1992	1993	1994
Sales	$10,000	$14,500	$18,850	$23,563	$27,097
Cost/Expenses					
COG	3,000	4,350	5,655	7,069	8,129
G & A	2,000	2,900	3,770	4,713	5,419
Mktg	3,500	5,075	6,598	8,247	9,484
	8,500	12,325	16,023	20,028	23,032
Net Income	$1,500	$2,175	$2,828	$3,534	$4,065

Generic Quality Corporation
Five Year Forecast

$30,000
$25,000
$20,000
$15,000
$10,000

Save the Word document, Excel worksheet, and chart with the same file names that were used during the linking process.

When you change the cost percentage numbers in the Word document, Excel recalculates the forecast, draws a new chart, and sends updated results to the Word document.

Ordering Microsoft Word for Windows

You may buy Microsoft Word for Windows through a local software dealer. To find out more about Word for Windows, contact Microsoft at the following address:

Microsoft Corporation
One Microsoft Way
Redmond, WA 98052-6399
(206) 882-8088

INDEX

801

Y-Z

More Computer Knowledge from Que

Lotus Software Titles

1-2-3 Database Techniques	24.95
1-2-3 Release 2.2 Business Applications	39.95
1-2-3 Release 2.2 Quick Reference	7.95
1-2-3 Release 2.2 QuickStart	19.95
1-2-3 Release 2.2 Workbook and Disk	29.95
1-2-3 Release 3 Business Applications	39.95
1-2-3 Release 3 Quick Reference	7.95
1-2-3 Release 3 QuickStart	19.95
1-2-3 Release 3 Workbook and Disk	29.95
1-2-3 Tips, Tricks, and Traps, 3rd Edition	22.95
Upgrading to 1-2-3 Release 3	14.95
Using 1-2-3, Special Edition	24.95
Using 1-2-3 Release 2.2, Special Edition	24.95
Using 1-2-3 Release 3	24.95
Using Lotus Magellan	21.95
Using Symphony, 2nd Edition	26.95

Database Titles

dBASE III Plus Applications Library	24.95
dBASE III Plus Handbook, 2nd Edition	24.95
dBASE III Plus Tips, Tricks, and Traps	21.95
dBASE III Plus Workbook and Disk	29.95
dBASE IV Applications Library, 2nd Edition	39.95
dBASE IV Handbook, 3rd Edition	23.95
dBASE IV Programming Techniques	24.95
dBASE IV QueCards	21.95
dBASE IV Quick Reference	7.95
dBASE IV QuickStart	19.95
dBASE IV Tips, Tricks, and Traps, 2nd Edition	21.95
dBASE IV Workbook and Disk	29.95
dBXL and Quicksilver Programming: Beyond dBASE	24.95
R:BASE User's Guide, 3rd Edition	22.95
Using Clipper	24.95
Using DataEase	22.95
Using Reflex	19.95
Using Paradox 3	24.95

Applications Software Titles

AutoCAD Advanced Techniques	34.95
AutoCAD Quick Reference	7.95
AutoCAD Sourcebook	24.95
Excel Business Applications: IBM Version	39.95
Introduction to Business Software	14.95
PC Tools Quick Reference	7.95
Smart Tips, Tricks, and Traps	24.95
Using AutoCAD, 2nd Edition	29.95
Using Computers in Business	24.95
Using DacEasy	21.95

Using Dollars and Sense: IBM Version, 2nd Edition	19.95
Using Enable/OA	23.95
Using Excel: IBM Version	24.95
Using Generic CADD	24.95
Using Harvard Project Manager	24.95
Using Managing Your Money, 2nd Edition	19.95
Using Microsoft Works: IBM Version	21.95
Using PROCOMM PLUS	19.95
Using Q&A, 2nd Edition	21.95
Using Quattro	21.95
Using Quicken	19.95
Using Smart	22.95
Using SmartWare II	24.95
Using SuperCalc5, 2nd Edition	22.95

Word Processing and Desktop Publishing Titles

DisplayWrite QuickStart	19.95
Harvard Graphics Quick Reference	7.95
Microsoft Word 5 Quick Reference	7.95
Microsoft Word 5 Tips, Tricks, and Traps: IBM Version	19.95
Using DisplayWrite 4, 2nd Edition	19.95
Using Freelance Plus	24.95
Using Harvard Graphics	24.95
Using Microsoft Word 5: IBM Version	21.95
Using MultiMate Advantage, 2nd Edition	19.95
Using PageMaker: IBM Version, 2nd Edition	24.95
Using PFS: First Choice	22.95
Using PFS: First Publisher	22.95
Using Professional Write	19.95
Using Sprint	21.95
Using Ventura Publisher, 2nd Edition	24.95
Using WordPerfect, 3rd Edition	21.95
Using WordPerfect 5	24.95
Using WordStar, 2nd Edition	21.95
Ventura Publisher Techniques and Applications	22.95
Ventura Publisher Tips, Tricks, and Traps	24.95
WordPerfect Macro Library	21.95
WordPerfect Power Techniques	21.95
WordPerfect QueCards	21.95
WordPerfect Quick Reference	7.95
WordPerfect QuickStart	21.95
WordPerfect Tips, Tricks, and Traps, 2nd Edition	21.95
WordPerfect 5 Workbook and Disk	29.95

Macintosh/Apple II Titles

The Big Mac Book	27.95
Excel QuickStart	19.95
Excel Tips, Tricks, and Traps	22.95
Using AppleWorks, 3rd Edition	21.95
Using AppleWorks GS	21.95
Using dBASE Mac	19.95
Using Dollars and Sense: Macintosh Version	19.95
Using Excel: Macintosh Verson	22.95
Using FullWrite Professional	21.95

Using HyperCard	24.95
Using Microsoft Word 4: Macintosh Version	21.95
Using Microsoft Works: Macintosh Version, 2nd Edition	21.95
Using PageMaker: Macintosh Version	24.95
Using WordPerfect: Macintosh Version	19.95

Hardware and Systems Titles

DOS Tips, Tricks, and Traps	22.95
DOS Workbook and Disk	29.95
Hard Disk Quick Reference	7.95
IBM PS/2 Handbook	21.95
Managing Your Hard Disk, 2nd Edition	22.95
MS-DOS Quick Reference	7.95
MS-DOS QuickStart	21.95
MS-DOS User's Guide, Special Edition	29.95
Networking Personal Computers, 3rd Edition	22.95
Norton Utilities Quick Reference	7.95
The Printer Bible	24.95
Understanding UNIX: A Conceptual Guide, 2nd Edition	21.95
Upgrading and Repairing PCs	27.95
Using DOS	22.95
Using Microsoft Windows	19.95
Using Novell NetWare	24.95
Using OS/2	23.95
Using PC DOS, 3rd Edition	22.95

Programming and Technical Titles

Assembly Language Quick Reference	7.95
C Programmer's Toolkit	39.95
C Programming Guide, 3rd Edition	24.95
C Quick Reference	7.95
DOS and BIOS Functions Quick Reference	7.95
DOS Programmer's Reference, 2nd Edition	27.95
Power Graphics Programming	24.95
QuickBASIC Advanced Techniques	21.95
QuickBASIC Programmer's Toolkit	39.95
QuickBASIC Quick Reference	7.95
SQL Programmer's Guide	29.95
Turbo C Programming	22.95
Turbo Pascal Advanced Techniques	22.95
Turbo Pascal Programmer's Toolkit	39.95
Turbo Pascal Quick Reference	7.95
Using Assembly Language	24.95
Using QuickBASIC 4	19.95
Using Turbo Pascal	21.95

For more information, call

1-800-428-5331

All prices subject to change without notice. Prices and charges are for domestic orders only. Non-U.S. prices might be higher.

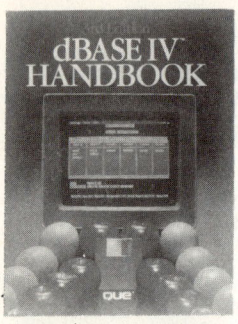